EARLY RUBENS

EARLY RUBENS

EDITED BY

SASHA SUDA
AND
KIRK NICKEL

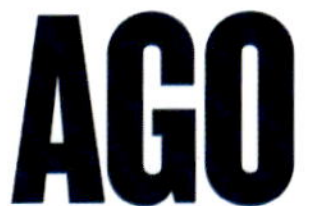

de Young \
\ Legion of Honor
fine arts museums
of san francisco

DelMonico Books • Prestel
Munich London New York

CONTENTS

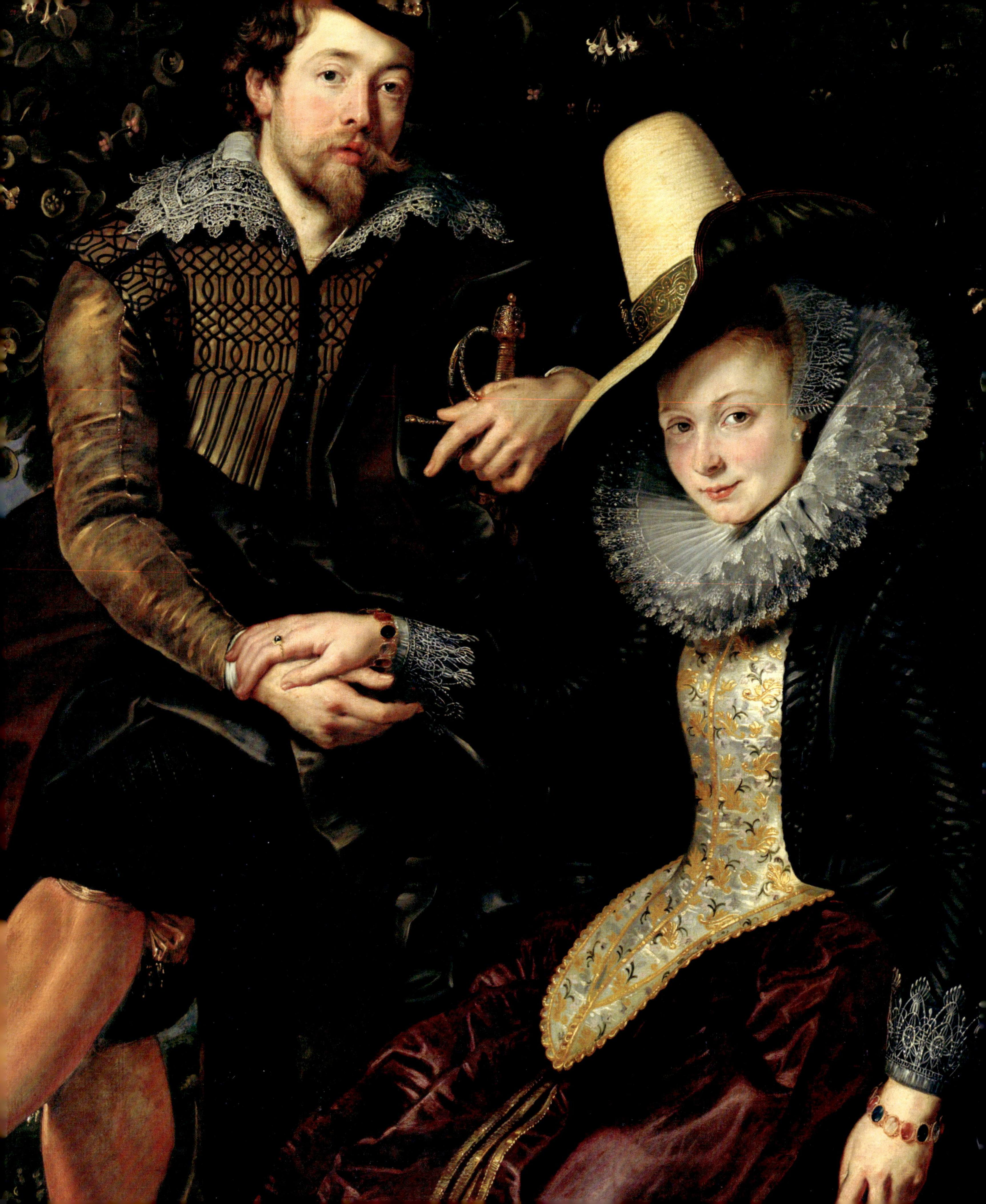

DIRECTORS' FOREWORD

Early Rubens represents a singularly ambitious collaboration between the Art Gallery of Ontario and the Fine Arts Museums of San Francisco. Though Peter Paul Rubens is a household name, his work has been infrequently exhibited in North America, and few have attempted to organize an exhibition that focuses on his oeuvre alone. *Early Rubens* shines a light on what is arguably the most generative, ambitious phase in the artist's professional life—the twelve years after he returned to Antwerp from Italy, when he built the foundation for his prolific career as an artist, businessman, and diplomat.

In 1600, when Rubens left Antwerp for Italy, Northern Europe had been devastated by religious warfare. Clashes between Catholics and Protestants had claimed thousands of lives and the related Iconoclastic Furies had destroyed innumerable artworks adorning the region's churches. Conflict was hardly absent when Rubens returned to Antwerp in 1608, but hope was on the horizon. The Twelve Years' Truce brought peace to the Low Countries (modern-day Belgium and Holland) for as many years, and provided Rubens with the stability he needed to build a business and a life in Antwerp that would change the art world forever. In these years, Rubens became court painter to the Hapsburg archdukes in Brussels, archdukes in Brussels, established his workshop, led the production of Counter-Reformation painting throughout the North, and re-established Antwerp as a social, economic, and cultural capital.

As custodians of extraordinary works of art from this period in Rubens's career, the Art Gallery of Ontario and the Fine Arts Museums of San Francisco are logical partners in this endeavour. *The Massacre of the Innocents* (1611–1612), donated to the AGO in 2008 by the legendary collector Ken Thomson, and *The Tribute Money* (c. 1610–1615), purchased in 1944 by the M.H. de Young Memorial Museum, now part of the Fine Arts Museums, are both under-studied paintings that will be seen anew in the context of *Early Rubens*.

An exhibition of this scale would not have been possible without the work of the talented staff at the AGO and at the Fine Arts Museums. We would like to acknowledge the contributions of staff across our museums, including Sasha Suda, Curator, European Art and R. Fraser Elliott Chair, Print and Drawing Council at the AGO during the development of this project, and now the Director and CEO of the National Gallery of Canada; and Kirk Nickel, Assistant Curator of European Paintings at the Fine Arts Museums; as well as Julian Cox, Chief Curator and Founding Curator of Photography at the Fine Arts Museums when the project started and Chief Curator and Deputy Director at the AGO when it was executed.

At the Art Gallery of Ontario, we extend thanks to Corrinne Chong, Research Assistant; Alexa Greist, Assistant Curator of Prints and Drawings; Carolyn Mensing, Gelber Fellow; Wendy Hebditch, Curatorial Administrative Assistant, European Art and Prints and Drawings; Devyani Saltzman, Director of Public Programming; Jessica Bright, Director of Exhibitions, and Laura Comerford, Project Manager; Gillian McIntyre, Interpretive Planner; the Edward P. Taylor Library & Archives team, including Amy Furness, Donald Rance, and Larry Pfaff; Katy Chey, Exhibition Designer; and the Publications team led by Jim Shedden. At the Fine Arts Museums, we gratefully acknowledge Max Hollein, former Director and CEO (now Director of The Metropolitan Museum of Art, New York), who supported this exhibition at its inception; Melissa E. Buron, Director of the Art Division; Martin Chapman, Curator in Charge of European Decorative Arts and Sculpture and Interim Curator in Charge of European Art; Krista

Opposite page

Peter Paul Rubens
The Artist and His First Wife, Isabella Brant, in the Honeysuckle Bower (detail)
1609–10
Oil on canvas
178 × 136.5 cm

Alte Pinakothek, Munich
Photo © bpk Bildagentur/Bayerische Staatsgemaeldesammlungen/Art Resource, NY

Brugnara, Director of Exhibitions, and Hilary Magowan, Exhibitions Manager; Kimberley Montgomery, Chief Registrar, and Nadia Ghani, Registrar; Sheila Pressley, Director of Education; Abigail Dansiger, Head of Library and Archives; and Natasha Coleman and Natalie Pellolio, Joseph F. McCrindle Interns in European Paintings in 2018 and 2017 respectively. Special thanks are also given to Esther Bell, the Robert and Martha Berman Lipp Senior Curator at the Sterling and Francine Clark Art Institute, Williamstown, who helped to initiate this project while Curator in Charge of European Paintings at the Fine Arts Museums.

Outside our institutions, we would like to thank the authors, for their perceptive insights on this subject, and also those who advised during the catalogue's early development and throughout its planning, including David Jaffé, Koen Bulckens, and Adam Harris Levine.

An ambitious project such as this relies on the generosity of a community of supporters. The AGO is grateful to Hans and Susan Brenninkmeyer for their remarkable support of both the exhibition and the research leading up to it. Special thanks to Robert Harding & Angel Yang, noting—with appreciation—that Robert is also President of the AGO Board of Trustees.

The Fine Arts Museums extend their gratitude and appreciation to the following donors: John A. and Cynthia Fry Gunn, Diane B. Wilsey, Government of Flanders, Gladyne Kenderdine Mitchell, The Bernard Osher Foundation, San Francisco Auxiliary of the Fine Arts Museums, The Diana Dollar Knowles Fund, Phoebe Cowles and Robert Girard, George and Marie Hecksher, the Robert Lehman Foundation, and The Gladys Krieble Delmas Foundation. The presentation at the Legion of Honor is supported in part by an award from the National Endowment for the Arts. The Legion's showing is also made possible by an indemnity from the Federal Council on the Arts and the Humanities.

The following institutions and individual collectors have shown their support of this exhibition through the extraordinary artworks that they have generously agreed to lend. We are deeply grateful to them for contributing their expertise as well as their works of art: Albertina, Vienna; Art Institute of Chicago; Bibliothèque Nationale de France, Paris; British Museum, London; Cincinnati Art Museum; Cleveland Museum of Art; Cummer Museum of Art and Gardens, Jacksonville, Florida; Detroit Institute of Arts; Flint Institute of Arts, Michigan; Galleria Borghese, Rome; Kunsthistorisches Museum, Vienna; Gemäldegalerie der Akademie der bildenden Künste Wien; Gemäldegalerie, Staatliche Museen zu Berlin; J. Paul Getty Museum, Los Angeles; Richard and Mary L. Gray; Hammer Museum, Los Angeles; The Hearn Family Trust; The John and Mable Ringling Museum of Art, Sarasota, Florida; Liechtenstein, The Princely Collections, Vaduz-Vienna; Los Angeles County Museum of Art; Mauritshuis, The Hague; The Metropolitan Museum of Art, New York; Moravian Art Gallery in Brno, Czech Republic; The Morgan Library and Museum, New York; Muscarelle Museum of Art, Williamsburg, Virginia; Musée des Beaux-Arts de Marseille; National Galleries of Scotland, Edinburgh; National Gallery of Art, Washington, DC; New York Public Library; Rijksmuseum, Amsterdam; Royal Museum of Fine Arts, Antwerp; Royal Museums of Fine Arts of Belgium, Brussels; Wallraf-Richartz-Museum, Cologne; Yale University Art Gallery, New Haven; and private collections.

The Art Gallery of Ontario and the Fine Arts Museums of San Francisco are proud to present this exhibition, further illuminating this key period of Rubens's life and work.

Stephan Jost
Michael and Sonja Koerner Director, and CEO
Art Gallery of Ontario

Thomas P. Campbell
Director and CEO
Fine Arts Museums of San Francisco

Opposite page

Peter Paul Rubens
Self-Portrait in a Circle of Friends at Mantua (detail)
c. 1602–05
Oil on canvas
77.5 × 101 cm

Wallraf-Richartz-Museum & Fondation Corboud, Cologne
Photo: Rheinisches Bildarchiv Köln, Walz, Sabrina

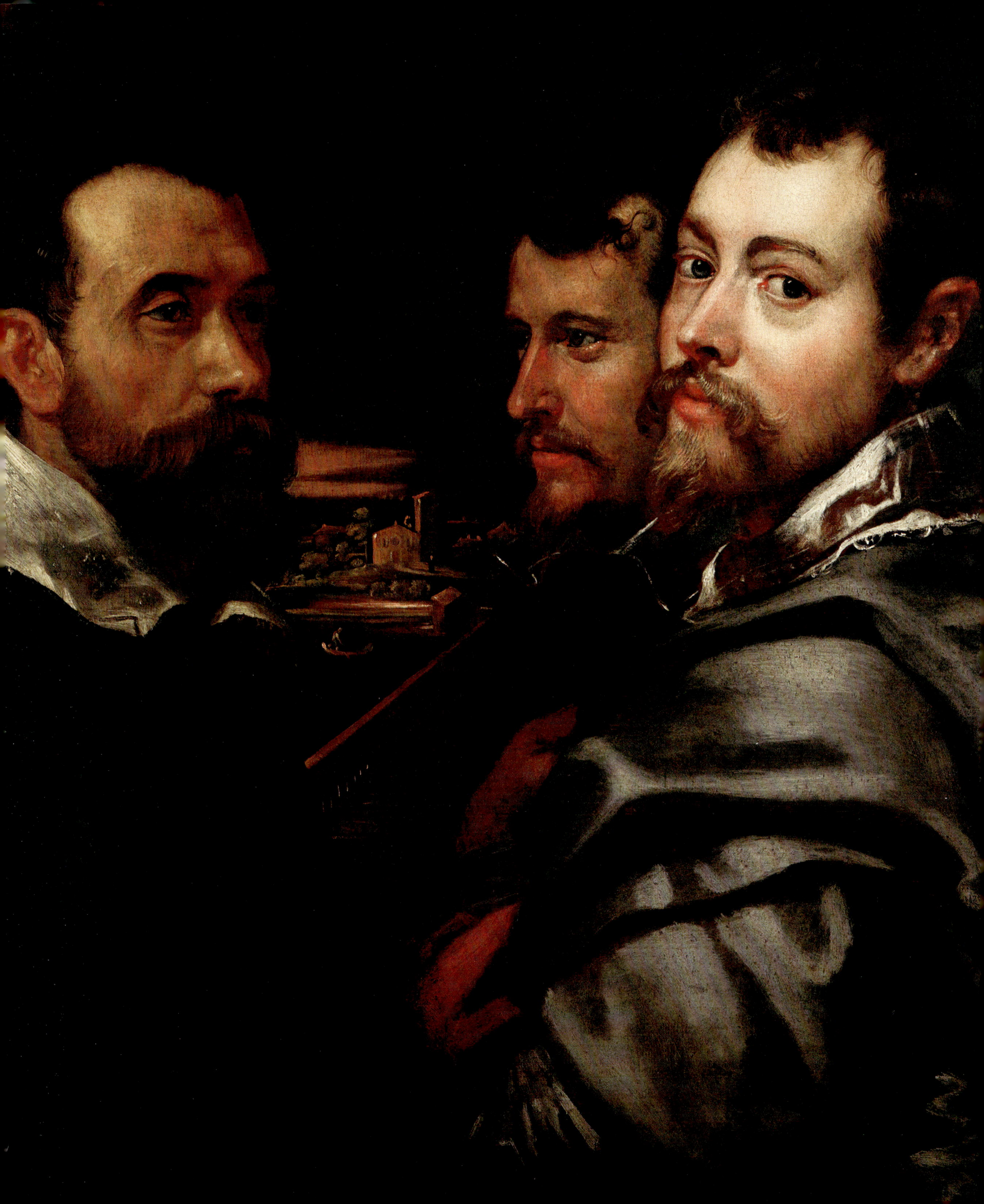

RUBENS: THE JEWEL OF ANTWERP'S RING

SASHA SUDA

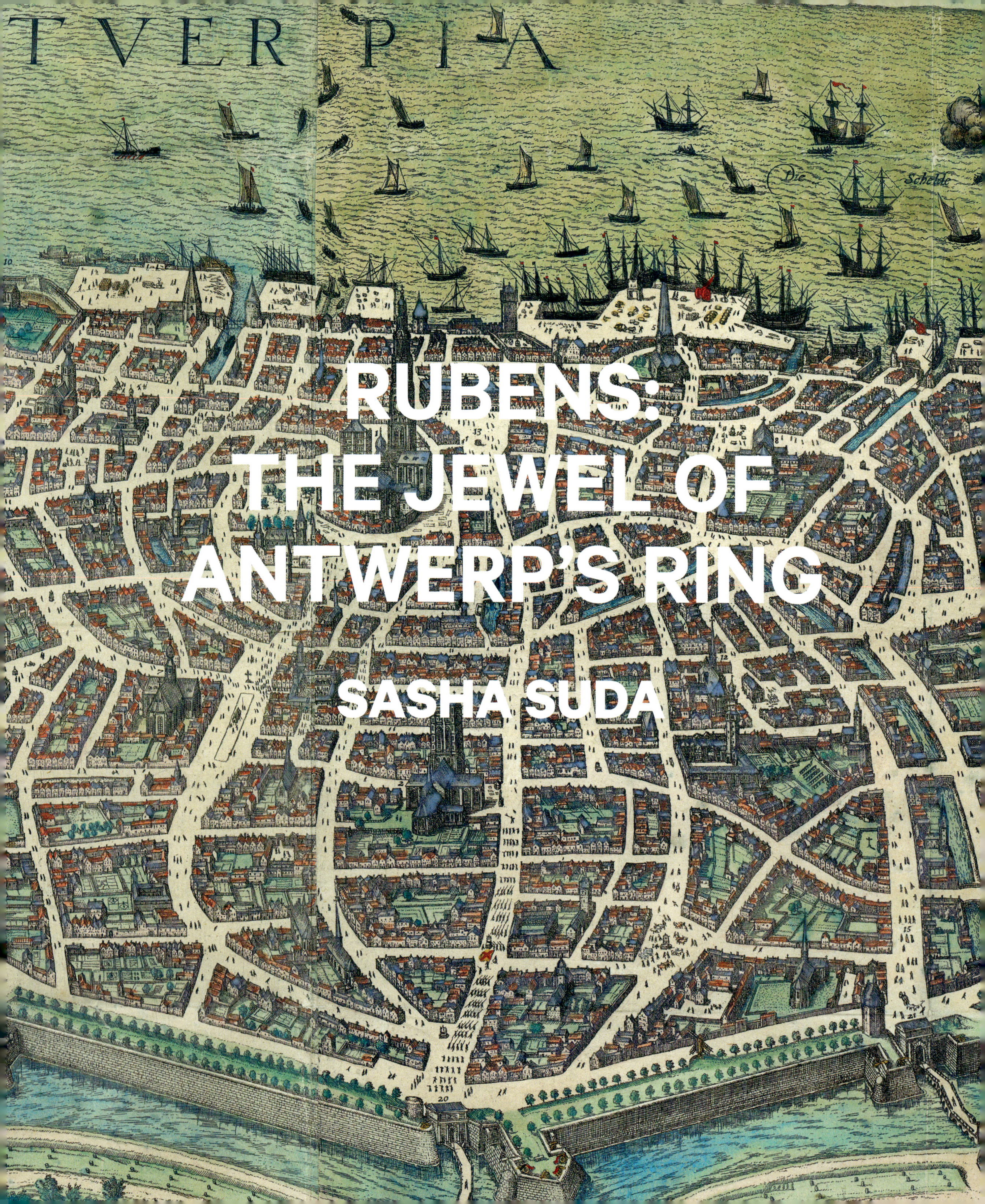

Fig 1 Joris Hoefnagel, Antverpia, *Bird's-eye View with the Citadel* (detail), c. 1598. Coloured etching, 46 × 78.8 cm. Plantin-Moretus museum/print room, Antwerp. PK.OP.21306. Museum Plantin-Moretus, Antwerp (collection Printroom)—UNESCO, World Heritage.

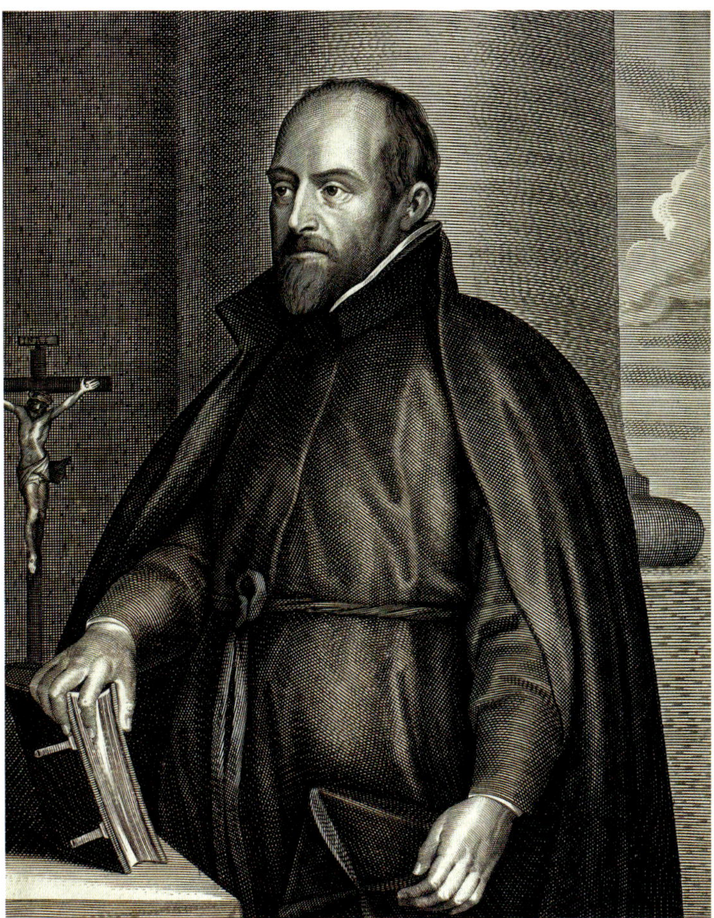

Fig 2 Peeter Clouwet (after Anthony van Dyck), *Carlo Scribani*, date unknown. Engraving on laid paper, mounted on laid paper, 23.5 × 19 cm. National Gallery of Canada, Ottawa, purchased 1948. 5476. Photo: NGC.

BELGIVM orbis ANNVLVS,
Belgium is the world's ring,
ANNVLIQVE huius GEMMA
And the jewel of this ring is
ANTVERPIA.
Antwerp.
BELGIVM orbis OCVLVS,
Belgium is the world's eye,
OCVLIQVE huius PVPVLA
And the pupil of this eye is
ANTVERPIA.
Antwerp.
BELGIVM orbis PARADISVS,
Belgium is the world's paradise,
PARADISIQ huius DELICIAE
And the pleasure of this paradise is
ANTVERPIA.
Antwerp.
BELGIVM orbis CAELVM,
Belgium is the world's heaven,
CAELIQ huius SOL
And the sun of this heaven is
ANTVERPIA.
Antwerp.[1]
(fig. 1)

IN HIS 1610 TREATISE *Antverpia*, the Jesuit Carlo Scribani (1561–1629) describes the city of Antwerp as the gem of Belgium,[2] itself the world's ring (fig. 2).[3] It is an evocative metaphor because this region of the Southern Netherlands was, between the mid-1400s and into the late 1500s, the European gateway for luxury goods imported from Africa, the Far East, and the Americas. By 1610, the city had long ceased to enjoy the status implied in the text; indeed, Scribani's words best describe Antwerp at least two decades *before* the poem was written. At the time of Scribani's arrival, Antwerp was a shell of its former self, having been gutted by the first half of the Eighty Years' War (1568–1648).[4] This decades-long conflict displaced large populations and segregated faith communities while devastating the Northern European trade economy.

Not long before the publication of *Antverpia*, Peter Paul Rubens (1577–1640) returned to Antwerp after eight years in Italy. While he recognized the challenges faced by the war-torn region, Rubens nevertheless expressed optimism about the city's future, were violence to come to an end:

> Antwerp and its citizens would satisfy me, if I could say farewell to Rome. The peace, or rather, the truce for many years will without a doubt be ratified, and during this period it is believed that our country will flourish again.[5]

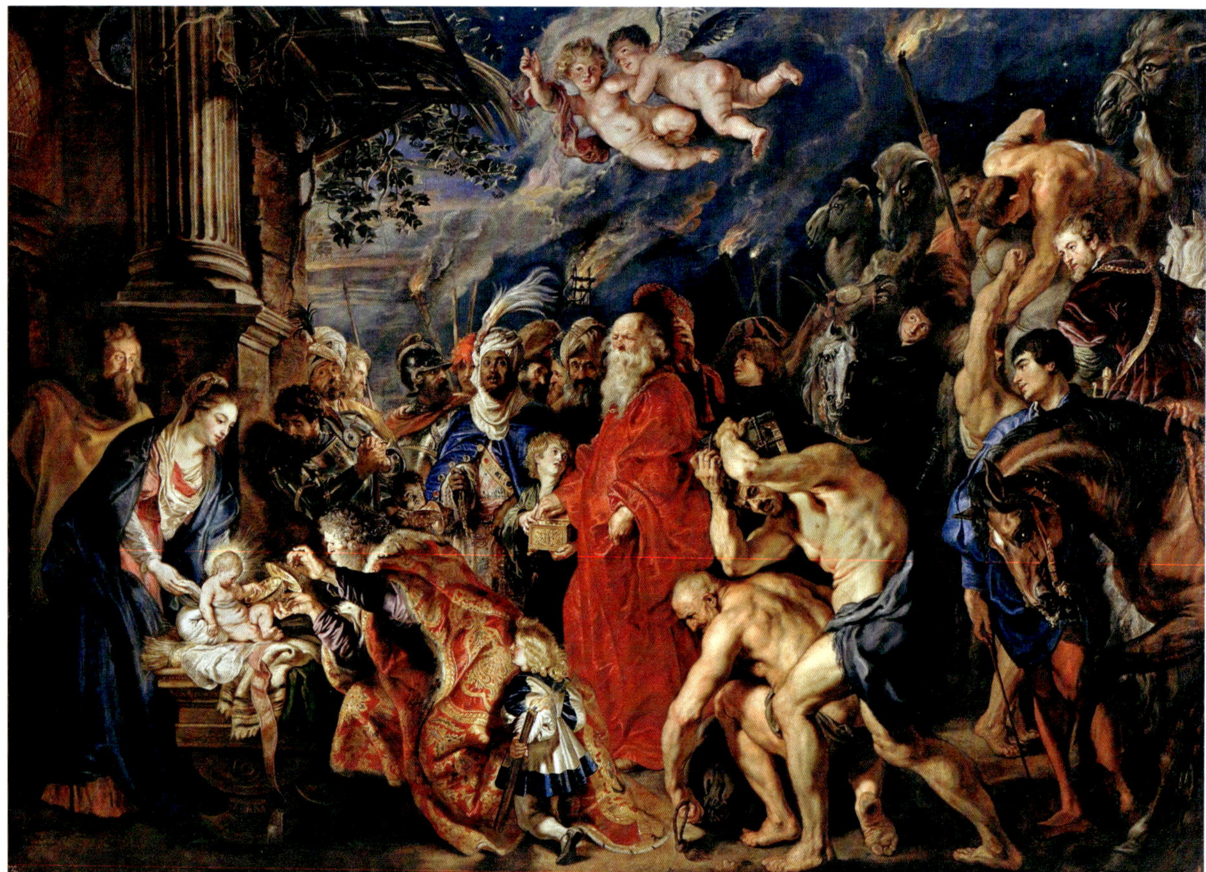

Fig 3 Peter Paul Rubens, *The Adoration of the Magi*, 1609 (enlarged in c. 1628–29). Oil on canvas, 355.5 × 493 cm. Prado National Museum, Madrid. P001638. Photo © Prado National Museum.

Indeed, the Twelve Years' Truce was signed in Antwerp on April 9, 1609, and Rubens painted *The Adoration of the Magi* (fig. 3) for the very room in the town hall where the truce was ratified. His painting is a celebration of Christianity, and its iconography makes a claim for the faith's universal significance, as evidenced by the three wise men, who travelled "from the east" to worship "the King of the Jews."[6] Conversely, the Magi model the acceptance and coexistence of faiths beyond Christianity, no doubt an allusion to the truce's expressed tolerance for Protestant values.

Painted one or two years later, Rubens's *The Massacre of the Innocents* (page 176) captures the next significant episode in Christ's life, and hits a significantly different tone. When King Herod, the Roman king of Judea, learned that the Magi had travelled to visit the newborn Christ, he ordered that all male babies be killed so that his own reign would be protected. Rubens pictures the young children as they suffer at the hands of Herod's soldiers; some infants having already succumbed to death, while others are about to receive their fatal blows. The boys' mothers react violently and out of desperation to save the lives of their children. Among the painting's most visceral images is that of a mother grasping at her own hair, in the lower right side of the painting. This desperate woman is lost in her loss, her nose just visible from behind her tangle of hair, as she grieves over her son, whose blue pallor confirms that he is dead. The old woman biting the hand of a soldier who plunges his sword toward her body and the blonde mother who scratching the face of a soldier trying to kill her boy are equally intense and confrontational moments in the painting. Presumably painted to hang above a mantlepiece in an Antwerp home, the *Massacre* showcased the artist's incredible technique while referencing his artistic education abroad.[7] It must have also served as a reminder of the loss incurred by religious warfare and the trauma that it caused in the very city where, and for which, it was painted.[8]

Scribani's poem makes no mention of Antwerp's recent history; it might, therefore, be better understood as a nostalgic reflection or aspirational musing on the city in which the Jesuit lived and worked. A prolific writer, Scribani published the book *Politico-Christianus* and dedicated it to the Spanish King Philip IV (1605–1665) in 1624.[9] The treatise outlines the ideal qualities and conduct of Christian princes and assumes the foundation of Catholic rule.[10] The publication's frontispiece, designed by Rubens, pictures two female figures, one symbolic of Christian rule (on the left) and the other depicting Abundance holding her cornucopia (on the right) (fig. 4).[11] Correspondingly, the text relays Antwerp's desire to resurrect its good fortune within a changing geopolitical landscape, a desire shared by both Scribani and Rubens. The twelve years of the truce offered a moment for Antwerp's residents to reflect on what their city had once been before violence broke out, but it also afforded the opportunity to consider what the city could become. By the time *Politico-Christianus* was published, the truce was over and the text could have been seen as aspirational, a call for good governance so that peace could be revisited. Scribani and Rubens, friends and colleagues, were part of a broader community who saw the city's potential to rebuild itself; today we might call them civic builders or boosters—Scribani, as a Jesuit and career Catholic, and Rubens, as an artist and entrepreneur who led the revitalization of Antwerp and its economy through art. Rubens's leadership in this moment of transition is remarkable—his entrepreneurial, diplomatic, intellectual, and artistic abilities eclipse those of any artist throughout Western history. Antwerp was Rubens's stalwart partner in the artist's endeavour to revitalize the city; it was her residents, history, infrastructure, and resilience that provided the platform for civic and artistic transformation. In our story, there are two protagonists: Rubens and Antwerp. Without one, the other would never have achieved the singular success that the two enjoyed together.

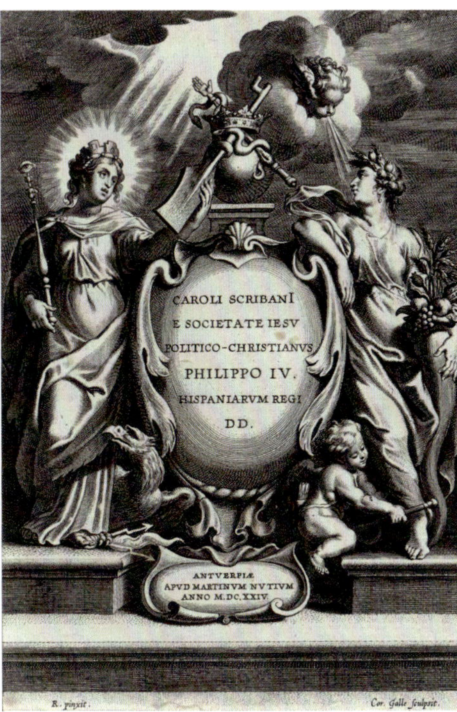

Fig 4 Cornelis Galle, after Rubens, Title page with title written on an oval cartouche at centre, flanked by female personifications of Politics and Abundance; title to Carolus Scribani's "Politicus-Christianus," c. 1624. Engraving, 20 cm × 136 cm. British Museum, London. 1858,0417.1215. Photo © The Trustees of the British Museum.

ANTWERP AND THE WORLD

Beginning in the Middle Ages, the Mediterranean Basin drove the European economy, with Venice as the main gateway for the import and export of international goods.[12] Over time, international trade moved north as new trade routes opened and provided easier access to the Atlantic Ocean and North Sea. The presence of Northern European cities on the international market can be traced to the 1100s, from whence they grew and dominated between the 1400s and the late 1500s. Bruges was the first major centre for trade. Its strategic location along the shipping channel the Zwin, otherwise known as the Golden Inlet, gives way to the Atlantic Ocean via the North Sea. International merchants, the majority from Spain, England, and Portugal, accessed the city accordingly and set up their own trading houses to serve their merchants.

When Bruges's main waterway became inaccessible in 1500 due to ongoing silting, Antwerp became queen and enjoyed truly singular success as the "centre of the *entire* international economy."[13] When the international trading communities that were established in Bruges moved to Antwerp seeking the new economic opportunities, the city's economy grew significantly. The Portuguese spice trade and English wool trade, were among those that chose Antwerp as their entrepôt.[14] With the economic shift from Bruges, Antwerp had established the fairs of Brabant, a series of important textile fairs at which locally produced tapestries and fabrics were sold.[15] These markets then naturally expanded to host English and Castilian textile merchants, the latter of which had previously been boycotted elsewhere in the Low Countries. Together, the ocean access and active trade networks helped Antwerp to develop a robust commercial infrastructure, which paved the way for a diverse and resilient economy that attracted continental European consumers who travelled to the city to purchase goods.[16] As a result, the city appeared in travel books and on maps that piqued the imaginations of potential visitors and incentivized travel there.[17]

The growing and resilient artistic community within Antwerp benefited greatly from the popularity of the *Pand*, a luxury goods market at which artists sold their works on spec rather than on order.[18] A *Pand* emerged in Bruges and in Antwerp around the same time that the European economy shifted north, from the

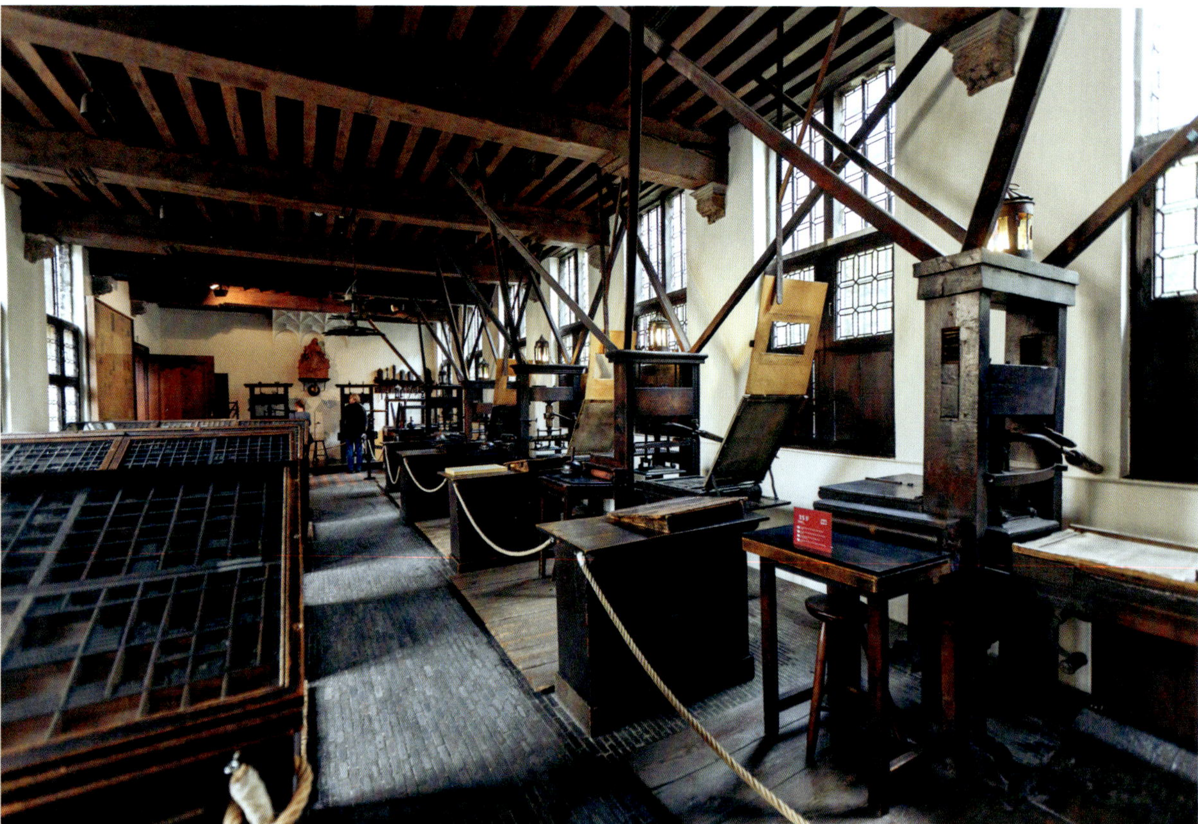

Fig 5 The Plantin-Moretus museum in Antwerp, Belgium, September 2014. Photo by Jorge Tutor/Alamy Stock Photo.

Mediterranean to the Atlantic Ocean.[19] As early as 1435, a Spanish traveller named Pero Tafur described Antwerp's *Pand* with awe: "The market that is held in this city is the most important one in the world . . . the most beautiful merchandise of this earth is on display here, the greatest wealth, and superb entertainment."[20] Within the next decade, the Medici were sending their own agents to Antwerp to buy paintings and tapestries that they had sent back to Florence.[21] By the sixteenth century, a *schilderpand*, or art market, was built to incorporate a network of specialized spaces and sales rooms for artwork. This art *Pand* was built adjacent to the New Bourse. The building and its infrastructure literally helped to form a sophisticated industry fuelled by artists and demand for their work, and facilitated by opportunistic dealers and middlemen.[22]

INTELLECTUAL LIFE IN ANTWERP

Logically, the book industry grew alongside the economy and the art market. The French book printer and publisher Christophe Plantin left Paris in the late 1540s and established Antwerp's most prolific and successful printing houses (fig. 5). At the time, the Plantin press specialized in popular Humanist texts that echoed the interests of those artists who travelled to Rome. Later, the press benefited acutely from the Counter-Reformation's demand for devotional books that helped to clarify every aspect of Catholic doctrine challenged by the Protestants. Throughout its existence, the press made use of Antwerp's incredible access to trade and distributed its publications across the globe. When Plantin died in 1589, his son-in-law Jan Moretus took over the company and it became the Plantin-Moretus press. The Plantin-Moretus press was one of the institutions within Antwerp that Peter Paul Rubens partnered with shortly after his return to the city. Childhood friends with Balthasar Moretus, Rubens was commissioned to paint The *Resurrection* from c. 1613–14 (page 50), which commemorated the deaths of Jan Moretus and his wife Martina Plantin in 1610 and 1616 respectively. Rubens partnered with the family soon after his eight-year journey through Italy, completing designs for frontispieces of books published by the Plantin-Moretus press soon after returning to Antwerp from Rome (see Jaco Rutgers's essay, page 102). Indeed, most Antwerp painters completed such work for money at the time, as the demand for artistic output was constant—as it had been for decades, even in conflict.

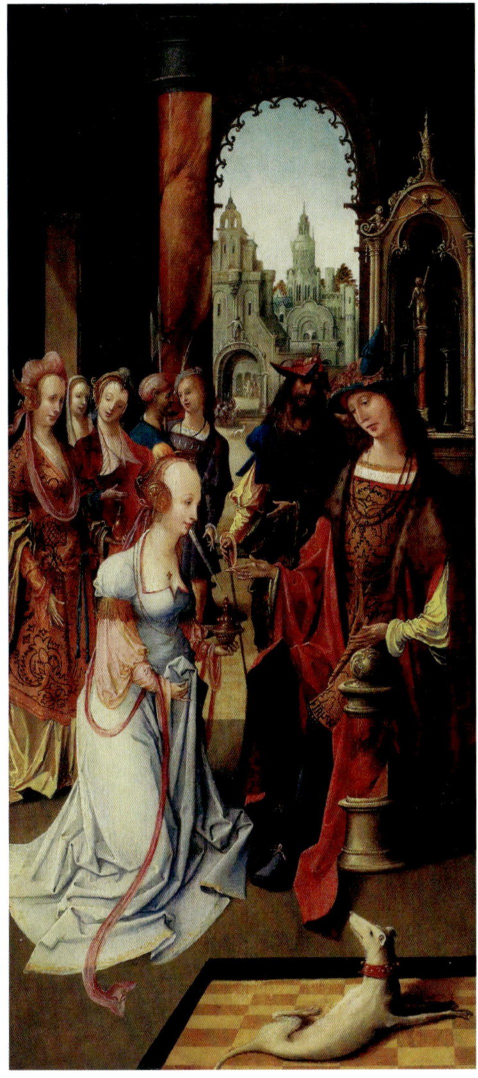

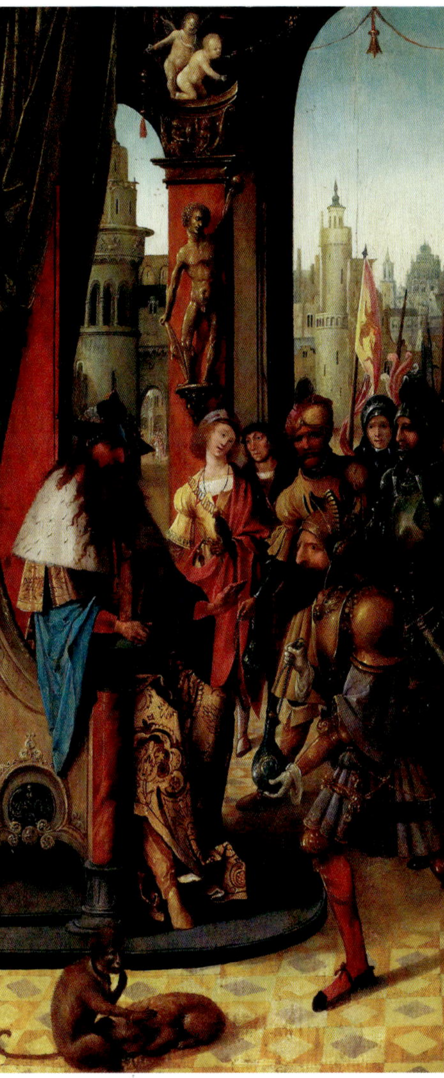

Fig 6 Pseudo Blesius, *The Queen of Sheba Visiting King Solomon*, c. 1515–20. Oil on panel, 55.4 × 26.3 cm. Art Gallery of Ontario, gift from the collection of Dr. Anne Tanenbaum to the Government of Ontario, on long-term loan to the Art Gallery of Ontario, 1995. 19525.

Fig 7 Pesudo Blesius, *The Messengers with the Water before David*, c. 1515–20. Oil on panel, 55.5 × 26.4 cm. Art Gallery of Ontario, gift from the collection of Dr. Anne Tanenbaum to the Government of Ontario, on long-term loan to the Art Gallery of Ontario, 1995. 19536.

Rubens's arrival in Antwerp did not signal the beginning of the city's artistic tradition. A long history of artistic production and consumption preceded him. Antwerp's artistic community was well established when the city experienced its economic boom in 1500. Quentin Massys and Jan de Beer were among the most well-known and highest-ranking within the city's guild of painters during that period. Massys mastered the influence of important predecessors, such as Hans Memling from Bruges and the Brussels-based Rogier van der Weyden of Tournai, while adding contemporary Italian fashions to his religious works; this helped the latter play a critical role in establishing a style described by some as Antwerp Mannerism.[23] The so-called Antwerp Mannerists painted religious subjects in contemporary contexts, referencing the material culture of the city, which was filled with imported fabrics and exotic wares that were available on the market. In a triptych wing depicting Queen Sheba before King Solomon from around 1515, the Antwerp painter Pseudo-Bles depicted a city filled with sumptuous textiles, fashion, and accoutrements imported from distant locales (fig. 6). The same is true of the *Messengers with the Water before David* (fig. 7), wherein the background cityscape depicting Old Testament Jerusalem echoes aspects of Antwerp's own flamboyant Renaissance-style architecture.

The next generation of Antwerp painters included Pieter Brueghel the Elder, who in 1551 became free master of Antwerp's painters guild, called the Guild of Saint Luke. Brueghel's genre paintings and surreal allegorical images, in the vein of Hieronymus Bosch, were a sharp contrast to the work created by his contemporaries in Antwerp, the so-called Romanists, including Jan Gossaert and Frans Floris, who had earned the moniker as a result of their travels to Rome. In Italy, the Romanists studied High Renaissance artists, including Michelangelo and Raphael.

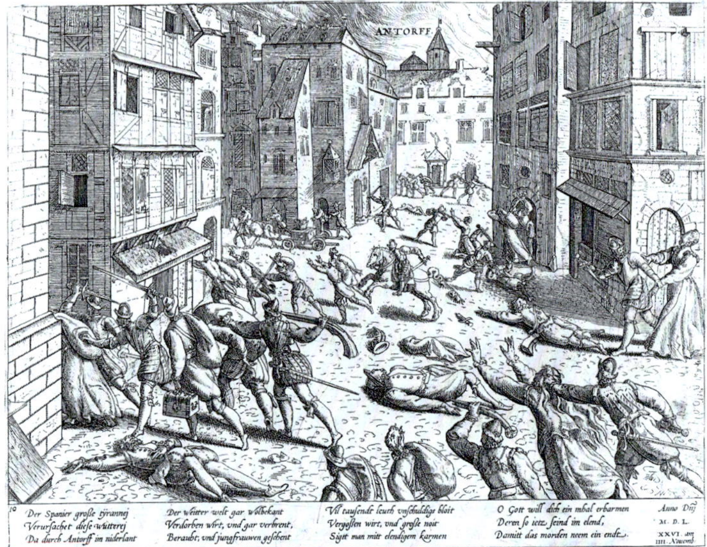

Fig 8 Frans Hogenberg, *The Sack of Antwerp from Events in the History of the Netherlands, France, Germany and England Between 1533 and 1608*, sixteenth century. Engraving, 28.6 × 35.6 cm (book cover). The Metropolitan Museum of Art, New York, The Elisha Whittelsey Collection, The Elisha Whittelsey Fund, 1959. 59.570.200(26).

Floris's *The Fall of the Rebel Angels* pays homage to Michelangelo's Sistine Chapel *Last Judgement*: both paintings present a tangle of muscular figures dynamically and dramatically intertwined in pursuit of good in the face of evil.

The influence of the Italian High Renaissance on Netherlandish culture was not limited to painting—artists working in all media travelled south. Upon returning from Italy in 1604, the Netherlandish painter, poet, and art historian Karel van Mander (1548–1606) wrote 250 biographies of Netherlandish artists in a volume called the *Schilder-Boeck*, based on Giorgio Vasari's Italian treatise *Lives of the Most Excellent Painters, Sculptors, and Architects*, first published more than fifty years earlier. Just as Vasari aimed to canonize Italian artists, van Mander hoped to celebrate a roster of past and present Netherlandish creators. Rubens's teacher Otto van Veen is among those Antwerp artists mentioned by van Mander and noted for his important work in the courts of Rudolf II in Prague and William V in Bavaria.[24] Marten De Vos is another painter who dominated the Antwerp scene before Rubens's arrival. Upon his return, Rubens worked alongside contemporaries, including Hendrik van Balen, famed for producing small cabinet paintings, and Jan Brueghel the Elder, one of his frequent collaborators.[25]

RULE AND CONFLICT IN THE LOW COUNTRIES

The Low Countries is a region in Northern Europe along the northwest coast, which mostly comprises modern-day Belgium and the Netherlands. Until the mid-fifteenth century, this region was part of the Frankish Empire and fell largely under the influence of the Kingdom of France and then the French Dukes of Burgundy. When Mary of Burgundy married Archduke Maximilian of Austria in 1477, control over the region shifted to the Hapsburg family, who had been exploiting the inextricable link between Church and State for several decades as the seat for the Holy Roman Emperor. In 1549, the grandson of Maximilian, Holy Roman Emperor Charles V, organized the Low Countries into one indivisible territory (roughly corresponding to the modern-day Netherlands and Belgium), which he called the Seventeen Provinces. When Charles abdicated the throne of Holy Roman Emperor in 1556, he split the rule of his kingdom into two. His son, the Spanish King Philip, inherited rule over the Seventeen Provinces, while Charles's younger brother, Ferdinand, the archduke of Austria, inherited the crown of the Holy Roman Empire.

Philip II lived in the Netherlands for the first three years of his rule, returning to the Spanish court in 1559. Leading Spain from afar proved challenging for Philip, as religious tensions peaked and Netherlanders increasingly resisted Spanish Catholic rule. Iconoclastic revolt in 1566 led to tensions and resentment, which were stoked by Protestant success at the Port of Brielle in 1572. In 1576, Antwerp was sacked by Spanish soldiers in the so-called Spanish Fury (fig. 8). During this harrowing incident, Antwerp was plundered by soldiers who had not been paid by Philip's court for many months. It was one of a series of brutally violent events experienced by Netherlanders between 1568 and 1648, during what became the Eighty Years' War. Indeed, the Fury only stoked tensions between the Spanish and their northern subjects, who increasingly sought religious freedom and political independence.[26] By 1582, the wool industry disappeared from Antwerp because of the city's increasing instability. In response to increasing Netherlandish dissidence, on August 17, 1585, Philip sent Alexander Farnese, Duke of Parma, to assert full Spanish control over Antwerp.[27]

The so-called Fall of Antwerp was a violent event that gutted the city and physically shut down the Scheldt river, making the city's port inaccessible (fig. 9). An engraving in Famiano Strada's

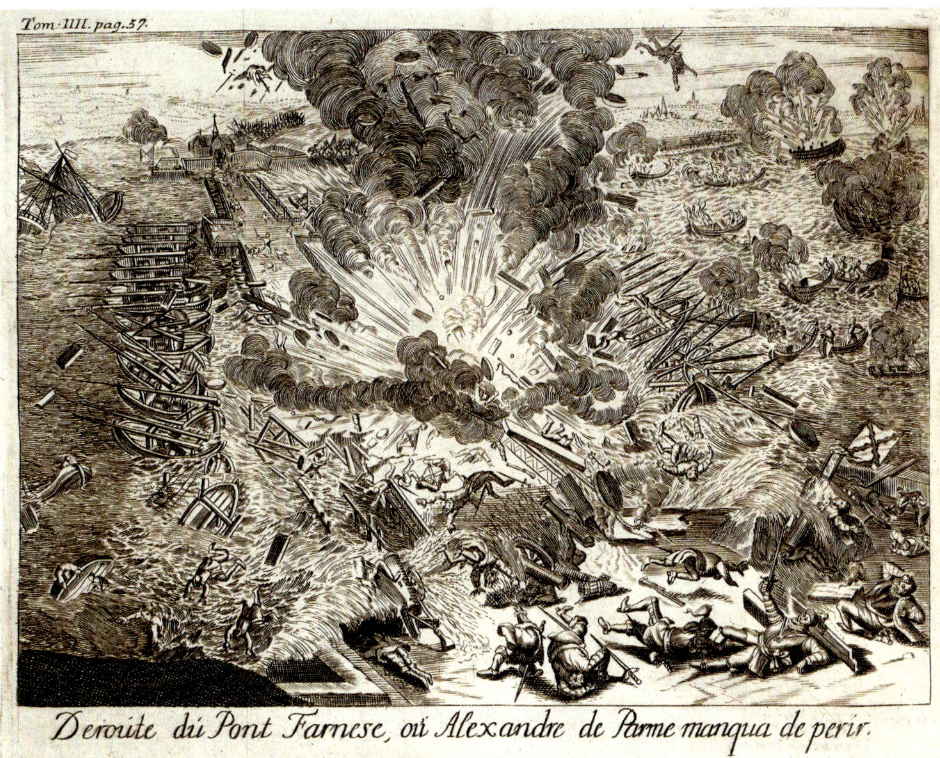

Fig 9 Famien Strada, *Pontoon Bridge by Alexander Farnese Was Blown-up during the Siege of Antwerp, 1585*, 1727. In *Histoire de la guerre des Païs-Bas (Lambrecht Cause)*, vol. 5, p. 57. Etching on paper, 12.8 cm × 16.7 cm. Bibliotheek van het Vredespaleis, The Hague, The Netherlands. MG 8932.

History of War in the Low Countries depicts the explosion that closed the Scheldt, aptly conveying the event's violent force and destruction of the city's lifeline. The siege chased out those who were left in Antwerp and the city's population dropped by almost a third immediately.[28] This decline in trade persisted well into the seventeenth century, allowing Amsterdam to take the lead from Antwerp, just as it had once taken over from Bruges. Amsterdam enjoyed the benefits of a trade network established on the North Atlantic coast of the Netherlands by the cities of Bruges and Antwerp up until the beginning of the eighteenth century: the so-called Golden Age. Peace was perhaps Amsterdam's greatest contributor to success, thanks to the northern Netherlandish provinces gaining political and religious independence from the Spanish court in 1648.

THE REFORM AND RISE OF THE CATHOLIC CHURCH

Without a doubt, the Reformation provided a complicated backdrop against which sixteenth-century Antwerp's politics and economy ebbed and flowed. Northern Europe had been the hotbed for Christian frustration with the perceived misuse of power and material wealth by the Catholic Church, dating back to the second half of the fifteenth century. Notably, Catholic reform sentiment manifested in the 1517 publication of Martin Luther's *Ninety-Five Theses*, which was distributed and much discussed throughout the Low Countries. Luther viewed many Catholic policies, including indulgences (the reduction of punishment for sin through sale) as a theologically dubious misuse of Catholic authority representative of broader Church policies. Many joined in the fight against the Church's abuses, including the French Reformer John Calvin, whose theology was followed by the majority of Antwerp's reformers. Unlike mainstream Protestantism, Calvinism denied the existence of Christ's real presence in the Eucharist—the bread and wine consumed during Mass. Christ's real presence was a central tenet of the Catholic faith, and thus its denial was a lightning rod for theological and social conflict between Antwerp's Calvinists and the ruling Catholic Hapsburgs. Tension between the two groups was inevitable and resulted in the 1566 Iconoclastic revolt, wherein a great number of works of art were removed from churches by mobs

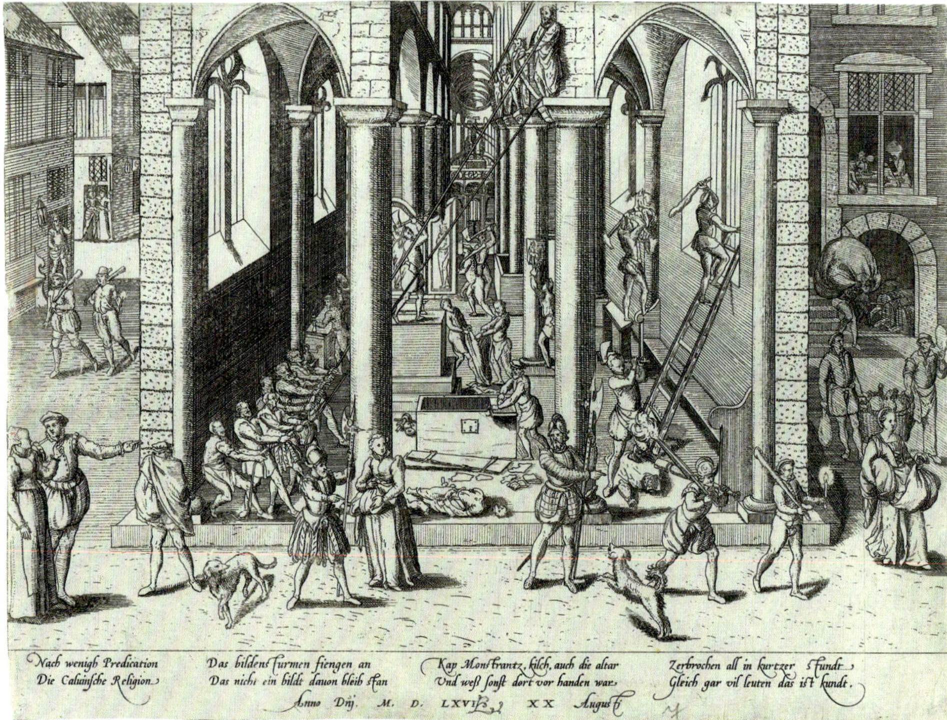

Fig 10 Frans Hogenberg, *Iconoclasm and Plunder*, 1566. Etching, 20.8 cm × 27.8 cm. British Museum, London. 1989,0930.167. Photo © The Trustees of the British Museum.

with torches (fig. 10). Franz Hogenberg provides a first-hand account in his print depicting the *Iconoclastic Fury of 1566*. The viewer is confronted by the violent acts of iconoclasts inside a large church, where they use bats to physically destroy architecture, stained-glass windows, and paintings. Ominously, outside the church, well-dressed rioters chat as they seek out their next target, reminding viewers of the social acceptability of iconoclastic sentiment.

The incessant pressure of Spanish rule eventually drove Antwerp's reformers north. Netherlandish Protestants, including Antwerp's Calvinists, had been moving north to the Republic of the United Provinces as early as the late 1570s.[29] Population displacement was both the cause and effect of the withdrawal of international investment and trade from Antwerp in the 1580s and it left the city devoid of the active economy it had for so long enjoyed. This significant loss nevertheless provided the Spanish Hapsburgs and the Catholic Church with an opportunity to reassert themselves. Unless they reconverted to Catholicism, Protestants had to leave Antwerp, leading them to become religious refugees who fled north. With the Spanish court based in Brussels, the recently thriving Antwerp became a logical foothold for the Catholic Church. Two religious orders in particular saw the opportunity in Antwerp: the Augustinians and the Jesuits, to which Scribani belonged. Later in this volume, Bert Timmermans and Koen Bulckens discuss how these orders contributed considerably to the economic and cultural life of the city. Indeed, the inexplicably violent iconoclasm of 1566, and the "quiet" iconoclastic event of 1581, left the city bereft of art and architecture, providing the newly stable city with an opportunity to redefine and reassert itself visually.[30] The artistic production required to repopulate the city's churches would become the city's largest economic engine as well as its ideological tool to demonstrate its relevance, presence, and vitality.

The Counter-Reformation facilitated the redecoration of churches across Europe within years of their destruction by Protestants. In Antwerp, this was very good for business and employed a generation of artists, who were afforded extraordinary opportunities after artworks produced by earlier generations were destroyed. Indeed, Antwerp's welcoming, friendly, and collaborative artist community is well documented during this period. It was a moment when the Church, guilds, and confraternities that commissioned significant, and expensive, works of art (see Bert Timmermans's essay, page 62) were not alone in fuelling Antwerp's art market.[31] A dynamic, less-exclusive market was very much alive and growing, for example, at the aforementioned *Pand*.

RUBENS'S RETURN

Rubens was born in Siegen, Westphalia (modern-day Germany), in 1577 to the magistrate Jan Rubens (1530–1587) and Maria Pypelinckx (1538–1608). Residents of Antwerp, Jan and Maria fled the city in 1568, when hostilities toward Protestants by the ruling Catholics began to peak.[32] The family found exile in Cologne, but moved to Siegen when Jan was appointed the legal adviser to Anna of Saxony, the second wife of the powerful Prince William of Orange, who would become the leader of the Dutch revolt against the Spanish Hapsburgs.[33]An affair between Jan and Anna resulted in his imprisonment in 1577, the same year that Peter Paul was born. One year later, Jan received a pardon and the family returned to Cologne, where Jan died in 1587. Soon thereafter, Maria moved the family back to her hometown of Antwerp, where she raised Peter Paul and his siblings, Christina and Philip, as Catholics.

Rubens began studying the classics in Latin school at the age of ten, when his family moved to Antwerp, and this is where he met Balthasar Moretus, among other contemporaries. He did not start his artistic training until the 1590s, when he apprenticed for the landscape painters Tobias Verhaecht and Adam van Noort. Rubens's most influential teacher was the Antwerp painter Otto van Veen, who had been a court artist for the Archduke Albrecht and Archduchess Isabella. Van Veen had travelled to Italy for around five years and, thus, his many large public commissions contain obvious Italian Renaissance influences.[34] It's possible that van Veen inspired Rubens to travel from Antwerp to Italy for an eight-year period.[35] Rubens studied with van Veen until his departure for Italy on May 9, 1600, and entered the court of Vincenzo Gonzaga, the duke of Mantua, shortly thereafter. Rubens's *Self-Portrait in a Circle of Friends at Mantua* (page 120) strongly suggests that the painter viewed his arrival in Mantua as a significant step forward in his education. In the painting dated around 1602 to 1605, Rubens pictures himself alongside his brother Philip, possibly the polymath Galileo Galilei, and his Humanist teacher, the Flemish scholar Justus Lipsius.[36] With Mantua as his home base, Rubens travelled to Venice, Rome, Genoa, and Florence.[37] Beginning in November 1605, Rubens lived in Rome with his Humanist brother Philip, who was the librarian to a high-ranking cleric. In these years, Rubens continued to engage his brother's intellectual social circle and to build on the foundation of his education in the Classics. A second friendship portrait, *The Four Philosophers* (fig. 11), once again pictures Rubens alongside his brother Philip and his teacher Justus Lipsius, only adding the scholar Jan van den Wouwer. The inclusion of Rubens's own antique sculpture of the Roman philosopher Seneca, is now believed to be a portrait of the Greek poet Hesiod.

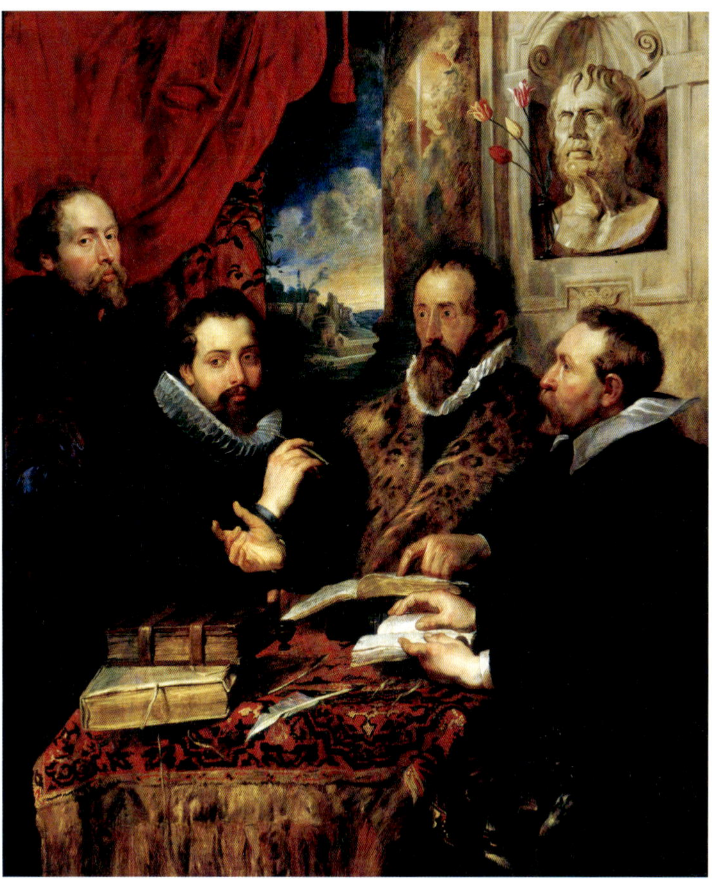

Fig 11 Peter Paul Rubens, *The Four Philosophers*, 1611–12. Oil on panel, 167 × 143 cm. Galleria Palatina, Palazzo Pitti, Florence, Italy. 1912, n.85. Photo © Alinari/Art Resource, NY. Photo: Nicola Lorusso.

On October 26, 1608, Rubens left Rome, having received word that his mother had fallen ill.[38] He arrived in Antwerp in early December, after she had already passed away.[39] The artist's first commission, *The Adoration of the Magi*, came very soon after his return, a testament to his immediate immersion in the city's artistic milieu. Rubens wrote to Johann Faber describing the archduke and archduchess's offers to hire him as a court painter on many occasions even before he returned to Antwerp: "Their offers are very generous, but I have little desire to become a courtier again."[40] He was, nevertheless, officially appointed to their court on September 23, 1609.[41] The terms of his appointment were generous, including a 500 guilder salary and privileges, including

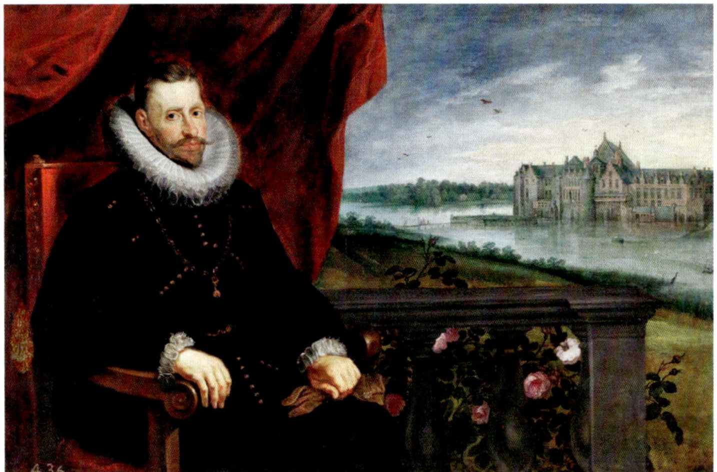

Fig 12 Peter Paul Rubens and Jan Brueghel the Elder, *Archduke Albert of Austria*, c. 1615. Oil on canvas, 113.5 × 177.5 cm. Prado Museum, Madrid. P001683. Photo © Museo Nacional del Prado/Art Resource, NY.

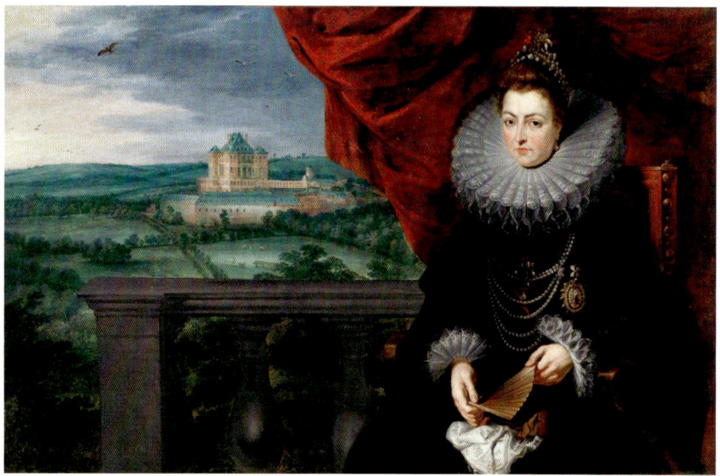

Fig 13 Peter Paul Rubens and Jan Brueghel the Elder, *The Infanta Isabella Clara Eugenia*, c. 1615. Oil on canvas, 113 × 175.8 cm. Prado Museum, Madrid. P001684. Photo © Museo Nacional del Prado/Art Resource, NY.

fiscal immunity, otherwise given only to members of the ducal household. Additionally, Rubens would be compensated separately for any artworks that he made for Albrecht and Isabella.[42] Rubens's portraits of the pair, dating to roughly 1615, present the rulers in complementary fashion (figs. 12, 13). Both paintings depict a royal Netherlandish property—the archduke's includes Tervuren Palace near Brussels, which was the residence of the former duke and duchess of Brabante (suggesting dynastic continuity). The infantas includes Mariemont, which was her favourite.

Not long before securing employment at the court, Rubens became a member of the Romanists, the aforementioned club of clerics, merchants, artists, and scholars who'd visited Rome, including his brother Philip.[43] Philip Rubens had moved back to Antwerp in late 1606, three years before his younger brother, after enjoying a successful academic and clerical career in Italy. By 1609, Philip was appointed secretary to the city of Antwerp; shortly thereafter, he married Marie de Moy, the daughter of another important city official. Peter Paul painted a beautiful portrait of his brother in 1610 or 1611 (page 124), wherein the young man's pink skin evokes youth and health. Philip nevertheless died at the young age of thirty-seven, on August 28, 1611.[44] Familial ties were doubtless a major draw for Rubens in returning to Antwerp. Establishing his own roots was central to the artist's early ambitions.

Rubens married Isabella Brant, the daughter of a prominent Antwerp city official named Jan Brant, on October 3, 1609. The painter captured their union in a stunning double portrait (page 6), in which the two are shown holding right hands in a gesture symbolic of their marital union.[45] This painting provides a stunning impression of how Rubens saw himself during his early days in Antwerp, and also where he aspired to situate his family within the city's social hierarchy. Both parties are wearing aristocratic costume, underscored by the inclusion of the sword on which Rubens rests his left hand. The portrait was likely meant as a gift for Isabella's father, Jan Brant, and pictured for him the loving union into which his daughter entered, as symbolized by the *jardin d'amour* in which the newlyweds are ensconced.[46] A later, more intimate portrait of Isabella (page 128) pictures her more than ten than years later, after the births of the couple's three children behind her: Clara Serena (b. 1609), Albert (b. 1614), and Nicolaas (b. 1618). The *Portrait of Clara Serena* is a touching image of Peter Paul and Isabella's five-year-old daughter. The young girl looks directly at the viewer, suggesting an intimate relationship between the sitter and her father, the painter. Clara Serena and Isabella both died of the bubonic plague—the former at age twelve, in 1622, and the latter three years later, at the age of thirty-five, having played a critical role in the establishment of Rubens's life and career in Antwerp.

Two years after marrying Isabella, on January 4, 1611, Rubens purchased a home on the Wapper Square in central Antwerp, off the city's main thoroughfare, the Meir. Surviving today as the Rubenshuis, Rubens's home included a studio that would serve him throughout his career. It is likely the place where he worked alongside studio assistants, producing an unfathomable number of works.[47] There can be no doubt that Rubens hosted artists alongside family and patrons, as there does not appear to have been a delineation between relations in the artist's life. Significant and wealthy benefactors were among those who helped to establish Rubens on his "home turf."

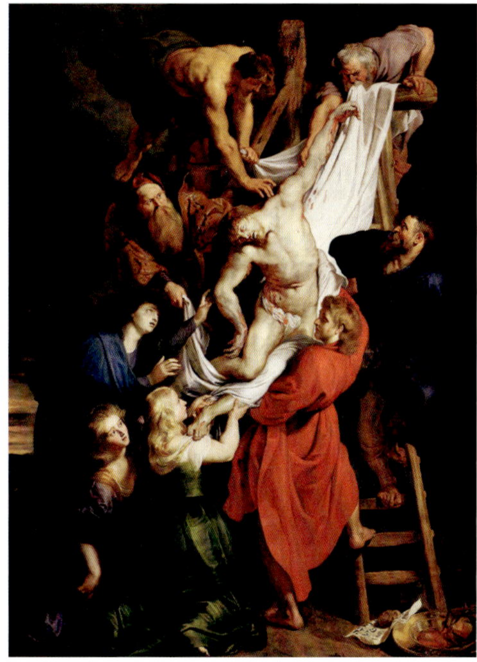

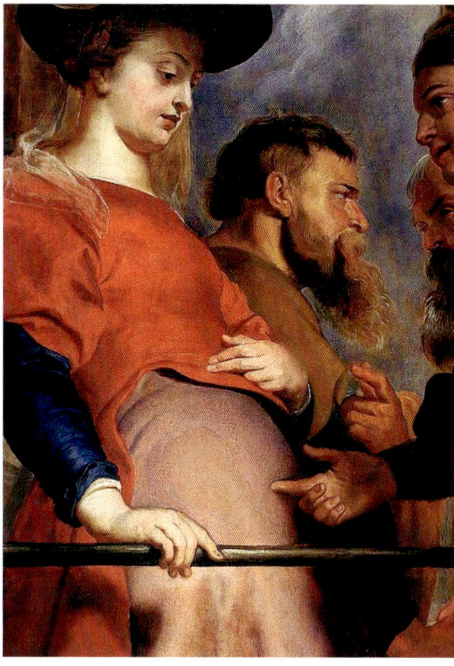

Fig 14 Peter Paul Rubens, *The Descent from the Cross*, 1612–14. Oil on panel, 420.5 × 320 cm. Cathedral of Our Lady, Antwerp.

Fig 15 Peter Paul Rubens, *The Descent from the Cross* (detail of left wing), 1612–14. Oil on panel, 420.5 × 320 cm. Cathedral of Our Lady, Antwerp.

The mayor of Antwerp, Nicolaas Rockox, invested his trust and confidence in Rubens upon his arrival. The 1609 *Adoration of the Magi*, painted by Rubens in honour of the signing of the Twelve Years' Truce for Antwerp's city hall, was paid by Rockox from private funds. Moreover, Rockox commissioned Rubens's *Descent from the Cross* for the Arquebusiers' Guild's altar in the Cathedral of Our Lady (fig. 14). A portrait of Rockox is featured on one wing of the massive altarpiece (the viewer's left-hand side), where he stands in profile, bearded and with close-cropped hair (fig. 15). He also commissioned several works from the artist for his own collection, which was on view in his home. Rockox's collection, which was immense, also included one of Rubens's most significant private commissions, *Samson and Delilah* (page 166), which the artist conceived through several studies (pages 154–156).

Cornelis van der Geest, a wealthy beneficiary of Antwerp's once-successful spice trade, was another of Rubens's significant patrons. Van Haecht's painting of van der Geest's art collection pictures a room teeming with paintings, sculpture, and audience. At once, the painting demonstrates the importance of collecting art in Antwerp society, the influential position of the collector, and the richness of artistic holdings in the city. Moreover, this work features one of the most famous paintings completed by Rubens for his patron, *Battle of the Amazons*. This painting's iconic composition was captured in an engraving designed by Rubens's collaborator, the printmaker Lucas Vorsterman (page 234). In addition to asserting a formative influence on Rubens's career, van der Geest should be considered a civic builder. He paid for the majority of the monumental altarpiece, depicting the raising of the cross, for the no-longer-standing Church of Saint Walburga, which helped to launch the artist's career and to establish the authority and momentum for Counter-Reformation rebuilding. Rubens completed this monumental altarpiece within two short years of returning to Antwerp, an accomplishment that suggests how quickly he won the trust and support of such a central supporter of the arts. Rubens's friendship with van der Geest endured throughout their lives. In 1638, the year the collector died—and two years before Rubens's own death—the artist published a beautiful print depicting the early commission in honour of his patron. The ambitious large-scale engraving (page 193) has an inscription that reads:

> Upper centre (on a sheet attached to Christ's Cross): *IESVS NASARENVS/REX IVDORVM* (last word partially obscured) and the same lines in Hebrew and Ancient Greek.
>
> Below: *D. CORNELIO VANDER GEEST VIRORVM OPTIMO ET AMICORVM VETVSTISSIMO SVOQVE AB ADOLESCENTIA PERPETVO FAVTORI ARTISQVE*

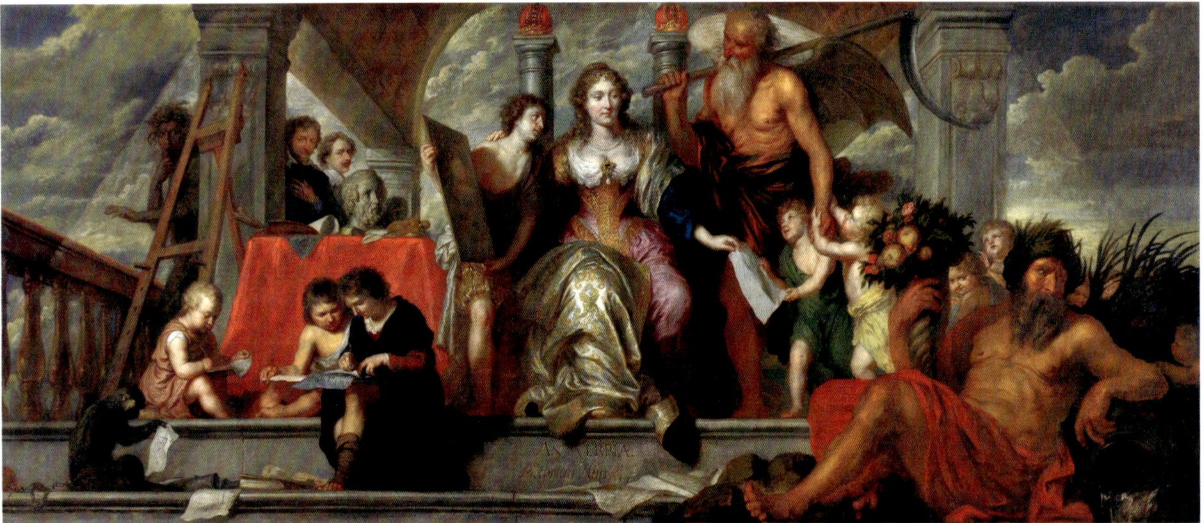

Fig 16 Theodoor Boeyermans, *Antwerp, Nourishing the Painters*, 1665. Oil on canvas, 454 × 188 cm. Koninklijk Museum voor Schone Kunsten, Antwerp. 23. Photo © Lukas-Art in Flanders.

> *PICTORIÆ SVMMO DVM VIXIT ADMIRATORI MONVMENTVM HOC AETERNÆ AMICITIÆ QVOD SVPERSTITI DESTINARAT DEFVNCTO L.M.D.D.Q./ Ex Tabula Walburgensis Ecclesiæ cuius ipse præcipuus Author et prmotor fuit.*
>
> Lower left: *P P Rubens pinxit./H. Withouc sculpsit A.° 1638.*
>
> Lower right: *Cum priuilegiis Regis Christianissimi/Principum Belgarum et Ordinum Batauiæ.*

It is possible that the oil sketch for said engraving (page 192), which survives in a remarkably finished state, was intended as a gift for van der Geest. Nostalgic for his early days, Rubens may have wanted to credit his long-time patron for having made such great contributions to the artist's career.

Indeed, Rubens had the most prolific and successful career of any artist in history. He died wealthy, with an inventory of belongings that would help to support his children and their children as well. He had been so successful that his offspring were not allowed to be painters themselves, lest they attempt to sell their father's work as their own. Still, there is something mysterious about his career: *How* did he become such a smashing success? *When* did he become such a smashing success? So much of what he achieved has been credited to Italy, to what he learned there and, in turn, accomplished at home. Indeed, there is a sort of alchemy that occurs when Rubens brings his learnings back to his hometown and homeland. It is more than a matter of an education, however. The art historian Svetlana Alpers writes: "When an internationalist in art and politics like Rubens returns home and paints a picture in the native tradition of his own country there is probably some link to be drawn between his art and his life."[48] Alpers was thinking about Rubens's later career, his decision to return home after serving at the court for so many years abroad and in diplomatic service. Indeed, he always returned home when he least needed to, suggesting that, in fact, he wanted to.

Rubens's achievements cannot be measured by his artistic output alone. He was a wildly successful entrepreneur, a trusted friend and collaborator, a stalwart diplomat, and a family man. His efforts, at least in the early years, centred on his hometown, Antwerp, where he built a home and a thriving business. In so doing, he also helped to create a thriving artistic community, which would become the city's economic backbone. Twenty-five years after Rubens died, in 1665, the Antwerp history painter Theodoor Boeyermans produced an homage to Antwerp's painterly past in *Antwerp, Nourishing the Painters* (fig. 16), executed for the ceiling of the Antwerp Academy's main meeting space. In the painting, Antwerp is personified as a beautiful and matronly woman seated at the centre and flanked by the god Chronos on her left and the river god Scaldis (representative of the city's Scheldt river) in front of him. The former helps young students present the city with their artworks, while the latter holds a cornucopia, symbolic of the riches of the city and its artistic tradition. This tradition is embodied by Peter Paul Rubens and Anthony van Dyck, who watch over the future of Antwerp, inherently linked to its artistic community, from an architectural niche to the side.

Thanks goes to Adam Harris Levine (Columbia University) for his research assistance, Dr. Carolyn Mensing (Art Gallery of Ontario) for her research assistance and early feedback, Dr. Corrinne Chong for her research assistance, and to Koen Bulckens for his wise counsel and collaboration.

1 Carlo Scribani, *Antverpia* (Antwerp: Apud Ioannem Moretum, 1610), 136, cited in Raingard Esser, "The Diamond of the Netherlands: Histories of Antwerp in the Seventeenth Century," in *Trading Values in Early Modern Antwerp*, ed. Christine Göttler, Bart Ramakers, and Joanne Woodall (Leiden: Brill, 2014), 349. Translation by Sasha Suda with assistance from Professor Seth Bernard (University of Toronto, Classics Department).

2 The modern state of Belgium was founded in 1830 as an outcome of the Belgian Revolution. Used in the seventeenth century, the term "Belgium" refers to the Latin *Gallia Belgica*, an ancient Roman province that was inhabited by the *Belgae*. Regional pride and an interest in ancient history inspired the use of the word in the seventeenth century by academics, politicians, and nobility aiming to strengthen their identity by connecting it with the Roman past. In *De Bello Gallico*, book 1, chap. 1, the Roman Emperor Julius Caesar states: "Gaul is divided into three parts, one of which the Belgae inhabit, the Aquitani another . . . the Gauls, the third . . .Of all of these, the Belgae are the strongest." See "History of Belgium," Wikipedia, https://en.wikipedia.org/wiki/History_of_Belgium.

3 Esser, "The Diamond of the Netherlands," 349.

4 Wilhelm Ribhegge, "Counter-Reformation Politics, Society and Culture in the Southern Netherlands, Rhineland and Westphalia in the First Half of the 17th Century," in *Humanistica Lovaniensi*, 49 (2000): 189.

5 Letter from Peter Paul Rubens to Johann Faber, Antwerp, April 10, 1609, in *The Letters of Peter Paul Rubens*, ed. and trans. Ruth Saunders Magurn (Cambridge, MA: Harvard University Press, 1955), 53–54.

6 Matthew 2: 1–2

7 David Jaffé asserts that the painting was completed for the Carenna family in Antwerp, whereas Hans Devisscher and Hans Vlieghe disagree and propose that the painting's earliest owner might have been Jan-Baptista Anthoine, whose probate inventory lists a *Massacre of the Innocents* on March 28, 1691 (no. 304). See Hans Devisscher and Hans Vlieghe, *Corpus Rubenianum Ludwig Burchard, Part V: The Life of Christ Before the Passion; I\; The Youth of Christ*, 2 vols. (London: Harvey Miller, 2014), 1:24.

8 Carlo Scribani, *Politico-Christianus* (Antwerp: Apud Martinum Nutium, 1624).

9 Carlo Scribani, *Politico-Christianus*.

10 Julius S. Held, "Carolus Scribanius's Observations on Art in Antwerp," *Journal of the Warburg and Courtauld Institutes* 59 (1996): 174.

11 Ribhegge, "Counter-Reformation Politics," 189.

12 Michael Limberger, "Economic Growth: Antwerp," in *Urban Achievement in Early Modern Europe: Golden Ages in Antwerp, Amsterdam, and London*, ed. Patrick O'Brien (Cambridge: Cambridge University Press, 2001), 40.

13 Fernand Braudel, *La Dynamique du Capitalisme* (Paris: Arthaud, 1985), 143.

14 Jan van der Stock, ed., *Antwerp: Story of a Metropolis* (Ghent: Snoeck-Ducajo und Zoon, 1993), 22, exh. cat.

15 Frans Baudouin, *Antwerp's Golden Age: The Metropolis of the West in the 16th and 17th Centuries* (Antwerp: J. E. Buschman, 1973), 11, exh. cat.

16 Filip Vermeylen, *Painting for the Market: Commercialization of Art in Antwerp's Golden Age* (Turnhout: Brepols, 2003), 16.

17 Jan van der Stock paints a rich image of the city in his book *Printing Images in Antwerp: The Introduction of Printmaking in a City; Fifteenth Century to 1585* (Rotterdam: Sound & Vision Interactive, 1998).

18 Vermeylen, *Painting for the Market*, 7.

19 Vermeylen, *Painting for the Market*, 15.

20 Pero Tafur quoted in Jan Albert Goris, *Lof van Antwerpen: Hoe reizigers Antwerpen zagen van de XVe tot de XXe eeuw* (Brussels: Standaard Boekhandel, 1940), 24–27, as cited in Vermeylen, *Painting for the Market*.

21 Dan Ewing, "Marketing Art in Antwerp, 1460–1560: Our Lady's *Pand*," *Art Bulletin* 72, no. 4 (December 1990): 560.

22 Vermeylen, *Painting for the Market*, 1999.

23 Peter van den Brink and Maximilian P.J. Martens, eds., *ExtravagAnt! A Forgotten Chapter of Antwerp Painting*, 1500–1530 (Antwerp: BAI: Bonnefantenmuseum; Koninklijk Museum voor Schone Kunsten, 2005), exh. cat.

24 Karel van Mander, *Schilder-Boeck*, 1604, s.v. "Otto van Veen."

25 See Anne T. Woollett and Ariane van Suchtelen, eds., *Rubens and Brueghel: A Working Friendship* (Los Angeles: J. Paul Getty Trust, 2006), exh. cat.

26 Sovereignty came only to the northern provinces, which became the Dutch Republic, and not until 1648.

27 R. Baetens, "Between Hope and Fear," in *Antwerp: Twelve Centuries of History and Culture*, ed. Karel van Isacker and Raymond van Uytven (Antwerp: Fonds Mercator, 1986), 164.

28 Baetens, "Between Hope and Fear," 164.

29 For a succinct overview of Antwerp's role in the Counter-Reformation, see Thomas L. Glen, "Rubens and the Counter Reformation: Studies in His Religious Paintings between 1609 and 1620" (PhD diss., Princeton University, 1975), 5–17.

30 For a thorough, reflective discussion of the Counter-Reformation and its relationship to painting in the seventeenth century, see David Freedberg, "Painting and the Counter-Reformation in the Age of Rubens," in Peter C. Sutton et al., *The Age of Rubens* (Boston: Museum of Fine Arts, 1993), 131–45, exh. cat.

31 Filip Vermeylen provides a thorough and readable summary of the history of the *Panden* in *Painting for the Market*.

32 Jan Rubens was a Calvinist.

33 A turning point in William's leadership of the Dutch came in 1572, when he was named Stadtholder of Holland and Zeeland after an outbreak of Calvinist revolt. See Jonathan Israel, *The Dutch Republic: Its Rise, Greatness, and Fall*, 1477–1806 (Oxford: Oxford University Press, 1995), 31–35.

34 David Jaffé and Minna Moore Ede, "A Master in the Making," in *Rubens: Master in the Making*, ed. David Jaffé and Elizabeth McGrath (London: National Gallery Company Ltd. 2005), 11, exh. cat.

35 Rubens's career in Italy has a rich bibliography, including Michael Jaffé, *Rubens and Italy* (Ithaca, NY: Cornell University Press, 1977); Frances Huemer, *Rubens and the Roman Circle: Studies of the First Decade* (New York: Garland, 1996); David Jaffé and Elizabeth McGrath, *Rubens: A Master in the Making* (London: National Gallery Company Ltd., 2005); various essays in Jochen Sander, Stefan Weppelmann, and Gerlinde Gruber, eds., *Rubens: The Power of Transformation* (Vienna: Kunsthistorisches Museum, 2015), exh. cat.

36 For a thorough discussion of Rubens's relationship to his brother Philip and Justus Lipsius, see Huemer, *Rubens and the Roman Circle*, esp. 29–54 (chap. 2, "Philip Rubens and Lipsius"). For Frances Huemer's compelling argument in favor of identifying Galileo in the Cologne painting, see *Source: Notes in the History of Art* 24, no. 1 (Fall 2004): 18–25.

37 Jaffé and McGrath, *Rubens*, 2005.

38 Filip Vermeylen, "Antwerp Beckons," in *Rubens and the Netherlands*, ed. Jan de Jong, Bart Ramakers, Frits Scholten, Mariët Westermann, and Joanna Woodall (Zwolle: Waanders, 2004), 16.

39 Vermeylen, "Antwerp Beckons," 17–18.

40 Rubens to Faber, Antwerp, April 10, 1609, in Magurn, *The Letters of Peter Paul Rubens*, 53–54.

41 Vermeylen, "Antwerp Beckons," 19.

42 Vermeylen, "Antwerp Beckons," 19.

43 On June 29, 1609, Rubens joined the Romanists, where he reconnected with Van Veen and Brueghel. Vermeylen, "Antwerp Beckons," 19.

44 Vlieghe, *Rubens Portraits*, 179–80.

45 Hans Vlieghe, *Flemish Art and Architecture, 1585–1700* (New Haven, CT: Yale University Press, 1998), 121–22.

46 Hans Vlieghe, *Corpus Rubenianum Ludwig Burchard, Part XIX: Portraits of Identified Sitters Painted in Antwerp*, 2 vols. (London: Harvey Miller, 1987), 1:163.

47 Anne Woollett, "Two Celebrated Painters: The Collaborative Ventures of Rubens and Brueghel, ca. 1598–1625," in Woollett and Suchtelen, *Rubens and Brueghel*, 5.

48 Svetlana Alpers, *The Making of Rubens* (New Haven, CT: Yale University Press, 1995), 26.

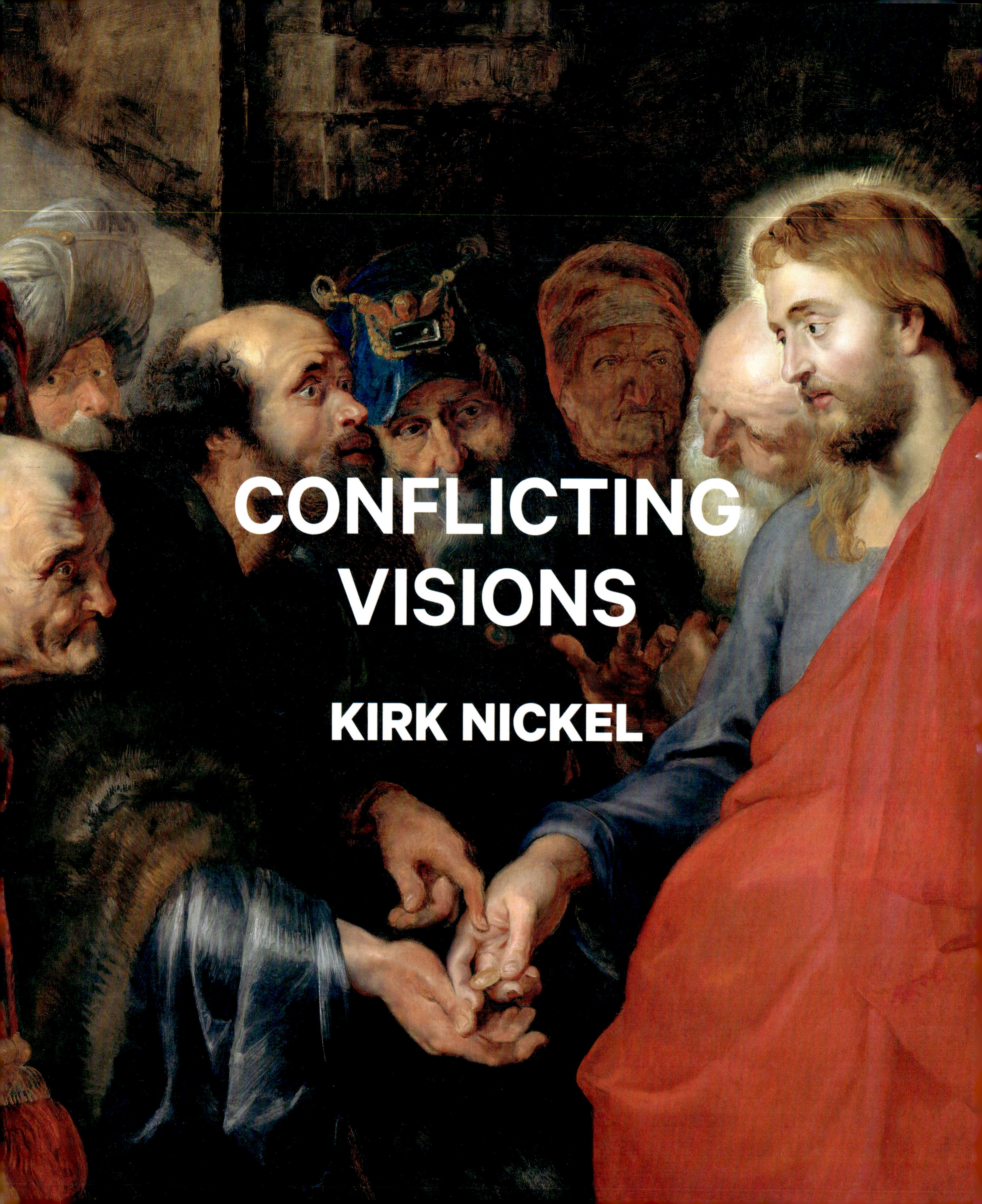
CONFLICTING
VISIONS
KIRK NICKEL

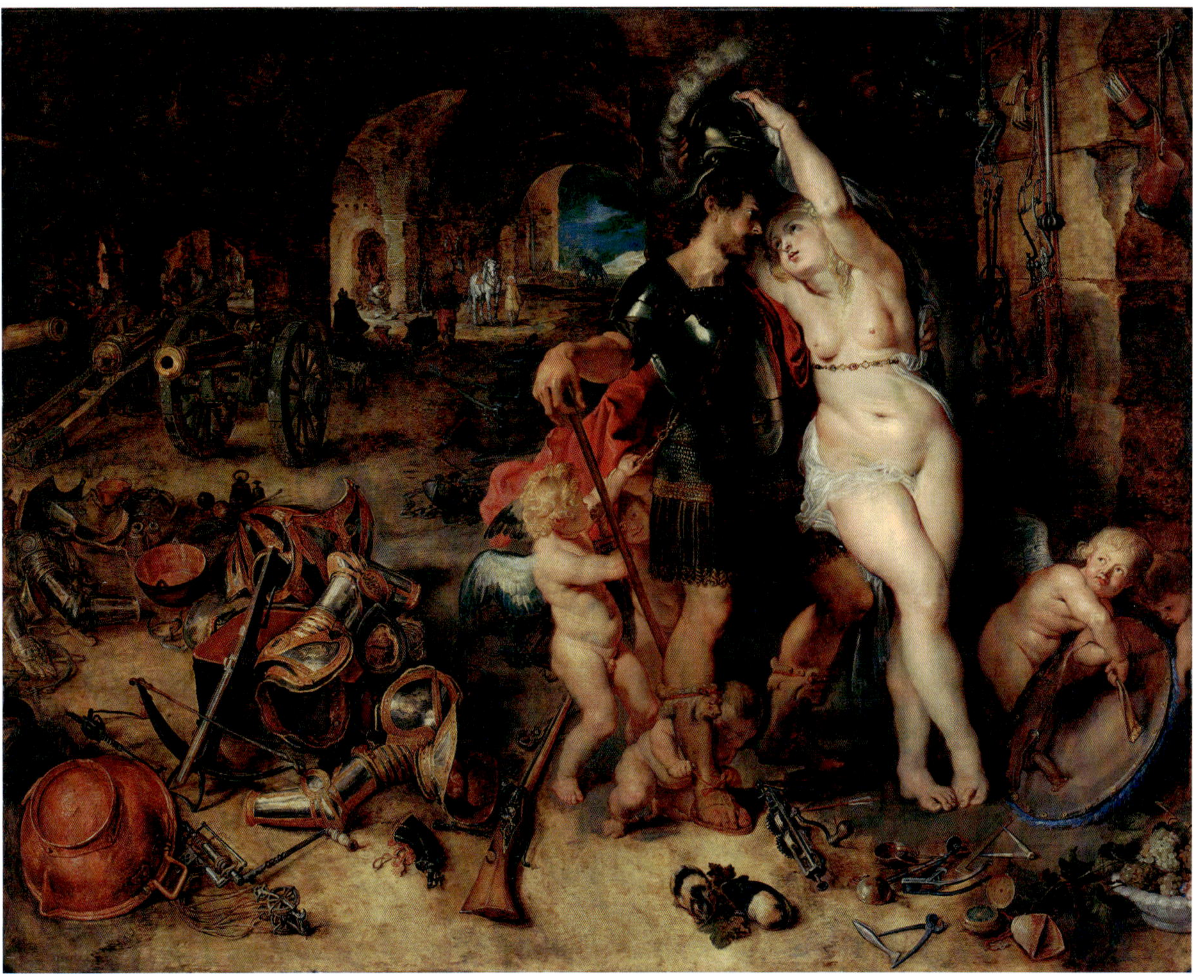

Fig 1 Peter Paul Rubens and Jan Brueghel the Elder, *The Return from War: Mars Disarmed by Venus*, c. 1610–12. Oil on panel, 127.3 × 163.5 cm. The J. Paul Getty Museum, Los Angeles, acquired in honour of John Walsh. 2000.68.

WHEN RUBENS RETURNED TO ANTWERP in the autumn of 1608, the city was anxious for peace. After four decades of open strife that began with Iconoclasm and the bloody tribunals of the Duke of Alba in the 1560s, the fractured Netherlands were at last negotiating a resolution. The Twelve Years' Truce was signed the following April and compelled the Catholic Southern Netherlands, including Antwerp, to acknowledge the Protestant northern provinces as a newly autonomous Dutch Republic with the right to trade in the southern lands. There was reason for all to hope that peace would bring increased commerce and prosperity. The region's artists, in particular, could expect the suspension of hostilities to energize the market for art and encourage more ambitious commissions. Even before a truce was imminent, the artist and writer Karel van Mander had hoped to induce peace through the visual arts themselves, exhorting his fellow painters to turn away from "descriptions of the ... tragedies of our Netherlandish bloodstained theatre" and to remember that pleasant "brushstrokes and paintings are your province."[1]

These hopes seem to take form in *The Return from War: Mars Disarmed by Venus* (fig. 1). Painted in the early 1610s, the scene is set among the arcades and barrel vaults of a large armoury, with metalsmiths working the forge and stable hands tending horses. Beautifully wrought arms and armour cover the ground between the distant workers and the principal action where the god of war is relieved of his battle dress and invited to embrace Venus, and thereby beauty and pleasure. The painting was a collaboration between Rubens and his good friend Jan Brueghel the Elder (1568–1625), and since both painters were employed by the archdukes in Brussels, the allegory may have been executed for the archducal court as a celebration of the recent truce.[2] The painting's action, though, is not as plainly encouraging as it appears at first. Because Brueghel's high horizon line and workshop vignettes draw our attention into the depth of the picture, we may be slow to recognize the drama playing out between the two lovers. As Venus lifts Mars's helmet, she looks longingly into his eyes; Mars remains entirely unmoved. He half-mechanically reaches his left

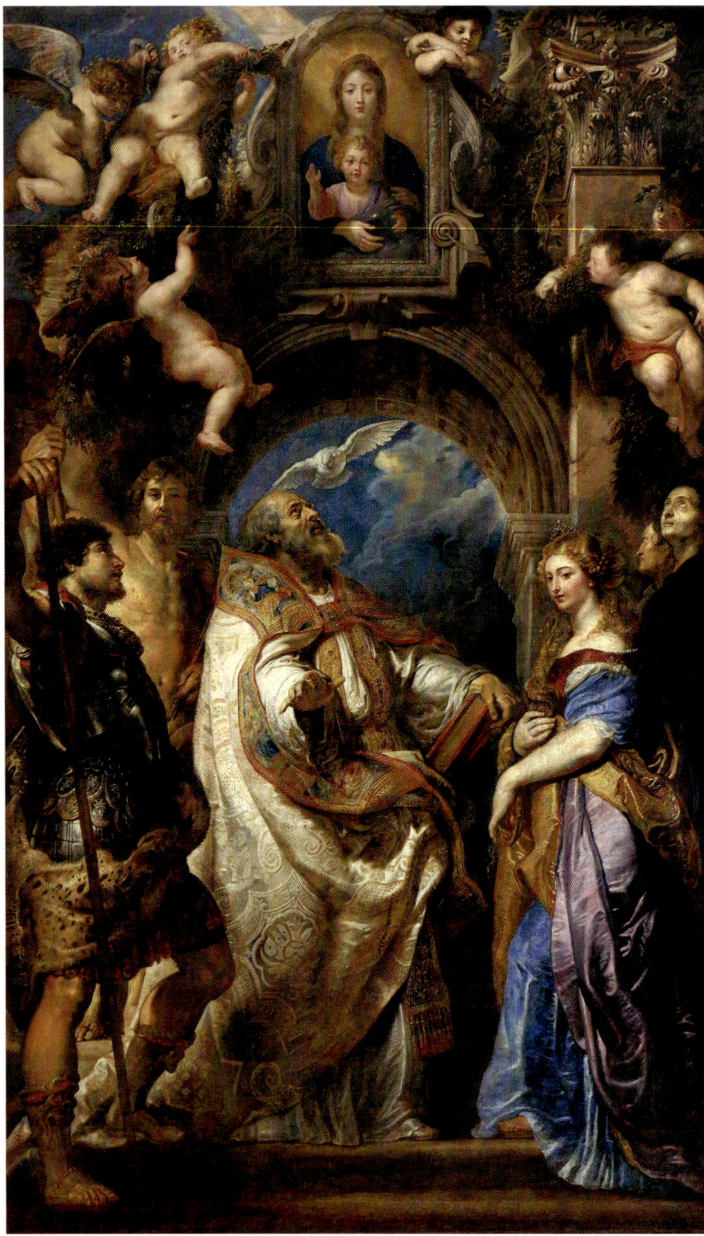

Fig 2 Peter Paul Rubens, *Saint Gregory Surrounded by Saints, Adoring the Madonna of Valicella*, 1606–1607. Oil on canvas, 477 × 288 cm. Musée des Beaux-Arts, Grenoble. MG 97.

arm to embrace Venus but cannot separate his own gaze from the weaponry hanging on the wall behind her. Venus's raised arms and veil may momentarily interrupt Mars's field of vision, but his rapt stare betrays his reluctance to leave the battle. And, indeed, Mars would have his way when the truce ended in 1621.

It is a commonplace of art history that Rubens's return to Antwerp initiated in the Low Countries a triumphalist Catholic art steeped in the priorities of the Roman Church, which valued, above all, the clear expression of orthodoxy. Yet, routinely in Rubens's paintings from the first years after his homecoming, we find him encouraging the viewer to question the relationship between visual appearance and essential truth. Often these paintings find their dramatic resonance in the sort of narrative misalignments present in *The Return from War*. In these decisive moments, we find acts of recognition or misrecognition that set the course for peace or conflict. The burden of interpretation that Rubens's pictures place on viewers is often substantial, and I hope to draw attention to the many ways his paintings troubled assumptions about a simple relationship between sight and truth.

In significant ways, Rubens's portrayal of vision as a polemical human faculty reflected contemporary experience in the Netherlands. The ability to distinguish between essence and appearance was a persistent concern for the region's inhabitants. Fierce allegiances to Catholic or Protestant doctrine had torn families apart and caused many to move to more accommodating cities, but there were continual fears of dissimulators living among communities seemingly unified in their beliefs.[3] The role of images in Christian worship had been fiercely contested from the beginning of the region's conflict, with Catholics understanding images as a means of directing adoration toward God and many Protestants believing it inevitable that the visible object would be misused as the actual focus of adoration and, therefore, become an idol. And this tension between appearance and essence founds its most persistent outlet in the controversy over the consecrated Eucharist, which, depending on one's confessional stance, might be understood as the sacrificial body of Christ in the flesh or as a thin wheaten disc of merely symbolic importance. None of these problems was resolved with the Twelve Years' Truce. Navigating the complicated relationship between the way the physical world presented itself and the true meaning of objects and events loomed large in the collective conscience of the Netherlands. It was to Rubens's great advantage that he quickly understood the appeal of pictures that addressed the uncertainties of visual experience in a city on the front line of Catholic counter-reform.

Among the more remarkable aspects of Rubens's professional re-entry to Antwerp was the fact that he arrived in the city bearing one of the most remarkable altarpieces painted in the new century (fig. 2). This was the rejected first version of his altarpiece for Santa Maria in Vallicella (also known as the Chiesa Nuova), which Rubens would shortly install near his recently deceased mother's tomb in the church at Saint Michael's Abbey.[4] The canvas, nearly five metres in height, depicts Pope Gregory

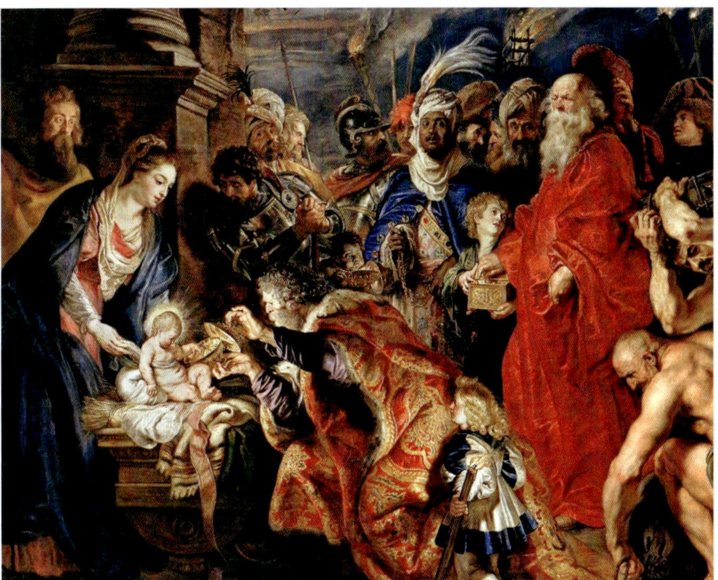

Fig 3 Peter Paul Rubens, *The Adoration of the Magi* (detail), 1609 (enlarged c. 1628–29). Oil on canvas, 355.5 × 493 cm. Prado National Museum, Madrid. P001638. Photo © Prado National Museum.

the Great viewing the Chiesa Nuova's miracle-working image, the Madonna della Vallicella, enframed above an antique Roman arch and honoured with a garland carried by a band of winged putti. In its original context, Rubens's painting would have shown one of the Chiesa Nuova's two patron saints, Gregory, gazing at the other, the Virgin Mary, in the form of the church's favoured Marian icon. Transported to Antwerp, the picture of the awestruck Gregory, who was revered by Catholics and Protestants alike, could be understood as making a more fundamental statement about the legitimacy of religious images in Christian worship.

Antwerp had been among the first cities in the Netherlands to suffer the "Beeldenstorm" in 1566, when Protestant iconoclasts destroyed or otherwise removed thousands of paintings, sculptures, and furnishings from churches throughout the Low Countries in a matter of weeks.[5] Some of Antwerp's altars had received new images in the intervening years of Catholic control, but with the Twelve Years' Truce, the repristination of the city's churches became an acknowledged cause. Seen in this environment, Rubens's picture of Gregory—the Roman pontiff most closely associated with the destruction of pagan idols in Late Antique Rome—became a charged statement in support of Christian image use. Moreover, the altarpiece presented the Marian icon in the terms that legitimize the Christian viewer's veneration of it. At the centre of the sixteenth-century debate over the role of images in Christian worship was the concern that devotees might honour the physical image and not the person represented, thus turning the image into an idol. Rubens's representation of the Vallicella Madonna undercut this concern, presenting the image as a vision emanating from the heavens. The putto just to the right of the Madonna passes its proper right arm through and around the stone frame, guaranteeing that the image that has prompted Gregory's adoration is immaterial. This further suggests that the light streaming down from heaven does not merely shine upon the Madonna della Vallicella but actually carries the image to earth and makes it perceptible to human vision, much as the form of the dove hovering near Gregory's head makes the ineffable Holy Spirit perceptible to human eyes.[6] This altarpiece, which might never have left Italy, spoke especially poignantly to concerns in Antwerp by presenting the mechanics of orthodox image use, distinguishing what one sees from the proper aim of his or her devotion.

The responsible use of Christian images required a devotee to be cognizant of a separation between representation and being. But some occasions demanded an acknowledgement of the presence of divinity in the humble materials of mundane existence. Shortly after his return, Rubens secured the commission to paint a life-sized *Adoration of the Magi* (fig. 3) to decorate the room in Antwerp's city hall where the truce with the northern United Provinces would be signed. The subject of the magi's encounter with the newborn Prince of Peace was well-suited to the occasion, echoing both the emissaries' journey to end hostilities and the wealth that Antwerp hoped would once again flow into the city as a result. Rubens's depiction of the gospel episode is unusual, however, for its representation of the magi's doubt about the king they have journeyed so far to find. At the centre of the composition, the youngest magus, wearing a plumed headdress, looks warily toward the eldest, whose hand hovers above the golden casket containing the gift he has brought Jesus. The eldest's knitted brow and concerned regard for the infant, meanwhile, threaten to derail the narrative. The biblical account of the magi's arrival in Bethlehem describes how "falling down they adored him; and opening their treasures, they offered him gifts..." (Matthew 2:11).[7] Rubens presents the encounter not as unmitigated celebration but rather as a transformational event marked by the magi's passage from hope to skepticism to recognition as they realize the king they sought has indeed begun his life in a manger.

The recognition of Christ's presence in the world, specifically his real bodily presence in the humble appearance of the consecrated Eucharist, was the single most pressing issue in the political and religious life of the Southern Netherlands. In the months after the truce was signed, the free passage of individuals between

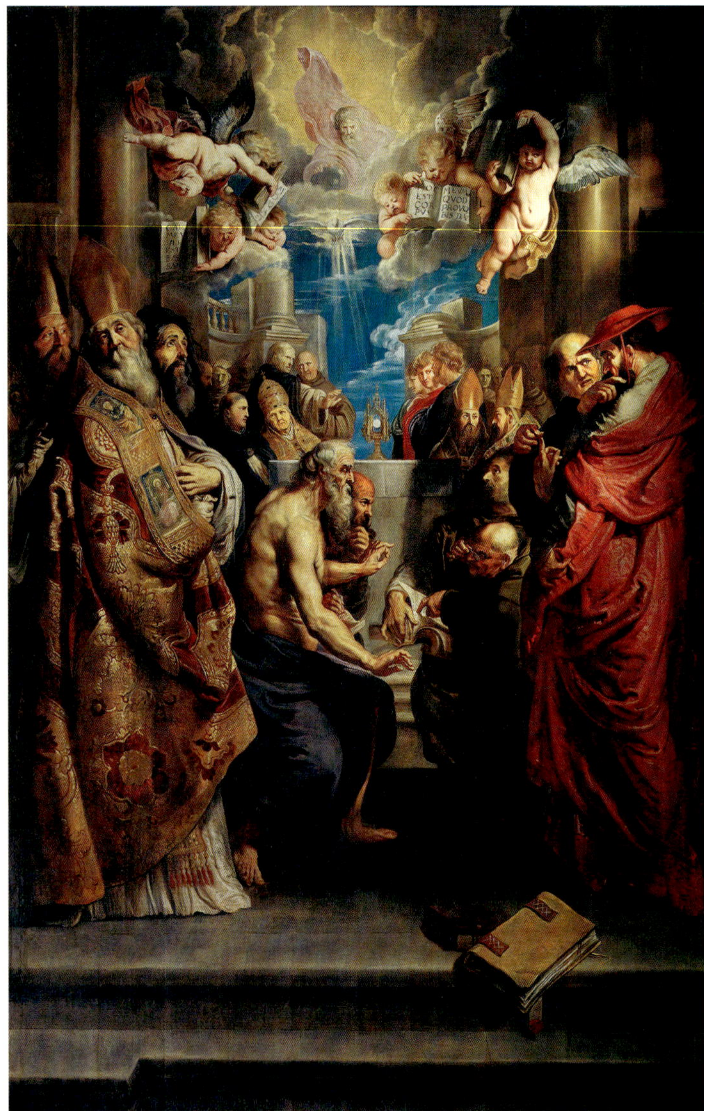

Fig 4 Peter Paul Rubens, *The Real Presence in the Holy Sacrament*, 1609–1610. Oil on panel, 309 × 241.5 cm. Saint Paul's Church, Antwerp. © Lukas-Art in Flanders, photo Hugo Maertens.

the Dutch Republic and the Spanish Netherlands brought an influx of Protestant preaching to the southern cities. For a time, this produced relatively amicable conversation, with the Jesuits of Antwerp and other communities hosting debates with Protestant ministers over the true nature of the Eucharist.[8] By the end of 1609, however, the archdukes came to feel that the potential threat to the region's stability was untenable, and the public expression of heterodox beliefs was again suppressed.[9] In the midst of this volatile debate, the confraternity of the Holy Sacrament housed in Antwerp's Dominican church commissioned Rubens to paint an altarpiece for its chapel. *The Real Presence in the Holy Sacrament* (fig. 4) depicts a hypothetical church council composed of bishops, cardinals, monks, and popes from Late Antiquity to the Middle Ages.[10] The scriptures brought into evidence by the winged sprites circling above the council clarify that the group's principal concern is the ratification of the Eucharistic wafer, seen at the centre of the painting's composition, as being the body of Christ:[11]

> *For my flesh is food indeed: and my blood is drink indeed.* (John 6:56)
> *This is my body, which is given for you.* (Luke 22:19)
> *Take ye, and eat. This is my body.* (Matthew 26:26)

These quotations relate to the gospels' descriptions of the moment in the Last Supper when Christ took the bread of the Passover feast, broke it, and shared it with his disciples. That what appears to be unleavened bread could *be* Christ's body would seem counterfactual; however, this apparently unreconcilable truth is the foundation of the sacrament of communion. In the sixth chapter of John's gospel, Christ's followers refer to his abstruse declaration about his body and blood as a "hard" saying. What Rubens has rendered for his patrons is a single scene that condenses the Church's history of working through these difficult claims in order to illuminate the full truth of Christ's words. The painting's emphasis on the process of evaluation and discernment was hardly a Counter-Reformation dictate. The decree on images issuing from the Council of Trent had stressed clarity of meaning, not ambivalence or debate. The desire to evoke the process by which consensus was built and the truth discerned seems, in this case, to derive from both the context of this particular church's learned monastic community and the urgency of the Eucharistic debate in Antwerp.

Most of Rubens's pictures considered so far were designed for public display, but Rubens's domestically scaled history paintings are an especially interesting class of image in which to consider his desire to interrogate sight and its connection to the discernment of truth. In the middle of Rubens's Italian sojourn, the Haarlem-based Karel van Mander published his *Schilder-Boeck* (1603–1604), roughly translatable as "Book on the Art of Picturing" and the source of the artist-poet's previously quoted thoughts on the need for a more pacific sort of painting in the Low Countries. Like many of his contemporaries, van Mander felt the noblest painters were those who specialized in figures and histories, the production of which were great achievements attainable "without danger, battle, or bloodshed."[12] But an accomplished painter of histories would need to have mastered landscape painting as well, because for van Mander,

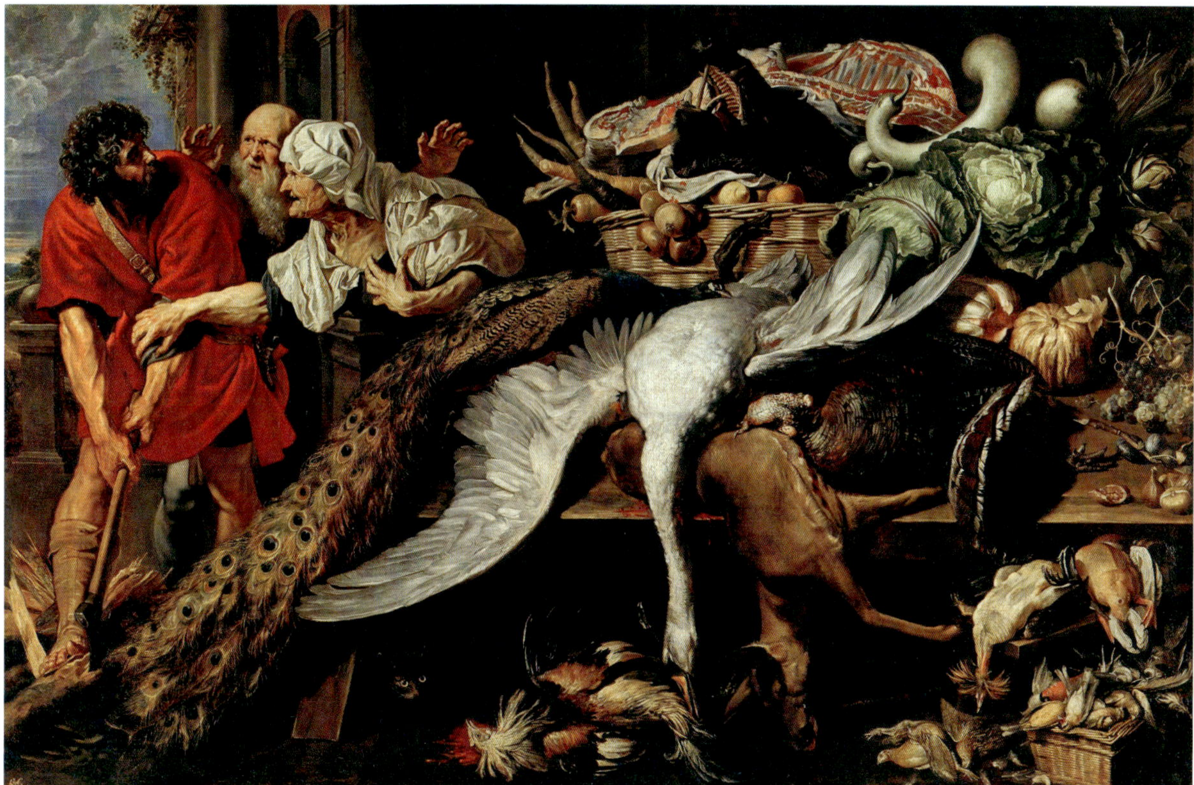

Fig 5 Peter Paul Rubens and Frans Snyders, *The Recognition of Philopoemen*, c. 1609. Oil on canvas, 201 × 313.5 cm. Prado National Museum, Madrid. P001851. Photo © Prado National Museum.

the depiction of histories was inextricably bound to the creation of landscape views. To follow his line of thought, the comprehension and enjoyment of a historical scene depended on the eye's ability to penetrate into a landscape and to move freely across the terrain, selecting small vignettes of figures to attend to in a sequence guided by the painter but ultimately chosen by the viewer. In his study of the *Schilder-Boeck*, Walter Melion summarizes the mechanisms that underlie the visual experience van Mander sought:

> To ensure that the eyes will linger attentively, [van Mander] advises the painter to devise a deep landscape setting into which the eyes may roam, and he adds that it is this panoramic vista, rather than figures proper, that centers the image . . . It is the magnetic pull exerted over the eyes by fully articulated *verschieten*, "distances," that will engage viewers, compelling them to "plough" into the image. In this formulation, sight itself, penetrating deep into the landscape, constitutes the history's action, and seeing displaces the story told as history's principal event.[13]

Under this rubric, the successful execution of a historical scene depended on the freedom allowed for a viewer's attention to move unencumbered through the depth of the pictorial space and to take pleasure in the variety of artistic creation that populated the landscape.[14] Jan Brueghel's contribution to *The Return from War* (fig. 1) is an accomplished example of the pictorial mode van Mander describes, and Rubens himself had experience designing histories in this way.[15] Based on the paintings Rubens made in the wake of his return to Antwerp, however, he had little interest conjuring the sort of pastoral experience van Mander promoted, at least not for the sake of tranquility alone. Rubens would reintroduce seeing as a fundamental narrative action and, frequently, a confrontation that implicated the viewer's own act of vision.

The Recognition of Philopoemen (fig. 5) is an excellent example of how Rubens broke with the compositional style van Mander promoted while taking advantage of the viewing habits engendered by those deep and absorbing landscapes. Plutarch tells the story of a banquet where the virtuous military commander Philopoemen was to be the honoured guest. Dressed modestly and arriving without retinue, the general was mistaken by his hostess for a servant and put to work chopping wood for the feast. Rubens captures the moment when, after her husband has realized the error, the woman stares into Philopoemen's face to determine if in fact this is the great man she had meant to honour.

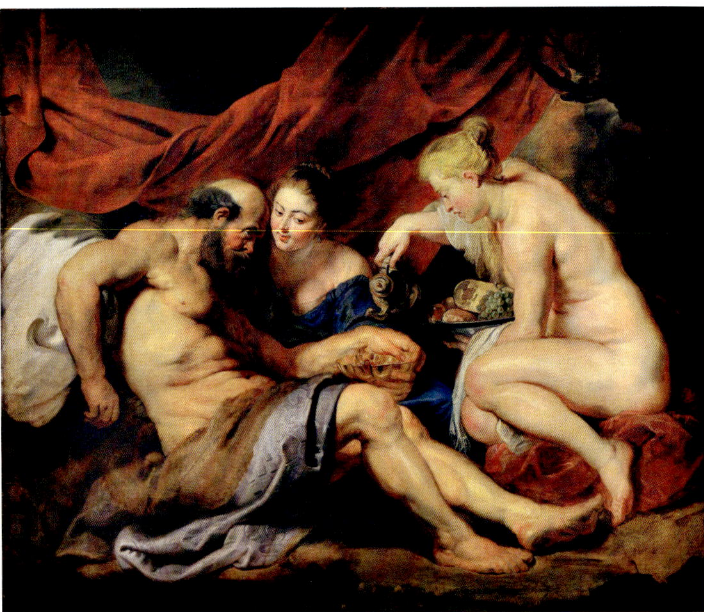

Fig 6 Peter Paul Rubens, *Lot and His Daughters*, c. 1613–14. Oil on canvas, 190 × 225 cm. Collection of an anonymous charitable foundation.

The magnificent peacock feathers that sweep down off the kitchen table and fall at the feet of the Greek general signal the painting's investment in the idea of visual attentiveness. According to myth, the "eyes" of the peacock's tail feathers came from the decapitated head of Argus, whose death came when he had fallen asleep while guarding the nymph-turned-heifer Io. Rubens, who laid out the scene's composition in an oil sketch, left to Frans Snyders the execution of the peacock and all of the fruits, vegetables, and game that fill the painting's right side.[16] This profusion of flora and fauna offers as much pictorial variety and visual interest as any landscape could, and it brings each element to the immediate foreground for the viewer's delectation. As one becomes increasingly absorbed in the act of viewing, a parallel develops between the viewer's experience of the picture and the picture's narrative, relegated to the far left of the canvas, where Rubens added his three figures. Taken as an *exemplum* of virtuous action, Philopoemen's humility is the point of Plutarch's account. This aspect of the narrative is still present in the painting, but Rubens constructed the scene's profusion of appealing visual details to align the viewer's experience with that of the stunned hostess, who had been so distracted by her immediate task that the meaning of her work had all but eluded her.

Rubens was playing a subtle game with the viewer in *The Recognition of Philopoemen*, and the small shock he achieved by catching the viewer between registers of pleasurable visual absorption and narrative conflict was aided by the collaboration with Snyders. On his own, Rubens tended to situate the problematic visual experience directly before the viewer. For instance, the crucial action in *Lot and His Daughters* (fig. 6) is the father's leering gaze, which Rubens emphasizes by allowing the three figures to fill the shallow foreground space. Shown in strict relief-like profile, the silent interaction of Lot and his hesitant daughter becomes almost diagrammatic. The book of Genesis describes how Lot's two daughters, fearful that their family line would end, conspired to inebriate their father and have sexual intercourse with him. On successive nights, Lot impregnated each of them, though the biblical account reports that "he perceived not neither when his daughter lay down, nor when she rose up" (Genesis 19:33-35). Rubens's version of the episode is far more ambiguous about Lot's complicity in the seduction and incest. At issue is what the drunken Lot thinks he sees when he looks at the nude woman refilling his drinking bowl, and Rubens further complicates a viewer's ability to answer that question by basing the painting's composition on Michelangelo's design for *Leda and the Swan* (fig. 7), where Jupiter seduces the swooning Leda after he had assumed the appearance of a white swan.[17] This added layer of artistic reference introduces the possibility that, even as Lot's culpability seems inescapable, he is both seducer and seduced.

Rubens had used the compositional scheme of Michelangelo's *Leda and the Swan* previously in the *Samson and Delilah* (fig. 8) for Nicolaas Rockox, Antwerp's multi-tenured burgomaster. In that picture, the critical misprision has already occurred, and the viewer witnesses the fateful cutting of Samson's hair that will result in his capture by the Philistine soldiers waiting outside the bedroom door. Overcome by Delilah's frequent appeals that he divulge the source of his superhuman strength, Samson has misjudged her beauty for innocence and revealed to her that his powers would leave him if his hair was ever shorn. The pernicious quality of Delilah's beauty is signalled by the statuette standing in a niche on the bedroom's rear wall. This idol of Venus and Cupid define Delilah and her domestic space as possessing a beauty that is potent but superficial and as false as the gods of the Gentiles. Rockox was a trained lawyer and a leading political figure in Antwerp, and he had helped guide the city through complicated political and economic times. Rubens's painting hung above the mantel in Rockox's home and must have functioned, at least in part, as an instructive parable warning against the

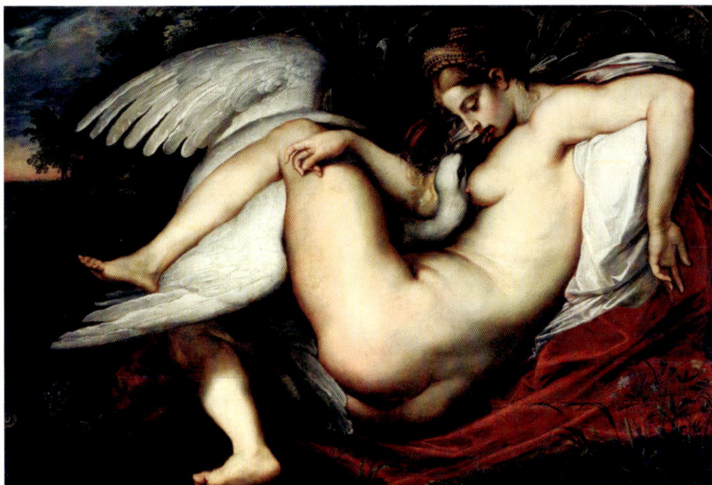

Fig 7 Peter Paul Rubens (after Michelangelo), *Leda and the Swan*, c. 1598–1600. Oil on panel, 122 × 182 cm. Gemäeldegalerie Alte Meister, Staatliche Kunstsammlungen, Dresden. 71. Photo © bpk Bildagentur/Gemaeldegalerie Alte Meister/Hans-Peter Klut/Art Resource, NY.

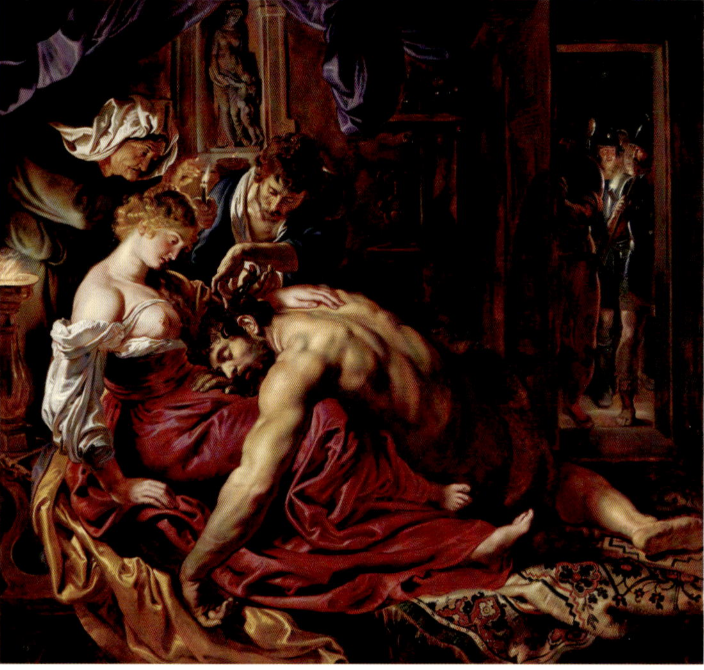

Fig 8 Peter Paul Rubens, *Samson and Delilah*, c. 1609–10. Oil on panel, 185 × 205 cm. National Gallery, London. Bought, 1980. NG6461. Photo © National Gallery, London/Art Resource, NY.

threat of miscalculation based on alluring appearances. Knowing that Rockox was behind Rubens's commissions for both the *Adoration of the Magi* and *Samson and Delilah*, it is perhaps not surprising that Rubens's invention for Rockox's funerary epitaph likewise centres on the complicated role of sight in securing Christian faith.

No episode from Christian history more closely associated vision and belief than the account of the apostle Thomas overcoming his doubts about the Resurrection upon seeing Christ's living body. It was this revelatory moment that Rockox and his wife Adriana Perez had Rubens paint as the central image of their funerary epitaph, originally installed in Antwerp Cathedral (fig. 9).[18] Upon presenting himself to Thomas and the other disciples, Christ differentiated between the faith required of those who have access to the proof of sight and those that believe even in the absence of such proof: "Because thou hast seen me, Thomas, thou hast believed: blessed are they that have not seen, and have believed" (John 20:29). As Barbara Haeger has emphasized, Rubens used the winged structure of the epitaph to embody this evidentiary gap. Unlike the apostles' direct sight of Christ's body, Rockox and Perez are portrayed on the epitaph's wings at one remove from the historical scene, acknowledging that their access to Christ (aside from his presence in the Eucharist) was limited to their meditative visions aided by the prayer book and rosary beads Rubens placed in their hands.[19] The Antwerp couple trust their faith to grant them direct sight of Christ's resurrected body at the Last Judgment, and in as much as the epitaph's central panel is a proxy for visual access to Christ's physical body, it is significant that Rubens chose to present *The Doubting of Thomas* in a format that cropped its figures. During his time in Rome, Rubens had come to know and appreciate the paintings of Caravaggio (1571–1610), whose half-length narratives, ranging from biblical episodes—including *The Doubting of Thomas*—to genre scenes of fortune tellers and card cheats, were highly regarded for their mirror-like reflection of reality. But fears persisted that perhaps accurate visual appearance was all these scenes contained. Precisely at the time Rubens chose to employ this cropped format for Rockox's epitaph, many artists wondered whether the half-length scene could convey anything of a spiritual nature.

Based on the accounts of contemporary painters, as well as that of Caravaggio's later biographer Giovan Pietro Bellori (1613–1696), we know there were serious concerns over the capacity of the half-length format to represent narrative action at all, much less narrative content that directed the viewer's thoughts toward an edifying ideal. Complaints circulated that Caravaggio merely depicted his models *as they were*: humble denizens of Rome, perhaps dressed in character, and holding poses in his studio as he recorded their external appearances. His priority in recording

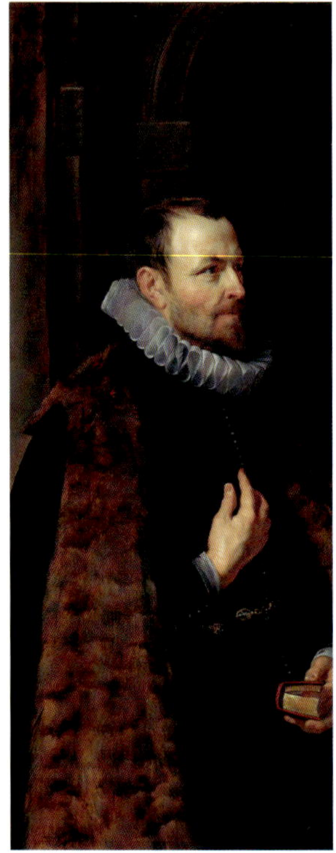
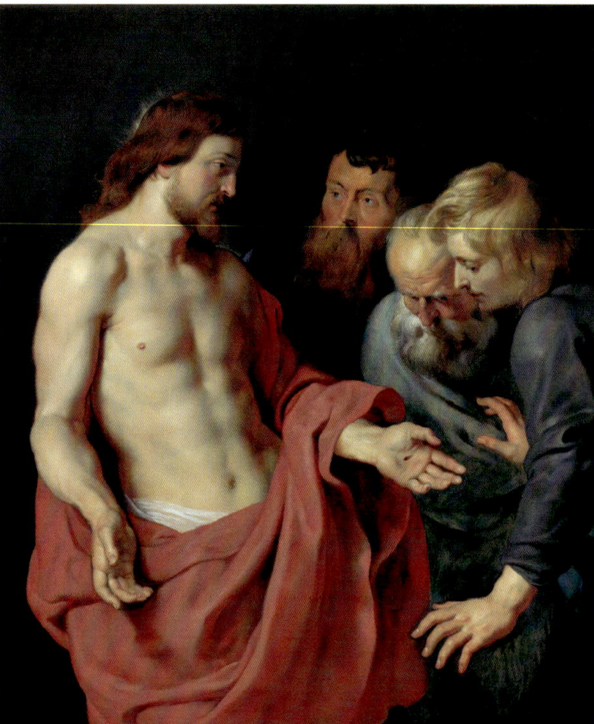
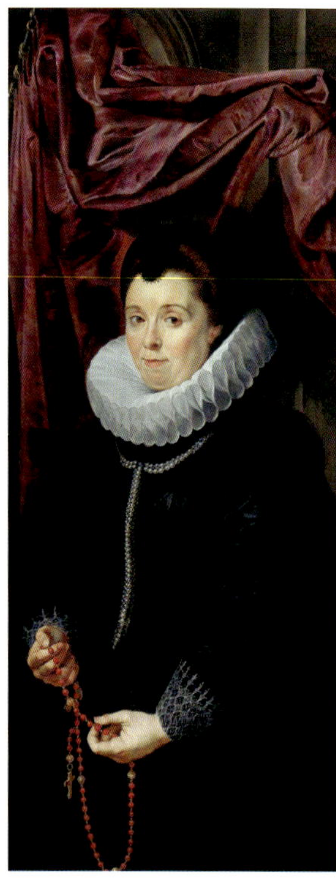

Fig 9 Peter Paul Rubens, *Rockox Epitaph (The Doubting of Thomas)*, 1613–15. Oil on panel, 143 × 123 cm (central). Royal Museum of Fine Arts Antwerp. © Lukas-Art in Flanders, photo Rik Klein Gotink.

the visible fact seemed to drain his figures, and thereby his narrative scenes, of meaningful action.[20] For many of Caravaggio's contemporaries, no matter how adept his skill at capturing surface appearance, his refusal to transform raw visual perception into an idealized expression kept his paintings from the beauty that defined artistic achievement.

The problem was worse still for half-length history paintings. Francesco Albani (1578–1660), a painter active in Rome at the same time as Caravaggio and Rubens, believed the failure of the half-length format as a vehicle for historical narrative lay in its clipped presentation of the human figure, which "as it only appears from the waist up, is disconnect from the thighs, rid of the legs and the ground it stands on, bereft of perspective, concepts, and expression."[21] For Albani, this sort of painting revealed

> the weakness of a painter more suited to painting senseless fruits than to representing stories, etc. Quite another thing is to devote oneself to a subject that requires a multiplicity of figures and this is why one must elucidate concepts in the same manner as the poet, because concepts are necessary in reading poetical compositions, and without this nobody will excuse skillful hands for their weakness in composing.[22]

Bellori, writing after Albani but well-versed in the art critical debates of early seventeenth-century Rome, would also lament Caravaggio's influence in popularizing the half-length narrative, suggesting that the format was best suited merely to the portrayal of heads studied from life.[23]

In the early 1610s, as Rubens continued to pursue compositional strategies that placed visual confrontations at the fore, the half-length was an obvious format to take up. Yet, the half-length's perceived deficiencies help illuminate the precarious balance that Rubens's cropped narrative scenes attempted to achieve. Rubens valued life studies, particularly studies of heads, as a component of his creative process, but he was also a painter committed to an art that transformed nature in order to elucidate concepts that reached beyond the mere facticity of natural appearance. In *The Doubting of Thomas,* the half-length format helps to present Christ's nude torso as a focus of devotion—nearly as an icon—set within the cropped view of the narrative scene.[24] In representing Christ this way, the half-length picture could be imbued with referential meaning that reached well beyond the immediate visual data provided by models, and several of Rubens's epitaph paintings took advantage of this strategy.[25] It is notable, though, that Rubens's activity as a painter of half-length scenes is limited almost exclusively to the 1610s, and it is not entirely evident that he felt comfortable with the format when composing a history for public view.

The half-length narratives considered part of Rubens's corpus are an uneven group ranging from workshop products to a few

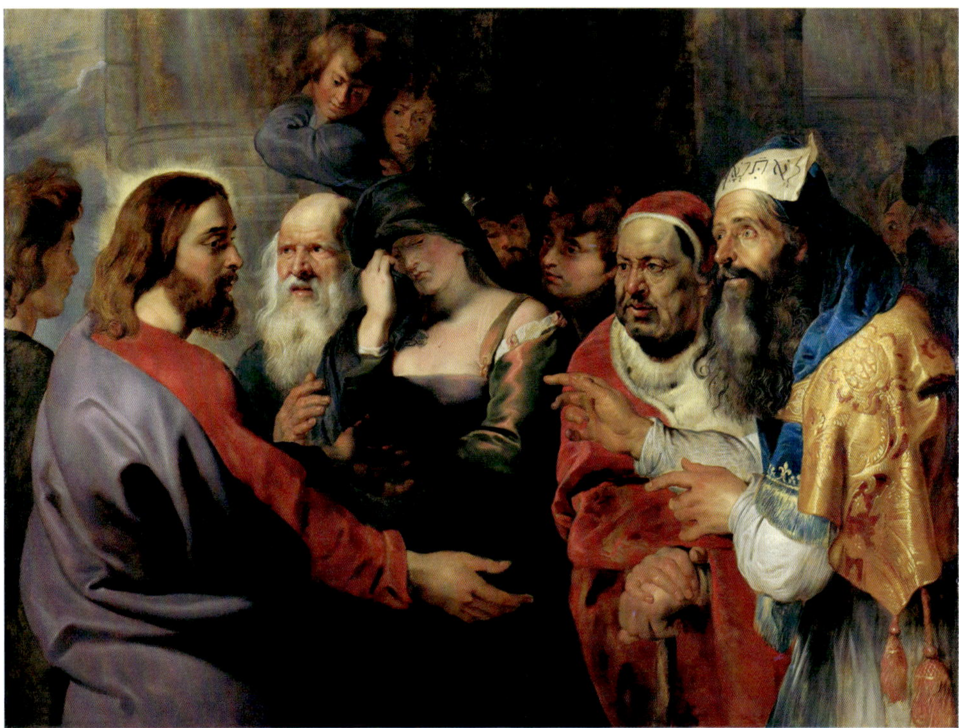

Fig 10 Peter Paul Rubens, *Christ and the Woman Taken in Adultery*, c. 1610–15. Oil on panel, 143 × 194 cm. Royal Museums of Fine Arts of Belgium, Brussels. © Royal Museums of Fine Arts Belgium, Brussels/photo: Grafisch Buro Lefevre, Heule.

fully or nearly fully autograph paintings.[26] In some cases it is possible that Rubens did little more than suggest a narrative subject.[27] Still, the thematic coherence of the group indicates that the master had clearly communicated to his assistants and collaborators the sort of scenes that he felt most appropriate to the format. A number of the half-length pictures, including the epitaphs, depict moments from ancient history—pagan and biblical alike—that enact a philosophical debate or an obscure action or statement, not unlike the "hard sayings" included in *The Real Presence in the Holy Sacrament*. Elizabeth McGrath has described these scenes as each representing an "instructive dilemma," and it may be added that the dilemma in question is frequently that of discerning an internal essence from superficial appearances.[28] Episodes such as *Diogenes Seeking a True Man* and *The Devotion of Artemisia*, Artemisia having become the "living tomb" of her husband, Halicarnassus, after imbibing his ashes, urge the viewer to recognize a meaningful difference between outward appearance and internal content.

Among the half-length narratives recognized as most fully by Rubens himself are *The Tribute Money* (page 184) and *Christ and the Woman Taken in Adultery* (fig. 10), two scenes of Jesus revealing his transcendence of the "Old Law" while debating with Jewish elders. In each, Rubens has caught the narrative in the instant when, as the crowd of elders stare at Jesus's radiant countenance, his words create a moment of potential insight into his divine nature. These scenes possess a marked tension between the close observation of reality and the need to surpass superficial appearance. Each painting includes several heads that originated from Rubens's life studies and that are arranged across the composition in a way that could facilitate further study and reproduction by a workshop assistant. But each picture also includes details that gloss the scene's action through metaphor or reference to external texts or pictures and that enrich the painting's possible interpretations. In recent remarks about *Christ and the Woman Taken in Adultery*, Tine Meganck has noted the significance of Rubens's decision to render Jesus's face in profile, a form that refers to a class of profile portraits of Christ that trace their origin to a supposed first-hand account of his physical appearance.[29] In the Brussels painting, this visual access to the "true likeness" of Christ is set against the spiritual blindness of the shocked Pharisee at the far right, whose incredulity in Jesus's divinity Rubens juxtaposed with a literal transcription of the Mosaic Law's prohibition against adultery. And in a brilliant stroke of visual metaphor, Rubens has the disbelieving Pharisee's accusing finger direct the viewer's eye to the flash of pink threads momentarily visible through the dominant green of the adulteress's shot silk dress. The fabric, like this potentially transformative encounter, reveals an unexpected truth when viewed from the proper angle.

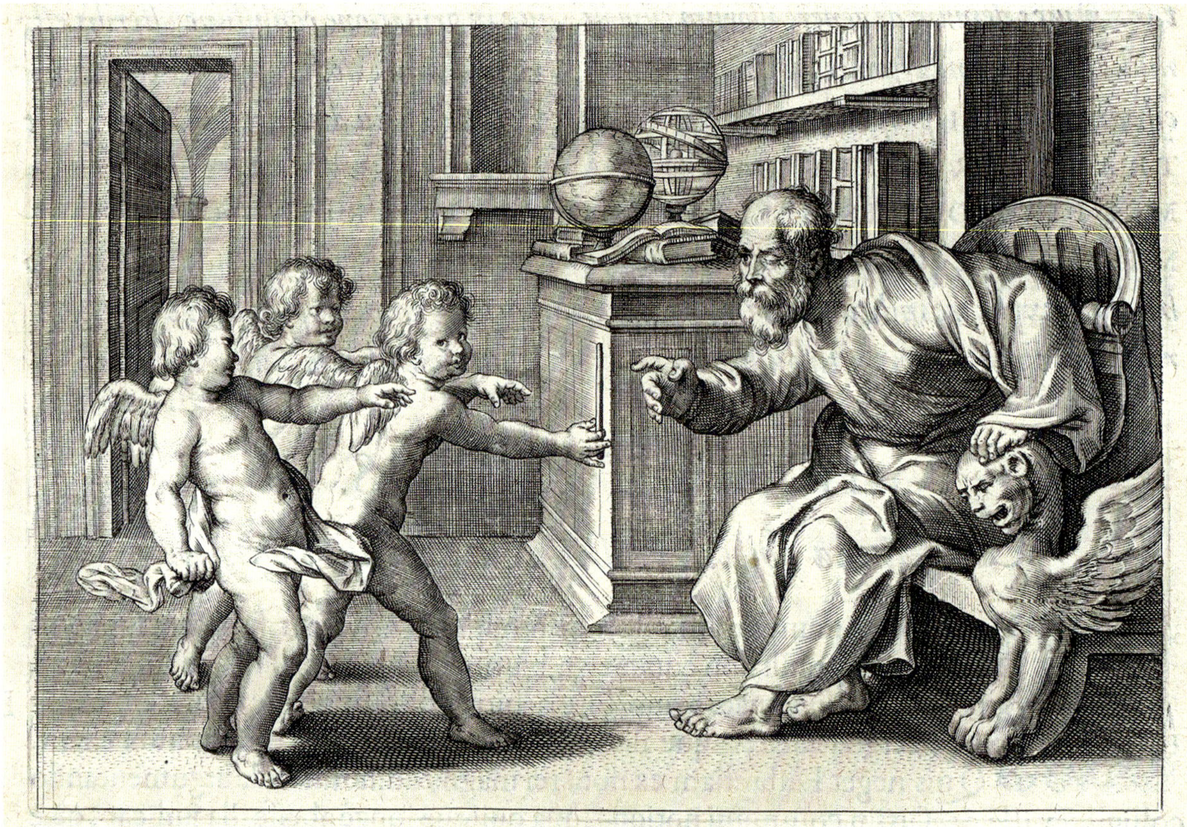

Fig 11 François d'Aguilon and Theodor Galle, after Sir Peter Paul Rubens, vignette of putti and aged scholar learning of binocular vision in *Opticorum Libri Sex*, published 1613. One of six headpieces engraved by Theodor Galle after Peter Paul Rubens, 35 × 22.1 cm (page size). National Gallery of Art, Washington, D.C., Ailsa Mellon Bruce Fund. 1989.36.1. Image courtesy National Gallery of Art, Washington, D.C.

The Tribute Money likewise uses the "true likeness" of Christ's profile to highlight the blindness of the Pharisees, though here the object under discussion is not scripture but image. As the coin used to pay the Roman tax is impressed with Caesar's image, so that which belongs to God bears the image of God.[30] The Pharisees fail to recognize Christ for who he is, and Rubens embodies this incapacity in the elderly man with the sunken mouth who presses forward to examine Christ and whose wandering right eye—focused indistinctly between Christ's face and the coin—compromises his ability to ascertain the full truth of what he seeks to know visually. This strained pose is reminiscent of the elderly scholar in Rubens's illustration for Book III of Franciscus Aguilonius's *Opticorum Libri Sex* (pub. 1613) who cannot properly locate an object in space when his vision is limited to the use of only one eye (fig. 11).[31] Rubens's depiction of the man's compromised sight can be taken as the sort of closely observed physical detail fostered by the three-quarter length format, but it also functions conspicuously as a metaphor for the blindness of those who cannot properly judge the meaning of what they see and who cling to the written word of the Law. Protestant reformers had insisted on seeking spiritual insight in the text of the Bible, to the exclusion of much else. Paintings such as the *The Tribute Money* and *Christ and the Woman Taken in Adultery* present the written Law as a hindrance to the full apprehension of Jesus's divinity, even when that divinity is revealed before one's eyes. While these two pictures were never intended for a religious context, it would not have taken an especially sophisticated viewer to read them in terms of the local religious and political divisions between the southern Catholics and northern Protestants, the new "people of the word."[32]

Having set to work in the Netherlands' northernmost bastion of Roman Catholicism, Rubens quickly recognized the attraction of pictures that addressed local concerns about the need to discern truth from visible appearance. In the first years after his return to Antwerp, Rubens regularly brought episodes of conflicted vision to the centre of his pictures, at times guiding interpretation, at times leaving the viewer with an unsettling sense of ambiguity. Such subtlety was not always well-suited to monumental public commissions, but the discernment of invisible

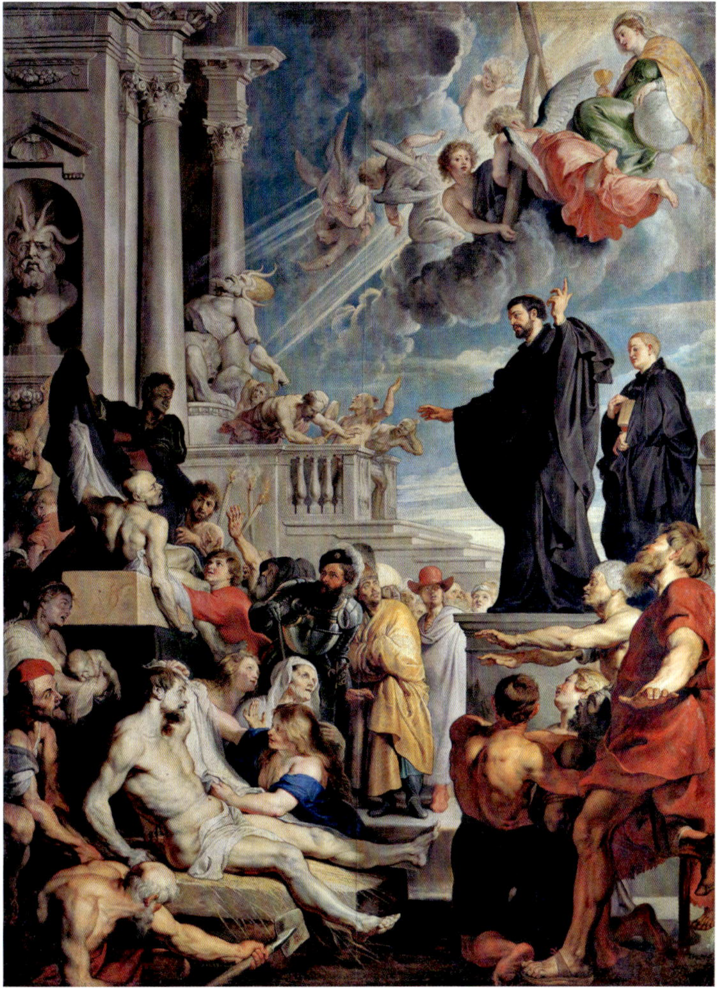

Fig 12 Peter Paul Rubens, *The Miracles of St. Francis Xavier*, c. 1617–18. Oil on canvas, 535 × 395 cm. Kunsthistorisches Museum, Vienna. Photo © Kunsthistorisches Museum, Vienna.

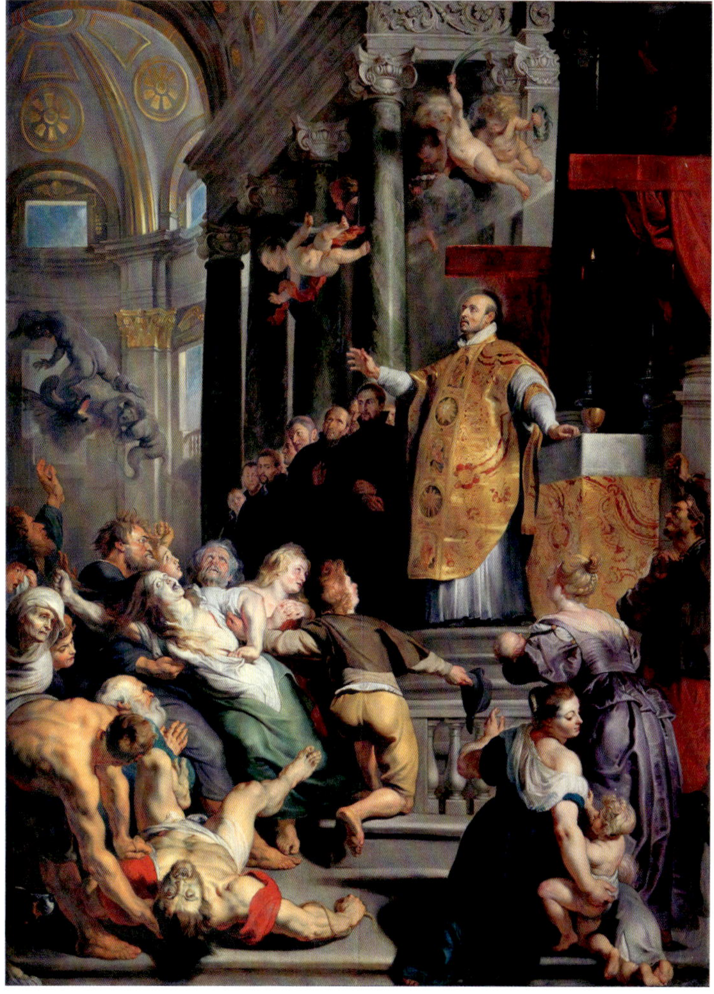

Fig 13 Peter Paul Rubens, *The Miracles of St. Ignatius of Loyola*, c. 1617–18. Oil on canvas, 535 × 395 cm. Kunsthistorisches Museum, Vienna, acquired for the Imperial Picture Gallery in Vienna in 1776. Photo © Kunsthistorisches Museum, Vienna.

character from visible appearance would dominate Rubens's enormous twin altarpieces for Antwerp's Jesuit church, arguably his most influential paintings of the decade (figs. 12, 13). Depicting miracles worked by Francis Xavier and Ignatius of Loyola, respectively the two altarpieces were intended to help promote each man's case for sainthood. Illuminated by the light of faith (depicted as an allegory in *The Miracles of Francis Xavier*), each Jesuit reveals the fraudulent appearances masking hidden forces. Ignatius casts evil spirits out of a man and woman still in the final throes of the demonic possession that operated their bodies against their wills. Francis Xavier—assuming a pose that recalls that of Christ in *The Tribute Money*—brings destruction on a pagan idol whose crumbling form exposes the would-be deity as nothing more than inert stone operated by the illicit spirit that now seems to animate the worried bust sitting in an adjacent niche. These altarpieces were designed as monumental statements of Counter-Reformation Catholicism intended to articulate the powers of spiritual discernment that all Jesuit missionaries streaming from the order's seminaries would hope to emulate throughout the world. For Antwerpers they must have seemed grand and yet still as relevant to the immediate life of the city as anything Rubens had painted.

Thanks go to Caitlin Haskell for her judicious comments on an early version of this essay.

1 Karel van Mander, *The Lives of the Illustrious Netherlandish and German Painters, from the First Edition of the Schilder-Boeck* (1603–1604), vol. 1, *The Text*, ed. and trans. Hessel Miedema (Doornspijk: Davaco, 1994).

2 On the creation of the painting and its early context, see Anne T. Woollett and Ariane van Suchtelen, *Rubens and Brueghel: A Working Friendship* (Los Angeles: J. Paul Getty Trust, 2006), exh. cat. no. 2, 52–59.

3 For background on Nicodemism in the Netherlands and the burgeoning categories of "public" and "private," see Natasha Constantinidou, "Public and Private, Divine and Temporal in Justus Lipsius' 'De Constantia' and 'Politica,'" *Renaissance Studies* 26, no. 3 (June 2012): 345–64, esp. 359–64.

4 Rubens was allowed to install the painting over the altar of the Holy Sacrament in 1610. Hans Vlieghe, *Corpus Rubenianum Ludwig Burchard, Part VIII: Saints*, 2 vols. (Brussels: Arcade Press, 1972), vol. 2, cat. no. 109, 50.

5 David Freedberg, "Painting and the Counter Reformation in the Age of Rubens," in Peter C. Sutton et al., *The Age of Rubens* (Boston: Museum of Fine Arts, 1993), 131–45, exh. cat.; see also the lectures published in Koenraad Jonckheere and Ruben Suykerbuyk, eds., *Art after Iconoclasm: Painting in the Netherlands between 1566 and 1585* (Turnhout: Brepols, 2012).

6 On Rubens's representation of the Madonna della Vallicella as a painting and a vision, see Ilse von zur Mühlen, *Bild und Vision: Peter Paul Rubens und der "Pinsel Gottes"* (Frankfurt: Peter Lang, 1998), 139–76. For further discussion of the painting's address to representation of the sacred, see Klaus Krüger, *Das Bild als Schleier des Unsichtbaren:* Ästhetische *Illusion in der Kunst der frühen Neuzeit in Italien* (Munich: Wilhelm Fink Verlag, 2001), 144–52.

7 All biblical citations refer to the Douay-Rheims translation of the Vulgate.

8 Cynthia Lawrence, "Confronting Heresy in Post-Tridentine Antwerp: Coercion and Reconciliation as Opposing Strategies in Rubens' 'Real Presence in the Holy Sacrament,'" *Netherlands Yearbook for History of Art* 55 (2004): 92–94.

9 Lawrence, "Confronting Heresy in Post-Tridentine Antwerp," 94–96. For background on the archdukes' edict, see A. Pasture, "Le Placard d'Hérésie du 31 décembre 1609: sa portée juridique et son application pendant le règne des archiducs Albert et Isabelle 1609–1633," *Mélanges d'histoire offerts à Charles Moeller*, vol. 2 (Leuven and Paris, 1914), 301–10.

10 On this altarpiece and the proposed identity of the figures, see Vlieghe, *Saints*, vol. 1, cat. no. 56, 73–78; see also Lawrence, "Confronting Heresy in Post-Tridentine Antwerp."

11 The inscriptions read: "CARO [ENIM] MEA VERE EST CIBVS ET SANGVIS MEVS VERE [EST POTVS]"; "HOC EST CORPVS MEVM QVOD PRO VOBIS DA[TVR]"; "ACCIPITE ET COMEDITE: HOC EST CORPVS MEVM."

12 For Van Mander, "figures and histories" [*figuren en historiestukken*] hold the supreme position in the art of schilder-const [*de opperheerschappij in onze kunst*], and their attainment does not require "danger, warfare, or bloodshed" [*gevaar, oorlog of bloedvergieten*]; Van Mander, Den grondt der edel vry schilder-const, ed. Hessel Miedema, vol. 1 (Utrecht: Haentjens Dekkeer & Gembert, 1973), 46.

13 Walter S. Melion, *Shaping the Netherlandish Canon: Karel van Mander's* Schilder-Boeck (Chicago: University of Chicago Press, 1991), 7–8.

14 Van Mander valued this sort of viewing experience as an antidote, or at least an escape, from the recent horrors of war, for which see Melion, *Shaping the Netherlandish Canon*, 7.

15 Before he left Antwerp for Italy, he had collaborated with Brueghel on two versions of *The Battle of the Amazons* that could hardly hew closer to Van Mander's notion of pleasing narrative composition, and a painting such as Rubens's *Aeneas and His Family Departing from Troy*, painted while in Italy, presents multiple narrative vignettes and distant points of visual interest that allow the viewer's eye to wander through the landscape.

16 Friso Lammertse and Alejandro Vergara, *Rubens: Painter of Sketches* (Madrid: Museo Nacional del Prado; Rotterdam: Museum Boijmans van Beuningen, 2018), 90, cat. no. 14.

17 Jeremy Wood, *Corpus Rubenianum Ludwig Burchard, Part XXVI: Copies and Adaptations from Renaissance and Later Artists; III: Artists Working in Central Italy and France*, 2 vols. (New York: Harvey Miller, 2011), vol. 1, nos. 199, 200, 221–33.

18 David Freedberg, *Corpus Rubenianum Ludwig Burchard, Part VII: The Life of Christ after the Passion* (London: Harvey Miller, 1984), cat. no. 18, 81–87.

19 Barbara Haeger, "Rubens' Rockox Triptych: Sight, Meditation, and the Justification of Images," *Netherlands Yearbook for History of Art* 55 (2004): 135–41.

20 Elizabeth Cropper, "Caravaggio and the Matter of Lyric," in *Caravaggio: Realism, Rebellion, Reception*, ed. Genevieve Warwick (Newark, DE: University of Delaware Press, 2006), 47–48, provides an excellent summary of Bellori's concerns with Caravaggio's art.

21 Quoted and translated in Lorenzo Pericolo, *Caravaggio and Pictorial Narrative: Dislocating the* Istoria *in Early Modern Painting* (London: Harvey Miller, 2011), 16.

22 Pericolo, *Caravaggio and Pictorial Narrative*, 16.

23 Giovan Pietro Bellori, *The Lives of the Modern Painters, Sculptors and Architects*, ed. and trans. Alice Sedgwick Wohl, Hellmut Wohl, and Tomaso Montanari (New York: Cambridge University Press, 2010), 185.

24 Haeger, "Rubens' Rockox Triptych," 133–34. For the origins of the half-length narrative in the late medieval bust-length devotional image, see the classic study by Sixten Ringbom, *Icon to Narrative: The Rise of the Dramatic Close-Up in Fifteenth-Century Devotional Painting* (Doornspijk: Davaco, 1984).

25 On the half-length epitaph pictures, see David Freedberg, *The Life of Christ after the Passion*, 11.

26 See the entry on *The Tribute Money* in this catalogue, page 184.

27 For instance, *The Seven Sages Disputing over the Tripod* is preserved in a oil sketch likely produced by the workshop, and Rubens's execution of a lost oil sketch that served as this sketch's model is almost entirely conjectural, see McGrath, *Corpus Rubenianum Ludwig Burchard, Part XIII: Subjects from History*, 2 vols. (London: Harvey Miller, 1997), vol. 2, cat. nos. 1, 9–14.

28 McGrath, *Subjects from History*, 2:11.

29 Tine Meganck, "Rubens on the Human Figure: Theory, Practice, and Metaphysics," in *Rubens: A Genius at Work*, ed. Joost vander Auwera and Sabine van Sprang (Tielt: Lannoo, 2007), 76.

30 Christopher J. Nygren, "Titian's *Christ with the Coin*: Recovering the Spiritual Currency of Numismatics in Renaissance Ferrara," *Renaissance Quarterly* 69 (2016): 449–88, provides a thorough analysis of the exegetical tradition around this confrontation, with special emphasis on the devotional resonances of the coin. The patristic interpretations that Nygren adduces, while brought to bear here on Titian's painting for the Este court, were still important for Rubens's contemporaries in the Spanish Netherlands when considering this moment from Christ's ministry.

31 J. Richard Judson and Carl van de Velde, *Corpus Rubenianum Ludwig Burchard, Part XXI: Book Illustrations and Title Pages*, 2 vols. (London: Harvey Miller—Heydon and Son, 1978), vol. 1, cat. no. 13, 109–10, fig. 65. See also Tine Meganck, "Peter Paul Rubens and the Antwerp Jesuit Church," in Vander Auwera and Van Sprang, *Rubens: A Genius at Work*, 219.

32 On the phenomenon of medieval and early modern Christians defining their communities through representations of Jews and Jewish history, see Herbert L. Kessler and David Nirenberg, eds., *Judaism and Christian Art: Aesthetic Anxieties from the Catacombs to Colonialism* (Philadelphia: University of Pennsylvania Press, 2013).

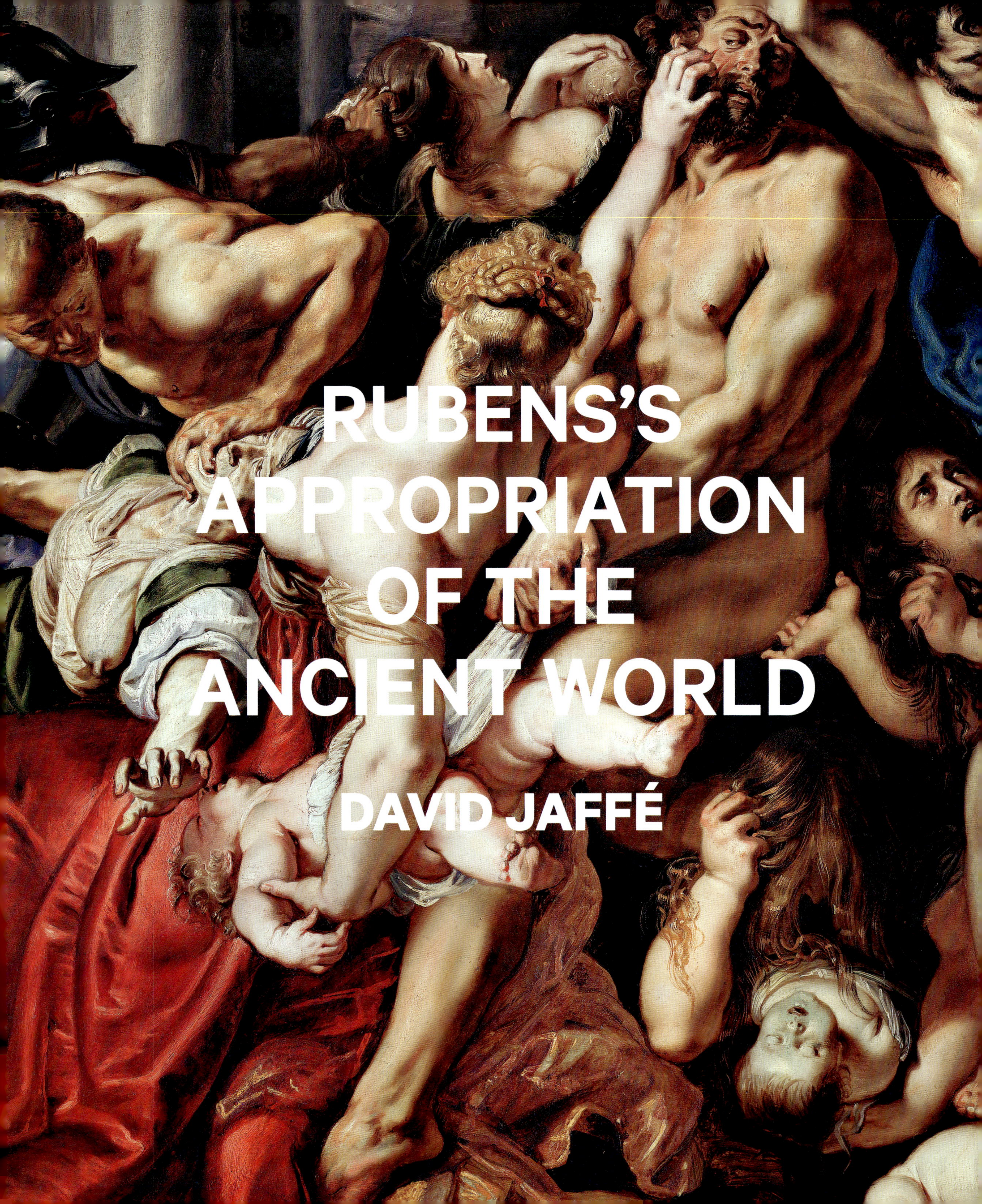

RUBENS'S APPROPRIATION OF THE ANCIENT WORLD

DAVID JAFFÉ

RUBENS'S VISION OF ANCIENT ART had a particular origin and character. He probably began by studying Roman engraved gems and coins, a subject of great interest in the Netherlands in the late sixteenth century, learning from discussions within Humanist circles in Antwerp about the ancient world in general, and about its coinage and textual interpretation. His principal teacher, Otto van Veen (widely known by his Latinized name, Vaenius), was himself a scholar, as well as an artist. Schooled in Latin, Rubens was to become not only an expert in classical antiquity but part of an international Republic of Letters, with wide interests in politics as well as archaeology.

He was generally curious about other cultures.[1] He reported with interest in 1628 that the Dutch had discovered Australia,[2] and he painted an Indigenous "Native American" quiver in his *Diana and the Nymphs Spied upon by Satyrs*.[3] In addition, the legendary Amazons had fired Rubens's imagination from an early age, even before he had seen any of the great representations of this subject in classical reliefs. One such from the Royal Ontario Museum shows the hero, Achilles, supporting the Amazon, Penthesilea; he has mortally wounded her, but finds himself overcome with love for the dying queen.[4] For Rubens, fragments of the ancient world offered the challenge of reconstructing from texts and images the feelings and emotions of his ancient heroes.

Visiting Rome for the first time in 1602, and again from 1605 to 1608, must have been a revelation to him as he pieced together the ancient art he previously knew largely from fairly crude and schematic engravings, such as those in Giovanni Battista de'Cavalieri's compendium of sculptures, or other secondary reproductions. Before he left Antwerp in 1600, Rubens would already have studied small bronzes and even plaster casts of some of the most famous ancient works. Kings like Francis I of France, the Hapsburg emperor Charles V, and Britain's Charles I, had the means to order life-sized metal casts, but others may have managed to obtain plasters made from the same moulds, not to mention wax and graphic versions. Whether or not these were widely available, there is ample evidence that Antwerp collections of the period included small bronze reductions, and these statuettes did supply completed visions. Of course, seeing the texture and scale of the original marbles in Rome would have been another matter.

Unfortunately, the surviving sculptures were battered. Headless torsos had to be rebuilt. Rubens would have welcomed the challenge of visualizing and repairing lost limbs or of improving on earlier Renaissance reconstructions of famous ancient statues. We get an impression of this in Rubens's *Laocoön* (fig. 1, 2), where he tries out a version of the missing right arm of the Trojan priest who battles with the serpents strangling his sons.[5] The prevailing solution was a raised straight arm, but Rubens intuitively supplied the bent arm (fig. 3), which we now know to be correct. He then explored different viewpoints and multiple variations, and was to return repeatedly to his drawings—and his memories—of the sculpture.

It could be argued that the the Laocoön group left its imprint on most of High Renaissance art, starting with Michelangelo, who was consulted about the restoration when it was discovered in 1506. Rubens became almost obsessed with the "boys with snakes" theme, as well as the design potential of triplet groupings—the threesomes in *The Massacre of the Innocents* are a distant echo (page 176). His fascination with the *Laocoön* played out in gender exploration, in Hell scenes, and in the formulae of struggling figures migrated to Amazon battles.[6] He drew inspiration

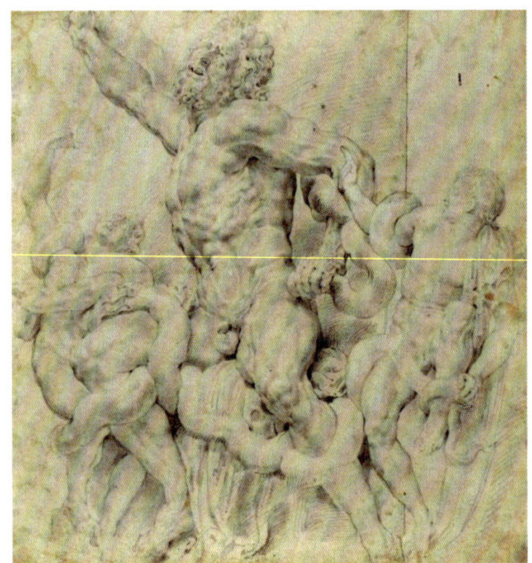

Fig 1 Peter Paul Rubens, *Laocoön and His Sons*, 1601–02. Black chalk with white heightening and wash, 47.5 × 45.7 cm. Veneranda Biblioteca Ambrosiana, Milan. From the Resta 2 Codex. F 249 inf. Sheet 4. Photo © Veneranda Biblioteca Ambrosiana/Mondadori Portfolio/Bridgeman Images.

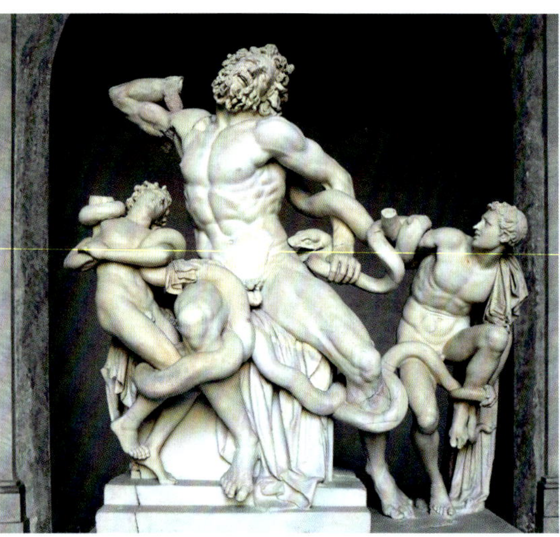

Fig 2 Hagesandros, Athenedoros, and Polydoros, *Laocoön and His Sons*, also known as the *Laocoön Group*. Marble, copy after an Hellenistic original from c. 200 BC, 208 × 163 × 112 cm. Vatican Museums. 1059, 1064, 1067.

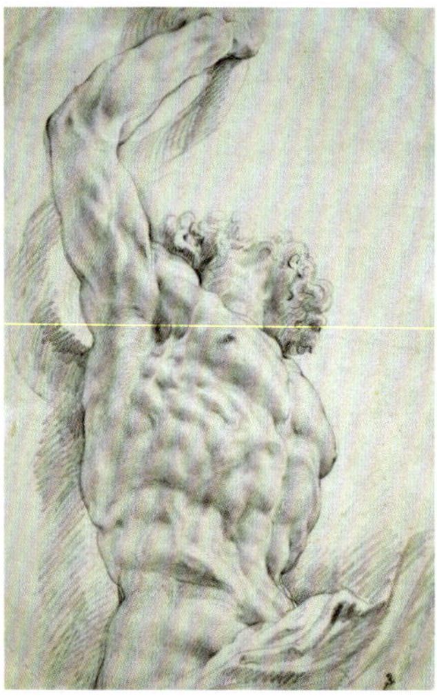

Fig 3 Peter Paul Rubens, *Laocoön*, c. 1601/02. Black chalk, 45.6 × 29.6 cm. Kupferstichkabinett, Staatliche Kupferstich-Kabinett, Dresden. C 1874-22 a. Photo © bpk Bildagentur/Kupferstichkabinett, Staatliche Kunstsammlungen, Dresden/Herbert Boswank/Art Resource, NY.

from the sculpture in less confrontational contexts as well, for example, in *The Triumph of Venus* (fig. 4),[7] and in the famous *Sea Nymphs Towing Maria de' Medici's Ship into Marseilles* (Musée du Louvre).[8]

For Rubens, art was above all the designing of interacting and sometimes struggling figures. He was notably inventive in his reworkings of and variations on the poses of the great sculptures of antiquity—and in his drawings of the *Laocoön*, he literally untangled the group into its separate component figures, and then quoted the individual parts to remake them in his own style. Moreover, it is hard to imagine another artist so immersed in the emotional charge of an ancient statue. The almost feral energy of the deep undercutting and drill-work in sculptures like the *Laocoön*, especially evident in the priest's beard and pulsating arteries, were obsessively captured in Rubens's early drawings of the statue. The revelation of how these vibrant pitted surfaces could amplify expression flowed into the iron-spring locks of hair in his early oil sketches and his own Hermitage *Ecce Homo*.[9] The turbulent Angel Gabriel in the Vienna *Annunciation*, included in this exhibition, springs from this ancient expression.

When Rubens returned to Antwerp in 1608, his challenge was to fuse the antique sources he had studied so avidly with the demands of narrative painting. Sometimes this integration was done so well that the antique building blocks need to be teased out of the composition. For example, *Jupiter Tonans* is the model for Christ armed with a thunderbolt, as Saint Dominic envisaged him, in the painting *Saint Dominic and Saint Francis Protecting the World from Christ's Wrath* (Lyon Musée des Beaux-Arts).[10] The pose may have been adulterated through a Giambologna bronze—which facilitated the angle of the aerial viewpoint—but the power of ancient authority underpins it.[11] For Rubens, the art of Michelangelo and his followers was essentially an extension of the classical world; these modern artists became for him gifted interpreters of a very fragmentary heritage.

Rubens's huge high altar for the Jesuit church in Antwerp (Saint Charles Borromeo), *The Miracles of Saint Francis Xavier* (fig. 6), is another example of his flawless integration of classical influences.[12] The torso of the marble statue the *Old Centaur Tormented by Eros* (Musée du Louvre) is quoted for the bound man kneeling on the right (figs. 5, 6), a reference that has been overlooked because it is so seamlessly integrated in style with the other protagonists in the miracle. Rubens must have expected his audience to recognize some of his references to the famous examples of ancient art, familiar through prints and guidebooks.

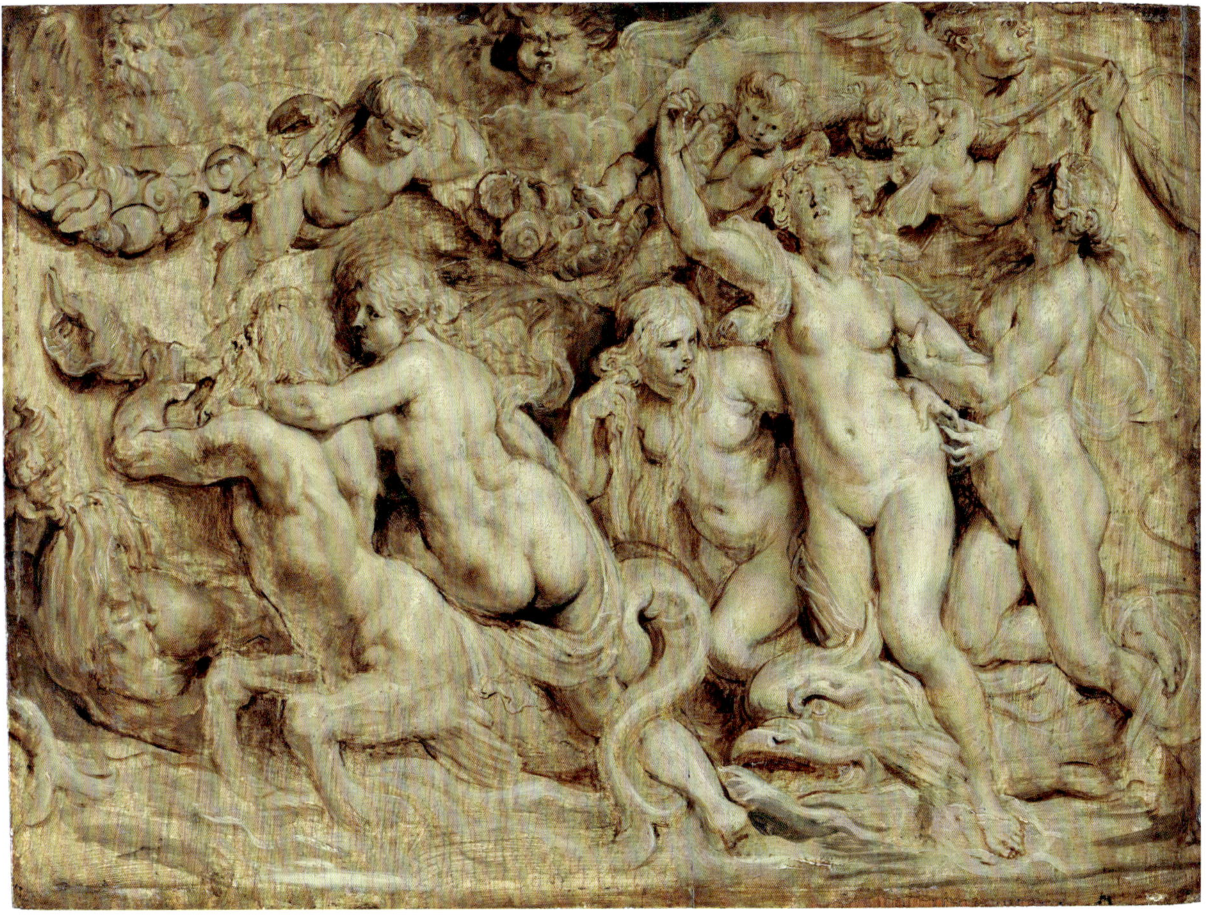

Fig 4 Peter Paul Rubens, *The Triumph of Venus*, 1628. Grisaille oil over black chalk indications on panel, 34.5 × 48.5 cm. Fitzwilliam Museum, Cambridge, UK. PD.7-2012. Photo © The Fitzwilliam Museum, Cambridge.

But many of them were assimilated and absorbed to a degree that they must have become almost an unconscious practice.

Rubens's public profile was bolstered through reproductions. Already by 1612, his *Santa Helena* of ten years earlier had been engraved by Jacques Callot.[13] By this time, Rubens already had a plan to publish reproductions of his inventions and had arranged for Cornelis Galle to engrave his *Judith and Holofernes*;[14] there followed, among others, Lucas Vorsterman's 1620 *Raising of the Cross*, and the great *Battle of the Amazons* in 1623 (pages 234–235). The last two, both exhibited here, were dedicated respectively to the Earl of Arundel and to his wife, Alethea Talbot. The dedications indicate that by 1620 Rubens was reaching out to an international audience, and his choice of the subject suggests he was marketing himself as a recreator of the ancient world. In tracking Rubens's development as a painter, it is easy to neglect his promotional interest in reproductions and their use for understanding his art. His *Self-Portrait* of 1622–1623 would come to be engraved by Paulus Pontius and released in 1630.

Perhaps the least considered group of Rubens engravings are his earliest. The book he illustrated for his brother Philip, which was produced as *Electorum libri II* in 1608, shows various antiquities needed to elucidate special antiquarian issues, such as the precise appearance of Roman togas; the size of the *mappa;* or cloth, that was dropped to start races, and instruments of sacrifice.[15] The Farnese *Flora* (fig. 7) was illustrated in the brothers' book simply to make a point about costume, but the suggestive transparency of the dress around her ankle and her gesture of raising her skirt were to reverberate throughout his art. Rubens used form-clinging drapery to great effect in his religious as well as secular paintings, including the sensuous posteriors of Magdalenes or allegorical figures and works like *The Flight of Lot and His Family from Sodom* (page 154), in which the see-through

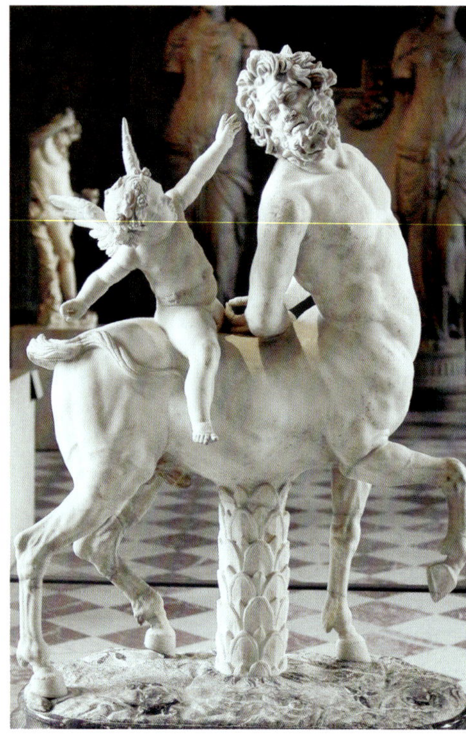

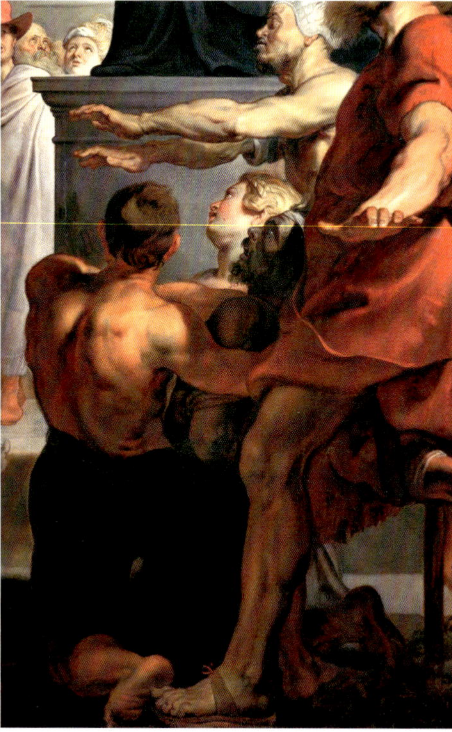

Fig 5 Artist unknown, *Old Centaur Tormented by Eros*. Roman copy (first and second centuries AD) of a Greek original of the second century BC. Marble, 147 × 107 × 52 cm. Musée du Louvre, Paris, Borghese Collection, purchase, 1807. MA 562 (MR 122). Photo by Jastrow.

Fig 6 Peter Paul Rubens, *The Miracles of Saint Francis Xavier* (detail), c. 1617–18. Oil on panel, 535 × 395 cm. Kunsthistorisches Museum, Vienna. 519. Photo © Kunsthistorisches Museum, Vienna.

dress reveals the outline of the angel's leg. Flora's back view already appears in the inner circle of heaven in his image of *All Saints* for the illustrated breviary of 1614 (page 280).

Perhaps the drawing *Two Wrestlers*, after the Roman marble in the Medici collection, is an illustrative example of the process of dismantling a classical composition and then rebuilding it (figs. 8, 9).[16] Rubens made a thumbnail pen sketch in the lower right, including his ideas for the missing heads. A somewhat different reconstruction of the ancient group is included in the Rubens/Brueghel 1617 *Sense of Sight*, and, as any visitor to the Uffizi Tribuna will recall, this restoration is still canonical today.[17] The ancient group itself had survived only as two legless torsos.[18] In the Fitzwilliam sheet, Rubens raises the group and adds alternative arms and legs. In other drawings, Rubens then challenged himself to build different wrestlers from it, showing one man leaning back and throwing another in an off-balance action.[19] The downward thrust on the bent arm still haunts his *David Slaying Goliath*.[20] The back view of the group again as the devil in the 1620 Fogg drawing for *Saint Gregory* for the Jesuit church in Antwerp,[21] and, about a decade later, in the kneeling servant setting down the tripod in *Briseis Given Back to Achilles* (fig. 10.[22] Rubens was engaged in the challenge of first, discovering what the ancient artist's piece might have really looked like and then hijacking its message.

In *Briseis Given Back to Achilles*, the back of the wrestler diagonally leads us into the tent, where the dead Patroclus is being mourned by two distressed women.[23] Achilles springs forward, mimicking the *Apollo Belvedere* pose, to meet his returned love, who modestly gathers her "toga-powered" dress, which dominates the composition. The scene is flanked by herms of Peace herself, and by Mercury, the bringer of Peace. Is the prominent athletic back also meant to foreshadow the sporting contests that characterized peace in ancient times?

Rubens's predilection for allowing figures sufficient space for movement is evident in his raising of the lower figure from his flattened pose in the *Wrestlers*, and can be seen again in his copy of an ancient gem, the *Triumph of Licinius*.[24] In Rubens's drawing after the *Licinius* (British Museum), he uncoils the crushed man just as he does for the lower wrestler. Even at the end of his life, Rubens perhaps had *The Wrestlers* in mind in his design for *The Fall of the Giants*, a work executed for him by Jacob Jordaens, emphasizing the desperate resistance to being crushed.[25]

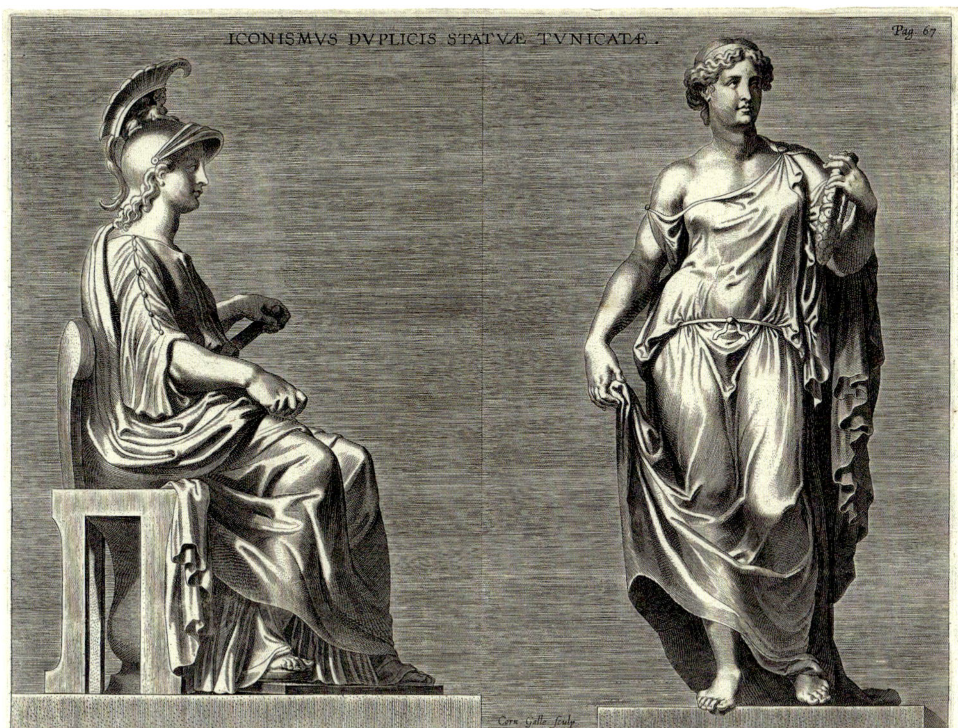

Fig 7 Philip Rubens, after Peter Paul Rubens, Iconismus Duplicis Statuae Tunicatae, illustration of *Roma* and the Farnese *Flora* statues on page 67 of the first book of Philip Rubens's "Electorum Libri II" (Antwerp: 1608), 1608. Engraving, 20.4 × 27.6 cm. British Museum, London. 1891,0414.1245. Photo © The Trustees of the British Museum.

Here Rubens is engaging with a Northern Renaissance visual commentary by Pieter Coecke van Aelst, which he knew from his own copy of the drawing, but the core problem remained the stone group.[26]

There is often a challenge in identifying precise antique sources in Rubens's work, because of the influence of views of statuettes by Willem Danielsz van Tetrode and Giambologna, but these essentially function as modern sculptors' guides for Rubens to aid in the interpretation of the ancient visual language, and were filters used to supplement the direct use of ancient sources.

We do not know exactly when Rubens made the drawings for his brother's *Electorum libri II*, but he may have begun gathering the material that was used in the book around 1602–1603. The plate of *Roma* and the Farnese *Flora* (fig. 7) may even suggest the artist had the idea of making a publication of his own on antique sculpture, with much superior engravings to those in the available compendia of antiquities. If so, such a publication would surely have included the *Laocoön*, and also the Farnese *Hercules*, as well as works such as those drawn in the sketchbook now in the Ambrosiana. It would also have included the Borghese marble *Centaur Tormented by Cupid*. Certainly, Rubens was fascinated by this invention. He played with a free variant of the back view of Cupid in his putto riding a goat on the Solomonic column in the 1602 *Saint Helena Discovering the True Cross*, Grasse.[27] Rubens added a literal quote in the angel below the Virgin in his *Assumption of the Virgin* from the 1614 *Breviarium Romanum* (fig. 13), and the figure reappears in many later variations.[28]

It is clear that the bulky figure style he produced for his final Roman altarpiece is really an adaptation of the lessons the artist learned copying classical statues. The massive presence of the male figure (*togatus*) in the plate in Philip's book, with its majestically folded drapery, ostensibly drawn to show how the folds in a toga worked, has a visual impact that suggests a grander artistic aim (fig. 11). The monumental simplification seen here was to be the foundation of Rubens's narrative paintings and tapestries of the 1610s. In taking his inspiration in this way from ancient art, Rubens was following in the footsteps of earlier painters, especially Raphael, in his tapestry cartoon designs. But there are other clues in his own work showing how classical art provided him with his essential first principles. Artists of previous generations, such as Hendrik Goltzius and Frans Floris, may have grasped the potential of muscle men, but Rubens understood the

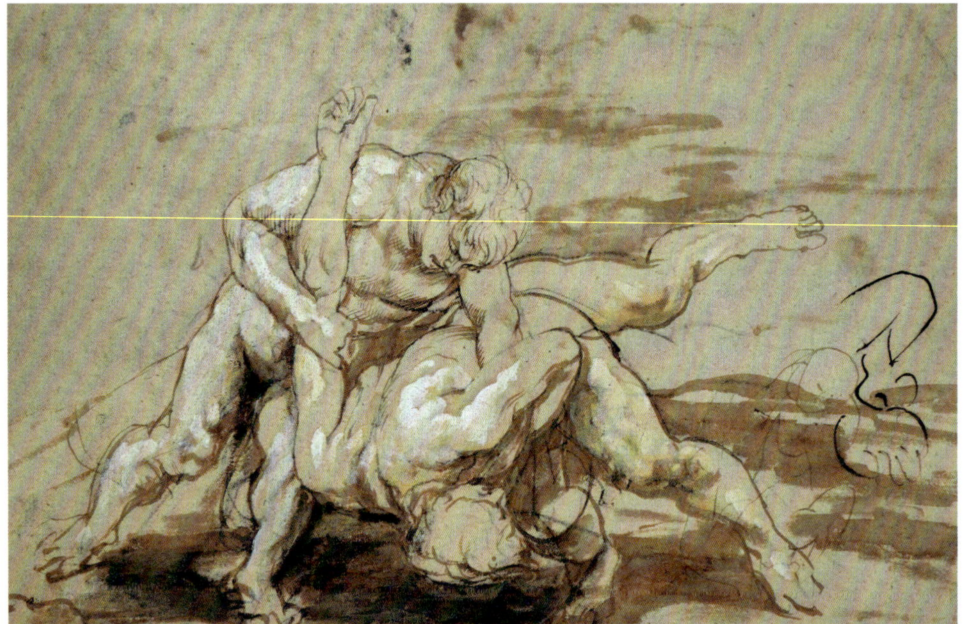

Fig 8 Peter Paul Rubens, *Two Men Wrestling*. Charcoal, pen and bistre ink, point of the brush, brown wash, heightened with white and yellow ochre on buff paper, 23.5 × 36.6 cm. The Fitzwilliam Museum, Cambridge, UK. 2181. Photo © The Fitzwilliam Museum, Cambridge.

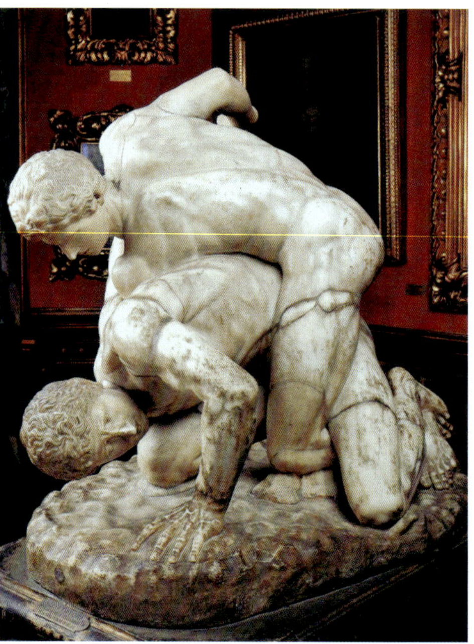

Fig 9 Unknown Roman artist, Lateral view of the sculpture group depicting the *Wrestlers*, copy from the bronze original from Pergamum, first century AD. Parian marble, lychnite variant, 89 cm (height). The Uffizi Galleries. 1914 no. 216. Photo: George Tatge, 1999, © Alinari/Art Resource, NY.

power of massed folds. Proof of this can be seen in the drawing for his late *Self-Portrait* in the majestic, Bernini-like massing of the folds of the cloak (fig. 12). (The effect is less readable in the finished painting, as the blacks have become sunken.)[29]

Rubens's relationship with ancient statues can be tracked in an interesting way in the *Triptych with the Resurrection of Christ* (*Moretus Epitaph*) in the Antwerp Cathedral (fig. 13), designed as an epitaph and featuring the *Resurrection* with, to either side, the name saints of Jan Moretus and Martina Plantin. *Saint Martina* is dressed *all'antica*, as was testified in the reproduction of the figure by Rubens's engraver Lucas Vorsterman (in which she was turned into Saint Catherine).[30] The Moretus epitaph, made for the publishing family with which Rubens worked, has another ancient reference—an antique statue of Apollo emerging out of the gloom on the top right. This is featured as a pagan idol that Saint Martina destroyed by her prayers.

Rubens was perhaps uncomfortable about showing the actual destruction of ancient art. He paints Apollo still standing and intact, even though his temple is drastically collapsing around him, adding drama to the central *Resurrection* next to it. Again, in the *Martyrdom of Saint Catherine* in Lille, the Apollo statue is still proudly erect. Apollo may not have appreciated musical competition, as Midas and Pan discovered, but he was a figure representative of classical culture in the painter's world, and he appears explicitly as such in Rubens's designs for title pages for books, among other things—for example, that of the poems of Sarbievius ("the Polish Horace").[31]

Rubens's allegiance to the pagan world is illustrated in his design of the Eucharist tapestries commissioned for Spain by his patron, the archduchess of the Spanish Netherlands, Isabella. In *Triumph of the Catholic Faith*, the personification of the Catholic faith is shown holding the host—but, typically for Rubens, both the putto and Catholic Faith herself look back almost wistfully at the trailing procession of ancient wisdom walking behind her chariot. In this case, a man carrying a sphere has been identified as ancient "Astronomy," a Socrates type as representing "Philosophy," and a younger man is associated with secular poetry. These figures have indeed been identified as Plato and Socrates themselves, along with Virgil.[32] Good Christians trample dragons, devils, and even heretics, but the inherited learning of antiquity is another matter. Astronomy was a reminder of the then-current controversy. Rubens's friend Nicolas-Claude Fabri de Peiresc

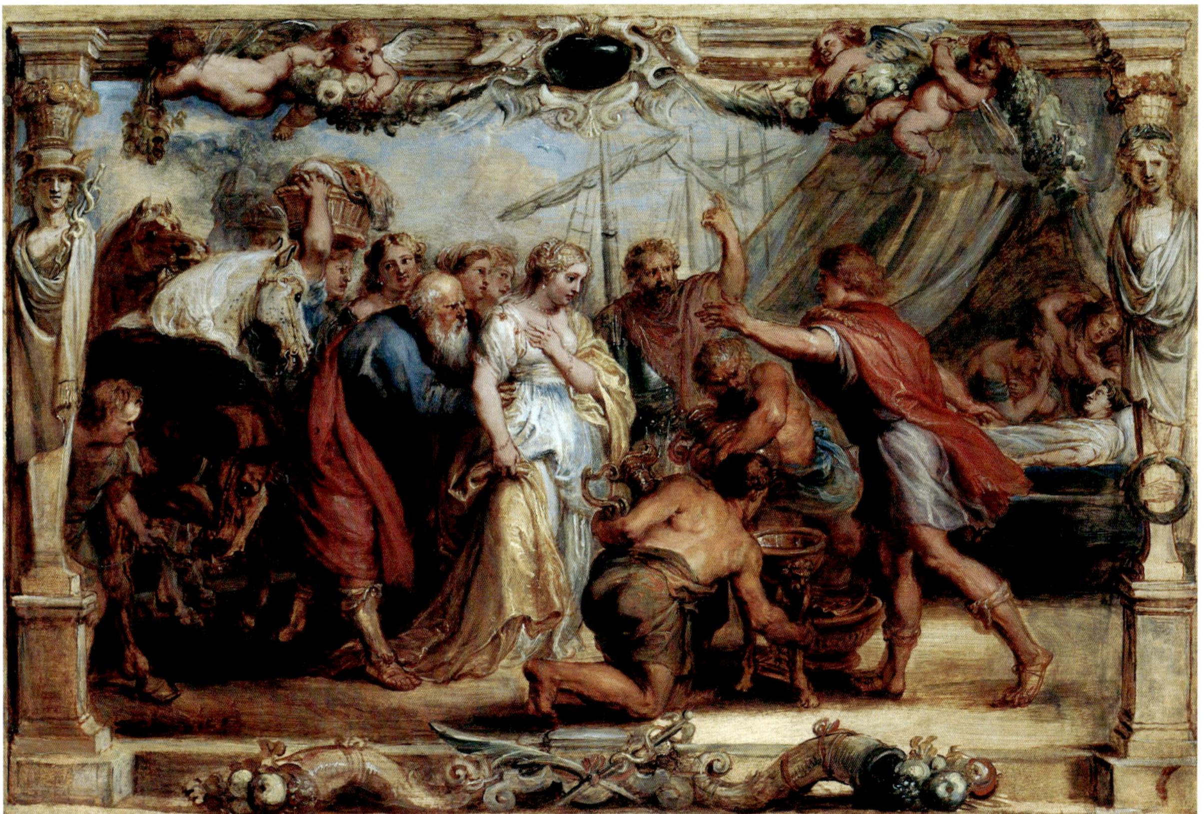

Fig 10 Peter Paul Rubens, *Briseis Given Back to Achilles*, c. 1630–31. Oil on oak panel, 45.4 × 67.6 cm. The Detroit Institute of Arts, bequest of Mr. and Mrs. Edgar B. Whitcomb. 53.356.

had boldly written about the persecution of Galileo, "The fathers might be acting in good faith but they will have trouble convincing the world."[33]

These two images, that of Apollo and that of the representatives of pagan wisdom in the Eucharist tapestry, illustrate a tension in Rubens's art, whereby respect, even adulation, of antique culture can affect his representation of Christian themes.

Rubens's portrait of Gaspar Gevartius with a bust of Marcus Aurelius (Antwerp, Royal Museums), his portrait of Ludovicus Nonnius with a bust of Hippocrates (London, National Gallery), or of Theodore Turquet de Mayerne with a statue of Aesculapius (Raleigh, North Carolina Museum of Art), not to mention Van Dyck's portrait of Nicolaas Rockox with a bust of Jupiter (Saint Petersburg, Hermitage), remind us how closely his friends identified with their ancient heroes.

Rubens's Antwerp circle lived in two worlds. Rubens went to check a Greek manuscript on Marcus Aurelius in the Escorial for Gevartius.[34] A gold coin owned by Rockox showing the empress Faustina giving out education scholarships to poor girls was included in the *Electorum libri II*.[35] As Rockox was an almoner engaged in similar charity work himself, the compliment was clear, as in the paintings Rubens later made for his friend. And, of course, Rubens depicted himself with his brother Philip, their friend Woverius, and their teacher Lipsius below a bust of their hero Seneca (Florence, Palazzo Pitti).

Rubens's *Death of Seneca* (Munich, Alte Pinakothek) perhaps exemplifies his attitude best.[36] Constrained by the necessity of using as his model the figure of an old fisherman identified and restored as Seneca bleeding to death, Rubens sought to endow his painted figure of the Stoic philosopher with an ecstatic vision as he imparts his last thoughts to a scribe while waiting for the heat of the bath to drain the blood from his severed veins. Seneca sharing his last thoughts, is made all the more poignant because we now have no record of the words that might have enlightened us. Much later, it was discovered that Rubens's identification of the ancient statue as Seneca was misplaced, but the message about the importance of human thought is still relevant. Rubens's creation of this image of a pagan visionary triumphing over the

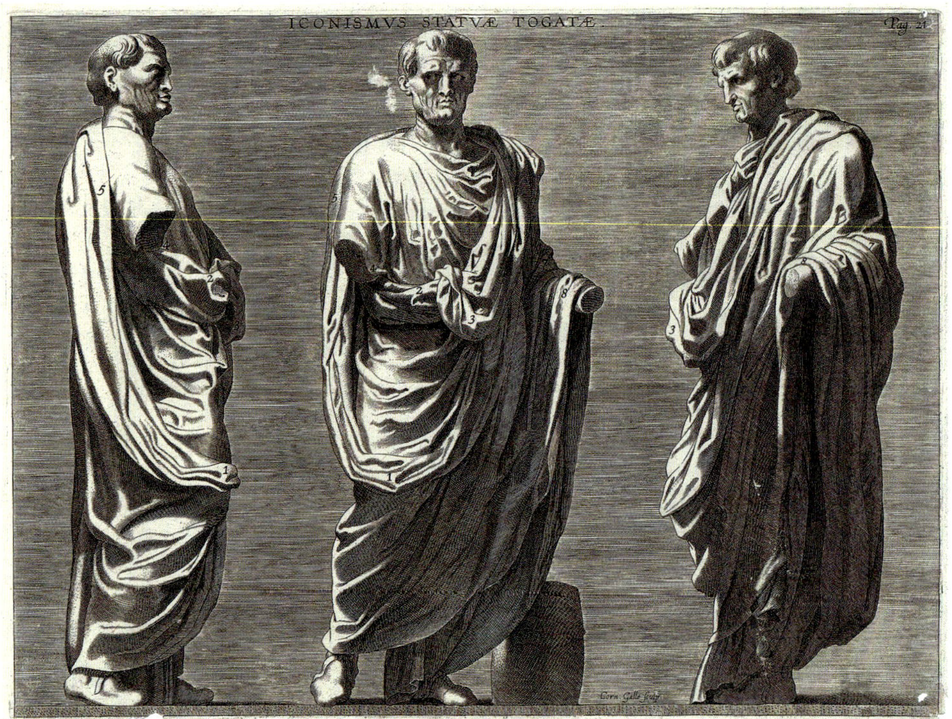

Fig 11 Philip Rubens, after Peter Paul Rubens, *Iconismus Statuae Togatus*, from the first book of Philip Rubens's "Electorum Libri II" (Antwerp: 1608), 1608. Engraving, 19.9 × 27.2 cm. British Museum, London. 1891,0414.1243. Photo © The Trustees of the British Museum.

trials of earthly existence seems no less intense than his images of Christian martyrdom.

For Rubens and his brother, ancient art was not just a curiosity, it was a way of reconnecting with the culture and thought of an age they admired above all else. It was a code of behaviour. The brothers and their friends sought to endow the surviving ancient texts, at times partial and fragmentary, with a greater veracity by finding visual parallels that might serve as keys to understanding. As an artist, Rubens could connect and transfer emotions, from anger to modesty, from passages recalled from one classical writer or another when he was interpreting antique sculptural reliefs.

A valuable clue as to Rubens's readings is found in the fragment from his Roman "Itinerary,"[37] in which he describes scenes on sarcophagi, shuffling the order of events in the carved relief for narrative consistency. For example, when describing the *Rape of Proserpina*, he pays attention to dress ("night, who has wings and billowing veil or drapery"), describing the cloth that curiously floats in front of the personification; then, much later, he adapts this flying figure for the *Flight of Maria de' Medici*.[38]

Further describing the Proserpina sarcophagus in the Palazzo Altemps, he writes: "Mercury finds Proserpina beside Pluto. She has her head completely covered by a veil, as if to hide her shame, wanting by this action to make it understood she prefers to stay rather than leave. As Penelope did, when she covered her head when her father asked her if she would rather follow Odysseus."

Rubens recalled this scene when he showed Proserpina veiled in his *Orpheus and Eurydice*, perhaps now to suggest that she wanted to hide that she longs to return to the Earth with them. In the finished painting, Rubens changes her gesture and gives her greater décolletage, in a manner that seems to lend a more positive indication of her relationship with Pluto, the god of the Underworld, despite his antisocial three-headed dog.[39] Thus, a covered head could convey female modesty or sensitivity about leaving a parent or husband, even when he had been her abductor, but Rubens responded to other uses of the veil to represent inexpressible grief. From a textual account, he recreated a lost painting by the Greek painter Timanthes, which showed Agamemnon with his head covered, the artist hesitating to find a way to show the grief of a father at the execution of his daughter. But Rubens may also have imagined that Agamemnon veils his head in shame as well as distress, rather than witness the event,

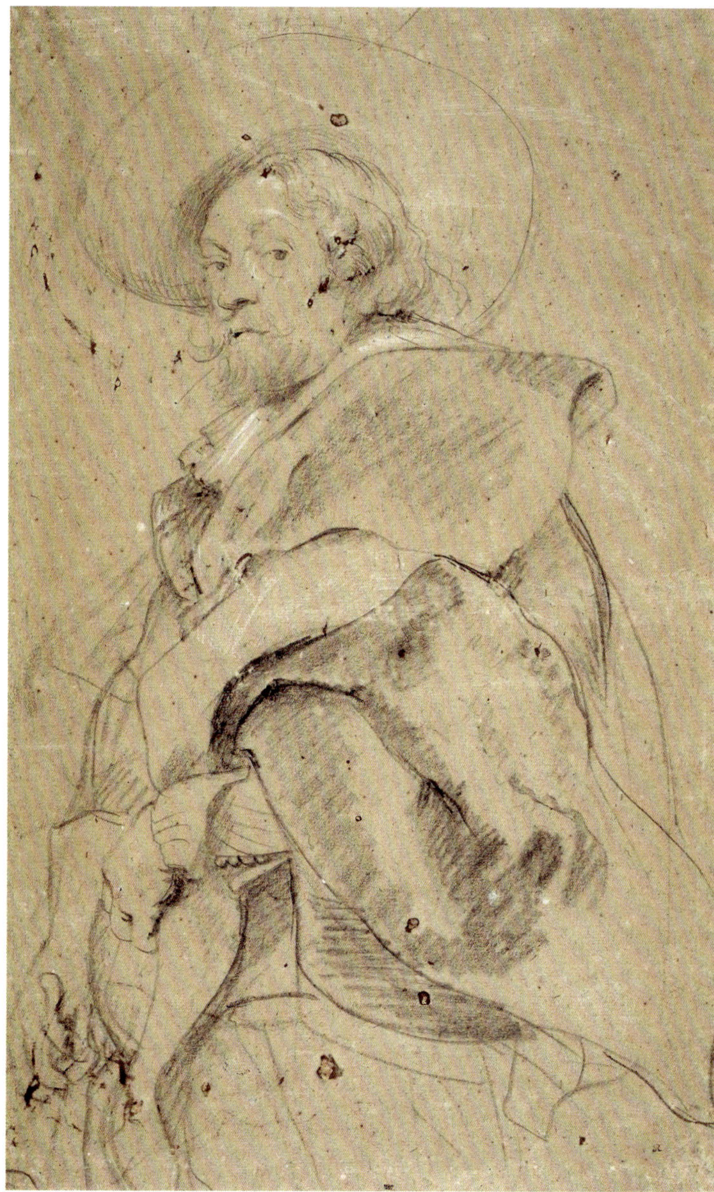

Fig 12 Philip Rubens, Self-portrait, c. 1635/38. Black chalk, heightened with white, on beige paper, 46.0 × 28.5 cm. Louvre Museum, Paris. 20195.

a sacrifice which he supposedly acquiesced to in order to allow the becalmed fleet to sail against Troy. The *Sacrifice of Iphigenia* was painted by Rubens on the façade of his own house,[40] among many other recreations from written descriptions of ancient paintings. The exercise demonstrates that Rubens was struggling to envisage and perhaps match the images that Greek and Roman artists were famed for, but which survive only as phantoms, reflected faintly in the compositions of narrative scenes on reliefs and sarcophagi as well as in surviving literary accounts.

A famous comment that Rubens once made, in response to the gift of a book by Franciscus Junius about the painting of the ancients, is a further reminder of the power of the ancients over the imagination of his generation. He wrote of how the great paintings by Apelles and other masters "present themselves to us only in the imagination, like dreams" and that attempting to reconstruct them is "insulting or alien to the dignity of the ancients."[41] Yet he actually mimics Lucian's description of Repentance "deep in mourning clad in black garments that are torn to shreds" when he writes a key to his own painting of the *Horrors of War* (Florence, Palazzo Pitti), describing Europa "in tearful mourning dressed in black with veil torn."[42] It is a matter of total immersion in the culture. His monstrous Furies and his voluptuous goddesses may be from a different script, but the ambition is ancient, just as much as is the two-headed Janus figure above the door of the temple, kept closed in time of peace. In this splendid painting, Rubens was looking back to Virgil's Golden Age in a plea for peace that allows society, human relationships, and the arts to flourish.

In the *Horrors of War*, Venus pleads with Mars tearfully, but with poignant dignity. In the decorum of Rubens's ideal ancient world, only slaves and women of low status would be shown resorting to extravagant gestures, such as the biting of executioners or abductors. We see arm-biting in the Munich *Massacre of the Innocents*, face-scratching in the Toronto *Massacre* (page 176), and a calf-biting old woman in his late sketch for *The Rape of the Sabine Women*. It is a matter of class as to who can express distress as violent anger by such means, as Roger de Piles clearly recognized in his commentary on the picture.[43] Instead, his heroines endure with well-bred composure and bear any trials with stoic dignity. Rubens's *Iphigenia* is a pagan version of a Catholic martyr.[44] The painter's determination to recreate an authentic ancient world must have been, in part, driven by his belief that it could be an exemplar for his own times. He was convinced that the power of ancient art and its literature could be harnessed to create a better world.

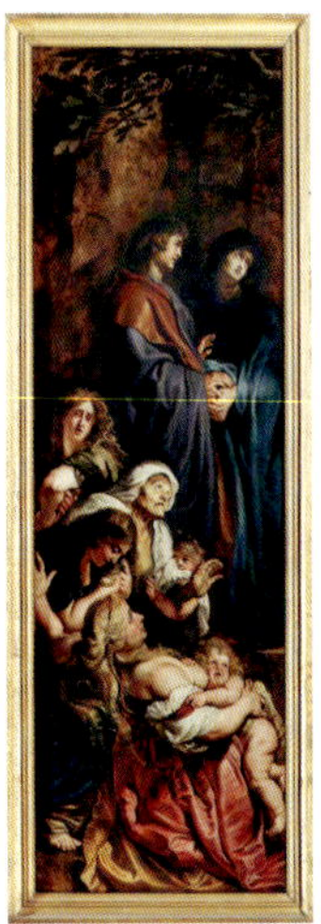
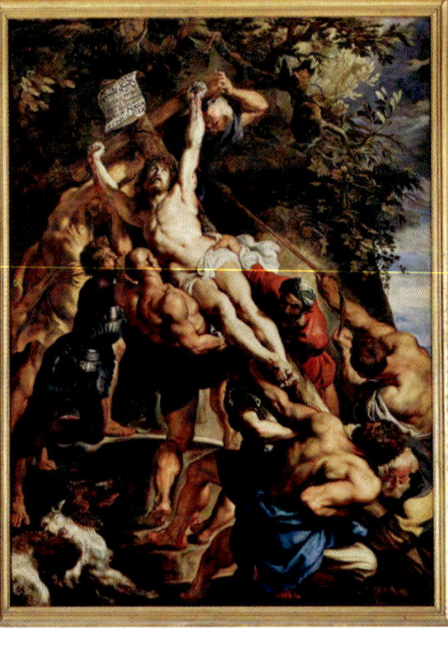
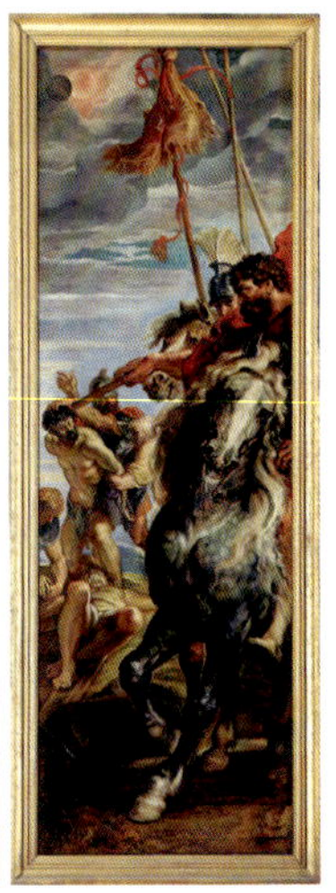

Fig 13 Peter Paul Rubens, *Triptych with the Resurrection of Christ (Moretus Epitaph)*, 1612. Oil on panel, 40 × 136 × 98 cm. Antwerp Cathedral. Photo © Lukas–Art in Flanders.

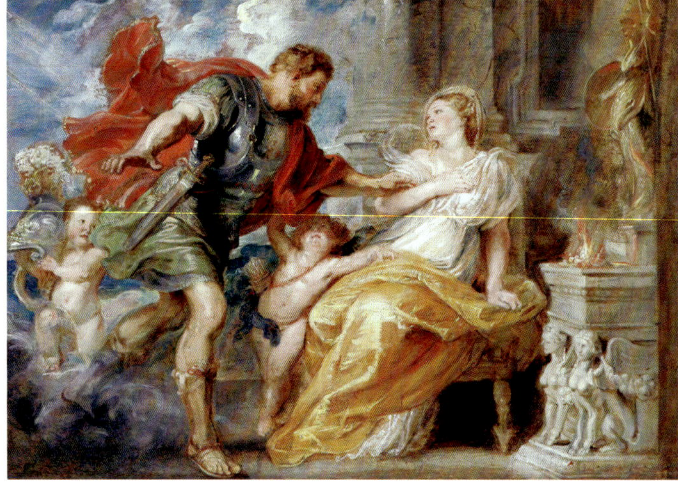

Fig 14 Peter Paul Rubens, *Mars and Rhea Silvia*, c. 1616–17. Oil on canvas, 46 × 66 cm. Liechtenstein, The Princely Collections, Vaduz-Vienna. GE115. Photo © LIECHTENSTEIN. The Princely Collections, Vaduz-Vienna/Scala, Florence/Art Resource, NY (2018).

Where possible, Rubens sought to soften the many ancient stories of outrageous seduction into what might now be called "speed dating" or even "falling in love," but he did seem to side with the victims and condone female vengeance.

In this exhibition, *Mars and Rhea Silvia* (page 250) illustrates Rubens's fully extended narrative capacity to rewrite the god's seduction of the vestal virgin as a love story with a happy outcome: the conception of Romulus, the founder of Rome.[45]

COROLLARY: RUBENS'S CONNECTION TO ANTIQUITY AS AN INDICATOR OF HIS INVOLVEMENT IN PRODUCTION

The practicalities of running a large workshop meant Rubens could not maintain the charged intensity he had found in Greek and Roman carving, but something of the electrical energy continues in his oil sketches and a few rare, fully autographed paintings he made after 1610.

The translation or mistranslation of these template sketches into large machines is a valuable key to allow us to measure the extent of his workshop intervention. Viewing from the perspective of Rubens's own engagement with the ancient world creates a basis to assess the competence of the scaled-up interpretation.

An example of the impulse and how it subtly gets dissipated is seen in *Mars and Rhea Silvia* (page 250).[46] The executioner of the large painting cannot be Rubens. Faced with the sketch's structural ambiguity, the pupil panicked over the perspective of the altar and made the wrong guess in his positioning of altar sphinxes. The corner pentimenti of the base is misaligned with the top, further evidence of the creator's lack of skill. This muddled masonry was partly rooted by Rubens's initial idea in the sketch (Fig 14): one can glimpse an homage to the bronze Greek tripod his friend Peiresc had just discovered, though the master later painted over the still-visible design with a more appropriate Roman marble altar.

This is not to dismiss the large version. It has impressive wall power and carries the artist's brand, but is tame in the handling of details. Even the sea dragons on the hem of Mars's skirt and impressionistic pommel mask and helmet dragon are a little weak, and not the work of the master: they are more optical in a Venetian way, almost anticipating Velasquez's abbreviations. Similarly, the clouds are flat and fail to give Mars his required entrance cover or even convincingly float across the column. The putto holding Mars's helmet now has an aimless expression. Unlike in the small sketch, Mars no longer slides down a light beam and breaks in a dusty racing-speed stop.

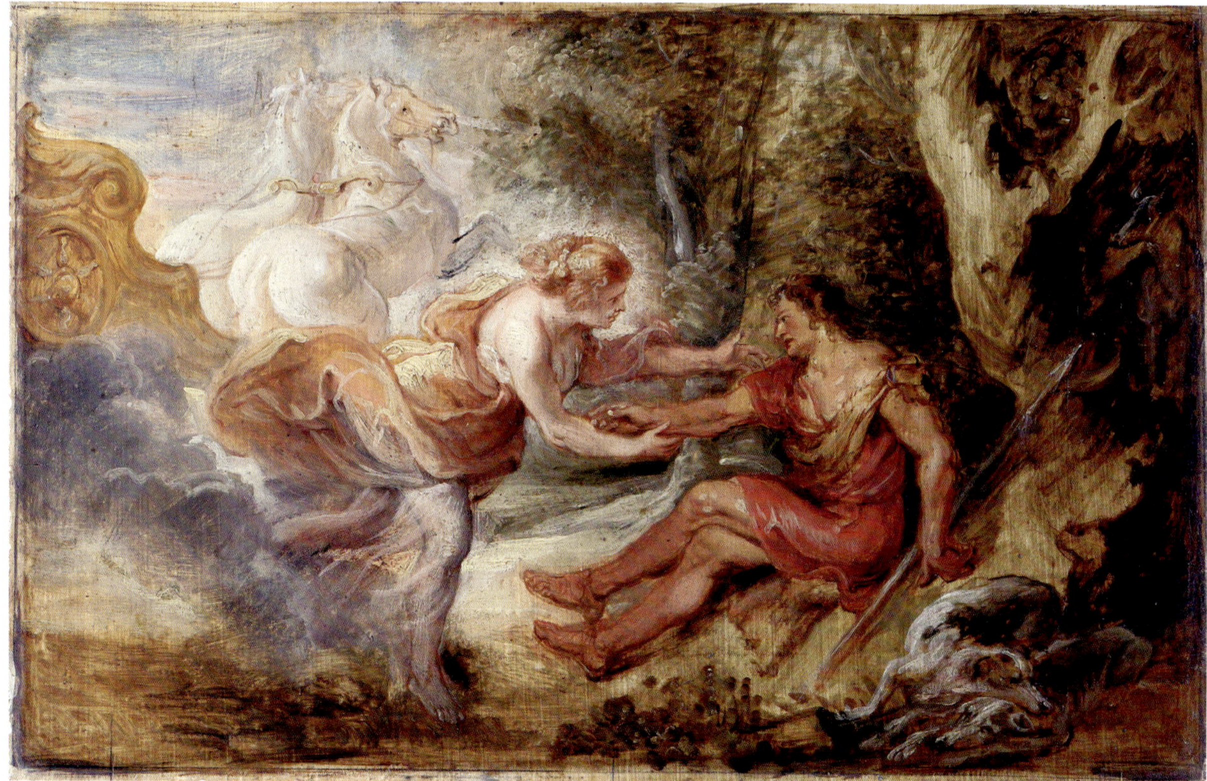

Fig 18 Peter Paul Rubens, *Aurora Abducting Cephalus*, 1636–37. Oil on oak, 30.8 × 48.5 cm. National Gallery London, Salting Bequest, 1910. NG2598. Photo © National Gallery, London.

The encounter recalls the London *Aurora Abducting Cephalus* (fig. 15), in which Dawn is trying to quickly seduce an exhausted hunter, despite her tight schedule caused by the sun-god Apollo's hot pursuit. In the London sketch, the clouds of morning mist and the break-dust are more evident, as the painting has not been bruised by a transfer to canvas, yet the same hasty descent and pit stop can be detected in the small *Rhea*. In the full-scale version *Rhea*, the enveloping mist has been dispersed and Mars and the seated woman are more solidly planted. In the final painting, she adopts a calmer, more monumental, demeanour with greater weight on her supporting arm.

Spatially, Mars, deprived of surprise, enthusiastically approaches her rather than crashing into her. The Cupids in both versions are simply accessories who give wardrobe assistance to aid the coupling. Subtly, the vestal virgin is changing her status as Rubens indicates by the knotted band slipping down. She is now in transition to becoming the mother of Romulus and Remus and so makes eye contact with her first suitor. When asked how she knew the father was Mars and not just some random soldier, she responds that he was in armour and just appeared out of the mist. Rubens embraces her account and chooses to have her fully awake, and anticipates the outcome by showing her virginal headgear already slipping. Rubens, as Elizabeth McGrath has pointed out, wants this to be a mutual Ovidian engagement, even if somewhat hasty.

As we see in the two *Holy Families* from Los Angeles and The Metropolitan Museum in this exhibition (pages 180–181), a copyist can generally be separated from the inventor by a diminution in the sense of three-dimensional reality. In the case of Rubens, a misunderstanding of the story behind an image (and the ancient culture that underpins that story) can mean that his workshop products leave the observant viewer with a sense that something has been lost in translation.

1 For the quiver, see Christopher White, *The Later Flemish Paintings in the Collection of Her Majesty the Queen* (London: Royal Collection Publications, 2008), 228, cat. no. 64.

2 Peter Paul Rubens to Pierre Dupuy, [Paris], June 29, 1628, in *The Letters of Peter Paul Rubens*, ed. and trans. Ruth Saunders Magurn (Cambridge, MA: Harvard University Press, 1955), 272.

3 White, *The Later Flemish Paintings*, 228, cat. no. 64.

4 For the Toronto museum example, see Dagmar Grassinger, *Die Mythologischen Sarkophage*, vol. 12, Part 1, *Achill, Adonis, Aeneas, Aktaion, Alkestis, Amazonen* in the series *Die Antiken Sarkophagreliefs* (Berlin: Gebr. Mann Verlag, 1999), 245, cat. no. 114, figs. 103.2 and 106–7. This example was found at Ostia *c.* 1831–34 and thus would not have been known to Rubens.

5 Marjon van der Meulen, *Rubens' Copies after the Antique* (London: Harvey Miller, 1994), 3 vols., cat. nos. 76–104, and David Jaffé, *Rubens: A Master in the Making* (London: National Gallery Company, 2005), 42, 88–91. Also see Ludwig Pollak, "Der rechte arm des Laokoon," *Römische Mitteilungen* 20 (1905): 277–82. Pollak found the right arm of the priest around the beginning of the twentieth century, but his discovery was not accepted as part of the original sculpture until a decade after his death. (Pollak perished in Auschwitz in 1943.)

6 Jan Garff and Eva de la Fuente Pedersen, *Rubens Cantoor: The Drawings of Willem Panneels; A Critical Catalogue* (Copenhagen: Royal Museum of Fine Arts, 1988), 178–79, cat. nos. 241 and 243, figs. 244 and 246. Rather than quoting the composition, the sixteenth-century painters Giulio Romano and Gaudenzio Ferrari rewrote the problem of the priest being attacked by Neptune's serpents; see Gemma Sena Chiesa and Elisabetta Gagetti, *Laocoonte in Lombardia* (Milan: Viennepierre, 2007), figs. 1–3.

7 Julius S. Held, *The Oil Sketches of Peter Paul Rubens: A Critical Catalogue* (Princeton, NJ: Princeton University Press, 1980), 357–60, cat. no. 266 and 358–60, fig. 357.

8 David Jaffé, "From Youthful Violence to Pleas for Peace: Rubens's Political Development, and the Influence of His Master Otto van Veen," in Eckhard Leuschner, *Rekonstruktion der Gesellschaft aus Kunst* (Petersberg: Michael Imhof, 2016), 167–83, figs. 5 and 6.

9 For examples of the Corsini's and Hermitage's *Studies of Old Men*, see Jaffé, *Rubens: A Master in the Making*, cat. nos. 85–86 and 186–87. The black-haired man holding the base of the cross in the *Raising of the Cross* (at Antwerp Cathedral) is the closest large-scale echo of this energization.

10 See Michael Jaffé, *Rubens catalogo completo* (Milan: Rizzoli, 1989), 250, cat. no. 542, for the Saint Paul's Church, Antwerp altar, where it was painted in around 1619. See also Hans Vlieghe, *Corpus Rubenianum Ludwig Burchard, Part VIII: I. Saints*, 2 vols. (Brussels: Arcade Press, 1972), 1:134–36, cat. no. 88, fig. 151.

11 For example, Giambologna's 1562 marble of *Samson and the Philistine*, which Rubens saw in Spain in 1604, or his *c.* 1580–1600 bronze statuette *Hercules Wielding the Club* are suitable models. See Charles Avery and Anthony Radcliffe, *Giambologna, 1529–1608* (London: Westerham Press, 1978), 13, fig. 15, and 135, fig. 90.

12 Vlieghe, *Saints*, 2:26–28, cat. no. 104a, fig. 6.

13 See David Freedberg, *Saints* 2:61, cat. no. 110, fig. 32. 1For the rest of the engravings in Jacques Callot, *Tableaux de Rome* (1609–11), see Anna Grelle in Paulette Choné, Daniel Ternois, and Jean-Marc Depluvrez et al., *Jacques Callot, 1592–1635* (Paris: Réunion des musées nationaux, 1992), 134–39, exh. cat.

14 See, most recently, Hans Jakob Meier, "Peter Paul Rubens and His Brother Philip's Poems on 'Samson' and 'Judith,'" *Journal of the Warburg and Courtauld Institutes* 77 (2014): 241.

15 The book was begun in 1601–1604, then worked on back in Rome in 1605 or early 1606 with Colonna; in May 1607 Philip returned to Antwerp; see Van der Meulen, *Rubens' Copies after the Antique*, 1:100.

16 For the Fitzwilliam drawing, see Ludwig Burchard and Roger Aldof d'Hulst, *Rubens Drawings* (Brussels: Arcade Press, 1963), cat. nos. 45 and 78–79. For the sculpture, see Van der Meulen, *Rubens' Copies after the Antique*, vol. 1, cat. nos. 100 and 101.

17 For the Fitzwilliam drawing, see Burchard and d'Hulst, *Rubens Drawings*, cat. no. 45, as at note 16.

18 The fragmentary state is recorded in de' Cavalieri, see p. 1593, cat. no. 11. Found in 1583; for the history, see Francis Haskell and Nicholas Penny, *Taste and the Antique: The Lure of Classical Sculpture, 1500–1900* (New Haven, CT: Yale University Press, 1981), 176. Rubens archaeological record of the *Wrestlers* is copied by Panneels. See Garff and Pedersen, *Rubens Cantoor*, 166, plates 226–27, nos. 224–25, where Rubens records the group as still headless. See Van der Meulen, *Rubens' Copies after the Antique*, vol. 1, cat. nos. 100 and 101.

19 See Jaffé, *Rubens: A Master in the Making*, 94–95, under cat. no. 29.

20 Burchard and d'Hulst, *Rubens Drawings*, 142–43, cat. no. 70.

21 John Martin, *The Ceiling Paintings for the Jesuit Church in Antwerp* (London: Harvey Miller, 1968), cat. no. 25a, fig. 133. Echoes of the top wrestler can be seen in the Cologne *Draught of Fishes*. Held, *The Oil Sketches of Peter Paul Rubens*, 462, cat. no. 335, fig. 330.

22 Held, *The Oil Sketches of Peter Paul Rubens*, 177–78, cat. no. 124, fig. 128; compare with Panneels in Garff and Pedersen, *Rubens Cantoor*, cat. no. 224, fig. 226.

23 The mourners seem to be borrowed from Held, *The Oil Sketches of Peter Paul Rubens*, 356, cat. no. 361; 497. Rubens's *Lamentation of Christ*, Berlin, dated early by Julius Held, to 1598–1602. Held, *The Oil Sketches of Peter Paul Rubens*.

24 See Van der Meulen, *Rubens' Copies after the Antique*, vol. 3, cat. nos. 167 and 185, fig. 321.

25 Svetlana Alpers, *The Decoration of the Torre de la Parada* (Brussels: Arcade Press, 1971), cat. nos. 25 and 25a and figs. 107–8.

26 *Grand Design: Pieter Coecke van Aelst and Renaissance Tapestry* (New York: Metropolitan Museum of Art, 2014), 94, cat. no. 20; Rijksmuseum, *The Fall of the Giants*, cat. no. 21, Cornelis Bos, *c.* 1540, after cat. no. 19 (p. 95), print after *Revolt of the Giants*; compare with Jeremy Wood, *Corpus Rubenianum Ludwig Burchard, Part XXVI: Rubens; Copies and Adaptations from Renaissance and Later Artists; Italian Artists*, 2 vols.; vol. 1, *Raphael and His School* (London: Harvey Miller, 2010), 357–61, cat. no. 77, fig. 195.

27 For Grasse, *Saint Helena*, see Christopher White, *Rubens: Man and Artist* (New Haven, CT: Yale University Press, 1987), 22, fig 35. Vlieghe, *Saints*, 2:59–61, cat. no. 110, fig. 31.

28 See J. Richard Judson and Carl van de Velde, *Corpus Rubenianum Ludwig Burchard, Part XXI: Book Illustrations and Title Pages*, 2 vols. (London: Harvey Miller; Philadelphia: Heydon & Son, 1978), vol. 2, cat. no. 27, fig. 92; and Gregory Martin, *Rubens in London: Art and Diplomacy* (London: Harvey Miller, 2011), cat. no. 169, fig. 82; compare with Van der Meulen, *Rubens' Copies after the Antique*, vol. 1, figs. 124–32, cat. nos. 65–69. For other echoes of the mounted cupid, see, finally, the boy riding the tiger in the 1634 Banqueting Hall *Procession*, and the 1622 Berlin *Perseus and Andromeda*, in Jaffé, *Rubens catalogo completo*, 279, cat. no. 757.

29 White, *Rubens: Man and Artist*, 291; Julius S. Held, *Rubens: Selected Drawings* (Oxford: Phaidon, 1986), 177, figs. 32 and 1606, Pierpont Morgan, *Portrait of a Lady*, and fig. 33, Metropolitan, *Saint Catherine*, are drawn examples of this extreme bulking of drapery.

30 The print is inscribed "... ex marmore Antiquo." See David Freedberg, *Corpus Rubenianum Ludwig Burchard, Part VII: The Life of Christ after the Passion* (London: Harvey Miller, 1984), 31–37, cat. nos. 1–3, figs. 3–5. Panneels's drawing is in Garff and Pedersen, *Rubens Cantoor*, cat. no. 97.

31 Judson and Van de Velde, *Book Illustrations and Title Pages*, vol. 2, cat. no. 62. Rubens was more amenable to depicting the destruction of ancient art for his favourite order, the Jesuits. See, for example, Saint Eugenia and Saint Chrysostom; see John Martin, *The Ceiling Paintings*, cat. nos. 35, 27.

32 Elizabeth McGrath, *Corpus Rubenianum Ludwig Burchard, Part XIII: I. Rubens; Subjects from History*, 2 vols. (London: Harvey Miller, 1997), 1:99–100 and fig. 31.

33 David Jaffé, "Rubens Peiresc and His Picture Collection," *Australian Journal of Art* 5 (1986): 22–46, esp. 25 and 37n8, citing letter of June 2, 1633, Peiresc to Holstenius.

34 Rubens wrote to Caspar Gervaerts (Brussels) on December 29, 1628, about the manuscripts on his Emperor in *San Lorenzo*; see Saunders Magurn, *The Letters of Peter Paul Rubens*, 293, letter no. 181. On his regret that he did not have time to research "this intimate sanctuary of the muses" for all the portraits, see Jaffé, *Rubens catalogo completo*, 153; "Four Philosophers," 922; "Gervaerts," 923; "Nonnius," 991; "Theodore," 2218.

35 Antonius Pius endowed free education to orphan girls in honour of his wife, Faustina, in AD 141; see Van der Meulen, *Rubens' Copies after the Antique*, 1:110.

36 See Elizabeth McGrath, *Rubens: Subjects from History* (London: Harvey Miller, 1997), vol. 2, cat. no. 54, fig. 195.

37 Van der Meulen, *Rubens' Copies after the Antique*, vol. 1, cat. nos. 82–84, and Appendix 1.2, 154. (This survives only in a French translation.)

38 Van der Meulen, *Rubens' Copies after the Antique*, vol. 1, cat. nos. 85 and 80.

39 Held, *The Oil Sketches of Peter Paul Rubens*, 288–89, cat. no. 206, plate 215, fig. 9. Held notes the Altemps Rospigliosi sarcophagus of the Petit Palais *Abduction of Proserpina* in the same volume, cat. no. 262, plate 246. See also Elizabeth McGrath, "The Painted Decoration of Rubens's House," *Journal of the Warburg and Courtauld Institutes* 41 (1978): 245–77 and 288, cat. no. 11.

40 McGrath, "The Painted Decoration of Rubens's House," 257.

41 Peter Paul Rubens to Franciscus Junius (London), August 1, 1637, in Saunders Magurn, *The Letters of Peter Paul Rubens*, 407, letter no. 241.

42 For the parallel, see McGrath, "The Painted Decoration of Rubens's House," 250n22; Rubens to Justus Sustermans (Florence), March 12, 1638, in Saunders Magurn, *The Letters of Peter Paul Rubens*, 408–9, letter no. 242.

43 Quoted in Elizabeth McGrath, *Rubens: Subjects from History*, 1:121; 2:187, cat. no. 40.

44 In "The Painted Decoration of Rubens's House," Elizabeth McGrath characterizes Iphigenia as displaying the "serenity of some virgin saint for martyrdom, though with pagan resignation."

45 See McGrath's *Rubens: Subjects from History*, 2:141, in which she discusses the artist changing the appearance of the Palladium to Minerva in contrast to Lipsius's idea. The sphinx reinforces the importance of the Palladium, as it predicts the empire that will result from this union. In chapter 5 of the first volume of this series, McGrath discusses whether Rhea was asleep, touching on the slipping veil and her claim that Mars came in armour, out of the mist.

46 See Elizabeth McGrath in Marco Chiarini, Michael Douglas-Scott, Kristina Herrmann-Fiore, David Jaffé, et al., *Rubens and the Italian Renaissance* (Canberra: Australian National Gallery, 1992), 118–20. Here, she points out that the finished painting is not really an autograph, noting that, "in fact, the liveliness and psychological subtlety of the sketch is rather lost in the large-scale picture." See also Held, *The Oil Sketches of Peter Paul Rubens*, 336–37, cat. no. 248, fig. 244.

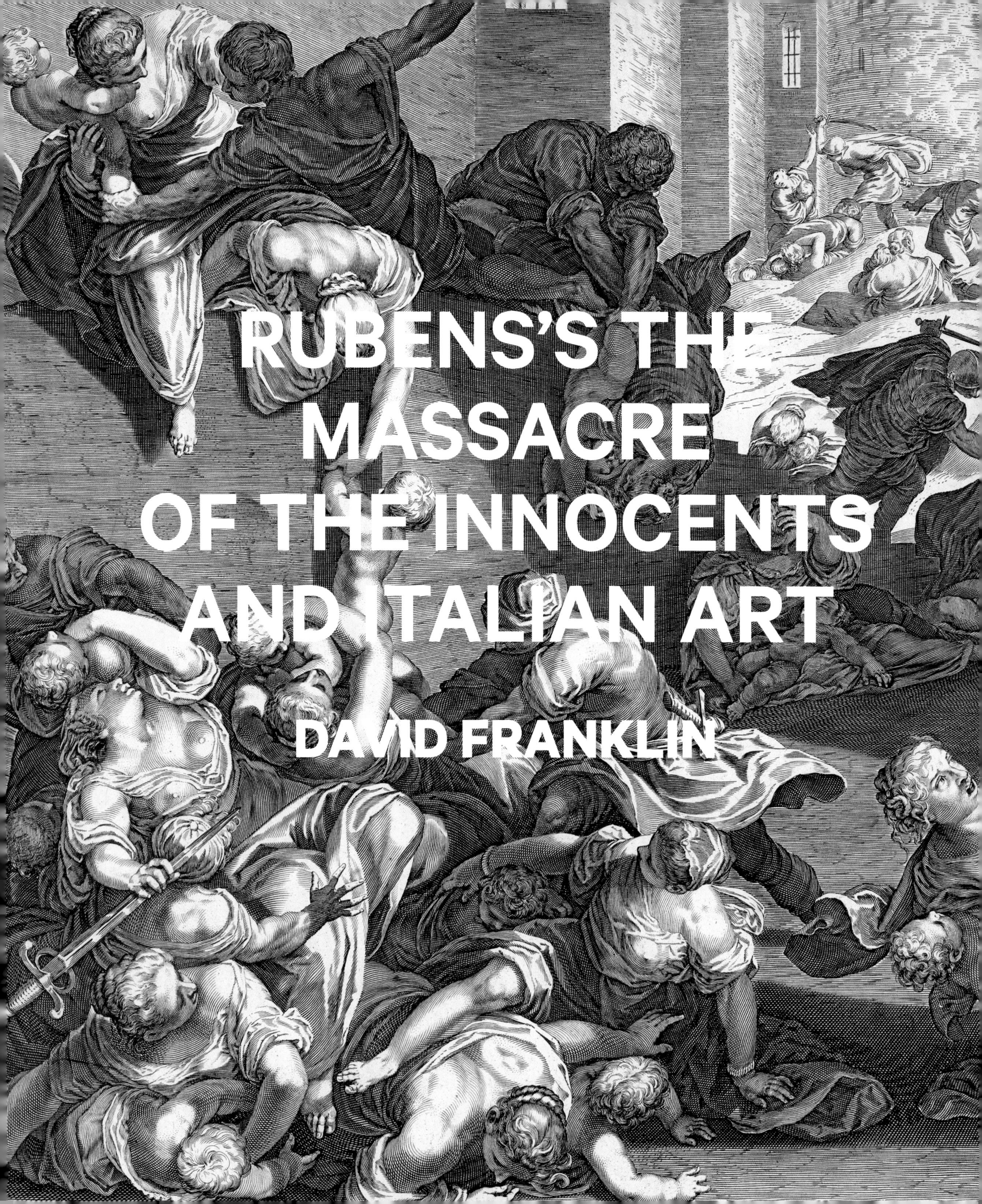
RUBENS'S THE MASSACRE OF THE INNOCENTS AND ITALIAN ART
DAVID FRANKLIN

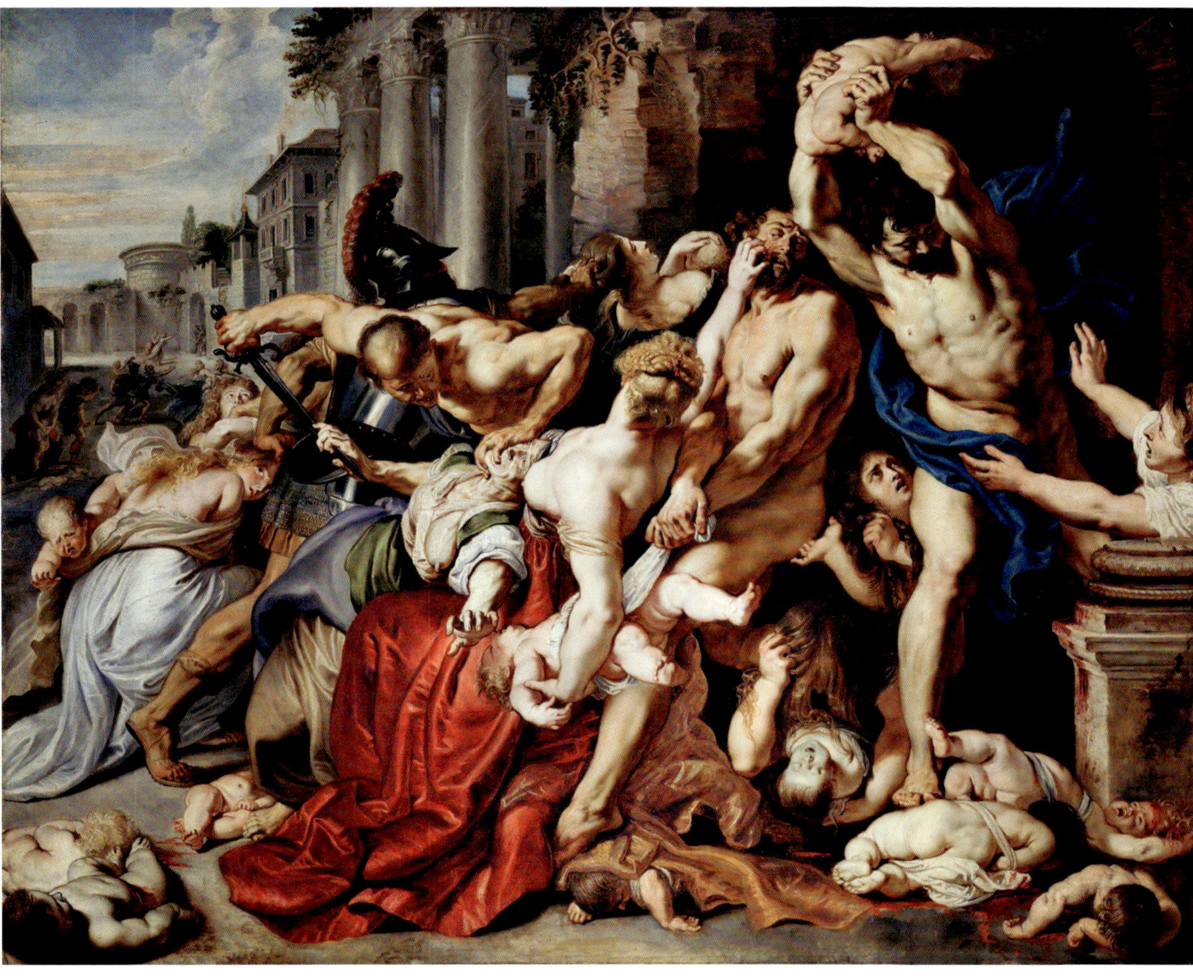

Fig 1 Peter Paul Rubens, *The Massacre of the Innocents*, c. 1611–12. Oil on panel, 142 × 182 cm. The Thomson Collection, Art Gallery of Ontario, Toronto. 2014/1581.

THE MASSACRE OF THE INNOCENTS by Rubens in the Art Gallery of Ontario (fig. 1) is a virtual index of his experience of Italy, painted following his return from an extended stay there, in the period around 1610, when he established artistic dominance in Antwerp.[1] This monumental panel, with its violent subject matter, presented his new approach to narrative and style, suffused with Italian accents. There are no preparatory sketches or oil sketches surviving for the painting, so we must work from the image itself to discover its source material. Rubens would have developed the painting in his Antwerp studio from the numerous copy drawings made in Italy of art past and present, as well as from the prints of the same subject he might have owned. He was fully at ease in blending and exploiting the principal duality of Italian sixteenth-century art: the sensual painterly softness of the Venetians and the graphic sculptural hardness of the Florentines. Only a non-Italian artist could have embraced these contradictions. Yet *The Massacre of the Innocents* is deliberately less Venetian than he could have emulated, intending more to demonstrate his absorption of a tougher manner of Central Italy, in keeping with the subject matter.

The painting features about a dozen monumental adult bodies, all deployed in dynamic poses along a foreground plane, with numerous dead and dying children displayed around. The terrible biblical story, one of the most heart-wrenching narratives in the history of religious art to represent, is broken into a series of separate but overlapping and independently conceived sequences: there is no single moment on which the viewer can fixate. It is a painting that attracts attention to each aspect of itself.

The stage-like platform on which the actions take place and the dense clustering of form reveal relief sculpture as one inspiration for Rubens's design. Certain figures are, without disguise, reprised from statues. The standing male soldier dominating the right edge of the panel appears to emerge from a niche, as if a sculpture brought suddenly to life. The helmet of the soldier toward the upper left has sinister red reflections, in contrast to the monochromatic ancient statuary Rubens studied—he intended

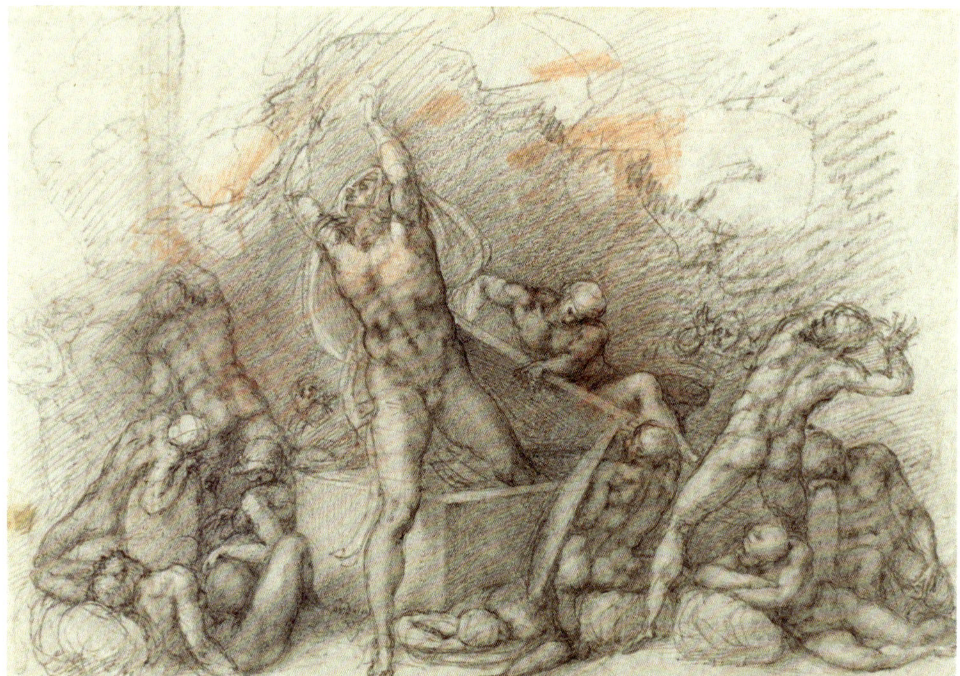

Fig 2 Michelangelo Buonarroti, *The Resurrection*, c. 1532. Black chalk over traces of stylus, with some red chalk offsetting, 24 × 34.7 cm. Royal Collection, Windsor. RCIN 912767. Royal Collection Trust/© Her Majesty Queen Elizabeth II 2018.

to reimagine antiquity in an eternal present moment. The painter exploited the power of sidewise, non-frontal poses from the experience of sculpture, which allows the trauma to be viewed in more aspects. The suspended child, pulled and held in the middle of the composition, recalls the famous Meleager sarcophagus that inspired many Renaissance artists, but in this context elicits feelings of pity, not heroic sacrifice. Implicit in Rubens's painting is a *challenge* to sculpture, in the tactile details, introducing touch and pain, as well as the textures of the sumptuous draperies. Fabric and hair have the equivalent movement and scintillating opalescent qualities, achievable only in oil paint.

The composition is centrifugal, predicated on a tumultuous torrent of bodies, some entirely naked for reasons of pure formal display. The general visual disorder is a metaphor for pain and brutality. Two soldiers stand not on the ground but precariously on other bodies to add to the gruesome spontaneity of the image. Poses are notable for their stressed tension and flexibility, from which the electrifying display results—again, importantly, something possible only in painting as opposed to sculpture. While the women attempt valiantly to save their children, the artist already anticipates mourning in some of their postures, long hair covering faces in inexpressible despair. The violence causes a single ribbon to unfurl spontaneously on the woman in the topmost centre: beauty born of cruelty.

While horror in the image is undeniable, the numerous complicated foreshortenings were introduced as demonstrations of pure artistic skill and to measure the pictorial space for the viewer—a deliberate response to the challenge and weight of Italian art history. Similarly, nudes or partial nudes of both genders are included, not very plausible to the story, but historical licence allowed Rubens to present his artistic range and evoke many responses, cerebral as well as visceral. Indeed, the slightly less than life-sized figures preserve some decorum and mercifully distance the spectator from the violence.

In addition to antique sculpture, *The Massacre* also contends with the painting and drawing of Rubens's time. Nearer contemporary sources, accessible to Rubens in Rome, are detectable in Italian masters of the early sixteenth century, who, not by coincidence, shared a deep predilection for sculpture and interpreted similar sources in their painting: Michelangelo and Polidoro da Caravaggio. To approach the ancients, Rubens made his own direct copies, but he also valued intermediate sources in his respect for antiquarian artists like Polidoro; Andrea Mantegna; and those more emotionally invested in the material as conscious rivals to it, above all, Michelangelo. Not only was it more expedient for Rubens to study modern translations of the past than always to rely directly on original sources, but it provided him with indications of what to value. With so little ancient painting surviving to emulate, with the exception of decorative grotesques, these artists also supplied Rubens with substitute ancient narrative paintings. In this case, Rubens adapted the pose of the soldier holding the child aloft from the figure of Christ in the Resurrection, extracted from a drawing like one now at Windsor,

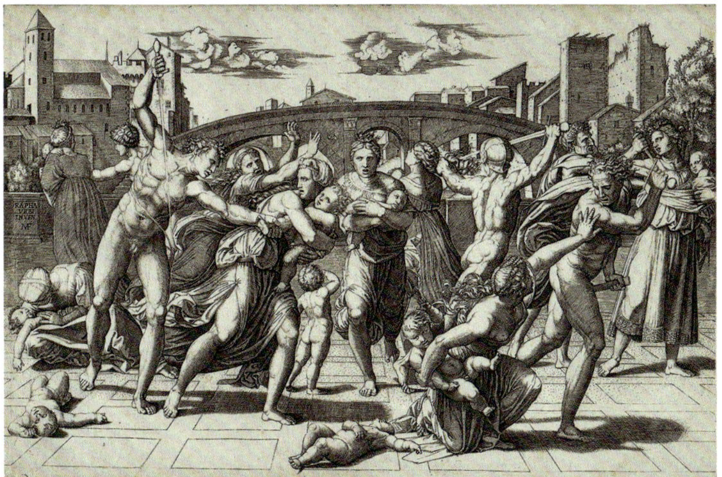

Fig 3 Marcantonio Raimondi, after Raphael, *The Massacre of the Innocents*, c. 1512–13. Engraving, 28.1 × 43 cm. The Metropolitan Museum of Art, New York, Rogers Fund, 1922. 22.67.21.

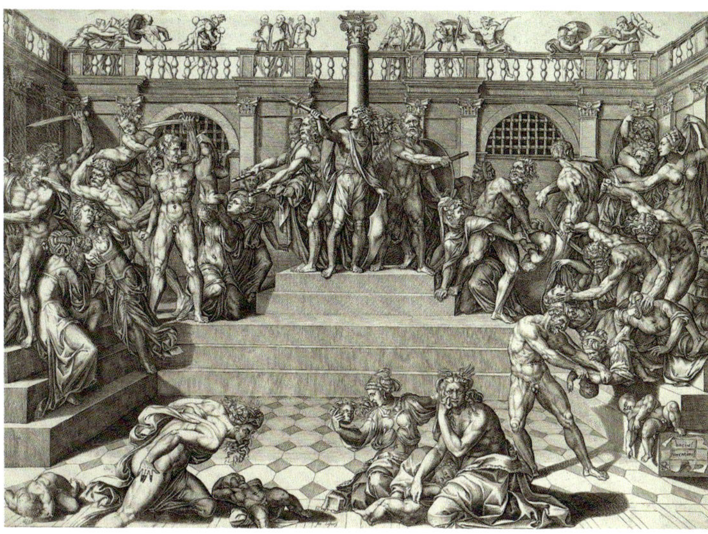

Fig 4 Marco Dente, after Baccio Bandinelli, *The Massacre of the Innocents*, no date. Engraving, 41 × 58.5 cm. The Metropolitan Museum of Art, New York, The Elisha Whittelsey Collection, The Elisha Whittelsey Fund, 1949. 49.97.618.

thought to have been intended for a fresco in the church of Santa Maria della Pace in Rome (fig. 2).[2] The general sense of tumult, arranged in a lateral frieze, recalls the Roman façade frescoes of Polidoro, who had a more rugged version of Raphael's graceful style.[3] Rubens's painting seems entranced mainly by these reference points from the previous century, but the treatment of monumental bodies lit from the side and in cascading rhythms is further indebted to the contemporary Baroque painter Caravaggio's approach, if in a hurried and dissonant time signature.

Print sources were especially important for this challenging theme and presented an esteemed lineage to Rubens. These mostly point away from Venice to Central Italy. This specific Old Testament narrative had already generated its own literate history as a demonstration piece in drawing, as recorded by a corresponding print, initiated in this case by Raphael. This helps explain why Rubens and his patron desired such an upsetting subject for a prominent location in the house. Whatever local resonance it had in Antwerp, the content was an art historical topos to address unto itself. Painting himself into this art history was a prime motivation for Rubens in tackling this particular subject and carefully replaying his source material. The confidence and self-consciousness of the artist's presentation gives the spectator some ability to cope with the awful details. Rubens had reworked Italian prints into paintings from the start of his career, and so this approach was practically a juvenile exercise. Rubens had already used this strategy as a young artist: another Raphael invention printed by Marcantonio Raimondi of the *Judgement of Paris* served as the model for a painting now in the National Gallery, London.[4] *The Massacre of the Innocents* arrogantly realized on a monumental scale what for Raphael was only a small paper print of the subject—the ambition to enlarge and supply a surrogate for a never-executed Renaissance masterpiece, so to fulfil that fictional promise. The dialogue between a monumental painting and several engravings of the same subject provides evidence for the high respect given to prints in the period, in both Italy and Northern Europe.

It was not the first print of *The Massacre of the Innocents*, but the first one relevant in this sequence for Rubens is Raphael's, executed by Marcantonio Raimondi around 1511 (fig. 3). Importantly, it was already a demonstration piece, prepared by a non-Florentine directly in response to the Florentine challenge, embodied by Leonardo and Michelangelo, to create a rich narrative with active nude bodies, but without sacrificing Raphael's own distinctive fluidity and elegance. It seems literally designed to be copied, to judge from its helpful aggregate quality. Raphael presented the story all on one level, like the Rubens, and while specific references are not explicit, they might include the nudity of the soldiers, the women's flowing hair, and the positioning of some babies. A pair of struggling figures in the background of Rubens's painting has also been pointed to as a quotation.[5]

In a relatively swift response to Raphael's print, the Florentine Baccio Bandinelli made one of the same subject, engraved by Marco Dente around 1520 (fig. 4). It was a yet larger print, now on two sheets of paper, measuring 41 by 58.5 cm. This fact alone

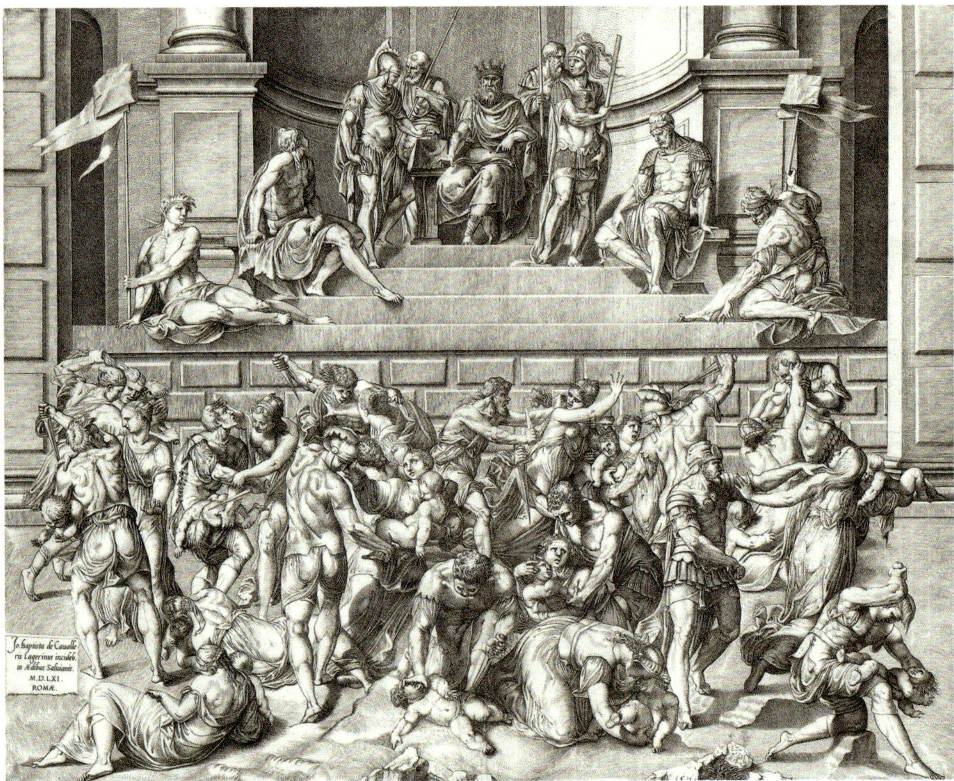

Fig 5 Giovanni Battista de' Cavalieri, *The Massacre of the Innocents*, 1561. Engraving, 47 × 59 cm. Photo © 2012 Christie's Images Limited.

betrayed its ambition to challenge the already venerated prototype of Raphael's print. Bandinelli's concentrates more on surface anatomy and musculature. Specifically, it may have inspired Rubens's choice to represent more of the dead babies lying around on the ground and the raised child about to be hurled to the ground. Rubens is known to have copied this majestic print in sketches in his notebooks. The image is now more flagrantly violent and justifies the licence Rubens would exploit in treating the repulsive subject.

Yet another large engraving of the subject was produced in Rome in 1561 by Giovanni Battista de'Cavalieri, as the theme was believed to have commercial appeal (fig. 5). It presumably records the invention of another artist, long considered to be Bandinelli again, but possibly Francesco Salviati.[6] The story is depicted on two levels, like Bandinelli's print, but it is more chaotic, taking on even further the character of a demonstration piece, with a densely populated foreground, closer in that way to what Rubens would attempt half a century later. Otherwise, it is difficult to locate any specific quotations.

Source spotting in the case of the Rubens *Massacre of the Innocents* perhaps misses the point of his intention, however. There are few precise borrowings from these prints, as Rubens was rarely copying their inventions but reworking them and the same sources they exploited. We can differentiate between two different types of influence: direct quotations intended to be perceived by knowledgeable viewers or knowingly pointed out, compared with a subtle distillation where Rubens sublimated the style into his own painting.[7] The intrinsic artistic challenge and producing a uniquely blended response, even improving on these precedents, all mattered most.

Rubens was attracted to the distribution of his inventions in print, but *The Massacre of the Innocents* was itself never turned into an engraving, perhaps because he felt the bold and intricate composition could not be successfully transcribed in a formal, technical sense. He might have hesitated from a commercial angle too, because the content was so repugnant. More than many of his paintings, with so much emphasis on non-frontal poses and site-specific illusionistic effects, it was a work to experience only in person. Perhaps the patron also wanted privacy and sense of an exclusive in this instance rather than seeking broader public glory.

As portable objects, Italian prints representing *The Massacre of the Innocents* would have been known in Northern Europe to both artists and patrons (and thus have been more relevant), in contrast to the painted sources in Italy, which only itinerant artists like Rubens could have recently seen. Prints were relatively cheap to purchase and easy to share and had a greater public relevance than more difficult-to-see paintings often in private locations. Few of the monumental Italian treatments of the subject had an impact on what Rubens would paint in Antwerp. Unlike the prints (which were a greater influence), these were created without much awareness of the others and present a less coherent group. The earliest was a fresco by Michele Alberti in the Della Rovere chapel in the church of Santissima Trinità dei Monti in Rome, based presumably on a design by Daniele da Volterra, who supplied the high altarpiece. Rubens specifically admired Daniele da Volterra, citing him, along with Bandinelli, on a page in his notebooks. Dating to the 1550s, this robust choreography was especially close in style to Michelangelo, almost as a surrogate work. For Rubens it was an important lesson for the grandiose scale and the tumbling, three-dimensional violence of his own large panel.

In an entirely contrary style, Tintoretto painted the story on a large canvas of the 1580s, in the Scuola Grande di San Rocco in Venice, a version Rubens must have seen. As much as he admired Tintoretto, Rubens's intent with his *Massacre* was not to emulate this furious approach. One awful motif of a woman bravely attempting to prevent a thrust sword with her bare hand is traceable, however, to the Venetian picture.[8] Significantly, Tintoretto's painting was made into a print by the Antwerp-born Aegidius Sadeler, which has to be dated on stylistic grounds but could predate Rubens's Toronto picture and may have supplied him with a memory aide for the Venetian canvas, in an easier-to-transcribe graphic format (fig. 6).

It is relevant to observe that Rubens's painting was assumed to have been designed for above a fireplace on a chimney, in the main room of a palace, to judge from the *di sotto in su* viewpoint. The original placement of the panel, elevated as a chimney piece respecting the Antwerp custom, had implications for how the composition is approached in illusionistic terms. As a chimney piece, because of the visual static of the real wall, the pictorial image needed to assert itself. It was also placed unusually high up relative to the proportions of the room so that the bottom margin of the painting provided real dramatic potential for the artist and impacted how the composition was developed. When the panel was in situ, the figures would have appeared precarious, as if about to fall out of the image, and one can imagine the spectator shifting involuntarily to avoid the confrontation in real physical space. Rubens learned this device not from local painting but from Italian frescoes and altarpieces in chapel settings, such as the Daniele da Volterra and Tintoretto treatments.

Closest in time, another northern Italian artist, Giovanni Battista Paggi, painted the *Massacre of the Innocents* in Genoa, 1604—a lost work recorded in an original fragment in a provincial museum and in copies including those made by Rubens in his notebooks, dateable to 1606.[9] As Paggi was living when Rubens was in Italy, they may well have met in Genoa and could have discussed approaches to this theme. This is the only importance of Paggi's painting for the Rubens of the same subject.

Accumulating examples, it is clear that Rubens was thoroughly aware of the subject in Italy before he returned to Antwerp and so perhaps convinced his patron that it was an ideal choice to demonstrate his new skills, rather than fulfilling a prior established commission purely relevant to the donor. The Holy Innocents was a feast day in the Catholic calendar, on December 28, and an altar dedication, but how relevant that was for a domestic work is not clear. Details, such as the gold highlights in the women's hair like Catholic martyr saints, recall an ecclesiastical setting and reinforce how it is at least appropriate to look at visual sources for the picture in churches.

Upon his return to Antwerp, Rubens found himself in the unusual role as both destroyer and creator of local tradition. Italy provided him with the necessary raw material. The *Massacre of the Innocents* was also represented in Northern European art. Rubens defied the best-known sixteenth-century precedent for the representation of this subject, by Frans Floris in the Antwerp Town Hall, dating to the middle of the sixteenth century. This now-lost work is recorded in a print by Philippe Galle, dated to the 1570s.[10] As someone who also respected Italy, Floris's painting was classicizing in general intent, like Rubens's panel, but to a static, staccato result that the younger artist surpassed with his fluency. Twice as large as the Toronto panel, another painting, by Cornelis van Haarlem, survives in the Rijksmuseum. A Dutch royal commission, it dates to around 1590. In this case, the painter produced an overtly political version of the subject with reference to recent Spanish atrocities. One soldier is even killed by a vengeful woman. Whether Rubens also intended a contemporary resonance for this work is not so obvious.

While Rubens was inspired by Italian artists for many formal considerations reviewed here, he was also consciously countering long-held Italian prejudices against Northern Europeans. He did this by thoroughly embracing the nude human figure in action and surface anatomy, on a campaign to elevate his national style, to demonstrate that a Northerner could work fluently in this more austere, cerebral manner. Yet if *The Massacre* is a compellingly hybrid painting, it does not finally resemble any Italian work of

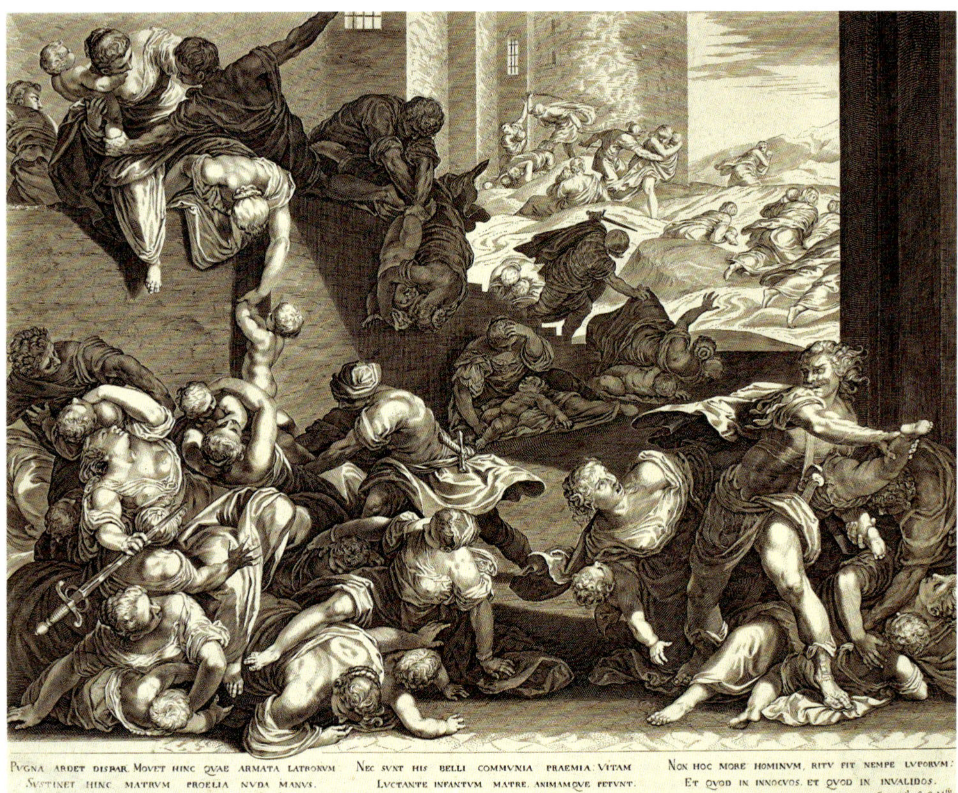

Fig 6 Aegidius Sadeler II, after Jacopo Tintoretto, *Massacre of the Innocents*, c. 1600. Engraving, 39.2 × 49.3 cm. The Metropolitan Museum of Art, New York, The Elisha Whittelsey Collection, The Elisha Whittelsey Fund, 1949. 49.95.2295.

art, and in its specifically Flemish aspects, it survived the near irresistible pull of Italy. To stress: these include the painting's uncomfortably graphic realism and attention to different textures, its glistening technique, as well as the inclusion of an elaborated background. The introduction of disturbing violence owes as much to traditions of Northern European religious and secular art as to ancient sculpture, Michelangelo, or Polidoro, in a tradition traceable to artists such as Hieronymus Bosch and Pieter Brueghel the Elder, who also painted *The Massacre of the Innocents* in a wintery setting. The unnervingly sharp contrast of beauty and ugliness, which accentuates both, was a deliberate device, recalling numerous images of the *Mocking of Christ* in Northern European painting. Certain details, such as the transfer of blood from one figure to another, a stark device Rubens often employed, would have been too graphic for an Italian artist to contemplate (with the exception of Caravaggio).

The background, defined by a receding diagonal into the left corner of the panel, contains separate narratives on a small scale, like the predella in an altarpiece. It provided the space to portray architectural ruins that reconstruct the antique setting in Bethlehem, locating the image in a historical time.[11] The smoke emitting from the chimneys indicate that the season is winter, a period of more severe emotions. The sensitive treatment of weather is more a Northern European than an Italian preoccupation in art. The relatively large amount of panel devoted to the background is also more in the Northern manner, as is the "faded" treatment of colour. The thin liquid handling portrays movement and distance. These recall the retrograde approach of Frans Floris and a German painter for whom Rubens had great respect, Adam Elsheimer, more than any Italian example. The nacreous surface is purely ornamental in finish and evokes something precious like mother of pearl or a satiny fabric, an entirely Northern appearance.

The original patron of the panel is not firmly documented. The tantalizing suggestion that it was an Italian merchant named Giacomo Antonio Carenna, long a resident in Antwerp, has been challenged.[12] Nonetheless, the Rubens is one of the first truly international paintings in art history, addressing different tastes equally. As a luxury object in Antwerp, it placed as much value on the foreign as the native. If the Toronto *Massacre of the Innocents* is a profoundly retrospective object, it points equally in many stylistic aspects to the direction of Rubens's mature career as a dominant painter in Europe.

1 On the painting see David Jaffé, *Rubens's Massacre of the Innocents: The Thomson Collection at the Art Gallery of Ontario* (London: Skylet Publishing/Art Gallery of Ontario, 2009), and Hans Devisscher and Hans Vlieghe, *Corpus Rubenianum Ludwig Burchard, Part V: The Life of Christ Before the Passion; I: The Youth of Christ*, 2 vols. (London: Harvey Miller, 2014), vol. 2: 241–45, cat. no. 52. On the vast subject of Rubens and Italy, start with Michael Jaffé, *Rubens and Italy* (Ithaca, NY: Cornell University Press, 1977), and Jeremy Wood, *Corpus Rubenianum Ludwig Burchard, Part XXVI: Copies and Adaptations from Renaissance and Later Artists, Italian Artists; II: Titian and North Italian Art*, 2 vols. (London: Harvey Miller, 2011).

2 Jaffé, *Rubens's Massacre of the Innocents*, 83, 85.

3 For Polidoro's façades in general, see now Franklin, *Polidoro da* Caravaggio (New Haven and London: Yale University Press, 2018), 39–67.

4 David Jaffé and Elizabeth McGrath, *Rubens: A Master in the Making* (London: National Gallery Company Ltd., 2005), 25–26.

5 Jaffé, *Rubens's Massacre of the Innocents*, 81.

6 Suzanne Boorsch, "Correction," *Print Quarterly* 17, no. 2 (2000): 190.

7 On the subject of Rubens's absorption of influence, see especially the comments of Joost vander Auwera in Joost vander Auwera and Sabine van Sprang, *Rubens: A Genius at Work* (Tielt: Lannoo: 2007), 66–70, exh. cat.

8 Jaffé, *Rubens's Massacre of the Innocents*, 77.

9 Jaffé, *Rubens's Massacre of the Innocents*, 82–83.

10 Jaffé, *Rubens's Massacre of the Innocents*, 84–85.

11 See the fine analysis of the background by Barbara Uppenkamp and Ben van Beneden, "Rubens and Antiquarianism: New Thoughts on the Two Versions of *The Massacre of the Innocents*," *Fragmenta* 5 (2011): 139–76.

12 See Devisscher and Vlieghe, *Corpus Rubenianum*, 244, who counter the suggestion for provenance made in Jaffé, *Rubens's Massacre of the Innocents*.

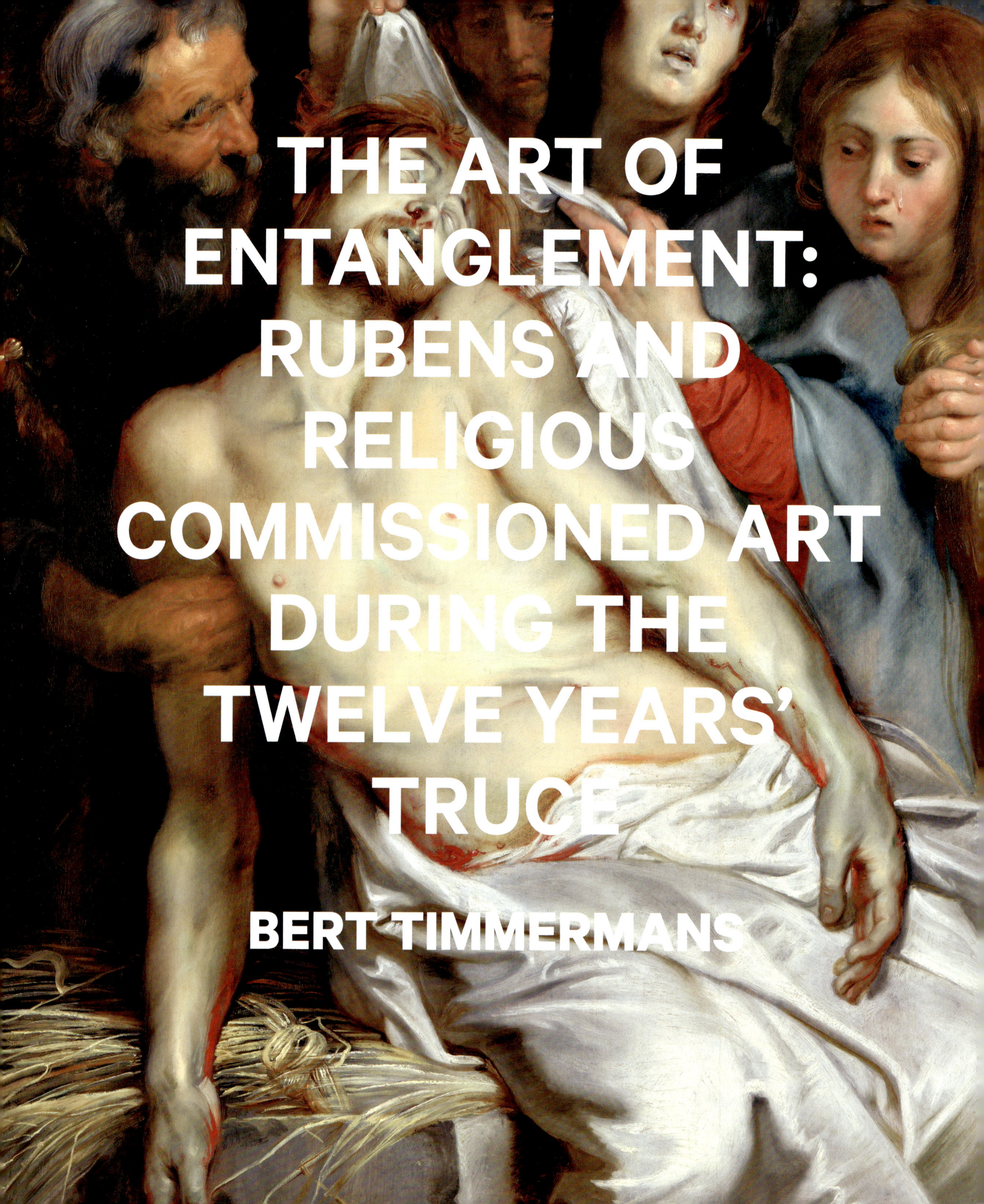

THE ART OF ENTANGLEMENT: RUBENS AND RELIGIOUS COMMISSIONED ART DURING THE TWELVE YEARS' TRUCE

BERT TIMMERMANS

PROLOGUE

A detailed reconstruction of Rubens's network within the circuit of ecclesiastical art patronage is beyond the scope of this essay. This article highlights Peter Paul Rubens's networking within elite groups in Antwerp, ability to take on a dominant market position, and his shift into a more multimedia approach. It covers network configurations, commission situations, and art decision-makers, as well as Rubens's contribution to the development of an urban media-architecture apparatus that transformed the character of many artworks and their platforms.Obviously, this trajectory was not unilinear, and Rubens's route to success contained more uncertainties than implied by the narrative below.[1]

RUBENS'S *ENROLMENT* AS THE ANTWERP PAINTER OF ALTARPIECES

On September 23, 1609, Archduke Albert and his wife, Isabella Clara Eugenia, chose Rubens as their court painter.[2] Though this appointment held significant symbolism for the artist, who had recently returned to the Low Countries from Italy, Rubens did not expect to receive a large number of commissions from the title. Instead of living in Brussels, where the court was located, Rubens requested a special status that would allow him to settle in Antwerp and establish a studio exempt from the regulations of the Antwerp Guild of Saint Luke, which represented painters and other artists.[3] By moving to Antwerp, Rubens had his eyes on the circuit of commissioned ecclesiastical art in the city.

In 1585, Antwerp returned to the rule of Hapsburg Spain following a failed revolt. This led to a significant paradigm change: the city on the Scheldt began to transition from a Calvinist republic into a stronghold of the Counter-Reformation.[4] Church infrastructure was severely damaged during the iconoclasms by the Protestants of 1566 and 1578, which also undermined the confidence of patrons of ecclesiastic art. Although the effects of those traumatic events continued to be felt for many years, recovery took place between 1585 and the conclusion of the Twelve Years' Truce in 1609. During this time, Catholic propaganda campaigns, new guidelines concerning the decoration of church interiors, and new juridical frameworks relegitimized and revitalized the model of *Christian patronage* and *salvation economy*. They had to persuade potential financiers to provide money for the salvation of their souls by acting as contributors and buyers of religious services. The Catholic Church stressed the fact that support for building and refurbishment projects counted as care for the *bonum commune* (the common welfare).[5] In this way, the conditions for the mobilization of financial resources, available again after the reconversion of the Antwerp economy in the last decade of the sixteenth and the first of the seventeenth centuries, were being shaped.[6] With a growing number of public events, such as processions and seasonal celebrations, and the increased proliferation of religious buildings, church institutions once again became the most extensive communication network in the city, (re)producing scenographies and dramaturgies and distributing images. Taking this into account, it is hardly surprising that the local secular government and the different social groups within the Antwerp social arena showed strong interest in these platforms, positioning themselves within the urban media-architecture apparatus. For artists, highly frequented ecclesiastic sites functioned as exhibition places, where huge altarpieces drew the attention of potential patrons and helped the artist build a reputation.[7]

For the successful *enrolment* of Rubens into the circuit of commissioned ecclesiastical art in Antwerp, it was essential to create a platform for his work in strategic places. This was especially crucial given that Rubens had only recently arrived in the city on the Scheldt, so only a small number of his paintings were given public display. Moreover, during Rubens's stay in Italy,[8] other Antwerp master-painters had built their reputation and networks, particularly in fraternities and artisanal corporations. After 1585, these milieus became the most important patrons of commissioned altarpieces,[9] which had become the renewed focal points of liturgical and devotional practice.[10]

Through support and financing from allies such as Antwerp mayor Nicolaas II Rockox and businessmen Louis Clarisse and Cornelis Van der Geest, grand altarpieces by Rubens were soon introduced to prominent ecclesiastical spaces, such as the church of the Dominicans, the Saint Walburga parish church and significantly, the Cathedral of Our Lady.[11] In record time, Rubens became a consecrated artist. Among potential patrons from French Flanders searching for an altarpiece, Rubens topped the list of recommended artists as early as 1611, only two years after his return from Italy.[12] In the same year, the selection committee of the Cathedral, led by dean Johannes del Rio, chose Rubens's design proposal for the high altar over that of his former teacher Otto Van Veen, who was still at the peak of his fame upon Rubens's return.[13]

Rockox[14] and Van der Geest[15] were key figures in Rubens's Antwerp network in those days. They were both important agents within artistic and information flows, enrolling and translating material and immaterial elements that stabilized the Rubens patronage assemblage. Rockox, especially, frequently acted as a decision-maker. From 1608 to 1609, Rockox, as mayor, was the driving force behind the commission of *The Adoration of the Magi*, a monumental work for the prestigious Hall of States inside the Antwerp city hall, where international delegations signed the Twelve Years' Truce in 1609.[16] Rockox regularly acted as commissioner within delegation procedures, which oversaw the artist selection process of church institutions, corporations, and fraternities, as well as of the city administration.[17] A political heavyweight, he also took up management positions outside of city council, such as presidency of the Guild of the Harquebusiers. As a driving force behind the (material) (re)territorialization process of the Counter-Reformation, he also kept in close contact with several prominent members of the Antwerp clergy. Yet his part in Rubens's *enrolment* went beyond that. Shortly after Rubens settled in Antwerp, Rockox privately ordered a showpiece, *Samson and Delilah*, for his *groote saleth*, the big ground-floor room of his urban estate.[18]

As collector-connoisseurs, Rockox and Van der Geest were owners of a *Constkamer* (art cabinet) annex and *Wunderkammer* (chamber of wonder)—a collection of paintings, sculptures, drawings, engravings, and plaster casts, but also precious gems, sundry scientific objects, minerals, and curiosities—that housed a haptic microcosm of the world.[19] These cabinets triggered the sensuous intelligence of visitors and acted as a forum for conversation, introducing collectors to new ideas and recently acquired works of art. They influenced the norms of reception and taste of art.[20] Putting themselves and their reputation behind an artist and offering a curated platform for the artist's oeuvre, collector-connoisseurs like Rockox and Van der Geest became *symbolic bankers*. Rubens proved to be a profitable investment, as his works soon became status symbols. Early patronage guaranteed prestige, even posthumously, as the notoriety of Rockox nowadays illustrates.[21] In the milieu of collectors-connoisseurs, informal, symbolic, and monetary economies were often intertwined.

During the second decade of the seventeenth century, the community around art cabinets largely overlapped with the Antwerp branch of the Republic of Letters, a long-distance intellectual community in Europe and the Americas with a strong interest in antiquity.[22] This late-Humanist intellectual scene[23] was the core of Rubens's earliest web of alliances in Antwerp.[24] Rubens also secured access to the political elite through his family background and marriage.[25] At the time, countless *grand seigneurs de commerce*, like Louis Clarisse, identified with the socio-cultural ideal of the cultivated businessman (*mercator sapiens*), which helped Rubens integrate with the also commercial elite as well.[26]

By participating in common projects and financial transactions, Rubens strengthened his social position and consolidated an ever-closer network of mutual obligations.[27] Moreover, soon after settling in Antwerp, he joined elite associations such as the Jesuit *Sodales latina maior*—or the fraternity of Romanists—an extremely exclusive society of political, commercial, clerical, and artistic elites who had lived in Italy.[28] Rubens participated in personal engagements and gatherings such as religious celebrations and banquets, and was often seen as generous by other members.[29] Interlocking connections enabled assemblies like these to act as catalysts within the Antwerp art world, mobilizing the capital of different Antwerp elite groups.

The entanglements did not, however, prevent tensions from developing between the different elite groups. During the seventeenth century, they went through a number of major transitions, the most important being the institutionalization of the commercial elite 's power within city government, and the emergence of a new urban nobility from circles of the commercial elite. Competition between old patrician families—the traditional arbiters of status—and emerging leaders of new wealth engendered feelings of uncertainty in both groups. This resulted in the increasing importance of cultural capital, as shown in a growing sensitivity toward genealogy, status honour, and displayed attachment to the *bonum commune*.[30] Patronage of the arts created platforms for representing individual, familial, and collective identities, as well as political and religious convictions. In the course of the 1610s, Rubens's income and capital, self-image, aristocratic lifestyle, and leisure activities began to coincide more and more with the financially well-off Antwerp elite, allowing him to penetrate the core of that configuration.[31]

RUBENS AND THE "RUBENSIZATION" OF ALTAR PAINTING

When Rubens first settled in Antwerp, he adopted the inventive Italian artistic techniques that he had developed over the previous decade, in accordance with the aesthetic expectations of patrons in the Antwerp milieu described above. It soon became clear that artistic innovations needed an incubation period. Different factors constrained the embedding and elaboration of innovative concepts from abroad: the attachment to their operative knowledge by the involved artists and artisans; the inertia of established practices and conventions of the fraternities and their wardens; and the material legacy represented by cherished pieces of art.[32]

For instance, Rubens complied with the opinions of the Saint Walburga church wardens, who refused to give up the traditional triptych for their high altar. At the same time, Rubens extended the enclosing limits of the frame. Having become familiar with the new Italian portico altars, which used only one large painting, Rubens likely preferred this sophisticated solution.[33] Yet he produced triptychs for two parish churches in Mechelen as late as 1619. Despite setbacks, Rubens was able to introduce new formal elements, monumentality, and increased verisimilitude of figures and textures.[34] By 1617, a new type of altar containing a vertical orientation, flanked by monumental columns, had gained acceptance. Even though Rubens did not introduce the portico altar to the Low Countries,[35] he played a key role in its acceptance by commissioners and adaptation by other painters.[36] In 1619–1620, for example, two portico altarpieces were commissioned by Rockox and silk merchant Gaspar Charles for the Antwerp Friars Minor.[37]

Paintings for epitaphs retained the triptych format longer than altarpieces. The relatives of Jan Moretus in 1611 and 1612, Rockox and his wife, Adriana Perez, from 1613 to 1615, and the couple Jan Michielsen and Maria Maes in 1617 all opted for this format. These epitaphs hailed back to a tradition in which the founders' figures were accompanied by their patron saints.[38] Yet even at the time, alternatives existed. Between 1615 and 1620, Rubens painted an epitaph for the merchant Alexander Goubau and his spouse, Anne Anthony, that depicted the couple in the eternal adoration of Virgin Mary and a child on one panel. From the 1610s onward, sculpted memorials also grew in popularity, and sculptors gained a more monumental vision under the influence of Rubens's creations.[39]

Rubens's activities were not limited to Antwerp. Prints of his large altarpieces drew the attention of potential patrons and enhanced the artist's reputation in other cities.[40] Soon enough, Rubens was able to establish connections outside of the Antwerp art world. In that respect, the city on the Scheldt proved to be an excellent choice of location: seventeenth-century Antwerp was an important information and financial hub in Europe. It was also an active centre for internationally oriented art trade.[41] During the second decade of the seventeenth century, Rubens extended his reach across the Southern Netherlands and its neighbouring regions, including French Flanders from 1612 onward,[42] Mechelen, Lier, Ghent, and Brussels after 1615, and to areas further abroad. Around that time, Rubens found a way into the international network of Jesuit communities. Rubens received Jesuit commissions from beyond Antwerp—from Genoa and Neuburg on the Danube, among others. Prominent Jesuits even acted as intermediaries for commissions from third parties abroad.[43] As such, Rubens's artworks became symbolic referents, creating vehicles for Antwerp art into other German states.[44]

In the meantime, the Antwerp program for rebuilding and renovating church buildings was running smoothly, and the *invasion conventuelle*—the establishment of convents—was stepping up gear. Intermediary institutions such as sodalities and confraternities also proliferated.[45] Since most of these organizations were setting up projects of (re)decoration, they created a constant stream of commissions for altarpieces. Rubens created twenty-two altarpieces in Antwerp between 1609 and 1620. During this period, his total output for religious buildings in Antwerp and abroad was no less than sixty-three works.[46] Production on such scale was made possible only by setting up a large studio around 1615, following the examples of painters Frans Floris and Tintoretto.[47] Through procedural and product innovations, Rubens's studio dominated in the field of monumental religious painting to such an extent that other artists, like Abraham Janssens and Cornelis de Vos, were forced to focus on provincial commissions in smaller towns and villages, with negative financial consequences.[48]

RUBENS AND THE ART OF ENTANGLEMENT

Around 1616 and 1617, Rubens created two large paintings for the main altar of the Saint Ignatius church, which was under construction at that time.[49] They were meant to be shown alternately by a rotation system in a monumental portico altar that was still to be constructed. The Antwerp Jesuits opted for a spatial arrangement that conformed to Charles Borromeo's 1577 tract on Christian living, which stated that the high altar should capture the eye as soon as a visitor entered a church building. These two altarpieces were overtures for a larger-scale project, in which Rubens could partly realize his ambitions as a painter-architect by integrating his painting in an architectural context.[50] This innovative mobilization of media was part of an emergent *media-architecture apparatus*, in which cultural, perceptual, and technological shifts, alongside new aesthetic and spatial forms, manifested themselves.

The reason many artistic and architectural innovations with an affective material productivity were realized in the site of the Saint Ignatius complex had to do with the Antwerp Jesuits' mindset. The international Society of Jesus was fighting two wars as the spearhead of a spiritual counteroffensive against Protestantism: a war of knowledge and a war of images.[51] The Antwerp hub played a major role in this fight, gaining the reputation of being a frontline city.[52] As the Society was convinced that a *culture of spectacle* and an *aesthetics of astonishment* had a greater influence than sermons on the illiterate masses, they used media devices as an integral part of their spiritual war machine.[53] The Antwerp Jesuits were exceptionally successful at implementing this internationally developed strategy, impressing both the Antwerp flock and visitors from foreign Protestant countries with dynamism and a "marble temple." The sensuous textures of the new church and the way its building materials juxtaposed with the tactility of natural light created an atmosphere previously unknown in the city on the Scheldt.[54] The Antwerp Jesuits produced a *haptic visuality*, the interpenetration of touch and vision, making embodied contact with its beholder and drawing the spectator into the work of art.[55] This approach required adopting and developing an *ars combinatoria* (art of entanglement), the integration of different media like small architecture, sculpture, and painting within an overall spatial concept. This relied on complex and cross-disciplinary artistic cooperation that employed the knowledge and skills of multiple individuals.

In their ambition to pool wide-ranging artistic knowledge to construct the Saint Ignatius church, the Jesuits employed Rubens as the *pictor doctus* (painter-intellectual) and painter-architect.[56] Rubens worked with the architect duo Pieter Huyssens, S.J., and François d'Aguilon, S.J., as well as a sculpture studio, leading to the realization that "architecture, sculpture and painting speak with one voice."[57] Due to this collaborative approach, Rubens's precise contribution to the architectural and sculptural dimensions of the Saint Ignatius project is difficult to gauge,[58] though his studio was indisputably responsible for two imposing paintings for the high altar and an impressive series of thirty-nine ceiling paintings.[59] Rubens had never before worked on a project with such complexity and monumental scale.[60]

The construction of the Saint Ignatius complex was unseen in terms of sheer bravado and unprecedented in its speed of realization, cost (535,734 florins in 1621), and reliance on borrowed money.[61] This led to growing concerns from the Roman headquarters of the Jesuit order. Nonetheless, the Antwerp Jesuits heedlessly continued their policy of deficit spending, leading to rising interests and debts. As a result, Antwerp carried, at 514,681 florins, 71.1% of the total debt held by the Flandro-Belgian province, threatening to drag the entire region into bankruptcy. Facing this crisis, the Antwerp Society of Jesus counted on the goodwill of artists like Rubens, who waited years before being paid the considerable sums owed for their labour.[62] The Jesuits were eventually able to stabilize their finances thanks to the patronage assemblage set up by the Society. Despite alarming reports on the threatening bankruptcy, wealthy individuals and merchant families lent large amounts of money (including 64,200 florins from the Houtappel-Grevens family and 4,560 florins from Nicolaas Rockox). Those donors retained trust in the Society and/or enabled the financial reorganization imposed by Rome through donations and bequests.

Even before 1585, during the Calvinist republic (1578–1585), the Antwerp Society secured a place in the network of Catholic families that would later become the Antwerp political and economic elite, some of whom were in exile in Cologne at the time.[63] Back in Antwerp, prominent Jesuits such as rector P. Carolus Scribani, S.J., further widened and strengthened this network.[64] In addition, the Jesuits could rely on a structure of sodalities of Our Lady—congregations with either an inclusive or elitist character—to support their activities and patrimony. Those sodalities became important patrons of the Society while also acting as intermediaries for private patrons. Prominent artists such as Rubens and Antony van Dyck and wealthy benefactors such as mayors Gillis Gerardi and Nicolaas Rockox all contributed to the Jesuits through their membership in sodalities. Rockox donated 4,300 florins and financed Rubens's altarpiece for the Saint Joseph church.[65]

EPILOGUE: VECTORS INTO THE FUTURE

The multimedia concept of the Antwerp Jesuit church, with its already extensive integration of (small) architecture, sculpture, and painting within an overall spatial frame and rich use of material textures, constituted an influential answer to the merger of decoration and architecture, an artistic question confronting many ecclesiastical buildings in the seventeenth-century Southern Netherlands. This also had its consequences for the Antwerp patronage assemblage and influenced Rubens's career.

As a painter-architect, Rubens played a significant role in designing and decorating the Saint Joseph altar in the Saint Ignatius church during the 1620s. The space was inspired by the concept of the Italian *capella gentilizia*, a semi-autonomous enclosed entity.[66] The elaborate construction, the interplay of different media, and the abundance of luxuriant materials like polychrome marble surfaces, colours, and textures demanded the involvement of the worshippers and made the Houtappel a milestone in the revival of the family chapel in Antwerp. This form of capital-intensive patronage often became a trans-generational, mostly familial project in ecclesiastical art and architecture. The Houtappel family—who only employed the most prestigious artists of the day, such as Rubens and the De Nole sculpture studio—invested an amount of at least 91,000 florins, facilitating an elaborate artistic program.[67] This created platforms for the artists to realize new concepts within the context of an *ars combinatoria*, the art of entanglement. In this way, the multimedia approach that built the Houtappel Chapel influenced later chapel realizations of the 1630s.[68]

To create the portico altar of the Houtappel Chapel, Rubens collaborated with Andreas Colyns de Nole's sculpture studio. Around that time, the relationship between small architecture, sculpture, and painting was beginning to change. Architectural motifs became integrated with figure sculpture, and painting, and artists deliberately extended one art form into the other. This led to more complex forms in seventeenth-century altars, generating an inter-sensorial texture of perception.[69] More than before, product innovation and changes in taste claimed their place within Antwerp altar production. High altars became more monumental and more sumptuous, while their lifecycle became shorter. This was made by competition between patrons, which set new and more expensive standards for consumption.

Finally, another element of the Saint Ignatius project needs to be viewed in light of changes in the *media-architecture apparatus* from the growing importance of the *ars combinatoria*: a series of ceiling paintings produced by the Rubens studio for the lower and upper galleries of the church. It was a commission in the Italian style, demanding capital-intensive patronage and centralized power of decision. The project allowed Rubens to prove that he was capable of managing a project of such scope, and it became a stepping stone to prestigious commissions in foreign courts.[70]

1 I wish to express my gratitude to Dr. Alexandra Suda and Koen Bulckens for their invitation to contribute to the present publication.

2 Frans Baudouin, *Rubens en zijn eeuw* (Antwerpen: Mercatorfonds, 1972), 12-13; Nils Büttner, *Herr P. P. Rubens: Von der Kunst, berühmt zu werden* (Göttingen: Vandenhoeck & Ruprecht, 2006), 39-40.

3 For the Counter-Reformation in Antwerp, see: Alfons K.L. Thijs, *Van Geuzenstad tot katholiek bolwerk. Maatschappelijke betekenis van de Kerk in contrareformatorisch Antwerpen* (Turnhout: Brepols, 1990); M.J. Marinus, *De Contrareformatie te Antwerpen* (1585-1676) (Brussels, 1995).

4 For the *war of images* in the Low Countries and their different phases: David Freedberg, *Iconoclasm and Painting in the Revolt of the Netherlands, 1566–1609* (New York-London: Garland, 1988); Koenraad Jonckheere, *Antwerp after Iconoclasm. Experiments in decorum, 1566–1585* (New Haven, London: Yale University Press, 2012); Christine Göttler, *Die Kunst des Fegefeuers nach der Reformation. Kirchliche Schenkungen, Abla® und Almosen in Antwerpen und Bologna um 1600* (Mainz: Verlag Philipp von Zabern, 1996). For the after-effects: Björn Schmelzer,"Singers in the Church: Implications of Voice, Sound and Movement in Post-Iconoclastic Interiors by Van Steenwijck, Grimmer and Neeffs," in *Divine Interiors. Experience churches in the age of Rubens*, ed. Claire Baisier (Kontich: BAI, 2016), 38–55.

5 Important studies concerning the Antwerp *Indian Summer* are: Wilfried Brulez, "Anvers de 1585 à 1650," *Vierteljahrschrift für Sozial-und Wirschaftgeschichte* 53, (1967): 75–99; Eddy Stols, *De Spaanse Brabanders of de handelsbetrekkingen der Zuidelijke Nederlanden met de Iberische wereld 1598-1648* (Brussels, 1971), 2 vols; Roland Baetens, *De nazomer van Antwerpens welvaart. De diaspora en het handelshuis De Groote tijdens de 1ste helft der 17de eeuw* (Brussels, 1976), 2 vols.

6 Bert Timmermans, *Patronen van patronage in het zeventiende—eeuwse Antwerpen. Een elite als actor binnen een kunstwereld* (Amsterdam: Amsterdam University Press, 2008).

7 Frans Baudouin, "Iconografie en stijlontwikkeling in de godsdienstige schilderkunst te Antwerpen in de zeventiende eeuw," in *Antwerpen in de XVIIde eeuw*, ed. W. Couvreur (Antwerp: Mercurius, 1989), 335; Ulrich Heinen, *Rubens zwischen Predigt und Kunst: Der Hochaltar für die Walburgenkirche in Antwerpen* (Weimar: Verlag und Datenbank für Geisteswissenschaften, 1996), 96–97.

8 Frederik Verleysen, "*Pretense Confrerieën?* Devotie als communicatie in de Antwerpse corporatieve wereld na 1585," *Tijdschrift voor Sociale Geschiedenis* 26 (2001): 153–74.

9 Ulrich Becker, *Studien zum flämishen Altarbau im 17: und 18. Jahrhundert* (Brussel, 1990), 101–19; Annick Delfosse, "Le dispositif de l'autel: normes liturgiques," in *Machinae spirituales: Les retables baroques dans les Pays-Bas méridionaux et en Europe; Contributions à une histoire formelle du sentiment religieux au 17e siècle*, ed. Brigitte D'Hainaut-Zveny and Ralph Dekoninck (Brussels: IRPA, 2014).

10 At the church of the Dominicans: *The Real Presence in the Holy Sacrament*; at St. Walburga Church: *The Raising of the Cross* (1610–11) (cost 2,600 florins); at the cathedral: *The Descent from the Cross* (1612–14) (cost 2,400 florins) for the Guild of the Harquebusiers. J.R. Martin, *The Antwerp Altar Pieces* (London: Thames & Hudson, 1969), R.A. D'Hulst, *De kruisoprichting van Pieter Paul Rubens* (Brussels: Roularta Books, 1992); Heinen, *Rubens zwischen Predigt und Kunst*.

11 A. Monballieu, "P.P. Rubens en het *Nachtmael voor Sint-Winoksbergen* (1611), een niet uitgevoerd schilderij van de meester," *Jaarboek Koninklijk Museum voor Schone Kunsten*, 1965: 186–97.

12 Carl van de Velde, "Rubens Hemelvaart van Maria in de kathedraal te Antwerpen," *Jaarboek Koninklijk Museum voor Schone Kunsten* 1975: 245–77.

13 H. van Cuyck, *Levensschets van Nicolaas Rockox den jongere, burgemeester van Antwerpen in de XVIIde eeuw* (Antwerp, 1882); Frans Baudouin, *Nicolaas Rockox, "vriendt ende patroon" van Peter Paul Rubens* (Brussels: Kredietbank, 1977); Leen Huet and Jan Grieten, *Nicolaas Rockox, 1560–1640: Burgemeester van de Gouden Eeuw* (Antwerp: Meulenhoff/Manteau, 2010).

14 A.J.J. Delen, "Cornelis Van der Geest: Een groot figuur in de geschiedenis van Antwerpen," *Antwerpen: Tijdschrift der Stad Antwerpen* 5 (1959): 57–72.

15 B. Welzel, "Rubens' Anbetung der Könige 1608 und 1628/29: die Gestaltung für verschiedene Patrone," in *Sponsors of the Past: Flemish Art and Patronage, 1550–1700*, ed. Hans Vlieghe and Katlijne van der Stighelen (Turnhout: Brepols, 2005), 229–38.

16 These special committees chose the artist, subcontracted the commission, and took responsibility for any follow-up, deciding on a number of elements, including format, place of exposition, theme, and financial arrangements. Timmermans, *Patronen van patronage*, 250–51.

17 David Jaffé, "Rubens" *Samson en Delila*, het verhaal achter een schoorsteenstuk," in *Samson en Delila: Een Rubensschilderij keert terug* (Antwerp, 2007), 10–17.

18 Barbara M. Stafford, "Technologies/Magical Domains," in *Devices of Wonder: From the World in a Box to Images on a Screen*, ed. Barbara M. Stafford and Frances Terpak (Los Angeles: Getty Publications, 2001), 6–7, 11–12; Horst Bredekamp, *The Lure of Antiquity and the Cult of the Machine: The Kunstkammer and the Evolution of Nature, Art and Technology*, trans. Allison Brown (Princeton, NJ: Markus Wiener, 1995), 72–73, 113.

19 Jeffrey M. Muller, "De verzameling van Rubens in historisch perspectief," in *Een huis vol kunst: Rubens als verzamelaar*, ed. Kristin Lohse Belkin and Fiona Healy (Schoten, 2004), 63–66, exh. cat.; J. Briels, "Amor Pictoriae Artis: De Antwerpse kunsthandelaar Pieter Stevens (1590–1668) en zijn constkamer," *Jaarboek Koninklijk Museum voor Schone Kunsten*, 1980: 203–26.

20 Heinen, *Rubens zwischen Predigt und Kunst*, 93–96; Büttner, *Herr P. P. Rubens*, 143–44.

21 H. Bots and F. Waquet, *Commercium litterarium: La communication dans la République des Lettres, 1600–1750; Forms of Communication in the Republic of Letters* (Amsterdam: APA–Holland University Press, 1994); Arjan van Dixhoorn and Susie Speakman Sutch, ‹*The Reach of the Republic of Letters: Literary and Learned Societies in Late Medieval and Early Modern Europe* (Leiden: Brill, 2008).

22 Mark P.O. Morford, *Stoics and Neostoics: Rubens and the Circle of Lipsius* (Princeton, NJ: Princeton University Press, 1991).

23 Among them were Rubens's older brother Philip; his father-in-law, Jan Brant; and Hendrik de Moy, all three of them important technocrats within the city administration; Jan van de Wouwere, who would build a diplomatic career; and his brother-in-law Louis Clarisse, businessman-banker and later alderman and Amman; Balthasar Moretus, manager of the important Antwerp publishers *Officina Plantiniana*; the Jesuit Andreas Schott and Canon Laurens Beyerlinck. Büttner, *Herr P. P. Rubens*, 42–43, Nils Büttner, "Rubens & Son," in *Family Ties: Art Production and Kinship Patterns in the Early Modern Low Countries*, ed. Koenraad Brosens, Leen Kelchtermans, and Katlijne van der Stighelen (Turnhout: Brepols, 2012), 131–44.

24 Rubens's father had been an alderman in the 1560s. In October 1609, Rubens married Isabella Brant, daughter of Jan Brant.

25 Christopher White, "Rubens en de klassieke oudheid," in *De eeuw van Rubens*, ed. Peter Sutton (Antwerp: Mercatorfonds, 1994), 147–58.

26 Büttner, *Herr P. P. Rubens*, 68–73.

27 Rijksarchief Antwerpen, Kerkelijk Archief, Sint Joris 63. Rekeningen van de oudermannen van de gilde van de Romanisten, 1574–1785; E. Dilis, *La confrérie des* romanistes (Antwerp, 1923); Timmermans, *Patronen van patronage*, 257.

28 Büttner, *Herr P. P. Rubens*, 67–68.

29 Roland Baetens and Bruno Blondé, "A la recherche de l'identité sociale et de la culture bourgeoise anversoise aux temps moderne," *Histoire, Economie et Société* 13 (1994): 531–39; Bert Timmermans, "The 17th Century Antwerp Elite and Status Honour: The Presentation of Self and the Manipulation of Social Perception," in *On the Edge of Truth and Honesty: Intersections; Yearbook for Early Modern Studies* 2 (2002): 149–65, and Bert Timmermans, "(Family) Portraits in the Construction of a Visual Family Tree and a Social Identity: Anticipating the Aspirations of Elite Clientele in Seventeenth-Century Antwerp," in *Pokerfaced: Flemish and Dutch Baroque Faces Unveiled*, ed. Katlijne van der Stighelen and Bert Watteeuw (Turnhout: Brepols, 2011), 175–92.

30 Büttner, *Herr P. P. Rubens*, 68–71, 74–75.

31 Becker, *Studien*, 91; Joost van der Auwera, "Conservatieve tendensen in de contrareformatorische kunst: Het geval Abraham Janssens," *Zeventiende eeuw* 5 (1989): 32–43, Natasja Peeters, "Diversité et originalité d´une expérience formelle de transition: Les triptique des corporations dans la cathédrale d´Anvers (1609)," in *Machinae spirituales: Les retables baroques dans les Pays-Bas méridionaux et en Europe; Contributions à une histoire formelle du sentiment religieux au 17e siècle*, ed. Brigitte D'Hainaut-Zveny and Ralph Dekoninck (Brussels: IRPA, 2014), 45–59.

32 Martin, *The Antwerp*, 40–43; d'Hulst *De kruisoprichting*, 59; Hans Vlieghe, "Rubens back in Antwerp: Reflections on the Change of His Style and the Taste Pattern of His Public," in *Actes du XXVIIe Congrès International d'Histoire de l'Art (1989)* (Strasbourg, 1993), 49–54; Heinen, *Rubens zwischen Predigt und Kunst*, 88–90.

33 Thomas L. Glen, *Rubens and the Counter Reformation: Studies in His Religious Paintings between 1609 and 1620* (Ann Arbor, MI: University Microfilms, 1978), 2–3, 12–15; Baudouin, *Iconografie en stijlontwikkeling*, 339; Hans Vlieghe, *Flemish Art and Architecture, 1585–1700* (New Haven, CT: Yale University Press, 1998).

34 Valérie Herremans, "Italië als inspiratiebron voor het zeventiende-eeuwse Zuid-Nederlandse retabel?" in *Relations Artistiques entre Italie et anciens Pays-Bas (XVIe et XVIIe Siecles): Bilan et Perspectives*, ed. R. Dekoninck (Brussels: Belgisch Historisch Instituut te Rome, 2012), 116–24.

35 Baudouin, *Rubens en zijn eeuw*, 73–91; Becker, *Studien*, 31–32, 64–84.

36 Baudouin, *Rubens en zijn eeu* : 75.

37 C. Eisler, "Rubens' Uses of the Northern Past: The Michiels Triprych and His Sources," *Bulletin van de Koninklijke Musea voor Schone Kunsten van België* 16 (1967): 43–77; David Freedberg, "Rubens as a Painter of Epitaphs, 1612–1618," *Gentse Bijdragen tot de Kunstgeschiedenis* 24 (1976–78): 51–71.

38 Cynthia Miller Lawrence, *Flemish Baroque Commemorative Monuments, 1566–1725* (New York: Garland, 1981), 135–37, J.S. Held, *Rubens and His Circle* (Princeton, NJ: Princeton University Press, 1982), 80–93.

39 Baudouin, *Rubens en zijn eeuw*, 14.

40 R. Pieper, "Informationszentren im Vergleich. Die Stellung Venedigs und Antwerpens im 16 Jahrhundert," in *Kommunikationsrevolutionen: Die Neuen Medien Des 16; Und 19; Jahrhunderts*, ed. Michael North (Cologne: Böhlau, 1995), 45–60; Roland Baetens, "Le rôle d'Anvers dans la transmission de valeurs culturelles au temps de son apogée (1500–1650)," in *17e Colloque international: Spa, 16–19; V. 1994; La ville et la transmission des valeurs culturelles au bas moyen âge et aux temps modernes; Actes* (Brussels: Crédit Communal de Belgique, 1996), 37–72.

41 Jan Białostocki, "The Descent from the Cross in Works by Peter Paul Rubens and His Studio," *Art Bulletin* 46, no. 4 (1964): 511–24.

42 Jeffrey Chipps Smith, "Rubens, Veit Adam von Gepeckh, and the Freising High Altar, 1623–1625," in *The Age of Rubens: Diplomacy, Dynastic Politics and the Visual Arts in Early Seventeenth-Century Europe*, ed. R. Malcolm Smuts and Luc Duerloo (Turnhout: Brepols, 2016), 265.

43 Jeffrey Chipps Smith, *Sensuous Worship: Jesuits and the Art of the Early Catholic Reformation in Germany* (Princeton, NJ: Princeton University Press, , 2002), 190.

44 Timmermans, *Patronen van patronage*, 117–46.

45 Glen, *Rubens and the Counter Reformation*, 20.

46 Baudouin, *Rubens en zijn eeuw*, 45, 62.

47 Katlijne van der Stighelen and Hans Vlieghe, *Cornelis de Vos (1584/5–1651) als historie- en genreschilder* (Brussels, 1994), 52; Vlieghe, *Flemish Art*, 42.

48 Baudouin, *Rubens en zijn eeuw*, 109–18, Christine Göttler, "*Actio* in Peter Paul Rubens' Hochaltarbilder für die Jesuitenkirche in Antwerpen," in *Barocke Inszenierung*, ed. Joseph Imorde (Emsdetten: Edition Imorde, 1999), 10–31.

49 For the sixteenth- and seventeenth-century tradition of painter-architect, see Becker, *Studien*, 56–57.

50 Manuel DeLanda, *War in the Age of Intelligent Machines* (New York: Zone Books, 1991), 187–88; Steven J. Harris, "Confession-Building, Long-Distance Networks, and the Organization of Jesuit Science," *Early Science and Medicine* 1, no. 3: 287–318.

51 Barbara Haeger, "The Façade of the Jesuit Church in Antwerp: Representing the Church Militant and Triumphant," in *Innovation and Experience in the Early Baroque in the Southern Netherlands: The Case of the Jesuit Church in Antwerp*, ed. Piet Lombaerde (Turnhout: Brepols, 2008), 97–124.

52 This policy of the Jesuits markedly differed from that of the Protestant Reformation, which preferred the Word over images and intellectual apprehension over bodily perception. For the Southern Netherlands, see Jeffrey Muller, "Jesuit Uses of Art in the Province of Flanders," in *The Jesuits II: Cultures, Sciences, and the Arts, 1540–1773*, ed. J.W. O'Malley, G.A. Bailey, S.J. Harris, and T.F. Kennedy (Toronto: University of Toronto Press, 2006), 113–55. Muller also points out that the Antwerp Society of Jesus, in the realization of the St. Ignatius church, deviated from the previous, more sober mode of decoration that was characteristic of Jesuit churches in Italy.

53 Ria Fabri, "Light and Measurement: A Theoretical Approach of the Interior of the Jesuit Church in Antwerp," in Lombaerde, *Innovation and Experience*, 175–86; Léon Lock, "Rubens and the Sculpture and Marble Decoration," in Lombaerde, *Innovation and Experience*, 155–74.

54 John Rupert Martin, *Baroque* (London: Penguin, 1977), 45–55 and 73, 155–56, on Loyola's sensual and emotive routes towards piety and co-extensive space. See Mieke Bal, *Quoting Caravaggio: Contemporary Art, Preposterous History* (Chicago: University of Chicago Press, 1999), 28, 30, and 140–41, for the concept of a correlativist aesthetics that demands the feeling, vision, and thought of the beholder. See also Laura U. Marks, *Touch: Sensuous Theory and Multisensory Media* (Minneapolis: University of Minnesota Press, 2002), 6–7, 12–16, 132.

55 August Ziggelaar, S.J., "Peter Paul Rubens and François de Aguilón," in Lombaerde, *Innovation and Experience*, 31–40; Ria Fabri and Piet Lombaerde, "Appendix I: Architectural Treatises, Books and Prints in the Libraries of the Jesuits in Antwerp," in Lombaerde, *Innovation and Experience*, 187–200.

56 Katharine Fremantle, *The Baroque Town Hall of Amsterdam* (Utrecht: Haentjens Dekker & Gumbert, 1959), 131.

57 This collaboration likely did not follow the strict modern demarcation of authorship. On the question of what can be ascribed to whom, see Frans Baudouin, "Peter Paul Rubens and the Notion 'Painter-Architect,'" in *The Reception of P.P. Ruben's Palazzi di Genova during the 17th Century in Europe: Questions and Problems*, Architectura Moderna, vol. 1, ed. Piet Lombaerde (Turnhout: Brepols, 2002), 15–36. See also Piet Lombaerde, "Introduction," in Lombaerde, *Innovation and Experience*, 15–30 and Piet Lombaerde, "The Façade and the Towers of the Jesuit Church in the Urban Landscape of Antwerp during the Seventeenth Century," in Lombaerde, *Innovation and Experience*, 77–96.

58 For a bibliography and in-depth discussion of this series, I refer to the contribution by Koen Bulckens on page 84.

59 Martin, *The Antwerp*, 39.

60 Timmermans, *Patronen van patronage*, 135–43, with archival and bibliographic references.

61 Even though the book project had promised Rubens 3,000 florins in April 1617, he had to wait for years before actually getting paid.

62 J.B. Kettenmeyer, *Die Anfänge der Marianischen Sodalität in Köln, 1576–1586* (Münster: Aschendorff, 1928), Bert Timmermans, "Mapping the Role of Commemorative Space in Processes of (Re)Territorialization: Elite Families and Spatialities of Enclosure in Counter-Reformation Antwerp," in *Reformations and Their Impact on the Culture of Memoria*, ed. Truus van Bueren, Paul Cockerham, Caroline Horch, Martine Meuwese, and Thomas Schilp (Turnhout: Brepols, 2016), 290–94

63 Familiar with the ins and outs of trade, they advised merchants and bankers on ethical matters, acted as confidant, and were sought out for spiritual assistance, for instance by the Houtappels, among other groups. Alfred Poncelet, S.J., *Histoire de la Compagnie de Jésus dans les anciens Pays-Bas: établissement de la Compagnie de Jésus en Belgique et ses développements jusqu'à la fin du règne d'Albert et d'Isabelle* (Brussels: Lamertin, 1927), 2:95–97; Jos Andriessen, *De jezuïeten en het samenhorigheidsbesef in de Nederlanden, 1585–1648* (Antwerp, Nederlandsche Boekhandel, 1957), 100–3, 171–73; Louis Brouwers, *Carolus Scribani S.J., 1561–1629: Een groot man van de Contra-Reformatie in de Nederlanden* (Antwerp: Ruusbroecgenootschap, 1961), 155, 108–9, 187, 279–82, 501.

64 R. Mannaerts, *De artistieke expressie van de mariale devotie der Jezuïeten te Antwerpen (1562–1773): Een iconografisch onderzoek* (Leuven: master's thesis, KUL, 1983), 2:237–79, 243; W. Scheelen, "De rol van de jezuïeten bij het tot stand komen van hun kunstpatrimonium," *De zeventiende eeuw* 5 (1989): 60–66.

65 Bert Timmermans, "The Chapel of the Houtappel Family: The Privatisation of the Church and the Extension of the House in Seventeenth-Century Antwerp," in Lombaerde, *Innovation and Experience*, 175–86.

66 Bert Timmermans, "*Siet wat een vrucht dat baert hen kercken te vercieren:* Family, Agency and Networks of Patronage; Towards a Mapping of the Revival of the Family Chapel in Seventeenth-Century Antwerp," in Brosens, Kelchtermans, and Van der Stighelen, *Family Ties: Art Production and Kinship Patterns in the Early Modern Low Countries* (Turnhout: Brepols, 2012), 189–224.

67 Becker, *Studien*, 68–72

68 John Rupert Martin, *The Ceiling Paintings for the Jesuit Church in Antwerp* (London: Phaidon, 1968), 42–43, Baudouin, *Rubens en zijn eeuw*, 14.

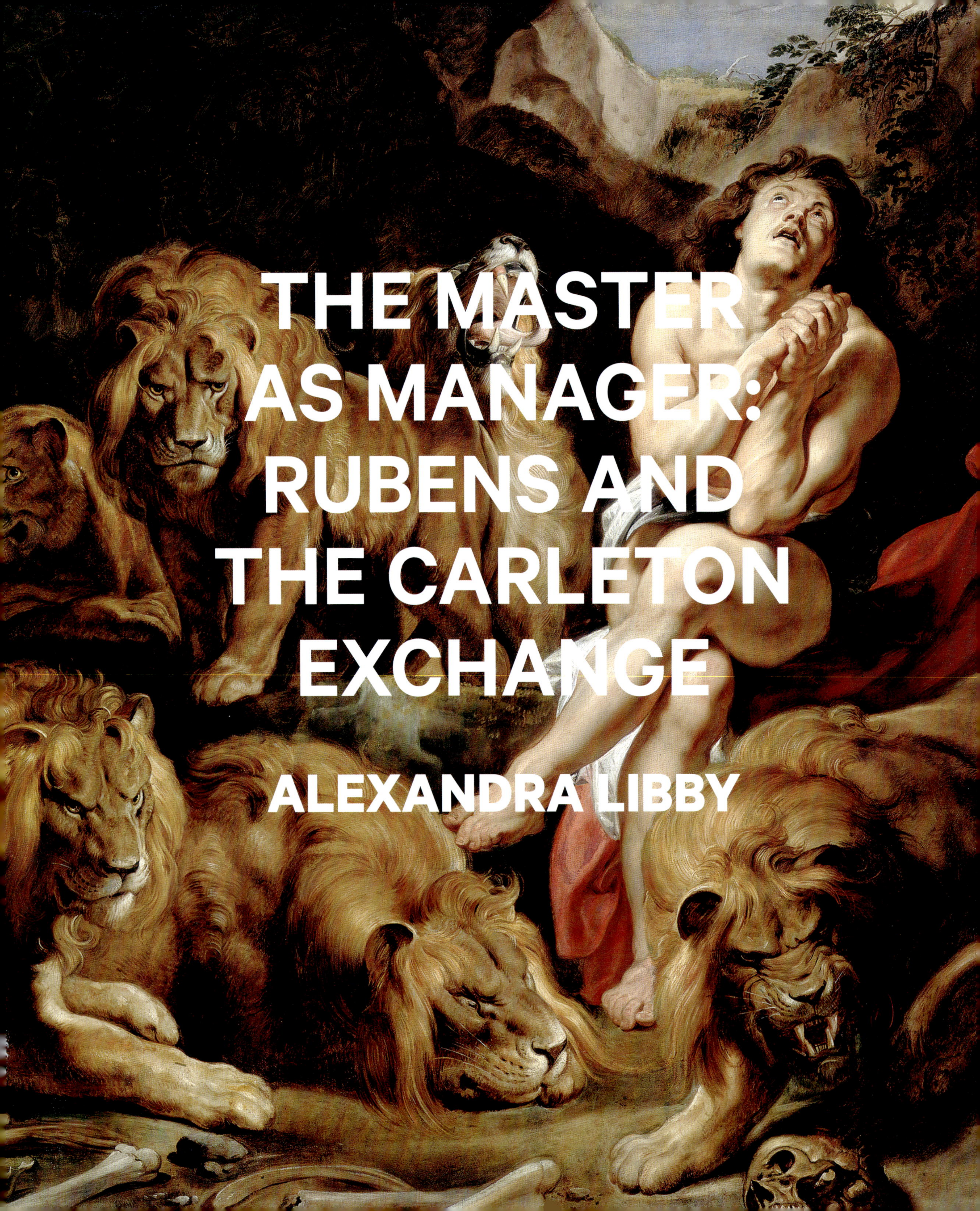
THE MASTER AS MANAGER: RUBENS AND THE CARLETON EXCHANGE
ALEXANDRA LIBBY

BY 1617, PETER PAUL RUBENS WAS VERY BUSY. Although he had returned to Antwerp only nine years earlier, having spent nearly as many years in Italy, he had already painted more than sixty altarpieces with the assistance of his studio (see essay by Bert Timmermans in this volume, page 62–70), completed a series of civic commissions, and executed a number of private works, such as his magnificent *Michielsen Triptych* for the Antwerp merchant Jan Michielsen and his wife, Maria Maes, (page 208) and his *Samson and Delilah* for the Antwerp alderman Nicolaas Rockox (1560–1640) (page 166). He had also been appointed court painter to the Archduke Albert (1559–1621) and the Infanta Isabella Clara Eugenia (1566–1644) with special dispensation that allowed him to remain in Antwerp rather than the court city of Brussels, and, finally, was managing a studio so full that he was forced to turn away scores of aspiring young artists. "From all sides applications reach me," Rubens told his friend Jacob de Bie in 1611. "Some young men remain here for several years with other masters, awaiting a vacancy in my studio . . . I can tell you truly, without exaggeration, that I have have [sic] to refuse over one hundred, even some of my own relatives or my wife's, and not without causing great displeasure among many of my best friends."[1] Around that time he had also purchased and undertaken the renovation of a large home and garden in one of Antwerp's most prestigious neighbourhoods and was actively enlarging his personal collection of art. With Rubens's attention pulled in so many directions, one cannot help but wonder how he managed it all.

The case of the collector and entrepreneur Sir Dudley Carleton, English ambassador to The Hague (1573–1632), may provide some clues. If Rubens was busy by 1617, Carleton was in a bind. During his previous ambassadorship in Venice from 1612 to 1614, he amassed a substantial collection of antique sculpture that he had intended to use as gifts to curry favour at the Stuart Court.[2] By the time Carleton shipped the collection from Venice to London in the spring of 1615, however, the unpredictability of court life meant that the intended recipient, Robert Carr, Earl of Somerset (c. 1587–1645), was no longer the principal favourite of King James I (1566–1625) but instead a prisoner in the Tower of London.[3] Thus Carleton set off to find a new buyer for his twenty-nine cases of antique marbles, eventually connecting with Rubens. The ensuing communication between Carleton and Rubens is one of the great artist-patron correspondences of the 1600s, replete with all the flatteries and careful language of negotiation and persuasion. Perhaps more importantly, though, it is also a valuable glimpse into how Rubens managed people and commissions. Describing the scope of his output, the makeup of his atelier, and the values of his painting, the letters reveal how he collaborated, delegated, priced, and marketed. They reveal, in short, the keys to his success.

THE CARLETON EXCHANGE

The earliest mention of Rubens vis-à-vis Carleton's collection comes by way of George Gage (c. 1582–1638), an English diplomat and art agent, who wrote to Carleton on November 1, 1617: "I delivered to Sig^{r} Rubens what y$^{[ou]r}$ L[ordship]. wrightes to mee concerning y^{r} heads and statuaes . . . if by any occasion y^{r} Ld should bee removed from [The Hague] before the sommer Sig^{r} Rubens entreateth y^{r} L. to cause him to bee certified in a worde therof, and hee will not faile himself alone to wait on you."[4] It is

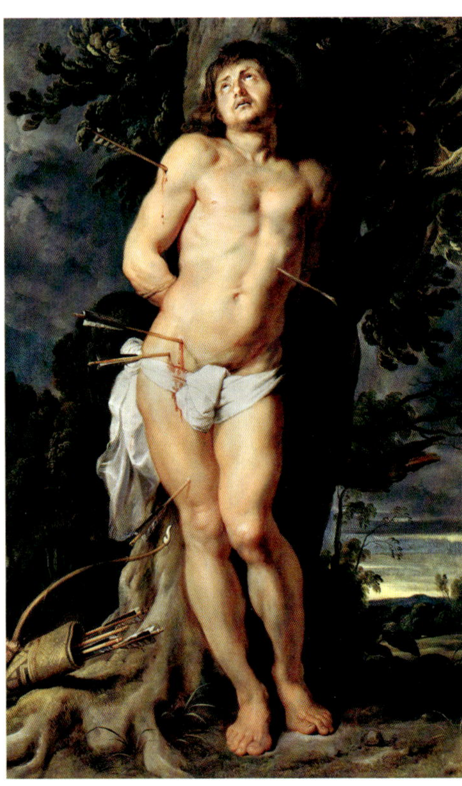

Fig 1 Peter Paul Rubens, *St. Sebastian*, c. 1618. Oil on canvas, 203.5 × 131.1 cm. Gemäldegalerie, Berlin. 798H.

unclear whether Gage was acting on his own initiative or under Carleton's direction in discussing the "heads and statuaes" with Rubens. However, both Gage and Carleton would have understood Rubens to be a natural choice. Not only did he possess an abiding love of the antique world (see essay by David Jaffé in this volume, page 40–53), but Carleton and Rubens had also done business before. Just one year earlier, in September 1616, Carleton and Gage had visited Rubens's studio and soon thereafter Carleton purchased a *Wolf and Fox Hunt* by the master's hand, offering as partial payment a chain of diamonds.[5]

This transaction was an important first step for their future dealings. Not only did it establish a relationship between the men, but it must also have suggested to Carleton Rubens's willingness to barter, and, to Rubens, Carleton's sense of fair trade.[6] When Rubens followed up with Carleton on March 17, 1618, about the antiquities, he mentions another such arrangement, offering an "exchange of these marbles for pictures by my hand."[7]

More specific details about the proposed trade emerge the following month when, on April 28, Rubens wrote again to Carleton. Rubens's agent, the Haarlem artist Frans Pietersz de Grebber (c. 1603–1652/53), had just returned from The Hague, where he viewed the ambassador's sculpture. His positive report encouraged Rubens to pursue the venture:

> By the advice of my agent, I have learned that Your Excellency is very much inclined to make some bargain with me concerning your antiquities . . . I find that at present I have in the house the flower of my stock, particularly some pictures which I have kept for my own enjoyment; some I have even repurchased for more than I had sold them to others. But the whole shall be at the service of Your Excellency, because I like brief negotiations, where each party gives and receives his share at once. To tell the truth, I am so burdened with commissions, both public and private, that for some years to come I cannot commit myself.[8]

Because Carleton's collection contained some ninety figures, heads, urns, sarcophagi, and stele valued at the not insignificant amount of 2,000 ducats, Rubens included a list of paintings from which Carleton could choose up to the corresponding value of 6,000 florins.[9] Remarkably, though all were supposed to be by Rubens's hand, as per his letter of March 17, the list, which included twenty-three paintings, distinguished several different types of production: there were originals by his hand; originals by his hand on which he had collaborated with a genre specialist (animal or landscape); copies by pupils after his work but retouched by him; an unfinished copy begun by a pupil that he would retouch so broadly it could be original; and finally, a pupil's original he had already retouched (see Appendix 1).

Carleton responded to Rubens within a few weeks, commenting that one of the paintings, a *Crucifixion* Rubens described as "perhaps the best thing I have ever done. — 12 × 6 ft." was too big for the "low buildings" in the Netherlands and England, but that he would accept a *St. Sebastian* by Rubens's hand in its place (fig. 1).[10] He would also not dispute the prices, "as I believe they are reasonable because they are not copies or works by your students, but entirely by your hand, just as my antiques are equally the hand of a master."[11] Carleton went on to state that he would, in fact, agree to take only paintings Rubens described as original and by his hand or those done in collaboration with a specialist. The acceptable works thus included the *St. Sebastian*, a "Daniel among many lions" (page 150); a "Prometheus bound on Mount Caucasus . . . the eagle done by Snyders" (fig. 2); a "Leopards, taken from life, with Satyrs and Nymph . . . [the] most beautiful landscape, done by the hand of a master skillful in that department;" a "Leda, with the swan and a cupid;" and a "St. Peter taking from the fish the coin to pay the tribute, with other fishermen around" (fig. 3).[12] Because these six paintings amounted only to 3,000

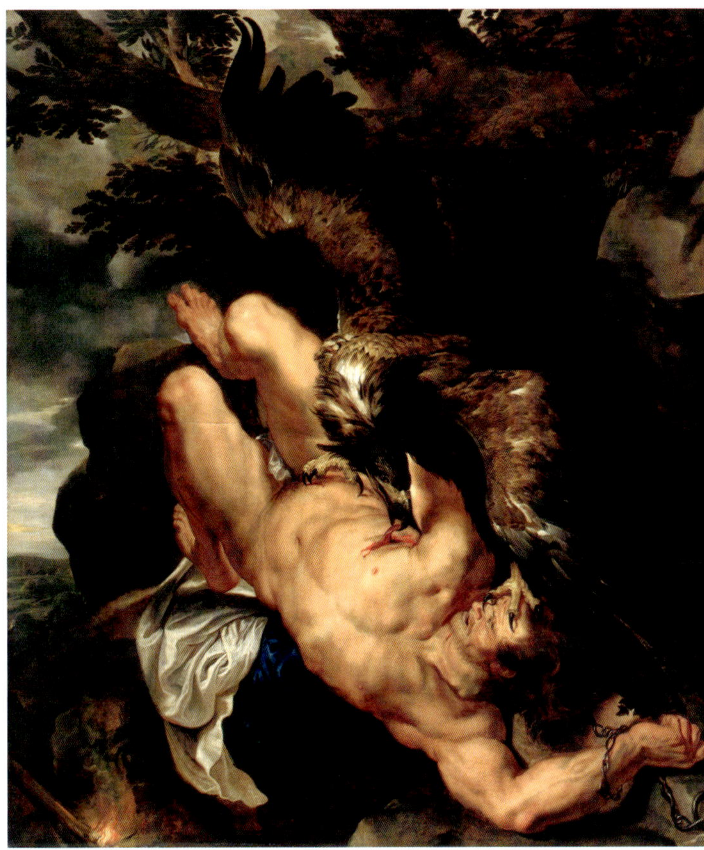

Fig 2 Peter Paul Rubens and Frans Snyders, *Prometheus Bound*, begun c. 1611–12, completed by 1618. Oil on canvas, 242.6 × 209.6 cm. Philadelphia Museum of Art, purchased with the W.P. Wilstach Fund, 1950. W1950-3-1.

florins, Carleton suggested a compromise in which Rubens paid him the remaining sum in tapestries.

Surprisingly, Rubens agreed, but not without clarifying the matter of the pupil-copies. In his letter, which is worth quoting at length, Rubens explained:

> Your Excellency has taken only the originals, with which I am perfectly satisfied. Yet Your Excellency must not think that the others are mere copies, for they are so well retouched by my hand that they are hardly to be distinguished from originals. Nevertheless, they are rated at a much lower price. I do not wish to influence your Excellency by fine words, because if you persist in your first idea I could still furnish pure originals up to this amount. But to speak frankly, I imagine that you haven't the desire for such a quantity of pictures. The reason I would deal more willingly in pictures is clear: although they do not exceed their just price in the list, yet they cost me, so to speak, nothing. For everyone is more liberal with the fruits that grow in his own garden than with those he must buy in the market. Besides, I have spent this year some thousands of florins on my estate, and I should not like, for a whim, to exceed the limits of good economy. In fact, I am not a prince, *sed qui manducat laborem manuum suarum* [but one who lives by the work of his hands].[13]

When all was said and done, Rubens convinced Carleton to accept nine paintings in total, the six entirely by his hand or done with collaborators, and then another three, including a "hunt of men on horseback and lions begun by one of my pupils . . . but all retouched by my hand;" a "Susanna, done by one of my pupils, but the whole retouched by my hand;" and another "trifle," later identified as *Hagar Leaves the House of Abraham* (fig. 4), as well as a set of tapestries after Giulio Romano's *History of Scipio* designs.[14]

RUBENS THE BUSINESSMAN

The most illuminating details to emerge from Carleton's and Rubens's correspondence are those that reveal Rubens's business strategy. It has become something of a cliché to refer to his workshop as a well-oiled machine, and the complexities of his atelier are an important, ever-growing area of study.[15] The fact remains, however, that Rubens was, by his own admission, a man who lived by the work of his hands, and to capitalize fully on his exhaustive talents and creativity, he needed to develop a model for operations, marketing, and communication, to use a bit of contemporary jargon, which would help ensure the success of his enterprise. This strategy emerges in the Carleton exchange, beginning with the trade itself.

According to Rubens, he maintained a pictorial supply comprising paintings that he had enjoyed so much they had never left his studio, as well as others that had left and that he bought back, the so-called "flowers" of his stock. Such colourful language reflects Rubens's sense of salesmanship and may cast doubts on his own claim—however, maintaining such a stock made good business sense. Between the twenty-three pictures, sixteen were subjects from the New Testament, four were from ancient myth, two were from the Old Testament, and one was a picture of a hunt. Diverse in subject matter, this stock provided Rubens with a range of pieces he could easily market, sell, or, as in the Carleton case, trade. They minimized the potential of lost opportunity

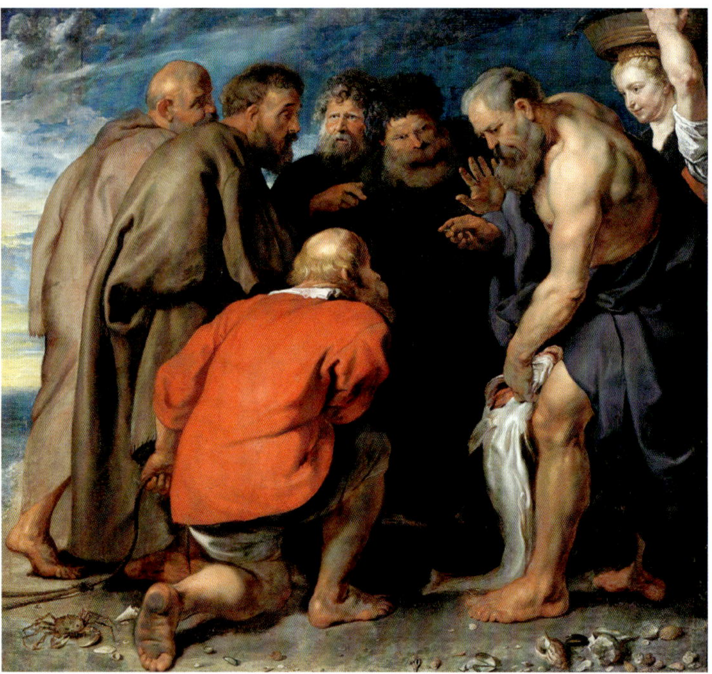

Fig 3 Peter Paul Rubens, *Saint Peter Finding the Tribute Money*, 1617–18. Oil on canvas, 199.4 × 218.8 cm. National Gallery of Ireland, Dublin, purchased, 1873. NGI.38. Photo © National Gallery of Ireland.

and saved him from spending extra time and cost—two valuable commodities given how "burdened" he claimed to have been by commissions and the recent expenditure on his estate. More time- and cost-efficient, still, was the fact that the paintings making up his stock were not exclusively by him.

It is generally known that Rubens maintained a large workshop. In the Carleton letters its members are referred to as "pupils," which, misrepresents, perhaps purposefully, the wide differences among them as well as their diverse responsibilities (an artist like Anthony van Dyck [1599–1641], for example, who was active in Rubens's atelier at that time, was hardly a student whose groundwork would need to be gilded by Rubens's touch). It is also well known that Rubens collaborated with other masters, most famously Jan Brueghel the Elder (1568–1625), with whom he executed nearly two dozen works over the course of twenty-five years.[16] He also worked with Frans Snyders (1579–1657), author of the eagle in the *Prometheus Bound*; Jan Wildens (1586–1653), master of the landscape in *Hagar Leaves the House of Abraham* and, likely, the picture of the leopards, nymphs, and satyrs, and many others still.[17] To both collaborate and delegate in the early decades of the 1600s, however, was unusual.

Collaborative production was a distinctly northern phenomenon deeply embedded within the Antwerp tradition.[18] The origins of the practice in which two artists combined their specialized talents—for figures, flowers, animals, landscapes—in a single image were tied largely to the economics of the venture. Not only did it allow artists to execute images more quickly, it was also cost-effective. The practice existed among artists of all abilities and along a spectrum of partnerships, from prestigious cooperation to mass production. At the lower end, artists simply unskilled in certain areas would work in tandem to execute images they could not otherwise produce alone. In a landscape painting, for example, one artist might create the features of the land and then pass the painting to a second artist to add figures. Commonly commissioned by a dealer but sometimes also a third-party artist,[19] these paintings tended to be small, formulaic and cheap to produce—an artist often earned less than one florin for his participation.[20] Working quickly and efficiently, these painters supplied a modest market, where an overall effect was more desirable than a single painter's hand.

At the "high end," however, collaborations were self-consciously precious commodities. Particularly with painters like Rubens, Brueghel, and Snyders, the most revered and desired artists of the time, collectors placed enormous value on cooperative paintings as connoisseurial treasures that would provide them with the experience of viewing the work of multiple acclaimed masters at once.[21] Remarkably, while the back-and-forth between artists as each perfected his invention likely made these collaborations somewhat less time-efficient to produce than those among artists of the lower tier (who simply left vague open zones for the other to fill in), the cost of high-level collaborations was still relatively low while the profit remained high. In most cases, one painter would initiate a project with a colleague in mind. He would pay him for his contribution and then sell the painting through his studio or to the patron who commissioned it. Although no such contracts between Rubens and his collaborators survive, the account books of other high-level Antwerp painters reveal that artists might pay each other as little as 12 florins for their contribution to a painting that could sell for 300 florins.[22]

While living in Italy, Rubens had scornfully rejected the thought of such collaboration, saying he would never "tolerate" a mixture of hands in a painting and that he had "always guarded against being confused with anyone, however great a man."[23]

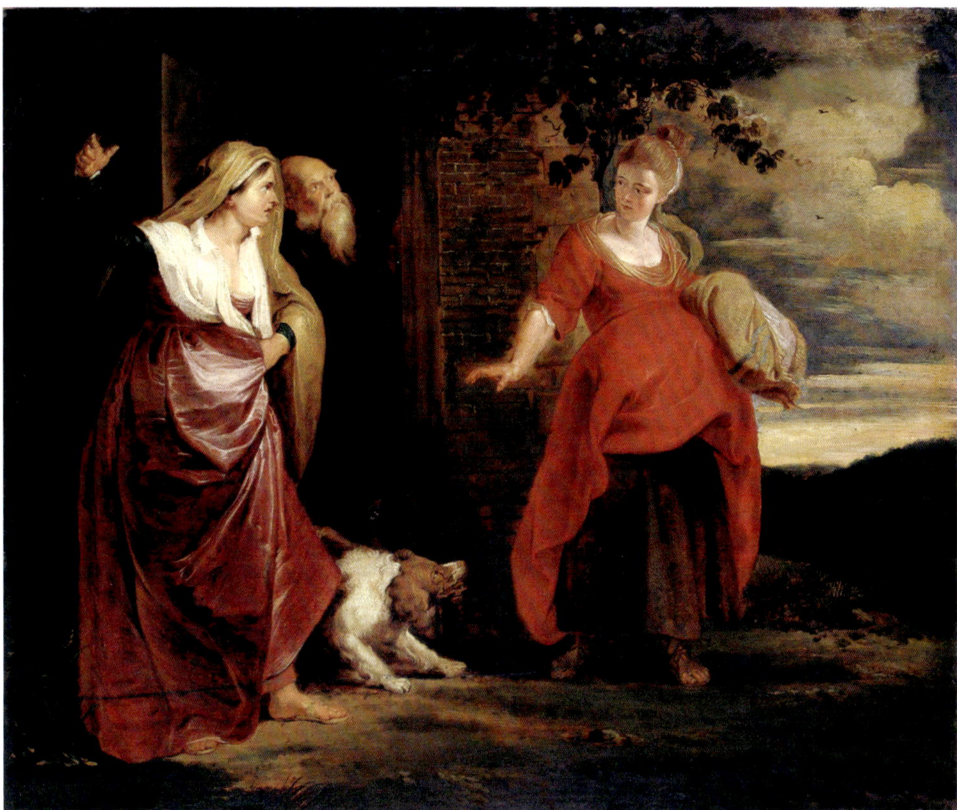

Fig 4 Peter Paul Rubens, *Hagar Leaves the House of Abraham*, c. 1615–17. Oil on panel, 62.8 × 76 cm. The State Hermitage Museum, Saint Petersburg, acquired from the collection of L.A. Crozat, Baron de Thiers in Paris. ГЭ-475.

Rubens hardly had access to collaborative endeavours, let alone a large studio in Italy, so his apparent disdain for that practice may actually have been defensive marketing. Either way, upon his return to Antwerp, he embraced the enormous artistic and economic potential of collaboration. Among the earliest works he created after moving back was a magnificent large-scale work with Snyders, *The Recognition of Philopoemen*, in which Rubens painted the narrative figures while Snyders executed a sweeping still life of dead game.[24] An independent master with a highly compatible technique, Snyders went on to become one of Rubens's most important collaborators, joining him also on *The Head of Medusa* (page 224), and, of course, on Carleton's *Prometheus*.

Rubens's change of heart is probably best understood vis-à-vis his other approach to production, which emerges in the Carleton exchange—an arrangement somewhat less common in painting studios of the Low Countries but typical of Italian atelier practice dating to the Renaissance: the separation of invention and execution.[25] In this tradition, the master generated the creative material for each piece, but could delegate the actual execution to an assistant highly trained in his style and technique, the rationale being that a painting good enough to be by him was as good as a painting *actually* by him. The master would preside over the execution of the work and add final touches at the end, as the highest value was placed on the intellectual labour of his invention. In this separation of duties, unlike in collaboration, all manners but one were effaced and the final composition had to look as if it was produced by the master's hand.

Rubens would have encountered this workshop practice during the years he spent in Italy, and would certainly have recognized its enormous potential when, upon his return to Antwerp, he was immediately overcome by demand.[26] Particularly given his exemption from the regulations of the Guild of Saint Luke, which would have had him register his assistants, he could engage a host of young artists to lay-in paintings, enlarge compositions he had executed in drawing or oil sketch, or provide copies of works already finished.[27] This workshop structure left him free to focus his artistic energies on the creative process and gave him the flexibility to participate in a variety of projects depending on their importance or the stipulations of a contract.

While these northern and southern workshop practices are distinct in premise—in the one, the artist's hand is the most important aspect, while in the other, the artist's idea is the core value—Rubens seemed to recognize that a combination of both traditions offered the highest potential for marketplace success. Approaching collaboration and delegation as two sides of the same coin, he assembled a team of associates and acolytes who ensured that his enterprise operated at maximum capacity and covered all manner of production.

Through this extremely efficient division of labour Rubens developed a brand, so to speak, that kept costs low and profits high. According to the list of the paintings in his stock, whether a work was fully original, produced in collaboration, or one in which his intervention was limited to the compositional sketch with final touches added at the end, it was worth the same amount.[28] He listed "A hunt of men on horseback and lions, begun by one of my pupils, after one that I made for His Most Serene Highness of Bavaria, but all retouched by my hand. — 8 × 11 ft." for 600 florins, the same price as the nearly identically sized and representationally similar *Daniel in the Lions' Den* "taken from life. Original, entirely by my hand. — 8 × 12 ft." (Appendix 1). He also valued both the *St. Sebastian*, "nude, by my hand. — 7 × 4 ft." (fig. 1) and "A Susanna, done by one of my pupils, but the whole retouched by my hand. — 7 × 5 ft." for 300 florins. Twelve paintings of the Apostles "with a Christ, done by my pupils, from originals by my own hand" also cost nearly the same as the *Crucifixion*. Only a *Last Judgment*, which Rubens described as "begun by one of my pupils, after one which I did in a much larger size for the Most Serene Prince of Neuburg, who paid me 3500 florins cash for it; but this one, not being finished, would be entirely retouched by my own hand, and by this means would pass as original. — 13 × 9 ft." was valued at a reduced price of 1,200 florins, though it is still twice as expensive as any other work on the list, likely owing to the subject's complexity.[29]

In general, these prices were consistent with those of Rubens's contemporaries. In around 1617 he was one of twelve painters engaged in the decoration of the Dominican Church of Saint Paul in Antwerp. The commission comprised fifteen paintings of identical size, and it was not Rubens who received the highest pay, but rather Hendrik van Balen (1575–1632), who earned 216 florins for an *Annunciation*, while Rubens received 150 florins for a *Flagellation*—the same fee also paid to Anthony van Dyck (1599–1641) for his *Christ Carrying the Cross* and to Jacob Jordaens (1593–1678) for his *Crucifixion*.[30] Indeed, although he was among the most sought artists in Europe during the 1600s, studies of Rubens's finances show that his immense wealth did not come from charging exceedingly high prices, but rather from setting prices that were moderate and firm.[31] Carleton would have been particularly well-versed in this matter during his first transaction with Rubens, which saw Carleton lose the first version of the *Wolf and Fox Hunt* to Philippe-Charles d'Arenberg, Duke of Aerschot (1587–1640), when he tried to haggle with the master.[32] Carleton received a hunt scene of his own only once he accepted Rubens's terms.

As a business strategy, this approach to pricing made good sense. It weighed competitor actions and market conditions above the cost-base, which meant that Rubens could charge high sums for his brand no matter who wielded the brush, all the while making patrons feel that they had not exceeded the limits of good economy, even for a Rubens. Nevertheless, Rubens seems to have been aware of its potentially negative perception given that patrons were not technically always receiving a Rubens. As the Carleton letters reveal, Rubens attempted to shape his patron's expectations about studio participation, which may have been ever more important in the Carleton case since he had been to Rubens's studio and seen the atelier in action (though it was hardly a secret given the hundreds of would-be students he was forced to turn away and how openly he spoke of their presence).[33] When it came to the works by pupils on his list, which amounted to two-thirds of the total offering, Rubens justified their prices with declarations that each would possess a high degree of his finish, descriptions about their subjects, estimations about their quality, and, if a copy, information about the prototype's provenance—a sort of pedigree by proxy. The same information was not given to the collaborations or originals, with the exception of the *Crucifixion*, which Rubens described, to no avail, as the best he ever did.

The description of the pupil-copy of his *Last Judgement*, as we have seen, contained a lengthy explanation of the original painting's owner as well as details of its transaction. Rubens further included his assurance that his intervention would be so substantial that it would pass as original. His "hunt of men on horseback and lions" and "The Twelve Apostles," also works of the studio, were similarly given ennobling, surrogate pedigrees: the original hunt went to the Elector Maximilian of Bavaria (1581–1651), while the apostle series was done for the favourite of

King Philip III of Spain (1578–1621), Francisco Gómez de Sandoval, Duke of Lerma (1553–1625). Meanwhile, a picture of Achilles among the daughters of Lycomedes, Rubens guaranteed, was not only done by the *best* of his pupils (Van Dyck), it was also "a most delightful picture, and full of many very beautiful young girls."[34]

That Carleton would initially reject studio-involved works may say more about Carleton's ultimate aim to use the paintings for gain rather than personal enjoyment than of Rubens's powers of persuasion.[35] However, despite his best efforts, Rubens did sometimes mistake where his buyers stood along the consumer spectrum. In 1621, Henry Danvers (1573–1643) contemptuously refused a hunting scene executed largely by Rubens's studio that the master had supplied unaware of Danvers's intention to give it to Charles, Prince of Wales (1600–1649). Perhaps owing to the rise of the discerning connoisseur-collector, the assurance that work was "by his hand" became increasingly frequent as Rubens's career progressed.[36] He made explicit guarantees in 1620 to execute the *modelli* for the project decorating the ceiling of the Jesuit church in Antwerp, while leaving the canvases to his students (see essay by Koen Bulckens in this volume, (page 84), and contracted his personal involvement when he accepted Marie de' Medici's commission for the series celebrating her life in 1622 by agreeing that the figures in the compositions be designed by his own hand.[37]

Though there were certainly instances in which Rubens misjudged a patron's expectations—as in the Danvers affair and in other correspondence and contract negotiations in the years that followed the Carleton exchange—in the decade within Rubens's return from Italy there was a concerted strategy for marketing, pricing, and managing expectations. For an artist as accomplished as Rubens, the point that he was also a deliberate businessman may not come as a surprise and does not detract from the unparalleled scale of his talent and creativity. Yet, as the Carleton case reminds us, Rubens's success was not a happy accident, but the result of careful, strategic thinking.

APPENDIX I

Peter Paul Rubens to Sir Dudley Carleton, 28 April 1618
List of the pictures which are in my house

500 florins	A Prometheus bound on Mount Caucasus, with an eagle which pecks his liver. Original, by my hand, and the eagle done by Snyders.	9 × 8 ft.
600 fl.	Daniel among many lions, taken from life. Original, entirely by my hand.	8 × 12 ft.
600 fl.	Leopards, taken from life, with Satyrs and Nymphs. Original, by my hand, except a most beautiful landscape, done by the hand of a master skillful in that department.	9 × 11 ft.
500 fl.	A Leda, with the swan and a cupid. Original, by my hand.	7 × 10 ft.
500 fl.	Crucifixion, life-sized, considered perhaps the best thing I have ever done.	12 × 6 ft.
500 fl.	A Last Judgment, begun by one of my pupils, after one which I did in a much larger size for the Most Serene Prince of Neuburg, who paid me 3500 florins cash for it; but this one, not being finished, would be entirely retouched by my own hand, and by this means would pass as original.	13 × 9 ft.
500 fl.	St. Peter taking from the fish the coin to pay the tribute, with other fishermen around; taken from life. Original, by my hand.	7 × 8 ft.
600 fl.	A hunt of men on horseback and lions, begun by one of my pupils, after one that I made for His Most Serene Highness of Bavaria, but all retouched by my hand.	8 × 11 ft.
50 fl. each	The Twelve Apostles, with a Christ, done by my pupils, from originals by my own hand, which the Duke of Lerma has, these need to be retouched by my own hand throughout.	4 × 3 ft.
600 fl.	A picture of an Achilles clothed as a woman, done by the best of my pupils, and the whole retouched by my hand; a most beautiful picture, and full of many very beautiful young girls	9 × 10 ft.
300 fl.	A St. Sebastian, nude, by my hand.	7 × 4 ft.
300 fl.	A Susanna, done by one of my pupils, but the whole retouched by my hand.	7 × 5 ft.

I would like to thank Melanie Gifford, Henriette Rahusen, and Lara Yeager-Crasselt for their thoughtful comments and insights during the preparation of this essay.

1 Peter Paul Rubens to Jacob de Bie, May 11, 1611, in Ruth Saunders Magurn, trans. and ed., *The Letters of Peter Paul Rubens* (Cambridge, MA: Harvard University Press, 1955), 55.

2 Robert Hill and Susan Bracken, who have examined the relationship between Rubens and Carleton, compellingly argue that contrary to the long-held belief that Carleton was an astute connoisseur who amassed his collection of antiquities for the love of sculpture, his motives were, in fact, self-promotional. These motives similarly inform his exchange with Rubens, as Carleton immediately used the paintings to gain favour at the English court. See Robert Hill and Susan Bracken, "The Ambassador and the Artist: Sir Dudley Carleton's Relationship with Peter Paul Rubens; Connoisseurship and Art Collecting at the Court of the Early Stuarts," *Journal of the History of Collections* 26, no. 2 (2015): 171–91. See also Robert William Hill, "Works of Art as Commodities: Art and Patronage; The Career of Sir Dudley Carleton, 1610–1625" (PhD diss., Nottingham Trent University and Southampton Institute, 1999).

3 Somerset had been implicated in a scandal involving the murder by poisoning of his friend Sir Thomas Overbury, who disapproved of Somerset's close relationship with the married Frances Howard.

4 George Gage to Sir Dudley Carleton, November 1, 1617, in Max Rooses and C. Reulens, *Correspondance de Rubens et documents épistolaires concernant sa vie et ses œuvres*, 6 vols. (Antwerp: Veuve de Backer, 1887–1909), 2:120.

5 Arnout Balis, *Corpus Rubenianum Ludwig Burchard, Part XVIII: Rubens Landscapes and Hunting Scenes*, (London: Harvey Miller, 1986), 98. The painting may be the version in the collection of Mr. James Methuen-Campbell of Corsham Court, Wiltshire. See Hill and Bracken, "The Ambassador and the Artist," *Journal of the History of Collections*, 185n26. On Carleton's offer, see Rooses and Reulens, *Correspondance de Rubens*, 2:93–103.

6 Jeffrey M. Muller has also made this observation in "Rubens's Museum of Antique Sculpture," *Art Bulletin* 59, no. 4 (December 1977): 575.

7 Peter Paul Rubens to Sir Dudley Carleton, March 17, 1618, in Saunders Magurn, *Letters of Peter Paul Rubens*, 59.

8 Peter Paul Rubens to Sir Dudley Carleton, April 28, 1618, in Saunders Magurn, *Letters of Peter Paul Rubens*, 59–60.

9 Jeffrey M. Muller has published a transcription of the inventory of the twenty-nine cases of sculpture Carleton sent from Venice to London in "Rubens's Museum of Antique Sculpture," *Art Bulletin* 59, no. 4 (December 1977): 581–82.

10 "Trovo chi'il crucifisso è troppo grande per queste fabriche basse et quelle ancora d'Inghilterra." Sir Dudley Carleton to Peter Paul Rubens, May 8, 1618, in Rooses and Reulens, *Correspondance de Rubens*, 2:145.

11 "Non dispute il pretio d'essi stimandolo ragionevole poi che non sono copie ni opera de discepoli ma tutti di man sua come queste mie antiquita tutte mostrano la man del maestro." Sir Dudley Carleton to Peter Paul Rubens, May 8, 1618, in Rooses and Reulens, *Correspondance de Rubens*, 2:145.

12 For Rubens's description of the pictures, see Peter Paul Rubens to Sir Dudley Carleton, April 28, 1618, in Saunders Magurn, *Letters of Peter Paul Rubens*, 60–61; for Carleton's selection, see Sir Dudley Carleton to Peter Paul Rubens, May 8, 1618, in Rooses and Reulens, *Correspondance de Rubens*, 2:145.

13 Peter Paul Rubens to Sir Dudley Carleton, May 12, 1618, in Saunders Magurn, *Letters of Peter Paul Rubens*, 62.

14 Of the objects exchanged, six paintings are known today: *Daniel in the Lions' Den* at the National Gallery of Art in Washington, D.C.; *St. Sebastian* at the Gemäldegalerie, Berlin; Philadelphia Museum of Art's *Prometheus Bound*; *Saint Peter Finding the Tribute Money* at the National Gallery of Ireland; *Hagar Leaves the House of Abraham* at The Hermitage, St. Petersburg; and possibly the "hunt of men and lions," which Arnout Balis has identified in a private collection in Madrid. See Arnout Balis, *Hunting Scenes*, 44, 127, no. 6. There is great debate as to whether the *Achilles Discovered by Ulysses and Diomedes* at the Museo del Prado, Madrid, is the same "Achilles" offered by Carleton to Rubens, and whether the paintings of the *Twelve Apostles* series at the Galleria Pallavicini-Rospigliosi also matches Rubens's list. Gregory Martin thoroughly summarized the divergent opinions regarding *Achilles* and concluded, with supporting technical information furnished by Alejandro Verara, that the Prado picture is likely a variant of that original (now lost) first version. See Gregory Martin, "Achilles on Scyros: No. 1. *Achilles Discovered among the Daughters of Lycomedes*; Painting," in Elizabeth McGrath et al., *Corpus Rubenianum Ludwig Burchard, Part XI: Rubens; Mythological Subjects; Achilles to the Graces*, 2 vols. (London: Harvey Miller, 2016), 1:71–80n1. Hans Vlieghe has also concluded that the Pallavicini-Rospigliosi is a different copy from that listed by Rubens in *Corpus Rubenianum Ludwig Burchard, Part VIII: Saints*, 2 vols. (London: Phaidon, 1972), 1:34–38.

15 The forthcoming dissertation by Koen Bulckens (PhD diss., Brown University) is the most recent in a series of important studies to deal with the character and functioning of Rubens's atelier. See also Hans Vlieghe, "Rubens's Atelier and History Painting in Flanders: A Review of the Evidence," in Peter C. Sutton et al., *The Age of Rubens*, (Ghent: Ludion Press, 1993), 159; Arnout Balis, "'Fatto da un mio discepolo': Rubens's Studio Practices Review," in *Rubens and His Workshop: The Flight of Lot and His Family from Sodom*, ed. Toshiharu Makamura, vol. 2 (Tokyo: National Museum of Western Art, 1994), 107–8; Arnout Balis, "Rubens and His Studio: Defining the Problem," in *Rubens: A Genius at Work*, ed. Joost vander Auwera and Sabine van Sprang (Tielt: Lanno, 2007), 30–43; Joost vander Auwera and Bert Scheepers, "Rubens as Entrepreneur: Better Suited to Very Large Works Than Small Curiosities," in Vander Auwera and Van Sprang, *Rubens: A Genius at Work*, 213–14.

16 On Rubens and Brueghel, see Anne T. Woollett and Ariane van Suchtelen, eds., *Rubens and Brueghel: A Working Friendship* (Zwolle: Waanders, 2006); Christine van Mulders, *Corpus Rubenianum Ludwig Burchard, Part XXVII: Rubens; Works in Collaboration*, 2 vols. (London: Harvey Miller, 2016).

17 Wildens is most often identified as the landscape artist involved in the "Leopards" picture and may also be the painter of the tree in the *Prometheus Bound*. See Gregory Martin, "Review: *L'Europe de Rubens*," *Burlington Magazine* 145 (September 2013), 643.

18 On collaboration in the seventeenth-century Flemish tradition, see Katherine van der Stighelen, "Produktiviteit en samenwerking in het Antwerpse kunstenaarsmilieu, 1620–1640," *Gemeentekrediet: Driemaandelijks tijschrift van het Gemeentekrediet van België* 172 (1990): 5–15; Peter C. Sutton, "Painting in the Age of Rubens," in Sutton et al., *The Age of Rubens*, 35–37; Woollett and Van Suchtelen, *Rubens and Brueghel*; and Susan Merriam, *Seventeenth-Century Flemish Garland Paintings: Still Life, Vision, and the Devotional Image* (London: Routledge, 2012), 48–53.

19 Jan Brueghel the Younger (1601–1678) was known to organize collaborations between a landscape specialist and a figure specialist and then sell the work himself. See J. Denucé, *Letters and Documents Concerning Jan Brueghel I and II* (Antwerp, 1934), 82; Melanie Gifford, "Landscape Painting Style and Technique: Fidelity to the 16th Century Tradition in Early 17th Century Landscape Production," *La peinture dans les Pays-Bas au 16e siècle*, ed. Hélène Verougstraete and Roger van Schoute (Leuven: Peeters, 1999), 184.

20 Elizabeth Honig, *Painting and the Market in Early Modern Antwerp* (New Haven, CT: Yale University Press, 1998), 179–81. In this indispensable study on the Antwerp market, Honig further notes that a "lower tier" staffagist named Willemsen received twenty stuivers per painting, while another low-end artist, "sr. Angilo," received only eighteen. See Honig, *Painting and the Market in Early Modern Antwerp*, 272n22. See also Gifford's study of efficiency in sixteenth- and seventeenth-century landscape production in "Landscape Painting Style and Technique," esp. 182–85.

21 Anna Tummers has written thoughtfully about the practice of connoisseurship in the 1600s in "'By His Hand': The Paradox of Seventeenth-Century Connoisseurship," in *Art Market and Connoisseurship: A Closer Look at Paintings by Rembrandt, Rubens and Their Contemporaries*, ed. Anna Tummers and Koenraad Jonckheere (Amsterdam: Amsterdam University Press, 2008), 31–66. See also Christine van Mulders, "The Collaboration between Peter Paul Rubens and Jan Brueghel the Elder," in Vander Auwera and Van Sprang, *Rubens: A Genius at Work*, 109–10.

22 Frequent Antwerp collaborators Hendrick van Balen (1575–1632) and Jan Brueghel the Younger (1601–1678) paid each other between twelve and twenty florins for their collaborations. See Honig, *Painting and the Market in Early Modern Antwerp*, 185.

23 Peter Paul Rubens to Annibale Chieppio, May 24, 1603, in Saunders Magurn, *Letters of Peter Paul Rubens*, 33.

24 Peter Paul Rubens and Frans Snyders, *The Recognition of Phililpoemen*, c. 1609, oil on canvas, 201 × 313.5 cm, Museo del Prado, Madrid, inv. no. P001851.

25 Tapestry production, on the other hand, relied on the separation of invention and execution. Models and cartoons for the narrative designs were produced by specialists, while the tapestries themselves were executed by weavers who remained largely anonymous. See Guy Delmarcel, *Flemish Tapestry from the 15th to the 18th Century* (Tielt: Lannoo, 1999).

26 See note 15.

27 Because Rubens was exempt from guild regulations requiring a master to register his pupils, thanks to his arrangement with the Archdukes Albert and Isabel Clara Eugenia, it is extremely difficult to arrive at a comprehensive list of Rubens's studio assistants at any given time. However, important studies to address this question include Arnout Balis, "'Fatto da un mio discepolo,'" 108–18; Vlieghe, "Rubens's Atelier and History Painting in Flanders," 158–70; and Balis, "Rubens and His Studio," 43–48.

28 On Rubens's pricing, see Nils Büttner, "Aristocracy and Noble Business: Some Remarks on Rubens's Financial Affairs," in *Munuscula Amicorum: Contributions on Rubens and His Colleagues in Honour of Hans Vlieghe*, ed. Katherine van der Stighelen, 2 vols. (Turnhout: Brepols, 2006), 1:67–75, and Nils Büttner, *Herr P. P. Rubens: Von der Kunst, berühmt zu warden* (Göttingen: Vandenhoeck & Ruprecht, 2006), 128–30.

29 Peter Paul Rubens to Sir Dudley Carleton, April 28, 1618, in Saunders Magurn, *Letters of Peter Paul Rubens*, 60–61.

30 Zirka Zaremba Filipczak, *Picturing Art in Antwerp* (Princeton, NJ: Princeton University Press, 1987), 79.

31 Filipczak, *Picturing Art in Antwerp*, 78–81.

32 See note 5.

33 Nils Büttner has written that Rubens may have conspicuously promoted the size of his studio to emphasize the intellectual level of his involvement. See Nils Büttner, "The Hands of Rubens: On Copies and Their Reception," *Kyoto Studies in Art History* 2 (2017): 43.

34 Balis, "'Fatto da un mio discepolo,'" 110.

35 See note 2.

36 In the contract for the Medici Cycle (Musée du Louvre) of February 26, 1622, Rubens guarantees that he will "make, perfect and paint each and every one of the figures with his own hand." Max Rooses, "Les contrats passes entre Rubens et Marie de Médicis concernant les deux galleries du Luxembourg," *Bulletin-Rubens* 4 (1910): 216–20. Arnout Balis also discusses how several large altarpieces may have stipulated similar demands in their contracts based on Rubens's extant receipts of payment, such as that for the *Adoration of the Magi* for St. John's Church in Mechelen (1617) and for his *Last Communion of St. Francis* (1619). See Balis, "'Fatto da un mio discepolo,'" 102–3, 122n57.

37 On the Medici Cycle, see Jacques Thuillier, *Le storie di Maria de' Medici di Rubens al Lussemburgo* (Milan: Rizzoli, 1967), translated by Robert Erich Wolf as *Rubens' Life of Marie de' Medici* (New York: Harry N. Abrams, 1970), 97. For the Antwerp ceiling, see John Rupert Martin, *Corpus Rubenianum Ludwig Burchard, Part 1: The Ceiling Paintings for the Jesuit Church in Antwerp* (London: Phaidon, 1968), 213–19.

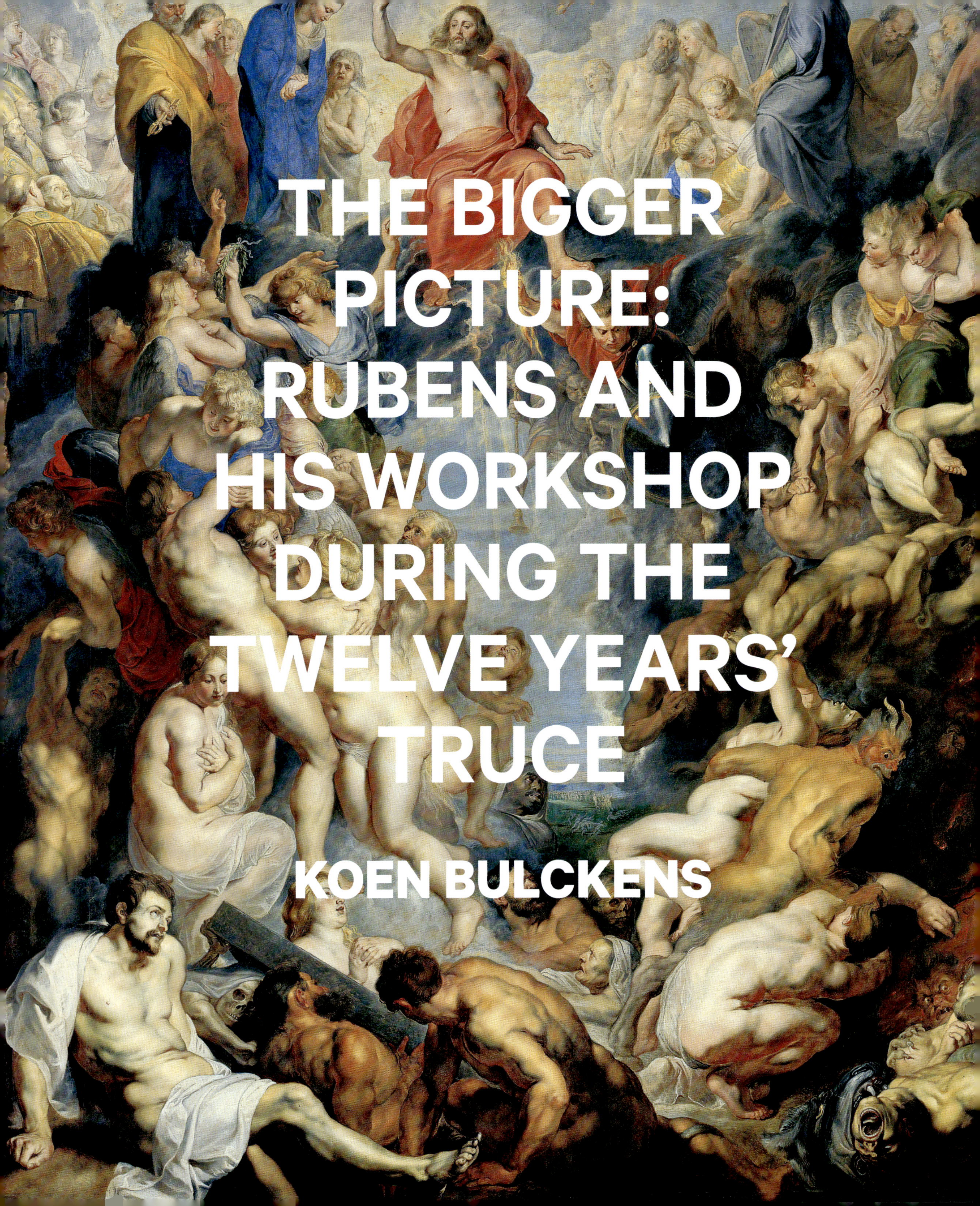
THE BIGGER PICTURE: RUBENS AND HIS WORKSHOP DURING THE TWELVE YEARS' TRUCE
KOEN BULCKENS

Fig 1 Peter Paul Rubens, *The Great Last Judgement*, 1617. Oil on canvas, 608.5 × 463.5 cm. Bayerische Staatsgemäldesammlungen, Alte Pinakothek München. 890. Photo © bpk Bildagentur/Bayerische Staatsgemäldesammlungen/Art Resource, NY.

WHEN PETER PAUL RUBENS SOUGHT TO SECURE the commission for the high altar of Saint Bavo's Cathedral in Ghent in 1614, he promised that the work "would be the largest and most beautiful ever painted in these lands."[1] Beauty may seem like the obvious selling point, but the artist's reference to size is as significant. Rubens indeed painted altarpieces that were noticeably larger than those of his Netherlandish predecessors,[2] and the scale of these works truly is impressive. *The Great Last Judgement* in Munich (fig. 1), which depicts over thirty bodies as they ascend into heaven and fall into hell, towers over six metres.[3]

The story of these big pictures and Rubens's workshop is a classic episode in the history of European art.[4] After decades of decline due to religious and political wars, Antwerp experienced an economic revival due to the Twelve Years' Truce (1609–1621), resulting in a wave of artistic patronage. The city saw a boom in the decoration of churches—newly built ones as well as those disfigured during Protestant uprisings of the previous century. There was a large demand for altarpieces. Rubens returned to Antwerp at the dawn of the Truce, after a period in Italy during which he developed an artistic vision for monumental paintings. The artist used his connections to obtain his first commissions, and once his reputation was established, patrons came looking for him. As Rubens's fame grew, Antwerp briefly enjoyed a renewed status as a leading artistic centre. While the monumental altarpieces constituted only a fraction of the city's artistic output at the time,[5] the narrative outlined above is nevertheless an accurate one.

Many studies have examined the historical context of the demand for large pictures.[6] This essay, by contrast, will provide observations on how Rubens managed to supply those paintings.

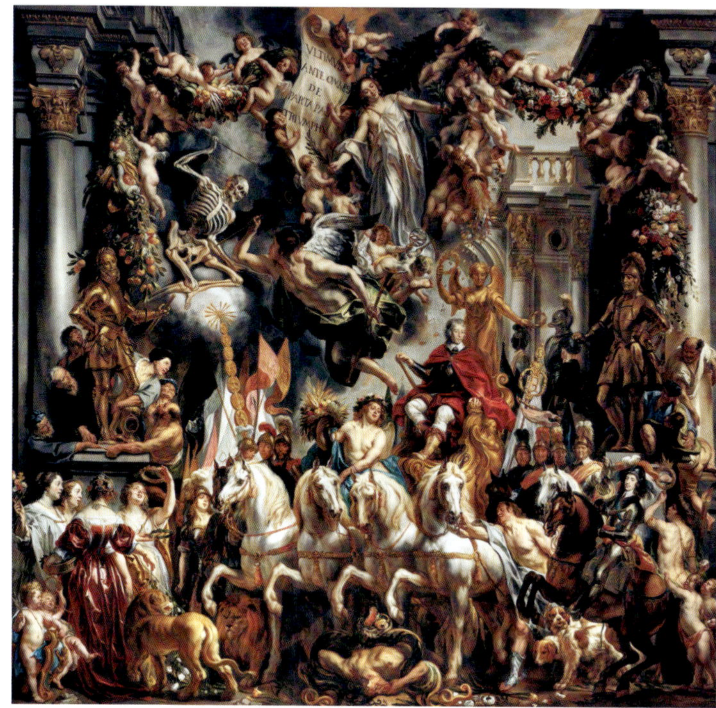

Fig 2 Jacob Jordaens, *The Triumph of Frederik Hendrik*, 1647–52. Oil on canvas, 728 × 755 cm. Oranjezaal, Royal Palace Huis ten Bosch, The Hague.

I will show that Rubens's production of monumental altarpieces increased when he moved to a larger workshop around 1615–1616. Self-evident as this connection may seem, this is the first analysis to fully explore the subject. Rubens's big paintings allow us to study dynamics between oeuvre and workspace in detail, as many of them are properly dated and their dimensions can be compared to those of the physical workshop. This essay will make a case for the impact of space on artistic activity, a relationship that has not been widely acknowledged.[7]

LARGE-SCALE PREDICAMENTS

Painting large pictures is a complex endeavour that requires careful planning and the right infrastructure. Several historical anecdotes reveal how artists experienced the scale of large paintings before they arrived at their final destination. When Jacob Jordaens (1583–1678) painted *The Triumph of Frederik Hendrik* (fig. 2), the canvas was so big that he could not fully span it in

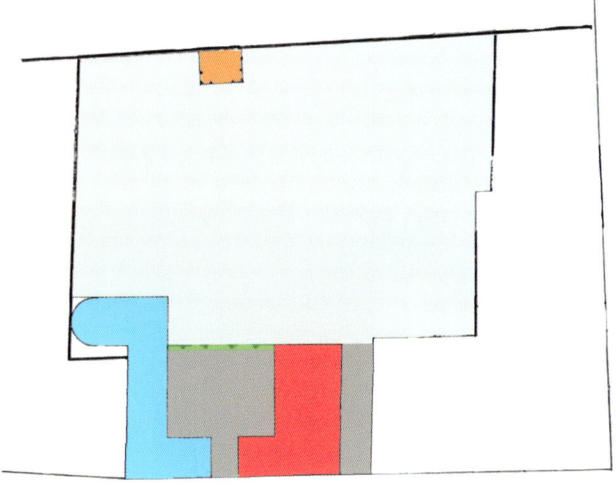

Fig 3 Author's image after a drawing by Emiel van Averbeke. An east-oriented view of the Rubens site, showing the north wing with living quarters (blue) and south wing with painting studio (red). Other highlighted elements are the courtyard and entrance ways (dark grey), portico or garden screen (green), garden (light grey), and garden pavilion (orange).

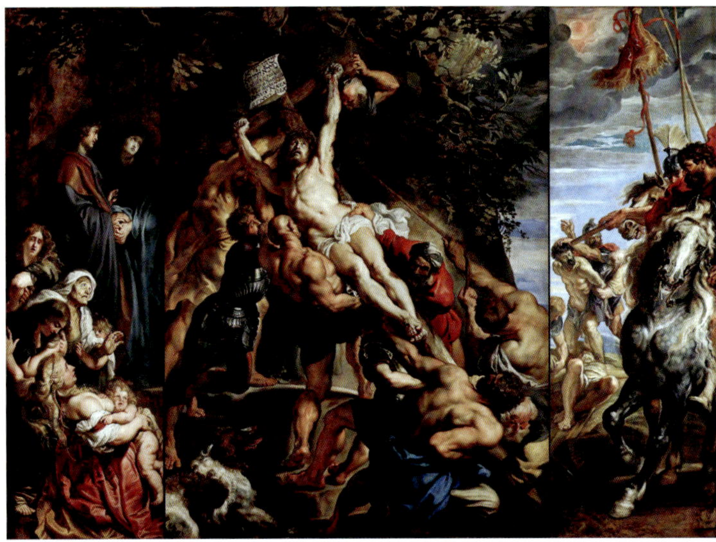

Fig 4 Peter Paul Rubens, *The Raising of the Cross*, 1610–11. Oil on panel, centre: 460 × 340 cm, wings: 460 × 150 cm. Cathedral of Our Lady, Antwerp.

his workshop.[8] The artist reported that it was difficult to create the work piece by piece. Without seeing it as a whole, he had to rely on his mind instead of his sight.[9] The painting bares traces of this self-confessed struggle: sudden changes in the colouring indicate that parts of the canvas were rolled up while others were painted.[10] While there are records of other strategies resembling that of Jordaens's, which allowed painters to work on large supports piece by piece,[11] it was preferable to work in spaces that fit oversized paintings in their entirety.[12]

Sometimes artists rented or created spaces ad hoc for large works. In 1634, Rubens directed a band of Antwerp artists to execute the decorations for the Joyous Entry of the Cardinal-Infante Ferdinand (1609–1641).[13] Some of these triumphal arches, consisting of wood and canvas mounted on a timber frame, were over twenty metres tall. They could be assembled, in part, in two large spaces rented for the occasion, the galleries of the Old Bourse and the refectory of the Calced Carmelites convent, both a stone's throw from Rubens's house.[14] Bas Dudok van Heel noted that Rembrandt built a warehouse at the back of his Amsterdam studio around the time he painted *The Night Watch* (1642; originally about 4.2 m × 4.8 m).[15] Rembrandt's regular workshop, equipped for producing smaller portraits and history paintings, could not have contained the large group portrait.

Plus-sized paintings could also be done in situ, at their final destination. Churches, for example, were popular worksites.[16] This method bypassed restrictions from studio size or transport practicalities. Moreover, it allowed artists to see how their works interacted with their surroundings. Over the course of the seventeenth century, artists increasingly paid attention to the relationship between artworks and environmental lighting conditions.[17]

Painters used ladders or scaffolds to reach the tops of their projects, which sometimes led to regrettable accidents. Michiel Coxie (1499–1592) died after he dropped from a scaffold in the Antwerp city hall.[18] Jordaens experienced a less dramatic but nonetheless unfortunate mishap. He fell off a ladder while painting *The Triumph of Frederik Hendrik* in his studio, leaving him immobilized and in fear of gangrene for a month.[19]

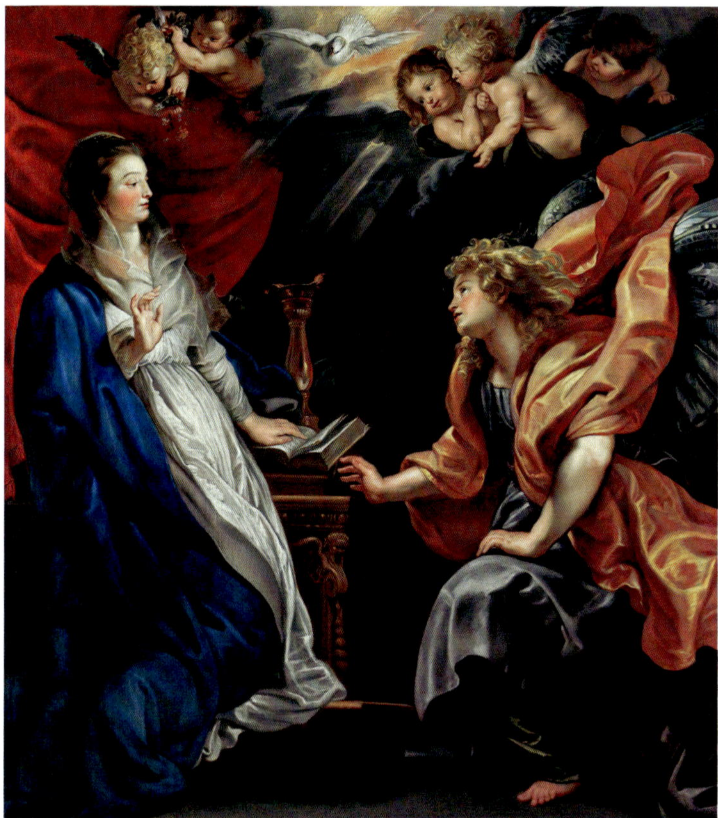

Fig 5 Peter Paul Rubens, *The Annunciation*, c. 1610. Oil on canvas, 224 × 200 cm. Gemäldegalerie, Kunsthistorisches Museum, Vienna. 685. Photo © Kunsthistorisches Museum, Vienna.

THE EARLY WORK AND SHOP (1609–1614)

In November 1610, Rubens bought a sixteenth-century house and an adjoining bleachfield on De Wapper, which formerly belonged to a Calvinist family of cloth dyers.[20] Rubens renovated the building to house his family and art collection, and constructed a large workshop on its south side (fig. 3).[21] After purchasing the property, Rubens lived with his family-in-law for some years, before moving to his new residence around 1615.[22]

There are no sources on the precise location of the artist's workshop before the move, although records on two large works shed some light on Rubens's early practices. *The Raising of the Cross* (1610–1611, 4.6 m. high; fig. 4, page 192 is a later version) was painted directly in the parish church of Saint Walburgis. Right before the contract for this altarpiece was signed, according to the documentation, "the admiral's men delivered a sail to hang while Rubens worked on the high altar."[23] By contrast, an account book documenting expenses for *The Descent from the Cross* (1611–1614; 4.2 m. high) shows that the artist also owned or rented a workshop at the time. In 1612 and 1614, workers were paid to pick up parts of the triptych "at Rubens's" and move them to the Cathedral of Our Lady.[24] The 1612 report mentions that the workers "lowered the painting from the first level to the ground floor."[25] This two-storey (or second-floor) workshop could have been anywhere in the city.[26]

Rubens's predilection for painting big had already been developed in Italy. His altarpiece for the Oratorian church in Rome, *Saint Gregory Surrounded by Other Saints, Adoring the Madonna of Vallicella* (1606–1607), stood 4.8 metres tall.[27] It is generally assumed that he painted many more large pictures immediately after he returned to Antwerp. However, during his first years back in the city, his workshop mainly produced smaller paintings.[28] Apart from *The Raising of the Cross* and *The Descent from the Cross*, there is only one monumental painting that can be securely dated before Rubens's move to De Wapper: *The Adoration of the Magi*, now in Madrid.[29] The artist submitted grand designs for the high altars of the Antwerp and Ghent cathedrals in 1611 and 1612, but both were executed a decade later.[30]

Some of Rubens's smaller works were made for religious settings, such as epitaphs[31] or altarpieces with a height in the two-to-three-metre range, like the Vienna *The Annunciation* (fig. 5, page 174).[32] This portion of Rubens's oeuvre can be reconstructed with the help of archival documents, which often yield precise dates. The artist also created paintings for private galleries, both by commission and for the open market, although the documentation only occasionally mentions these works. According to a letter from 1611, for instance, we know Rubens had promised the *Juno and Argus* in Cologne to the engraver Jacob de Bie (1581–after 1637), but sold it to someone else as "a profitable occasion presented itself."[33]

Rubens signed and dated seven works around 1614, which provide us with more information about his gallery pictures. They most consist of small and medium-sized history paintings on panel[34]—among them was a variant of *The Lamentation*, included in this exhibition (fig. 6, page 202). From Rubens's letter to Archduke Albert in 1614, we learn that he was also making "great works" on canvas around this time. He offered to show some of them to

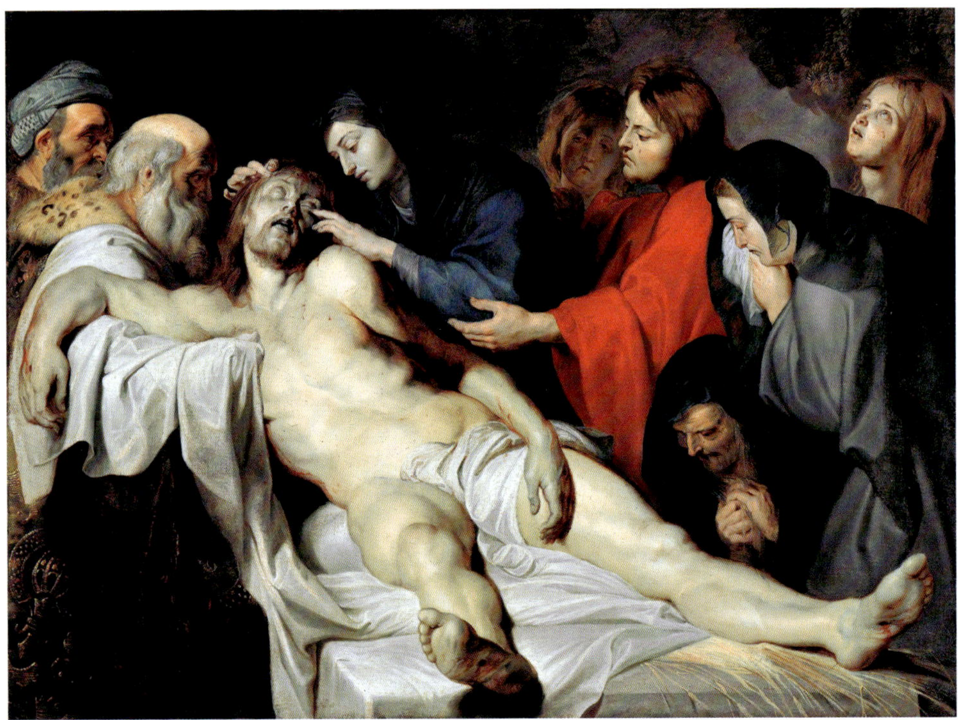

Fig 6 Peter Paul Rubens, *The Lamentation*, c. 1612. Oil on canvas, 150 × 204 cm. Liechtenstein Princely Collections, Vaduz-Vienna. GE 62. © LIECHTENSTEIN. The Princely Collections, Vaduz-Vienna.

the Archduke in Brussels.[35] I'm inclined to think that the works mentioned here were made for secular settings, as in the case of *Daniel in the Lions' Den* (fig. 7), rather than religious commissions.[36] In addition to high-quality works, Rubens's workshop also produced copies and cheaper paintings.[37] He was already running a busy shop, but there was still margin for growth.

THE MOVE TO DE WAPPER AND THE EVOLUTION OF RUBENS'S OEUVRE (1615–1621)

The date of Rubens's move to his new workshop can be deduced from circumstantial evidence. We know that he still lived with his family-in-law, the Brants, in 1614, as his son Albert was baptized in their parish in March of that year.[38] However, a document from February 1616 mentions the artist as living "on De Wapper,"[39] which implies that Rubens moved around 1615. Slaters were working on his roof and attic that year, suggesting that construction was well underway.[40] Payment for a wall at the east end of Rubens's garden, separating the estate from the neighbouring shooting range of the Guild of the Harquebusiers, was also dated 1615.[41] This may indicate that the Rubens site became more populated at that point, though renovations were not entirely finished. In November 1616, Rubens commissioned a large staircase,[42] likely the one pictured in the ground floor gallery in Jacobus Harrewijn's print (fig. 9). I believe the ground floor was already in use when Rubens went to live at De Wapper around 1615, and the workshop was fully operational after this staircase was finished.[43]

An additional argument in favour of this hypothesis can be found in Rubens's oeuvre, in the notable increase in his production of monumental paintings from 1615/1616 onward. Whereas only three tall works can be securely dated to the period between 1609 and 1614, twelve large pieces are documented between 1615 and 1620, and five more are attributed to this period on stylistic grounds.[44] Examples are *The Entombment* for the Capuchin Church in Cambrai (1616, 4 m. high),[45] *The Great Last Judgment* and the two side altars for the Jesuit church in Neuburg (fig. 1, 1617, 6.1 m. tall; 1619, both 4.7 m. tall),[46] and *The Miracles of Francis Xavier* and *Ignatius of Loyola* for the Jesuit church in Antwerp (c. 1618, both 5.35 m. tall).[47] Paintings like *The Last Judgment* and the Antwerp Jesuit altars were also taller than anything Rubens had painted previously. Importantly, the artist did not stop producing smaller works. Rather, the portion of large works within

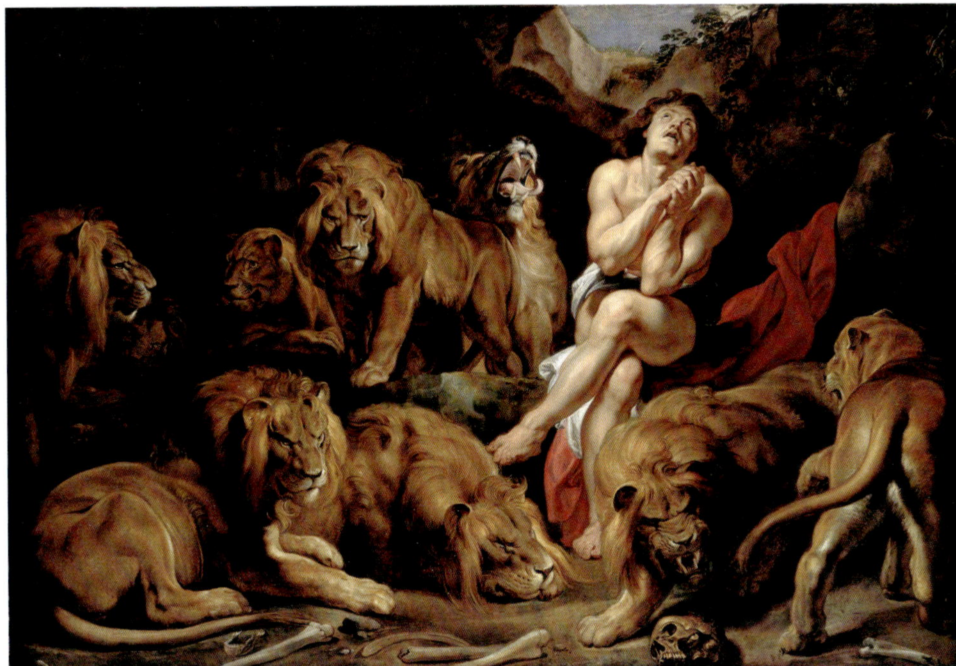

Fig 7 Peter Paul Rubens, *Daniel in the Lions' Den*, c. 1614–16. Oil on canvas, 224.2 × 330.5 cm. National Gallery of Art, Washington, D.C., Ailsa Mellon Bruce Fund. 965.13.1. Image courtesy National Gallery of Art, Washington D.C.

his total output increased. He painted at least two of them per year around this time.

References to *The Raising of the Cross* and *The Descent from the Cross* describe obstacles that Rubens had to overcome while painting on a large scale before his move to De Wapper. A sail was hung to shield the painter from churchgoers, and workers were hired to lower a painting between floors. Once such barriers were removed, Rubens's production of monumental paintings skyrocketed. The artist's workspace, built for completing large works quickly, allowed him to corner a market niche. Rubens continued to work on-site occasionally, as when he finally obtained the commission for the high altar in the Antwerp cathedral in 1626.[48] However, from 1615–1616 onward, the artist increasingly worked for clients in far-away destinations, exporting paintings to present-day Germany, Italy, and France.[49] These works were evidently executed in Antwerp. While he sometimes outsourced commissions to his colleagues in the city,[50] this practice must have been rare for large altarpieces. As Katlijne van der Stighelen has noted, large freestanding studios like Rubens's were exceptional in the first decades of the seventeenth century.[51]

RECONSTRUCTING THE GROUND FLOOR OF RUBENS'S WORKSHOP

The Rubenhuis that stands in Antwerp today is largely a twentieth-century reconstruction.[52] While built in good faith, it has some defects. The following paragraphs draw on three sources to establish the original appearance of the ground floor, where Rubens likely painted his large pictures. The first source consists of a pair of engravings of Rubens's house by Jacobus Harrewijn, published in 1684 and 1692, roughly half a century after Rubens's death (figs. 8, 9, 10, pages 119). The second is a floorplan drawn by the Brussels Rubens aficionado François Mols, who visited the house before it was extensively renovated in 1763 (fig. 11).[53] Lastly, I will include notes from the archeological research that preceded the restoration of 1939–1945. These were made by Emiel Van Averbeke, the city architect overseeing the project, and Theo Ruyten, the on-site supervisor.[54]

Harrewijn's print and Mols's floorplan correspond fairly well. The exterior and interior views from the print can be located on the plan. The main goal of the research conducted by van Averbeke and Ruyten was to determine whether Harrewijn's and

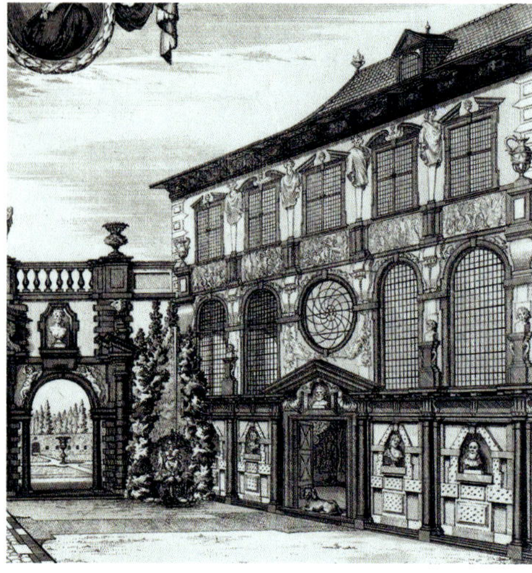

Fig 8 Jacobus Harrewijn, after J. van Croes, *View of the Rubenshuis in Antwerp* (detail), c. 1675–1732. Engraving, 28.7 × 35.7 cm. Metropolitan Museum of Art, New York, The Elisha Whittelsey Collection, The Elisha Whittelsey Fund, 1951. 51.501.7502.

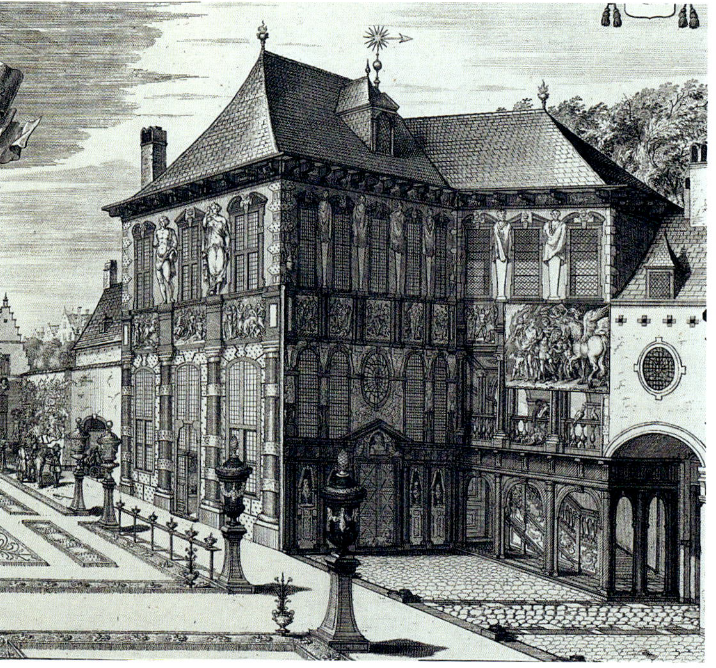

Fig 9 Jacobus Harrewijn, *The North and Garden Façades of Rubens's Workshop* (detail), 1692. Etching, 32.5 × 42.2 cm. University of Antwerp, print room. MP13.5.

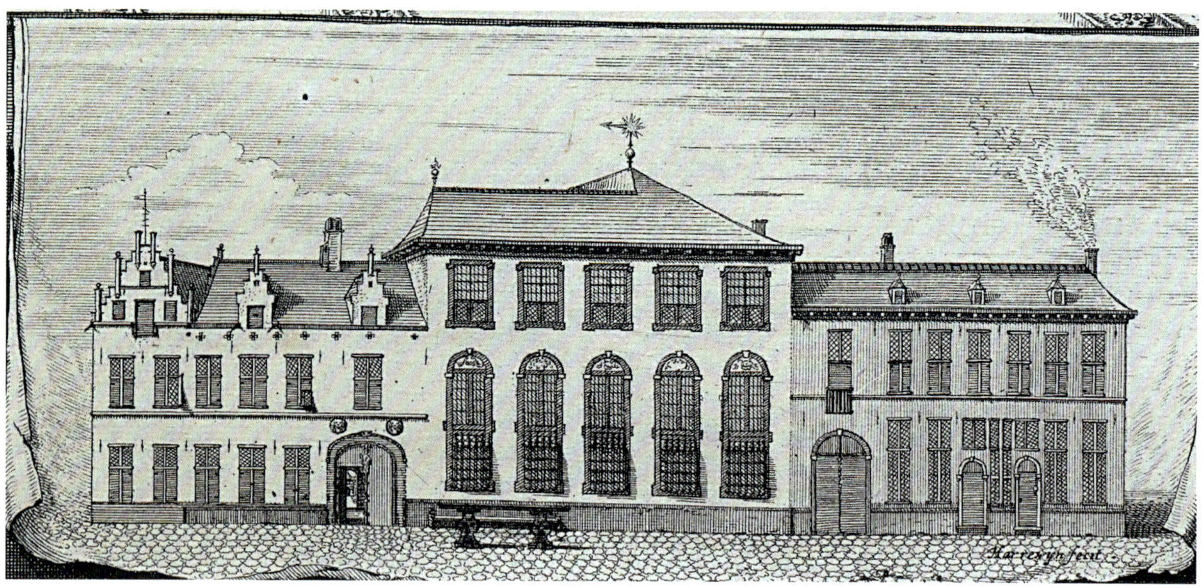

Fig 10 Jacobus Harrewijn, *The Street or West Façade of Rubens's House and Workshop* (detail of *The North and Garden Façades of Rubens's Workshop*), 1692. Etching, 32.5 × 42.2 cm. University of Antwerp, print room. MP13.5.

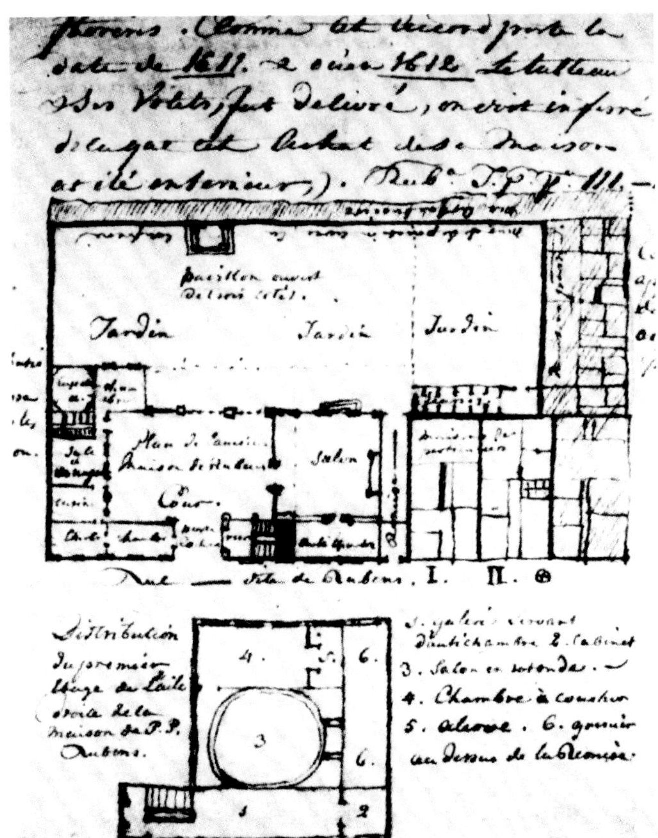

Fig 11 François Mols, Floorplan of Rubens's House drawn from memory, in François Mols, 'Rubeniana', II, 1 (Annecdotes, Lettres). Royal Library of Belgium, Brussels. Ms. 5726, fol. 10.

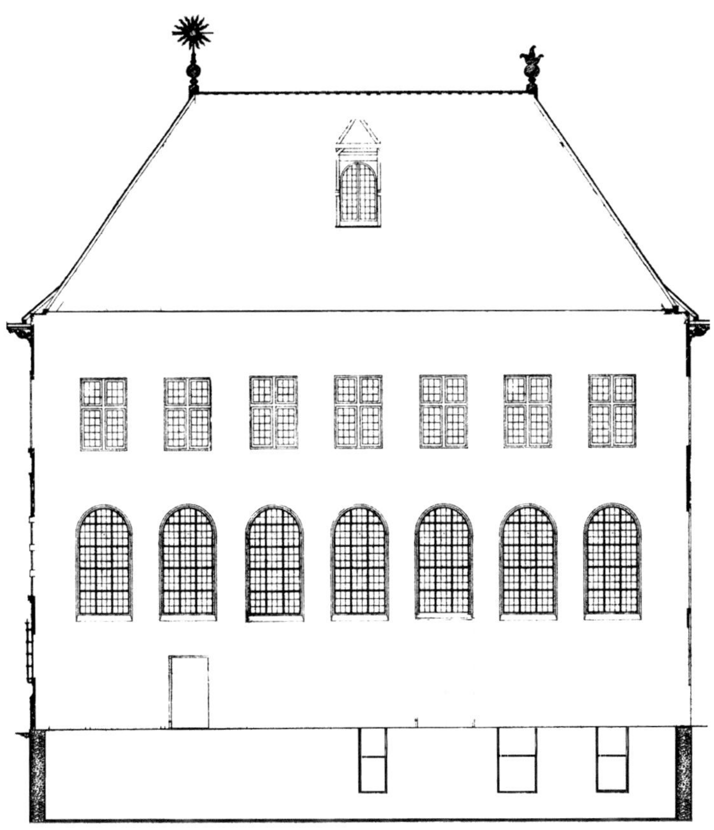

Fig 12 Author's image, after a drawing by Emiel van Averbeke, reconstruction of the south façade of Rubens's workshop, showing also the cellar and its windows.

Mols's images showed the building in its original state or after renovations.[55] An examination of the surviving masonry of the north wall confirmed that it was initially constructed as depicted by Harrewijn.[56] The garden and street façades were completely destroyed and rebuilt in 1763, so these passages could not be tested against material record.[57] Most scholars have nevertheless assumed that Harrewijn's engraving depicted the original street façade (fig. 10), while some, such as Van Averbeke, have considered his version of the garden façade (fig. 9) a later alteration.[58] Inspection of the south wall, invisible in Harrewijn's print, revealed the tracery of seven arched windows on each floor, at the same height as those on the north wall (fig. 12).[59] This means that the passageway on the building's south side, represented as closed in the images of Harrewijn and Mols, was originally open.[60] Foundation walls and their relation to other surviving architectural elements made it possible to deduce the dimensions of the workshop: it measured 8.5 metres from north to south and 19 metres from east to west. Rebates in the walls, into which beams for the ceiling were anchored, established the height of the ground floor at 6.8 metres.[61]

Only a few elements of the ground floor interior remained: some brick floor tiles,[62] a stove in the south east-corner,[63] and traces of the partition wall shown in Mols's plan in the foundation.[64] The ground floor was thus subdivided into a large hall at the garden side (five bays) and an antechamber at the street side (two bays). The antechamber may have been a presentation room for finished paintings, functioning as a sort of shop front.[65] This room could be accessed from a small door in the south façade (discovered in the masonry, see fig. 12) and from two doors in the loggia on the north side (shown by Harrewijn, fig. 9).[66] The hall east of the antechamber must have been where Rubens created his biggest paintings. The area could be entered from the

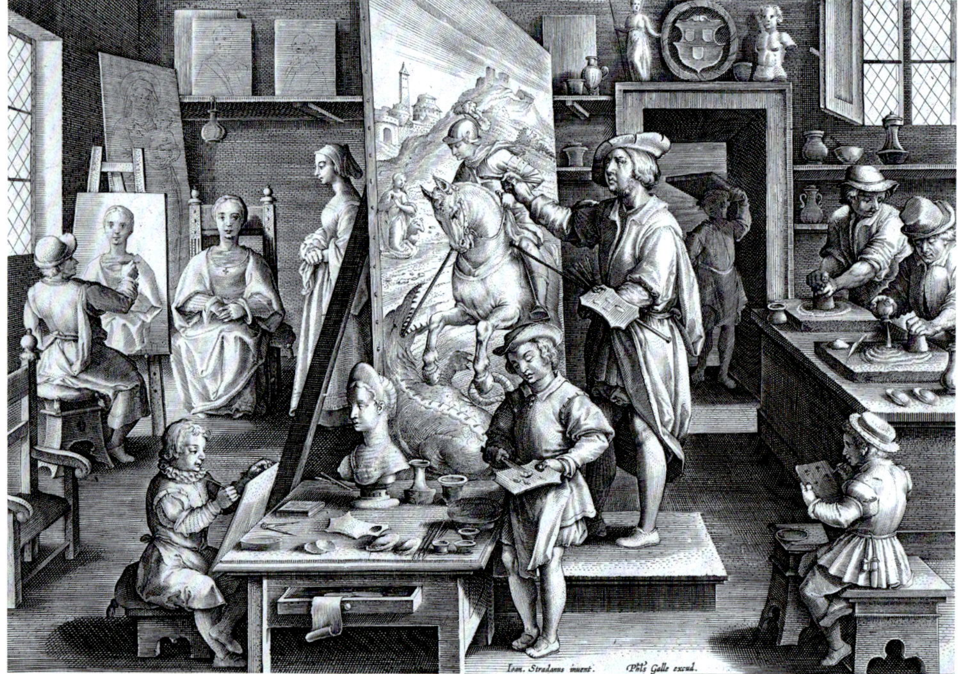

Fig 13 Philip Galle, after Jan van der Straet, *Color olivi* in *Nova Reperta*, 1580–1605. Engraving, 20.4 × 27.1 cm. British Museum, London, bequeathed by Sir Hans Sloane. 1948,0410.4.204. Photo © The Trustees of the British Museum.

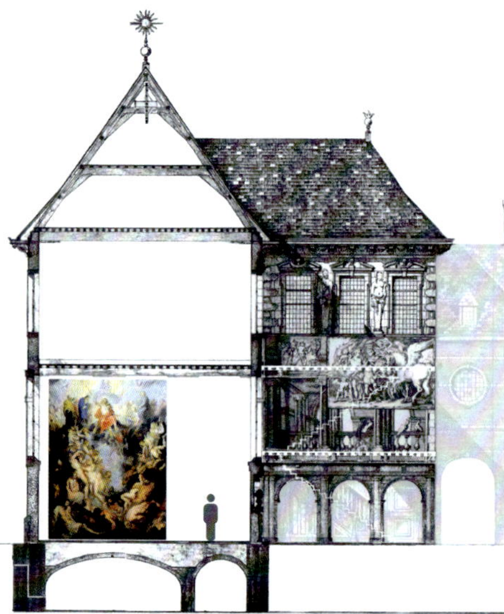

Fig 14 Author's image, after Emiel van Averbeke: East-west section of Rubens's workshop, showing *The Great Last Judgement* and a person on scale for comparison.

antechamber, and from a wide door at the courtyard beneath the rosette. There was probably a higher door too, either in the east or south façade,[67] so that large pictures could be moved in and out easily without crossing the courtyard (see fig. 3).

Any further claim about how the ground floor was used will inevitably be speculative, but it is nevertheless an interesting exercise in thought. Pictures up to two or three metres tall could be painted on easels, as shown in Stradanus's (1523–1605) idealized rendition of a painter's workshop (fig. 13). However, this approach would not have sufficed for the largest and heaviest works. Depictions of artists working on oversized paintings are rare, but Hélène Dubois spotted one example in a gallery picture by Cornelis De Baellieur (1607–1671) in Rohrau. It shows a painter on a scaffold completing a canvas mounted on a stretcher that is leaning against the back wall. I think that Rubens used such a setup: *The Great Last Judgement*, his tallest altarpiece, is about as tall as the ground floor of his workshop (fig. 14), so he was not required to roll his canvases like Jordaens once did.[68] If Rubens's largest panels and canvases were indeed painted as a whole, they would have rested against a partition wall. The outer walls of his workshop all included arched windows positioned three metres up.[69] Architectural theorists since Vitruvius had recommended northern light for working spaces,[70] so Rubens's preference for windows all around may be significant. Perhaps he simply wanted to take in all the daylight he could get—the days are notoriously gloomy and short in Antwerp half of the year.[71] On the other hand, Dubois has suggested that Rubens may have used these windows to emulate lighting conditions at the destinations of his works.[72]

ABOUT SPACE AND CHANGE

The evolution in the productivity of Rubens's shop during the Twelve Years' Truce is truly spectacular. After his return from Italy, the artist spent around ten months designing and executing *The Raising of the Cross*.[73] By 1621, he needed only eleven

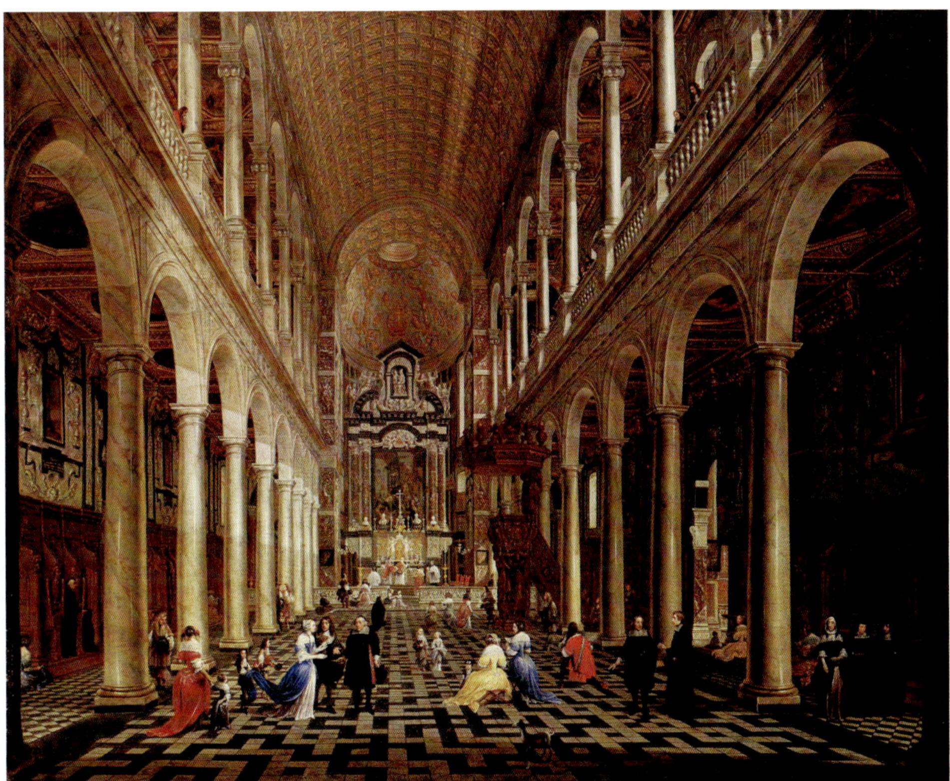

Fig 15 Anton Günther Gheringh, *A View of the Antwerp Jesuit Church*, 1665. Oil on canvas, 113 × 141 cm. Kunsthistorisches Museum, Vienna. 602. Photo © Kunsthistorisches Museum, Vienna.

months to deliver a series of thirty-nine ceiling paintings for the Antwerp Jesuit church (see fig. 15), a surface area more than ten times as large as that of *The Raising of the Cross*.[74] Rubens devised multiple strategies to cope with the growing demand for his paintings, including delegating work to skilled assistants and developing economical design and painting processes. I hope to have shown that his workshop also played a vital role in the bigger picture. Financial gain was not the sole motivator for increasing efficiency.[75] Rubens pursued visibility and recognition by creating challenging works for prominent places. His workspace was instrumental in achieving his vision.

In 1621, Rubens stated that he was "by natural instinct, more fit to execute very large works than small curiosities."[76] This moment of self-realization must have been triggered by the recently completed Jesuit ceiling paintings, and it signalled a turning point in the artist's oeuvre. Rubens's most ambitious works in the two following decades were not large altarpieces but rather decorative cycles, paintings as well as tapestries. He was able to adapt his workspace and procedures to the specific needs of individual commissions. The ceiling paintings for the Banqueting Hall in the Palace of Whitehall (executed c. 1633) were the first and only of Rubens's canvases that did not fit into the artist's studio. This led Gregory Martin to believe that they were painted in an ad hoc space.[77] In around 1636, when Rubens was under pressure to deliver sixty paintings for the hunting lodge of the king Philip IV of Spain (1605–1665), he subcontracted many of them to different Antwerp workshops.[78]

However, I am inclined to think that Rubens initially created cycles in-house. The first time that he spread his story over multiple narrative surfaces was in 1617, when he created a tapestry series depicting *The Life of Decius Mus*.[79] Around the same time, the large staircase in his space was completed, expanding the surface area of his workshop[80]—this may be another significant correspondence in the chronologies of the artist's work and workspace.

This essay draws on research for my dissertation on Rubens's workshop, supervised by Jeffrey Muller, who I want to thank for his inspiring guidance. I am also grateful to Petra Maclot and Nora De Poorter, both preparing books on Rubens's workshop, for their sharp observations on earlier drafts of this text.

1 "*Sarebbe . . . la più grande i bella che mai si facesse in questi paesi.*" Letter from Peter Paul Rubens to Archduke Albert, March 16, 1614; Max Rooses and Charles Ruelens, *Correspondance de Rubens et documents épistolaires concernant sa vie et ses œuvres*, 6 vols. (Antwerp: Veuve de Backer, 1887–1909), vol. 2, doc. 138, 69. Rubens had made the design for the altar two years earlier, at the request of Bishop Charles Maes (1559–1612). When Maes died, his follower was reluctant to proceed with the project, so Rubens called on Archduke Albert (1559–1621) to pressure him. If Albert made any attempt to help Rubens, he was unsuccessful. The artist obtained green light for the commission only in 1623, after Antoon Triest (1576–1657) became the bishop of Ghent. Hans Vlieghe, *Corpus Rubenianum Ludwig Burchard, Part VIII: Saints*, 2 vols. (Brussels: Arcade, 1972–73), 1:107–9, no. 72.

2 This has been observed by, for example, e.g. Frans Baudouin, "Iconografie en stijlontwikkeling in de godsdienstige schilderkunst te Antwerpen in de XVIIde eeuw," in *Antwerpen in de XVIIde eeuw*, ed. Walter Couvreur (Antwerp: Genootschap voor Antwerpse Geschiedenis, 1989), 339; Alfons K.L. Thijs, *Van Geuzenstad tot katholiek bolwerk. Maatschappelijke betekenis van de Kerk in contrareformatorisch Antwerpen* (Turnhout–London: Brepols, 1990), 120, 122; David Freedberg, "Painting and the Counter Reformation in the Age of Rubens,", in *The Age of Rubens*, ed. Peter Sutton (Boston: Museum of Fine Arts, 1994), exh. cat., Museum of Fine Arts, Boston, 141. These authors all note that while although there was a tradition of monumental painting in the Low Countries, Rubens pushed the boundaries in size. Baudouin links the increased height with Rubens's preference for portico altars over the traditional triptych format.

3 On this work, see Konrad Renger, *Peter Paul Rubens: Altäre für Bayern* (Munich: Bayerische Staatsgemäldesammlungen, 1990), 25–62, exh. cat. Throughout this essay I define large works as anything taller than 3.5 metres, about the height of the tallest altarpieces of the previous generation of Antwerp history painters, including Frans Floris (c. 1519–1570), Maerten de Vos (1532–1603), and Otto van Veen (1556–1629). Rubens's paintings regularly exceeded this size.

4 An example within a general art historical survey is the chapter "Vision and Visions: Catholic Europe in the Seventeenth-Century" in Ernst Gombrich, *The Story of Art*, 1st ed. (London: Phaidon, 1950). Academic texts include Frans Baudouin, "Altars and Altarpieces before 1620," in *Rubens before 1620*, ed. John Rupert Martin (Princeton, NJ: Princeton University Press, 1972), 45–91; Filip Vermeylen, "Antwerp Beckons: The Reasons for Rubens' Return to the Netherlands in 1608," *Netherlands Yearbook for History of Art* 55 (2004), 17–33; Bert Timmermans, *Patronen van Patronage in het zeventiende-eeuwse Antwerpen: Een elite als actor binnen de kunstwereld*, Studies Stadsgeschiedenis (Amsterdam: Amsterdam University Press); for large paintings, esp. 194–95 and the literature cited under note 2.

5 Some art historians have emphasized that these works and their creators have received disproportionate attention. The city was also a bustling production centre for smaller paintings, a field in which the likes of Jan Brueghel the Elder excelled. For a discussion on the scale of these works and habits of collecting and display, see especially Elizabeth Honig, *Jan Brueghel and the Senses of Scale* (University Park, PA: Penn State University Press, 2016). Apart from high-end painters, there were shops that specialized in the bulk production of second-rate works. See, for example, Christina Currie and Dominique Allart, *The Brueg[H]el Phenomenon: Paintings by Pieter Bruegel the Elder and Pieter Brueghel the Younger, with a Special Focus on Technique and Copying Practice* (Turnhout: Brepols, 2012), 3 vols. Even within religious art, monumental paintings formed an exclusive niche. For a broader view of the material culture of the Counter-Reformation, see Jeffrey M. Muller, *St. Jacob's Antwerp Art and Counter Reformation in Rubens's Parish Church* (Leiden: Brill, 2016).

6 See the literature under notes 2 and 4.

7 Some overviews of workshop architecture or general infrastructure draw on treatises, depictions of workshops, and historical plans. See, for example, Hans Schwartz, *Das Künstlerhaus: Anmerkungen zur Sozialgeschichte des Genies* (Braunschweig: Vieweg & Sohn, 1990); Katja Kleinert, *Atelierdarstellungen in der niederländischen Genremalerei des 17. Jahrhunderts*, Studien zur internationalen Architektur und Kunstgeschichte 40 (Petersberg: Michael Imhof Verlag, 2006); and Ernst van de Wetering, *Rembrandt: The Painter Thinking* (Amsterdam: Amsterdam University Press, 2016), the comments in chap. 1, 3–60. Workshops have also been conceptualized as social spaces where knowledge was generated and exchanged, a scholarly tradition initiated by Pamela O. Long, *Openness, Secrecy, Authorship: Technical Arts and the Culture of Knowledge from Antiquity to the Renaissance* (Baltimore: Johns Hopkins University Press, 2001), and Pamela H. Smith, *The Body of the Artisan: Art and Experience in the Scientific Revolution* (Chicago: University of Chicago Press, 2004). A more archeological approach to the painting process of a specific artist, also envisioned in the present essay, is uncommon. One example is Hélène Dubois, "'Come s'usa di fare non volendo ingannarsi': The Execution of Large Altarpieces on Canvas in Rubens's Studio," in *Rubens: A Genius at Work*, ed. Joost vander Auwera and Sabine van Sprang (Tielt: Lannoo, 2007), exh. cat., 160–63.

8 Margriet van Eikema Hommes and Lidwien Speleers, "cat. no. 32," in *De Oranjezaal: Catalogus en Documentatie*, ed. Rudi Ekkart et al., http://oranjezaal.rkdmonographs.nl/, accessed July 2018. The work formed part of the Oranjezaal in Huis ten Bosch, which was decorated by the most prominent painters of the Low Countries.

9 "*Het alder moeyelyckxste dat ickt niet encan geheel in mijn huys wtspannen soo dat ickt meer met het concept int hooft dan met het gesicht het moet wtvoeren om sijn moeyelycke groote.*" ("The most difficult thing of all is that I cannot span it [the canvas] out in its entirety, so that because of its difficult size I have to work more from the concept in my mind than from sight.") Letter from Jacob Jordaens to Constantijn Huygens, November 8, 1651, in Johan H.W. Unger, "Brieven van Eenige Schilders aan Constantin Huygens," *Oud Holland* 9 (1891), 195–96.

10 Margriet van Eikema Hommes and Lidwien Speleers noticed this during the restoration of the Oranjezaal paintings. The column at the far right in Jordaens's *Triumph*, for example, suddenly changes color above the bald man's head. It proved impossible to reconstruct the artist's canvas rolling precisely, but restorers generally discerned two to three phases. The painting was also too wide for Jordaens's workshop, so the artist worked on two vertical strips of primed canvas separately and then sewed them together, later painting over the seam. Van Eikema Hommes and Speleers, "cat. no. 32," 2. Observaties en technische informatie" in Ekkart et al., *De Oranjezaal: Catalogus en Documentatie.*

11 Hélène Dubois mentions the existence of cylinder systems on which canvases could be rolled during the painting process, noting that an example is depicted in the self-portrait of Jacques Ignatius De Roore (1686–1747) in Hamburg. Dubois, "Come s'usa di fare non volendo ingannarsi,'" in Vander Auwera and Van Sprang *Rubens: A Genius at Work*, 161; the portrait is pictured on 278. Leonardo Da Vinci drew a similar setup for the panels in one of his manuscripts. The support could be lowered with a pully into a slot in a room below the workshop, allowing the painter to remain seated while the work moved. (Ms. A, Bibliothèque nationale de France, inv. 2038, fol. 4v; reproduced Jean-Paul Richter, "Lionardo da Vinci's Lehrbuch von der Malerei," *Zeitschrift für bildende Kunst* 17 (1882): 13.

12 This was recommended by the seventeenth-century critic Joachim von Sandrart (1606–1688) when he described the ideal artist's studio. He emphasized that an artist should be able to step back to appreciate his work. For these and other contemporary comments on studio size, see Kleinert, *Atelierdarstellungen in der niederländischen Genremalerei des 17. Jahrhunderts*, 34.

13 On this project, see John Rupert Martin, *Corpus Rubenianum Ludwig Burchard, Part XVI: The Decorations for the Pompa Introitus Fernandi* (Brussels: Arcade, 1972), and Anna C. Knaap and Michael C. J. Putnam, eds., *Art, Music and Spectacle in the Age of Rubens: The Pompa Introitus Fernandi*, Studies in Baroque Art 1 (London: Harvey Miller, 2013).

14 John Rupert Martin, *Decorations for the Pompa Introitus Fernandi*, 30–31. Documents on the commission were published by Pierre Génard in several issues of the Antwerpsch Archievenblad: Pierre Génard, "Intrede van den Prins-Kardinaal Ferdinand van Spanje te Antwerpen, op 17 April 1635," *Antwerpsch Archievenblad* 6 (1869): 400–72; 7 (1870), 1–113; 13(1876), 215–345. For the Beurs, see 7:56. For the refectory, see 7:54–55, 56, 60. In the convent, painters and carpenters disrupted daily life, staying up late, behaving noisily, and hogging the stove.

15 Sebastian A.C. Dudok van Heel, "De galerij en schilderloods van Rembrandt; of waar schilderde Rembrandt de 'Nachtwacht'?" *Amstelodamum* 74, no. 5 (September–October 1987): 103–6.

16 Two examples of Rubens working in situ are discussed below (see notes 24 and 49<I believe these are the notes being referred to; please confirm my changes>). Jennifer Montagu gave an account of young sculptors working in situ in Rome. Jennifer Montagu, *Roman Baroque Sculpture: The Industry of Art* (New Haven, CT: Yale University Press, 1992), 128–30; see also 36.

17 See Margriet Eikema Hommes, "Een triomfstoet belicht: De werkelijke en de geschilderde lichtinval in de Oranjezaal," in Margriet Eikema Hommes and Elmer Kolfin, *De Oranjezaal in Huis ten Bosch: Een zaal uit liefde* (Zwolle: Waanders, 2013), 179–254.

18 Karel van Mander, *Het Leven der Doorluchtige Nederlandtsche, en Hoogduytsche Schilders*, in *Het Schilder-Boeck* (Haarlem: Jacob de Meester, 1604), fol. 259r. On the artist's life, see Koenraad Jonckheere, ed., *Michiel Coxcie (1499–1592) and the Giants of His Age* (Turnhout: Brepols, 2013).

19 Transcribed in Johan H.W. Unger, "Brieven van Eenige Schilders aan Constantin Huygens," *Oude Holland* 9 (1891): 196.

20 Two documents regarding the sale are preserved, respectively dated November 1, 1610, and January 4, 1611. They are discussed in Frans Baudouin, "De fresco's op de gevels van Rubens' werkplaats: enkele addenda," *Mededelingen van de Koninklijke Academie voor Wetenschappen, Letteren en Schone Kunsten van België: Klasse der Schone Kunsten* 57, no. 1 (1998): 3–24. Rubens bought the house from Hans Thijsz I. (1556–1611), a descendant of a Protestant family that dispersed after the Fall of Antwerp in 1585; he became a wealthy merchant in the Dutch Republic. See John Michael Montias, "Art Collectors and Painters I: Rubens's Promise to Hans Thijsz." in *Art at Auction in 17th Century Amsterdam* (Amsterdam: Amsterdam University Press, 2002), 153–63, with earlier bibliography.

21 This has been commonly assumed since Ary J.J. Delen, *Het huis van Pieter Pauwel Rubens: Wat het was, wat her werd, wat het worden kan* (Brussels: L.J. Kryn, 1933). There are two main arguments in favour of this hypothesis. The first involves three sixteenth-century bird's-eye views of the city (Hieronymus Cock, 1557; Virgilius Bononiensis, 1565; Joris Hoefnagel, 1594), all of which show a small house on an otherwise empty lot. (For reproductions of Rubens's block, see Rutger Tijs, *P.P. Rubens en J. Jordaens: barok in eigen huis* (Antwerp: Stichting Mercator Plantin, 1984), 88–92; For more on the interpretation of the Bononiensis map, see Petra Maclot, "A Portrait Unmasked: The Iconology of the Bird's-Eye View of Antwerp by Virgilius Bononiensis (1565) as a Source for Typological Research of Private Buildings in Fifteenth- and Sixteenth-Century Antwerp," in *Portraits of the City: Representing Urban Space in Later Medieval and Early Modern Europe*, Studies in European Urban History (1100–1800), 31, ed. Katrien Lichtert, Jan Dumolyn, and Maximiliaan P.J. Martens (Turnhout: Brepols, 2014), 33–47. Second, there are transfer deeds. On September 16, 1660, when Rubens's house was sold to the merchant Jacomo van Eycke (Delen, *Het huis van Pieter Pauwel Rubens*, 49), a "painting studio" (*schilderhuys*) was listed as part of the estate, which was not mentioned when Rubens bought the house in 1610/1611. Some have warned, however, that not all elements described in Rubens's deed of purchase of 1611 have been identified, and perhaps a pre-existing structure was incorporated into the southern wing. Tijs, *P.P. Rubens en J. Jordaens* , 96 (argues that existing "galleries" were included in the painting studio); Annika Devroe, *Van Rubens' huis tot Rubenshuis: Een bouwhistorische studie* (master's thesis, Hoger instituut voor architectuurwetenschappen Henry van de Velde, 2008), 83–86 (general plea for caution) .

22 Rubens married Isabella Brant (1591–1626), daughter of Jan Brant (1559–1639), on September 29, 1609. Filips Rubens (1611–78), the artist's nephew and earliest biographer, mentions that the couple lived at Jan Brant's residence when Rubens painted *The Elevation of the Cross* (1610–11). ("*In contubernio soceri aliquot annos vixit, quo tempore fecit tabulam magni altaris exxlesiae Stae Walburgis Antverpiae, qua supplicium Domini nostri exhibit.*") For Filips's biography, see Frédéric de Reiffenberg, "Nouvelles Recherches sur Pierre-Paul Rubens, contenant une vie inédite de ce grand peintre," *Mémoires de l'Académie royale des sciences, des lettres et des beaux-arts de Belgique* 10 (1837), 3–19, for the above quote, 7. Filips's account is corroborated by the fact that the couple's first two children, Clara Serena (1611–1623) and Albert (1614–1657), were both baptized at the Church of Saint Andrew, in the parish of the Brant house. See Pierre Génard, *P.P. Rubens: Aanteekeningen over den grooten meester en zijne bloedverwanten* (Antwerp: P. Kockx, 1877), 414, for Clara Serena (baptized March 21, 1611) and 17 for Albert (baptized June 5, 1614). Génard, aware of Filips Rubens's biography, maintained that Rubens lived in the house of his deceased mother, Maria Pijpelinckx. However, Maria rented this residence from St. Michael's Abbey. The inventory of her estate (see Génard, *P.P. Rubens*, 434) listed an item for "eight months of rent of the house in which the deceased passed away." ("*Voor acht maenden huere vanden huyse, daerinne de afllijvige overleden is, betaelt. LXXXIII guld. VI s.t.*"). I do not consider it likely that Rubens renewed the lease, though he remained in close proximity: the Brant house was opposite the house in which Rubens's mother died.

23 "*Betaelt aen de gasten van den Admirael voor het seyl dat den capiteyn wel hadde geleent om te hangen terwylent den schilder Rubens den hoogen Autaer heeft geschildert.*" The expense is undated, but it is listed after funds for the altar were first collected on May 17, 1610, and before a contract that was signed in early June 1610. Max Rooses, *L'Oeuvre de P.P. Rubens* (Antwerp: Maes, 1886–92), vol. 2, 79–80, under nos. 275–85.

24 For the account book, see Max Rooses, "De Afdoening van het Kruis: Uit het Rekeningboek der Antwerpsche Kolveniersgilde," *Rubens-bulletijn* 5 (1910): 230–33; the centre panel September 12, 1612, the wings February 18 and March 6, 1614. The document states twice that workers picked up the parts of the triptych "*ten huyse vanden schilder*," which literally translates as "at the house of the painter." However, the wording did not necessarily signify "the place where Rubens lived"; it could have referred to a building that Rubens used for work.

25 "*Het afdoen vande schilderye vanden solder tot inden vloer.*" Max Rooses, "De Afdoening van het Kruis: Uit het Rekeningboek der Antwerpsche Kolveniersgilde," *Rubens-bulletijn* 5 (1910): 230. While the sentence could also be read as "from the attic to the [ground] floor," the above translation is more likely. The panels for *The Descent from the Cross* are 4.2 metres high, and they were made in one piece. The supports would not have fit in most seventeenth-century Antwerp attics, nor the windows and staircases commonly used to access them. I thank Petra Maclot for this observation.

26 Most have assumed that Rubens painted in the Brant house. See, for example, Frans Baudouin, "Altars and Altarpieces before 1620," in John Rupert Martin, *Rubens before 1620*, 62. I am hesitant, however, to assume that a prominent Antwerp citizen like Jan Brant would have allowed a proper artist's workshop to be set up in his house, even if he lived spaciously. The Brant residence is now destroyed, so any hypothesis on how Rubens fit his shop there (or whether he did so at all) could draw from archival research only. It is also worth considering whether the artist ran some of his activities in the sixteenth-century wing of his new estate.

27 The painting was refused, and Rubens took it back with him and installed it near his mother's tomb. For the intriguing controversy surrounding this work, see page 226; Ruth S. Noyes, *Peter Paul Rubens and the Counter-Reformation Crisis of the Beati Moderni*, Sanctity in Global Perspective 1 (London: Routledge, 2018).

28 See the comments about large and small paintings at the end of note 3. Size is always relative with Rubens. Susan Koslow remarked that *The Discovery of Pihiloemen* in Madrid (c. 1609; 2 × 3.1 m), a gallery painting by Rubens and the animalier Frans Snyders, was notably "larger than other surviving picture of this type." Susan Koslow, *Frans Snyders: The Noble Estate; Seventeenth-Century Still-life and Animal Painting in the Southern Netherlands* (Antwerp: Mercatorfonds, 1995), 74. In the present context, it is crucial to note that these works are in landscape format: while the surface is big, they are wide rather than tall.

29 This canvas was made for the *Staetencaemer* (Chamber of States) in the Antwerp city hall, where the Twelve Years' Truce would be signed. Hans Devisscher and Hans Vlieghe, *Corpus Rubenianum Ludwig Burchard, Part V: The Life of Christ before the Passion; I, The Youth of Christ*, 2 vols. (Turnhout: Brepols, 2014), 1:110–35, no. 23. Three more large Rubens works are occasionally dated to 1609–14 on the basis of style, namely *The Assumption of the Virgin*, now in Vienna (David Freedberg, *Corpus Rubenianum Ludwig Burchard, Part VII: The Life of Christ after the Passion*, [Turnhout: Brepols, 1984], 149–57, no. 37, "c. 1613"); *The Adoration of the Shepherds* in the Antwerp Dominican church (Devisscher and Vlieghe, *The Life of Christ before the Passion: I, The Youth of Christ*, 1:62–65, no. 10, "c. 1614"); and *St. Francis Receiving the Stigmata* in Cologne (Vlieghe, *Saints*, 1:138–40, no. 90), "shortly before or after the middle of the second decade" "recorded at the Capuchin Church ... in October 1616." Of *The Adoration* and the *St. Francis*, I believe that they might well have been painted in 1615. *The Assumption* is related to a complex cluster of works, and it is therefore impossible to critically evaluate the date here. Even if we accept that all three of these works were painted before 1615, the number of large altarpieces painted during the second half of the Truce remains significantly larger.

30 Rubens submitted two *modelli* for the high altar of the Antwerp cathedral on April 22, 1611. It is unclear why the commission was postponed until 1626. Freedberg, *The Life of Christ after the Passion*, 172–78, no. 43. When Rubens wrote to Albert to secure the Ghent commission, he mentioned that he had showed the duke a sketch for the altarpiece in 1612 ("two years ago"). See note 1 for this letter.

31 These works are discussed as a group in David Freedberg, "Rubens as a Painter of Epitaphs, 1612–1618," *Gentse Bijdragen tot de Kunstgeschiedenis* 24 (1977): 51–71.

32 Another well-known example is *The Disputa of the Holy Sacrament* (c. 1609; 3.1 × 2.4 m) for the Dominican church in Antwerp. See Vlieghe, *Saints*, 1:73–78, no. 56.

33 Letter from Peter Paul Rubens to Jacob de Bie, May 11, 1611, in Ruth Saunders Magurn, *The Letters of Peter Paul Rubens* (Cambridge, MA: Harvard University Press, 1955), 55, doc. 22; Carl van de Velde, "Rubens' brieven in het Nederlands," in *Munuscula amicorum: Contributions on Rubens and His Colleagues in Honor of Hans Vlieghe*, ed. Katlijne van der Stighelen (Turnhout: Brepols, 2005), 1:147–84, doc. 1. Rubens assured de Bie that another painting would come his way in due time. The fact that paintings could find a client before they were completed shows that the line between a commission and a market piece was blurred. The lack of documentation is not restricted to market paintings; it also holds true for gallery commissions. For example, we know that *Samson and Delilah* was done for Nicolaas II Rockox, as the latter is mentioned on an engraving after the composition, and because the work figures on a cabinet painting of Rockox's collection. Still, there is no contract or receipt to help us define the precise context for its creation.

34 For a quick overview of these works, see Michael Jaffé, *Rubens: Catalogo Completo* (Milan: Electa, 1989), nos. 196, 221, 232–36. The *Cupid Charging His Bow* in Munich (Jaffé, *Rubens: Catalogo Completo*, no. 235) is the only one of these works on canvas. *The Incredulity of St. Thomas* (Jaffé, *Rubens: Catalogo Completo*, no. 221) is the only one that was surely done for a religious setting.

35 "*Sono al presente più cargato d'opere grandissime che non fossi giamai, delle quali penso di portare alcune à Brusselles per monstrar a S.A. quando saranno finite poi chè si fanno in tela.*" Rooses and Ruelens, *Correspondance de Rubens et documents épistolaires concernant sa vie et ses œuvres* (Antwerp: Veuve de Backer, 1887–1909), vol. 2, doc. 138, 70n1. It is more sensible to read "*grandissime*" as "great" rather than as "huge," as Rubens uses the Italian *grande* to mean large size earlier in the letter.

36 Rubens mentioned to Albert that he was *cargato d'opere grandissime*, assuring him that he wasn't after the Ghent commission for profit (see note 1). No effort has been made to identify these works, presumably because of a lack of further information. All we know is that they were great, on canvas, painted in 1614, and possibly shown to the duke. These criteria indicate, however, that the paintings in question were gallery pictures rather than altarpieces. Some of Rubens's most splendid gallery canvases have been dated around 1614, such as *Daniel in the Lions' Den* and *The Flight of Lot and His Family*. Incidentally, a version of the *Daniel* was in the archduke's collection.) By contrast, no documented religious commissions fit the description. *The Adoration of the Shepherds* in Antwerp and *St. Francis* in Cologne (see note 29) are the only candidates dated to 1614 on stylistic grounds. I wonder, however, why Rubens would bring paintings like that to Brussels. An additional problem arises with the phrase *cargato d'opere*, which has been translated as "charged with commissions" in the authoritative English edition of Rubens's letters (Saunders Magurn, *Letters of Peter Paul Rubens*, doc. 24, 57). Strictly speaking, however, Rubens may have started these works on his own initiative. The word *cargato* is related to *caricato*, which means "full of" or "burdened with." (*Geladen* is translated as *cargato, caricato, gaurato* in Levinus Hulsius, *Dictionarium Teutsch Italiänisch und Italiänisch Teutsch* [Frankfurt: Wolfgang Hofmann, 1630], 4th ed., 127.) This would mean that Rubens "had his hands full with great works." In the context of the letter to Albert, Rubens would then have assured the archduke that he had a capital in the making, paintings that he could soon sell at a good price. The artist's offer to present such works at the court may have come with the option of a first pick for the archdukes.

Rubens employed "*cargato d'opere*" in two other letters, and I believe that a commission isn't necessarily implied in either case. (Letter to Ercole Bianchi, written on behalf of his friend Jan Brueghel, January 25, 1612, Giovanni Crivelli, *Giovanni Brueghel pittor fiammingo, o Sue lettere e quadretti esistenti presso l'Ambrosiana* [Milan: Ditta Boniardi-Pogliani di E. Besozzi, 1868], 198–99; letter to Dudley Carleton, April 28, 1618, Rooses and Ruelens, *Correspondance de Rubens*, vol. 2, doc. 166, 135–37.) The notion of commission may have been blurry even for gallery pictures, as these could be sold at varying stages of the production process (see note 33).

37 A systematic study of Rubens's copies has yet to be completed. For some introductory notes, see Arnout Balis, "'Fatto da un mio discepolo': Rubens's Studio Practices Reviewed," in *Rubens and His Workshop: The Flight of Lot and His Family from Sodom*, ed. Toshiharu Nakamura (Tokyo: National Museum of Western Art, 1994), 105–6, 112, exh. cat.; Nils Büttner, "The Hands of Rubens: On Copies and Their Reception," in *Appreciating the Traces of an Artist's Hand*, Kyoto Studies in Art History 2, (proceedings of the Kyoto Art History Colloquium, September 25, 2016), ed. Toshiharu Nakamura (Kyoto: Kyoto University, 2017), 41–53.

38 See note 22.

39 The document in question is the funerary scroll of Marina Plantin (1550–1616), mother of Rubens's childhood friend Balthasar Moretus (1574–1641). It states that Rubens lives *opden Wapper*. Nora De Poorter, "Chronology," *Rubens Privé: De meester portretteert zijn familie*, ed. Ben van Beneden (Brussels: Marot, 2015), 240, exh. cat. The scroll was dated 1617 in older literature, which led some authors to suppose that Rubens moved at a later date. Tijs is the only author to assert that Rubens began to use the large studio after 1621, arguing that the artist did not have the financial means to renovate the house before then. Tijs, *P.P. Rubens en J. Jordaens*, 110–13. However, Büttner has since shown that Rubens had a substantial fortune at his disposal soon after his return. Nils Büttner, "Aristocracy and Noble Business: Some Remarks on Rubens's Financial Affairs," in *Munuscula amicorum: Contributions on Rubens and His Colleagues in Honor of Hans Vlieghe*, ed. Katlijne van der Stighelen (Turnhout: Brepols, 2005), 1:67–78.

40 "To his joiners, who made his house in the year 1615, he also asked to make the attic and, at the same time, his roof which he had them cover with slates." ("*Aen syne timmerlieden, die gemaect hebben syne huysinge in den iaer 1615, oock hadden aenbesteedt te solderen ende bedeen syn dack dwelck hy heeft doen dechten in de schalien.*") This reference dates from 1621, when Rubens appeared with the joiner in front of a notary because the latter had not fixed the slates properly. The joiner agreed to finish his job, charging only for the cost of the nails. The document was discovered in 2017 by Ingrid Moortgat while conducting research for the Jordaens and Van Dyck Panel Paintings Project, and was published in translation in their online newsletter. Justin Davies, "The Botched Job on Rubens's Roof," in *Jordaens and Van Dyck Panel Painting Project*, ed. Joost vander Auwera and Justin Davies, http://jordaensvandyck.org/rubens-had-problems-with-his-roof, accessed July 2018.

41 Among the costs were 323 pots of beer for the workers, half of which covered by Rubens and the other half by the Guild. Max Rooses, "De Afdoening van het Kruis: Uit het Rekeningboek der Antwerpsche Kolveniersgilde," *Rubens-bulletijn* 5 (1910): 233. The earlier version of the wall can be seen in several bird's-eye-view representations of Antwerp (mentioned at note 21), and it is also mentioned in the deed of purchase. Tijs, *P.P. Rubens en J. Jordaens*, 90.

42 "*Twee houtte trappen ende laeynen.*". Published in Tijs, *P.P. Rubens en J. Jordaens*, 96–99. The contract was undersigned on November 2 by Jasper Billeau, a woodworker, and by Hans van Mildert, a sculptor acting on Rubens's behalf. See also note 80.

43 There are two additional references to Rubens's expenses on the house in 1618, but in light of the sources discussed above, I don't think these imply that the workshop was built from the ground up at that point. The expenses may be related to further embellishments (decoration, portico) or the payment of outstanding debts. In May 1618, Rubens wrote to a patron that he had already "spent several thousands of florins on his house that year." ("*Ho speso questo anno qualq. Migliaia di fiorini nella mia fabrica.*"). Letter to Sir Dudley Carleton, May 12, 1618, Rooses and Ruelens, *Correspondance de Rubens*, vol. 2, doc. 168, 149–60, quote on 149. The same year, Frans Sweerts—a Humanist, tapestry dealer, and friend of Rubens's—also commented on the costs of Rubens's renovations, writing that the latter "had already spent over 24,000 guilders on his house." ("[Rubens] *heeft alreede over 24 duysent guldens versnoept in sijn huys.*") Letter from Frans Sweerts to Janus Gruterus, July 18, 1618, in Jozef Duverger, "Aantekeningen betreffende de patronne van P.P. Rubens en de tapijten met de geschiedenis van Decius Mus," *Gentse Bijdragen tot de Kunstgeschiedenis* 24 (1977–78), doc. 2, 39. Rubens expanded his estate by purchasing eight adjoining houses after the Truce, which we don't need to be concerned with here. See Emiel van Averbeke, "De eerste bevindingen: Het plan van Blomme, de dwalingen van Mols, wat er dient gedaan te worden" *Het Huis van P.P. Rubens: Periodisch Bulletin* 1 (1938), 36, illus. 6, for a reconstruction plan of Rubens's block after the acquisition; Devroe, *Van Rubens' huis tot Rubenshuis*, 51–56 for references.

44 Six examples cited in the text; the remaining documented works are *The Assumption of the Virgin* in Dusseldorf (receipt of 1616–17) (Freedberg, *The Life of Christ after the Passion*; *The Descent from the Cross* in Lille (was "being made" in 1617); Richard J. Judson, *Corpus Rubenianum Ludwig Burchard, Part VI: The Passion of Christ* (Turnhout: Brepols, 2000), 192–97, no. 48; *The Last Communion of St. Francis* in Antwerp (completed in 1618); Vlieghe, *Saints*, 1:156–62, no. 102; *Lamentation with St. Francis* in Brussels (after 1617 "first decoration received"; before 1620 "altar consecrated"); Richard J. Judson, *The Passion of Christ*, 229–34, no. 70; *The "Coup de Lance"* in Antwerp (presented in 1620), Richard J. Judson, *The Passion of Christ*, 139–52, no. 37; *The Miracles of St. Ignatius of Loyola* in Genua (arrived in 1620); and Vlieghe, *Saints*, 2:78–82, no. 116. For the works dated to this period on stylistic grounds, see Michael Jaffé, *Rubens: Catalogo Completo* (Milan: Electa, 1989).

45 Judson, *The Passion of Christ*, 239–45, no. 74. The work reportedly arrived in the church in 1616.

46 These commissions are well documented. *The Last Judgement* arrived in Neuburg November 1617; the side altars were shipped from Antwerp December 1619. Renger, *Peter Paul Rubens*, 25–62.

47 Frans Baudouin, "De datering van de twee schilderijen van Rubens voor het hoofdaltaar van de Antwerpse Jezuïetenkerk en enkele aantekeningen over Hans van Mildert," in *Miscellanea Jozef Duverger: Bijdragen tot de kunstgeschiedenis der Nederlanden* (Ghent: Vereniging voor de geschiedenis der textielkunsten, 1968), 301–22 (started around April 13, 1617; completed before January 23, 1619); Vlieghe, *Saints*, 2:26–29, no. 104; 2:73–74, no. 115.

48 Such an operation called for measures from both parties. Rubens requested that the choir was dismissed while he painted the work, so that he would not be disturbed. Freedberg, *The Life of Christ after the Passion*, 172–78, esp. 176, no. 43. Balis also mentions that Rubens sent out assistants to retouch paintings completed in the workshop after they were installed in situ. Arnout Balis, "'Fatto da un mio discepolo': Rubens's Studio Practices Reviewed," in Nakamura, *Rubens and His Workshop*, 107n111.

49 Rubens mainly painted for patrons in and around Antwerp during the first half of the Truce. Some exceptions include commissions for people he met during his travels in Italy and Spain. Vincenzo I Gonzaga (1562–1612), duke of Mantua and former Rubens patron, ordered *Raising of Lazarus* from Rubens around 1611, as an epitaph for his wife, Eleonora de Medici (1566–1611). Koen Bulckens, *Corpus Rubenianum Ludwig Burchard, Part V (2): The Life of Christ before the Passion; The Ministry of Christ* (Turnhout: Brepols, 2017), 147–49, no. 32. Rubens also painted a series of apostles for the duke of Lerma, who he had met on a visit to Spain. The series is first mentioned in 1618, but it is usually dated earlier, around 1610. Vlieghe, *Saints*, 1:34–48, nos. 6–18. From 1615/1616, a substantial number of large altarpieces was exported to cities like Neuburg, Lille, Cambrai, and Genua (see the works listed under notes 44–46).

50 This appears to have been the case for some copies and series. Isabella Brant's estate lists a debt of forty-eight florins to the painter Cornelis de Vos (1584–1651) for "two copies." His colleague Cornelis Schut (1597–1655) was to be paid seventeen guilders for "delivered [blank]." Max Rooses, "Staat van goederen in het Sterfhuis van Isabella Brant," *Rubens-bulletijn* 4 (1890): 176. On these references, see Arnout Balis, "'Fatto da un mio discepolo,'" in Nakamura, *Rubens and His Workshop*, exh. cat., 112. For subcontracted series, see the comments on the *Torre de la Parada* below and at note 75.

51 The author concluded that most painters worked in the houses in which they lived. An exceptional precedent was the large workshop of Frans Floris (built in the mid-sixteenth century), which may have served as an example for Rubens. Unfortunately, only the building's façade is documented; no traces of its interior division remain. On Floris, see Edward Wouk, *Frans Floris (1519/20–70): Imagining a Northern Renaissance* (Leiden: Brill, 2018). Artists who built large workshops in Antwerp at a later date include Jordaens, Jan Cossiers (1600–1671) and Schut—three people who have been associated with Rubens's workshop. Katlijne van der Stighelen, "Van zelfbeeld tot ezel: kunstenaarsalaam op zestiende- en zeventiende-eeuwse zelfportretten" in *Concept, Design and Execution in Flemish Painting (1550–1700)*, ed. Hans Vlieghe, Arnout Balis, and Carl van de Velde (Turnhout: Brepols, 2000), 238–40. Van der Stighelen worked with the estate inventories of artists. Petra Maclot's forthcoming study of artists' workshops in Antwerp, by contrast, combines historical and archaeological methods. She informs me that the purposefully built studios mentioned above were larger than earlier ones, often installed in existing sixteenth-century houses. At present, however, she is hesitant to generalize too much about the size of the latter variant, above all stressing the great diversity of workshops. Kleinert mentions that the shops of Rembrandt (see also note 15) and Vermeer, two artists who mostly painted on a smaller scale, both had a height in the 3- to 3.5-metre range. Kleinert, *Atelierdarstellungen in der niederländischen Genremalerei des 17. Jahrhunderts*, 33.

52 Presenting a complete reconstruction of the workshop would not be possible within these pages. Moreover, it would always be partly hypothetical because of the fragmentary nature of the evidence. The most substantial study of the Rubens house remains Tijs, *P.P. Rubens en J. Jordaens*. The book is especially valuable as a compendium of sources, since Tijs at times draws odd conclusions from his rich documentation. Annika Devroe most recently assessed the available evidence anew in a lucid and systematic manner in *Van Rubens' huis tot Rubenshuis*</i >, available at the Rubenianum. The abovementioned studies are in Dutch. Thorough literature on Rubens's workshop in English is forthcoming: Petra Maclot is preparing a book on artist's workshops in Antwerp, and Nora De Poorter is working on a *Corpus Rubenianum* volume about Rubens's house.

53 Mols was aware of Harrewijn's print and noted deviations from it. For a transcript of the report from his visit, see Max Rooses, "La Maison de Rubens," *Rubens-bulletijn* 3 (1888), 235–36, Annex 4.

54 These notes are kept in the Rubenshouse Archive (RHA). Van Averbeke wrote two intermediary reports when research on-site was in progress: RHA, Documentation Ruyten, Emiel van Averbeke, "Eerste Verslag: Rubenshuis—Herstelling," April 30, 1938; RHA, box 3, folder 10, 4.2.3.; Emiel van Averbeke, "Tweede Verslag: De opzoekingen en de bevindingen in the Rubenshuis," July 23, 1938. A notebook by Ruyten, attributed to Van Averbeke in the inventory of the RHA, covers on-site discoveries chronologically: RHA, box 3, folder 11, 4.4.7., Theo Ruyten, "Notaboekje met verslag van de werken vanaf 10/01/1938 tot 15/09/1938," 1938. This document probably formed the basis of a later typed note by the same author: RHA, box 11, Theo Ruyten, "Nota's aangaande de opzoekingswerken welke de wederopbouw van het Rubenshuis voorafgingen," sd. (This is a copy of the document in box 4, folder 16, 6.4.2., now missing.) These sources were studied by Tijs and Devroe (see the above note), but fresh observations can still be drawn from them.

55 Although Van Averbeke was highly skeptical about the documentary value of both sources, they remained a crucial benchmark throughout the restoration process. See RHA, box 11, Theo Ruyten, "Nota's aangaande de opzoekingswerken welke de wederopbouw van het Rubenshuis voorafgingen," 1.

56 The tracery of the four arched windows was discovered in the masonry, as were parts of the rosette. One of the niches depicted by Harrewijn was also rediscovered. RHA, box 3, folder 10, 4.2.3., Emiel van Averbeke, "Tweede Verslag: De opzoekingen en de bevindingen in the Rubenshuis," July 23, 1938, 10–11.

57 The house was then bought by Carolus Nicolaes Josephus De Bosschaert, who allegedly renovated the whole site extensively. Along with rebuilding the garden and street façades, he also added an extra level on the ground floor of the workshop. Needless to say, these renovations destroyed valuable material clues. The 1763 changes were most recently discussed at length in Devroe, *Van Rubens' huis tot Rubenshuis*, 60–64.

58 To my knowledge, Harrewijn's rendition of the street façade has not raised any suspicion. However, Van Averbeke considered the architectural ornaments of the garden façade inconsistent. He was convinced that Canon Henricus Hillewerve (1621–1694), who owned the house when Harrewijn published his prints, had rebuilt it. RHA, box 3, folder 10, 4.2.3., Emiel van Averbeke, "Tweede Verslag: De opzoekingen en de bevindingen in the Rubenshuis," July 23, 1938, 27. See also note 67. Whatever the case, the garden wall was probably subdivided in three window bays, corresponding with those in the street façade.

59 RHA, box 3, folder 10, 4.2.3., Emiel van Averbeke, "Tweede Verslag: De opzoekingen en de bevindingen in the Rubenshuis," July 23, 1938, 28–29. Seven additional windows were found on the second floor.

60 Three cellar windows at the south side suggest that the passage was used for deliveries.

61 The walls of the north and south façades were still original, and the portico showed the position of the garden wall. The foundations of the walls around the entrance were also discovered, and these were aligned with the pilasters of the portico. There are no notations of the measurements on-site, but we can assume that these are generally reflected in Van Averbeke's renovation plans. RHA, box 3, folder 10, 4.2.3., Emiel van Averbeke, "Tweede Verslag: De opzoekingen en de bevindingen in the Rubenshuis," July 23, 1938, 14–15 (entrance ways), 27 (east façade), 29 (ceilings).

62 They formed part of the original studio floor. Emiel van Averbeke, "De eerste bevindingen: Het plan van Blomme, de dwalingen van Mols, wat er dient gedaan te worden," *Het Huis van P.P. Rubens: Periodisch Bulletin* 1 (1938), 37.

63 RHA, box 3, folder 10, 4.2.3., Emiel van Averbeke, "Tweede Verslag. De opzoekingen en de bevindingen in the Rubenshuis," July 23, 1938, 32–33. The stove was located between the two easternmost windows on the south façade.

64 RHA, box 3, folder 11, 4.4.7., Theo Ruyten, "Notaboekje met verslag van de werken vanaf 10/01/1938 tot 15/09/1938," 1938, fol. 1.

65 During the 1939–45 renovation, a suspended floor was installed in the antechamber. However, the masonry of the walls suggests that there was originally no such extra level. This means that the ceiling of the antechamber was probably as high as that of the adjoining workspace. RHA, box 3, folder 11, 4.4.7., Theo Ruyten, "Notaboekje met verslag van de werken vanaf 10/01/1938 tot 15/09/1938," 1938, fol. 5.

66 For the south door, see RHA, box 3, folder 11, 4.4.7., Theo Ruyten, "Notaboekje met verslag van de werken vanaf 10/01/1938 tot 15/09/1938," 1938, fol. 12. Harrewijn shows a door to the left of the staircase, and another one to its right side. The latter led to a small hallway, which gave access to the antechamber and cellars. (Ruyten notes in fol. 26 that the wall separating this hallway from the rest of the loggia "had always been there.")

67 Van Averbeke was convinced that this door would be in the south wall opposite of the rosette at the north end, creating symmetry in the floorplan. This way, paintings could be easily moved through the passageway and onto the street. RHA, box 3, folder 10, 4.2.3., Emiel van Averbeke, "Tweede Verslag: De opzoekingen en de bevindingen in the Rubenshuis," July 23, 1938, 29. The door was reconstructed where Van Averbeke thought it would be (it is depicted in a lighter shade in fig. 12), but he found no material evidence to support his intuitions. Ruyten reported that he searched for traces of the door in the south wall and noted no findings. RHA, box 3, folder 11, 4.4.7., Theo Ruyten, "Notaboekje met verslag van de werken vanaf 10/01/1938 tot 15/09/1938," 1938, fol. 29. Possibly all traces of the door had disappeared because a fireplace was later installed opposite the rosette (see Mols's floorplan, fig. 11). Alternatively, Van Averbeke (see also note 58) may have been wrong, and the tall door pictured in the east façade in Harrewijn's engraving may be original, as was suggested to me by Nora De Poorter. Paintings could then be handled and turned easily at the garden's edge, before moving onto the narrow passageway to the street.

68 "'Come s'usa di fare non volendo ingannarsi,'" in Vander Auwera and Van Sprang, *Rubens: A Genius at Work*, 162, fig. 4. Stretchers were especially necessary for priming, but they were also used to keep tension on the canvas during the painting process. For more on the stretchers and depictions of them, see Ernst van de Wetering, *Rembrandt: The Painter at Work* (Amsterdam: Amsterdam University Press, 1997), 117–21. *The "Great" Last Judgment*, specifically, has not been subjected to a thorough conservation campaign like Jordaens's *Triumph* (see note 10). Still, Von Sonnenburg briefly discussed the canvas and its seams without mentioning that painted pieces were joined at a later date, something he would have noticed. Hubert von Sonnenburg, "Rubens's Bildaufbau und Technik. I. Bildtraeger, Grundierung und Vorskizzierung," *Maltechnik-Restauro* 85 (1979), 84, also 88 and note 29. It would still be interesting to verify whether the canvas bears traces of rolling during the painting process. Around 1633, Rubens did make a canvas that did not fit into the shop for the ceiling of the Banqueting Hall in Whitehall Palace (see note 76). The system that Da Vinci drew for panels (see note 11) would not have worked in Rubens's workshop at De Wapper, as his cellars were not deep enough.

69 If not a wooden structure, this may have been the wall between the antechamber and the working area. This would have allowed for the largest possible viewing distance from the garden edge of the workshop. We have seen that the partition wall was partly rediscovered in the foundations in 1938 (see note 61). Ruyten noted that the pilasters against this wall were not original, and that two vertical wooden beams were initially worked into the masonry. RHA, box 3, folder 11, 4.4.7., Theo Ruyten, "Notaboekje met verslag van de werken vanaf 10/01/1938 tot 15/09/1938," 1938, fols. 6–7. Other than that, we know nothing about the partition wall's material characteristics. Mols (fig. 11) drew the passage to the adjoining studio in the centre, which would not have left enough wall space on either side to hold Rubens's large paintings. If Mols's partition wall were used for painting, the door would have been built on the side.

70 For Renaissance theories of light in places of creation and display, see Jeffrey M. Muller, "Rubens's Museum of Antique Sculpture: An Introduction," *Art Bulletin* 59, no. 4 (1977): 576–79. Joachim von Sandrart followed Leonardo Da Vinci in recommending northern light for the painter's studio. See Michèle-Caroline Heck, "The Reception of Leonardo da Vinci's Trattato della Pittura, or Traitté de la Peinture, in Seventeenth-Century Northern Europe," in *Re-reading Leonardo: The Treatise on Painting across Europe, 1550–1900*, ed. Claire Farago (Farnham, UK: Ashgate, 2009), 394.

71 Jordaens commented on the "*corte vuyle daege*" ("short and foul days") of winter that prevented him from working at full speed. Johan H.W. Unger, "Brieven van Eenige Schilders aan Constantin Huygens," *Oud Holland* 9 (1891): 196. For related references to artists' dependency on natural light, see Kleinert, *Atelierdarstellungen in der niederländischen Genremalerei des 17. Jahrhunderts*, 34.

72 Rubens could cover windows with blinds to achieve the desired effect. Dubois, "'Come s'usa di fare non volendo ingannarsi,'" in Vander Auwera and Van Sprang, *Rubens: A Genius at Work*, 160.

73 The sail was hung in the church in early June 1610, and the work was completed by March of the following year, when it was mentioned in a letter from Jan Legrand to Lieven Eeckhout dated March 12, 1611; Adolf Monballieu, "P.P. Rubens en het 'Nachtmael' voor St. Winoksbergen (1611)," *Jaarboek Koninklijk Museum voor Schone Kunsten Antwerpen* (1965), 195–96, doc. 2. There are other examples where we know the date the contract was signed and a work shipped, which generally happened within a span of eight to fifteen months. Presumably not all this time was spent on painting. It would also have included gathering materials and making studies, and perhaps waiting for the schedule to open up.

74 The contract, signed March 29, 1620, stipulated that Rubens would deliver the series "as soon as he possibly could, in any event before the end of the present year or at the beginning of the next" ("*soo haest het hem mogelijck sal syn immers voor het uytgaen van desen tegenwoordigen Jaere ofte met het beginsel van het toekomende Jaer*".) John Rupert Martin, *Corpus Rubenianum Ludwig Burchard, Part I: The Ceiling Paintings for the Jesuit Church in Antwerp* (London: Phaidon, 1968), App. 1, 213–19, the above quote on 213. Rubens would be paid 10,000 florins upon the delivery of the paintings (p. 214), 7,000 for the ceiling paintings, and 3,000 for two altarpieces that he completed earlier (see note 44). The artist apparently made the deadline: the Jesuits' account book notes a debt of 10,000 florins to Rubens on February 13, 1621 (App. 2, 221). Piet Lombaerde and Ria Fabri discuss Rubens's contributions to the church in a forthcoming volume of the *Corpus Rubenianum*.

75 A large Rubens altarpiece cost about 1,500 florins on average, roughly four times the yearly wage of a skilled laborer—a substantial sum. However, it appears that price was negotiable depending on circumstance, especially for large commissions. See Svetlana Alpers, *Corpus Rubenianum Ludwig Burchard, Part IX: The Decoration of the Torre de la Parada* (Brussels: Arcade, 1971), 32; Nils Büttner, "Ware Kunst: Zur ökonomischen Praxis des Malers Peter Paul Rubens," in "*Eigennutz" und "gute Ordnung": Ökonomisierungen der Welt im 17. Jahrhundert*, Wolfenbütteler Arbeiten zur Barockforschung 53, ed. Sandra Richter and Guillaume Garner (Wiesbaden: Harrassowitz, 2016), 241–56.

76 Rubens added that "no undertaking, however vast in size and diverse in subject matter, had ever surpassed his courage." Letter from Peter Paul Rubens to William Trumbull, September 13, 1621, in Rooses and Ruelens, *Correspondance de Rubens*, vol. 2, doc. 225, 286–88, and Saunders Magurn, *Letters of Peter Paul Rubens*, doc. 46, 77. In the letter, Rubens was lobbying for the commission to decorate the ceiling of the Banqueting Hall in Whitehall Palace (see below).

77 Gregory Martin, *Corpus Rubenianum Ludwig Burchard, Part XV: The Ceiling Decorations of the Banqueting Hall* (Turnhout: Brepols, 2005), 55–56.

78 Alpers, *The Decoration of the Torre de la Parada*, 30–33.

79 Reinhold Baumstark's volume on this series in the *Corpus Rubenianum* is due to appear shortly.

80 The contract for the staircase was signed on November 2 (see note 43), and it mentions that the workers would take an unspecified number of "weeks" to complete the project. The contract for the tapestries was signed on November 9. Duverger, "Aantekeningen betreffende de patronne van P.P. Rubens," 37–38. Nora De Poorter believes that a temporary staircase was installed before the contract was signed.

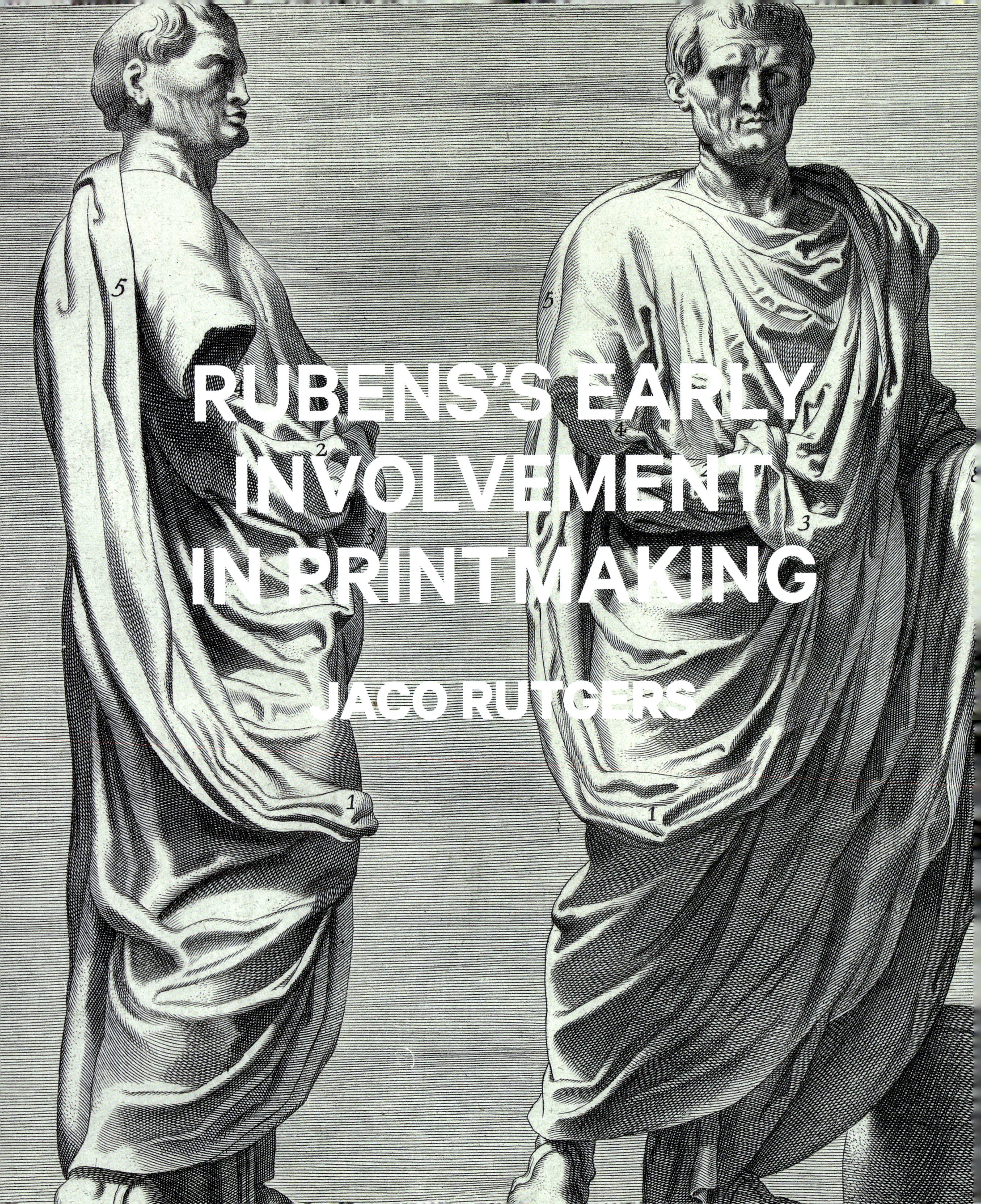
RUBENS'S EARLY
INVOLVEMENT
IN PRINTMAKING
JACO RUTGERS

Fig 1 Cornelis Galle, after Peter Paul Rubens, *A Roman Statue of an Orator Dressed in a Toga* (detail), an illustration for Philip Rubens's *Electorum Libri II*, 1608. Engraving, 20 × 27.3 cm. Rijksmuseum, Amsterdam. RP-P-OB-4305.

THE BUSINESS OF PRINTMAKING in Antwerp had already been the domain of professional publishers and entrepreneurial engravers for half a century when Peter Paul Rubens returned to the city from Italy in 1608. Painters seldom initiated print projects and generally only provided designs for engravers; this was also Rubens's role up to around 1618. He was involved in printmaking as a designer for frontispieces and illustrations for books, and provided engravers with detailed drawings based on his own paintings, which served as models for prints. Then, toward the end of the second decade of the seventeenth century, Rubens took matters into his own hands by starting his own printmaking enterprise and applying for print privileges, which provided legal protection against unauthorized copying, from the authorities in France, as well as in the Northern and Southern Netherlands. He would become the first Flemish painter to initiate a large-scale project to have his inventions engraved and published as a collaborative effort involving his own studio. Why exactly he became an entrepreneur is a question we can answer only after a thorough reconstruction of the events leading up to this decision. Rubens's start-up in the business of printmaking was a success story resulting in dozens of prints published on his initiative, and it brought him fame and fortune.

In the 1610s, Rubens started working regularly for the book publishing business of his friend Balthasar Moretus, grandson of the founder of the famous Plantin press, Christoffel Plantin. Earlier, in 1608, his designs were reproduced as five illustrations (fig. 1) in his brother Philip Rubens's *Electorum Libri II* (Two Books of Selections), which was published by Balthasar's father, Jan Moretus. However, this publishing activity was an isolated incident[1] and the drawings by Peter Paul were probably not intentionally created as models for engravings.[2] Philip likely chose the illustrations from his brother's drawings that he took with him as study material when he travelled back to Antwerp from Rome in May 1607.[3] Moreover, the book, including illustrations engraved by Cornelis Galle, was probably already published before Peter Paul returned from Italy in October 1608.[4]

The true beginning of Rubens's involvement in book publishing as a designer of book illustrations and title pages was in 1613. That year, Rubens collaborated on two books with Balthasar Moretus, who had taken over the business from his father in 1610. The books contain images based on drawings by Rubens undeniably made specifically for that purpose. One was a book on optics, François d'Aguilon's *Opticorum Libri Sex*, and the other was a new edition of the important liturgical text *Missale Romanum*. In both instances, the commission and the creative process followed practices typical for the many book projects that Rubens would be involved with for the next twenty-five years.

For the François d'Aguilon book, Rubens designed the title page and six vignettes at the start of every section of the book (figs. 2–5). The preparatory drawing for the title page is currently kept at the British Museum, London, and drawn *modelli* for two of the vignettes are preserved in the National Gallery of Art, Washington D.C.[5] Every vignette illustrates the subject matter of a section of the book (*liber*) in the form of a scholar in the act of doing an experiment helped by putti. Moretus or the author of the book provided Rubens with information about the contents of the publication to help him create designs reflecting its main ideas. The title page and the illustrations were engraved by Theodoor Galle, who carefully followed Rubens's preparatory work.[6]

Rubens's illustrations for the *Missale Romanum* were part of a more complex project that involved new plates for two of the most important liturgical texts in the Catholic Church. These books had an enormous impact for more than a century.[7] The *Missale* contained texts and instruction for celebrating the Mass as promulgated by Pope Pius V in 1570. Its use became obligatory throughout the Roman Church. In 1604 and 1634, small revisions to the book were prescribed by Pope Clement VIII and Pope Urban VIII respectively. The Plantin press began issuing illustrated editions of the *Missale* in 1571. The first run contained an engraved title-page vignette and woodcut illustrations based on designs by Peeter van der Borcht.[8] Many considerable printings in various sizes followed, and worn plates had to be regularly replaced. Taste in imagery also began to shift, and woodcuts were gradually replaced by engravings, which allowed more detail. In the 1613 *in-folio* edition of the *Missale,* two full-page images were added to the eight illustrations in the 1606 and 1610 editions. Rubens made the designs for these added scenes: *The Adoration of the Magi* (see page 266) and *The Ascension of Christ.*[9] He also followed the engraving process carefully, instructing the printmaker and retouching proof impressions using pen and brush with ink and white gouache.[10] Furthermore, Rubens made at least one drawing for a decorative frame for this publication, *The Tree of Jesse*, which surrounded the page next to the image with *The Annunciation* (figs. 6, 7).[11] The preparatory drawing for *The Tree of Jesse* is in the Louvre, Paris. Decorative frames surrounded text pages at the beginning of every new section, which were preceded by the full-page illustrations.[12]

A year later, in 1614, *The Adoration of the Magi* and *The Ascension of Christ* were reused for an edition of the *Breviarium Romanum*, another important liturgical text. The book contains canonical prayers, hymns, Psalms, readings, and notations for everyday use by the clergy in the Holy Office. This text became the standard from the Council of Trent (1568) onward.[13] For the 1614 Plantin-Moretus edition, Rubens designed a new title page (see page 262) as well as all other illustrations (see pages 264, 266, 268, 270, 272, 274), with the exception of the printer's device.[14] As three pages from the Plantin-Moretus archives show (fig. 8), Rubens received detailed guidelines from the publisher on figures to include on the title page, as well as a rough layout for the composition. On the basis of these instructions, Rubens composed a drawing, now in the British Museum, London, which was engraved by Theodoor Galle.[15] For the full-page illustrations, Rubens suggested slight adjustments to the engraver by retouching proof impressions.[16] The decorative frame Rubens designed for the *Missale* was not included in the *Breviarium*, nor were any of the other frames.[17]

Rubens's collaboration with Balthasar Moretus would continue along the same lines up to Rubens's death in 1640. Not much would change in the workflow, division of labour, or the nature of the commissions. Rubens's role was described by Moretus in a letter to Balthasar Corderius on September 13, 1630, after Corderius inquired about having a title page designed by the master. According to Moretus, patience was required when choosing Rubens as *inventor*. Book illustrations had to be ordered well in advance. Moretus himself usually gave more than six months—three months at the absolute minimum. Although the publisher implied that Rubens needed time to thoroughly think through the composition, it was more likely that this type of work was not of the utmost importance to him. Apparently, Rubens gave priority to his role as the head of a large studio specializing in large-scale history paintings, only doing book illustrations on Sundays and other holidays. He would have had to charge far too much for his designs—up to 100 florins—if they had interfered with his primary work.[18] The Plantin-Moretus press account books documented Rubens's fee for working on models on a holiday: twenty florins for a design *in-folio* and less for smaller sizes.[19] In comparison, the engraver was paid seventy-five florins for cutting a folio-sized copper plate.[20]

The only changes made to the collaborative process between Rubens and Balthasar Moretus stemmed from practical considerations. From 1628 onward, engravers increasingly worked from oil sketches on panel instead of paper drawings, and when Rubens suffered from gout in old age, his inventions were laid out by assistants instead of the master himself, although they followed his strict verbal instructions and quick sketches. One of Rubens's assistants was the painter Erasmus Quellinus II. The title page for Hieronymus de la Higuera's *Luitprandi Subdiaconi Toletaniticensis . . . Opera qvæ extant,* published by Moretus in 1640 in Antwerp (fig. 9), mentions Rubens as the *inventor* ("Pet. Paul. Rubenius inuenit"), while Quellinus was responsible for the actual preparatory drawing ("E. Quellinius delineauit"), which was engraved by Cornelis Galle the Younger ("Corn. Galleus iunior sculpsit").[21]

Before Rubens started collaborating with Balthasar Moretus, engravings that copied paintings by the master were already in circulation. Willem Isaacsz. van Swanenburg issued *The Supper*

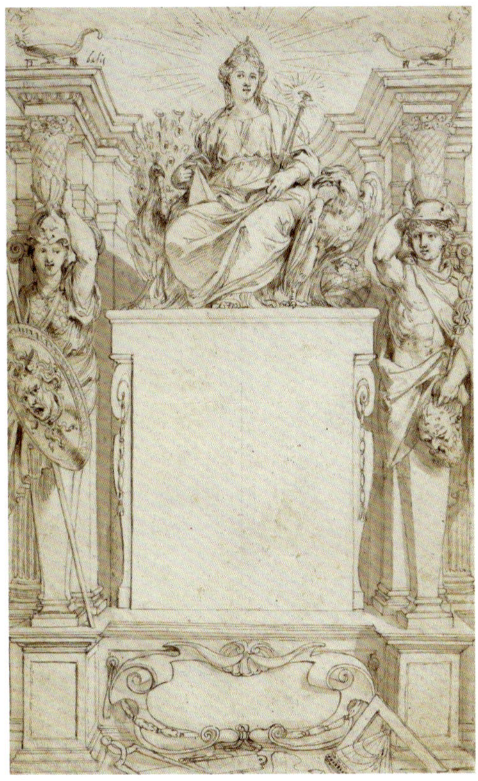

Fig 2 Peter Paul Rubens, Preparatory Drawing for the title page for François d'Aguilon's *Opticorum Libri Sex*, c. 1613. Pen and brown ink and wash, over black chalk, 30.4 × 19 cm, British Museum, London. 1861,0608.148. Photo © The Trustees of the British Museum.

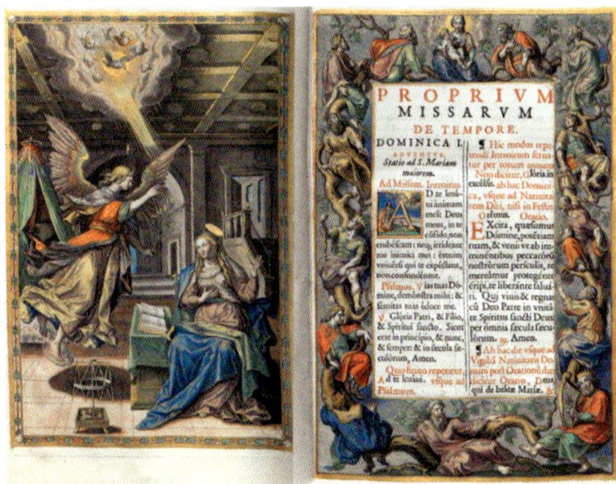

Fig 7 Theodoor Galle, after Peter Paul Rubens, *The Tree of Jesse*, decorative frame for the *Missale Romanum*, 1613. Engraving, 30.5 × 20 cm. Plantin-Moretus museum, Antwerp. A 1546.

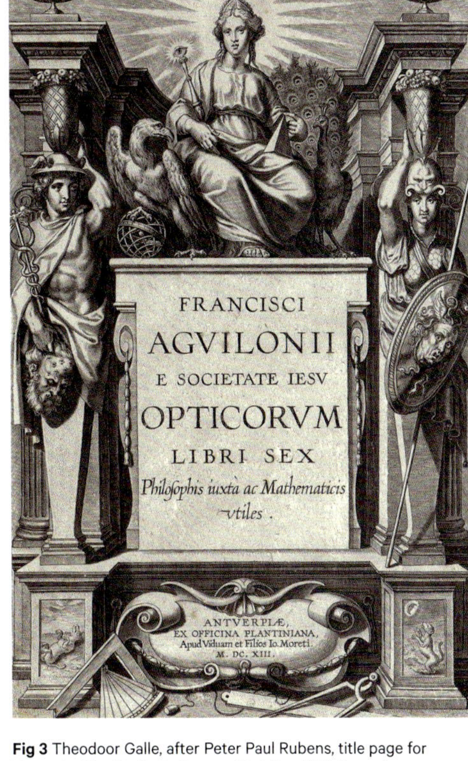

Fig 3 Theodoor Galle, after Peter Paul Rubens, title page for François d'Aguilon's *Opticorum Libri Sex*, 1613. Engraving, 31.4 × 19.4 cm. Rijksmuseum, Amsterdam. RP-P-OB-6889.

Fig 6 Peter Paul Rubens, preparatory drawing for *The Tree of Jesse*, decorative frame for the *Missale Romanum*, c. 1613. Pen and ink and wash, over black chalk, 30.9 × 20.2 cm. Cabinet des Dessins du Musée du Louvre, Paris. 20.216. Photo © RMN-Grand Palais/Art Resource, NY.

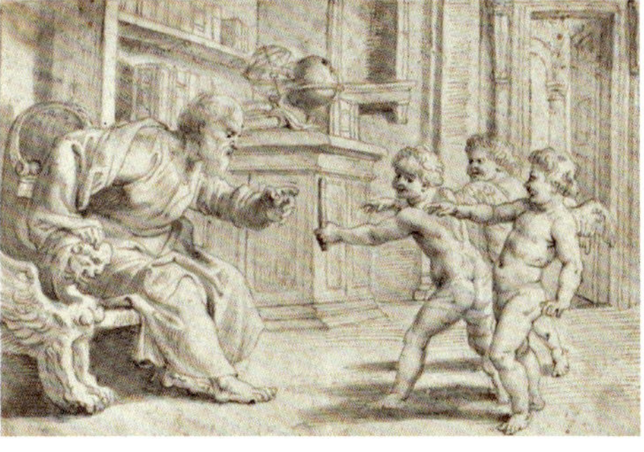

Fig 4 Peter Paul Rubens, preparatory drawing for *Putti Testing a Man's Perception of Depth*, c. 1613. Pen and brown ink and wash, over black chalk, heightened with white, laid on paper; indented with a stylus and chalked for transfer on the verso, 9.7 × 14.6 cm. National Gallery of Art, Washington D.C., Alisa Melon Bruce Fund. 1982.104.1. Image courtesy National Gallery of Art, Washington D.C.

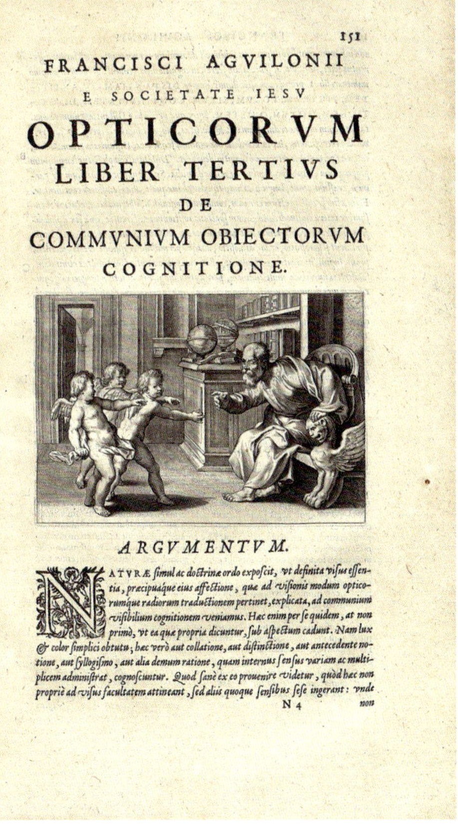

151

FRANCISCI AGVILONII
E SOCIETATE IESV
OPTICORVM
LIBER TERTIVS
DE
COMMVNIVM OBIECTORVM
COGNITIONE.

ARGVMENTVM.

NATVRÆ *ſimul ac doctrinæ ordo expoſcit, vt definita viſus eſſentia, præcipuaque eius affectione, quæ ad viſionis modum opticorumque radiorum traductionem pertinet, explicata, ad communium viſibilium cognitionem veniamus. Hæc enim per ſe quidem, at non primò, vt ea quæ propria dicuntur, ſub aſpectum cadunt. Nam lux & color ſimplici obtutu; hæc verò aut collatione, aut diſtinctione, aut antecedente notione, aut ſyllogiſmo, aut alia demum ratione, quam internus ſenſus variam ac multiplicem adminiſtrat, cognoſcuntur. Quod ſanè ex eo prouenire videtur, quòd hæc non propriè ad viſus facultatem attineant, ſed aliis quoque ſenſibus ſeſe ingerant: vnde*

N 4 *non*

Fig 5 François d'Aguilon and Theodor Galle, after Sir Peter Paul Rubens, vignette of putti and aged scholar learning of binocular vision in *Opticorum Libri Sex*, published 1613. One of six headpieces engraved by Theodor Galle after Peter Paul Rubens, 35 × 22.1 cm (page size). National Gallery of Art, Washington, D.C., Ailsa Mellon Bruce Fund. 1989.36.1. Image courtesy National Gallery of Art, Washington, D.C.

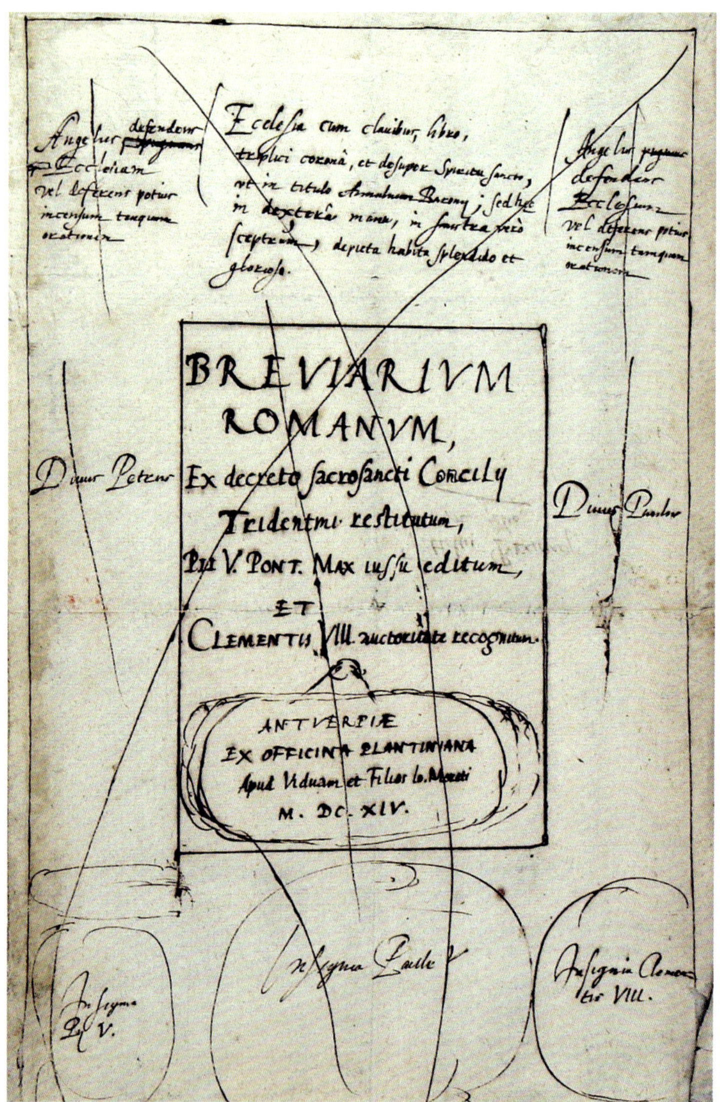

Fig 8 Balthasar Moretus, Instructions for the Title Page of the *Breviarium Romanum*, c. 1614. Pen and brown ink, 36.5 × 23.5 cm. Plantin-Moretus museum, Antwerp. Archief 118, F. 427.

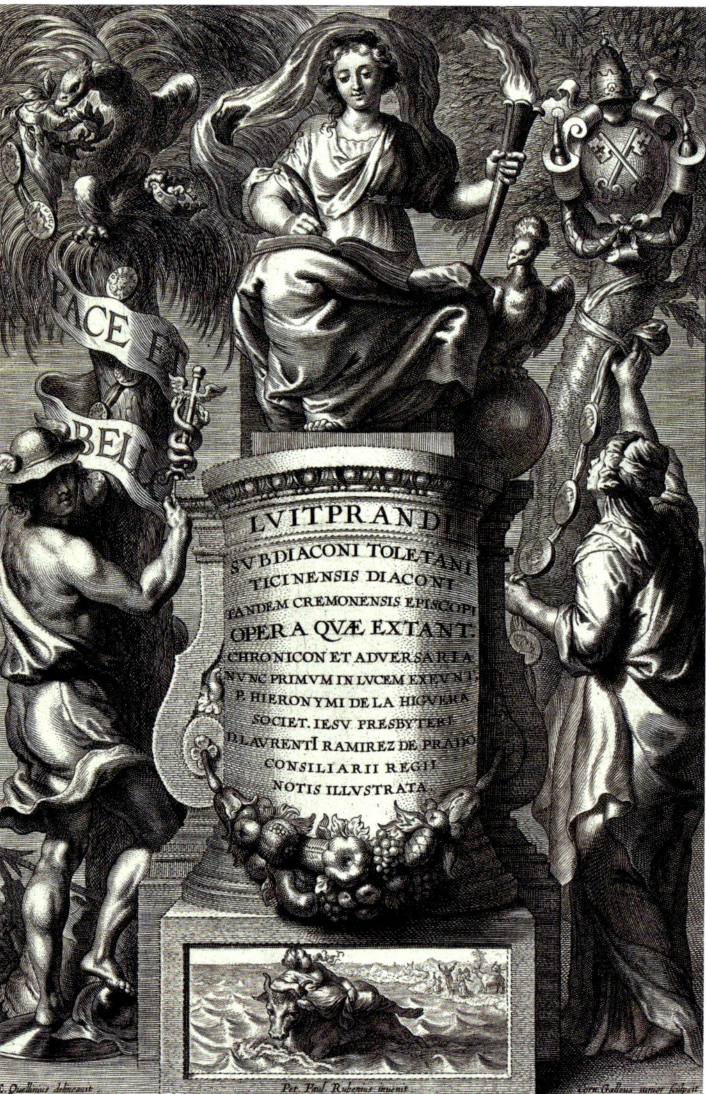

Fig 9 Cornelis Galle, after Peter Paul Rubens, Title Page for Hieronymus de la Higuera's *Luitprandi Subdiaconi Toletaniticensis*, 1640. Engraving, 27.3 × 18 cm. Rijksmuseum, Amsterdam. RP-P-OB-7061.

at Emmaus in 1611 (fig. 10) and *Lot and His Daughters* in 1612.[22] These two prints are often described as piracies of Rubens's inventions and the reason he started his own print business—to take matters into his own hands.[23] However, this interpretation is very unlikely. As modern copyright did not exist at that time, an engraving made after a painting, even without the consent of the painter, was not considered illegal. Even the print privileges that Rubens obtained in 1619 and 1620 did not protect the invention, whether it was a painting or drawing, on which the print was based. Print privileges covered only the investment of having an engraving produced—impressions of the respective print could not be copied.[24] Besides, in the first decades of the seventeenth century, prints were generally made at the instigation of professional publishers or engravers who also acted as publishers, who would request drawings from artists to cut into copper, and it is more likely that that is what happened in the case of these Swanenburg engravings.

Engravings that directly reproduced paintings were rare at the start of the seventeenth century. Swanenburg likely simply had asked Rubens to provide him with a drawing that he could engrave. He could even have offered Rubens a fee for the drawing. The working relationship involved in issuing single prints is similar to that between a book publisher and a designer of the illustrations, except the engraver was often also the publisher.

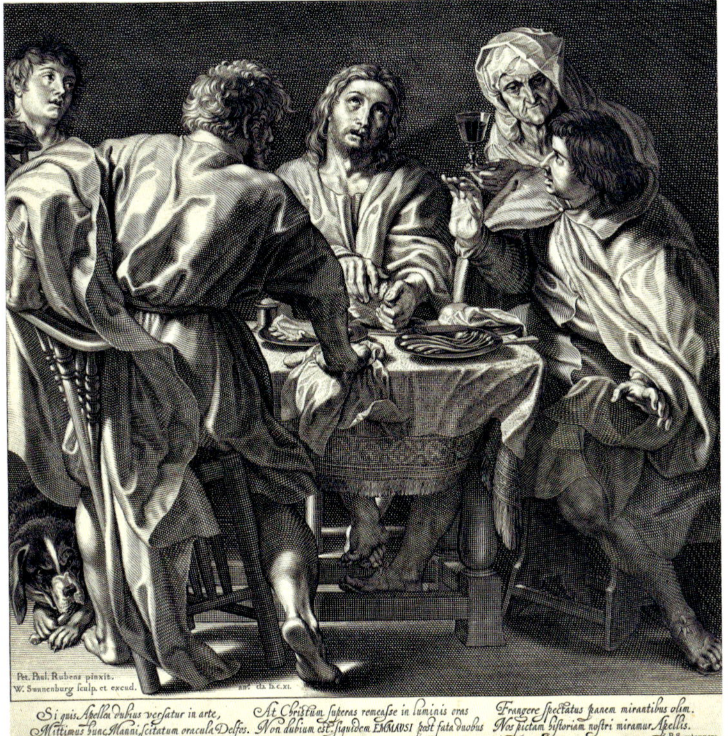

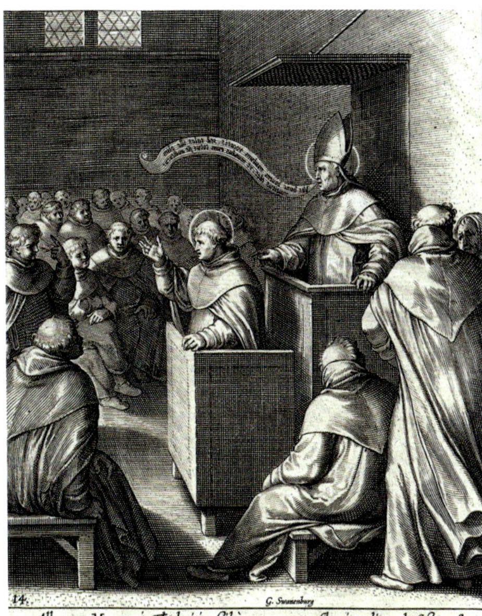

Fig 10 Willem van Swanenburg, after Peter Paul Rubens, *The Supper at Emmaus*, 1611. Engraving, 32.2 × 31.8 cm. Rijksmuseum, Amsterdam. RP-P-OB-4599.

Fig 11 Willem van Swanenburg, after Otto van Veen, *Albertus Magnus Preaching* (plate 14 of the *Vita D. Thomae Aquinatis*), c. 1610. Engraving, 21 × 14.9 cm. British Museum, London. 1935, 0413.242. Photo © The Trustees of the British Museum.

Rubens may have known Swanenburg because he had already made engravings based on the most prominent history painters in the North, like Abraham Bloemaert, Joachim Wtewael, and Paulus Moreelse. Based in Leiden, Swanenburg was also in close contact with the professors of Leiden University, whose portraits he engraved. One of these portraits is that of the Humanist scholar Justus Lipsius, who Rubens had studied under. Another is the portrait of Dominicus Baudius, who maintained a correspondence with Rubens.[25] Baudius also provided Swanenburg with texts for some of his other prints. The same Swanenburg engraved two plates for a series of prints, *Life of Saint Thomas Aquinas*, which was published in Antwerp in 1610 (fig. 11).[26] The designs were made by Rubens's teacher Otto van Veen, who grew up in Leiden and had probably been a pupil of Isaac Claesz. van Swanenburg, Willem's father. Thus, it is unlikely that Rubens and Willem van Swanenburg were complete strangers to each other.

There might have been a similar working relationship between designer and engraver with Jacob Matham's *Samson and Delilah* (pages 168–69).[27] The print was published and dedicated by the engraver himself under the privilege obtained by him from the Holy Roman Emperor in Prague. Rubens must have sent Matham a drawing, in accordance with the standard practice in printmaking at the time.[28] Rubens could have even corrected one of the proofs—the retouched impression of the first state is currently in the Rijksmuseum, Amsterdam—but this involvement does not automatically imply that Rubens initiated the print. Matham had a history of requesting drawings from painters that he engraved and published. He made prints from drawings provided by other Antwerp painters, including Sebastian Vrancx (1606) and Jan Wildens (1614, fig. 12), both particularly close with Rubens.[29]

Matham's print is generally assumed by art historians to be directly related to Rubens's trip to Holland in 1612. That year, Rubens travelled to the North accompanied by Jan Brueghel the Elder and Hendrik van Balen, and it has been proposed that he made the trip specifically in search of a printmaker who could engrave his paintings.[30] As a consequence, Matham's *Samson and Delilah* is usually dated to 1612–1613. However, Rubens did not seem to have been involved in printmaking at that time.[31] The print itself is not dated, and Matham's stylistic development as a printmaker offers no clue. The print could have been a product of the larger Matham studio, and was not necessarily engraved by Matham himself. The only clue as to the print's date is a text from the 1615 publication of writings by Rubens's brother Philip, which was posthumously collected by Rubens's father-in-law, Jan Brant, and published by the Plantin press: S.*Asterii, Episcopi Amaseae, Homiliae Graece et Latine nunc primum editae* ("Five Homilia by Saint Asterius, Bishop of Amasea, in Greek and Latin, now published for the first time").[32] This suggests that Matham's print dates to 1615 or slightly later.

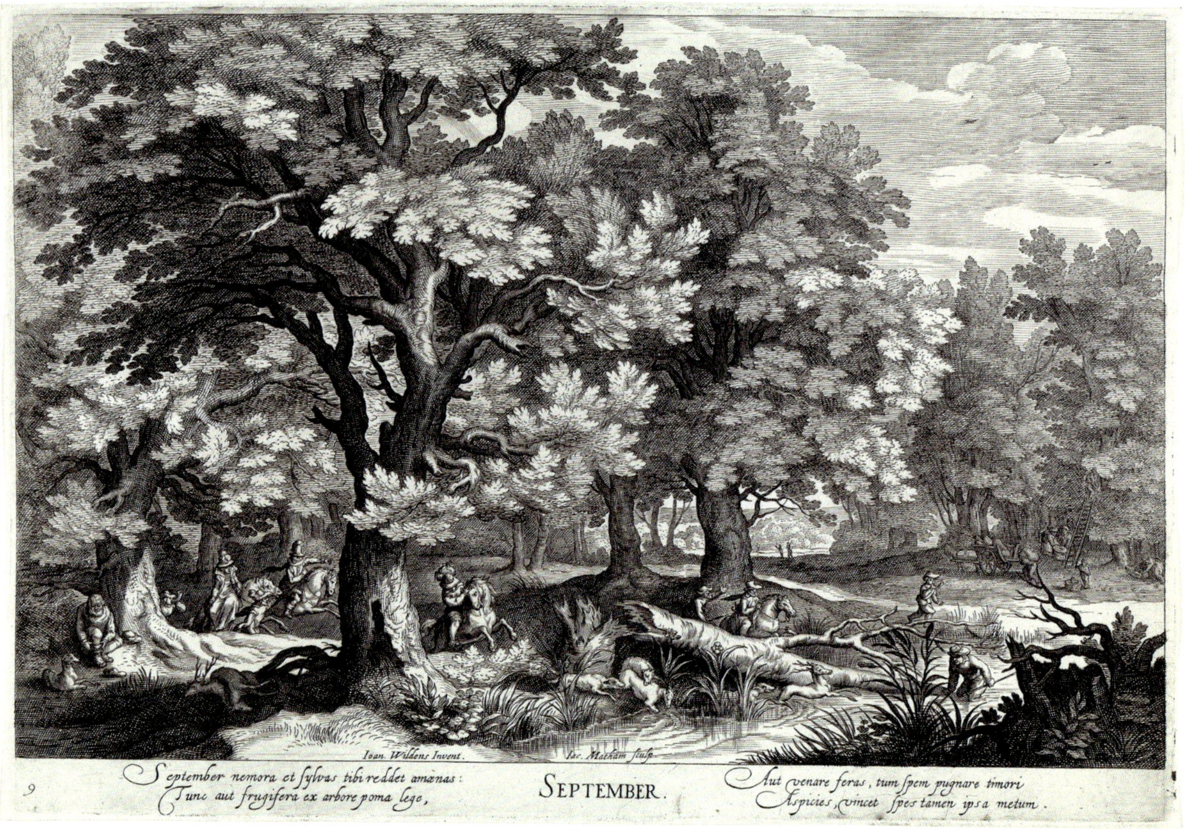

Fig 12 Jacob Matham, after Jan Wildens, *September*, 1614. Engraving, 29.1 × 43 cm. Rijksmuseum, Amsterdam. RP-P-OB-27.247.

The first print that Rubens was actively involved with as initiator is *Judith and Holofernes*, engraved by Cornelis Galle (fig. 13). This is suggested by the dedication from Rubens to his friend Jan de Wouwer, alias Woverius, which is included on the print: "To his dearest friend, the very famous gentleman Jan de Wouwer, does Peter Paul Rubens give this sheet, created under a prosperous constellation and he dedicates this first proof of the works printed from a copper plate engraved with one of his images as his recollection of a promise made long ago in Verona" ("*Clariss.° et amicissimo viro D. Ioanni Woverio paginam hanc auspicalem primumque suorum operum/typis aeneis expressum Petrus Paullus Rubenius promissi iam olim Veronae a se facti memor dat dicat.*").[33] Despite Rubens's claim that the print was his idea, it was published by Cornelis Galle (*Cornelius Galle sculp. et excud.*), who kept control of the copper plate and sold it soon after completion. The third state was issued with the address of Adriaen Collaert (*Cornelius Galle sculp. Adrian Collaert excud.*), Cornelis's brother-in-law, who died in 1618.[34]

The year of Collaert's death provides a firm *terminus antequem* for *Judith and Holofernes*, and the engraving was probably not produced much earlier. Galle was provided with a detailed preparatory drawing, likely made by a member of the Rubens workshop based on a Rubens painting (fig. 14). The painting did not survive, but the drawing is now in the Nationalmuseum in Stockholm. Since this *modello* is quite close to the ones used by Lucas Vorsterman for his Rubens prints dated 1620, it seems likely that the drawing for Galle was not created earlier than 1616. Incidentally, Rubens started collaborating with Cornelis Galle on a regular basis around 1615. Earlier dealings with the Galle family, such as the *Missale* and *Breviarium* projects, were with Cornelis's older brother Theodoor.[35] Moreover, six lines of verse in the margin, above the dedication to Jan de Wouwer, are taken from Philip Rubens's writings published in 1615 (and mentioned earlier). It is reasonable to assume that *Judith and Holofernes* was created around 1616, or just a few years before Rubens founded his own start-up in the printmaking business.

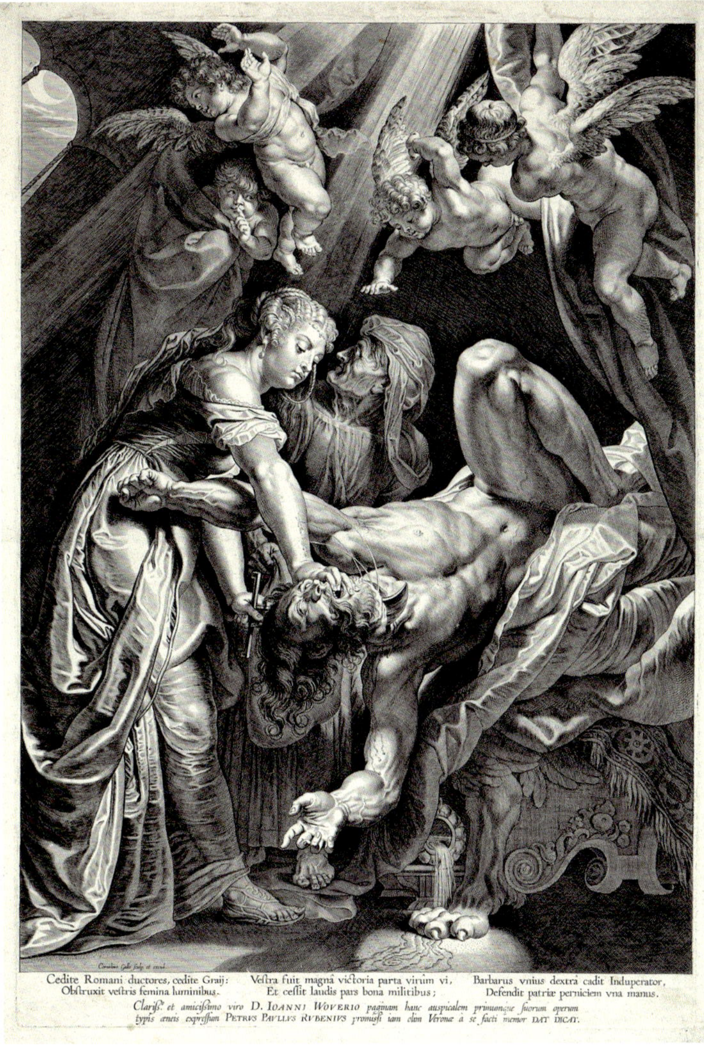

Fig 13 Cornelis Galle, after Peter Paul Rubens, *Judith and Holofernes*, c. 1616. Engraving, 65 × 37.9 cm. Rijksmuseum, Amsterdam. RP-P-OB-67.675.

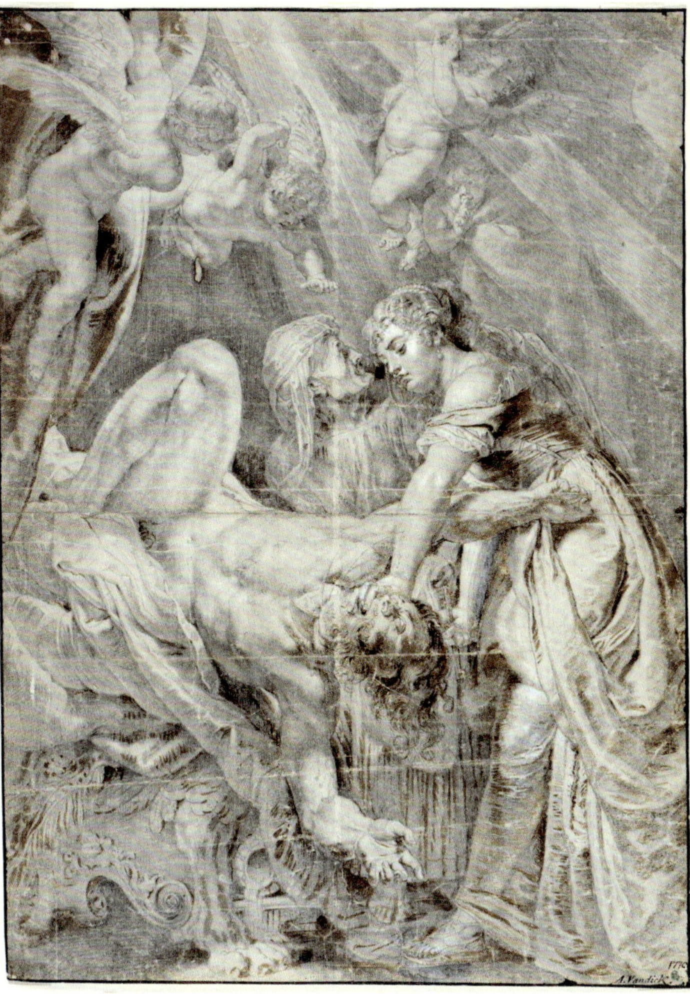

Fig 14 Peter Paul Rubens, *Judith Beheading Holofernes*, c. 1616. Black chalk and pen and brown ink and wash, 50.8 × 36.8 cm. Nationalmuseum, Stockholm. NMH 1963/1863. Photo: Hans Thorwid/Nationalmuseum.

The first prints from Rubens's own printmaking enterprise were published between 1620 and 1623, all of them done by the engraver Lucas Vorsterman, including *St. Francis Receiving the Stigmata* (1620, fig. 15), *The Tribute Money* (1621, see page 185, and *Battle of the Amazons* (1623, see page 234). From letters and resolutions by three state governments, it is clear that by early January of 1619, Rubens was establishing his printmaking business. On January 4, he asked Pieter van Veen, who was based in the Hague and was the brother of his teacher, Otto van Veen, to help him obtain a privilege for his prints from the States General of the United Provinces. Around that time, he likely filed similar requests to authorities in France and the Spanish Netherlands.

The process of having Rubens's paintings engraved, including the division of labour, stayed more or less the same for two decades. An assistant would make a drawing in black chalk (fig. 16) after an original painting (fig. 17) or a workshop copy, which remained in the artist's studio. The draftsman responsible would already have received instructions from Rubens on adjusting the composition to follow the requirements for engraving or to modernize the image. The *modelli* were seldom slavish copies after the originals.[36] In turn, these drawings were retouched by the master himself in pen and ink and wash, as well as white gouache, mostly slight adjustments to the compositions or modifications to the chiaroscuro. The corrected drawing was then

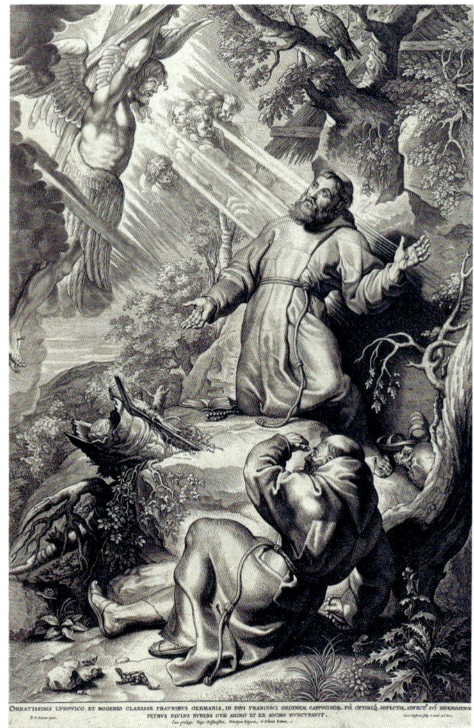

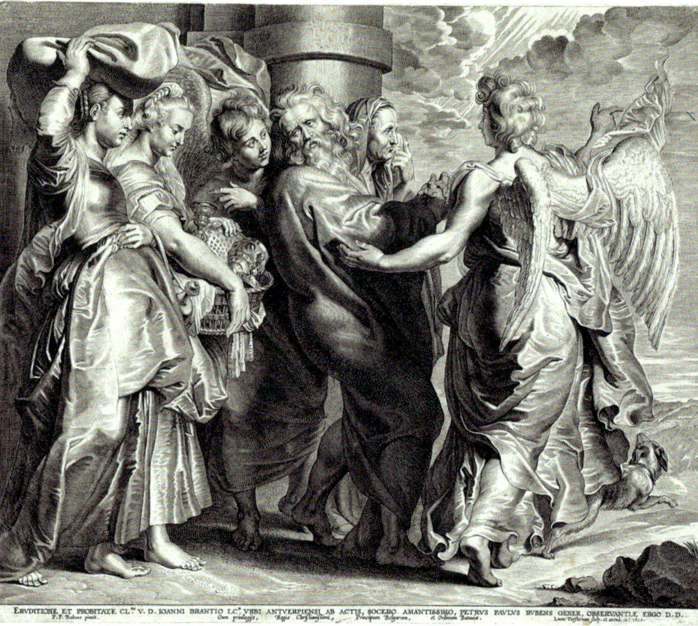

Fig 15 Lucas Vorsterman, after Peter Paul Rubens, *St. Francis Receiving the Stigmata*, 1620. Engraving, 524 × 350 cm. Rijksmuseum, Amsterdam. RP-P-OB-33.034.

Fig 16 Lucas Vorsterman, after Peter Paul Rubens, *The Flight of Lot and His Family from Sodom*, 1620. Engraving, 33 × 38.8 cm. Rijksmuseum, Amsterdam. RP-POB-33.000.

engraved onto a copper plate by the printmaker, often in several stages, giving Rubens another opportunity to suggest further changes. When the printmaker was finished, the copper plate would be sent to a professional letter engraver, who would furnish with the proper lettering. Finally, the plate was sent to a professional printer, who would pull thousands of impressions at a time, certainly not limited editions.[37] These prints were sold through agents who had wide networks of print- and booksellers all over Europe.[38]

This process allowed Rubens to monitor the production and guarantee the highest possible quality. It was modified around 1628, when oil sketches became the favoured preparatory material over drawings, as was the case with book illustrations. We may assume that carefully following the process was important for Rubens. However, this is likely not the only reason he got involved with the printmaking business himself, since he had also supervised projects that he had not initiated. By publishing prints himself, he was able to get the largest share in profits. Owning a copper plate was like owning a matrix to print money following the invention of banknotes. A blank sheet was printed with an image that dramatically increased its value, a value that was not intrinsic to the paper support.

There is indication that Rubens's enterprise was quite successful. Certainly, the prints did not come cheap. Just a few months after the first engravings were issued from Rubens's studio, the amateur Arnout van Bucchel stated in his diary that he attended a meeting of artists in Utrecht on July 16, 1620, where Vorsterman's prints of the master's work were discussed negatively: the quality of the prints was not the issue; they were just considered very expensive.[39] The prices for these engravings must have been exceptional, otherwise the remark would not have made sense. In the 1630s, during a lawsuit about a violation of his privilege, Rubens was accused of extracting enormous sums of money from France by means of his print business. Rubens denied this and stressed that he was the one who had been harmed—in terms of reputation and finances—by the unauthorized copying of one of his prints.[40] In any case, serious amounts of money had been involved, which is also confirmed by documented settlements after Rubens's death between his heirs and Jacques Moermans, who took care of the commercial side of Rubens's print business. The settlements mentioned numbers of up to 2,500 florins.[41]

Requesting print privileges from three governments allowed Rubens to protect his investments. His engravings could not be

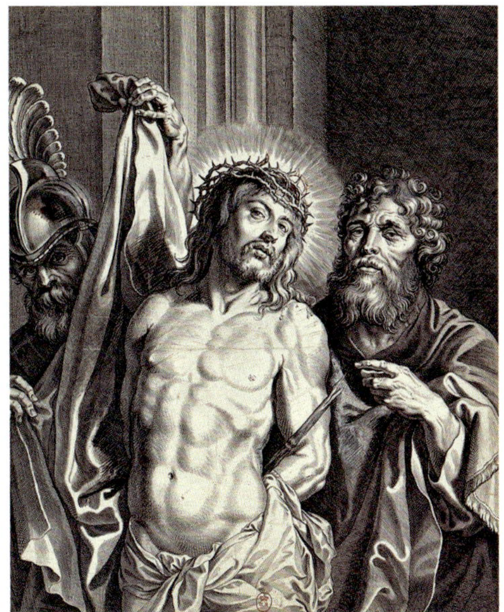

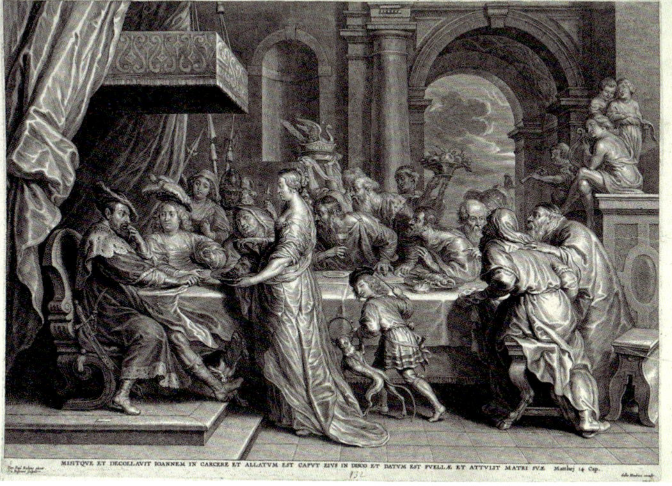

Fig 17 Cornelis Galle, after Peter Paul Rubens, *Ecce Homo*. Engraving retouched in pen and brown ink and wash, 37.5 × 28 cm, Bibliothèque Nationale de France, Paris. Réserve CC-34 (J: 1-2)-Boîte Fol. no. 9.

Fig 18 Schelte a Bolswert, after Peter Paul Rubens, *The Feast of Herod*, c. 1638. Engraving, 60.4 × 42.5 cm, Rijksmuseum, Amsterdam. RP-P-OB-67.524.

copied until his death in any of the three major centres for printmaking: Antwerp, Amsterdam, and Paris.[42] This did not prohibit anyone from making engravings directly from any of his paintings, but it was professional courtesy to not do so without the artist's consent, and it was foolhardy to upset such an influential artist.[43] This did not mean, however, that no prints based on Rubens's works were published outside of his studio. Even after setting up his own enterprise, Rubens continued collaborating on print projects for engravings not issued by him. For instance, Cornelis Galle's *Ecce Homo*—based on the composition now in the Hermitage, Saint Petersburg, and originally issued by Theodoor Galle—was finished from a proof state with retouchings ascribed to Rubens himself (fig. 17).[44] A drawing in a private collection for Schelte a Bolswert's *The Feast of Herod*, from the painting presently in the Scottish National Gallery, Edinburgh, was most likely made by a member of Rubens's studio as a model for an engraving before the painting was shipped off to its commissioner, Gaspar Roomer in Naples (fig. 18).[45] Rubens's willingness to collaborate with engravers and publishers outside of his own studio indicates that exclusivity was not a goal. By providing drawings and retouching proofs, he maintained some control over the appearance of the prints and assured a level of quality.

The high-quality engravings after Rubens's paintings, such as the ones by Lucas Vorsterman, considerably contributed to the international spread of Rubens's fame and knowledge about his oeuvre. They may have led to new commissions. The full scope of Rubens's printmaking enterprise, however, can only be fully understood after taking the financial side of the project into consideration. Rubens's experience in the years before 1620 showed him the benefits of monitoring the whole project closely, which ensured a high quality, and it also made him realize that taking printmaking into his own hands would give him the lion's share of the profits. The engraved work by Rubens's printmakers was of an extremely high quality, as looking at nineteenth-century impressions of the plates reveals. Very late impressions included in the so-called Recueil Hodges of 1808 show relatively little wear of the copper plate and still produced decent imagery, indicating that the engravers did an exceptional job.[46] The thousands of impressions pulled from copper plates produced in Rubens's workshop from 1620 onward brought Rubens not only fame but also great fortune.

This essay is a partial reflection of the research carried out by Simon Turner and me for the New Hollstein Rubens, a multi-volume catalogue raisonné *of the seventeenth-century prints of Rubens's creations to be published shortly. I want to thank my co-compiler Simon for valuable remarks, as well as the publisher, Frits Garritsen, and our editor, Ger Luijten, for making the project possible.*

1 Julius S. Held, among others, has suspected that Rubens was involved in a book published in Rome in 1609, *Vita Beati P. Ignatii Loiolae*. However, the preserved drawings related to this project—one at the National Galleries of Scotland, Edinburgh (inv. D 1695) and one in the Cabinet des dessins in the Musée du Louvre, Paris (inv. 22239)—are not by Rubens, as Christian Tico Seifert suspects, and no other evidence exists for his collaboration. See Julius S. Held, "Rubens and the Vita Beati P. Ignatii Loiolae of 1609," in *Rubens before 1620*, ed. John Rupert Martin (Princeton, NJ: Princeton University Press, 1972), 93–134, and Christian Tico Seifert, *Rubens & Company: Flemish Drawings from the Scottish National Gallery* (Edinburgh: National Galleries of Scotland, 2016), 52–53, nos. 17a–b (with further literature).

2 Marjon van der Meulen, *Petrus Paulus Rubens Antiquarius: Collector and Copyist of Antique Gems* (Alphen aan den Rijn: Canaletto, 1975), 10.

3 J. Richard Judson and Carl Van de Velde believe that Rubens did make designs specifically for the book. However, none of his actual drawings used for the illustrations has been preserved. See J. Richard Judson and Carl van de Velde, *Corpus Rubenianum Ludwig Burchard, Part XXI: Book Illustrations and Title Pages*, 2 vols. (Brussels: Arcade, 1977), 1:77–85, nos. 1–5, and 2, figs. 41–46; Marjon van der Meulen, *Corpus Rubenianum Ludwig Burchard, Park XXIII: Copies after the Antique*, 3 vols. (London: Harvey Miller, 1994–95), I, 97–113, text ills. 51–61, and Dirk Imhof in Dirk Imhof, ed., *De Boekillustratie ten tijde van de Moretussen* (Antwerp: Stad Antwerpen, 1996), 107–8, no. 18.

4 The manuscript was ready by November 1607, whereas the printing of the text probably took place in the early months of 1608. The engraver was paid for his work in August, and the publisher was charged for printing the illustrations in September. See Herman F. Bouchery and Frank van den Wijngaert, *Rubens en het Plantijnsche Huis* (Maerlantbibliotheek IV, Antwerp: De Sikkel; Utrecht: W. de Haan, 1941), 58; Judson and Van de Velde, *Book Illustrations*, 1:78; and Van der Meulen, *Copies after the Antique*, 1:98.

5 The inventory number for the title page in London is 1861,0608.148, and for the vignettes, 1982.104,1 and 1996.114.1. See also Judson and Van de Velde, *Book Illustrations*, 1:104–5, no. 10a, 107; no. 11a and 110; no. 13a and 2; figs. 56 and 62, Michael Jaffé, "Rubens and Optics: Some Fresh Evidence," *Journal of the Warburg and Courtauld Institutes* 34 (1971): 362–66, and Gitta Bertram, "Elevating Optics: The Title Page by Peter Paul Rubens of Franciscus Aguilonius's Opticorum Libri Sex (1613) in Its Historical Context," *Explorations in Renaissance Culture* 42, no. 2 (2016): 212–42.

6 Payments to Theodoor Galle are documented. On May 20 and June 22, 1613, he was paid for the vignettes at eighteen guilders each, and also received seventy-two guilders for the title page on June 22. Galle also took care of printing all copper plates for the book, as is clear from a settlement dated August 9, 1613. He was paid a total of seventy-eight guilders and eighteen stuivers. The exact date of a payment to Rubens is not known, since it was registered in the Plantin-Moretus accounts with four illustrations for the *Missale Romanum* and work for Justus Lipsius's edition of the Seneca works of 1615. See Judson and Van de Velde, *Book Illustrations*, 1:100–15, nos. 10-16a, and 2:447 and 453–54, nos. 1 and 12–14, and Dirk Imhof in Imhof, *Boekillustratie*, 137–38, no. 42.

7 Hans Gerhard Evers, *Rubens und sein Werk: neue Forschungen* (Brussels: De Lage Landen, 1943), 195–219; and Judson and Van de Velde, *Book Illustrations*, 1:85–100 and 118–51, nos. 6–9 and 18–28, and 2, figs. 47–54 and 71–97.

8 Christoffel Plantin was granted the right to print the reformed missal for the Netherlands, Hungary, and parts of Germany in July 1570. In February 1571, Philip II awarded him the initial contracts for the large Spanish market. Plantin often recycled copper plates for the many illustrated religious texts issued by his press, a practice his heirs, the Moretuses, would continue. Copper plates could be used for decades and were often restored. See Karen L. Bowen and Dirk Imhof, *Christopher Plantin and Engraved Book Illustrations in Sixteenth-Century Europe* (Cambridge: Cambridge University Press, 2008), 126, and Hans Mielke and Ursula Mielke, *The New Hollstein Dutch & Flemish Etchings, Engravings and Woodcuts, 1450–1700: Peeter van der Borcht—Book Illustrations, Part II*, ed. Ger Luijten (Ouderkerk aan den IJssel: Sound & Vision Publishers, 2003), 29, nos. 489–93.

9 The two subjects were illustrated in the 1605 *in-octavo* edition but not in the older *in-folio* editions. The older illustrations, engravings by the Collaert brothers from designs by Maarten de Vos, had been in use since 1596. Theodoor Galle was paid for engraving the two Rubens designs on February 13, 1613. See Judson and Van de Velde, *Book Illustrations*, 2:452, no. 9; Anne-Marie Logan, *Peter Paul Rubens: The Drawings* (New Haven, CT: Yale University Press, 2005), 169–71, no. 49; Karen Bowen in Imhof, *Boekillustratie*, 123–24, no. 32a; Karen L. Bowen and Dirk Imhof, "Book Illustrations by Maarten de Vos for Jan Moretus I," *Print Quarterly* 18 (2001): 259–89; and Bowen and Imhof, *Christopher Plantin*, 237.

10 A retouched proof impression for the *Adoration of the Magi* is at the Bibliothèque Nationale de France, Paris (inv. Réserve CC-34-boîte fol-1). However, most of the suggested changes were included in a later state only. See Judson and Van de Velde, *Book Illustrations*, 1:132–33, no. 22a.

11 The Plantin-Moretus account book mentions a payment to Rubens for four drawings for the Missale ("quatre du Missel"), but only three illustrations seem to be made from his design. He might have designed another frame that was never engraved. Six drawings for scenes from the New Testament used for the frame accompanying a full-page illustration of the *Adoration of the Shepherds*, now at the Morgan Library & Museum, New York, are sometimes attributed to Rubens. However, these diverge from his style of drawing and were more likely done by someone at the Galle studio. See Judson and Van de Velde, *Book Illustrations*, 1:92–96, nos. 7 and 7a, and 2, figs. 49–50, and Felice Stampfle, *Netherlandish Drawings of the Fifteenth and Sixteenth Centuries and Flemish Drawings of the Seventeenth and Eighteenth Centuries in the Pierpont Morgan Library* (New York: Pierpont Morgan Library; Princeton, NJ: Princeton University Press, 1991), 140–41, nos. 299–304.

12 Payments to Theodoor Galle for engraving the decorative frames are documented between September 1612 and March 1613. The names of the artists responsible for the preparatory drawings are not mentioned. All illustrations were ready by May 20, 1613, when Galle was payed for printing "heel af den missael in folio" ("the whole of the Missale, in folio"). See Judson and Van de Velde, *Book Illustrations*, 2:451–53, nos. 5–8 and 10–11.

13 Judson and Van de Velde, *Book Illustrations*, 1:118–19, and Karen L. Bowen in Imhof, *Boekillustratie*, 125–26, no. 33a.

14 Between 1610 and 1618, Rubens was paid 132 guilders to draw models for ten full-page illustrations and a frontispiece. One of his designs, *Christ Crucified between the Two Thieves* ("Crucifixus cum latronibus") was not engraved and *Christ Dead on the Cross* ("Crucifixus defunctus") was used only a few years later. On October 16, 1614, Theodoor Galle was paid for printing "heel af den brevier in folio" ("whole of the Breviarium in folio"). See Judson and Van de Velde, *Book Illustrations,* 2:447, no. 1, and 2:458, no. 25; Logan, *Peter Paul Rubens,* 172–73, no. 50; Stijn Alsteens in *Van Floris tot Rubens: Meestertekeningen uit een Belgische privéverzameling,* ed. Stefan Hautekeete (Ghent: Uitgeverij Snoeck; Brussels: Koninklijke Musea voor Schone Kunsten van België, 2016), 196–99, no. 68, and Ilona van Tuinen, *Power and Grace: Drawings by Rubens, Van Dyck, and Jordaens* (New York: Morgan Library & Museum; London: Paul Holberton, 2018), 40–43, no. 3.

15 Rubens did not follow the instructions very strictly and was allowed to make slight modifications. Theodoor Galle was paid seventy-five guilders for cutting the plate for the title page on May 15, 1614. See Judson and Van de Velde, *Book Illustrations,* 1:122–24, no. 18a–b, and 2:456, no. 20, figs. 75–77; and Christine van Mulders in Imhof, *Boekillustratie,* 126–27, no. 33b.

16 A few of these retouched full-page illustrations are at the Bibliothèque Nationale de France, Paris. See Judson and Van de Velde, *Book Illustrations,* 1:131–33, 142–43, 146, and 150–51, nos. 21b, 22a, 26b, 27b, and 28b.

17 The 1616 and 1618 editions of the *Missale Romanum* published by the Plantin-Moretus press do contain the decorative frames, including the one designed by Rubens. *The Adoration of the Magi* and *The Ascension of Christ* were designed for the 1613 edition and eight new full-page illustrations were included in the 1614 *Breviarium.* In addition, a new *Christ on the Cross,* based on Rubens's design (see note 16), replaced the old one from a Maarten de Vos drawing. See Judson and Van de Velde, *Book Illustrations,* 1:88–89.

18 Max Rooses and Charles Ruelens, eds., *Correspondance de Rubens et documents épistolaires concernant sa vie et ses oeuvres* 6 vols. (Antwerp: Jos. Maes, 1887–1909), 5:335–36, no. 687.

19 Much of the accounting paperwork is preserved at Museum Plantin-Moretus, in Antwerp. Documents on the production of book illustrations and title pages were published in, among others, Max Rooses, *Petrus-Paulus Rubens en Balthasar Moretus: Eene bijdrage tot de geschiedenis der kunst,* Antwerp (Drukkerij Wed. De Backer) and Ghent (Ad. Hoste), 1884, Bouchery and Van den Wijngaert, *Rubens en het Plantijnsche Huis,* and Judson and Van de Velde, *Book Illustrations.* As Rooses made clear, Rubens received twenty florins for a folio-sized design, twelve florins for a quarto-sized, eight florins for an octavo-sized, and five florins for one *in-240.* See Rooses, *Rubens en Moretus,* 25–26.

20 This is what Cornelis Galle was paid for many of the illustrations in the 1613 *Missale Romanum* and for the title page for the 1614 *Breviarium Romanum.* See Max Rooses, *L'oeuvre de P.P. Rubens: histoire et description de ses tableaux et dessins,* 5 vols. (Antwerp: Jos. Maes, 1886–92), 5:65.

21 Judson and Van de Velde, *Book Illustrations,* 78.

22 Dieuwke de Hoop Scheffer, George S. Keyes, and Ger Luyten, *Hollstein's Dutch and Flemish Engravings, Etchings and Woodcuts, ca. 1450–1700,* vol. 29, *Samuel de Swaef to Jan Thesing,* ed. Karel G. Boon (Blaricum: A.L. Van Gendt, 1984), 14–16, nos. 1 and 6.

23 For instance, Paul Huvenne talks about prints of Rubens's work from 1611 onward as "piracies" ("piraatdruk" and "roofdrukken"). See Paul Huvenne, "Inleiding," *Copyright Rubens: Rubens en de grafiek,* ed. Nico van Hout (Ghent: Ludion, 2004), 13.

24 The widespread idea that Rubens was particularly concerned about his intellectual property and issued prints to protect his inventions—for instance, as expressed by Nico van Hout—are completely ahistorical, as Antony Griffiths explains. See Nico van Hout, ed., *Copyright Rubens: Rubens en de grafiek* (Ghent: Ludion, 2004), 30, and Antony Griffiths, *The Print before Photography: An Introduction to European Printmaking, 1550–1820* (London: British Museum Press, 2016), 99–101.

25 A complete set of the 1609 portraits of the Leiden professors is kept at the British Museum, London (inv. 1983,U.2394.1-48). A set issued in 1613 is at the Rijksbureau voor Kunsthistorische Documentatie, The Hague (shelf mark PREC/17F16). See De Hoop Scheffer, *Hollstein* 42, no. 69 (Baudius), and 44, no. 86 (Lipsius).

26 De Hoop Scheffer, *Hollstein,* nos. 101–2.

27 Léna Widerkehr, *The New Hollstein Dutch & Flemish Etchings, Engravings and Woodcuts, 1450–1700: Jacob Matham,* ed. Huigen Leeflang, 3 vols. (Ouderkerk aan den IJssel: Sound & Vision Publishers, 2007–8), 1:23, no. 10.

28 It is unlikely that Rubens sent or brought the oil sketch—now at the Cincinnati Art Museum (inv. 1972.459)—to Holland, as has been suggested. However, the preparatory drawing, now lost, may have been based on the oil sketch rather than the larger painting. See Marjorie E. Wieseman, *Drawn by the Brush: Oil Sketches by Peter Paul Rubens,* ed. Peter Sutton and Marjorie E. Wieseman (New Haven: Yale University Press, 2004), 88–93, no. 2.

29 Jacob Matham seems to have already been in contact with Rubens's friend Jan de Wouwer, alias Woverius, in 1608. He provided text for the lines of verse underneath Matham's portrait of Domenicus Baudius, the Leiden professor with whom Rubens corresponded himself, as mentioned above. For the relevant print by Matham, see Widerkehr, *Jacob Matham,* 2:182, no. 228 (with further literature).

30 This was first suggested by Jan Gerrit van Gelder and later often presented as fact. Nico van Hout proposes that Rubens went "talent hunting" (*talentenjacht*) in Holland. See Jan Gerrit van Gelder, "Rubens in Holland in de zeventiende eeuw," *Netherlands Yearbook for History of Art* 3 (1950–51): 102–50, at 119–21; Van Hout, *Copyright Rubens* 33; and Widerkehr, *Jacob Matham,* 1:lvi.

31 As Andrew Hottle has stated, "There is little indication that Rubens seriously considered printmaking as a significant means of disseminating his designs prior to 1618 ... The claim that Rubens travelled to Haarlem in 1612 to find an engraver is enticing but unfounded." One should even ask why Rubens would have wanted to search for an engraver in Holland. Antwerp was still the leading centre in printmaking at the start of the seventeenth century, and many Northern Netherlandish engravers even moved to Antwerp for work. See Andrew D. Hottle, "Peter Paul Rubens and the Dedicated Print: Strategies in the Marketing of an Early Modern Master" (PhD diss., Temple University, 2004), 17–18.

32 The source of the lines of verse was discovered by Hans Jakob Meier. See Hans Jakob Meier, "Peter Paul Rubens and His Brother Philip on Samson and Judith," *Journal of the Warburg and Courtauld Institutes* 77 (2014): 241–45.

33 I am grateful to Jan-Willem van Haaften for help with translating these lines of verse from Latin.

34 Adriaen Collaert was married to the sister of Theodoor and Cornelis Galle, Justa. The fourth state was published by Adriaen's son Carel Collaert. See Ann Diels, *"Wat d'yser can bemaelen": Les estampes des graveurs anversois Collaert (1550–1630)* (Brussels: Bibliothèque Royale Albert I; Ouderkerk aan den IJssel: Sound & Vision Publishers, 2005), 22–26, and Ann Diels and Marjolein Leesberg, *The New Hollstein Dutch & Flemish Etchings, Engravings and Woodcuts, 1450–1700: The Collaert Dynasty*, ed. Arnout Balis and Marjolein Leesberg, 8 vols. (Ouderkerk aan den IJssel: Sound & Vision Publishers, 2005–6), 1:lv-lxvii and 8:11, no. 2095.

35 Also observed by Andrew Hottle. See Hottle, *Rubens and the Dedicated Print*, 96.

36 On the subject, see Konrad Renger, "Planänderungen in Rubensstichen," *Zeitschrift für Kunstgeschichte*, 37 (1974), 1–30.

37 In 1633, Christoffel Jegher produced woodcuts from Rubens's compositions, which were printed by the Plantin press with the details documented in its account books. On July 23, Rubens was charged for making no less than 2,000 impressions of "onse L. Vrouwe" ("Our Lady"), probably the *Rest on the Flight into Egypt*. From other woodblocks by Jegher, 500 impressions were printed, possibly restrikes. There is another note listing a debt by Rubens for 2,000 impressions of a woodblock dating between March 31, 1634, and April 12, 1636. See Rooses, *L'oeuvre de P.P. Rubens*, 5:137–38, and Bouchery and Van den Wijngaert, *Rubens en het Plantijnsche Huis*, 100–1.

38 Following Rubens's death, there were documented settlements between the heirs of Gabriel Tavernier, Rubens's representative in Paris and Jacques Moermans, who seemed to have taken care of the commercial side of the print business in the later part of the 1630s. See Pierre Génard, "De Nalatenschap van P.P. Rubens," *Antwerpsch Archievenblad/Bulletin des Archives d'Anvers* 2 (1865), 94–96, nos. 108, 115, and 116 (69–179); Pierre Génard, *P.P. Rubens: Aantekeningen over den grooten meester en zijne bloedverwanten* (Antwerp: Boekhandel van P. Kockx, 1877), 51–52; Henri Hymans, *La gravure dans l'école* de Rubens (Brussels: Académie royale de Belgique), 1878, 208 and 250; Ilja M. Veldman, *Crispijn de Passe and His Progeny (1564–1670): A Century of Print Production*, Studies in Prints and Printmaking 3 (Rotterdam: Sound & Vision Publishers), 2001, 267; and Ann Diels, *The Shadow of Rubens: Print Publishing in 17th-Century Antwerp; Prints by the History Painters Abraham van Diepenbeeck, Cornelis Schut and Erasmus Quellinus II* (London: Harvey Miller, 2009), 165.

39 This is confirmed in 1630, when Nicolas-Claude Fabri de Peiresc wrote a letter to thank Pierre Dupuy for buying him some prints with Lucas Vorsterman, and to also tell Dupuy that he wanted to wait after acquiring some prints by Rubens "où il va tant d'argent." See Rooses and Ruelens, *Correspondance de Rubens*, 5:266–67, no. 656; Aernout van Buchell, *Notae Quotidianae*, ed. J.W.C. van Campen (Utrecht: Kemink en Zoon, 1940), 1–2; and Gerdien Wuestman, "Prijzen van Rubensgrafiek in de zeventiende eeuw," *Delineavit et Sculpsit* 19 (1998): 1–7.

40 Hymans, *La gravure dans l'école* de Rubens, 201–4.

41 Génard, *Nalatenschap*, 94–96, nos. 108, 115, and 116; Génard, *Aantekeningen*, 51–52; and Hymans, *La gravure dans l'école* de Rubens, 208.

42 It is probably not a coincidence that the French engraver François Ragot requested a French privilege for copies of Rubens's prints in 1641, just after the master's death. In the Spanish Netherlands, Rubens's heirs were granted a twelve-year extension of his print privilege in 1644, after it had expired in 1642. See Marianne Grivel, *Le commerce de l'estampe à Paris au XVIIe siècle* (Geneva: Libraire Droz, 1986), 368, and Van Hout, *Copyright Rubens*, 38.

43 This was kindly pointed out to me by Antony Griffiths, who I am very grateful to for sharing his knowledge on the subject. One artist who did copy a Rubens print in his lifetime was Jacques Honervogt, and Rubens was dogged in pursuing him—albeit at a distance, through the French legal system. See Hymans, *La gravure dans l'école* de Rubens, 201–4, and Griffiths, *The Print before Photography*, 250–51.

44 It is possible that the print was made before 1619, though it is generally dated to the early 1620s. Since the publisher, Theodoor Galle, died in 1633, the etching certainly dates from Rubens's lifetime and is not a later reproduction after his work. See J. Richard Judson, *Corpus Rubenianum Ludwig Burchard, Part VI: The Passion of Christ* (London: Harvey Miller, 2000), 64–67, nos. 13 and 13a.

45 The draftsman may have been Schelte a Bolswert, who would have been allowed access to Rubens's studio to make the copy. See Logan, *Peter Paul Rubens*, 187–89, no. 57.

46 Charles Howard Hodges traced a number of copper plates for engravings based on creations by Rubens and Van Dyck, and published these in a *recueil* issued in Amsterdam in 1808. Copies of the complete *Recueil Hodges* are at the Rijksmuseum, Amsterdam, and at the Royal Library of Belgium in Brussels, among others. See Abraham Jacob van der Aa, *Biografisch woordenboek der Nederlanden:. Deel 8. Tweede stuk* (Haarlem: J.J. van Brederode, 1867), 848.

CATALOGUE

Jacobus Harrewijn
born Amsterdam, Netherlands, 1660;
died Brussels, Belgium, after 1732
After J. van Croes
View of the Rubenshuis in Antwerp
c. 1675–1732
Engraving
28.7 × 35.7 cm

Metropolitan Museum of Art, New York
The Elisha Whittelsey Collection, The Elisha Whittelsey Fund, 1951
51.501.7502

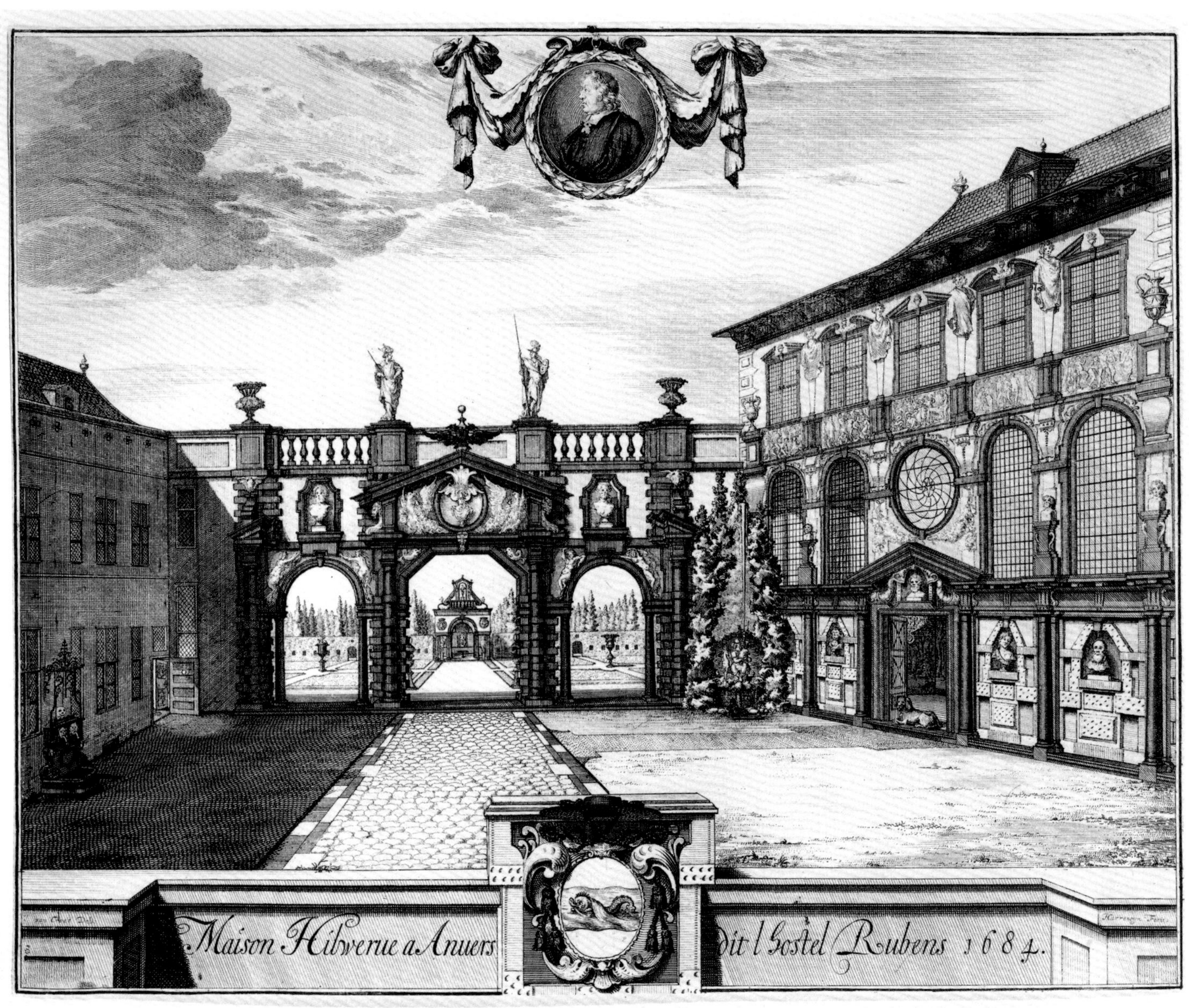
Maison Hilwerue a Anuers
dit l Gostel Rubens 1684.

Peter Paul Rubens
born Siegen, Westphalia (now Germany), 1577;
died Antwerp, Spanish Netherlands (now Belgium), 1640
Self-Portrait in a Circle of Friends at Mantua
c. 1602–05
Oil on canvas
77.5 × 101 cm

Wallraf-Richartz-Museum & Fondation Corboud, Cologne
WRM Dep. 248
Photo: Rheinisches Bildarchiv Köln, Walz, Sabrina

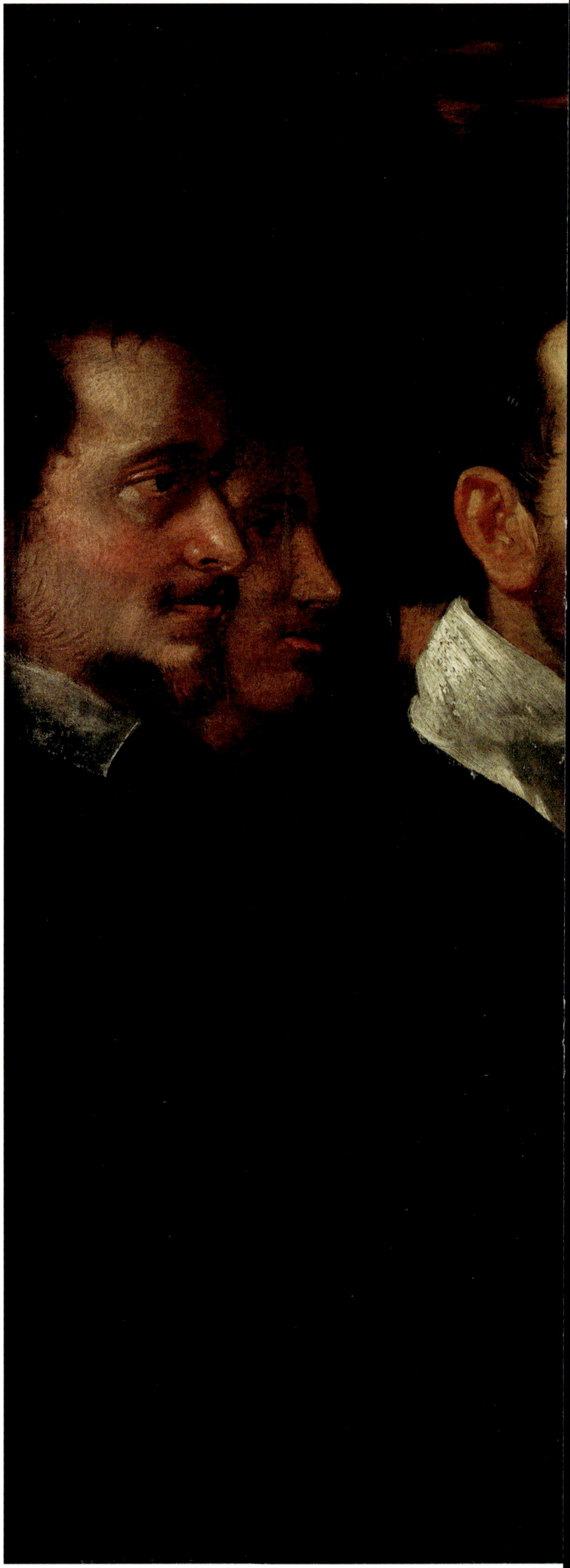

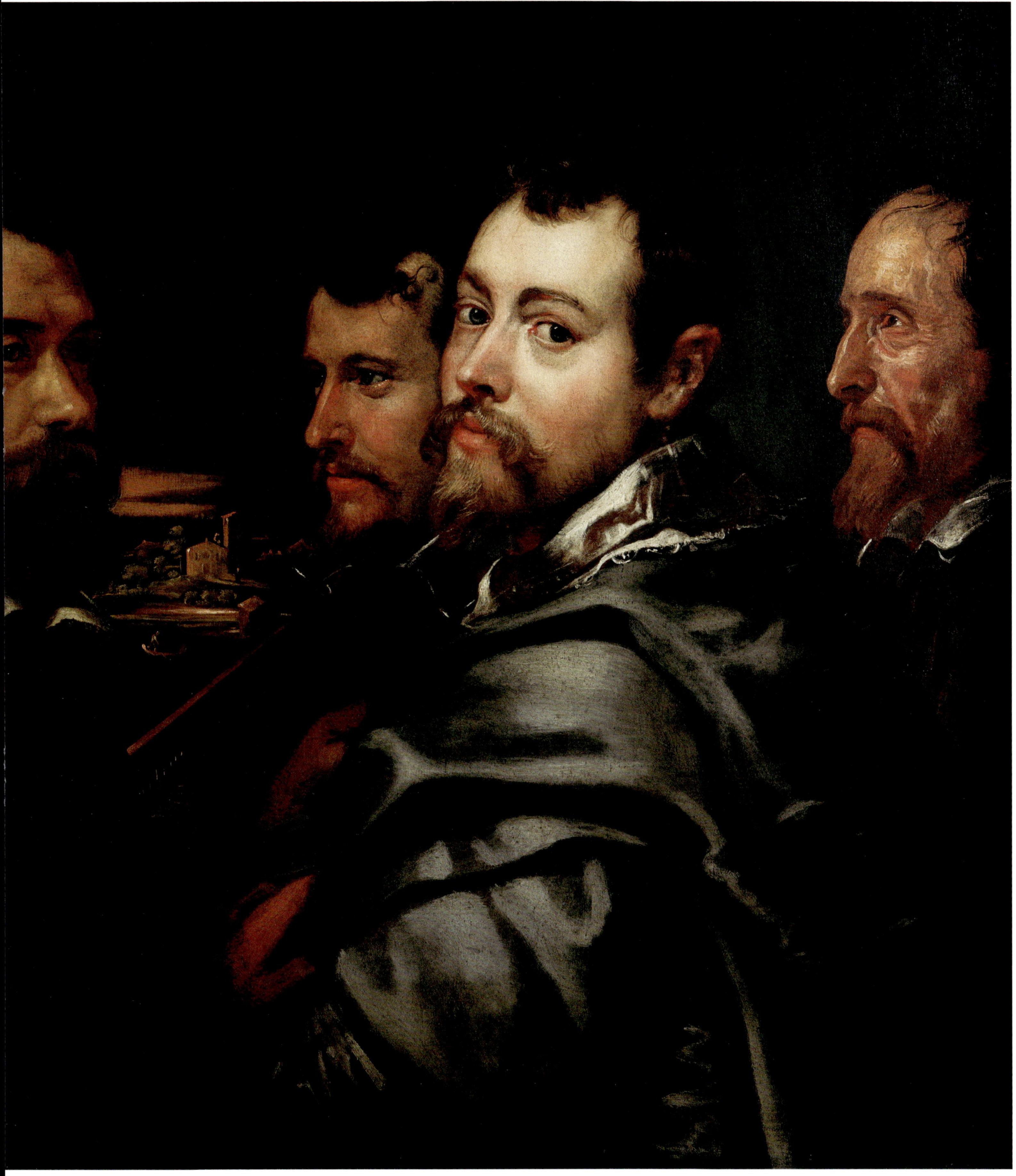

Peter Paul Rubens
Self-Portrait in a Circle of Friends at Mantua

In this earliest-known self-portrait by Rubens, the painter presents himself among a group of men at the court of the Gonzaga family in Mantua. Rubens's likeness, second from the right, is easily recognizable, and the Mantuan setting was identified by Ludwig Burchard on the basis of the background vista that records Mantua's Ponte San Giorgio leading to the church of San Giorgio in the far distance.[1] Much else about the painting, from its moment and place of execution to the identities of Rubens's five companions, remains open to debate.

Rubens's employment by Duke Vincenzo I Gonzaga seems to have come about through a felicitous encounter in Venice with the duke's secretary, Annibale Chieppio. But Rubens may well have hoped that Mantua would be a welcome landing spot even before he left Antwerp in the spring of 1600. Otto van Veen, with whom Rubens spent his final apprenticeship, had worked at the Gonzaga court during his own period of travel and study in Italy, and the duke was known to keep Flemish painters around the court, especially for the purpose of painting portraits. If, in fact, Rubens entered Duke Vincenzo's entourage more or less immediately after striking up a friendship with Chieppio in June, this did not dissuade the duke from writing to Brussels to secure the services of the portraitist Frans Pourbus the Younger, who would arrive in Mantua that autumn.[2]

The community of Netherlandish and German expatriates at the Gonzaga court seems to provide the context for Rubens's group scene. The vast majority of modern assessments of the picture have agreed that the individuals portrayed were friends or intellectually sympathetic acquaintances of Rubens and his circle in the Southern Netherlands, all or most of whom passed through Mantua during Rubens's time there. The attempts to identify each member of the group have varied widely. Rubens's own identity has never been in doubt, and there is general consensus that the man standing directly behind him is his older brother Philip, who met and travelled with the artist through northern Italy as early as 1602.[3] The figure in strict profile at the far right has been alternately identified as Joseph Scaliger, Pietro Bembo, Claudio Monteverdi, and Justus Lipsius, although Scaliger and Bembo are particularly unlikely candidates and Lipsius has garnered somewhat greater support than these other options.[4]

None of the three men at left have been positively identified. This lack of clarity has frustrated attempts to interpret the picture, especially since the foremost of these three places a reassuring (consoling?) hand on Rubens's arm and is presented as a sort of counterpart to the painter himself. This middle-aged figure, who is surely central to the portrait's occasion and meaning, has been connected to Johann Faber, Annibale Chieppio, and Frans Pourbus the Younger. The figure in profile at the extreme left has most often been identified as Gaspar Schoppius, although Burchard specifically rejected this notion. And the identity of the man second from left has been especially fugitive, prompting guesses ranging from the painter Adam Elsheimer to Guillaume Richardot, a pupil of Philip Rubens.

Greater confidence in the identities of the men Rubens assembled in the Cologne portrait would help clarify whether this group of six had actually reunited in Mantua, and, if so, this would further aid in ascertaining the painting's date. With the present understanding of the group's composition, persuasive scholarly interpretation has been muted, yet insightful approaches to the painting's meaning have been put forward. Justus Müller Hofstede described the picture as a painterly analogue to the scholar's *album amicorum* (book of friends), in which a university student would collect witty or erudite inscriptions from his close friends and likeminded peers during the course of his studies.[5] Martin Warnke offered a more specific, if controversial, analysis, claiming the Cologne portrait was created to commemorate Justus Lipsius following his death in 1606. This late date would require

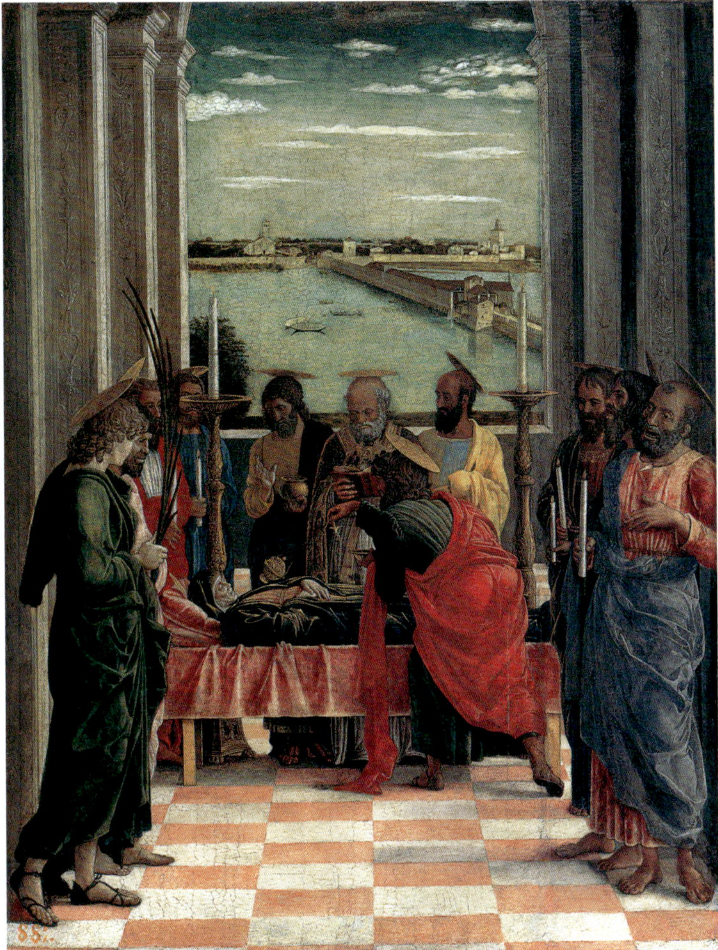

Fig 1 Andrea Mantegna, *Death of the Virgin*, c. 1462. Mixed technique on panel, 54.5 × 42 cm. Museo Nacional del Prado. P000248. Photo © Museo Nacional del Prado/ Art Resource, NY.

that Rubens painted the canvas while in Rome, a conclusion that few scholars have followed. However, Warnke's suggestion relates nicely to Rubens's decision to place himself and his compatriots in front of a view of Mantua's lakes and the Ponte San Giorgio. A very similar daytime view of this topography serves as the background in Andrea Mantegna's *Death of the Virgin* (fig. 1), a picture Rubens would have known from the Gonzaga collection.[6] If Rubens meant to reference Mantegna's panel, this would not only have commemorated the departed Lipsius as the hallowed leader of the group but would also have insinuated Rubens and his northern cohort into the apostles' shoes.

Kirk Nickel

1 For a concise account of the literature on the painting and its various interpretations, see Frances Huemer, *Corpus Rubenianum Ludwig Burchard, Part XIX: I, Portraits Painted in Foreign Countries* (Brussels: Arcade Press, 1977) 163–66, cat. no. 37.

2 Michael Jaffé, *Rubens and Italy* (Ithaca, NY: Cornell University Press, 1977), 9, 74.

3 See page 133 for Rubens's chalk study of Jan Woverius.

4 For these identifications and those following, see Huemer, *Corpus Rubenianum*, 164–65.

5 Justus Müller Hofstede, *Peter Paul Rubens, 1577–1640: Katalog I; Rubens in Italien; Gemälde, Ölskizzen, Zeichnungen* (Cologne: Museen der Stadt Köln, 1977), 80–82, exh. cat 82.

6 Martin Warnke, *Kommentare zu Rubens* (Berlin: Walter de Gruyter, 1965), 22–24.

7 For Mantegna's painting, now in the Museo Nacional del Prado, see Jane Martineau, ed., *Andrea Mantegna* (London: Royal Academy of Arts; New York: Metropolitan Museum of Art, 1992), 159–62, exh. cat. no. 17.

Peter Paul Rubens
Portrait of Philip Rubens
c. 1610–11
Oil on panel
68.5 × 53.5 cm

Detroit Institute of Art, Michigan
Gift of William E. Scripps in memory of his son,
James E. Scripps II
26.385

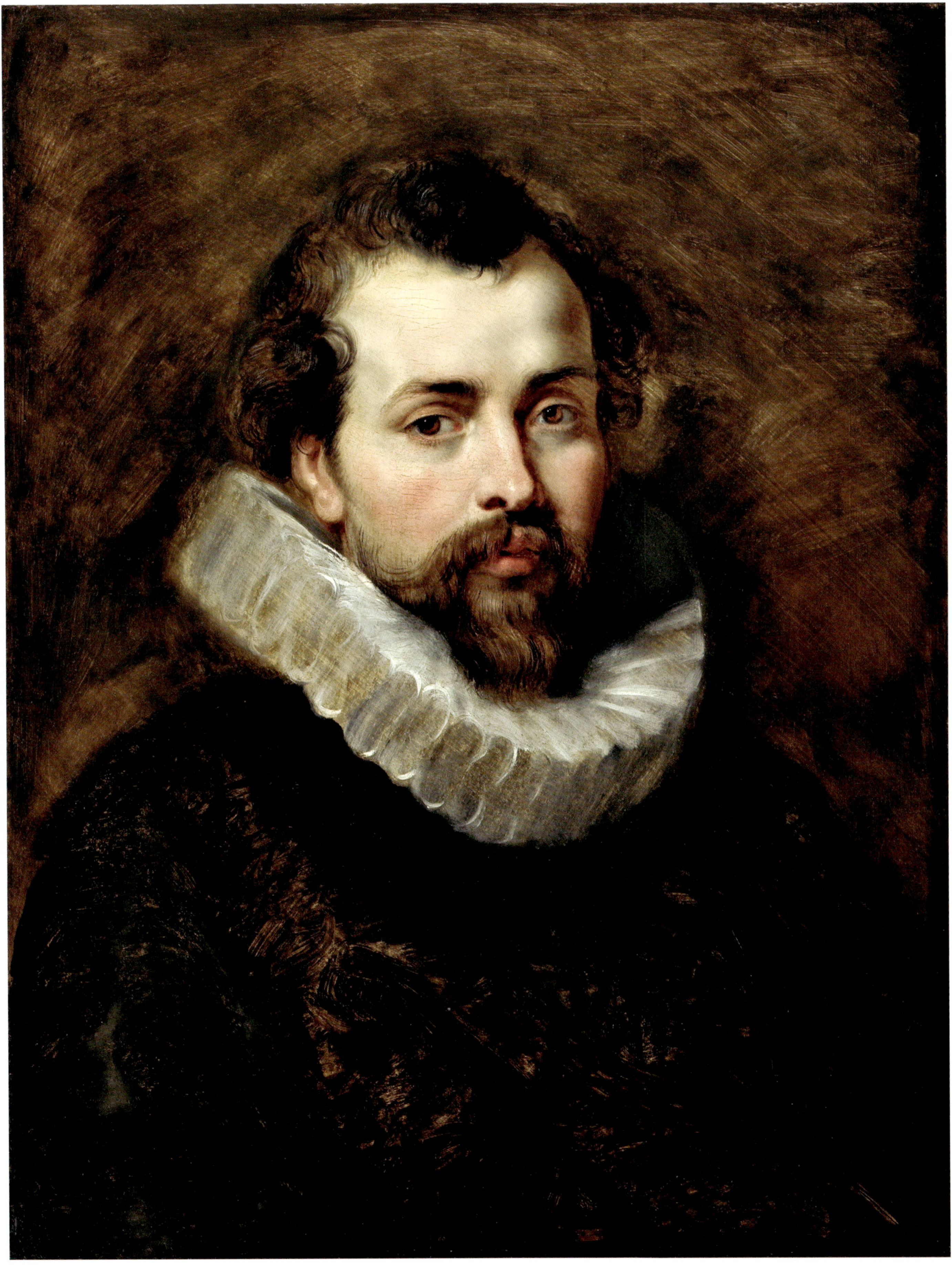

Peter Paul Rubens
Portrait of Philip Rubens

As prodigious and gifted as his brother Peter Paul, Philip Rubens (1574–1611) was a renowned jurist and Neo-Stoic scholar destined to succeed the foremost Humanist of his age, Justus Lipsius, had it not been for Philip's premature death at the age of thirty-seven. Following in the footsteps of Rubens, Philip travelled to Italy, where he would remain from 1601 to 1607. During this period, he earned a Doctor of Laws degree from the university in Rome, served as private secretary to the president of the privy council of the Spanish Netherlands, and was appointed librarian to Cardinal Ascanio Colonna. The remarkably short time in which he realized these accomplishments attests to the tremendous breadth of his intellect and erudition. Undoubtedly, the pinnacle of his Italian sojourn was his reunion with Rubens in 1606. While residing in Rome—the nexus for classical and antiquarian scholarship—the Rubens brothers immersed themselves in their research to produce a volume of philological studies entitled *Electorum libri II.*[1] Published by the Plantin-Moretus press in 1609, Rubens contributed five drawings of Roman sculpture (engraved by Cornelis Galle). But, as Philip affectionately acknowledged in the elegy, he was indebted to both the "skillful hand" and "keen and unerring judgement" of his learned brother.[2] After declining the coveted position of chair at the University of Pisa, Philip returned to the Netherlands in 1607 and was appointed municipal secretary of Antwerp in 1609. Through his political connections and eminence in the Neo-Stoic movement, he was instrumental in bringing Rubens into direct contact with the city's administrative and cultural elite.

The sitter is represented *en buste* in a simple black outfit with lace ruff and a fur-trimmed toga. The plasticity with which Rubens models Philip's markedly handsome face, and the rosy flush he adds to his complexion, impart an idealized youthfulness that typifies an homage. The slightly parted lips, almost carmine in colour, subtly enliven the sombre palette and mood. The Detroit portrait is generally believed to have decorated Philip's tomb in the church of Saint Michael's Abbey, but this opinion has been challenged on the basis of eighteenth-century French descriptions of the original portrait's oval shape.[3] However, scholars unanimously agree that the painting's stylistic vocabulary date it to around the time of Philip's death. In 1615, the portrait was engraved by Cornelis Galle for Jan Brant's biography of Philip in the posthumously published *S. Asterii Episc[opi] Amaseae Homiliae Graece et Latine*—an anthology of Humanist, epistolary, and poetic writings featuring the deceased's Latin translations of homilies by Asterius of Amaseae (fig. 1). Philip also appears in the celebrated group portrait *The Four Philosophers* at the Palazzo Pitti (page 19) and possibly in the *Self-Portrait in a Circle of Friends at Mantua* at the Wallraf-Richartz-Museum (page 120).[4] The Detroit painting is exceptional because it is the only individual portrait of Philip by Rubens.

Corrinne Chong

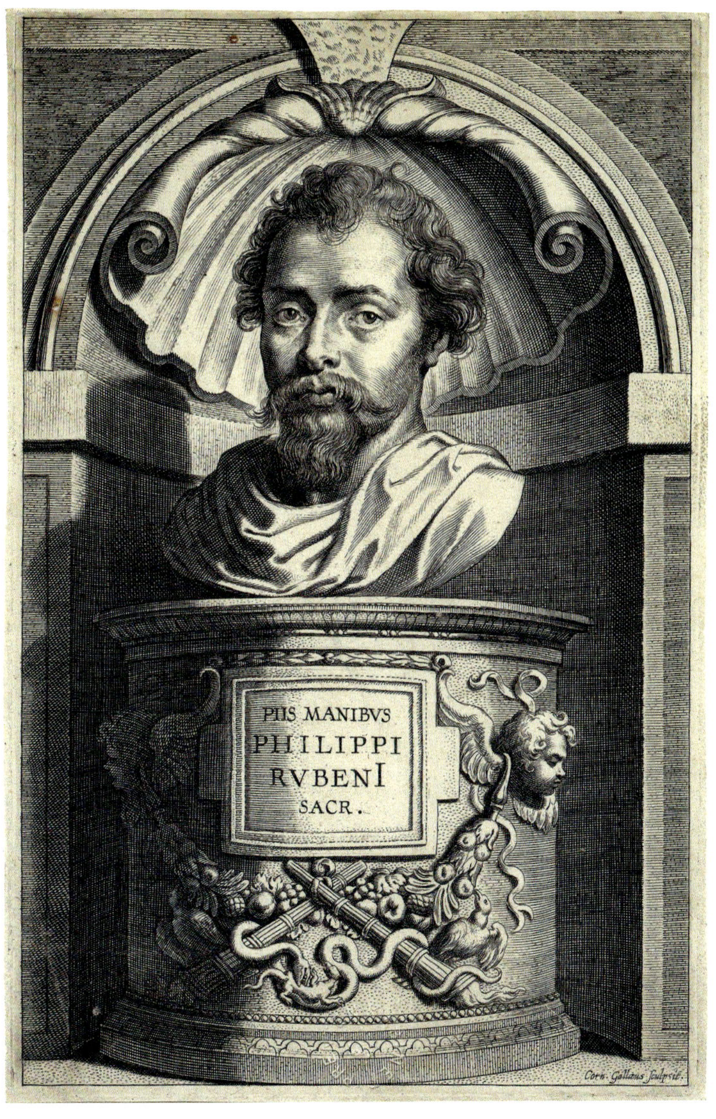

Fig 1 Cornelis Galle, after Rubens, *Portrait of Philip Rubens*, 1615. Engraving, 20 × 13.3 cm. Museum Plantin-Moretus, Antwerp. PK.OP07317.

1 For selections in English from the *Electorum libri II* and *S. Asterii Episc[opi] Amaseae Homiliae Graece et Latine*, see Frances Huemer, *Rubens and the Roman Circle: Studies of the First Decade* (New York: Garland, 1996), 149–228.

2 Nils Büttner, *Rubens in Private: The Master Portrays His Family*, ed. Ben van Beneden (London: Thames & Hudson, 2015), 160, exh. cat. no. 14.

3 Julius S. Held, *Flemish and German Paintings of the 17th Century*, The Collections of the Detroit Institute of Arts (Detroit: Detroit Institute of Arts, 1982), 81. Although there are no visible traces of a pre-existent oval frame, Vlieghe countered that this is expected given the extensive amount of restoration and over-painting. See Hans Vlieghe, *Corpus Rubenianum Ludwig Burchard, Part XIX: Rubens Portraits of Identified Sitters Painted in Antwerp*, 2 vols. (London: Harvey Miller, 1987), 2:180. Vlieghe's opinion is reiterated in *Rubens in Private*, 156, cat. no. 12.

4 With the exception of Rubens and Lipsius, the identification of the sitters depicted in *Self-Portrait in a Circle of Friends at Mantua* varies in the scholarship. For differing interpretations, see Frances Huemer, "Rubens' Portrait of Galileo in the Cologne Group Portrait," *Notes in the History of Art* 24, no. 1 (Fall 2004): 18–25; Hans Vlieghe in Arnauld Brejon de Lavergnée, ed., *Rubens* (Ghent: Snoeck, in association with Palais des Beaux-Arts de Lille, 2004), 36; and Nils Büttner, *Rubens in Private*, 146–47, exh. cat.

Peter Paul Rubens
Portrait of Isabella Brant
c. 1620–25
Oil on panel
53 × 46 cm

The Cleveland Museum of Art
Mr. and Mrs. William H. Marlatt Fund
CMA 1947.207

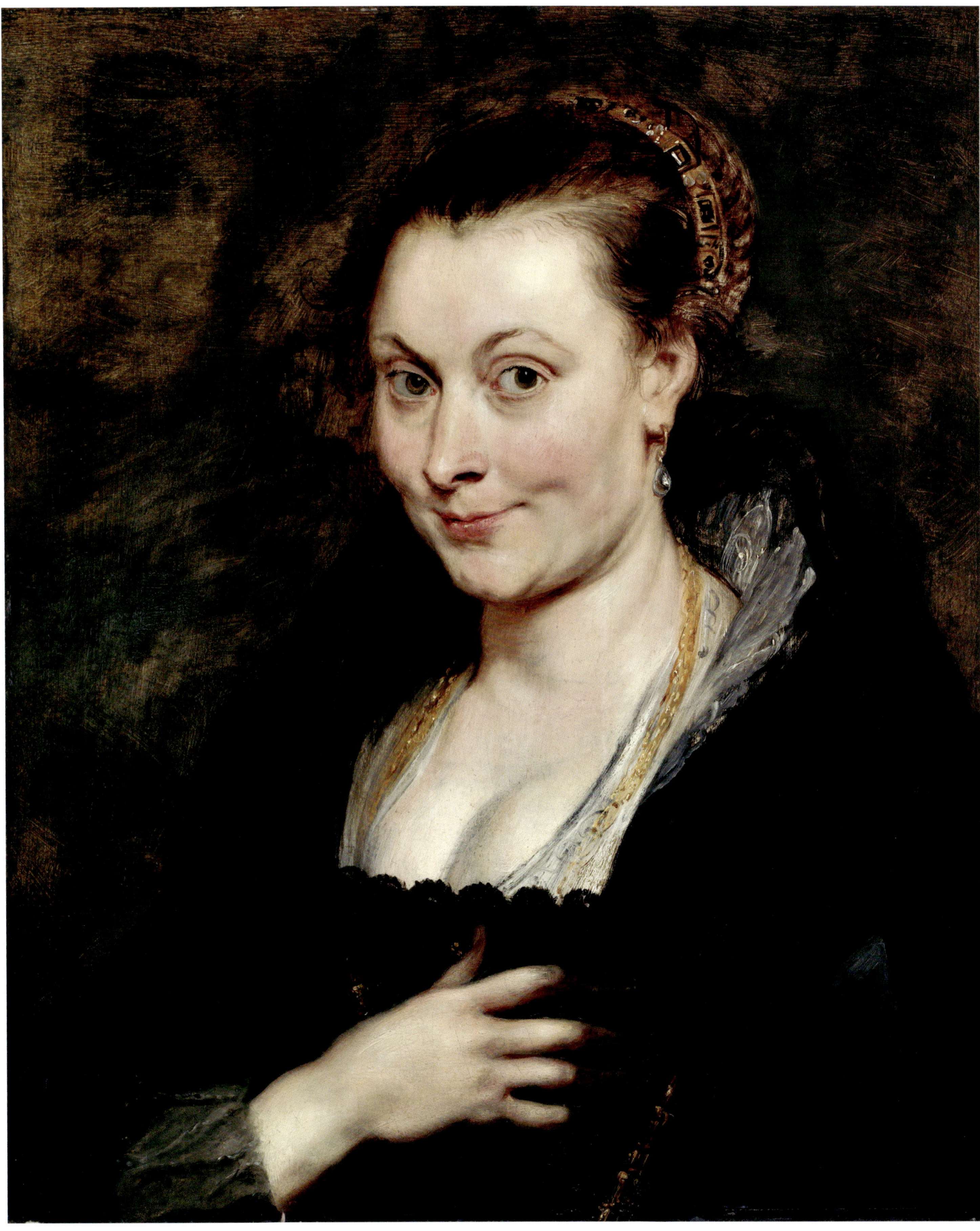

Peter Paul Rubens
Portrait of Isabella Brant

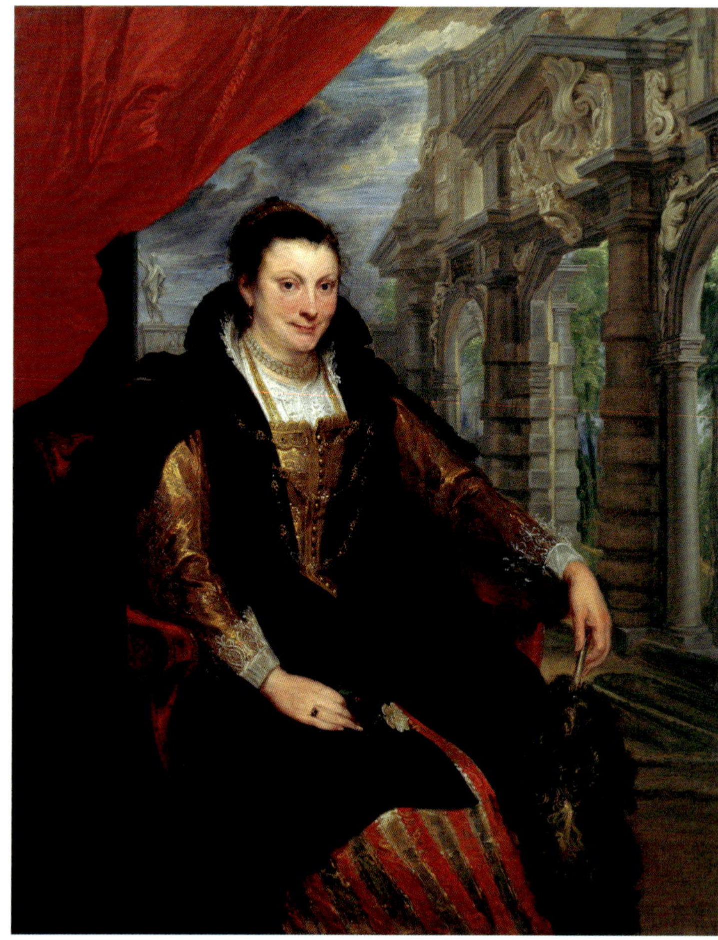

Fig 1 Anthony van Dyck, *Isabella Brant*, 1620–21. Oil on canvas, 153 × 120 cm. National Gallery of Art, Washington, D.C., Andrew W. Mellon Collection. 1937.1.47. Image courtesy National Gallery of Art, Washington, D.C.

Upon the marriage of his brother Philip to Maria de Moy on March 23, 1609, Rubens vowed that he, himself, would "not dare to follow him, for he has made such a good choice that it seems inimitable."[1] In October that same year, just ten days after his prestigious appointment as court painter to the Archdukes Albert and Isabella, he too would be "favored by Venus, the Cupids, Juno, and all the gods."[2] The wedding was held at Saint Michael's Abbey, where his mother had been buried more than a year earlier, and his bride was the eighteen-year-old Isabella Brant—the charismatic young woman depicted in the Cleveland portrait. The eldest daughter of a highly esteemed alderman, municipal clerk, and Humanist scholar, Jan Brant, and Clara de Moy, Isabella was likely well educated and cultured—an ideal match for Rubens. Her identity in the painting is confirmed by Anthony van Dyck's celebrated portrait in Washington, D.C. (fig. 1) and an exquisite drawing *aux trois crayons* at the British Museum (fig. 2).[3]

Intelligence, wit, and joie de vivre radiate from Isabella's confidant gaze and coy smile in the Cleveland portrait. Painterly touches such as the tiny dabs of lead white on her pupils intensify the vibrancy of her alert eyes, while heightened shadows in the hollows of her dimples draw out the playfulness in her expression. The fluidity of the artist's dynamic brushwork further animates the sitter's smiling visage, imbuing the portrait with an air of spontaneity and evoking the momentary. Her accoutrements—the luxurious gold diadem, filigree chain necklace, and pearl-drop earrings—are counterbalanced by a black veil (*huyck*) symbolizing her chastity and modesty.[4] With her voluminous veil wrapped around her shoulders and hand over her breast, Isabella is portrayed as a respectable, demure, and devoted companion.[5] In contrast to Rubens's second wife, Helena Fourment, who often donned the guise of eroticized muse or goddess, Isabella is presented as she is.[6] The frankness in expression and freshness of touch vividly convey the sitter's inner life: the source of the portrait's irresistible charm.

A letter written by Rubens and addressed to the French philosopher Pierre Dupuy can be read as a literary pendant to the portrait. After having given birth to three children—Clara Serena (b. 1609), Albert (b. 1614), and Nicolaas (b. 1618)—Isabella unexpectedly died, on June 20, 1626, at age thirty-five, of the bubonic plague. In the letter, which provides the most detailed account of

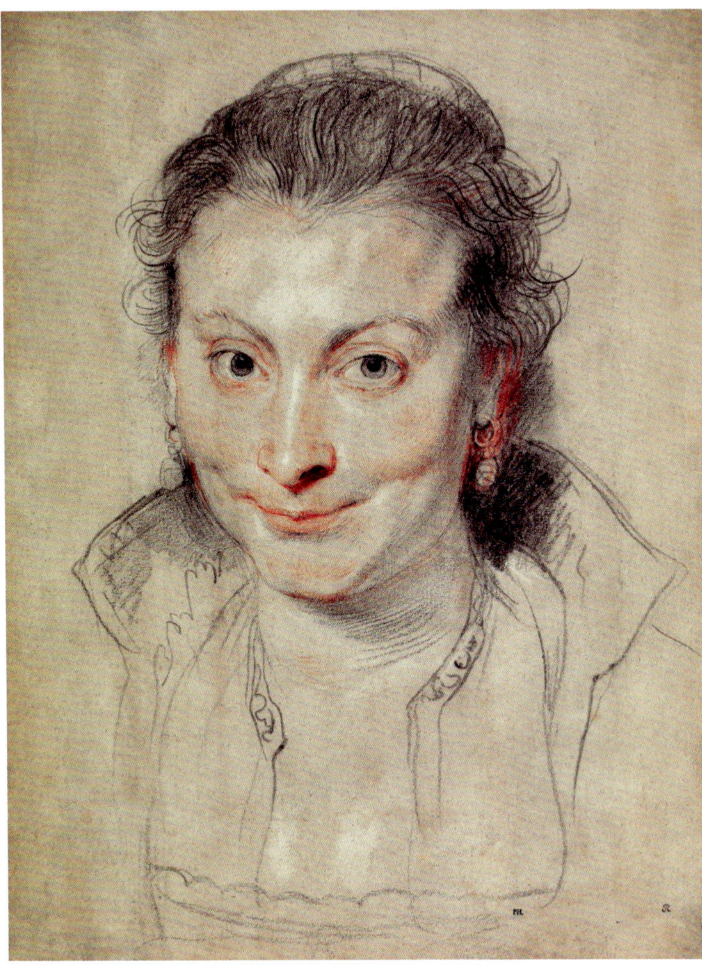

Fig 2 Peter Paul Rubens, *Portrait of Isabella Brant*, c. 1621. Coloured chalks with pale brown wash and white heightening, 38.1 × 29.4 cm. British Museum, London. 1893,0731.21. Photo © The Trustees of the British Museum.

the deceased, Rubens poignantly expressed his sorrow in the following words: "Truly I have lost an excellent companion, whom one could love—indeed had to love, with good reason—as having none of the faults of her sex. She had no capricious moods, and no feminine weaknesses, but was all goodness and honesty . . . I find it very hard to separate grief for this loss from the memory of a person whom I must love and cherish as long as I live."[7] The recourse from "relapses into grief" was travel, and by November of that year, Rubens would increasingly take on the role of fleet-footed artist and international diplomat.

Corrinne Chong

1 Letter from Peter Paul Rubens to Johann Faber, Antwerp, April 10, 1609, in *The Letters of Peter Paul Rubens*, ed. and trans. Ruth Saunders Magurn (Cambridge, MA: Harvard University Press), 52.

2 Rubens to Faber, Antwerp, April 10, 1609, in Magurn, *Letters*, 52.

3 Vlieghe remarks that both the Washington and Cleveland portraits rely on the same set of preliminary sketches by Rubens. The drawing from the British Museum likely belonged to the set and served as the prototype for the abovementioned works, given the pronounced physical resemblances. See Hans Vlieghe, *Corpus Rubenianum Ludwig Burchard, Part XIX: Rubens Portraits of Identified Sitters Painted in Antwerp*, 2 vols. (London: Harvey Miller, 1987), 2:55.

4 Bert Watteeuw, *Rubens in Private: The Master Portrays His Family*, ed. Ben van Beneden (London: Thames & Hudson, 2015), 175, cat. no. 19.

5 Technical imaging revealed that the original painting consisted of three vertical planks of wood with a horizontal member laid across them. These individual components were subsequently glued on to a Masonite panel by the restoration team led by Willian in the 1940s. The inconsistent painting technique and unconvincing execution of Isabella's hand and left arm in the lower part of the composition have led scholars to speculate that the horizontal plank was appended at a later date and overpainted either by Suhr or another artist. See Vlieghe, *Corpus Rubenianum*, 55; Watteeuw, *Rubens in Private*, 166; and Nancy Coe Wixom, *European Paintings of the 16th, 17th, and 18th Centuries*, Cleveland Museum of Art Catalogue of Paintings, Part Three (Ohio: Cleveland Museum of Art, 1982), 24–28.

6 For example, Christopher White interprets Rubens's relationship with Isabella as one founded on "admiration" and, for Helena, "infatuation." See Christopher White, *Peter Paul Rubens: Man and Artist* (New Haven, CT: Yale University Press, 1987), 237–39. This duality is also discussed in Susan Lawson, *Rubens* (London: Chaucer Press, 2006), 80–82.

7 Peter Paul Rubens, letter to Pierre Dupuy, July 14, 1626, in Magurn, *Letters*, 136.

Peter Paul Rubens
Portrait of Jan Woverius
1602
Black, red, and traces of yellow chalk, heightened with white chalk, stumped, brush and brown ink, pen and dark brown ink on brownish paper
29.6 × 24.3 cm

The Albertina Museum, Vienna
8264

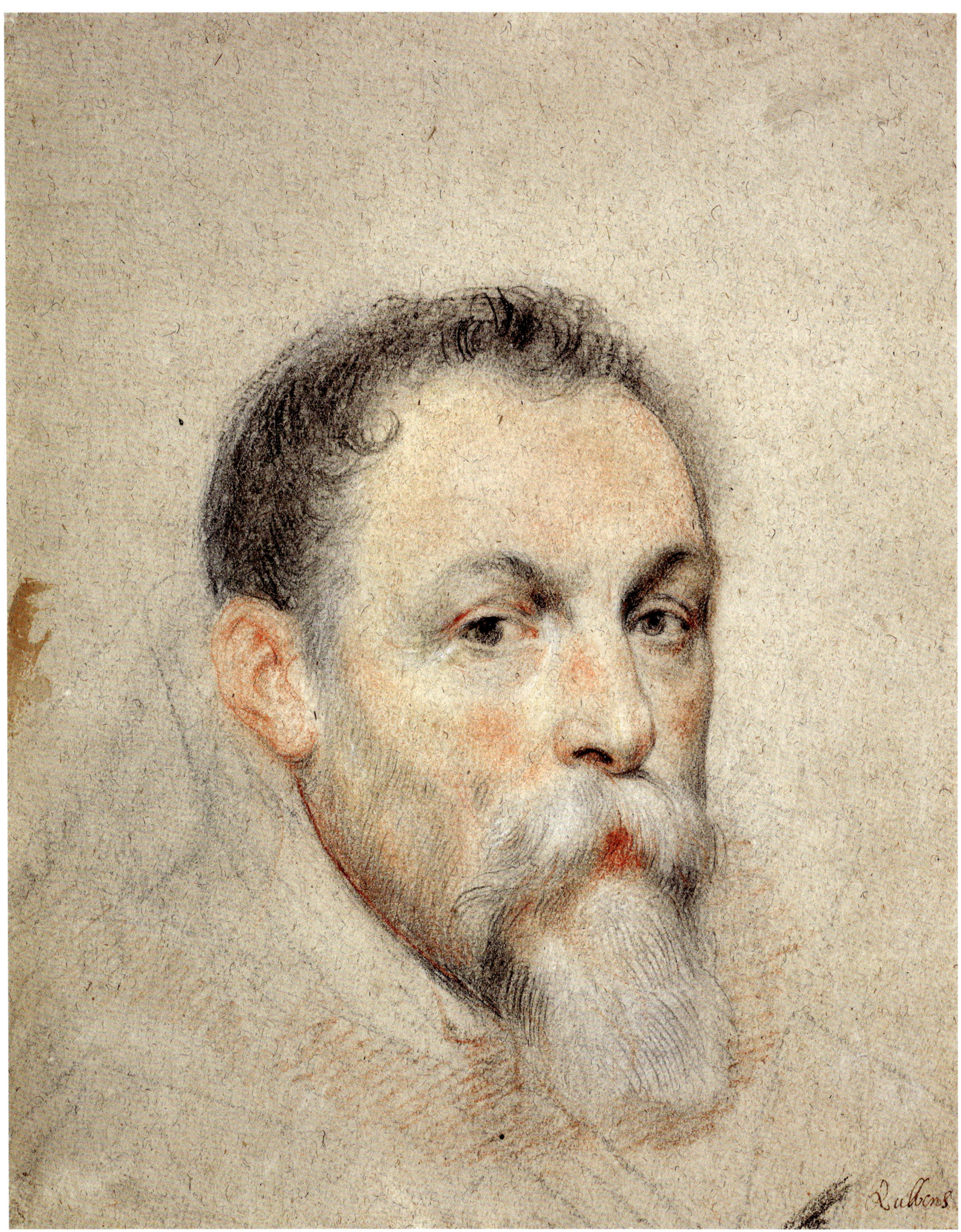
Rubens

Peter Paul Rubens
Portrait of Jan Woverius

This head study is one of two extant portraits by Rubens of his friend Jan van den Wouwere, better known to history by the Latinized "Woverius."[1] Educated by Jesuits before becoming a student of the Neo-Stoic philosopher and professor Justus Lipsius, Woverius became a close friend to fellow Lipsius disciple Philip Rubens and to the artist himself. These four—Peter Paul and Philip Rubens, Lipsius, and Woverius—would be commemorated famously in Rubens's group portrait known as *The Four Philosophers* (page 19).[2] In the painting, executed soon after Philip's death in 1611, the artist depicted himself standing between the open view onto nature and the scholars' table, where Philip and the slightly older Jan Woverius flank their mentor (also deceased by this time), who sits beneath a bust of the Stoic philosopher Seneca.

The present sheet likely documents an actual meeting between three of these "philosophers" that took place in July 1602, when the Rubens brothers travelled from Padua to visit Woverius in Verona. The likeness Rubens took of his friend is surely a single sitting's work, swift and competent in technique. Chalk was used with more regularity as a drawing medium in Italy than in the Low Countries, and Rubens shows here that a year into his Italian sojourn he had begun to master a range of strategies for developing lifelike volume and colour, from stumping and blending colours with his finger to licking the chalk in order to intensify hue. The deepening of shadow in the nostril and eyes with pen and ink may have happened well after the initial rendering. Whether this study was made in preparation for a painted portrait is unclear, but Rubens seems to have kept the drawing with him rather than present it to Woverius.[3]

The following year, Woverius returned home to Antwerp and married Marie Clarisse, the daughter of wealthy silk merchant Rogier Clarisse and Sara Breyel (pages 146–47). While he remained occupied with his study of letters, Woverius entered the political life of Antwerp in the 1610s, holding various judicial posts, as well as the prestigious office of alderman for multiple terms. His success in Antwerp was recognized by the archducal court, where he was appointed to several finance and secretarial posts, before being sent to Spain in 1622 to advocate for an extension of the Twelve Years' Truce.

It is clear that Rubens and Woverius remained close until the latter's death in 1636. Aside from the evidence provided by *The Four Philosophers*, their relationship is confirmed through several book and print projects on which they collaborated or in which they are otherwise named together. In 1615, the Plantin press printed the second edition of Lipsius's edited *Seneca*, for which Woverius contributed an introductory statement on Lipsius's erudition and the value of the volume's commentary; Rubens supplied drawings for engraved illustrations portraying Lipsius and Seneca. That same year, the Plantin press issued a volume of Philip Rubens's letters, poems, and discoveries, together with elegies by members of his Humanist circle, to which, again, Woverius contributed text and Rubens a drawing of his brother, to be engraved for publication.[4] Around 1616, Cornelis Galle published his engraving after Rubens's lost *Judith and Holofernes*, which included the statement that "mindful of his promise made long ago in Verona" Rubens dedicates this print to Woverius.[5] Finally, Paulus Pontius's engraved profile portrait of Christ (c. 1633) bears an elaborate inscription confirming that the engraving, after a drawing by Rubens, reproduces a panel that once was a cherished devotional image owned by Saint Ignatius Loyola in Rome, and furthermore, that the panel had come into the hands of Jan Woverius, who donated it to the chapel of Our Lady in Halle, near Brussels.[6] The inscription not only broadcast Woverius's generosity but also described the bringing together of two very special images—Ignatius's portrait of Christ and the miraculous statue of the Virgin at Halle, for whose sake Lipsius, many years before, had been mocked by Protestants, an incident about which Woverius had published an impassioned defence of this beloved teacher.[7]

Kirk Nickel

1 For a biographical sketch, see *Nationaal Biografisch woordenboek*, vol. 13 (Brussels: Paleis der Academiën, 1992), s.v. "Wouwere."

2 Hans Vlieghe, *Corpus Rubenianum Ludwig Burchard, XIX, pt. 2: Portraits of Identified Sitters Painted in Antwerp*. (London: Harvey Miller, 1987), 128–32, no. 117.

3 The "Rubbens" annotation connects the sheet to other drawings that remained together in Rubens's possession. See Anne-Marie S. Logan and Michiel C. Plomp, *Peter Paul Rubens: The Drawings* (New York: Metropolitan Museum of Art; New Haven, CT: Yale University Press, 2005), 86, exh. cat. no. 11.

4 On this volume, see J. Richard Judson and Carl van de Velde, *Corpus Rubenianum Ludwig Burchard, XXI: Book Illustrations and Title Pages*, 2 vols. (London: Harvey Miller and Heydon & Son, 1978), 1:151–54, no. 29.

5 The dedication lines read: *Clariss(im)o et amicissimo viro D. IOANNI WOVERIO paginam hanc auspicalem primumque suoram operum / typis aeneis expressum PETRVS PAVLLVS RVBENIVS promissi iam olim Veronae à se facti memor DAT DICAT.*

6 For this image of Christ, the print's inscription, and an outline of its content, see Hans Vlieghe, *Corpus Rubenianum Ludwig Burchard, VIII: Saints*, 2 vols. (Brussels: Arcade Press, 1972), 1:28–31, no. 2.

7 Mark P.O. Morford, *Stoics and Neostoics: Rubens and the Circle of Lipsius* (Princeton, NJ: Princeton University Press, 1991), 44n112.

Peter Paul Rubens
Portrait of Paracelsus
c. 1615–20
Oil on panel
77.5 × 54.5 cm

Royal Museums of Fine Arts of Belgium
3425

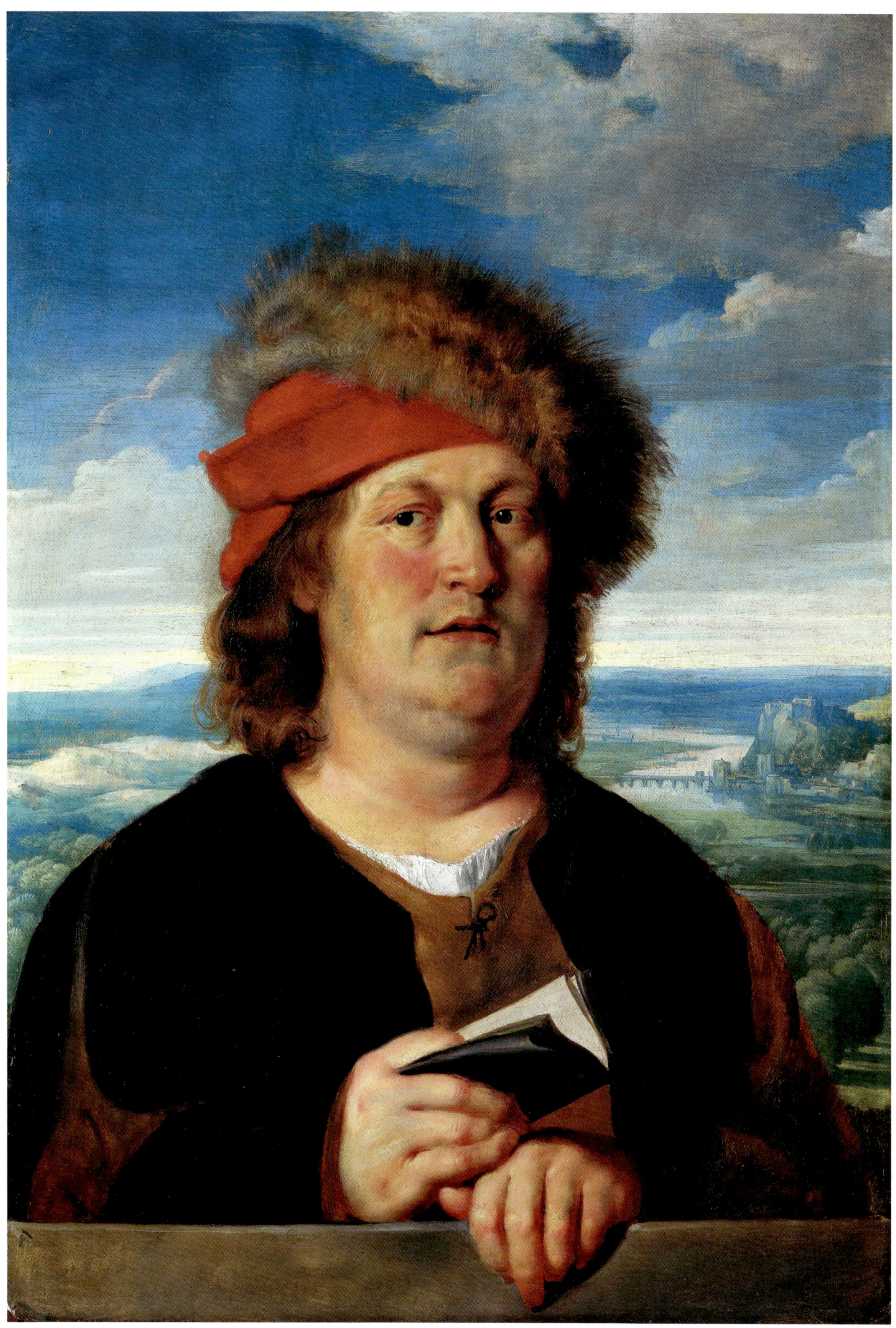

Peter Paul Rubens
Portrait of Paracelsus

The Swiss-born Paracelsus was a physician, alchemist, and prognosticator. He was also a wide-ranging thinker in the realm of natural philosophy, with a strong inclination toward explanations of natural phenomena grounded in sympathetic magic. Well known in his lifetime, Paracelsus became a rallying figure for later sixteenth-century mystics and hermetic philosophers, especially in Northern Europe. Rubens's portrait bears no inscriptions, but contemporary evidence supports the sitter's identification as Paracelsus. Multiple seventeenth-century copies of Rubens's picture are inscribed with Paracelsus's name or the Latin mottos associated with him, and a 1635 inventory that includes works from the Duke of Buckingham's collection lists a "Rubens, The Picture of Paracelsus."[1]

Portrait of Paracelsus is an intriguing mixture of artistic ambition and civic retrospection. Based on Rubens's brushwork, his handling of highlights, and the aggressively modulated skin tones, the painting can be plausibly dated to the latter half of the 1610s.[2] The overall scheme of the composition, however, has nothing to do with contemporary portrait painting in the Netherlands. The arrangement of the sitter behind a parapet is a compositional device common in portraits of the early 1500s, and the landscape tones that move from green near the viewer to a monochromatic blue at the horizon is also consistent with pictorial techniques of that time.

Rubens is known to have painted versions of portraits by artists many generations older than himself, and the artistic anachronisms in *Paracelsus* suggest that it was based on an actual painting from the early 1500s.[3] A painting with this composition appears in Willem van Haecht's *The Picture Gallery of Cornelis van der Geest* from 1628, although whether it is Rubens's painting, its prototype, or another copy is not clear. Van der Geest championed the paintings of Quentin Massys, who many art aficionados in Antwerp considered the founder of the local school of painting,[4] and this has bolstered an argument for imagining Rubens's prototype to have been a portrait by Massys. However, the landscape details in Rubens's painting led Larry Silver to suggest that the posited model was likely by an artist close to Joos van Cleve, an important contemporary of Massys.[5] Whoever painted the work Rubens copied, it is almost certain he understood the portrait to have been painted by an artist active in Antwerp a century before, at the dawn of a golden era in the city's history, when Antwerp became the most active art exporter in the world.

Why Rubens chose to portray Paracelsus is not obvious. Certainly, Rubens's version of the older portrait was an act of artistic emulation, and he may have appreciated the distinctive sitter as material for a creative head study to be reused in other contexts. Neither motivation excludes the other, and it is even possible that Rubens held a genuine interest in Paracelsus's ideas. Rubens was fascinated by systems of knowledge, rational and mystical, and he may have been introduced to Paracelsian theories by his former master, Otto van Veen.[6] And it is striking how comfortable Paracelsus was with couching his thoughts on natural processes in the terms of artistic creation, particularly when addressing the "Sign," his term for an external form that accurately expresses internal qualities:

> Nature does not practice her art like a painter, who produces an image and gives it no Sign, and indeed can give it none. For there is nothing in the picture, and so it has no Sign; it is like a shadow with no quality in it. However, those craftsmen who are skillful do something similar to Nature when they make an image [i.e., sculpture] . . . their art does proceed from the Maker of animate images. And the more the craftsman wishes to make accomplished images, the more he must discern the Sign.[7]

Paracelsus's description of nature crosses into artistic conversations about the relative merits of painting and sculpture and the ability of artists to convey mental and emotional states through a body's external disposition. Rubens was highly invested in both of these artistic preoccupations. It is tantalizing to imagine that in his reportrayal of the Swiss physician, Rubens may have actively sought to devise a Sign so attuned to Paracelsus's internal quality that painting's flat "shadow" might rise to the expressive potential that Paracelsus himself reserved for three-dimensional sculpture.

Kirk Nickel

1 Joost vander Auwera and Sabine van Sprang, eds., *Rubens: A Genius at Work* (Tielt: Lannoo, 2007), 79–80, exh. cat.

2 Vander Auwera and Van Sprang, *Rubens*, 80.

3 Kristin Lohse Belkin, *Corpus Rubenianum Ludwig Burchard, Part XXVI: Copies and Adaptations from Renaissance and Later Artists; German and Netherlandish Artists*, 2 vols. (London: Harvey Miller, 2009), 1:234–38.

4 Larry Silver, *The Paintings of Quentin Massys, with Catalogue Raisonné* (Montclair, NJ: Allanheld & Schram, 1984), 2.

5 Silver, *The Paintings of Quentin Massys*, 242, supp. E.

6 Tine Meganck, "Rubens on the Human Figure: Theory, Practice, and Metaphysics," in Joost and Van Sprang, *Rubens: A Genius at Work*, 52–64, esp. 57.

7 See this translation and further discussion in Michael Baxandall, *The Limewood Sculptors of Renaissance Germany* (New Haven, CT: Yale University Press, 1981), 161.

Peter Paul Rubens
Portrait of Michael Ophovius
1615–17
Oil on canvas
111.5 cm × 82.5 cm

Mauritshuis, the Hague
252
Photography: Margareta Svensson

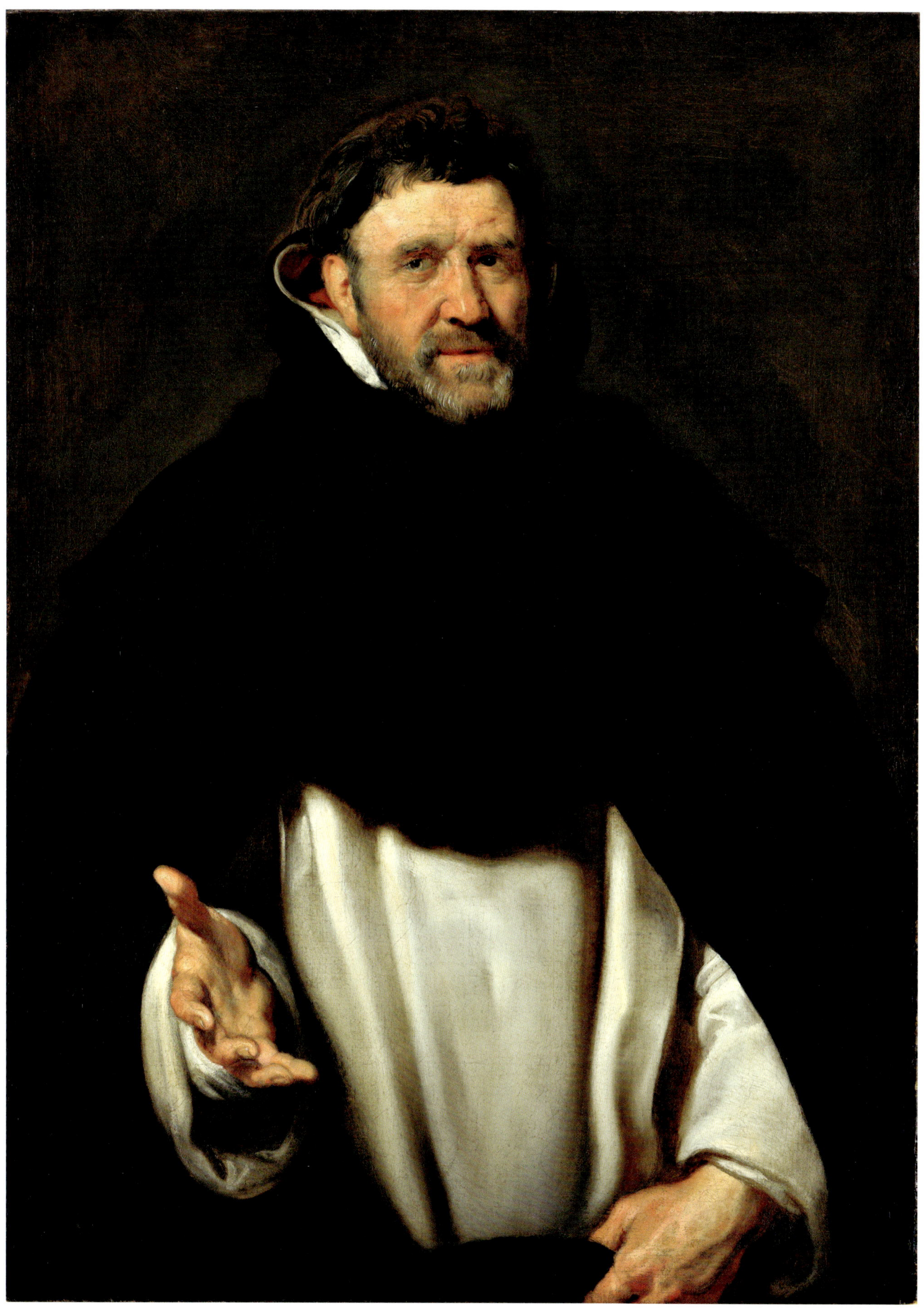

Peter Paul Rubens
Portrait of Michael Ophovius

Rubens's arresting portrait of his friend and purported confessor commands the beholder's attention. Depicted in the austere black and white habit of the Dominican order, Ophovius addresses the audience directly through his penetrating gaze, parted lips (as if in mid-speech), and the powerful thrust of his extended hand: the locus of the painting's drama. These details typify traditional representations of preachers in liturgical portraits and orators in secular images,[1] but more importantly, they exemplify Rubens's synthesis of Italian and Northern conventions. To illustrate, Ophovius's rhetorical hand gesture—the most expressive and dynamic element in the painting—draws on Renaissance representations of learned men, while the extreme foreshortening recalls precedents in early sixteenth-century Netherlandish art.[2] To express the sitter's inner life, Rubens highlights Ophovius's concentrated brow; the sculptural articulation of the drapery enhances his physical presence. Rubens's choice of an extended three-quarter length composition also imparts added weight and monumentality.

The portrait's plastic qualities are consistent with the artist's early style and date the painting to around 1615–1617, but much contention surrounds its origins. While some authors believe that the present portrait is the one that originally hung in the Dominican monastery in Antwerp, others argue that it is one of several replicas executed by Rubens's studio.[3] The question of the Mauritshuis painting's authenticity is also compounded by the existence of an almost identical variant at the Rubenshuis. But as Hans Vlieghe astutely concludes from his observation of the closed mouth in the latter, "The omission of this subtle detail, which so well fits the argumentative and didactic pose of the Dominican prior, can only be explained as a copyist's typical mistake."[4]

The son of a cloth merchant, Michael Ophovius was born in Den Bosch ('s-Hertogenbosch) in 1570, and at the age of fifteen, entered the Dominican order in Antwerp at Saint Paul's. In 1590, his formidable intellectual gifts led him to the universities of Louvain and Bologna, where he taught philosophy and studied theology. A year after he was granted the degree of magister, he was promoted from prior to provincial in 1611 and appointed prefect of a Dominican mission in 1615. Recognized for his fervent Catholicism and militant character, he became a confidential envoy for the Archduchess Isabella. During a diplomatic mission in 1623, he was arrested and held captive at The Hague for twenty-one months for bribing the commandant of Heusen to surrender the fortress town. On his release, Ophovius was ordained bishop of Den Bosch, prompting Rubens to remark, "He has done well to exchange bonds [chains] for the miter."[5] After failed peace talks with Frederik Hendrik during the siege of Den Bosch in 1629, Ophovius went into exile and spent his remaining years in Lier and Antwerp.

One can posit that the artist felt an immediate kinship with Ophovius in the devotional, diplomatic, and intellectual spheres. Both men were devout Catholics, indefatigable peacemakers, and lifelong scholars. The extent of their relations is illuminated by a diary entry of February 4, 1631, in which Ophovius recounts that he had met with Rubens to discuss the design of his funerary tomb (presently at Saint Paul's Church, Antwerp).[6] When Ophovius assumed the role of prior in 1608, he spearheaded an ambitious campaign to redecorate the Saint Paul's. Under Ophovius's auspices, Rubens carried out several high-profile commissions for the church, including *The Adoration of the Shepherds, The Real Presence in the Holy Sacrament,* and *Saint Dominic and Saint Francis Protecting the World from the Wrath of God.* Although evidence of Ophovius's role as the artist's confessor is scant, there is no doubt that Rubens's growing fame as the foremost painter of the Counter-Reformation was indebted to the infamous bishop's patronage.[7]

Corrinne Chong

1 See Marjorie E. Wieseman in Peter C. Sutton, ed., *The Age of Rubens* (Boston: Museum of Fine Arts, 1993), 279, cat. no. 23.

2 Hans Vlieghe, *Corpus Rubenianum Ludwig Burchard, Part XIX: Portraits of Identified Sitters Painted in Antwerp*, 2 vols. (London: Harvey Miller, 1987), 2:141.

3 For example, in their coauthored catalogue entry (cat. no. 52), Ben Broos and Hans Vlieghe identify the Mauritshuis portrait as the original, but in his individual entry (cat. no. 126) for the *Corpus Rubenianum*, Vlieghe casts doubt on the painting's origins. The latter point of view is also shared by Marjorie E. Wieseman. See Ben Broos and Ariane van Suchtelen, introduction to *Portraits in the Mauritshuis*, 1430–1790, ed. Rudy Ekkart (Zwolle: Waanders, 2004), 234.

4 Vlieghe, *Corpus Rubenianum*, 142.

5 Letter from Rubens to Pierre Dupuy, Antwerp, September 17, 1626, in *The Letters of Peter Paul Rubens*, ed. and trans. Ruth Saunders Magurn (Cambridge, MA: Harvard University Press, 1971), 142.

6 Cynthia Lawrence, "Rubens and the Ophovius Monument: A New Sculpture by Hans van Mildert," *Burlington Magazine* 29, no. 1014 (September 1987): 584. For a preliminary version of the previous article, see Cynthia Lawrence, "A New Source for Van Mildert's Effigy," *Notes in the History of Art* 5, no. 2 (Winter 1986): 28–31.

7 The earliest and most convincing evidence lies in an inscription at the bottom of an engraving of the portrait made by Nicholas van den Bergh in the eighteenth century. The inscription reads: P:P Rubenij Confessarius. See Broos and Vlieghe, *Portraits in the Mauritshuis*, 234.

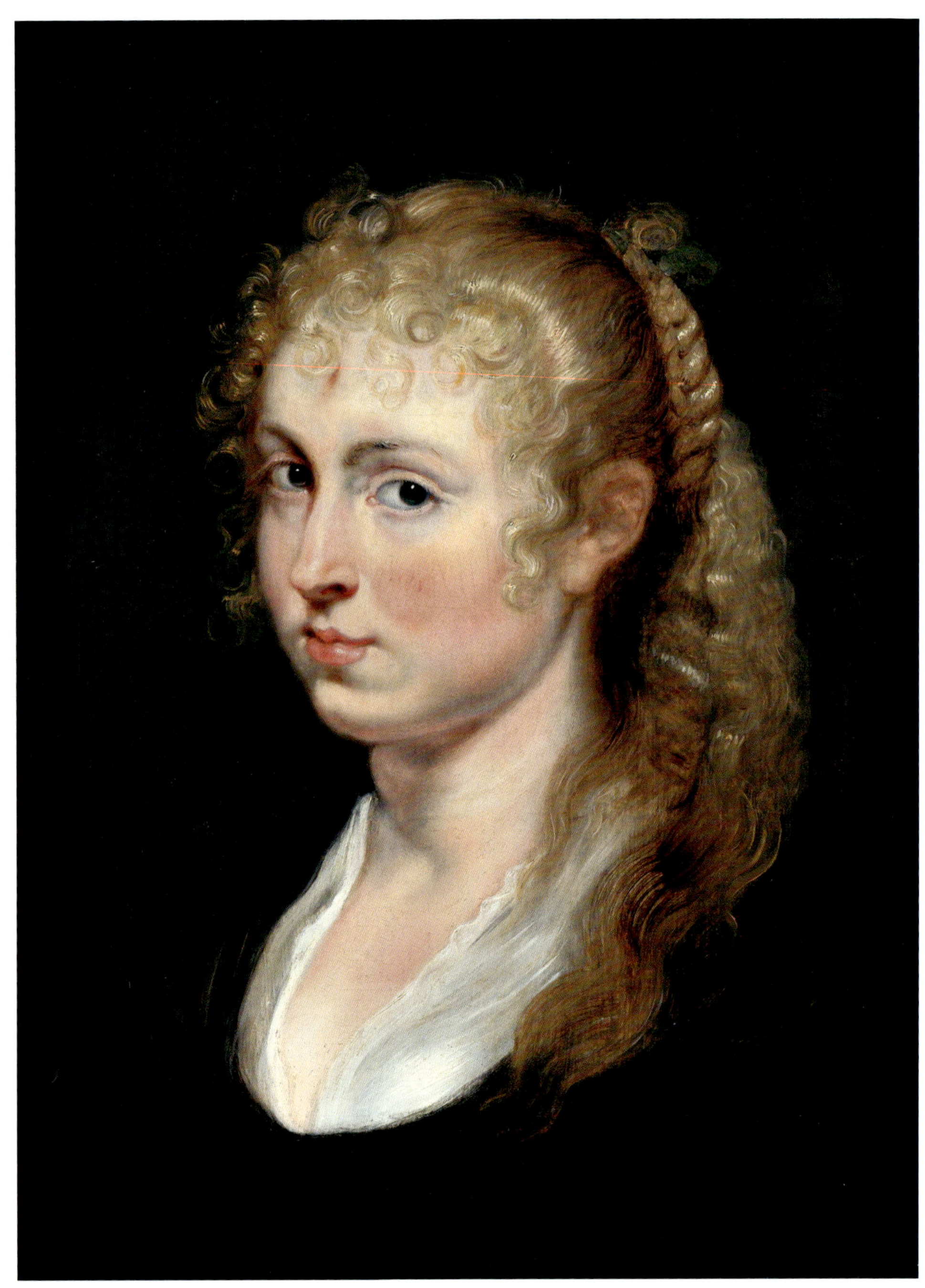

Peter Paul Rubens
Young Woman with Curly Hair
c. 1618–20
Oil on panel
43.3 × 33.5 cm
enlarged to 67.0 × 52.4 cm

Hammer Museum, Los Angeles
The Armand Hammer Collection,
gift of the Armand Hammer Foundation
A.H.C. no. 80,005

Peter Paul Rubens
Young Woman with Curly Hair

This charming rendering of a young woman points to the difficulty of categories such as "portrait" and "head study" when considering Rubens's bust-length pictures of individual figures. The slight tension in the turn of her head and the lively expression in her eyes make it easy to imagine that such a woman was part of Rubens's Antwerp milieu, and, indeed, his close attention to the light reflecting off her curling blonde hair and to her warm, glowing complexion suggest the painting was made in the presence of a live model. Yet no credible identity has been attached to this likeness, and that the image is so entirely devoted to recording a type of perfection of flesh and hair weighs in favour of the panel's status as a document of physical traits for future reference by Rubens and his workshop.[1] This is further supported by the tightly cropped appearance of the original panel (now enlarged), which extends from a few centimetres above the hair to just below the neckline of the sitter's dress.[2]

Rubens's production of head studies was limited largely to the 1610s.[3] Certainly, Rubens understood that his rapidly expanding workshop would benefit from physiognomic models that could both speed the production of paintings and provide standard points of reference for his many assistants and collaborators. The near absence of head studies made by Rubens after about 1620 is more difficult to explain. There may have been a feeling that the existing models (and the many copies made by pupils) were sufficient, although in these later years Rubens also turned toward projects that placed increasing emphasis on allegory and poetic allusion, where closely observed physiognomy may have seemed less necessary. Julius S. Held proposed to date the Hammer picture to the latter years of Rubens's consistent production of head studies, around 1618–1620, and this suggestion has not been seriously challenged. Still, even considering *Young Woman with Curly Hair* as a relatively late head study, it remains curious that this young woman's features do not seem to have been incorporated into any known painting by Rubens or his workshop.[4]

Despite apparently never having been used as the model for a head in one of Rubens's larger narrative scenes, the work was admired throughout the seventeenth and eighteenth centuries. Half a dozen painted copies of the head exist.[5] Perhaps the best of these—in the collection of the Museumslandschaft Hessen Kassel—is also the earliest. It shows the young woman to the bottom of her neckline, where the original panel also ended. The Hammer picture was subsequently trimmed slightly and fitted into an oval panel that was later pieced out to create its present form. The other five copies were all made after the *Young Woman with Curly Hair* in its present appearance.[6]

Kirk Nickel

1 For the proposed, and rejected, identities ascribed to the panel, see Julius S. Held, *The Oil Sketches of Peter Paul Rubens: A Critical Catalogue*, 2 vols. (Princeton, NJ: Princeton University Press, 1980), 1:613.

2 On the changes to the panel over its lifetime, see Armand Hammer Foundation, *The Armand Hammer Collection* (Los Angeles: Armand Hammer Foundation, 1985), 31, exh. cat. no. 9.

3 Held, *The Oil Sketches*, 597–99, provides an overview of Rubens's production and use of head studies, as well as of the critical concerns regarding their categorization.

4 Held, 613, put forward the Berlin *Perseus and Andromeda* as a possible reappearance of the Hammer study's model. In my opinion, Andromeda's head is rendered too summarily to claim a significant connection between the two paintings.

5 Held, 613–14.

6 Kenneth Donahue's entry in *The Armand Hammer Collection*, 31, exh. cat. no. 9, provides additional commentary on these copies not present in Held's list of copies.

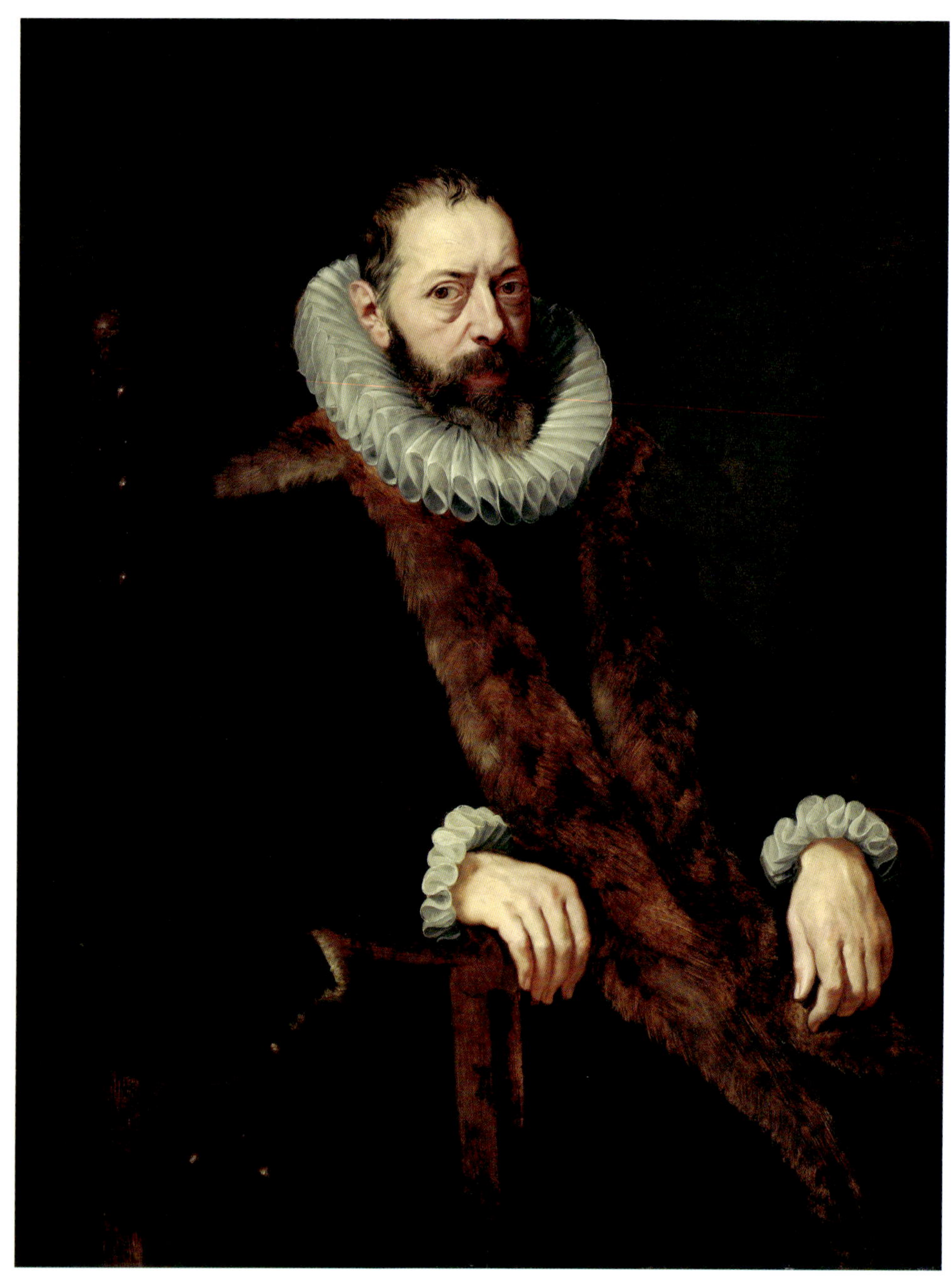

Peter Paul Rubens
Portrait of Rogier Clarisse
c. 1611
Oil on panel
118.1 × 90.8 cm

Fine Arts Museums of San Francisco, California
Roscoe and Margaret Oakes Collection
53.12

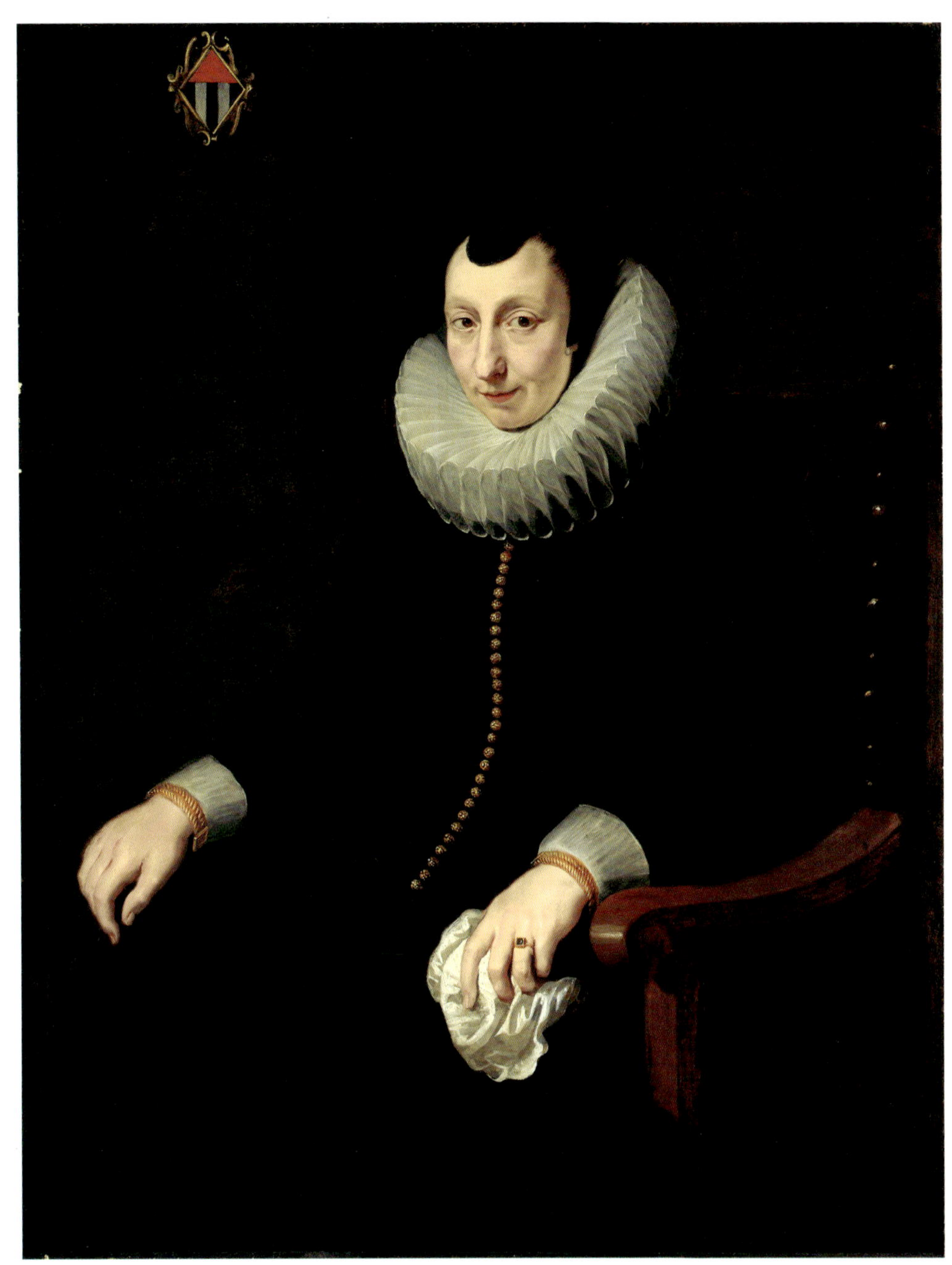

Peter Paul Rubens
Portrait of Sara Breyel
c. 1611
Oil on panel
118.1 × 91.9 cm

Fine Arts Museum of San Francisco, California
Gift of Ben N. Maltz
60.27

Peter Paul Rubens
Portrait of Rogier Clarisse

Peter Paul Rubens
Portrait of Sara Breyel

Rubens's pendant images of Rogier Clarisse and Sara Breyel are a study in restrained display. Seated in minimally adorned Spanish-style chairs against an unarticulated background, the couple present themselves in austere black wool and starched linen collars and cuffs, conservative in taste. The crumpled handkerchief in Sara Breyel's left hand is an oblique reference to the source of the family's immense wealth, earned from their trading in silk, which otherwise appears in subtle elements such as the thin line of gold buttons that close Breyel's dress, the bracelets that peek out from under her cuffs, and in Rogier's fur-trimmed cloak. In this last detail, Rubens took the opportunity to display his own skill through reduced means. Clarisse's richly textured collar is a remarkable passage of thin, loosely scattered brush marks that play over the visible ground layer to create a scintillating effect of light reflected through dense fur.

Excepting official likenesses of monarchs and Rubens's self-portraits with his wives, portrayals of married couples are relatively rare in the master's oeuvre. The notable instances tend to be couples with whom Rubens was familiar, such as the portrait of *The Family of Jan Brueghel the Elder* or Nicolaas Rockox and Adriana Perez, depicted on the Rockox epitaph (also known as *The Incredulity of St. Thomas*).[1] While the names Clarisse and Breyel do not figure as prominently in accounts of Rubens's Antwerp milieu as do Brueghel or Rockox, it is likely that the artist knew the couple quite well. Their daughter, Marie, was the wife of Jan Woverius (page 133), a close friend of Rubens. And their son, Louis, was a patron, contributing to the Guild of the Harquebusiers in 1611 to help fund Rubens's altarpiece *The Descent from the Cross*.[2] Around 1614, Louis commissioned Rubens to paint *The Flagellation of Christ*, part of a Rosary cycle meant to repristinate the side chapels in the Dominican church of Saint Paul's in Antwerp.[3] Rubens maintained a connection with the family throughout the decade. Among the first reproductive engravings that Rubens published in 1620 was a *Saint Francis Receiving the Stigmata* that bears a dedication to Louis Clarisse and his brother Rogier. Not long after, Lucas Vorsterman I executed an engraving after Rubens's *The Holy Women at the Grave*, dedicated to the wives of Louis and Rogier, Marie Noirot and Madeleine De Schotte.[4]

The Clarisse family had roots in Lille, but the elder Rogier's father, Louis, moved the family's silk-trading concern to Antwerp in the mid-sixteenth century.[5] Louis's success and his commitment to his new city were confirmed with the funerary epitaph that he and his wife, Marie le Batteur, installed over their tomb in Antwerp Cathedral. It portrayed husband and wife on wing panels (figs. 1, 2) that flanked an *Adoration of the Magi* attributed to Cornelis van Cleve.[6] For a viewer familiar with the Clarisse–Le Batteur epitaph, Rubens's portraits of Rogier Clarisse and Sara Breyel might seem a domestic version of that earlier monument, Rogier's appearance and even his address to the viewer is so similar to that of his father's donor portrait.

When, around 1611, Clarisse and Breyel commissioned their portraits from Rubens, the family had already begun to leverage its wealth to solidify a more prominent position in Antwerp society and in the eyes of the Spanish Crown. In 1608, the younger Louis Clarisse had purchased the castle and title of Dilbeek, near the archducal court at Brussels.[7] In 1614, Rogier Clarisse, our sitter, obtained a positive response from the archdukes to a petition for a coat of arms. This petition would have been granted on the basis of Clarisse's pure bloodlines and exemplary life, but it was surely aided by his support of the Capuchins, a reformed branch of the Franciscans favoured by the archdukes.[8] In his petition, Clarisse mentioned that his family had given a substantial donation to the Capuchins for the construction of a new monastery, ultimately erected in nearby Lier in 1628. Clarisse died in 1622, having secured the position of senator but not yet having taken office, and was buried in the Capuchin monastery in Antwerp, where Breyel would join him in 1635.[9]

By the twentieth century, the sitters' identities had been lost, until Michael Jaffé proposed Rogier Clarisse as the male sitter on the basis of a coat of arms added to his portrait, presumably in the mid-seventeenth century, and subsequently removed as part of a cleaning that took place shortly before the painting entered the collection of the M.H. de Young Museum.[10] The identification of Clarisse was soon confirmed with Jaffé's subsequent identification of the pendent portrait, its sitter identifiable as Sara Breyel with the aid of the Breyel family arms and the date 1611 painted in its upper left corner.[11] While not painted by Rubens, the Breyel arms and date were left intact during a 1959 restoration, as they were judged to be contemporary to the portrait itself.[12]

Kirk Nickel

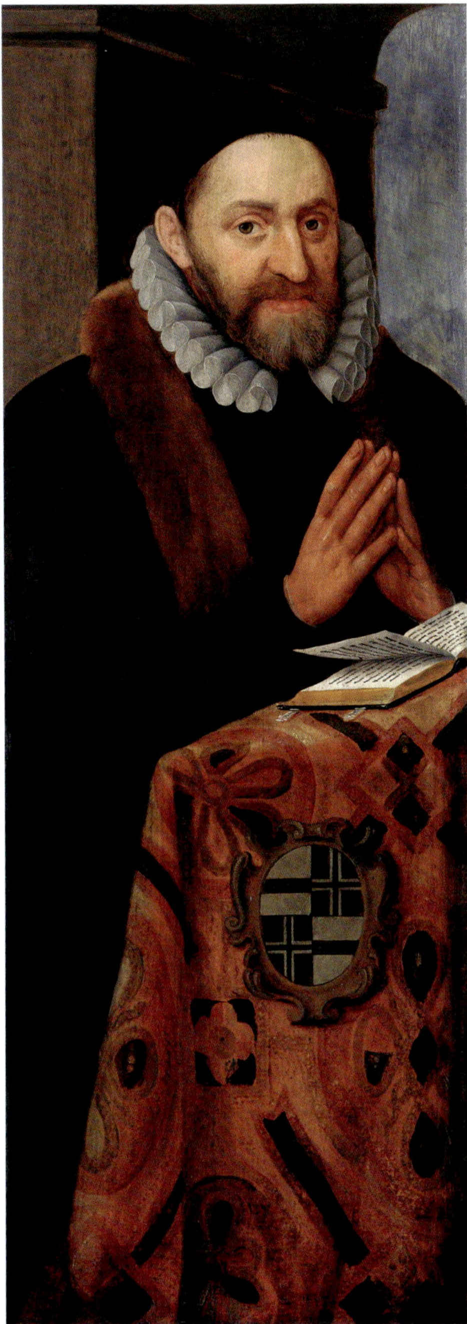

Fig 1 Abraham van Rijcke, *Portrait of Lodewijk Clarys (Louis Clarisse)*, last quarter of the sixteenth century. Oil on panel, 37.0 × 101.0 cm. Royal Museum of Fine Arts Antwerp.

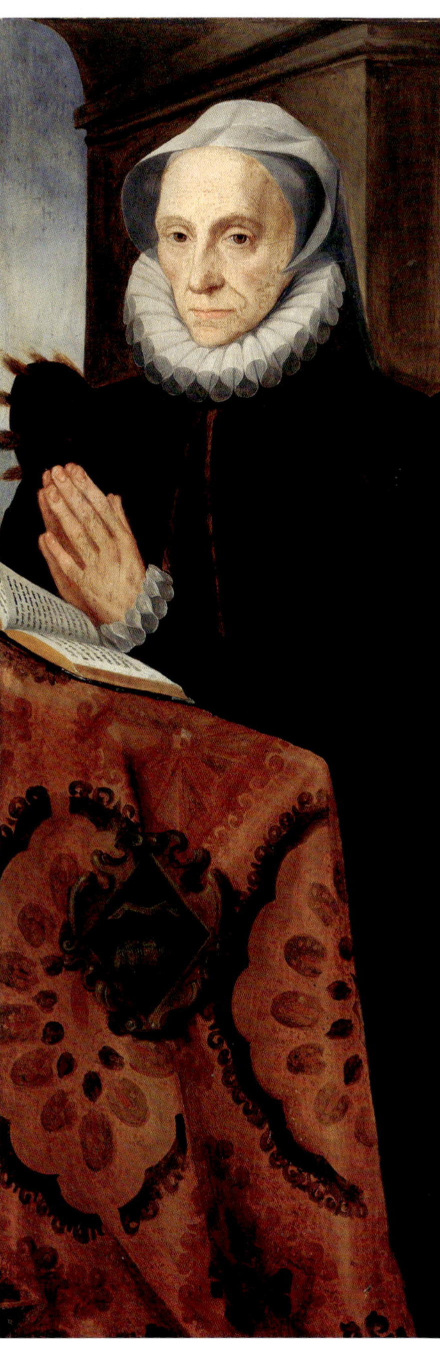

Fig 2 Abraham van Rijcke, *Portrait of Marie le Batteur*, last quarter of the sixteenth century. Oil on panel, 37.0 × 101.0 cm. Royal Museum of Fine Arts Antwerp.

1 Michael Jaffé first dated the portrait of Rogier Clarisse to "1612–1615" based on its stylistic affinities with the portrait of Rockox in the latter's epitaph. See Michael Jaffé, "Rubens' Portrait of Rogier Clarisse," *Burlington Magazine* 95, no. 609 (December 1953): 388.

2 J. Richard Judson, *Corpus Rubenianum Ludwig Burchard, Part VI: The Passion of Christ* (Antwerp: Harvey Miller, 2000), 27.

3 Judson, 59–62.

4 The *Saint Francis Receiving the Stigmata* is among the engravings mentioned in the famous letter to Pieter van Veen in January 1619, Rubens's first proclamation of his desire to publish prints after his paintings. For these two engravings and transcriptions of their dedications, see D. de Hoop Scheffer, *Hollstein, Dutch and Flemish Etchings, Engravings and Woodcuts, 1450–1700*, vol. 43, *Lucas Vorsterman I* (Roosendaal: Koninklijke van Pool in cooperation with the Rijksprentenkabinet, 1993), nos. 3 and 71 respectively.

5 For a biographical sketch of the Clarisse family and further bibliography, see Michael Jaffé, "Rubens' Portrait of Rogier Clarisse," 387–90.

6 Théodore van Lerius, *Notice sur le catalogue du Musée d'Anvers* (Ghent: L. Hebbelynck, 1851), 86, transcribes the inscription on the Clarisse–Le Batteur tomb. For the central panel of the *Adoration*, see, most recently, Hildegard van de Velde and Nico van Hout, *Het Gulden Cabinet: Koninklijk Museum bij Rockox te gast* (Antwerp: VZW Museum Nicolaas Rockox and KMSKA, 2013), 24.

7 Alphonse Wauters, *Histoire des environs de Bruxelles* (Brussels: Typographie de Ch. Vanderauwera, 1855), 1:191.

8 J. Theod. de Raadt, "Nederlandsche en andere oudheden: De heerlijkheden van het Land van Mechelen; Niel en zijne heeren," *Dietsche Warande* 2, no. 2 (1889): 401–2.

9 For the inscription on the couple's tomb, see de Raadt, 402.

10 See Jaffé, "Rubens' Portrait of Rogier Clarisse," which reproduces the now-removed coat of arms as figure 17.

11 Michael Jaffé, "The Companion to Rubens' 'Portrait of Rogier Clarisse,'" *Burlington Magazine* 103, no. 694 (January 1961): 2, 4–6.

12 Curatorial file, Fine Arts Museums of San Francisco.

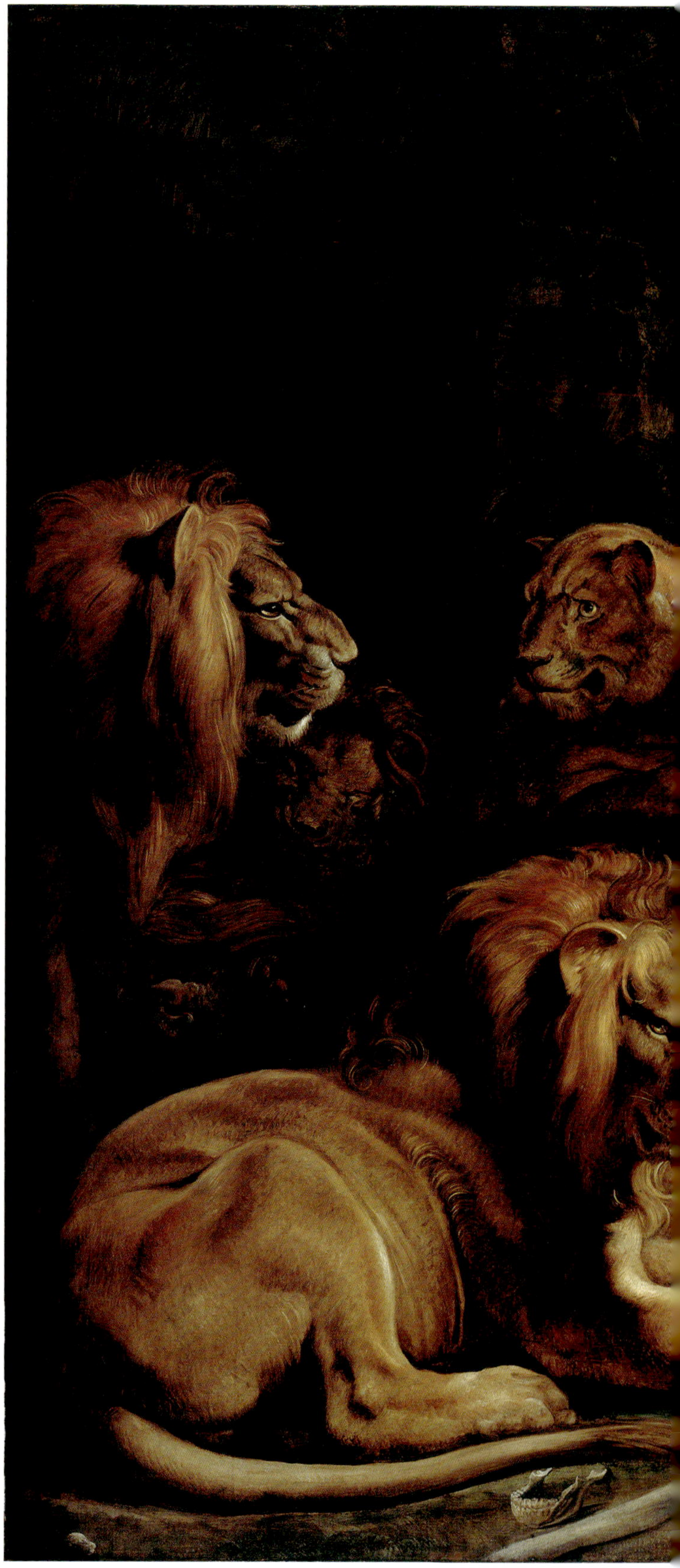

Peter Paul Rubens
Daniel in the Lions' Den
c. 1614–16
Oil on canvas
224.2 × 330.5 cm

National Gallery of Art, Washington, D.C.
Ailsa Mellon Bruce Fund
1965.13.1
Image courtesy National Gallery of Art, Washington D.C.

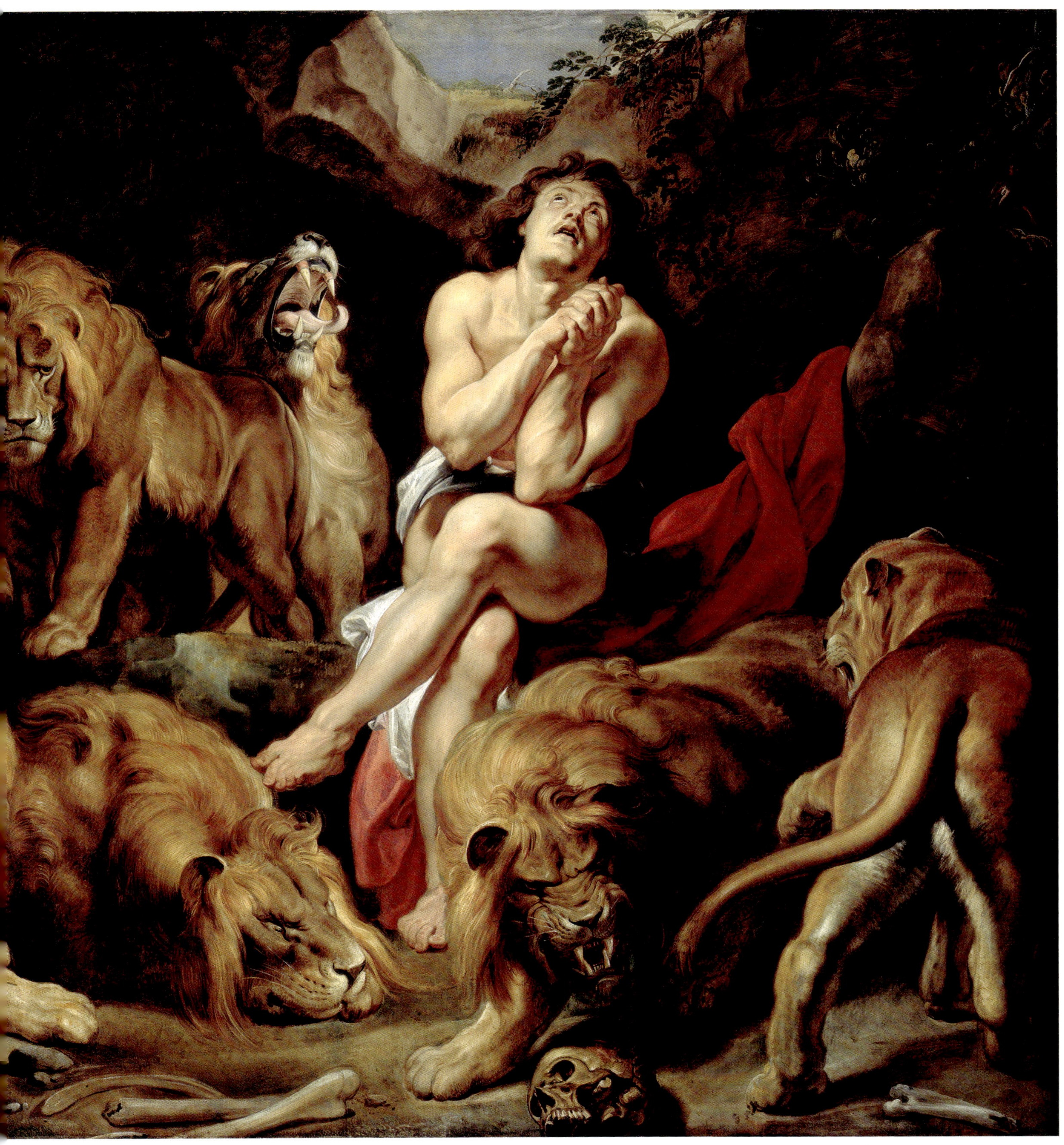

In the years following his return from Italy, Rubens painted several awe-inspiring, grand biblical epics. While usually commissioned by princes and priests and destined for the great palaces and churches of Europe, there were a handful of works that, according to Rubens, he kept for himself. *Daniel in the Lions' Den* was one such painting. The earliest mention of it comes in April 1618, when Rubens entered complex negotiations with the English ambassador to The Hague, Sir Dudley Carleton, to trade several of his paintings for Carleton's collection of antique sculpture (see my essay, page 72). Rubens described the paintings, which included a "Daniel among many lions," as the "flower of my stock, particularly some pictures which I have kept for my own enjoyment; some I have even repurchased for more than I had sold them to others." *Daniel*, he explained, was "taken from life. Original, entirely by my hand."[1]

Exactly why Rubens executed this enormous painting and kept it in his studio is not well understood.[2] Measuring just over seven feet high and almost eleven feet wide, the painting represents a dramatic episode from the Old Testament, in which Daniel is sentenced to death for praying to God and is thrown into a den of lions by order of King Darius. After a sleepless night, King Darius returns in haste to the den, and, as the Bible vividly recounts, "When he came near the den where Daniel was, he cried out anxiously to Daniel, 'O Daniel, servant of the living God, has your God whom you faithfully serve been able to deliver you from the lions?' Daniel then said to the king, 'O king, live forever! My God sent his angel and shut the lions' mouths so that they would not hurt me, because I was found blameless before him; and also before you. O king, I have done no wrong.'"[3]

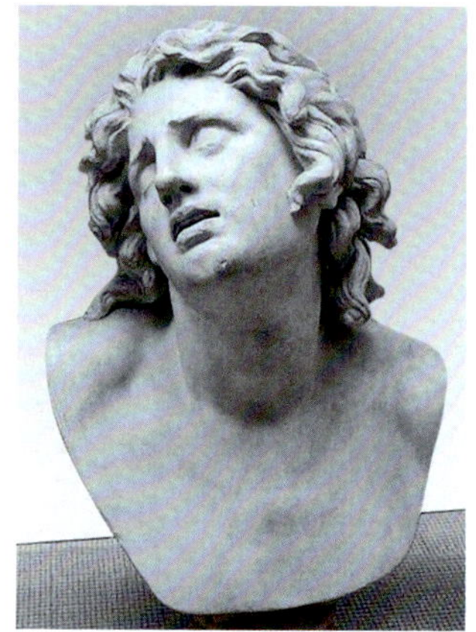

Fig 1 *Head of the "Dying Alexander."* Plaster cast, 87.6 (height) × 53.7 (width) × 33.5 cm (depth). Museum of Classical Archaeology, Cambridge. 374. Original: *Dying Alexander*, late third century or early second century BC. Marble, 42 cm. Uffizi Gallery, Florence. 338. © Museum of Classical Archaeology, University of Cambridge.

Here Rubens captures the moment of Daniel's deliverance from this harrowing test of endurance and faith. Nearly nude and more than life-sized, he looks heavenward with clasped hands and dewy, pleading eyes as a pride of ten lions encircles him. As Arthur Wheelock has written, Daniel's salvation would have been understood through the lens of Counter-Reformationist thought, in which Old Testament heroes prefigured the labours and triumphs of the New Testament, while standing as moral exemplars and paradigms of faith in their own right.[4] As a figure who survived persecution through the strength of his faith, Daniel would also have been a paradigm of Neo-Stoic philosophy, which espoused the endurance of suffering through constancy. Wheelock and Michael Jaffé have identified Daniel's beseeching visage in a series of antique and Renaissance sources, including the famous Hellenistic bust of *Dying Alexander* (fig. 1) and Girolamo Muziano's altarpiece *The Penitent Saint Jerome* in Bologna, both of which Rubens would have encountered in Italy and, in

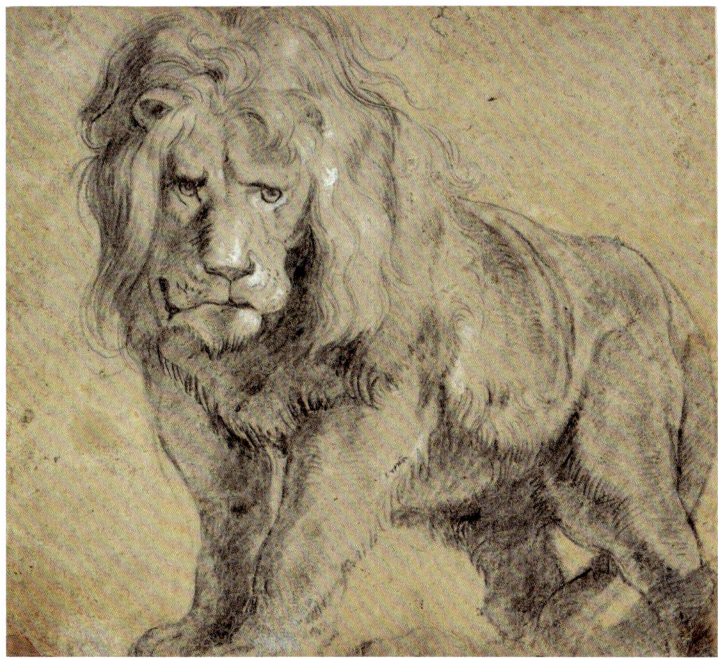

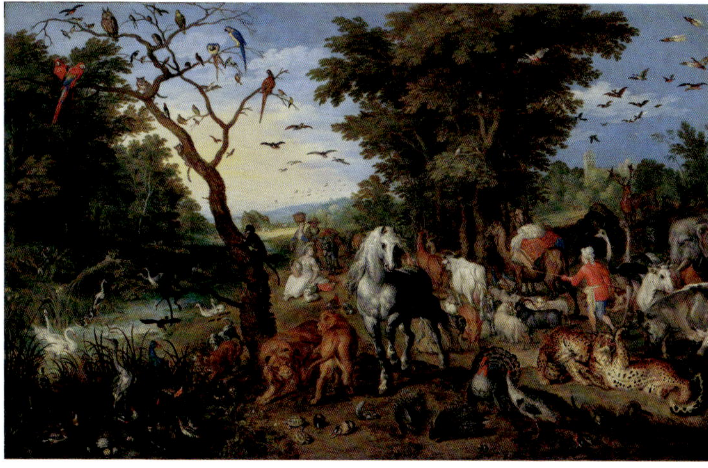

Fig 2 Peter Paul Rubens, *Lion*, c. 1612–13. Black chalked heighted with white chalk, 25.2 × 28.3 cm. National Gallery of Art, Washington D.C., Ailsa Mellon Bruce Fund. 1969.7.1. Image courtesy National Gallery of Art, Washington, D.C.

Fig 3 Jan Brueghel the Elder, *The Entry of the Animals into Noah's Ark*, 1613. Oil on panel, 54.6 × 83.8 cm. The J. Paul Getty Museum, Los Angeles. 92.PB.82.

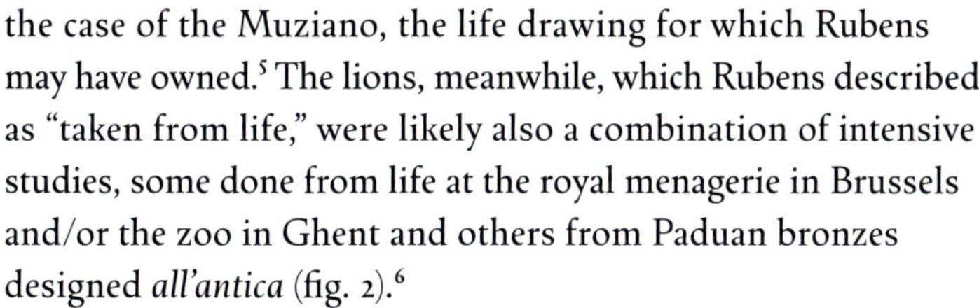

the case of the Muziano, the life drawing for which Rubens may have owned.[5] The lions, meanwhile, which Rubens described as "taken from life," were likely also a combination of intensive studies, some done from life at the royal menagerie in Brussels and/or the zoo in Ghent and others from Paduan bronzes designed *all'antica* (fig. 2).[6]

Combining Counter-Reformation principles with Neo-Stoic virtues and observations from life with studies from antique and Renaissance sources, *Daniel in the Lions' Den* is a masterful summation of the painter's intellectual and artistic breadth. Although the work and its preparatory drawings are undated, Rubens seems to have begun planning for the painting shortly after returning to Antwerp,[7] as the lions circling at Daniel's right appear in Jan Brueghel the Elder's *The Entry of the Animals into Noah's Ark*, which is signed and dated 1613 (fig. 3). It, thus, seems most likely that Rubens began to compose *Daniel* soon after his return from Italy. And though possibly conceived as a work to demonstrate the full scope of his abilities, it ultimately inspired patrons and painters alike.

Alexandra Libby

1 Peter Paul Rubens to Sir Dudley Carleton, April 28, 1618, in *The Letters of Peter Paul Rubens*, trans. and ed. Ruth Saunders Magurn (Cambridge, MA: Harvard University Press, 1955), 59–60.

2 Jeremy Wood has argued that, given its size, the painting must have been a failed commission. See Jeremy Wood, *Corpus Rubenianum Ludwig Burchard, Part XXVI: Copies and Adaptations from Renaissance and Later Artists, Italian Artists; III, Artists Working in Central Italy and France*, 2 vols. (New York: Harvey Miller, 2011), 1: 422. In a research dissertation on this painting, Rachel Aviva Pollock, on the other hand, claims that the painting was intended as a political statement about the Twelve Years' Truce and the agenda of the Spanish Hapsburgs in their efforts to maintain control over the Netherlands. See Aviva Pollock, "Peter Paul Rubens' *Daniel in the Lions' Den*: Its Sources and Its Political Significance" (PhD diss., University of Maryland, College Park, 2015).

3 Dan. 6:20–23.

4 Arthur K. Wheelock Jr., *Flemish Paintings of the Seventeenth Century* (Washington, DC: National Gallery of Art, 2005), 168.

5 Michael Jaffé, "Some Recent Acquisitions of Seventeenth-Century Flemish Painting," *Report and Studies in the History of Art* 3 (1969): 17.

6 Jaffé, "Some Recent Acquisitions," 9–13.

7 Wheelock speculates that the painting was executed between 1612 and 1617, "most likely about 1614/1616 ... [the] years that the artist was particularly interested in infusing his pictorial forms with sculptural qualities." See Wheelock, *Flemish Paintings*, 171.

Peter Paul Rubens
The Flight of Lot and His Family from Sodom
1613–15
Oil on canvas
220.3 × 243.8 cm

Collection of The John and Mable Ringling Museum of Art,
the State Art Museum of Florida, Florida State University,
Sarasota, Florida
Bequest of John Ringling, 1936
SN218

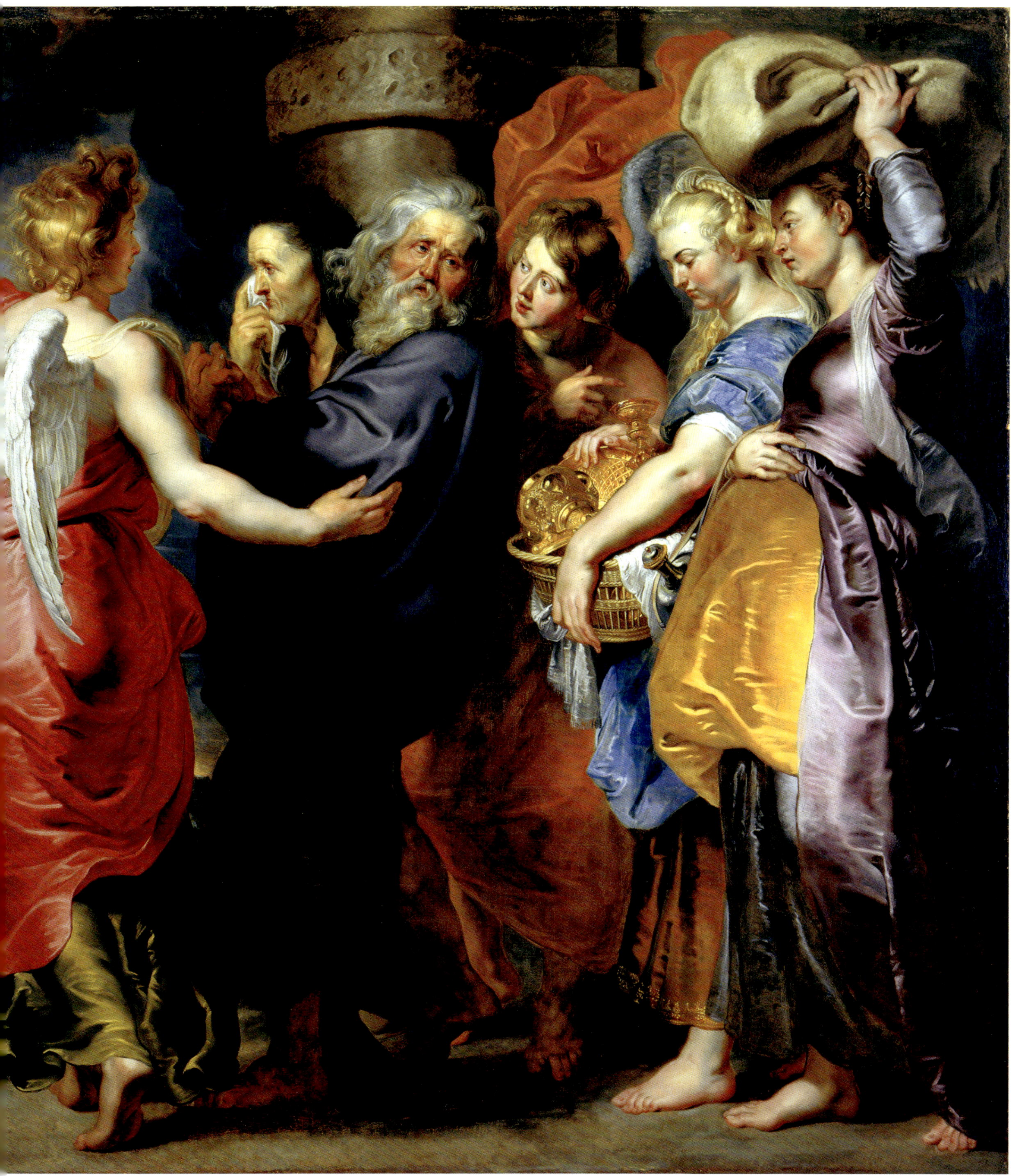

Peter Paul Rubens and Workshop
The Flight of Lot and His Family from Sodom

During the Counter-Reformation, the Old Testament underwent a revival as a rich source for paintings with moralizing undertones. The story of Lot was often used as a symbol to renounce carnal pleasures and to preserve one's soul for eternal life. Most painters—including Rubens—often chose to depict Lot and his daughters eating and drinking in a cave, as it afforded painters with an excuse to depict sensual female nudity. In that biblical passage, Lot's daughters, afraid that they are the last humans on earth, intoxicate their father with wine to lie with him in an attempt to produce progeny.

In *The Flight of Lot and His Family from Sodom*, Rubens depicts the moment the family leaves the doomed city, although he includes several references to future events. Two angels lead Lot and his family away from the burning city in the background; one pushes a reluctant Lot forward, while the other catches the attention of the patriarch, who has turned his head toward him. The angel's hand rests on a basket with golden vessels, carried by one of Lot's daughters. This gesture seems to serve a double meaning; a reminder of the renouncement of worldly possessions and an allusion to the imminent intoxication with wine.[1] Lot's grieving wife, drying her eyes with a handkerchief, is placed in front of a pillar; a reference to her looming disobedience to God's command not to turn around, an action that will transform her into a pillar of salt. The two beautiful daughters walk behind their parents with resignation, one carrying the basket with golden vessels, the other with a large bulk of cloth on her head, likely containing more of their household goods. The second daughter also carries a flask in her hand, perhaps holding the wine that will be served to her father in the cave. She presses her hand on her abdomen as if to allude to her later pregnancy.[2] The almost life-sized figures are placed parallel to the picture plain and draw the viewers into the composition, making them participants of this unfolding family drama.

The painting is exemplary for Rubens's extensive knowledge of antique sculpture, drawing from several ancient sources to create a highly original composition. The frontality and frieze-like composition is a testament to his encounter with architectural and sarcophagus decoration; the angel and Lot seem to relate to Triton and nereid depicted on the lid of a sarcophagus at the Badia at Grottaferrata. The face of Lot derives from the tortured visage of *Laocoön*, one of the most important and famous classical sculptural groups Rubens saw and copied during his stay in Rome. Rubens's familiarity with the work of Titian is revealed in the angel's swirling pose, recalling a female figure in *Bacchus and Ariadne*.[3]

The painting was part of the collection of art connoisseur Peter Stevens, a cloth merchant and almoner in Antwerp. Stevens's extensive collection was praised by a contemporary, stating that his "collection was the most beautiful [in the city]" ("*het frayste kaebinet dat hier te sien is*").[4] It included works by renowned painters from the fifteenth and sixteenth centuries, including Jan van Eyck, Hieronymus Bosch, Quentin Massys, and Pieter Brueghel the Elder. He owned several paintings by Rubens and commissioned his own and his wife's portraits from Rubens's former student, Anthony van Dyck. A fervent supporter of contemporary artists and a pious man with a strong sense of civic responsibility, Stevens must have been impressed by the strong aesthetic qualities and clear moralizing undertone of the painting.

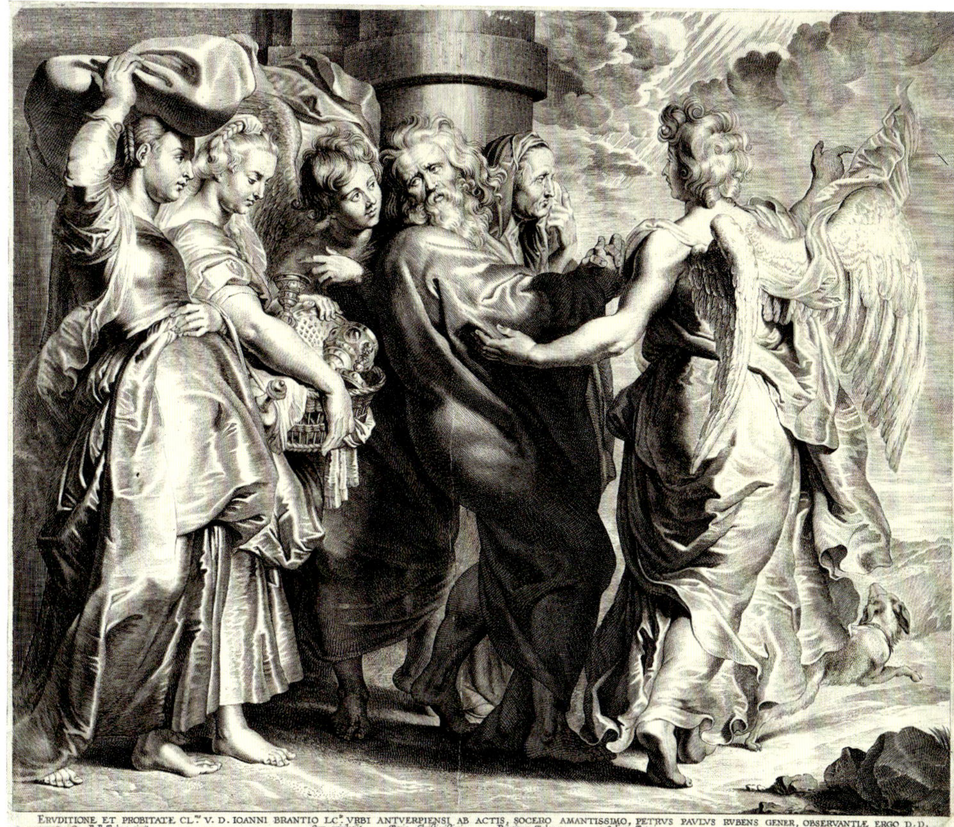

Fig 1 Anthony van Dyck, after Peter Paul Rubens, *The Flight of Lot and his Family from Sodom*, 1620. Engraving, 33 × 38.5 cm. The British Museum. R,3.7. Photo © The Trustees of the British Museum.

Three painted versions of *The Flight of Lot and His Family from Sodom* are known. Two are generally considered to be workshop copies (The Bass Museum of Art, Miami Beach, Florida; private collection) and one copy is attributed to Jacob Jordaens (National Museum of Western Art, Tokyo). Lucas Vorsterman I made a print after the painting based on a preparatory chalk drawing by Anthony van Dyck. The print, part of a series of nine large prints after Rubens, was published in 1620 and dedicated to Rubens's father-in-law, Jan Brant. There might have existed a preparatory (oil) sketch for the composition, as the Tokyo painting includes details not found in the Miami Beach version or the Vorsterman print. The print served as a model for several printed and painted versions, including a drawing by Rembrandt (Bibliothèque nationale de France, Paris), copying the movement and direction of the figural group.[5]

Carolyn Mensing

1 Virginia Brilliant, *Triumph and Taste: Peter Paul Rubens at the Ringling Museum of Art* (London and New York: Scala Arts Publishers 2011), 86–95.

2 Brilliant, *Triumph and Taste*, 89.

3 Roger-Adolf d'Hulst and Marc Vandenven, *Corpus Rubenianum Ludwig Burchard, Part III: The Old Testament* (London: Harvey Miller Publishers,1989), 40–44.

4 Bert Timmermans, *Patronen van patronage in het zeventiende-eeuwse Antwerpen: een elite als actor binnen een kunstwereld* (Amsterdam: Aksant, 2008), 234.

5 D'Hulst and Vandenven, *Corpus Rubenianum*, 40–44.

Peter Paul Rubens
Lot and His Daughters
c. 1613–14
Oil on canvas
190 × 225 cm
Collection of an anonymous charitable foundation

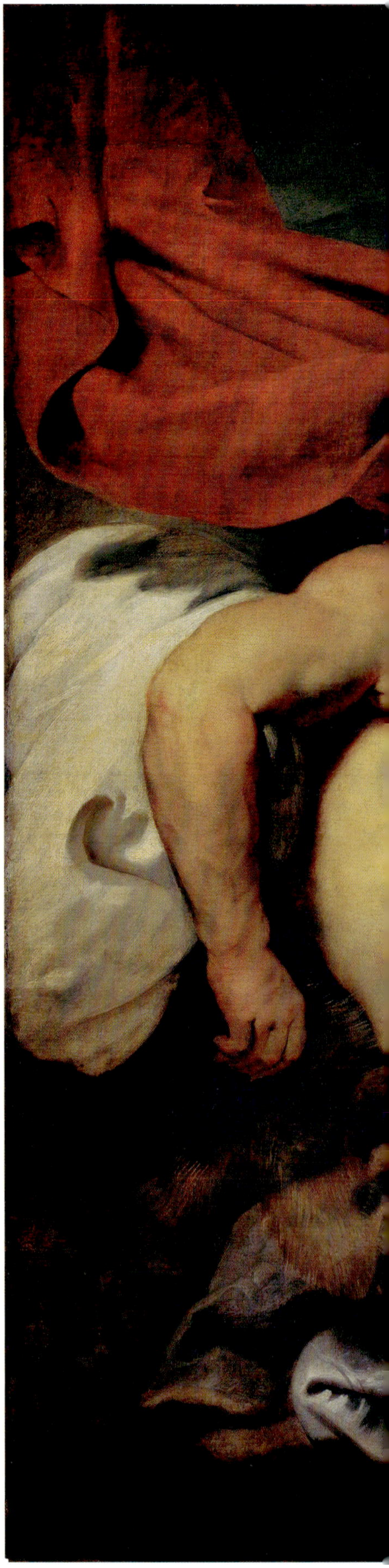

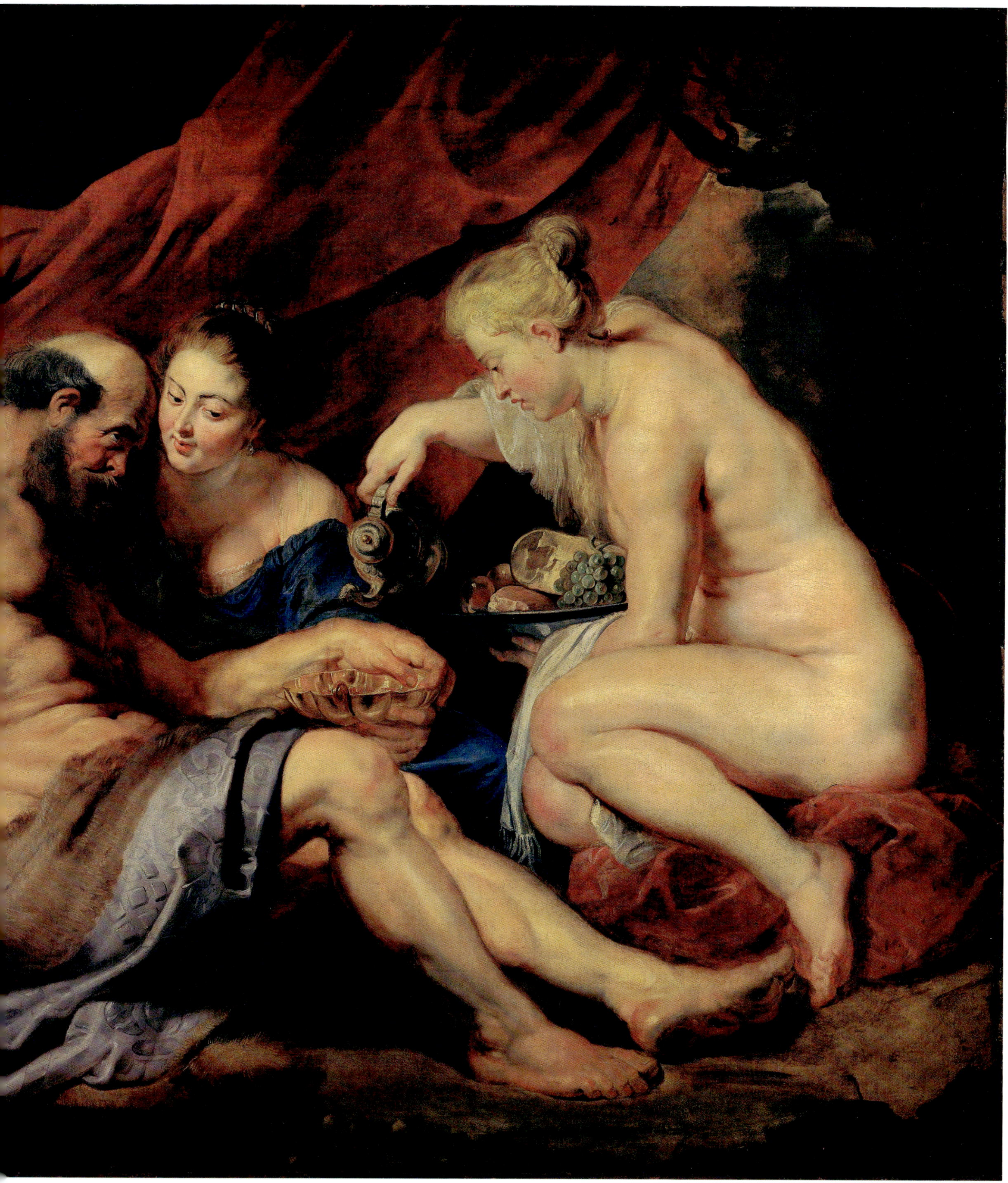

Peter Paul Rubens
Lot and His Daughters

Chapter Nineteen of Genesis tells of God's destruction of the cities of Sodom and Gomorrah and of the consequences for Lot and his family. Because of God's enduring protection of Lot's uncle, Abraham, Lot was warned to leave Sodom before fire and brimstone rained down from the heavens and consumed their home. Around 1613, Rubens painted *The Flight of Lot and His Family from Sodom* (page 154), a large canvas with six standing, full-length figures showing an ambivalent Lot, his sorrowful wife, and their two daughters led out of the city by the two angels sent to warn them. *Lot and His Daughters* depicts a subsequent moment in the same narrative and dates to roughly the same time in Rubens's career, although the artistic models that informed the creation of *Lot and His Daughters* imbue it—both erotic and sinister by virtue of its subject—with an unsettling ambiguity.[1]

While fleeing Sodom, Lot's wife defied the angels' instruction not to look back at the burning city, and she was turned into a pillar of salt. Scared of their own destruction, Lot and his two daughters took refuge in a mountain cave, and the two young women soon became concerned not only for their own lives but for the continuation of their father's lineage. Fearing that there may be no men left on Earth, they devised to get their father drunk on successive nights, allowing each daughter to become impregnated by him. Rubens's scene captures the fraught moral and psychological interaction between the three during the middle of one evening's seduction. As Lot reclines, he can barely support the weight of his drinking bowl or of his slumping head, yet his leering stare at the undressed daughter, who apprehensively replenishes his wine, suggests his complicity in the affair.

Rubens had previously painted this scene around 1610 (fig. 1), although the later version is more sophisticated in its artistic references and more resistant to characterizing Lot or his daughters as guilty or innocent. Rubens based his figure of Lot principally on two works of art, one antique and one modern. The physiognomy of Lot's head and upper torso were adapted from a Roman reproduction of the Hellenistic statue *Drunken Silenus Leaning against a Tree Trunk*, which Rubens copied in a chalk drawing that portrays Silenus in right profile.[2] At the same time, the supine pose, the arm nearest the viewer pulled well behind the body, and the shallow relief-like space that situates Lot opposite a crouching figure derive from Michelangelo's famous design for *Leda and the Swan*, a composition Rubens had emulated previously on at least two occasions.[3] Leda, a Greek princess, was seduced by Zeus when the king of the Olympic gods visited her in the form of a swan. This allusion sets up a precarious balance in Rubens's painting, between Lot's powerful musculature and Silenus-like intemperance and his vulnerability to his plotting daughters' scheme. For the knowledgeable viewer who recognized Rubens's artistic debts, Lot's complicity in the seduction and incest becomes less certain and a function of what the viewer believes Lot sees and can discern about his circumstances.

The first owner of *Lot and His Daughters* is not known. It has been suggested that the painting was a commission, and there is

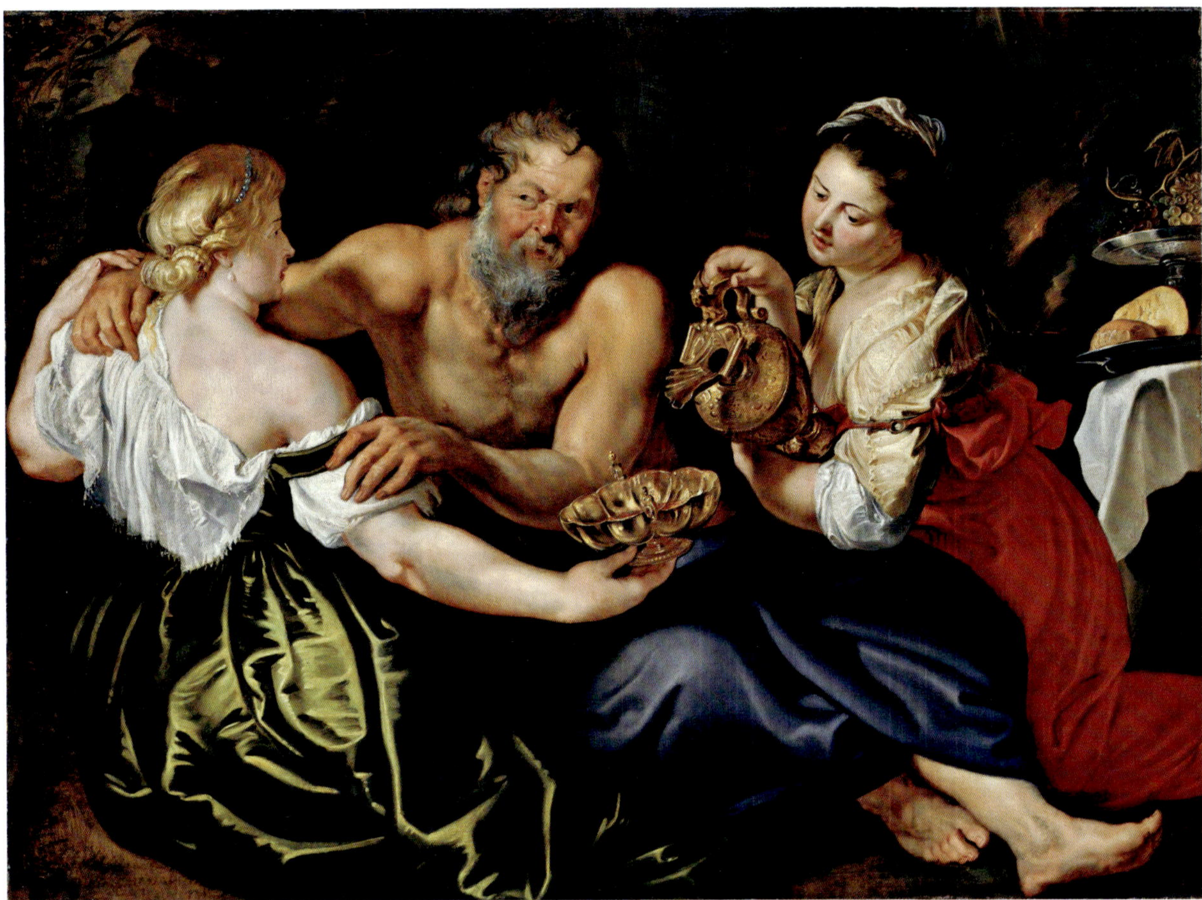

Fig 1 Peter Paul Rubens, *Lot and His Daughters in a Rock Grotto*, 1610. Oil on canvas, 108 × 146 cm. Staatliches Museum Schwerin. 3059.

no doubt that Rubens intended it to hang in a private residence or gallery rather than in a religious setting. Still, Rubens did not require the impetus of a commission to execute an ambitious picture of this scale, and the painting may have found a buyer only after Rubens made it.[4] By at least the mid-seventeenth century, the picture had been purchased by its first identifiable owner, the Antwerp merchant Balthazar Courtois.[5] Subsequently passing through the collections of the Elector of Bavaria and the Holy Roman Emperor in the early eighteenth century, *Lot and His Daughters* entered the collection of the first Duke of Marlborough some time before 1740 and was consequently installed at Blenheim Palace for nearly a century and a half. In the 1880s, the work was purchased for the collection of Baron Maurice de Hirsch, in whose family it remained—almost entirely off-view to the public—until it was purchased by its present owner in 2016.

Kirk Nickel

1 Due to modern scholars' limited access to the painting, the literature on the work is relatively small. See especially the Christie's catalogue *Rubens: Lot and His Daughters*, published in advance of the painting's inclusion in the Old Masters and British Paintings Evening Sale, London, Thursday, July 7, 2016. Also, R.A. d'Hulst and M. Vandenven, *Corpus Rubenianum Ludwig Burchard Part III: The Old Testament* (London: Harvey Miller Publishers, 1989), 50–51.

2 *Rubens: Lot and His Daughters*, 16.

3 On Rubens's copies after Michelangelo's design for Leda and the Swan, see David Jaffé and Elizabeth McGrath, *Rubens: A Master in the Making* (London: National Gallery Company Ltd., 2005), 96–97, cat. no. 30.

4 One thinks, for instance, of the many canvases Rubens mentions as available to Sir Dudley Carleton in their correspondence. See Alexandra Libby's essay in this catalogue, page 72.

5 For the work's provenance, see *Rubens: Lot and His Daughters*, 4, which includes early ownership unknown to d'Hulst and Vandenven.

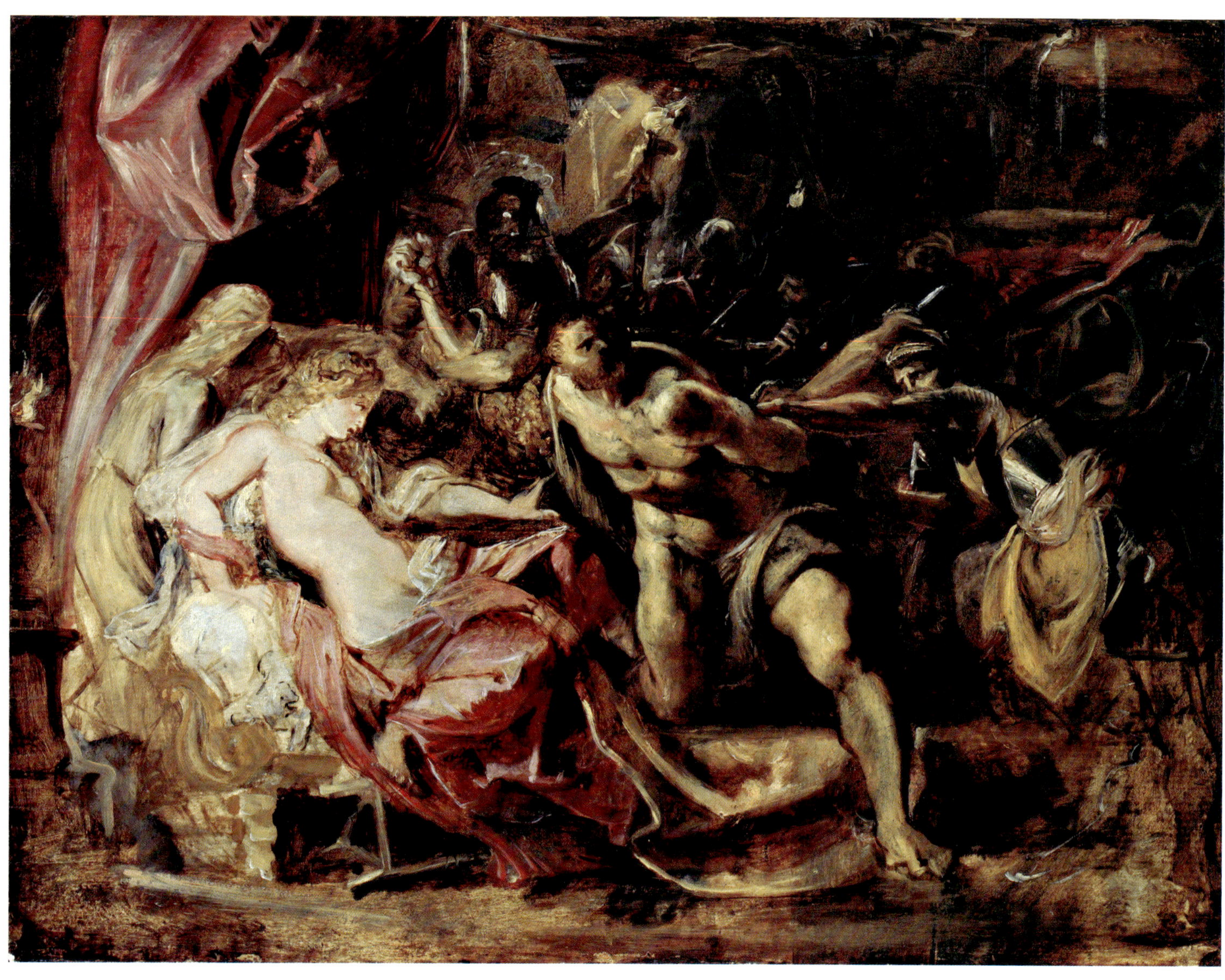

Peter Paul Rubens
The Capture of Samson
c. 1609
Oil on panel
50.4 × 66.4 cm

Art Institute of Chicago, Illinois
Robert A. Waller Memorial Fund
1923.551

Peter Paul Rubens
The Capture of Samson

According to the biblical book of Judges, Samson's parents consecrated their yet unborn child to God, who God promised that his divine strength would remain with Samson as long as the boy's hair was never cut. As he grew into manhood, Samson became a nearly invincible foe to the oppressive Philistine regime, setting their crops on fire and killing their men by the dozens. Having failed to overcome his superhuman strength in combat, the Philistine elders bribed Samson's lover, Delilah, to learn the secret of his power.

Rubens's oil sketch depicts the instant when the betrayed Samson, waking from Delilah's lap to find his head shorn, struggles to free himself from his Philistine captors (Judges 16:19–20). Delilah braces herself with her right arm and draws her right foot beneath her body as she repels the helpless Samson. A vaguely defined figure shields Delilah as the Philistine soldiers rush into the bedroom and restrain Samson.

In the upper right corner of the image, what at first appear as swags of red and blue drapery decorating Delilah's bedroom are, in fact, traces of an earlier composition—a rare instance of Rubens creating a new design on top of a previous oil sketch. Beneath the scene of Samson's capture is an unfinished sketch related to *The Adoration of the Magi* that Rubens painted for Antwerp's city hall in anticipation of the signing of the Twelve Years' Truce in April 1609.[1] The fact that the two designs are superimposed does not, in itself, determine the capture scene's precise moment of execution, but it does lend support for a date in the early months of 1609, when Rubens was planning the composition for *The Adoration*.

Along with *The Blinding of Samson* in Madrid and the *Samson and Delilah* in Cincinnati (page 166), the Chicago panel is one of three Samson-themed oil sketches that have interested scholars for their possible role in the development of Rubens's early masterpiece *Samson and Delilah*, painted in or around 1610 for the Antwerp burgomaster Nicolaas Rockox.[2] The dates of the three oil sketches, and even their relative chronological order, have been controversial. A finished painting of *The Capture of Samson* in the Alte Pinakothek, Munich, was based on the Chicago panel and dates to the second half of the 1610s.[3] Despite this close connection, there is strong agreement that the present oil sketch was produced soon after Rubens's arrival in Antwerp and that, several years later, it served Rubens and his workshop as an aid for the Munich canvas. In the catalogue for the recent exhibition of Rubens's oil sketches, Alejandro Vergara has suggested persuasively that the figure of Delilah in the Chicago oil sketch was the immediate source for the more clothed figure we see in the Cincinnati panel and in the final painting.[4]

Kirk Nickel

1 On this incomplete sketch and its relationship to *The Adoration of the Magi*, see Friso Lammertse and Alejandro Vergara, *Rubens: Painter of Sketches* (Madrid: Museo Nacional del Prado; Rotterdam: Museum Boijmans van Beuningen, 2018), 68, exh. cat. no. 6.

2 For Rockox's *Samson and Delilah*, see C. Brown, *Rubens: Samson and Delilah* (London: National Gallery, 1983); also see David Jaffé and Elizabeth McGrath, *Rubens: A Master in the Making* (London: National Gallery Company Ltd., 2005), 166, exh. cat. no. 77.

3 For a consideration of the Munich canvas in relation to the Samson oil sketches, see Jaffé and McGrath, *Rubens*, 161.

4 Lammertse and Vergara, *Rubens*, 68, cat. no. 6. For an alternative ordering of the Samson oil sketches prioritizing the Cincinnati panel, see Julius S. Held, *The Oil Sketches of Peter Paul Rubens: A Critical Catalogue*, 2 vols. (Princeton, NJ: Princeton University Press, 1980), 1:432.

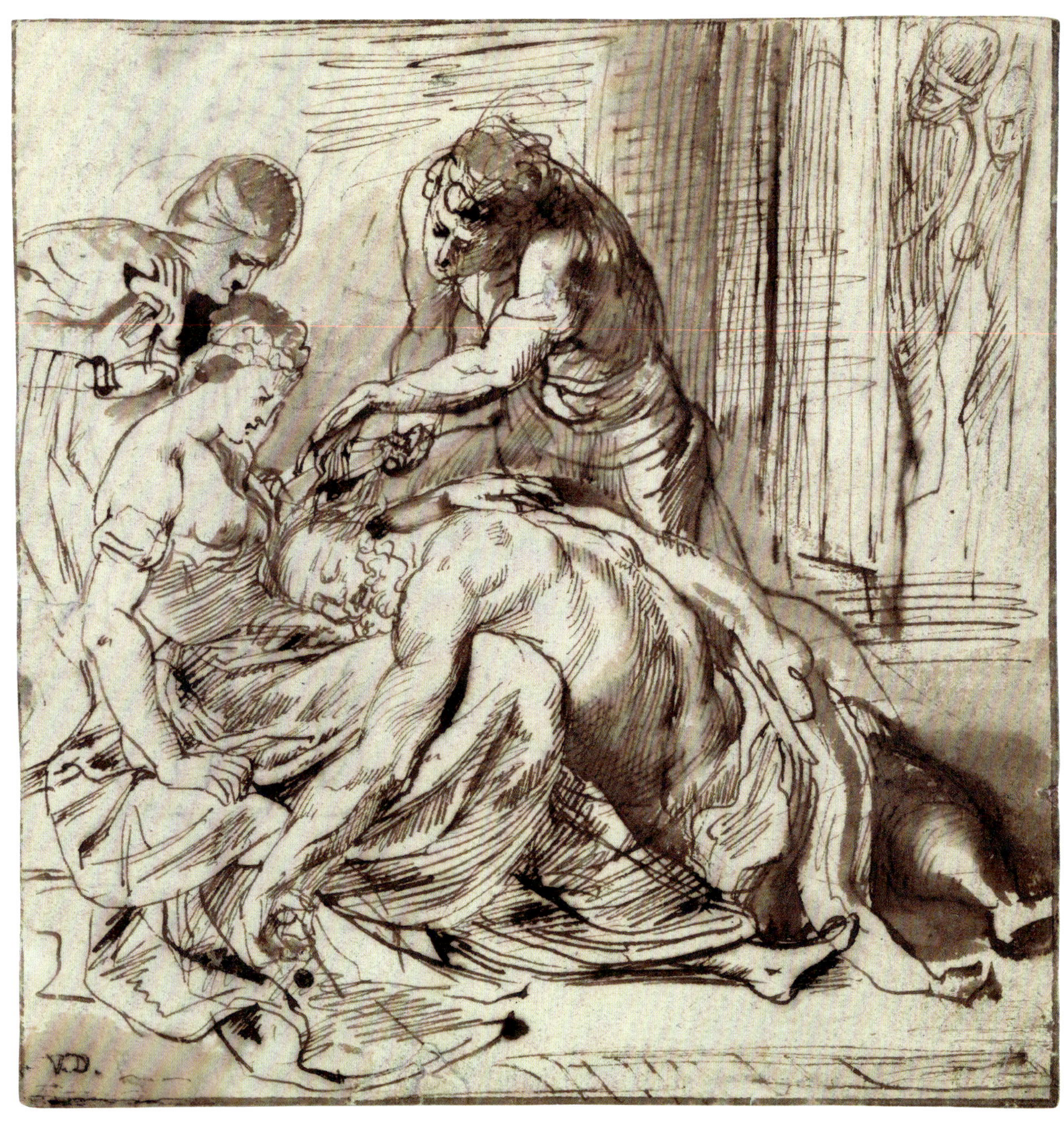

Peter Paul Rubens
Samson and Delilah
c. 1609–10
Drawing in pen, brush,
and brown ink
16.4 × 16.2 cm

Private collection

Peter Paul Rubens
Samson and Delilah

After agreeing to betray Samson to the Philistines, Delilah struggled to convince her lover to divulge the source of his invincibility. Only on her fourth attempt to learn his secret did Samson reveal the truth: "If my head were shaved, then my strength would leave me; I would become weak, and be like anyone else."[1] Informing the Philistine elders, Delilah allowed a barber to enter her chamber and strip the sleeping Samson of his divine strength.

In 1609 Rubens began planning a scene of Samson and Delilah for Antwerp's burgomaster, Nicolaas Rockox, and as Rubens's thoughts for the commission developed, his composition came to focus on the dramatically tense moment of the silent hair cutting. The present work is the only known preparatory drawing for Rockox's *Samson and Delilah* and represents our earliest glimpse of Rubens's ultimate compositional arrangement for that chimney piece.[2] In the drawing, Delilah's prominent right knee is fully bent, bringing her right foot beneath her body, as in the Chicago composition (page 162), rather than crossing her left leg and supporting the slumbering Samson, as in the subsequent Cincinnati oil sketch (page 166) and the final London painting.

If this drawing relied on certain aspects of the Chicago oil sketch, the very fact that Rubens returned here to pen and ink underscores his desire to work up a new scene from a distinct compositional foundation.[3] Rubens began the design with the interlocking forms of the seated Delilah and the sleeping Samson, an arrangement that allows the barber access to Samson's hair. Rubens's quill outlined the bodies and drapery with extreme economy, indicating shadow schematically with broad passages of rapid hatching. Even at this early stage, the artist intended multiple light sources; his use of brown wash indicates shadow cast by the torchlight of the Philistine soldiers entering through the back doorway and by another flame in the foreground that illuminates the barber's work. It may have been the need for additional foreground light that encouraged Rubens to fit the figure of Delilah's attendant—an analogue of the ill-defined attendant in the Chicago panel—into the scene.

When the drawing entered the collection of I.Q. van Regteren Altena in the 1920s, it carried an attribution to Anthony van Dyck.[4] This likely explains the initials "V.D." inscribed in pen in the lower left corner of the sheet.

Kirk Nickel

1 Judges. 6:17.

2 Anne-Marie S. Logan and Michiel C. Plomp, *Peter Paul Rubens: The Drawings* (New York: Metropolitan Museum of Art; New Haven, CT: Yale University Press, 2005), 124–27, exh. cat no. 28. For additional literature, see the entry for the drawing in Christie's sale catalogue *The I.Q. van Regteren Altena Collection*, part I, July 10, 2014, London, lot no. 9.

3 Logan and Plomp, *Peter Paul Rubens*, 126.

4 *The I.Q. van Regteren Altena Collection*, lot no. 9.

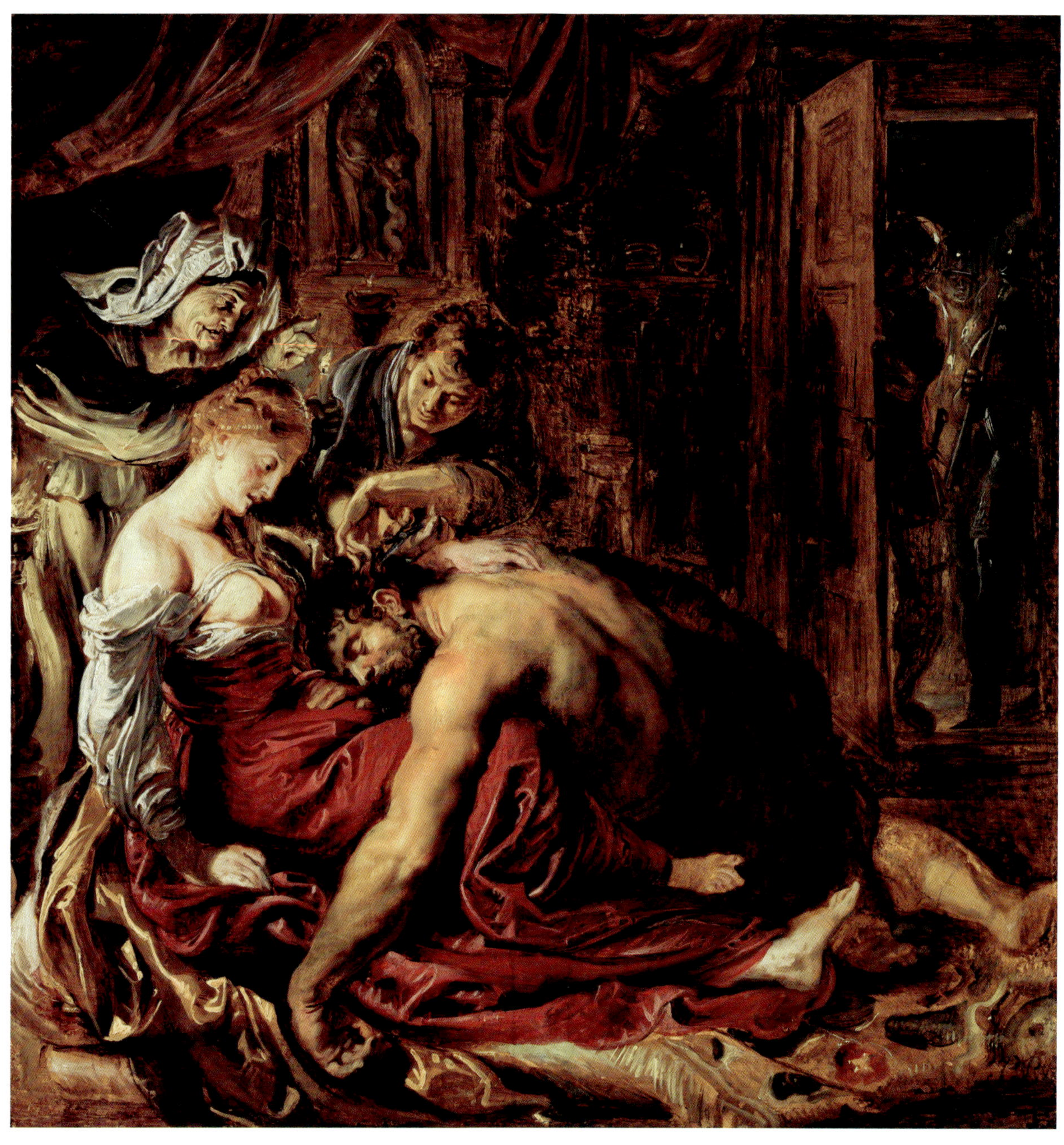

Peter Paul Rubens
Samson and Delilah
c. 1609–10
Oil on panel
52.1 × 50.5 cm

Cincinnati Art Museum
Mr. and Mrs. Harry S. Leyman Endowment
1972.459

Peter Paul Rubens
Samson and Delilah

Rubens's *Samson and Delilah* for Nicolaas Rockox is one of his few commissions for which we possess a preparatory drawing, an oil sketch, and the final painting, providing us a rare vantage on the artist's thoughts as the project developed.[1] The multiple light sources implied in the drawing (page 164) are further defined in this oil sketch and shown to emanate from the lampstand by Delilah's bed, the candle held by her elderly attendant, a small flame beneath the statue of Venus and Cupid on the back wall, and a torch carried by the Philistine soldiers standing ready just beyond the bedroom door. The heat from these four flames is nearly palpable, an effect Rubens achieved by allowing the honey-yellow ground layer to function as a mid-tone in the room's colouring, mediating between the dark brown of deep shadow and the local colour of surfaces seen in full light. Although the final painting is characterized by a cooler palette, it owes its vibrant effect of flickering lamplight to the interplay of surface colouring and exposed ground colour explored in the Cincinnati panel.

The oil sketch also clarifies the interlocking forms of Samson and Delilah as the centrepiece of the composition and of the scene's psychological drama. As he developed the figure group from the initial drawing, Rubens arranged the elderly female attendant and the barber further from the picture plane, which subtly isolates the central pair. By focusing attention on Delilah watching Samson, her deep ambivalence becomes more apparent as the viewer recognizes the tender worry visible on her face and the contrast of her hands, one tensed to brace herself in anticipation of Samson's rage, the other resting familiarly on her lover's back.

Sources for Rubens's figure of Delilah have been identified in sixteenth-century Italian works, including Michelangelo's sculpted *Night* and his painting *Leda and the Swan*.[2] The latter—now lost but known through copies, including two by Rubens (page 33)—is especially resonant with the interpersonal drama of *Samson and Delilah*.[3] In Michelangelo's relief-like composition, Zeus has assumed the guise of a large swan and is well advanced in his seduction of the swooning Leda. Rubens's central pair relates closely to Michelangelo's earlier design in details such as the position of Delilah's head, the long, straight nose that defines her profile, the rearward placement of her arm nearest the viewer, and, most significantly, the basic arrangement of a powerful male protagonist in the lap of a beautiful reclining female. Yet, in Rubens's transformation of his visual source, he reverses the imbalance of the original narrative: now, it is the supposedly invincible male who has fallen asleep and risks being overthrown by the female, whose greater power lies in her ability to mask her duplicity with beauty. The complex inversion at work in Rubens's emulation of Michelangelo is a striking example of poetic chiasmus and marks the *Samson and Delilah* as a major achievement of early Baroque painting.

Kirk Nickel

1 On the relationship between the three works, see Wieseman's entry on this panel in Peter C. Sutton and Marjorie E. Wieseman, with Nico van Hout, *Drawn by the Brush: Oil Sketches by Peter Paul Rubens* (New Haven, CT: Yale University Press, 2004), 88–92.

2 For a discussion of the Italian works proposed as sources for the *Samson and Delilah*, see R.A. d'Hulst and M. Vandenven, *Corpus Rubenianum Ludwig Burchard, III: The Old Testament* (London: Harvey Miller, 1989), 109–11.

3 On Rubens's copies after Michelangelo's design for *Leda and the Swan*, see David Jaffé and Elizabeth McGrath, *Rubens: A Master in the Making* (London: National Gallery Company Ltd., 2005), 96–97, cat. no. 30.

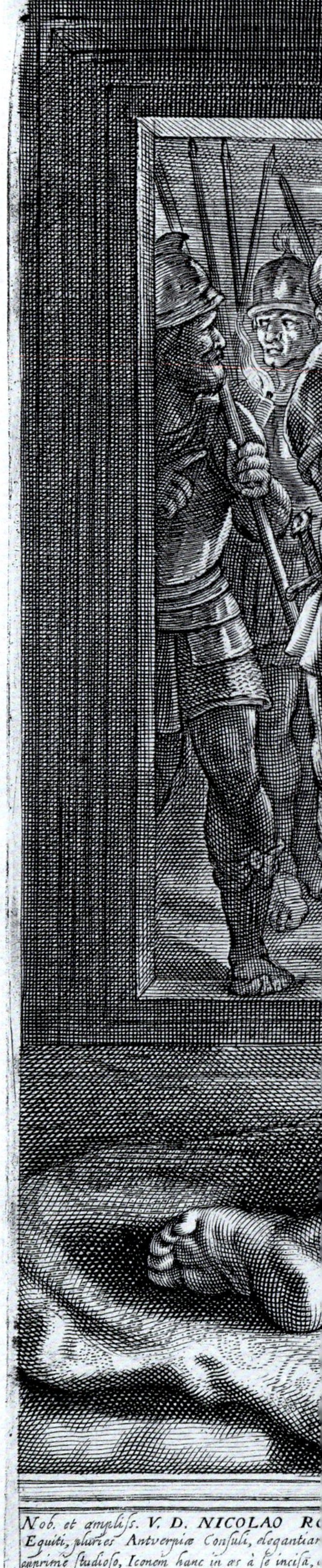

Jacob Matham
born Haarlem, Netherlands, 1571;
died Haarlem, Netherlands, 1631
After Peter Paul Rubens
Samson and Delilah
Likely c. 1615
Engraving
Between state ii/v and iii/v
(New Hollstein, Jacob Matham, I: no. 10, 23)
37.5 × 44.1 cm

The Hearn Family Trust
186.1
Photo by Arturo Sánchez

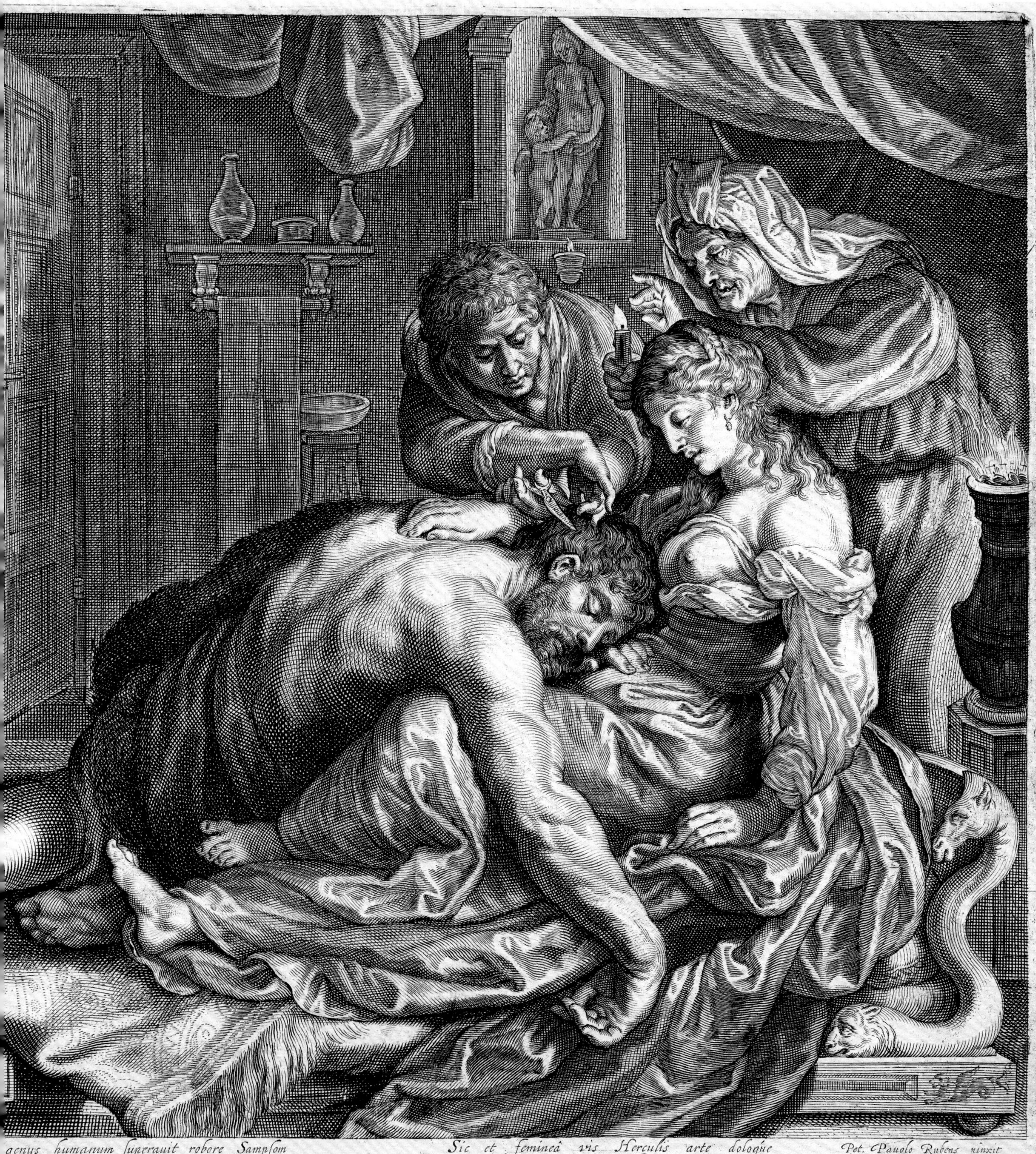
genus humanum superauit robore Sampsom
Femineis tandem vincitur insidijs.
Sic et feminea vis Herculis arte doloque
Occidit. ô summis sexus inique viris!
Pet. Paulo Rubens pinxit
Ja. Matham sculp. et excud.

Jacob Matham
After Peter Paul Rubens
Samson and Delilah

Signatures and address in margin at right: *Pet. Pauolo Rubens pinxit / Ja. Matham sculp. et excud.*

Imperial privilege in margin at left: *Cum privil. Sa. Caes. M.*

Dedication to Nicolaas Rockox in cartouche at lower left corner: *Nob. et ampliss. V.D. Nicolao Rocoxio/Equiti, pluries Antwerpiae Consuli, elegantiaru(m) omnium/apprime studioso, Iconem hanc in aes à se incisa(m), cultus et ob-/servantiae causa, tu(m) quòd archetijpa tabula artifice Pet. Pauli/Rubenij manu depicta apud ipsu(m) cu(m) admiratione spectatur, Matha(m)/L.M.D.D.*

Four lines of Latin text in two columns in margin: *Qui genus humanum superavit robore Sampson,/ Femineis tandem vincitur insidiis./ Sic et feminea vis Herculis arte doloque/ Occidit. o magnis sexus inique viris!*

Since the finished *Samson and Delilah* is thought to have gone directly into Nicolaas Rockox's home, and Jacob Matham is not known to have visited Antwerp in the 1610s, the appearance of the present engraving in that decade virtually presupposes Rubens's participation. Yet, the nature of Rubens's involvement in the print's production has been difficult to establish. Around 1619, Rubens collaborated with Lucas Vorsterman I to begin making engravings after several of his painted compositions, and it has been suggested that he similarly sought out Matham, in Haarlem, to engrave the *Samson and Delilah* at some earlier moment. Jaco Rutgers has recently proposed an alternative to this long-standing assumption. Rather that posit Rubens as the project's driving force, Rutgers suggests that Matham likely requested a copy of the composition from the painter for the purpose of reproduction. This scenario accords well with the knowledge that most of the period's reproductive prints were initiated by the engraver or publisher, not the painter, and that Antwerp was replete with competent engravers, had Rubens wished to underwrite the project himself.[1]

Publishing it in Haarlem with Matham's own privilege from the Holy Roman Emperor, the engraver took pains to situate the image in its Antwerp milieu. A cartouche in the lower left corner declares the composition to have been painted by Rubens and to belong to Nicolaas Rockox, the long-tenured burgomaster of Antwerp. The print's margin contains four lines of Neo-Latin verse composed by Rubens's brother Philip before his death in 1611 and first published in 1615.[2] The lines compare the fate of the depicted Jewish hero to that of his mythological counterpart:

> Samson, who surpassed the human race in strength, is finally conquered by a feminine trap. So, too, the force of Hercules succumbed to female craft and guile. You women, baneful to great men![3]

The poem couches the image as a moralizing tale about the deceptiveness of womankind, an enduring theme in Northern European printmaking especially.[4] However, Matham's interest in Rubens's painting and his inclusion of these verses likely went well beyond their superficial misogyny. No printmaker in Europe was more closely associated with Hercules and the muscular male nude than the legendary Hendrik Goltzius,

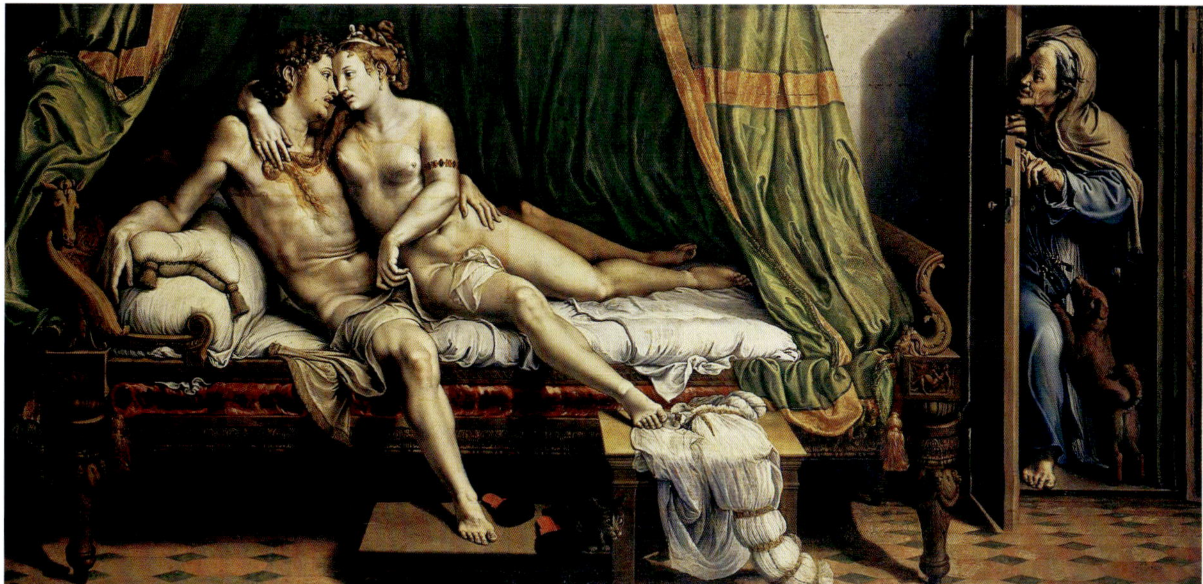

Fig 1 Giulio Romano, *The Lovers*, c. 1525. Oil on panel, transferred to canvas, 163 × 337 cm. The State Hermitage Museum, Saint Petersburg. ГЭ-223.

Matham's stepfather. With Rubens's return to the Low Countries, Matham may have recognized in Rubens's art an updating of the Herculean figure to which Goltzius's legacy was so closely tied. By 1618, an affinity between the two was explicitly recognized, when the poet Balthazar Gerbier's "Lament on the Death of Hendrik Goltzius" described Rubens as leading a fictive procession commemorating the elder artist.[5]

While the cartouche acknowledges Rockox as owning the *Samson and Delilah*, Matham's engraving is closest in detail not to the finished painting but rather to the oil sketch, now at the Cincinnati Art Museum (page 166).[6] Still, a drawn version of the composition must have mediated the oil sketch for the engraver's burin, and in this process of translation, details that may point to Rubens's own participation entered the scene. The carved ornamentation behind Delilah takes the form of a hybrid creature with two zoomorphic heads. The finished painting includes a similar horse-head ornament, although the creatures are entirely lacking from the Cincinnati oil sketch. Significantly, both these animal heads appear as ornaments to the bed frame in Giulio Romano's *Two Lovers* (fig. 1), which Rubens would have known from his residence at the Gonzaga court.[7] This recollection of Giulio's amorous scene, though cited inconspicuously in the engraving, may be telling of Rubens's inspiration for the motif of the silent watchers at the bedroom door.

Kirk Nickel

1 For background, see Jaco Rutgers's essay in this catalogue, page 102.

2 Rutgers's preference for a date close to 1615 is based, in part, on the posthumous publication of Philip Rubens's Latin verses in this year.

3 Hans Jakob Meier, "Peter Paul Rubens and His Brother Philip's Poems on 'Samson' and 'Judith,'" *Journal of the Warburg and Courtauld Institutes* 77 (2014): 241.

4 Lucas van Leyden's *The Power of Women* series is only one of the most outstanding examples of this common theme.

5 David Freedberg, "Fame, Convention and Insight: On the Relevance of Fornenbergh and Gerbier," *Ringling Museum of Art Journal*, 1983: 240–45.

6 F.W.H. Hollstein, *Jacob Matham, Part 1, The New Hollstein*, ed. Huigen Leeflang (Ouderkerk aan den Ijssel: Sound & Image Publishers in cooperation with the Rijksprentenkabinet, 2007), 23.

7 Tilmann Buddensieg, cited in R.A. d'Hulst and M. Vandenven, *Corpus Rubenianum Ludwig Burchard, Part III: The Old Testament* (London: Harvey Miller, 1989), 111–12.

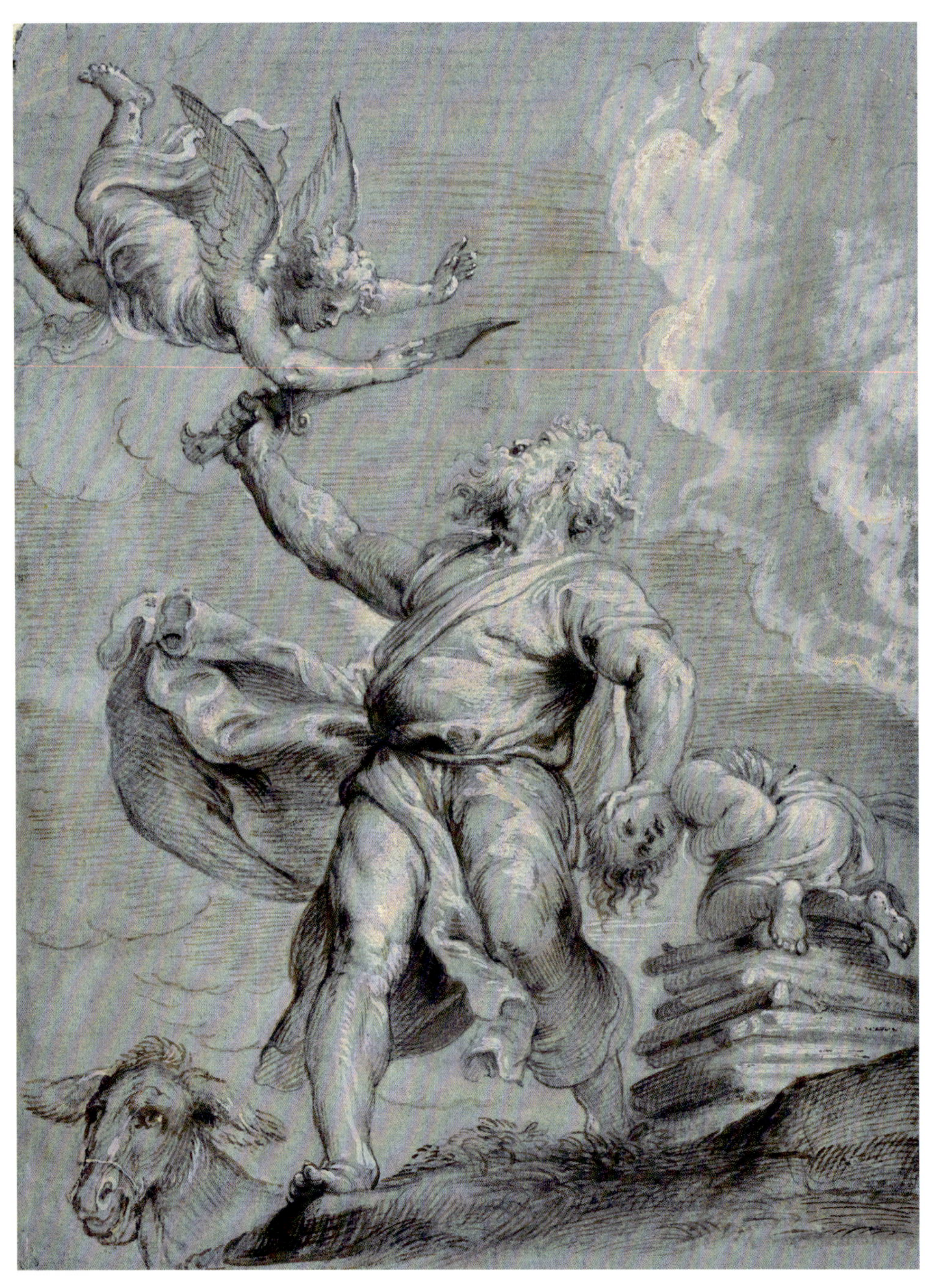

After Titian
born Pieve di Cadore, Italy, 1488;
died Venice, Italy, 1576
Retouched by Peter Paul Rubens
Study after "Abraham Sacrificing Isaac"
Perhaps c. 1600, with retouching by Rubens c. 1600–10
Black chalk on grey-green paper, retouched with
brown ink and white bodycolour
33.2 × 24.8

The Albertina Museum, Vienna
8203

After Titian
Retouched by Peter Paul Rubens
Study after Abraham Sacrificing Isaac

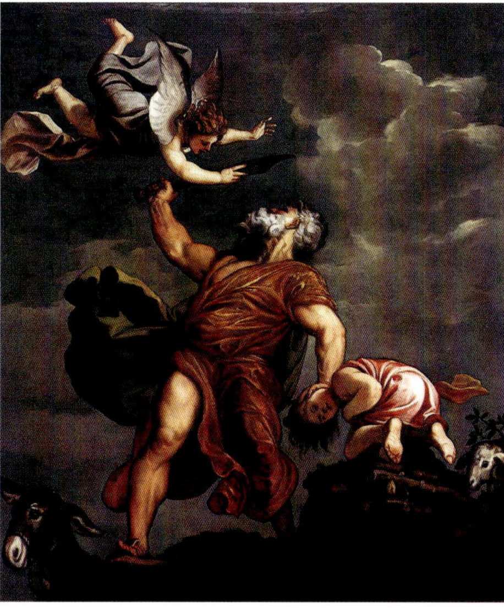

Fig 1 Titian, *Abraham Sacrificing Isaac*, 1542–44. Oil on canvas, 328 × 285 cm. Santa Maria della Salute, Venice.

Long before Rubens reached Venice, he may have known of Titian's accomplishments in foreshortening from seeing prints by the Antwerp-trained engraver Cornelis Cort. Engravings after Titian's *Tityus Chained to a Rock* and *The Martyrdom of Saint Lawrence*, for instance, portrayed the human figure in strenuous and highly foreshortened postures, a mark of consummate pictorial skill in the judgment of many sixteenth-century art critics.[1] Still, viewing these engravings would have done little to prepare Rubens for Titian's ceiling paintings for the church of Santo Spirito in Isola.

Study after "Abraham Sacrificing Isaac" copies one of three canvases that Titian executed for the Augustinian church in the 1540s (fig. 1), the other two paintings being *Cain Killing Abel* and *David Beheading Goliath*.[2] The drawing reproduces Titian's composition faithfully, the most significant differences being the cloud formations and the lack of a ram or thicket at right, although the latter elements may have been lost when the sheet was trimmed. The sheet once belonged to the collection of Everhard Jabach, where it was ascribed to Rubens, though this attribution has come under some criticism in recent decades.[3] Even if the initial record of Titian's scene is not Rubens's own, the drawing likely came into Rubens's possession during his Italian sojourn and was retouched by him at that time.[4]

Rubens's facility with foreshortening the human figure increased dramatically during his years in Italy. Paintings from his earliest years abroad, such as his *Passion* scenes for the chapel of Saint Helena in the Roman church of Santa Croce in Gerusalemme, display ambitious but not always convincing *scorti*, while the first version of the Chiesa Nuova altarpiece possesses masterful foreshortening not only in the bodies of the hovering putti but most conspicuously in Saint Gregory's right hand, dramatically extended toward the viewer (page 225). Rubens could have found no better school at which to learn these skills than his post at the Gonzaga court in Mantua, where the collection of paintings and frescoes by Andrea Mantegna constituted a veritable treatise on linear perspective and bodily foreshortening. However, for Rubens's execution of the ceiling scenes for the Jesuit church in Antwerp—his greatest achievement in foreshortened narratives seen from below—Titian's example at Santo Spirito in Isola would have been the more likely touchstone. The Jesuit ceiling project involved dozens of discrete scenes spread throughout the soffits of the aisles and upper galleries on the left and right sides of the church. Based on the extant oil sketches, it is clear that Rubens's intention with each scene was not to create an analytically coherent environment but, as in Titian's scenes from the Hebrew Bible, to evoke receding space through figures portrayed in lost profile and through overlapping forms that stand at a logical, if not a fully described, distance from the viewer.

Kirk Nickel

1 Manfred Sellink, compiler, and Huigen Leeflang, ed., "Cornelis Cort," in F.W.H. Hollstein, *The New Hollstein, Dutch & Flemish Etchings, Engravings and Woodcuts, 1450–1700* (Rotterdam: Sound & Vision Interactive; Amsterdam: Rijksprentenkabinet, Rijksmuseum, 2000), nos. 126–28 and 190.

2 For these three paintings, see Harold E. Wethey, *The Paintings of Titian*, 3 vols., *The Religious Paintings* (London: Phaidon, 1969), 1:120–21, cat. nos. 82–84.

3 Jeremy Wood, *Corpus Rubenianum Ludwig Burchard, XXVI: Copies and Adaptations from Renaissance and Later Artists, Italian Artists; II, Titian and North Italian Art*, 2 vols. (London: Harvey Miller, 2011), 1:105–11.

4 Wood, 108.

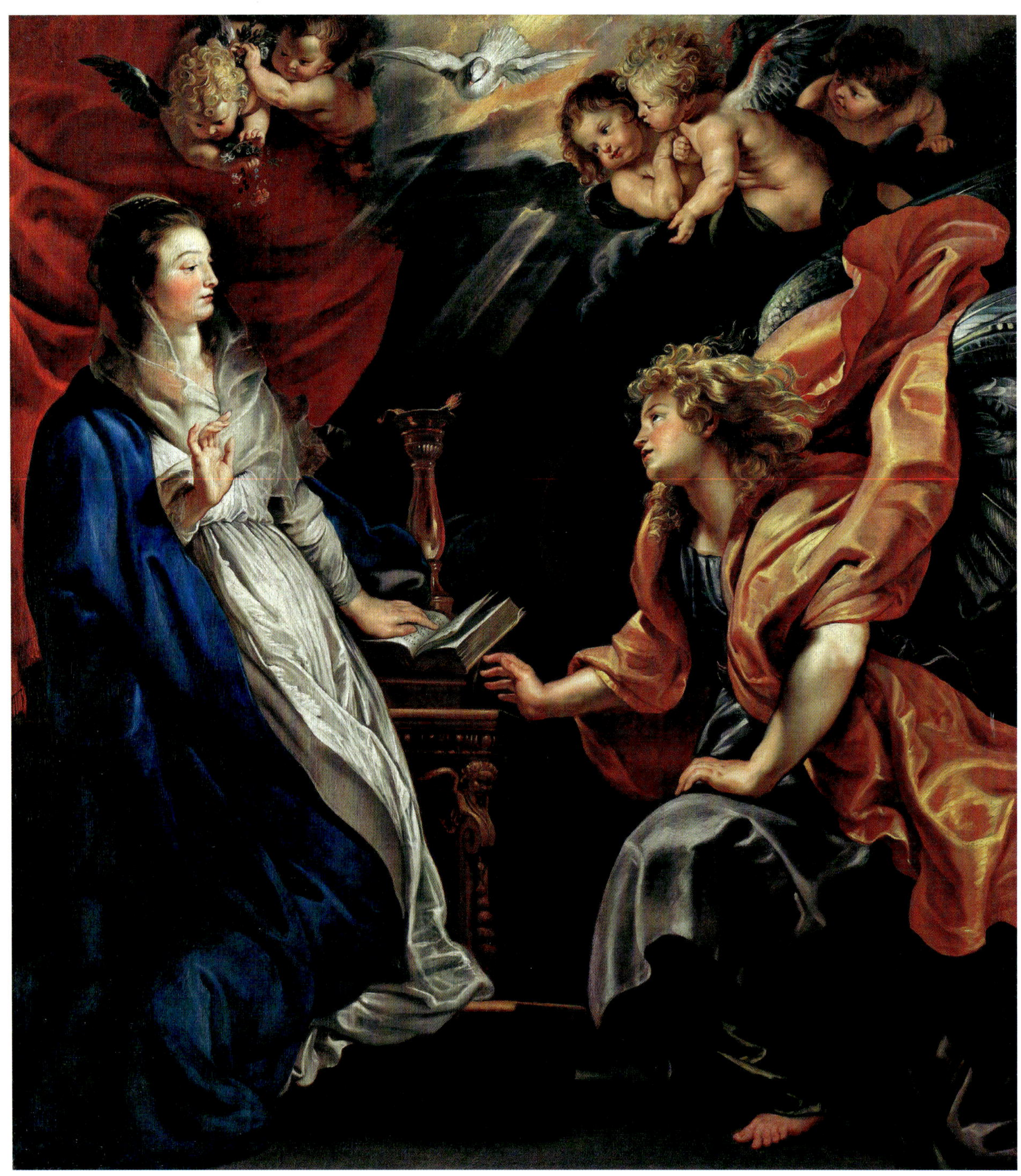

Peter Paul Rubens
The Annunciation
c. 1610
Oil on canvas
224 × 200 cm

Gemäldegalerie, Kunsthistorisches Museum, Vienna
685

Peter Paul Rubens
The Annunciation

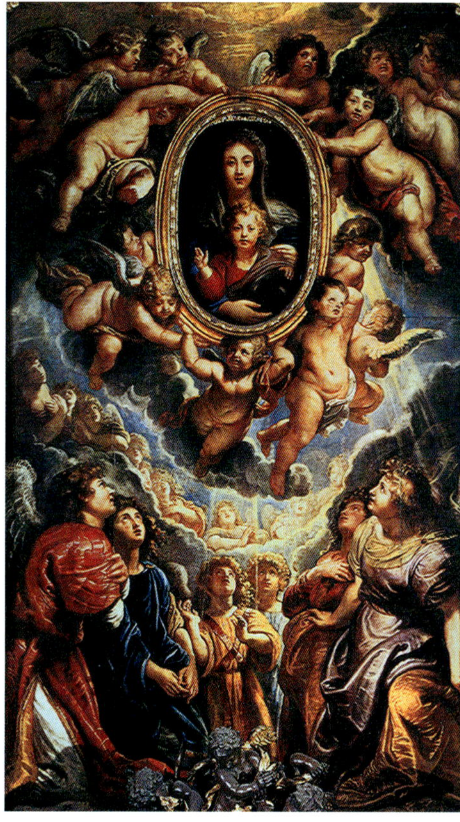

Fig 1 Peter Paul Rubens, *Madonna della Vallicella*, 1606–08. Oil on canvas, 250 × 425 cm. Santa Maria in Vallicella, Rome.

In this sumptuous *Annunciation*, Rubens painted the Virgin Mary being informed by the angel Gabriel that she would be the mother of God:

> The angel Gabriel was sent by God to a town in Galilee called Nazareth, to a virgin engaged to a man whose name was Joseph, of the house of David. The virgin's name was Mary. And came to her, and said, "Greetings favoured one! The Lord is with you." But she was much perplexed by his words and pondered what sort of greeting this might be. The angel said to her, "Do not be afraid, Mary, for you have found favour with God. And now you will conceive in your womb, and bear a son, and you will name him Jesus . . . The Holy Spirit will come upon thee, and the power of the Most High will overshadow you: therefore the child to be born will be holy; he will be called the Son of God."[1]

The painting was hung in the Latin Sodality of Married Men, which was adjacent to the Antwerp Jesuit College.[2] There has been some discussion about the date that the painting was executed because the Jesuits took possession of the sodality building in 1623, but scholars have reached the consensus that this work dates to roughly 1609–1610, shortly after the artist returned from his travels in Italy.[3] Indeed, *The Annunciation* is very Italianate—almost directly quoting the angel from Frederico Barocci's *Annunciation* from 1582–1584, which Rubens may well have seen during his time in Rome, as it hung in the basilica of Loreto.[4] Moreover, the robust figures, swathed in sumptuous folds of drapery, resemble those of Rubens's *Madonna della Vallicella* at the Chiesa Nuovo in Rome (fig. 1).

The figure of Gabriel is particularly dominant in this composition. Not only does the light emitted from the sky above fully illuminate him, but his dramatically sweeping red mantel forms what looks almost like a mandorla around him. His right hand crosses the centre line of the panel, penetrating the Virgin's space, presupposing the physical miracle that is about to happen. Mary steps back, shocked by the news, with her right hand up in a defensive position. With her cheeks flush and gaze cast toward Gabriel, it is clear that she has understood his message. She leans her body against the table, holding the prayer book under her hand, which suggests that the faith and its writings are helping her to grasp this new reality. The choice of this subject for the Sodality of Married Men is interesting: it underscored Mary's seminal role in the Incarnation, while it might also have suggested the passive role that women played in being vessels for Catholic belief.

Demonstrating the staying power of Rubens's Italian-style painting, an engraving was made after the painting, sometime between 1620 and 1640. As is necessitated by the medium, the scene in the engraving is pictured in reverse.

Sasha Suda

1 Luke 1:26–36.

2 Hans Devisscher and Hans Vlieghe, *Corpus Rubenianum Ludwig Burchard, Part V: The Life of Christ before the Passion; I, The Youth of Christ*, 2 vols. (London: Harvey Miller, 2014), 1:32.

3 Edmonds Geudens, *Plaatsbeschrijving der straten van Antwerpen en omtrek naar het charterboek van 1374 der H.-Geesttafel van O.L. Vrouwekerk* (Antwerp: Donk, 1904), quoted in Devisscher and Vlieghe, *Corpus Rubenianum*, 32.

4 Devisscher and Vlieghe, *Corpus Rubenianum*, 32.

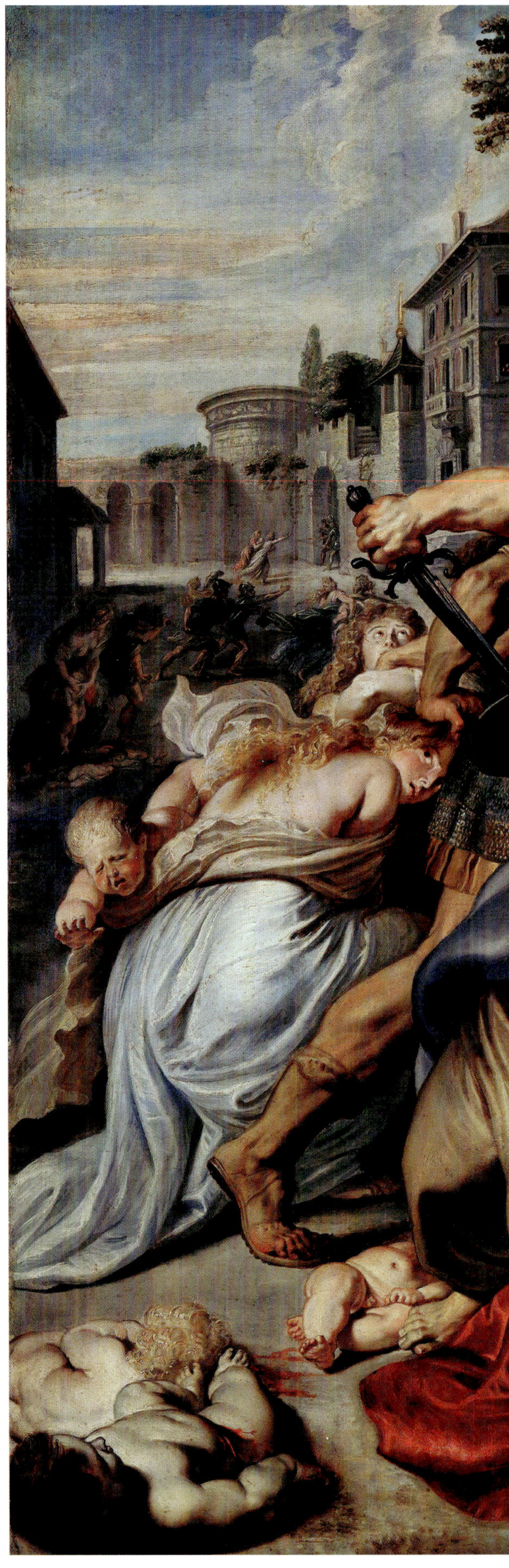

Peter Paul Rubens
The Massacre of the Innocents
c. 1611–12
Oil on panel
142 × 182 cm

The Thomson Collection
Art Gallery of Ontario, Toronto
2014/1581

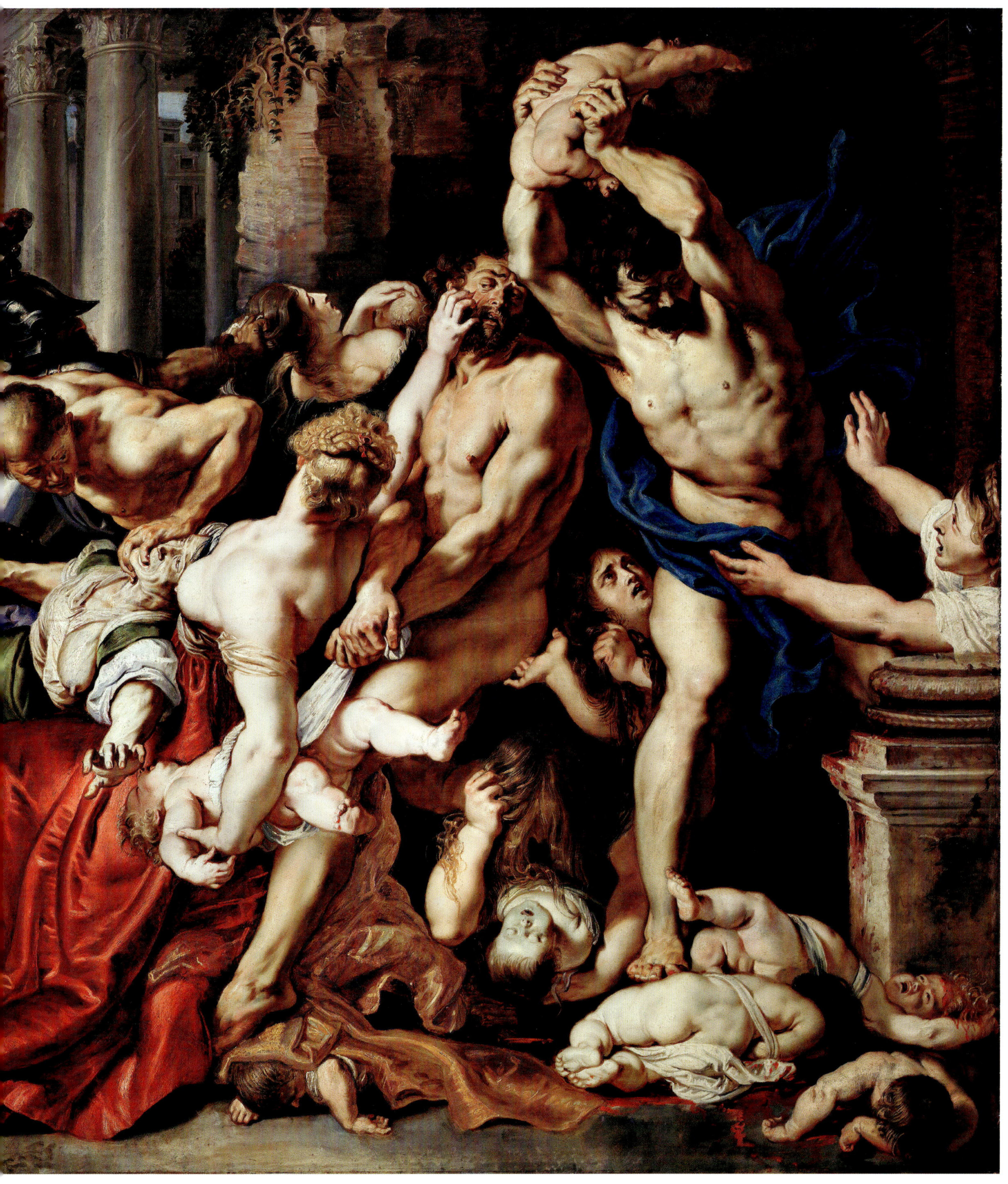

Peter Paul Rubens
The Massacre of the Innocents

Rubens's *The Massacre of the Innocents* illustrates the culmination of one of the New Testament's most gruesome stories. It is also an incredibly effective allegory for understanding the toxicity of humanity's need to wield and maintain power over others. As recounted in the Gospels, Herod, king of Judea, was informed by three wise men that the Christ child was born and would become king of the Jews:

> After Jesus was born in Bethlehem of Judea, wise men from the east came to Jerusalem, asking, "Where is the child who has been born king of the Jews? For we observed his star at its rising, and have come to pay him homage." When King Herod heard this, he was frightened, and all Jerusalem with him; and calling together all the chief priests and scribes of the people, he inquired of them where the Messiah was to be born.[1]

After finding and visiting with Christ, the wise men departed Bethlehem and an imminent threat was revealed to Joseph, the Christ child's father, in a dream:

> Now after they had left, an angel of the Lord appeared to Joseph in a dream and said, "Get up, take the child and his mother, and flee to Egypt, and remain there until I tell you; for Herod is about to search for the child, to destroy him." Then Joseph got up, took the child and his mother by night, and went to Egypt, and remained there until the death of Herod.[2]

Herod, in the meantime, sought the Christ child out vehemently: "Herod . . . was infuriated, and he sent and killed all the children in and around Bethlehem who were two years old or under"[3]

More so than any other painting of this subject from the history of Western art, Rubens's *The Massacre of the Innocents* captures the psychological nuances from Matthew's account—namely, the angst and fear of Herod. Rubens's tangle of figures is on the brink of explosion, composed in a knot of bodies so tight that a mere poke could detonate the picture. Matthew describes a king who has lost perspective, willing to end the lives of boys who represent his kingdom's future to hang onto its throne for, only a short time longer. Such a reading could be extended to Rubens's own composition and its implicit commentary on the reality in which he lived. Indeed, it foregrounds the senselessness of the killing and its unavoidable nature given Herod's blind hunger for power.

The original patron for *The Massacre* at the AGO in Toronto remains unknown. David Jaffé has proposed Antonio Carenna, while Hans Devisscher and Hans Vlieghe maintain that this is not possible.[4] Either way, it was presumably painted for an Antwerp residence, where it hung above the mantelpiece.

Scholars agree that the subject matter provided a wonderful opportunity for Rubens to show off his mastery and recent Italian education. The painting is described by Jaffé as a "bravura display of classical and artistic learning," quoting many of the sources that inspired Rubens while he was abroad.[5] Indeed, David Franklin builds on Jaffé's interpretation of the painting's Italian components in his essay within this catalogue.

Rubens returned to this subject matter in 1636–1638, when he painted another version of the subject, currently in the collection of the Alte Pinakothek in Munich (fig. 1). This composition is significantly different from the Toronto panel. It abandons the tight crop of the earlier version, zooming out to gain the feel of a history painting, in line with the evolution of Rubens's career and of his studio's approach to storytelling. Although the subject remains highly dramatic, it nevertheless loses some of the psychological urgency of the Toronto picture with its plethora of figures and groupings presented at different perspectival positions.

Deaccessioned by the original owner, then again by the Liechtenstein Princes, the Toronto *Massacre*, one of Rubens's greatest masterpieces, is perhaps best known for its reappearance on the world stage in 2001, when it was discovered again after several

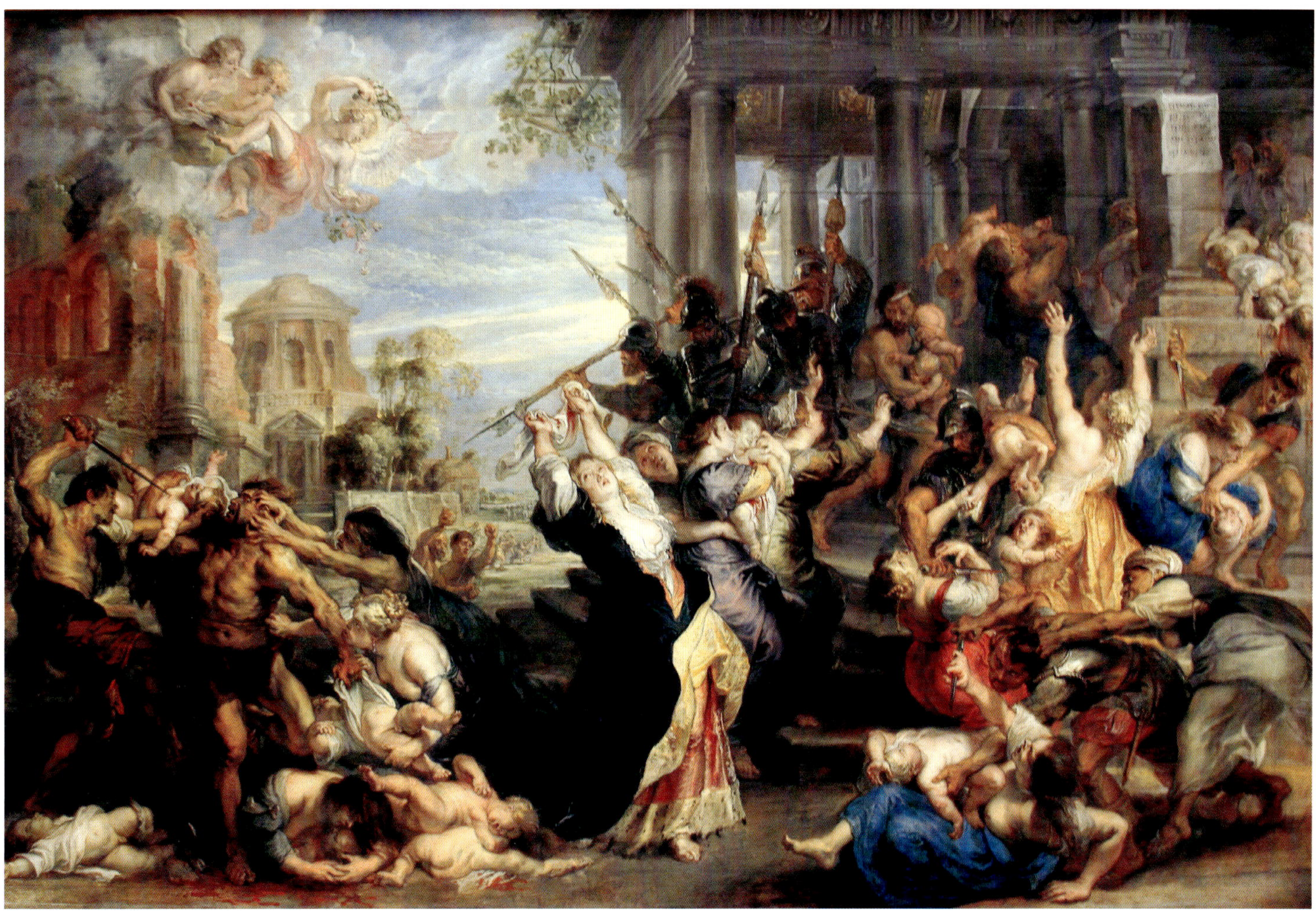

Fig 1 Peter Paul Rubens, *The Massacre of the Innocents*, c. 1637. Oil on panel, 198.5 × 302.2 cm. Alte Pinakothek, Munich. 572. Photo: José Luiz Bernardes Ribeiro/CC BY-SA 4.0.

centuries. The difficulty of the subject matter and its presentation may well have played a role in its centuries' long neglect. Albeit a tour de force of Italian sources and Northern realism, it nevertheless confronts the viewer in an unusually aggressive manner. Given the work's timeless resonance with humankind's most base instincts, there couldn't be a better moment for its reinterpretation and reintroduction to the canon.

Sasha Suda

1 Matthew 2:1–4.

2 Matthew 2:13–14.

3 Matthew 2:16.

4 Hans Devisscher and Hans Vlieghe, *Corpus Rubenianum Ludwig Burchard Part XIII Part V: II. The Life of Christ Before the Passion: 1. The Youth of Christ*, 2 vols. (London/Turnhout: Harvey Miller Publishers, 2014), I: 241-245.

5 See David Jaffé and Amanda Bradley, *Rubens's Massacre of the Innocents: The Thomson Collection at the AGO* (London: Paul Holberton Publishing, 2008).

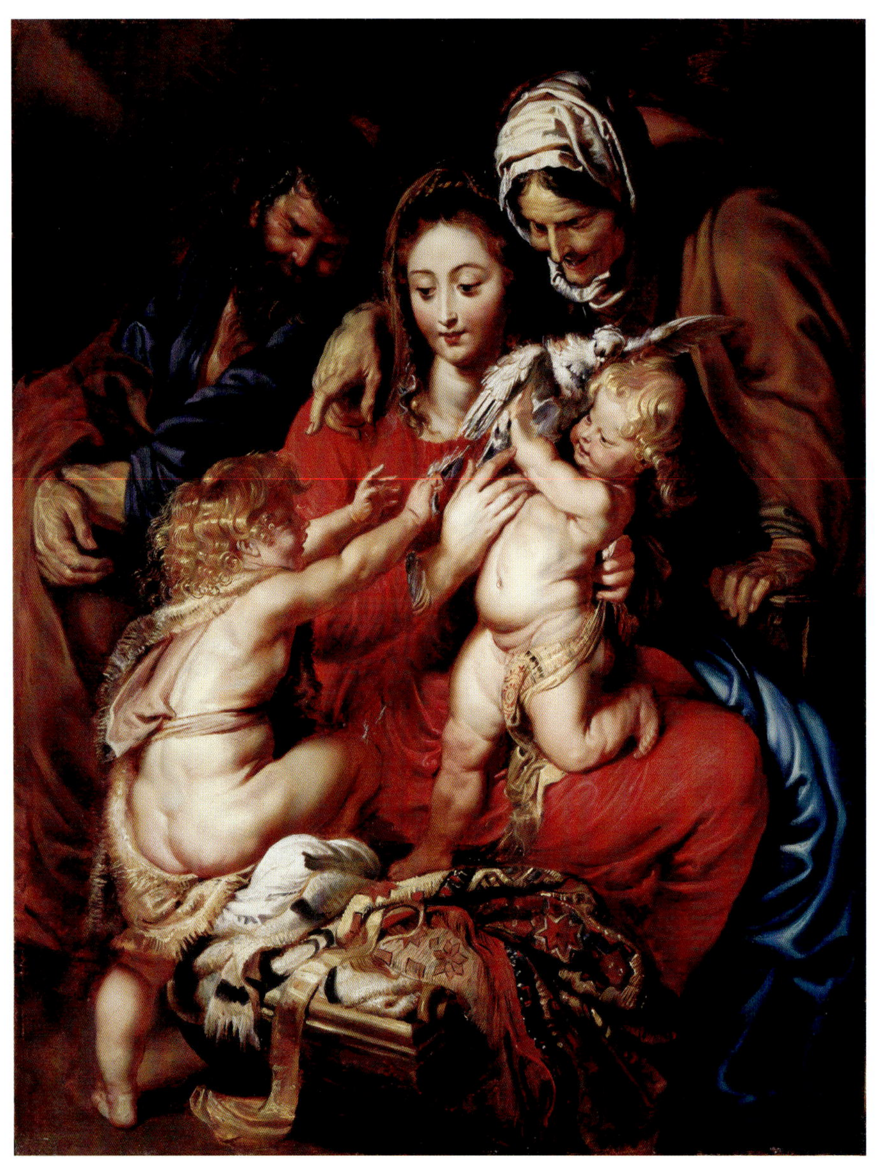

Peter Paul Rubens
The Holy Family with Saint Elizabeth, Saint John and a Dove
1608–09
Oil on wood
66 × 51.4 cm

Metropolitan Museum of Art, New York
Bequest of Ada Small Moore, 1955
55.135.1
Photo © The Metropolitan Museum of Art
Image source: Art Resource, NY

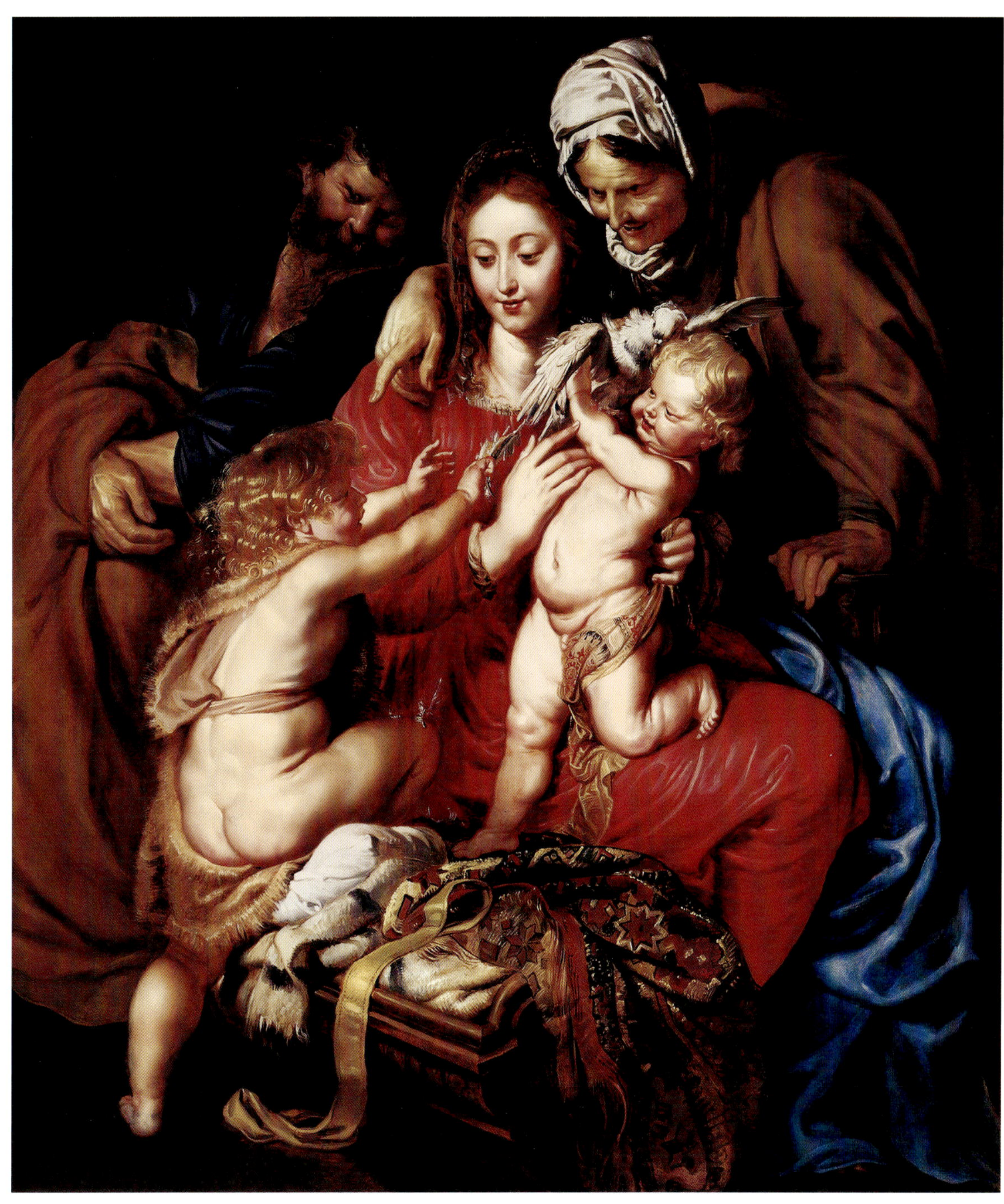

Peter Paul Rubens
The Holy Family with St. Elizabeth, St. John, and a Dove
c. 1609
Oil on wood
138.43 × 120.65 cm

Los Angeles County Museum, California
Colonel and Mrs. George J. Denis Fund
53.27

Peter Paul Rubens
The Holy Family with Saint Elizabeth, Saint John, and a Dove
The Metropolitan Museum of Art, New York

Peter Paul Rubens
The Holy Family with St. Elizabeth, St. John, and a Dove
Los Angeles County Museum of Art

This scene of the Holy Family strays from the traditional portrayal that was common in the Low Countries. Instead of using a static, centrally oriented composition with the figures integrated into the background, Rubens introduces an Italian aesthetic, using bold colours and a tightly packed dynamic configuration. The viewer's eye is led around the composition by a repetition of colours (in particular, the blue and brown of the robes), the triangular placement of the figures, and the gaze and hand gestures of the adults. The centrally placed Virgin dons a loving smile as she watches the two golden-haired toddlers tumble over her lap, completely unruffled by the scene, quite unlike the dove that Jesus has wrenched from the hands of John. John's pose is taken from the representation of a climbing boy in Raphael's *Fortitude* (Stanza della Segnatura, Vatican) or ancient putti on the columns of the old Saint Peter's in Rome.[1] Jesus, who is stepping toward the cradle—a reference to his later entombment—has roughly pulled the dove from John's hand, leaving behind only a few feathers in his grasp. The motif of the crudely handled dove, a symbol of the Holy Spirit, was introduced in Italy around 1611–1612, and might allude to Christ's Passion.[2] At least two Italian paintings from the same period reveal similarities: Orazio Borgianni's *Holy Family with St. Elizabeth and the Infant St. John* (c. 1611), which includes the two boys in playful fight; and Carlo Saraceni's *Madonna and Child with St. Anne* (c. 1610), in which Saint Elizabeth roughly lifts a dove by its wings. These paintings might share a literary source that is unknown to us today.[3]

To date, three versions of *The Holy Family with St. Elizabeth, St. John, and a Dove* are known (a third copy measuring 100 by 78 cm was found by Walter Liedtke in a private collection in Rome) but their exact relation is unclear.[4] Additionally, an anonymous engraving by Martinus van den Enden was made after its composition, a testament to its popularity.[5] The Los Angeles County Museum of Art painting has been convincingly attributed to Rubens, but there remains some uncertainty about the extent to which the master was involved in the production of the smaller version at The Metropolitan Museum. The latter includes more crudely painted passages, particularly in the children's lower legs, the drapery, and the cradle in the foreground. However, such rudimentary sections are not uncommon in Rubens's oeuvre around 1609–1610, and the handling of the paint is comparable to some sections in *Samson and Delilah* (page 33). Liedtke has suggested that the Metropolitan panel might have served as a *modello*, a detailed, preparatory study for a larger painting, prepared for a patron's approval.[6] Such a study could have been used in the workshop to produce several versions, a common studio practice in the 1600s. However, the panel is quite large and unusually finished to serve such a function. The Metropolitan Museum painting might have been Rubens's first attempt to integrate what he had seen in Italy into a dynamic composition, after which he continued to experiment in consecutive versions in different sizes.

Carolyn Mensing

1 David Jaffé and Elizabeth McGrath, *Rubens: A Master in the Making* (London: National Gallery Company Ltd., 2005), 116, exh. cat.

2 Walter A. Liedtke, *Flemish Paintings in The Metropolitan Museum of Art*, 2 vols. (New York: Metropolitan Museum of Art, 1984), 1:209–13.

3 Liedtke, 211.

4 Memo of Walter Liedtke, written to the European Paintings Department on July 26, 1996. Liedtke believed the Rome painting to be a period copy of The Metropolitan Museum of Art (MMA) work, probably made in Rubens's studio around 1609–1610. Based on this find, he concluded that the MMA panel may be considered a *modello* used for more than one studio version, rather than a first version of the Los Angeles painting. See also "The Holy Family with Saint Elizabeth, Saint John, and a Dove," Metropolitan Museum of Art, accessed November 12, 2018, https://www.metmuseum.org/art/collection/search/437529.

5 Max Rooses, *L'Oeuvre de P.P. Rubens: Histoire et description de ses tableaux et dessins*, vol. 1 (Antwerp: Conservateur du Musée Plantin-Moretus, 1886), n.p., cat. no. 232, plate 79.

6 Liedtke, *Flemish Paintings*, 209–13.

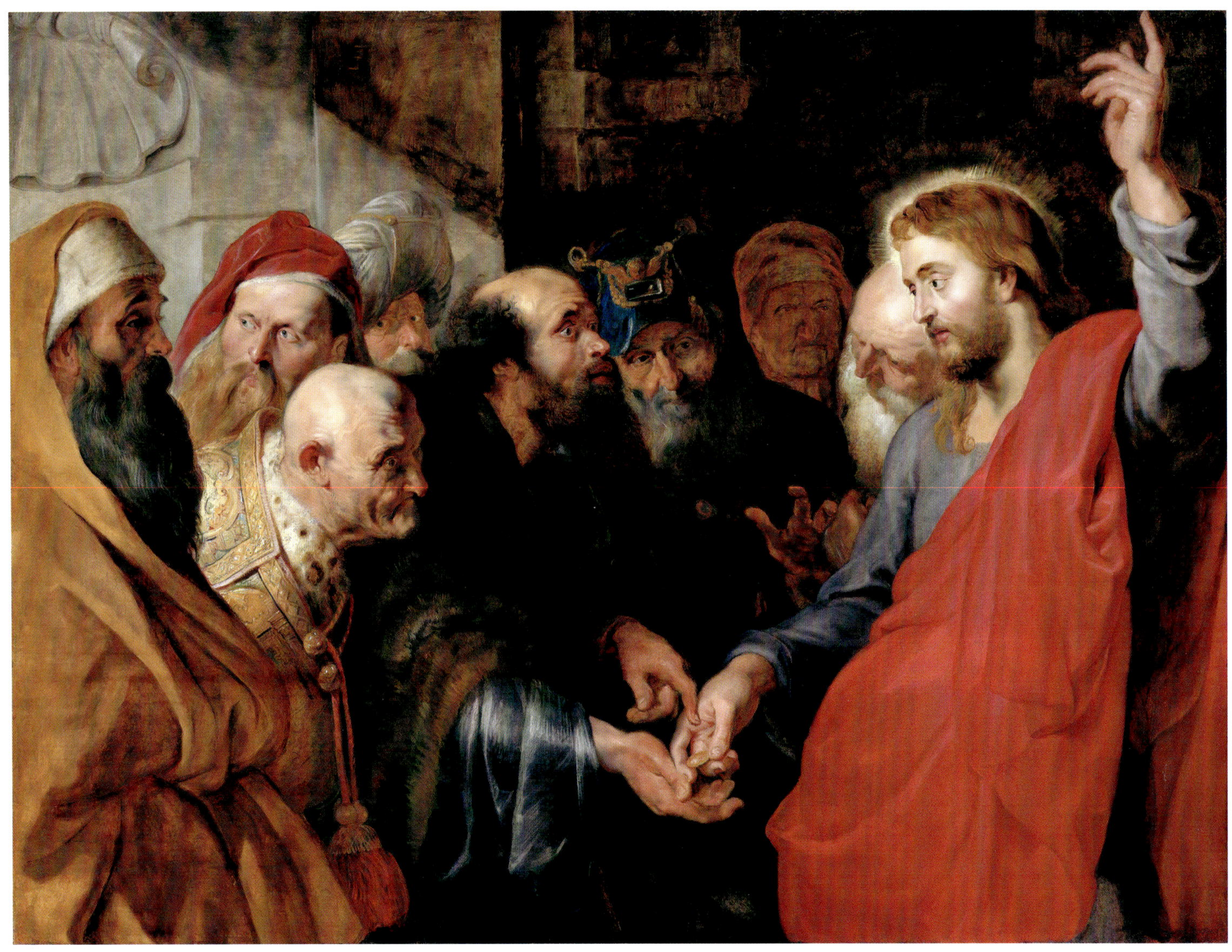

Peter Paul Rubens
The Tribute Money
c. 1610–15
Oil on panel
144.1 × 189.9 cm

Fine Arts Museums of San Francisco, California
Museum purchase, M. H. de Young Art Trust Fund
44.11

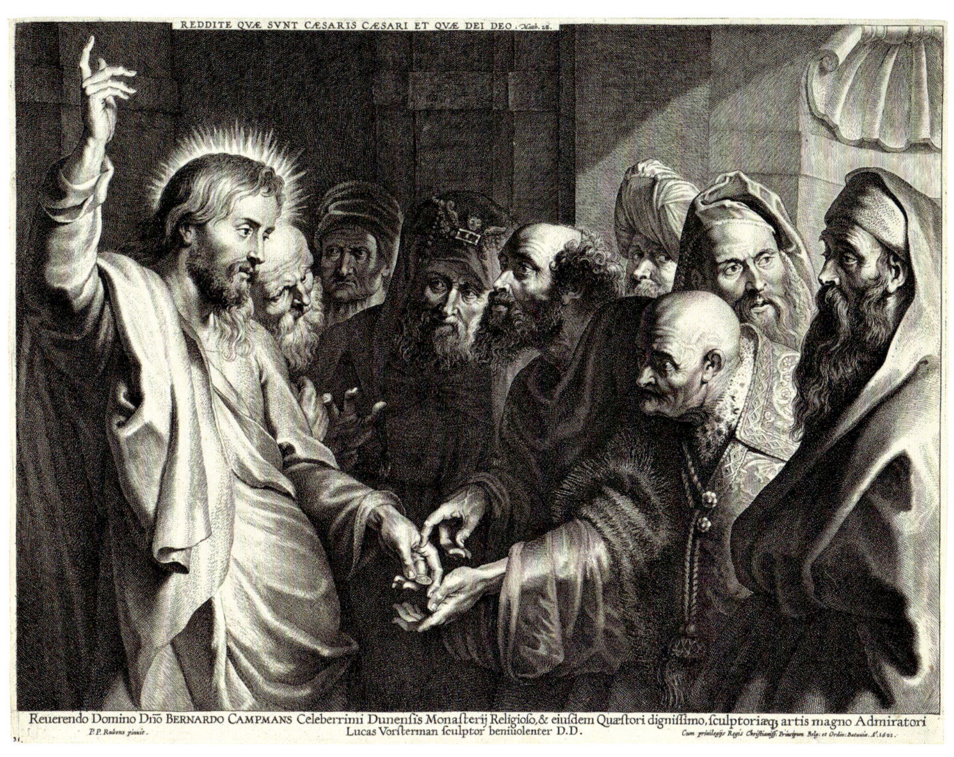

Lucas Vorsterman
born Zaltbommel, Netherlands, 1595;
died Antwerp, Belgium, 1675
after Peter Paul Rubens
The Tribute Money
1621
Engraving
27.5 × 36.4 cm

Rijksmuseum, Rijksprentenkabinet, Amsterdam
RP-P-OB-33.010

Peter Paul Rubens
The Tribute Money

Lucas Vorsterman I
The Tribute Money

Inscribed in plate above Christ: "*REDDITE QVAE SVNT CAESARIS CAESARI ET QVAE DEI DEO. Matth.* 22."

Two lines of dedication in margin: "*Reuerendo Domino D(omi)no Bernardo Campmans Celeberrimi Dunensis Monasterij Religioso, & eiusdem Quaestori dignissimo, sculptoriaeq(ue) artis magno Admiratori / Lucas Vorsterman sculptor beniuolenter D.D.*"

Left: "*P.P. Rubens pinxit.*"

Right: "*Cum priuilegijs Regis Christianiss: Principum Belg: et Ordin: Batauiae. A°.* 1621."

Jesus's confrontation with Jewish elders over the obligation of the Jewish people to observe Roman tax law is recounted in the three Synoptic Gospels (Matthew 22:15–22; Mark 12:13–17; Luke 20:20–26). Designed to entrap Jesus by having him declare exclusive allegiance to either God or the Roman government, the Pharisees' plan begins to unravel when Christ asks to be shown the coin used to pay the tribute. After noting that the Roman emperor's image appears on the coin, Jesus utters his famous dictum: "Render therefore to Caesar the things that are Caesar's, and to God the things that are God's."

Rubens's painting captures the scene in the instant after Jesus has spoken, his gesturing arms still distinguishing between the mundane and the divine. The gospels uniformly describe the would-be accusers as "astonished" by Jesus's response, but Rubens stretches the moment of reaction, exploring the internal states of mind of the various figures as they exhibit amazement, curiosity, or indifference, or as they search the faces of others (including the viewer) to determine how to react to the puzzling statement. Several of the heads in *The Tribute Money* are closely related to those of figures in other Rubens paintings.[1] At the picture's left, the bearded man in the red hat, whose attention has been distracted from Christ, is distinctly similar to the man supporting the dead Christ's proper right arm in *The Descent from the Cross* (1611–1614). In front of him, a bald man thrusting his head forward in an attempt to see resembles the *Saint Bartholomew* from Rubens's *Twelve Apostles* series (c. 1610–1612).[2] Behind these two, a partially seen turbaned figure peering at the viewer recalls a similarly dressed character looking out from behind the masonry wall in Rubens's *The Adoration of the Magi* for the city of Antwerp in 1609. And, near Christ, the older man who wears a blue hood and ornamented headgear favours the elderly turbaned figure who stands next to the oldest magus, also in *The Adoration of the Magi*.

Scenes with figures depicted in half or three-quarter length are relatively rare in Rubens's corpus, and his limited engagement with the format was a phenomenon largely of the 1610s. During these years, he painted a small but significant group of funerary epitaphs with narrative scenes portrayed in half length.[3] For works that could be classed as "gallery pictures," understanding their execution and use becomes more complicated. Multiple versions of *The Devotion of Artemisia* have been put forward as the primary composition that would have involved Rubens's direct participation, but even the best of these seem to be mostly workshop productions.[4] *Diogenes Seeking a True Man* and *The Seven Sages of Greece Disputing over the Tripod* exist only as productions of Rubens's studio or his close circle, the latter composition merely in the form of an oil sketch. The *Old Woman and Boy with Candles*, now at the Mauritshuis, *is* by Rubens, but this seems likely to have been kept as a workshop model since it was still in the master's possession at the time of his death.[6]

The Tribute Money and *Christ and the Woman Taken in Adultery* may be the earliest of Rubens's forays into half-length narratives.[7] Rubens organized the two scenes as near reflections of each other. In the mirrored arrangements and the emphasis on physiognomic variety within the pictures, we observe Rubens thinking through the possibilities of this cropped format; these paintings well may have begun as trial efforts in composing half-length narrative scenes and as a means of recording valued head studies for

Rubens's workshop. That *The Woman Taken in Adultery* appears to have stayed with Rubens to the end of his life lends some support to the notion that the workshop was, at least initially, the primary viewership for these pictures.[8]

Still, our understanding of the use and early reception of these paintings is far from settled. Elizabeth McGrath has made the perceptive suggestion that both *The Tribute Money* and *Christ and the Woman Taken in Adultery* are best considered, together with several of the half-length history paintings already mentioned, as belonging to a class of pictures that represent "instructive dilemmas" from antiquity.[9] As each of the gospel scenes focuses on the moment when Jesus's utterance resolves a rhetorical bind, it is conceivable that the pictures were designed for a Humanist viewership that not only enjoyed verbal jousting but also was amenable to considering Christ's wisdom within an expansive tradition of ancient philosophical thought.

The first record of *The Tribute Money* appears in 1687, in Nicodemus Tessin the Younger's account of his travels in the Low Countries. Tessin saw the painting in The Hague, in the the home of Johan Philip Silvercroon, adopted son of Pieter Spiering van Silvercroon, an art agent and procurer for Queen Christina of Sweden.[10] Whether the painting was at any point destined for Sweden is not known, but it did enter two royal collections. Until 1713, *The Tribute Money* was in the possession of William of Orange (King William III of England), and in the 1840s, it entered the collection of King William II of the Netherlands.[11]

To judge from its proliferation in the seventeenth and eighteenth centuries, *The Tribute Money* was among the most popular of Rubens's compositions during these years. More than fifty painted copies exist, several of which draw on knowledge of one or another of the seven prints that translated the composition, beginning with Lucas Vorsterman's engraving of 1621.[12] This print carries Rubens's "triple privilege" for publishing, but most of the lower margin is given to Vorsterman's dedication of the engraving to the Cistercian monk, Bernard Campmans.[13] Described there as "quaestor," Campmans oversaw revenue and expenditures for the Abbey of the Dunes, and would soon become abbot, when the abbey was reconstituted in Bruges a few years later.

Kirk Nickel

1 Koen Bulckens, *Corpus Rubenianum Ludwig Burchard, V, pt. 2: The Life of Christ before the Passion: The Ministry of Christ* (London: Harvey Miller, 2017), 140–45, no. 31.

2 Compare, also, the older head in *Study of Two Heads of Men* in an American private collection. See Julius S. Held, *The Oil Sketches of Peter Paul Rubens: A Critical Catalogue*, 2 vols. (Princeton, NJ: Princeton University Press, 1980), 1:606–07, cat. no. 440.

3 David Freedberg, *Corpus Rubenianum Ludwig Burchard, VII: The Life of Christ after the Passion* (London: Harvey Miller, 1984), 22.

4 Elizabeth McGrath, *Corpus Rubenianum Ludwig Burchard, XIII: I, Subjects from History*, 2 vols. (London: Harvey Miller, 1997), 2:73–81, esp. 77.

5 McGrath, 9–14, no. 1; 64–71, no. 12.

6 Jan van Meurs posthumous inventory of Rubens's estate, Antwerp 1640, no. 125.

7 Bulckens, *Corpus Rubenianum*, 135–45, nos. 30–31.

8 Joost vander Auwera, "Rubens and His Visual Sources," in Vander Auwera and Van Sprang, eds., *Rubens: A Genius at Work* (Tielt: Lannoo, 2007), 71–76, exh. cat.

9 McGrath, *Corpus Rubenianum*, 11.

10 Gustaf Upmark, "Ein Besuch in Holland 1687 aus den Reiseschilderungen des schwedischen Architekten Nicodemus Tessin d. J.," in *Oud Holland* 18, no. 3 (1900): 149–50.

11 Bulckens, *Corpus Rubenianum*, 140.

12 For all the known paintings and engravings after *The Tribute Money*, see Bulckens, *Corpus Rubenianum*, 140–42.

13 D. de Hoop Scheffer, *Hollstein, Dutch and Flemish Etchings, Engravings and Woodcuts, 1450–1700*, vol. 43, *Lucas Vorsterman I* (Roosendaal: Koninklijke van Pool in cooperation with the Rijksprentenkabinet, 1993), 23, no. 12. The final digit of the engraved date at times has been confused for a "2," rendering the date incorrectly as 1622.

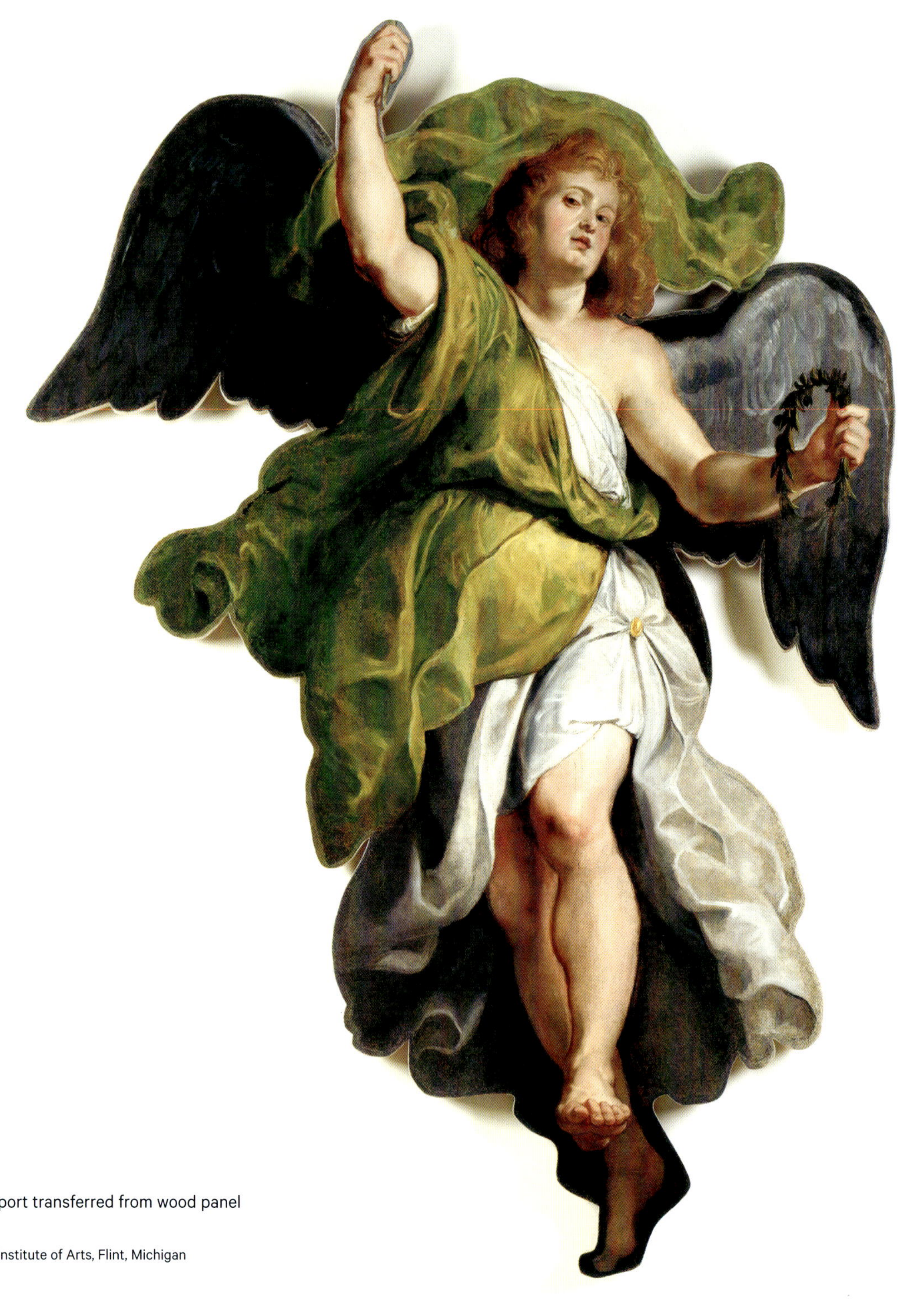

Peter Paul Rubens
Angel
c. 1611
Oil on modern support transferred from wood panel
204.5 × 144.8 cm

Collection of the Flint Institute of Arts, Flint, Michigan
Gift of Viola E. Bray
2005.158

Peter Paul Rubens
Angel

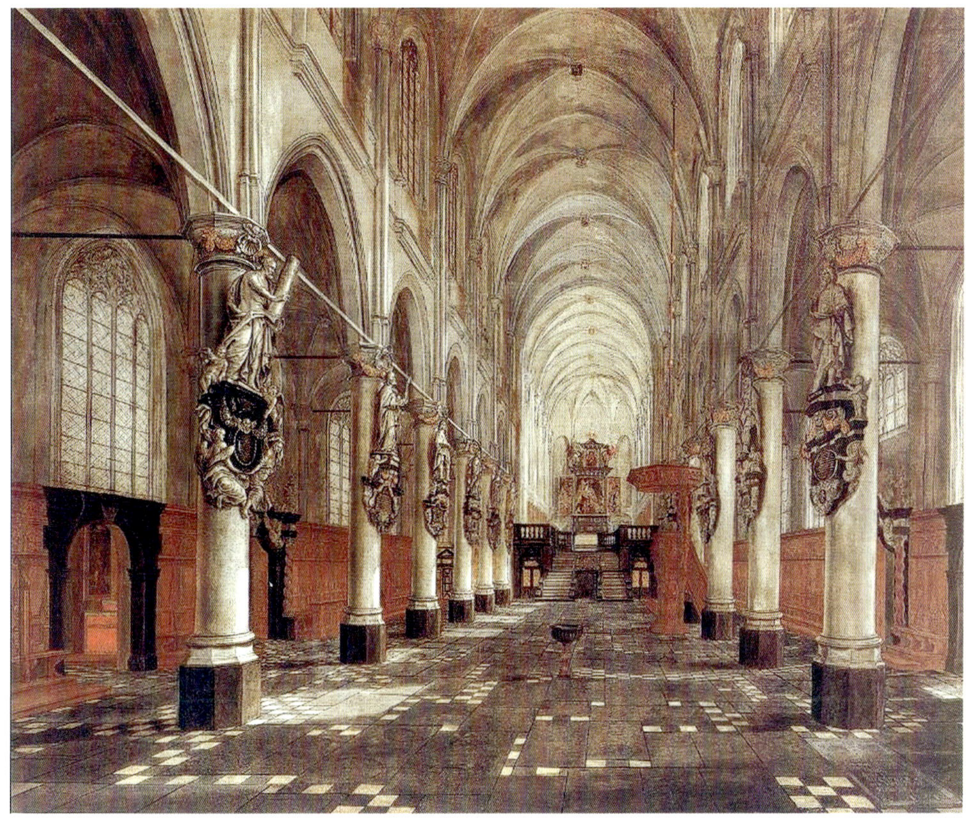

Fig 1 Anton Günther Gheringh, *The Interior of the Church of St. Walburga*, following the restoration of 1992, showing *The Raising of the Cross* in situ, 1664. Antwerp, Saint Paul. Photo: Abbus Acastra/Alamy Stock Photo.

This appealing cutout painting of an angel by Rubens was once part of the complex iconographic scheme surrounding his *The Raising of the Cross* triptych for the Church of Saint Walburga (now in the Cathedral of our Lady) in Antwerp.[1] Executed between 1610 and 1611, the altarpiece was financed and commissioned by Rubens's friend and patron Cornelis van der Geest. In 1794, the church was demolished during the French annexation of Belgium, but visual reconstructions are possible owing to Anthon Gunther Gheringh's *The Interior of the Church of St. Walburga*, 1661, the only extant representation of the high altar shown in situ (fig. 1).[2] The altarpiece had three tiers. Below the central panel of *The Raising of the Cross* were three *predellas* depicting *The Burial of Saint Catherine* (lost), *The Miracle of Saint Walburga in a Storm at Sea* (Museum der Bildenden Künste), and *Christ on the Cross* (lost). Above the panel, a gabled tabernacle, topped by a gold-gilt pelican sculpture, contained a picture of God the Father. A figure of a hovering angel on each side of the tabernacle completed the ensemble.

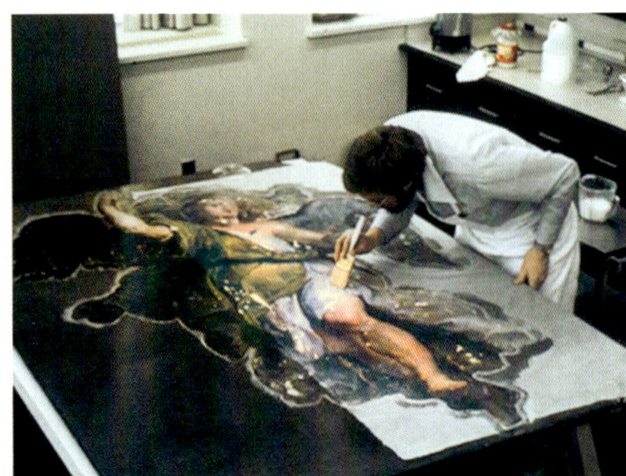

Fig 2 Restoration of the Flint Institute of Arts Rubens's *Angel* at Intermuseum Laboratory, Oberlin, Ohio. Image courtesy of the Flint Institute of Arts.

The Flint angel was situated to the left and is one of the only two subsidiary paintings recovered from the altarpiece when it was dismantled in 1733.[3] Originally painted on oak panel and cut along its contours, Rubens's angel was transferred to a rectangular canvas and painted with a sky backdrop in the eighteenth century. During an extensive four-year restoration at a conservation laboratory in Oberlin, Ohio, X-rays exposed the angel's original silhouette (fig. 2). The removal of varnish and overpaint revealed that more than eighty percent of the original paint remained.[4] Since the completion of its restoration in 1988, the painting has been supported by an aluminum honeycomb core in lieu of a wood panel.[5]

As noted by John Rupert Martin, cutouts such as Rubens's angel were a common form of vernacular decoration, known as *schrooyersels*, made for triumphal arches set up in Antwerp to honour the joyous entry of a prince or governor. The only other surviving cut out by Rubens is his *Jupiter and Juno Enthroned*, created for the entry of the Cardinal-Infante Ferdinand in 1635.[6] Such cut outs also appeared in ecclesiastical architecture of the sixteenth century, but whereas contemporary models were "static," Rubens's animates his angel with "a new sense of illusionistic motion."[7] An impression of movement is convincingly conveyed by the dynamism of the angel's fluttering drapery, outspread wings, and forward step. His imminent takeoff, as Martin keenly observed, is implied by the clear view of his left foot's heel and sole.[8]

Above all, Rubens's innovation lies in the unprecedented dramatic unity he achieves by transcending the concrete boundaries of the triptych's frame and by harmonizing the disparate elements of the high altar. The narrative moment cohesively unfolds across all three panels, the upward glance of the triumphant Christ is directed toward God the Father in the gabled niche, and the angel—with its downcast eyes—appears to address the laity. In addition, both Christopher White and Cynthia Lawrence have compellingly argued that the passage of light portrayed in the triptych corresponded with the natural sunlight entering from the south-facing lancet window.[9] Altogether, the triptych's immensity within the dark, confined space of the choir and the synchronization between representational and natural light created the illusion that the Crucifixion was transpiring in real time. Rubens's angel may be a peripheral figure within the larger scheme of the high altar, but it was nevertheless an active agent in the artist's masterful orchestration between temporal, spatial, and architectural elements—all of which amplify the verisimilitude and emotional profundity of the sacred moment.[10]

Corrinne Chong

1 In 1794, when the church was destroyed, the altarpiece was transferred to Paris. After its reinstitution to the Netherlands in 1815, it was relocated to the Cathedral of Our Lady in Antwerp, where it currently stands.

2 This painting is preserved at the Saint Paul's Church in Antwerp.

3 In 1733, with permission from the magistrate, all three predella paintings—*God the Father*, and the two angels—were sold to raise funds for a new altar. Save for *The Miracle of Saint Walburga* and the Flint angel, the locations of the other pieces remain unknown. An engraving of *God the Father* by Ignace Joseph van den Berghe provides the only evidence for the painting's appearance.

4 Tracee J. Glabb, *Magnificence and Awe: Renaissance and Baroque Art in the Viola E. Bray Gallery at the Flint Institute of Arts* (Flint, MI: Flint Institute of Arts, 2011), 87–89.

5 Glabb, *Magnificence and Awe*, 88.

6 John Rupert Martin, "The Angel from Rubens's 'Raising of the Cross,'" in *Rubens and His World*, ed. Roger Adolf d'Hulst (Antwerp: Het Golden Cabinet, 1985), 143.

7 J. Richard Judson, *Corpus Rubenianum Ludwig Burchard, Part VI: The Passion of Christ* (Antwerp: Harvey Miller, 2000), 121. Cynthia Lawrence postulates that the "victory angels" embellishing the spandrels in the nave arcade of Santi Nereo e Achilleo—restored by Cardinal Cesare Baronio at the end of the sixteenth century—were the most probable prototypes for Rubens's iteration. It is inconceivable that during his almost decade-long Italian sojourn, Rubens would not have seen the most important early Christian churches in person. See Cynthia Lawrence, "Rubens's *Raising of the Cross* in Context: The 'Early Christian' Past and the Evocation of the Sacred in Post-Tridentine Antwerp," in *Defining the Holy: Sacred Space in Medieval and Early Modern Europe*, ed. Andrew Spicer and Sarah Hamilton (London: Routledge Taylor & Francis, 2005), 271–72.

8 Martin, "Angel from Rubens's 'Raising of the Cross,'" 143.

9 Lawrence, "Rubens's *Raising of the Cross* in Context"; Christopher White, *Peter Paul Rubens: Man and Artist* (New Haven, CT: Yale University Press, 1987), 262–63.

10 Based on Lawrence's examination of the Gheringh painting, Rubens's iconographic program might have also encompassed the monumental sculpted apostles in the nave. His multimedia approach and manner of aligning elements along a linear axis anticipates Bernini. See Lawrence, "Rubens's *Raising of the Cross* in Context," 266.

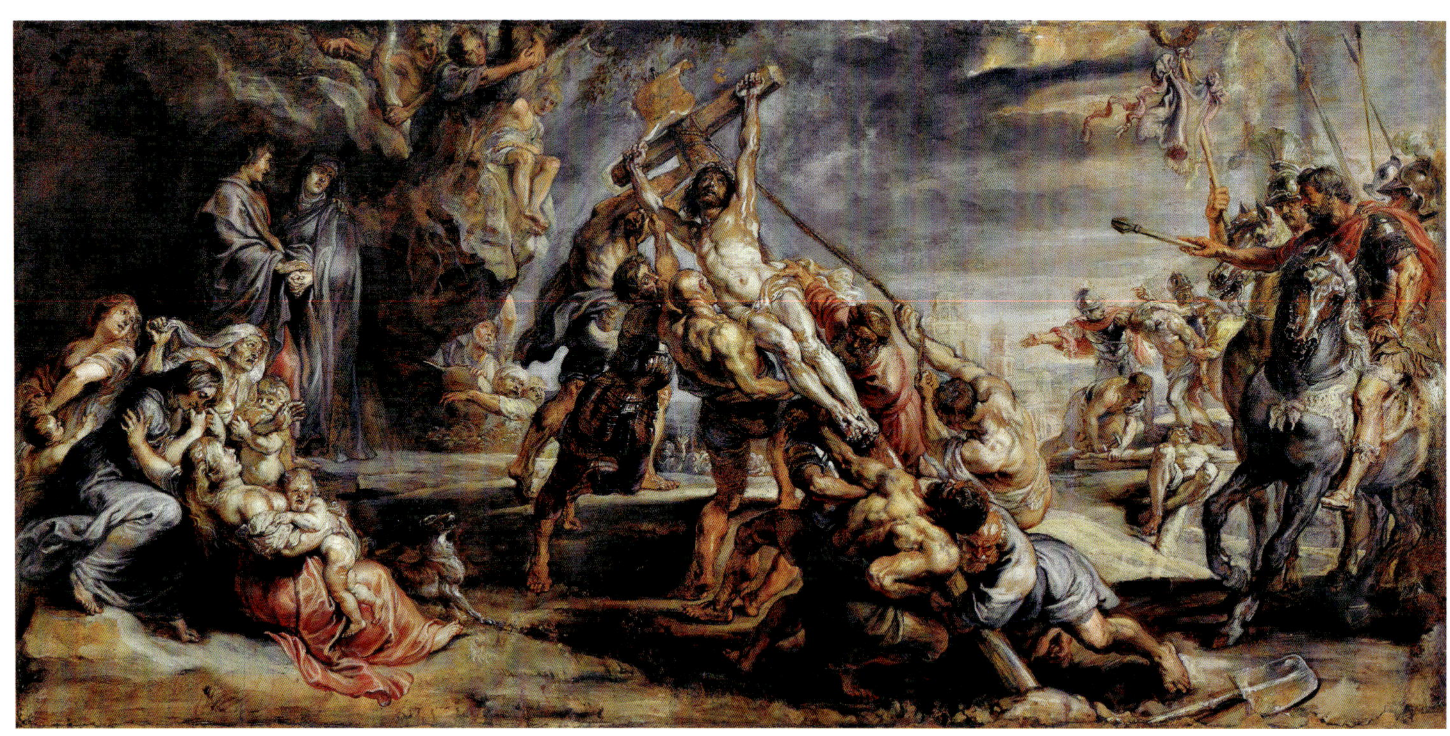

Peter Paul Rubens
The Raising of the Cross
1638
Oil on paper; later mounted on canvas
72.1 × 132.7 cm
Art Gallery of Ontario, Toronto
906

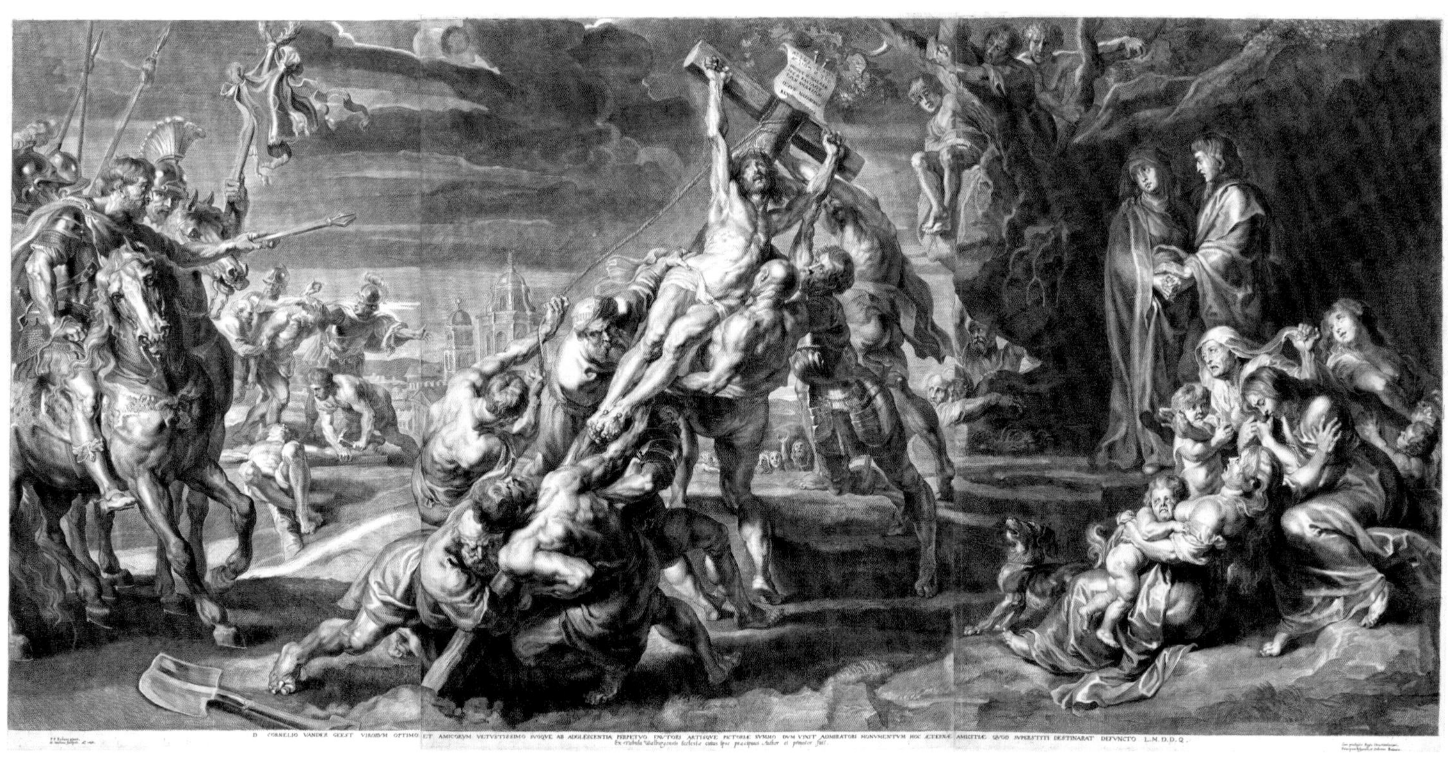

Hans Witdoeck
born and died Antwerp, Belgium, 1615–42
after Peter Paul Rubens
The Raising of the Cross
1638
Engraving
61.6 × 125.2 cm

Rijksmuseum, Amsterdam
RP-P-OB-103.801

Peter Paul Rubens
The Raising of the Cross

Hans Witdoeck
The Raising of the Cross

Upper centre (on a sheet attached to Christ's Cross): *IESVS NASARENVS/REX IVDORVM* (last word partially obscured) and the same lines in Hebrew and Ancient Greek.

Below: *D. CORNELIO VANDER GEEST VIRORVM OPTIMO ET AMICORVM VETVSTISSIMO SVOQVE AB ADOLESCENTIA PERPETVO FAVTORI ARTISQVE PICTORIÆ SVMMO DVM VIXIT ADMIRATORI MONVMENTVM HOC AETERNÆ AMICITIÆ QVOD SVPERSTITI DESTINARAT DEFVNCTO L.M.D.D.Q. / Ex Tabula Walburgensis Ecclesiæ cuius ipse præcipuus Author et prmotor fuit.*

Lower left: *P P Rubens pinxit. / H. Withouc sculpsit A.º* 1638.

Lower right: *Cum priuilegiis Regis Christianissimi / Principum Belgarum et Ordinum Batauiæ.*

It is believed that Rubens sent a studio assistant to the Church of Saint Walburga in 1638 to sketch the altarpiece depicting *The Raising of the Cross.*[1] This monumental altarpiece, created in 1610–1611, was one of Rubens's first significant commissions in Antwerp. It was paid for by the spice merchant Cornelis van der Geest, also an art collector, who owned the painting *Battle of the Amazons*.

Upon receiving the rough sketch of the altarpiece, Rubens adjusted the composition, ultimately overpainting the studio assistant's original sketch. The master unified the altarpiece's three panels into one composition by including a landscape that both harmonizes the three groups of figures and makes the composition feel less crowded. The changes made between the altarpiece and the oil sketch create a much more successful composition for translation to the linear and monochromatic medium of engraving, for which the oil sketch was a preparatory work. The sketches for other prints in Rubens's oeuvre are monochromatic, so this beautifully coloured example stands out. It has been speculated that the highly finished nature of the work is a result of Rubens's desire to gift the work to Van der Geest, a wonderful idea that is nevertheless unconfirmed.

Rubens had considered having an engraving made after the Saint Walburga altarpiece almost two decades earlier, and he mentioned the subject in a letter to Pieter van Veen of January 23, 1619.[2] This impressive engraving printed on three sheets of paper closely follows the oil sketch and is almost as large. The print is dedicated to Cornelis van der Geest, who died in 1638, before the print was published. The dedication reflected Rubens's desire to honour his constant patron while he was still living.[3]

Alexa Greist and Sasha Suda

1 Alejandro Vergara, "The Raising of the Cross, ca. 1638," in *Rubens: Painter of Sketches*, ed. Friso Lammertse and Alejandro Vergara (Madrid and Rotterdam: Museo del Prado and Museum Boijmans Van Beuningen, 2018), 204.

2 See *The Letters of Peter Paul Rubens*, ed. and trans. Ruth Saunders Magurn (Cambridge, MA: Harvard University Press, 1955), 69.

3 "[T]his souvenir of eternal friendship is dedicated, intended to be presented in his lifetime," trans J. Richard Judson and Carl van de Velde, in *Corpus Rubenianum Ludwig Burchard, Part VI: The Passion of Christ* (Antwerp: Harvey Miller, 2000), 108, fig. 78.

Peter Paul Rubens
The Lamentation of Christ
c. 1602–06
Oil on canvas
180 × 137 cm

Galleria Borghese, Rome
411
Photo © Scala/Art Resource, NY

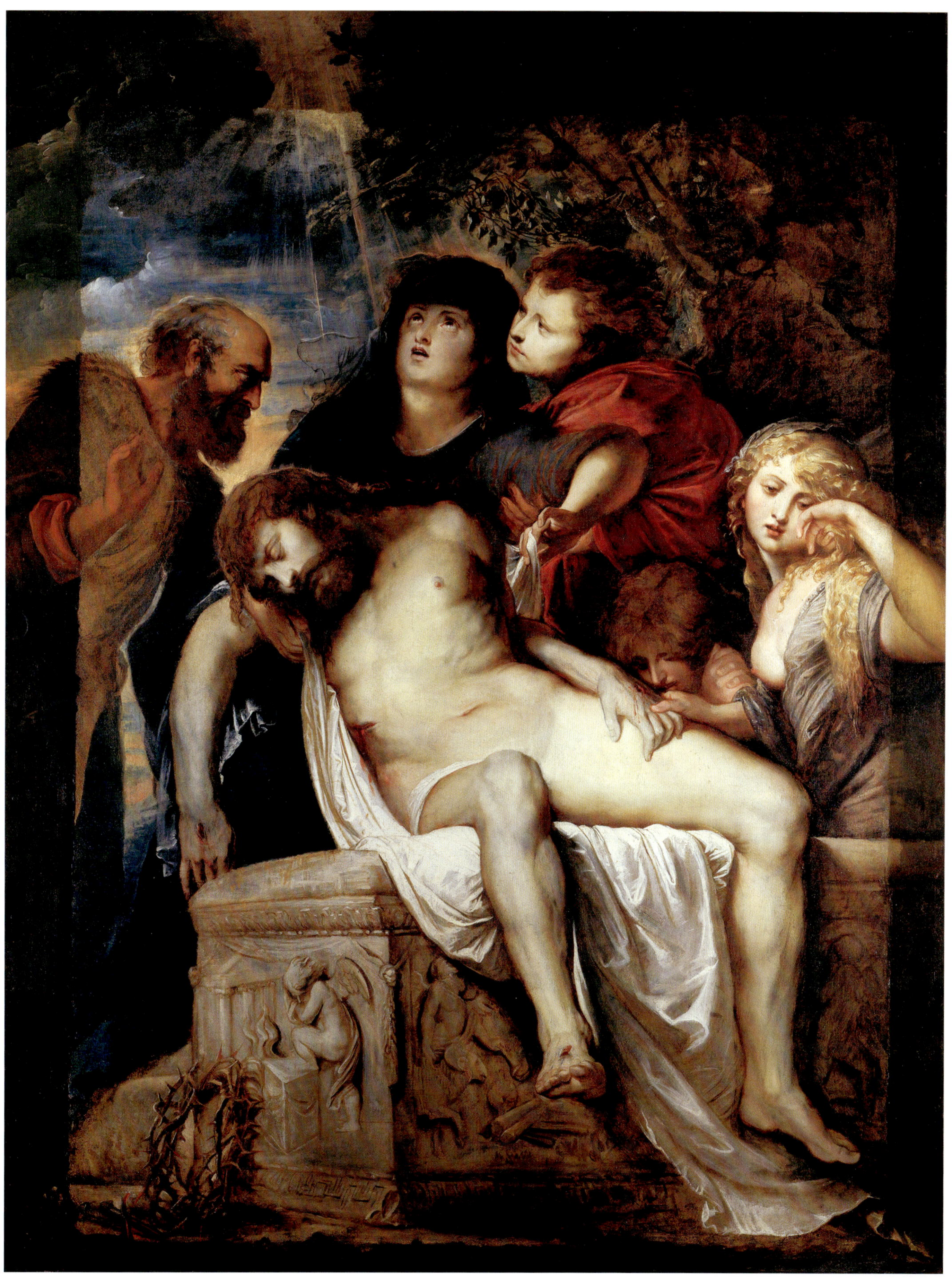

Peter Paul Rubens
The Lamentation of Christ

Rubens's *Lamentation* is one of the first altarpieces he produced. It was presumably destined for an Italian church, though for what original location remains undocumented. Even though the Borghese owned the canvas early on in its history, the family likely did not commission it. Upon his arrival in Rome, Rubens was recommended to Cardinal Alessandro Montalto, and as the latter had the social connections to interact with the Borghese family, the mostly likely explanation is that the prelate commissioned the altarpiece directly before deciding it was more advantageous to gift it, as suggested by Michael Jaffé. The nephew of Pope Sixtus V, Cardinal Montalto had special ties to the church of Sant'Andrea della Valle in Rome and Villa Lante a Bagnaia, two possible original locations to explore.

Whatever the intended destination for the painting was initially, it is quite possible that it was never installed. Its removal from an altar attests to the early fame of the painter, who created a public religious icon that quickly transformed into a private collector's object. On stylistic grounds, the painting dates to the first years of the seventeenth century, not long after Rubens reached Italy; it's slightly more mature in style than the altarpiece produced for Santa Croce in Gerusalemme in Rome, dateable to 1601–1602 and now in the cathedral in Grasse in Southern France. At a later date, the Borghese canvas was extended on all four edges to fit it into a new frame. Curiously, it was attributed to Anthony van Dyck in a nineteenth-century inventory.

The painting features the dead Christ, on a tomb, supported by mourners, while appearing to collapse backward. His mother glances heavenward, away from the pathetic scene, for divine sustenance and a powerful, warm light strikes her covered head. In an unusual detail, to bring more attention to her in the design, the Virgin Mary holds the white winding cloth with which Christ's body was removed from the cross. The youthful John the Evangelist supports her, just as she supports her son. Mary Magdalene is represented at the right edge in a complex serpentine pose with her under-chemise and one breast accidentally revealed in an arrangement Rubens would often return to in his religious paintings. Her contorted pose and hair sharply parted in the centre in an *all'antica* manner are evidence of a high stylization. Yet the tears and detail of some of Christ's blood on her finger reveals the artist was also striving for a genuine pathos with this counterpoint character in the drama. The gesture of her left hand to her cheek evokes traditional images of melancholy traceable to early fifteenth-century Netherlandish painting, which Rubens would have known well from his youth. Rubens did not introduce haloes but gave the figures relatively more naturalistic radiances around their heads.

Christ is held like an ancient hero on a reused ancient stone sarcophagus, already showing signs of wear, which will become his tomb. The two sculpted, faux classical reliefs featuring scenes of sacrifice and mortality mirror the main subject as in a predella panel. Rubens would have seen this motif in paintings by Titian, such as the Pesaro altarpiece that, by coincidence, survives in Antwerp. Instruments of the Passion—the crown of thorns and the nails from the Cross—are artificially arranged in the bottom left corner. That we can see the underside of Christ's foot suggests that, in its original placement, the canvas was elevated.

As so often in Rubens's work, pictorial influences are not obvious but adeptly reblended. Creative absorption, as opposed to direct quotation, was his preferred method. All suggestions of potential sources for Rubens's canvas from paintings of the same theme, including a range of Italian examples by Correggio, Giuseppe Porta, and Tintoretto, while evocative, are not completely convincing. Curiously, Andrea Mantegna's secular *Bacchanal* prints have also been cited as sources for the pose of Christ, and Rubens is known to have copied this print. This might be a coincidence, or unintentional; however, a closer and more likely model for the positioning of Christ's legs is Michelangelo's fresco of *Jonah* on the Sistine Chapel ceiling.

Even if the thick, muscular form of Christ illustrates the impact of ancient sculpture and Michelangelo, the pictorial style is distinctly northern Italian, inspired by the work of Titian and Tintoretto, for its supernatural lighting, dense atmosphere, and softly modulated, slightly out-of-focus bodies. The sense of tumult and fury possessing the scene conjures the Italian artists' paintings. As they did, Rubens painted rapidly with a detectable pace in the handling, as if life itself could be imitated in the movement of soft paint. The dark, restrained palette is only augmented by the dramatic red burst of John's robe. Somewhat unusually, this iconic scene takes place outdoors. There is no view to the distance, just the trees forming an enclosed, curtain-like background and the dramatic, appropriately tragic sky. Rubens is sensitive to indicate the temperature: it is cold enough for Joseph of Arimathea to wear fur, and this contributes to our melancholy feeling in looking at the painting.[1]

David Franklin

1 Selected Bibliography

Didier Bodart, Rubens (Milan: Mondadori, 1985).

David Freedberg, *Corpus Rubenianum Ludwig Burchard Part VII: The Life of Christ after the Passion* (London: Harvey Miller, 1984).

J. Muller Hofstede, "An Early Rubens Conversion of Saint Paul," *Burlington Magazine* 56 (1964), 95–98.

David Jaffé and Elizabeth McGrath, *Rubens: A Master in the Making* (London: National Gallery Company Ltd., 2005).

Michael Jaffé, *Rubens and Italy* (Ithaca, NY: Cornell University Press, 1977).

J. Richard Judson, *Corpus Rubenianum Ludwig Burchard Part VI: The Passion of Christ* (Antwerp: Harvey Miller, 2000).

Hans Vlieghe, *Corpus Rubenianum Ludwig Burchard Part VIII: I, Saints, 2 vols.* (Brussels: Arcade Press, 1972–73).

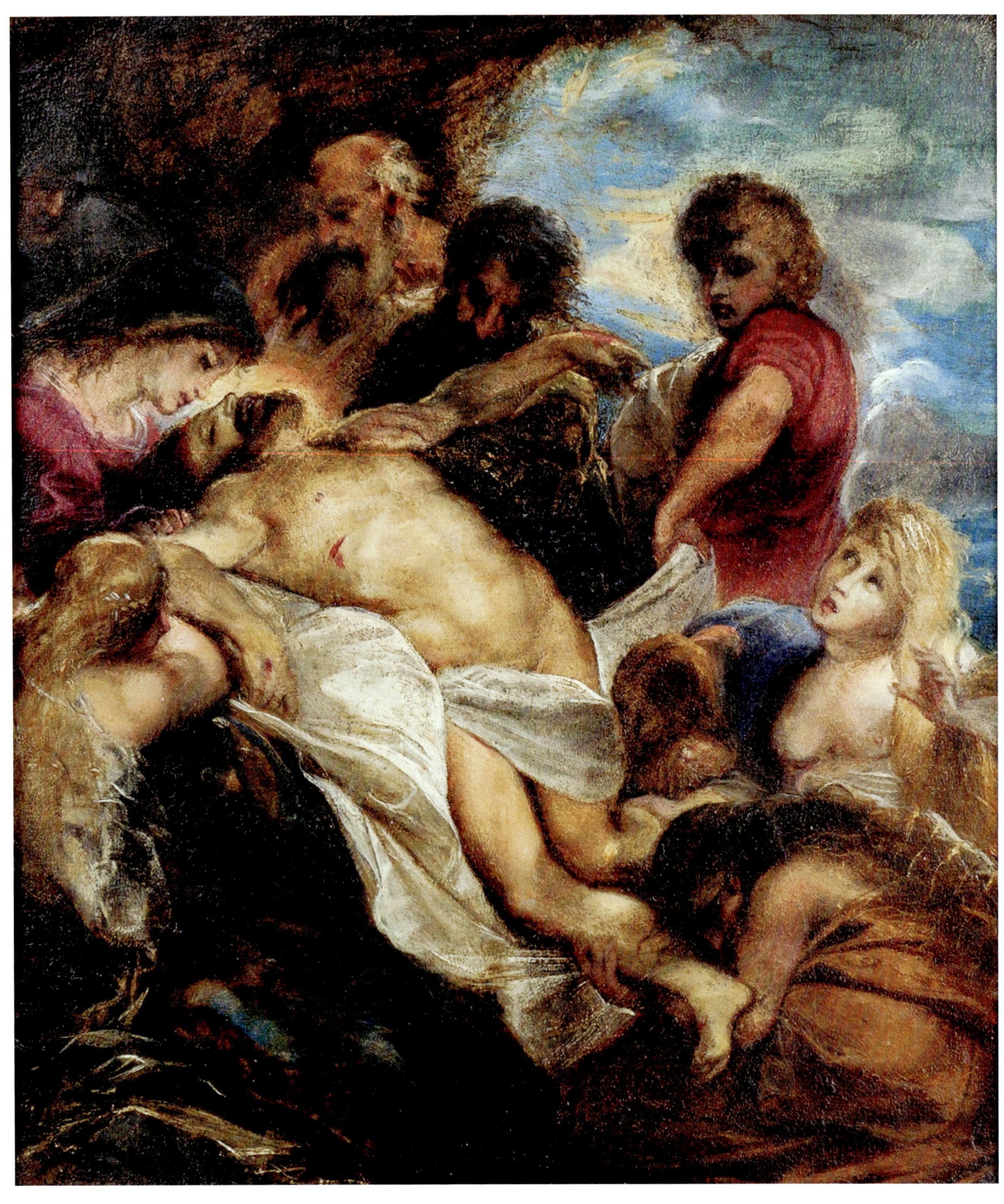

Peter Paul Rubens
The Lamentation
c. 1605
Oil on copper
27.9 cm × 24.13 cm

Cummer Museum of Art & Gardens, Jacksonville
Bequest of Ninah M. H. Cummer
C.0.131.1

Peter Paul Rubens
The Lamentation of Christ
Cummer Museum, Jacksonville

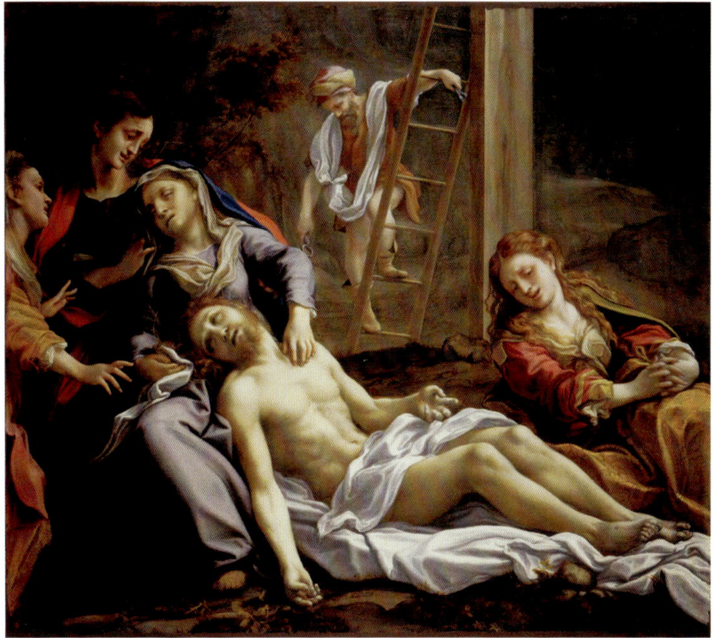

Fig 1 Antonio Allegri Correggio, *Lamentation*, c. 1524. Oil on canvas, 157 × 182 cm. Galleria Nazionale, Parma. Photo: Scala/Art Resource, NY.

The *Lamentation* at the Cummer Museum in Jacksonville, Florida, is an early example of Rubens's treatment of this subject, which became prolific in his oeuvre. This painting was in the collection of the Colonna family in Rome and is mentioned in their 1783 inventory.[1] Indeed, Philip Rubens worked for Cardinal Ascanio Colonna in 1605–1606, and it has been suggested that he arranged for the sale to his employer.[2] The small size and compromised surface of the Jacksonville picture have led some to believe that it was a preparatory work for a larger composition. Nevertheless, it seems more likely that the Cummer *Lamentation* was a finished work with a completed composition.[3] The composition itself is remarkably original for its time. Rubens breaks away from the typical iconography of the subject: Christ does not lie in the lap of the Virgin nor is he seated atop a sarcophagus, supported by her.[4] Rubens had not yet broken with convention when he painted the Borghese *Lamentation* (page 197). The Cummer painting also differs from the design of Correggio's 1524 *Lamentation* (fig. 1), which up to that point had represented the greatest departure from tradition.

In this painting, Rubens pictures Christ moments after he was removed from the Cross, with his left arm still in the position that it assumed during his Crucifixion. His body is splayed across a rocky outcropping and he is surrounded by seven mourners—Joseph of Arimathea, Nicodemus, Saint John the Evangelist, the three Marys, and the Virgin Mary. The glow emanating from Christ's halo connects his gaze to that of his mother and creates a sense of time stopping. This draws out the viewer's understanding of the special mother-son relationship shared by Christ and Mary and contrasts with the rest of the composition, wherein the sweeping brushstrokes and the circle of mourners suggest the emotional tumult of grief. Richard Judson has likened the intense sorrow of the figures in this composition to that of Yale's *Hero and Leander* (page 239).[5] The two intimately scaled works (both on view in this exhibition) appeal to the emotions, encouraging a viewer's contemplation of how one might react to the sudden death of a loved one. Appealing to the viewer's emotions was a basic premise of Counter-Reformation art. The Cummer *Lamentation* does so beautifully and perhaps most viscerally in the passage where Mary Magdalene buries her face in Christ's feet.

Sasha Suda

1 The copper panel bears the seal of the Colonna family on its reverse and is listed in the 1783 inventory of treasures from the Colonna palace.

2 Justus Müller Hofstede, *Rubens in Italien* (Cologne: Wallraf-Richartz-Museum, 1977), 159.

3 J. Richard Judson, *Corpus Rubenianum Ludwig Burchard Part VI: The Passion of Christ* (Antwerp: Harvey Miller, 2000), 210, no. 59.

4 Judson, 210.

5 Ibid.

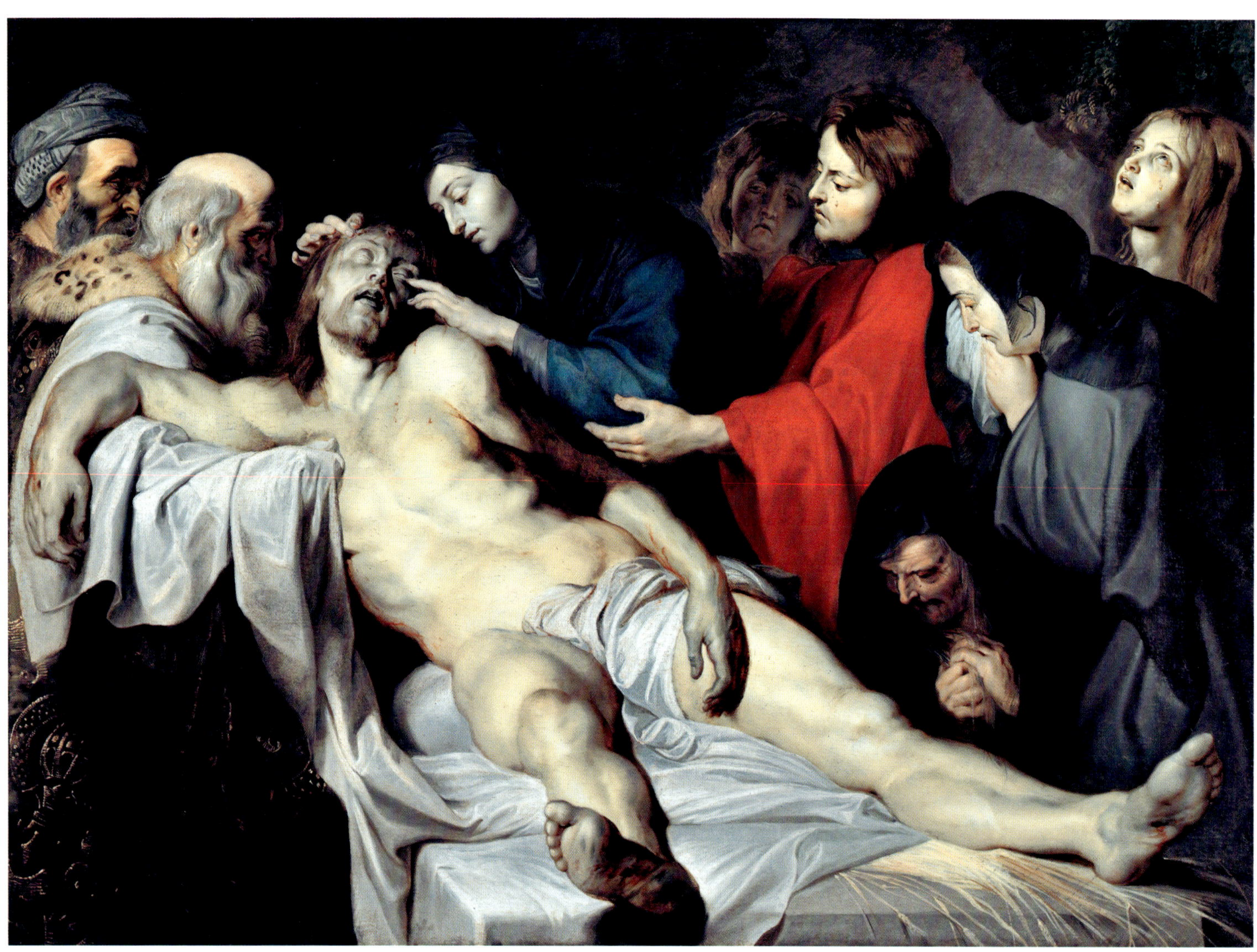

Peter Paul Rubens
The Lamentation
c. 1612
Oil on canvas
150 × 204 cm

Liechtenstein, The Princely Collections, Vaduz-Vienna
GE 62

Peter Paul Rubens
The Lamentation
Liechtenstein, The Princely Collections, Vaduz-Vienna

In the Liechtenstein *Lamentation*, Rubens presents a visceral image of the dead Christ, moments after he was removed from the Cross and before he was cleaned by his mother, the Virgin Mary. Christ's body confronts the viewers as it forms a strong, central diagonal line from the composition's top left to the bottom right, where his feet are effectively foreshortened. The body is laid atop the stone unction on which he will be prepared for burial, and has the blue hue of death that has taken full hold of his face. The Virgin Mary has a similar pallor as she closes Christ's left eye with one hand and pulls a thorn from his forehead with another. The similarity of their skin tones stands in stark contrast to the others pictured, whose faces are highlighted with a lively pink colour. The similitude of Christ's and Mary's pallor encourages the viewer to consider the closeness of their relationship and the unbearable experience of a mother's burial of her own child. Joseph of Arimathea features prominently in the image, his bald head reflecting light from above as he supports Christ's right arm and upper body. Joseph's body is draped in the white cloth mentioned in all four gospels:

> Then [Joseph] took [the body] down, wrapped it in a linen cloth, and laid it in a rock-hewn tomb, where no one had ever been laid.[1]

Indeed, the cloth's clean whiteness features prominently against the dark background of the painting and stands in contrast to Christ's uncleansed yellowish-blue skin. The sorrowful tenor of the painting aligns with Counter-Reformation ideals, wherein art had the express aim of engaging the empathy and emotions of its Catholic viewers. Like in the *Michielsen Triptych*'s central panel (pages 208–9) and the Getty's *Entombment*, Christ's body lies on wheat sheaves, or "straw." This reference to a key ingredient in bread proposes to viewers that Christ's body is present in the Eucharist. The real presence of Christ was a major tenet of Catholic post-reform faith, and one not shared by the Calvinists in particular. Rubens's extensive exploration of this particular subject suggests that it was popular with patrons. Acquired by the Prince of Liechtenstein between 1767 and 1780, the painting's original context is unknown.

Sasha Suda

1 Luke 23:53–54.

Peter Paul Rubens
The Entombment
c. 1612
Oil on canvas
131.1 × 130.2 cm.
J. Paul Getty Museum, Los Angeles
93.PA.9

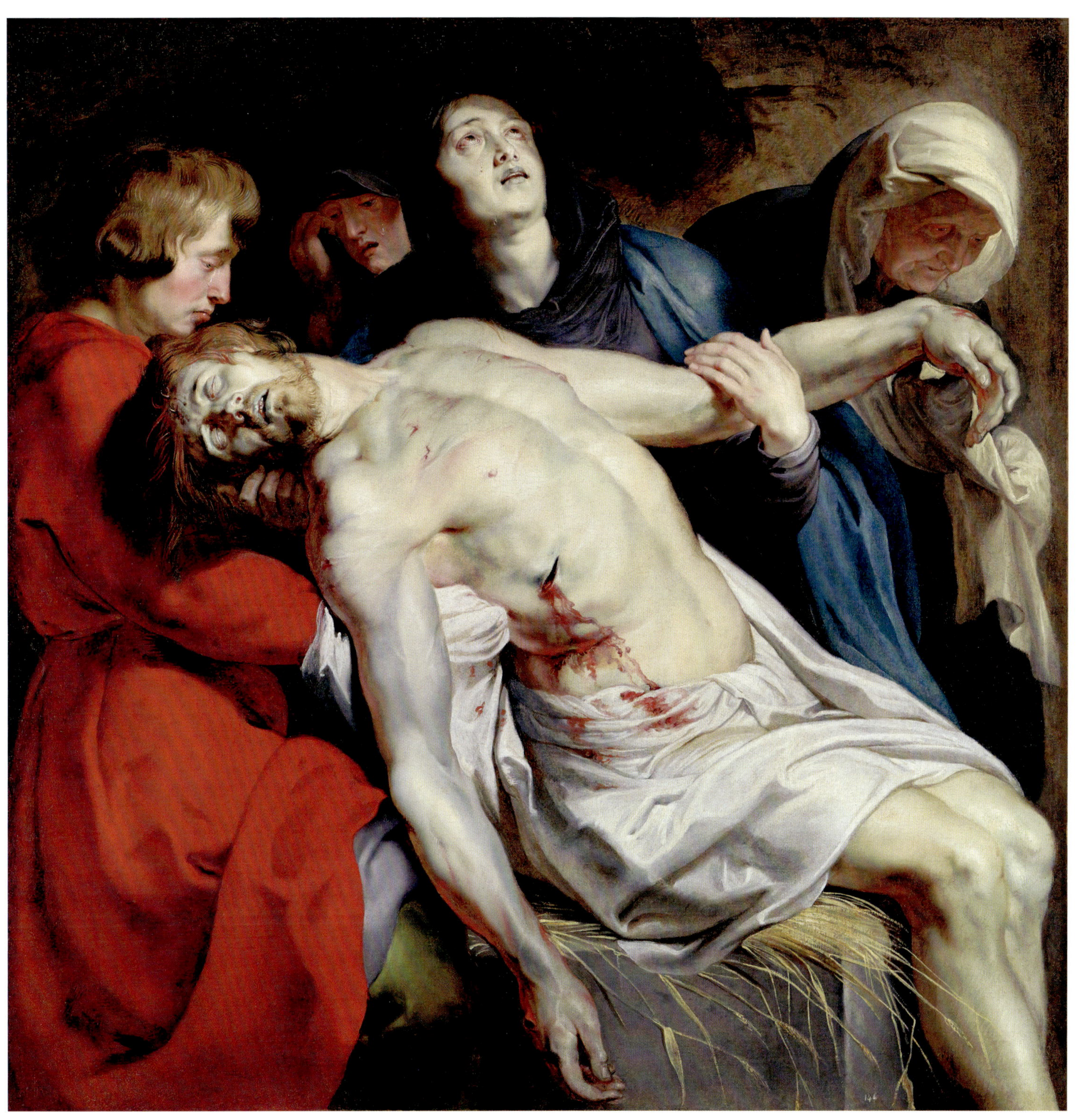

Peter Paul Rubens
The Entombment
J. Paul Getty Museum, Los Angeles

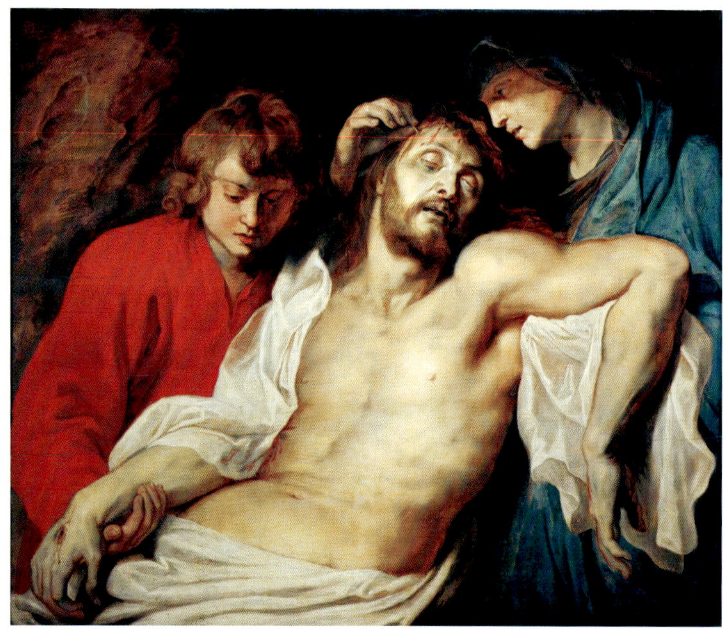

1 Peter Paul Rubens, *Deploration of Christ with Saints Mary and John the Apostle*, c. 1614–1615. Oakwood, 107.5 × 115.5 cm. Kunsthistorisches Museum, Vienna, Austria. 529. Photo: Erich Lessing/ Art Resource, NY.

The events following Christ's Crucifixion are consistently reported in all four gospel accounts. After Christ was removed from the Cross, Joseph of Arimathea assumed responsibility for his burial; Christ's body was cleansed by his mother and eventually laid to rest in a sarcophagus. Unlike other paintings of the same subject by Rubens, the Getty *Entombment* omits Joseph of Arimathea and focuses the story on those closest to Christ when he died. The liquid blood dripping out of Christ's chest wound suggests that Christ has *just* descended the Cross and that the work of cleaning the body and preparing for his burial is still ahead of the mourners. Saint John the Evangelist, a faithful apostle, stoically bears the weight of his upper body while the Virgin Mary grieves, her red eyes looking up to Heaven for an explanation of her son's death. The various tones of blue in the robes of the three Marys underscore the blueish pallor of Mary's own face and lips, which stand in stark contrast to the rosy-cheeked faces of the others in the image. As with other images of the subject, Rubens connects the Virgin Mary and Christ subtly to underscore their important relationship.

Compositionally, the Getty *Entombment* shares much in common with the *Michielsen Triptych* (page 208), which was painted roughly six years later. In the later work, the figures of Christ and Mary are almost identically composed, with the background figure of Mary Magdalene replaced by John the Evangelist in a very similar pose to her. Joseph of Arimathea makes a reappearance in the *Michielsen Triptych*, replacing the Getty panel's Saint John the Evangelist and creating a tighter grouping of figures. The Kunsthistorisches *Lamentation* (fig. 1) focuses this scene even further, cutting the cast of characters down to three: Saint John the Evangelist, the Virgin Mary, and the dead Christ. Indeed, Rubens painted two main types of *Lamentation* or *Entombment* scenes—the type featured here, presenting Christ somewhat upright and tightly framed by a smaller group of people; and another, in which he is laid out more prostrate, with a larger group surrounding him, as in the Liechtenstein *Lamentation*. The latter type relied heavily on Caravaggio's *Entombment of Christ* (fig. 2) from 1603/1604, for the Church of Santa Maria della Vallicella (the Chiesa Nuova)—a painting Rubens certainly would have seen, having himself painted the high altar for that church two to three years later. The Cummer *Lamentation* (page 200) and an *Entombment* from the National Gallery of Canada underscore this point well.

Of Rubens's surviving *Lamentation* and *Entombment* pictures, the Getty is one of the most affective images of the scene. Like others, it features him atop wheat sheaves to underscore his real presence in the Eucharist. The bloodiness of his chest and forehead further emphasize the reality of his death. Mary Magdalene's shock, the Virgin Mary's sorrowful gaze upward, and the elder Mary's resignation as she holds Christ's left hand all engage the viewer's own experience of death in a visceral way. These motifs, together with the beautiful surface of the painting, demonstrate Rubens's uncanny ability to make something so sad profoundly beautiful.

Sasha Suda

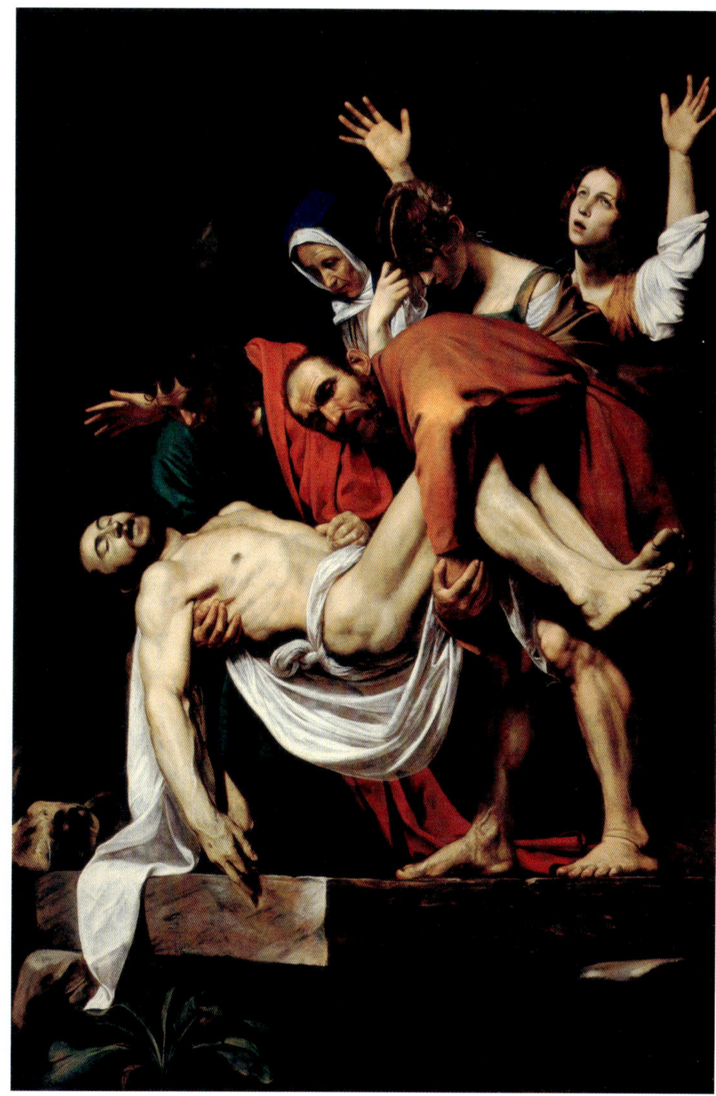

2 Michelangelo Merisi da Caravaggio, *The Deposition*, 1600–1604. Oil on canvas, 300 × 203 cm. Pinacoteca, Vatican Museums, Vatican State. Photo © Scala/Art Resource, NY.

Peter Paul Rubens
Michielsen Triptych,
known as *Christ on the Straw*
1618
Oil on panel
Centre panel: 138 × 108 cm;
side panels: 136 × 40 cm

Royal Museum of Fine Arts Antwerp
300-304

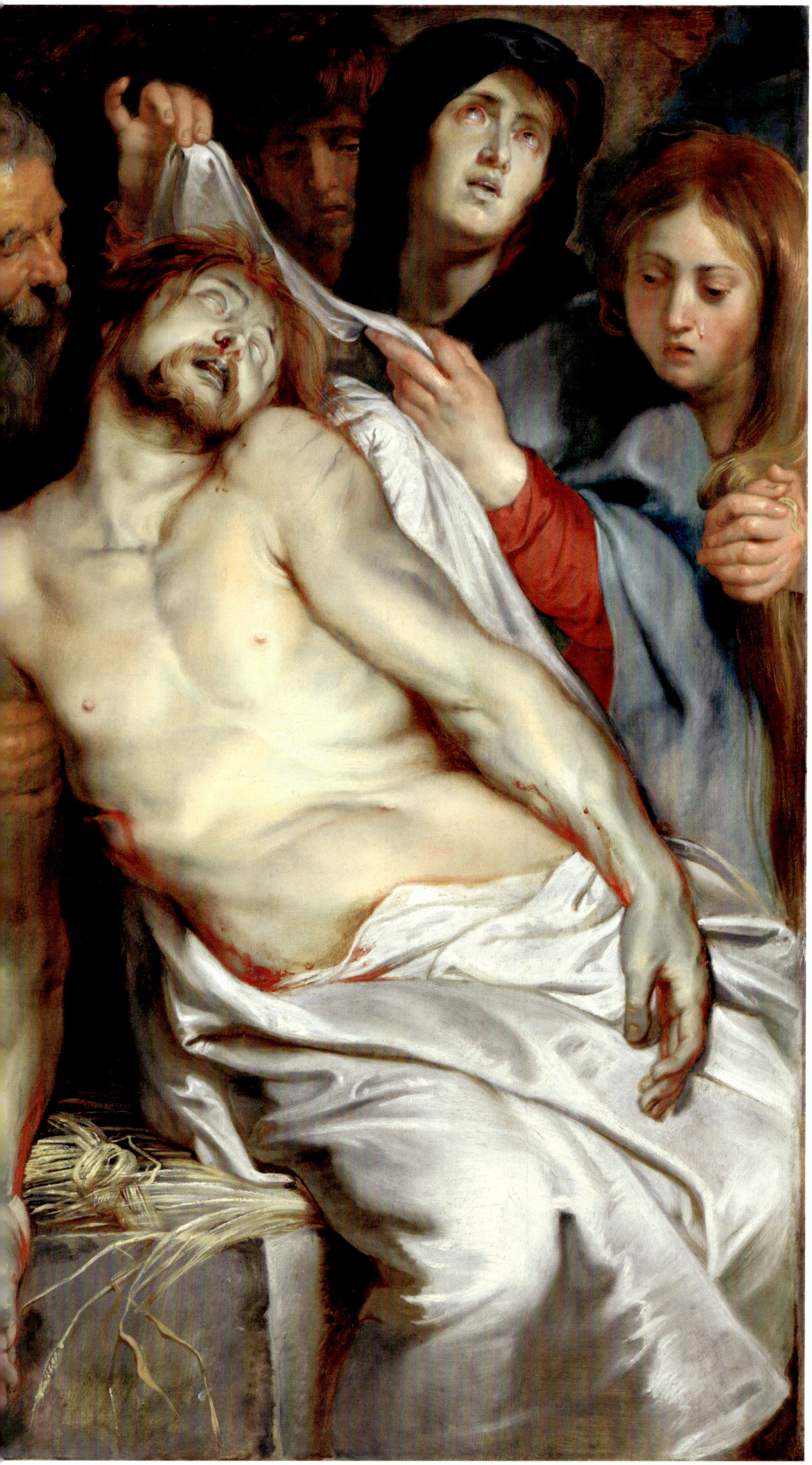

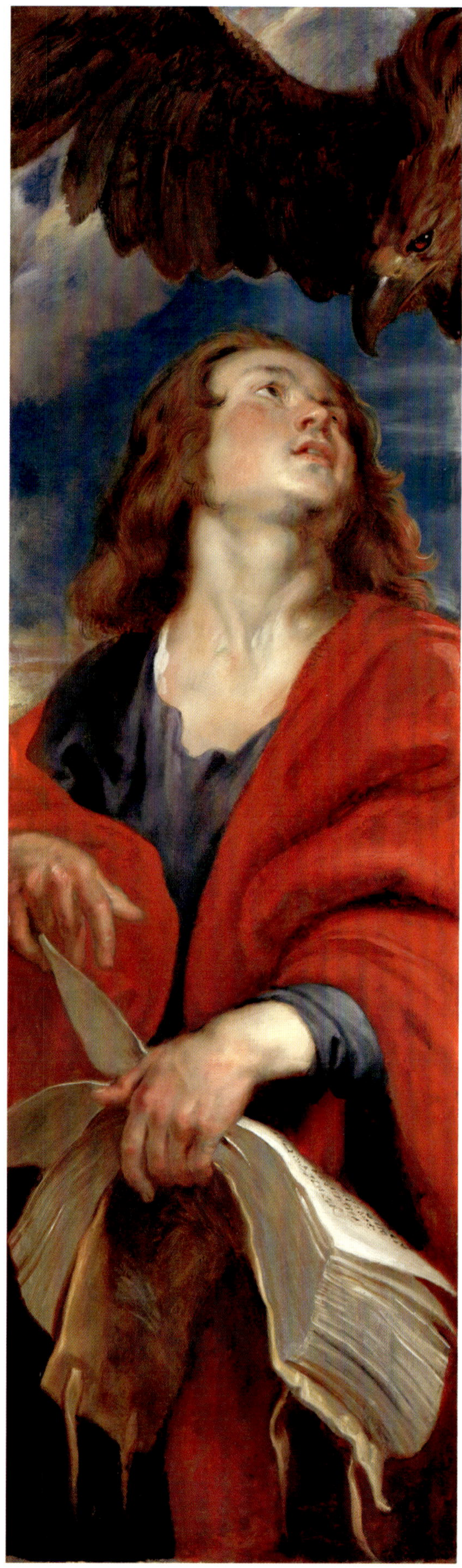

Peter Paul Rubens
Michielsen Triptych, Christ on the Straw

The Michielsen epitaph comprises a central panel depicting *The Lamentation with Mary, Joseph of Arimathea and Mary Magdalene* and two side wings: the left one portraying the *Virgin and Child* and the right one *St. John the Evangelist*. When the wings are closed, the reverse sides are visible and depict Christ as the Saviour of the World, or the Salvator Mundi (left), and Mary with the Christ Child (right) in grisaille. This triptych was painted by Rubens as a memorial epitaph for Jan Michielsen, who died on June 20, 1617. It was likely commissioned by his widow, Maria Maes, and completed sometime in 1618.[1] Both Michielsens are interred at Antwerp's Cathedral of Our Lady, where the triptych's presence was recorded as early as 1771.[2] Upon installation in the church, the triptych was accompanied by a Latin inscription that no longer exists but was transcribed in the eighteenth century:

> Dedicated to God the most Great and Good. Here lies [but] does not lie in [this] tomb—hidden- [but] not hidden-like John, that which was Michiels, for by the law of fate dead to the world [but] not to his wife Maria, chaste in mind with the countenance of Masia [*sic*], in whose heart, surviving himself, he lives, and breathes, living in his four children. Stop, rest, o traveler, pray for perpetual rest and long days. Died June 20th, 1617.[3]

The Lamentation pictures Christ on a stone, presumably meant to be the one on which, historically, after his death he was prepared for burial. It is covered in straw, which is why the work is often referred to *Le Christ à la Paille* or *Christ on the Straw*. The straw, or wheat sheaf, has been said to symbolize the inside of Christ's crib or the ground on which he lay as an infant in the manger where he was born. Indeed, his infancy is the subject of the left wing, where the young Christ stands, looking toward his lifeless adult body in the central panel. In both compositions, the body of Christ is featured prominently and undoubtedly refers to its Eucharistic function. Unlike the Calvinists, Catholic Christians believed in the real presence of Christ's body in the Eucharist, and this painting renders the belief explicit. An essential ingredient for bread, wheat is pictured with the body of Christ to proclaim their coexistence in the Eucharist.

The format of the triptych, with the figures close to the foreground pictured in three-quarter length, might be borrowed from Italian models that Rubens encountered during his southern travels. However, Colin Eisler and Lynn F. Jacobs have both convincingly argued for Rubens's reliance on fifteenth- and sixteenth-century Northern models in this and other contemporary epitaph triptychs. The former demonstrated Rubens's reliance on the work of Hugo van der Goes and other Flemish Primitives.

The latter connection is shown by sophisticated iconographic choices made by the painter—specifically, the use of "miraculous thresholds," whereby the three panels depict images simultaneously unified and divided in time and space.[4] In the *Michielsen Triptych* this threshold is best understood as it negotiates the relationship between Maria and Jan Michielsen and the featured saints who shared their names—Mary and John. The aforementioned inscription renders this connection explicit, as it likens [Saint] John to [Jan] "Michiels" and Maria [Michiels] to "Masia" (which, undoubtedly, was meant to read "Maria"). Rubens's use of the miraculous threshold might be described as in opposition to Counter-Reformation theology, which after the Council of Trent emphasized the importance of clarity and accessibility in painting and the truths that it conveyed. A part of the Council of Trent, the 1563 decree on sacred imagery, strictly forbade the veneration of idols.[5]

Sasha Suda

1 Colin Eisler, "Rubens' Uses of the Northern Past: The Michiels Triptych and Its Sources," *Musées Royaux des Beaux-Arts de Belgique Bulletin* 16 (1967): 55.

2 J.F.M. Michel, *Histoire de la vie de P.P. Rubens* (Brussels: AE. e Bel, 1771), 119.

3 J. Richard Judson, "64-68: The Lamentation: Triptych," in *Corpus Rubenianum Ludwig Burchard, Part VI: The Passion of Christ* (Antwerp: Harvey Miller, 2000), 222–28, quoted in and translated by Lynn F. Jacobs, "Rubens and the Northern Past: The Michielsen Triptych and the Thresholds of Modernity," *Art Bulletin* 91, no. 3 (September 2009): 302. Originally transcribed by F. Mols and preserved in a manuscript at the Bibliothèque Royale in Brussels (MS 5726).

4 Jacobs, "Rubens and the Northern Past," 304.

5 See David Freedberg, "Painting and the Counter Reformation in the Age of Rubens," in *The Age of Rubens*, ed. Peter C. Sutton (Boston: Museum of Fine Arts, 1993), 140–41.

After Correggio
born and died Correggio, Italy, 1489–1543
Extended and retouched by Peter Paul Rubens
Study after "Madonna of Saint George"
Possibly first decade of the seventeenth century, with later retouching by Rubens
Pen and ink with wash, retouched with brush and brown wash over black chalk, heightened with lead white, on a sheet of paper extended on all four sides
27.3 × 22.2 cm

The Albertina Museum, Vienna
8229

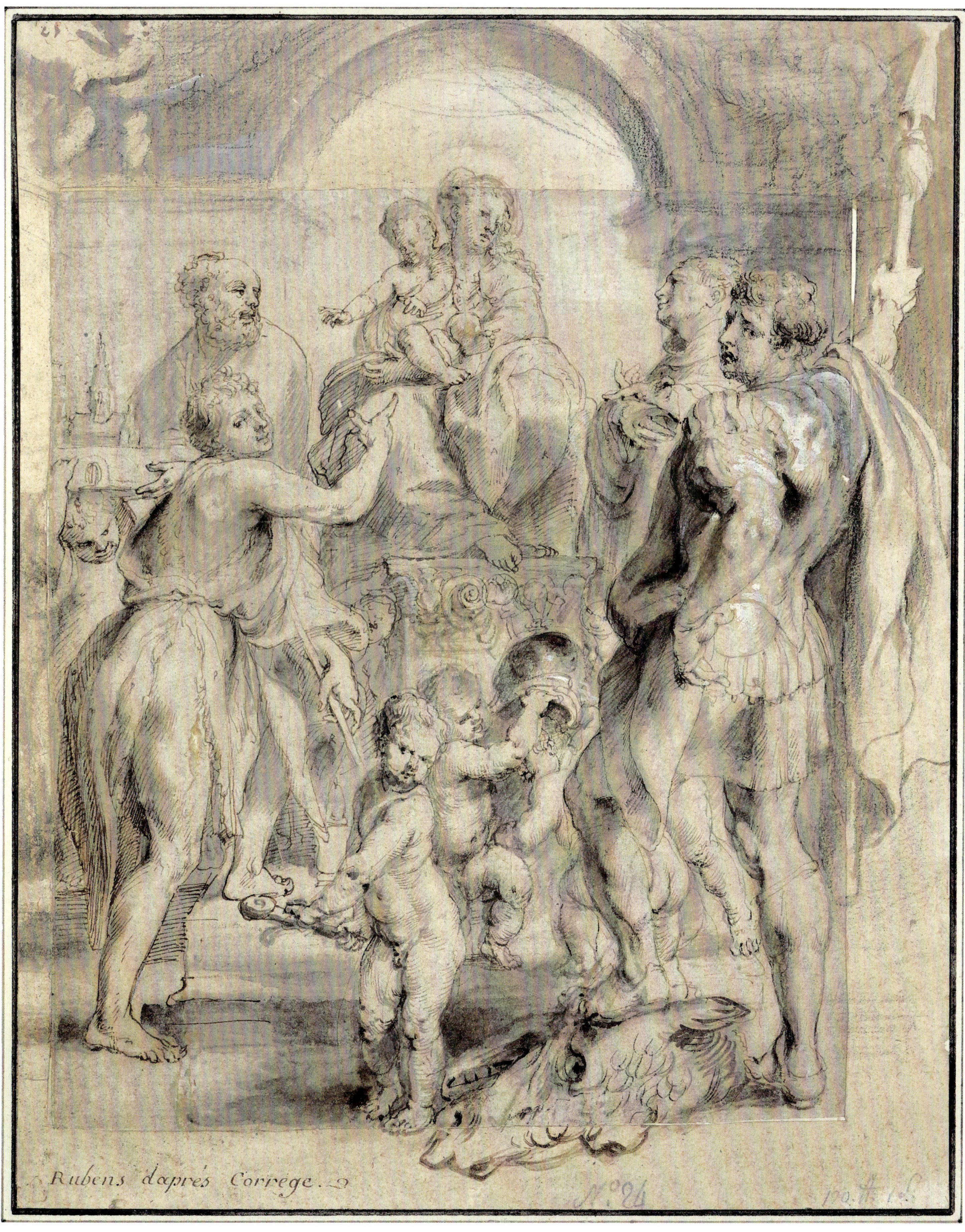
Rubens dapres Correge.
N.° 24

After Correggio
Extended and retouched by Peter Paul Rubens
Study after The Madonna of Saint George

Having arrived in Italy in the spring of 1600, Rubens seems to have made his first stop in Venice. Within days of his arrival in the lagoon, he befriended an agent of Duke Vincenzo I Gonzaga and secured a position as painter to the court of Mantua.[1] His role primarily involved painting portraits of the Gonzaga family and copies of works they wished to send out as gifts or have recorded for their own pleasure. These occasional tasks left Rubens time to travel and acquaint himself with northern Italian art of the previous century. This education would serve Rubens particularly well during his time in Rome, where the most astounding new painting was being produced by northern Italians, notably Annibale Carracci and pupils from his Bolognese academy on the one hand and Caravaggio on the other.

This drawing after Correggio's *Madonna of Saint George* was long held to be the work of Rubens alone, although the recent suggestion that it is an expansion and retouching of the work of another artist is supported by the current understanding of Rubens's drawing and collecting practices.[2] The work is constructed of two sheets: a core drawing that copies the figures of Correggio's *Madonna of Saint George* and a surrounding sheet split along the edges of a central cutout to allow the sketch to be fitted this window (fig. 1).[3] While delicate work, this manner of splicing together multiple sheets is not unknown among the drawings Rubens collected, manipulated, and retouched. Correggio's altarpiece, now in Dresden's Gemäldegalerie Alte Meister, was then still in Modena, and while the original ink drawing of the figures may have been sketched in the painting's presence, Rubens's additions relied on his memory of the altarpiece and his own sense of pictorial finish. For instance, the expansion allowed Rubens to resituate the Virgin and Child beneath the open arch that frames the figure group, but it also permitted him to intervene in Correggio's composition. Along the bottom edge, Rubens completed the dragon's head that Correggio had cropped in the altarpiece. Likewise, Rubens elevated Saint George's right hand and spear to accentuate how the soldier-saint occupies space, just as he deepened the shadow beneath George's left shoulder blade to set off the strongly foreshortened left elbow that protrudes so forcefully toward the viewer.

Correggio's art has been called "proto-Baroque," which is an imprecise description but one that indicates the profound importance of his persuasively fleshy figures and his handling of strong local colour for the artists—specifically the Carracci—who contributed to the inception of Baroque painting in Italy. Rubens would have seen Correggio's paintings in the Gonzaga collection, and from Mantua he had ready access to the Renaissance painter's masterpieces in Parma and Modena. Perhaps Rubens's interest in Correggio further intensified after arriving in Rome and learning of Annibale Carracci's stupendously successful frescoes in the Galleria Farnese. Certainly, Rubens's large oil sketch for the Chiesa Nuova's high altarpiece (page 225), makes apparent his investment in Correggio's forcefully posed figures: Saint Maurus stepping up from the lower left is a fairly faithful left-right transposition of Correggio's Saint George, with the rearward jutting elbow intact. For the finished painting, Rubens presented Maurus in profile but now conforming even more closely to Correggio's model, with the left leg raised and with lance in the right hand, allowing Saint Gregory's foreshortened gesture toward the viewer to take precedence.

Kirk Nickel

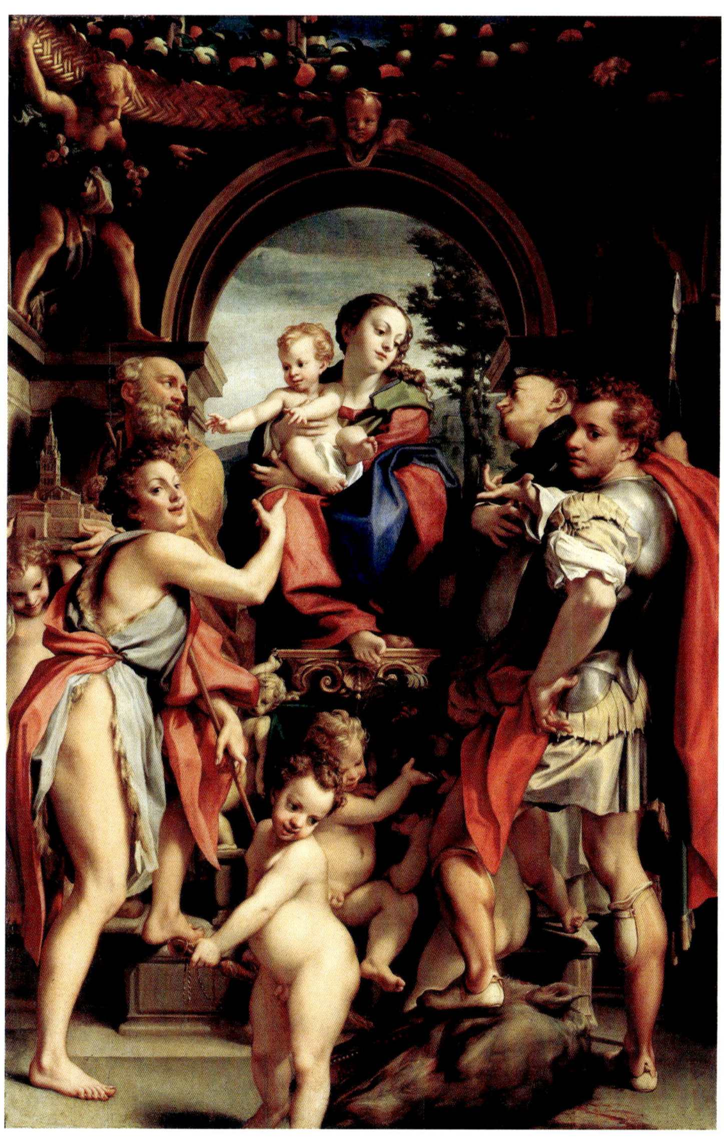

Fig 1 Correggio, *Madonna and Child with Saint George*, c. 1530. Oil on panel, 285 × 190 cm. Gemäldegalerie Alte Meister, Dresden. 153. Photo: bpk. Bildagentur/Gemäldegalerie Alte Meister, Dresden/Hans-Peter Klut/Art Resource, NY.

1 Michael Jaffé, *Rubens and Italy* (Ithaca, NY: Cornell University Press, 1977), 9.

2 Jeremy Wood, *Corpus Rubenianum Ludwig Burchard, XXVI: Copies and Adaptations from Renaissance and Later Artists, Italian Artists; II, Titian and North Italian Art*, 2 vols. (London: Harvey Miller, 2011), 1:370–71. On Rubens's retouching of other artists' drawings, see Anne-Marie S. Logan and Michiel C. Plomp, *Peter Paul Rubens: The Drawings* (New York: Metropolitan Museum of Art; New Haven, CT: Yale University Press, 2005), 15–18, exh. cat.

3 For Correggio's altarpiece, see David Ekserdjian, *Correggio* (New Haven, CT: Yale University Press, 1997), 183–92.

Peter Paul Rubens
The Conversion of Saint Paul
c. 1601–02
Oil on panel
72 × 103 cm

Liechtenstein, The Princely Collections, Vaduz-Vienna
GE40

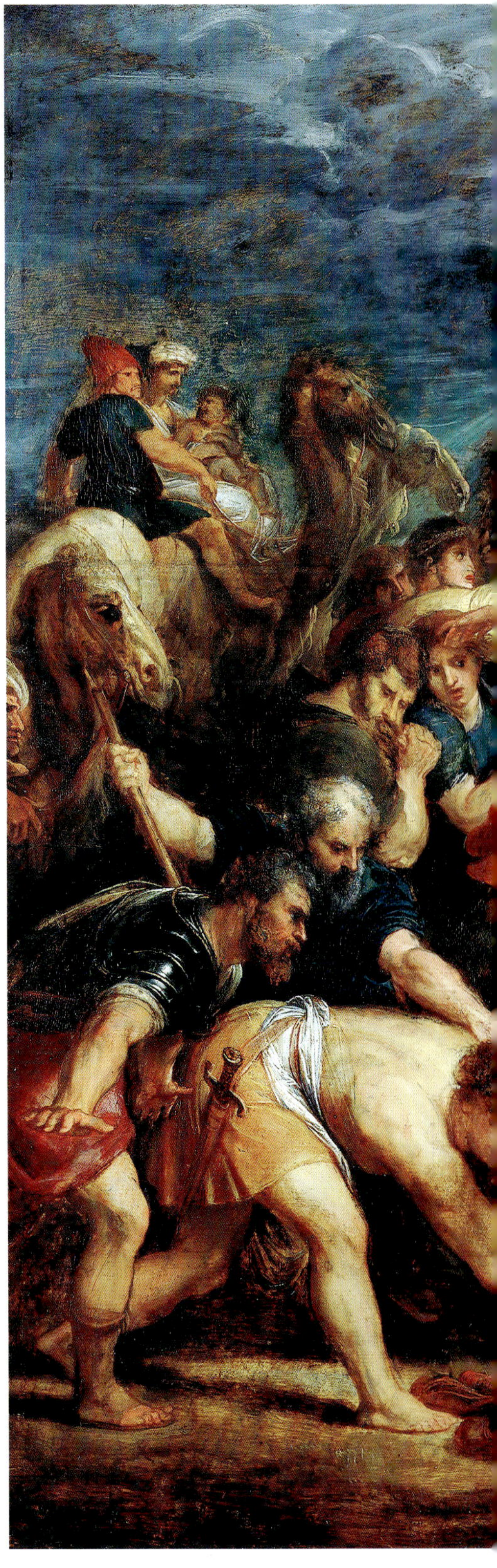

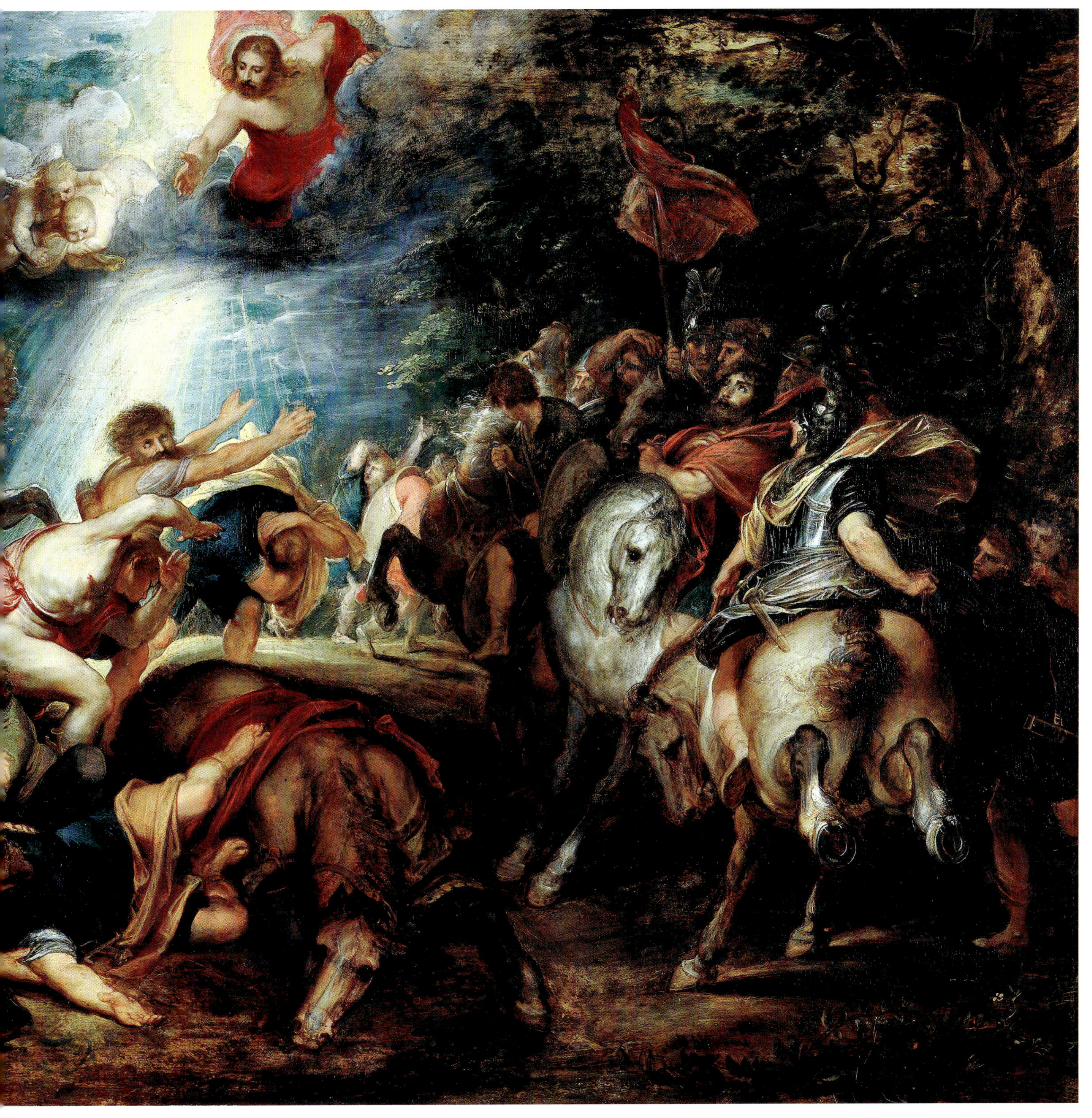

Peter Paul Rubens
The Conversion of Saint Paul

This work was first attributed to Rubens in 1964 by Justus Müller Hofstede, who noticed that a panel painting of this subject was recorded in 1641 in an inventory of the collection of the late mayor of Antwerp, Nicolaas Rockox. Assuming this is the same painting, as seems plausible, would circumstantially support the view that it was executed by Rubens in Antwerp prior to his departure for Italy in 1600. Certainly, it is a youthful work that had been dated to the start of the Italian period, until David Jaffé proposed an even earlier moment for it, the late 1590s. As a young artist, Rubens was rapacious for dramatic inventions, better the more exuberant and elaborate, and he attempted several multi-figured narrative paintings like this one, replete with action and trauma, and including various animals. A remarkable group of exotic camels appears here in the upper left.

The conversion of Saint Paul was a common subject in Italian art, but it is not evident that Rubens had yet seen in person the major painted versions by Michelangelo, Parmigianino, or Taddeo Zuccari for examples. Instead, he created a painting to challenge venerable Italian prints in the same lateral format with dense compositions, including Francesco Salviati's engraving cut by Enea Vico in 1545. This unusually large print even approached the painting in scale (53.5 by 93.5 cm). Another printed source was Cornelis Cort's engraving of *The Conversion of Saint Paul* after Giulio Clovio of 1576 (fig. 1). The latter features a figural style similar to the Salviati but is more atmospheric and so closer to the Rubens. Both prints filtered some of the Italian painted sources that Rubens had not yet experienced. Constructing an elaborate composition from multiple sources was a typical youthful exercise for him, an approach he became more adept at: *The Massacre of the Innocents* at the Art Gallery of Ontario developed from essentially the same principle. It is not yet rooted in an complex preparatory process involving oil sketches or life drawing, to judge from the malleable and collapsing bodies.

Told in the Acts of the Apostles (Acts 9:3–5), the story depicted in the painting is of the Roman persecutor of Christians, Saul, on the road to Damascus, where a divine light and the voice of Christ knocked him from his horse, leading to his conversion to Christianity. He became the apostle Paul after this revelation. By representing the scene at night and with Christ appearing in the sky, Rubens respected artistic conventions elaborated from a spare written account. In his treatment, Paul falls to the ground like an animal. He has a highly public revelation during which everyone reacts to the overpowering celestial light. The prostrate body of the soon-to-be saint allows for the usual demonstration of the artist's skill at foreshortening. While the subject matter was religious, it was a traditional excuse for formal pyrotechnics.

Rubens seems to have felt, as a young painter, that to be a great artist required painting involved scenes of conflict with

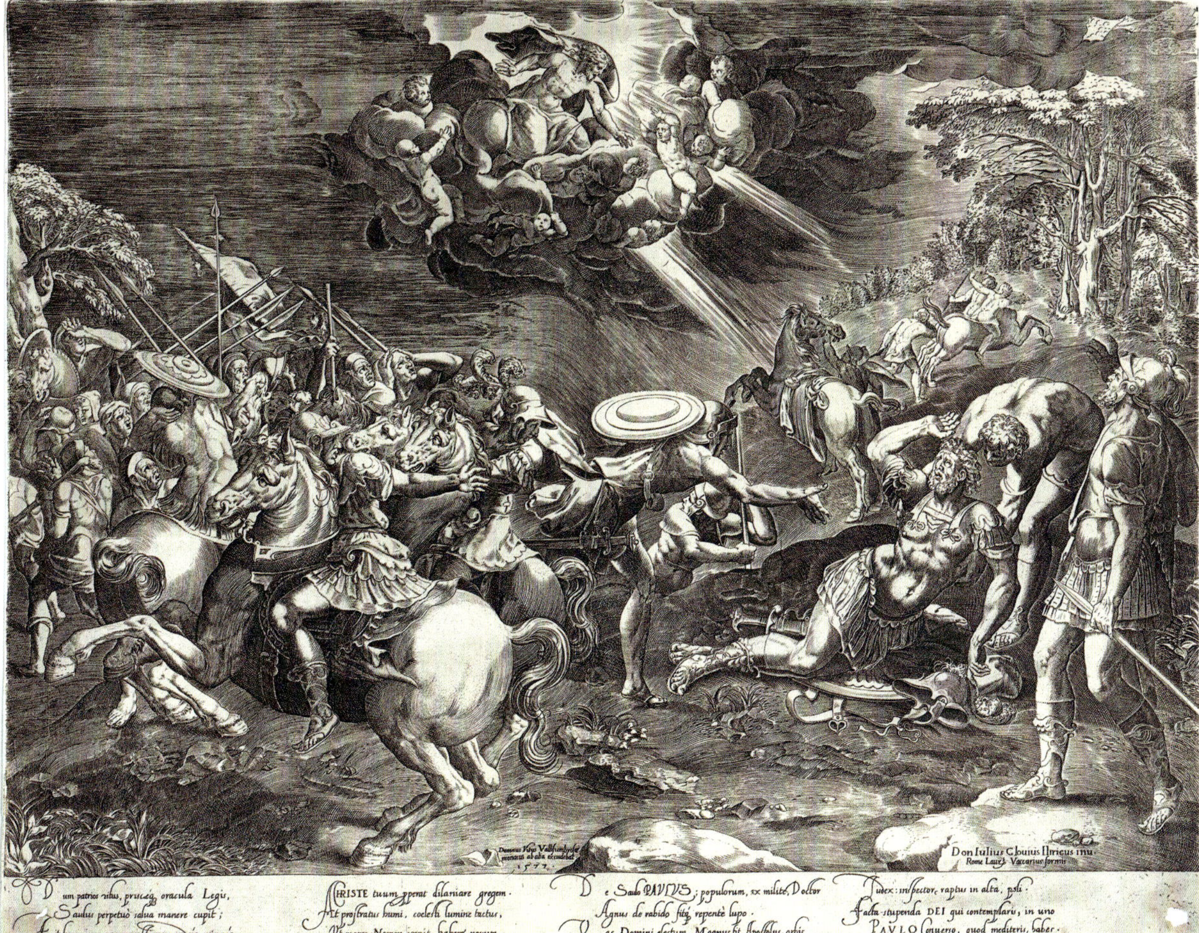

Fig 1 Giulio Clovio and Cornelius Cort, *The Conversion of Saint Paul*, 1576.. Engraving, 36 × 48.3 cm. British Museum, London, 1951. 0407.47. Photo © The Trustees of the British Museum.

myriad overlapping figures, including nudes, and he never lost this ambition. A certain amount of chaos was tolerable as a transmitter of visual and emotional energy. Rubens treated other narratives in this period with the same sentiment, such as in *Battle of the Amazons* or the Old Testament defeat of an Assyrian general in *The Defeat of Sennacherib*. He even reused some of the same poses and lighting effects. His approach to subject matter was entirely ambidextrous.

The Conversion of Saint Paul demonstrates how Rubens, as a young artist, was already making literate collector pictures, in an extemporizing style one imagines would inspire educated conversation in front of the work. Painted on panel, although the support could just as easily be copper, the work is closer in spirit to the Northern painters Rubens admired (such as his teacher Otto van Veen and, especially, the German painter Adam Elsheimer) in its tendency toward miniaturization, an artificial blue-green palette, and evaporating special light effects, than to Italian design or technique. It is a more muscular version of Elsheimer's extraordinarily exaggerated and original version of the same subject, now in Frankfurt, closely contemporary to this panel. Rubens might have felt he had much to improve on.[1]

David Franklin

1 For the selected bibliography relating to this entry, please see note 1 on page 199.

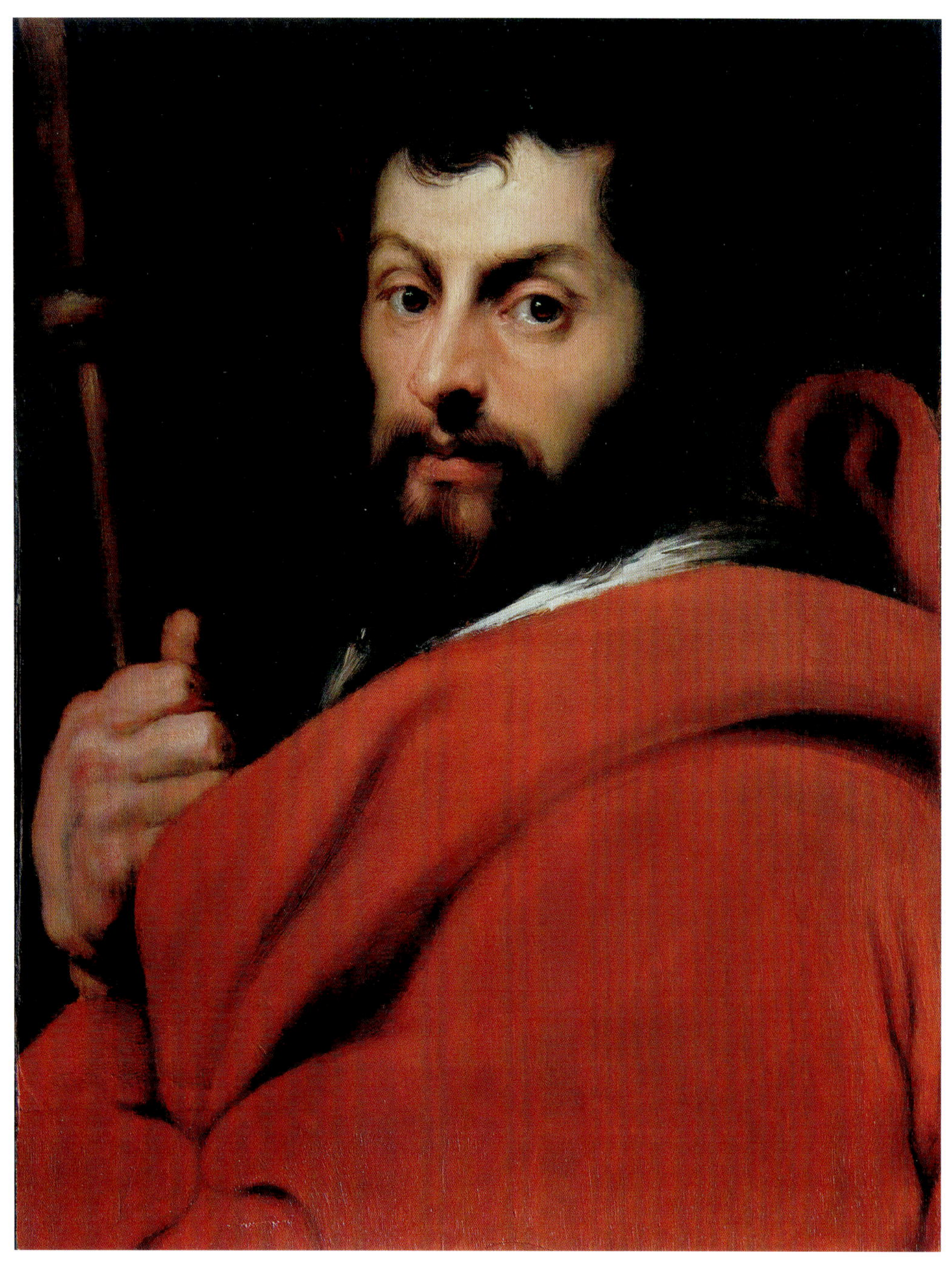

Peter Paul Rubens
Saint James the Greater
c. 1609
Oil on panel
62.5 × 48 cm

Muscarelle Museum of Art at the College
of William & Mary, Williamsburg, Virginia
Acquired with funds from the Board of Visitors
Muscarelle Museum of Art Endowment
2016.236

Peter Paul Rubens
Saint James the Greater

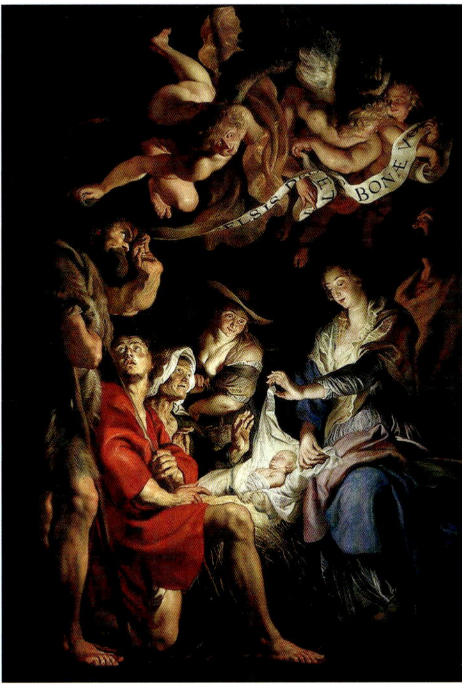

Fig 1 Peter Paul Rubens, *Adoration of the Shepherds*, c. 1609. Oil on canvas, 400 × 300 cm. Saint Paul's Church, Antwerp.

This vivacious portrait of the apostle Saint James the Greater shows strong stylistic affinities with the early works of Rubens, specifically his paintings from the years 1608–1609, around the end of his second visit to Italy and his arrival in Flanders. It is most likely that Rubens painted this work after his return to Antwerp. On the cradle backing of the present composition are fragments of the original panel, bearing the panel-maker's mark of Guilliam Aertssen and the castle and hands brand of Antwerp. Aertssen became a master of the Guild of Saint Luke in 1612 and remained active as a panel-maker until at least 1626.[1]

The animated features of this *Saint James the Greater* and the billowing red mantle are Correggio-esque qualities shared with Rubens's other paintings of this transitional period, and with two altarpieces of *The Adoration of the Shepherds*—the first in Fermo, Italy, in 1608 and the second in Antwerp in 1609. Rubens's 1608 altarpiece is clearly based on Correggio's lively proto-Baroque *Adoration of the Shepherds (La Notte)* in the church of San Prospero in Reggio.[2] In 1609, Rubens received a commission to paint the altarpiece for Saint Paul's in Antwerp. This altarpiece (fig. 1) is a replica of his earlier Fermo one.

From 1610 to 1612, Rubens painted a complete set of the twelve apostles for the Duke of Lerma in Spain. He based the pose of the *Saint James the Greater* (Museo Nacional del Prado) on the Muscarelle picture, but the Prado Saint James faces the opposite direction and shows both his hands (fig. 2). Before sending the finished series to Spain, Rubens's studio made several copies of the series for later study and sale.[3] In Rubens's mature style, as exemplified in the Lerma *apostolado*, Venetian naturalism has superseded Correggio's animation.

The Lerma *Saint James the Greater* serves as a *terminus ante quem* for the date of the present picture, which the Muscarelle discovered and acquired at Dorotheum (Vienna, Austria) in 2016. The auction house attributed this picture to the studio of Anthony van Dyck in response to the existence of two similar paintings of the same Saint James the Greater painted by Van Dyck around 1618 (Althorp House) and 1619–1620 (Stockholm, private collection). It is entirely plausible that Rubens kept the Muscarelle panel in his studio to serve as a model for his students and assistants, including the young Van Dyck. By the time Van Dyck painted his earlier version of *Saint James the Greater* (fig. 3), he had already been a part of Rubens's studio for two years. Van Dyck clearly applies his own artistic style to his earlier version of the saint, which is sketchier and more noticeably unfinished than the Muscarelle panel, while his later version (fig. 4) is a closer copy to Rubens's original picture. One of the most telling differences between Rubens's prototype and Van Dyck's two apostles are the drapery folds. In the present picture, it is clear that this knot of folds in the lower left of the painting conceals the grip of the saint's left hand. In Van Dyck's two replicas, these folds are unclear and appear less substantive.

John T. Spike, PhD with contributions from Aaron De Groft, PhD and Lauren Greene, MLitt

1 Anne T. Woollett and Ariane van Suchtelen, eds., *Rubens and Brueghel: A Working Friendship* (Los Angeles: J. Paul Getty Museum, 2006), 241.

2 Christina Corsiglia, ed., *Rubens and His Age: Treasures from the Hermitage Museum, Russia* (Toronto: Art Gallery of Ontario, 2001), 38. This canvas is now in the Gemäldegalerie Alte Meister in Dresden, Germany.

3 Arthur K. Wheelock Jr., *Flemish Paintings of the Seventeenth Century* (Washington, DC: National Gallery of Art, 2005), 212.

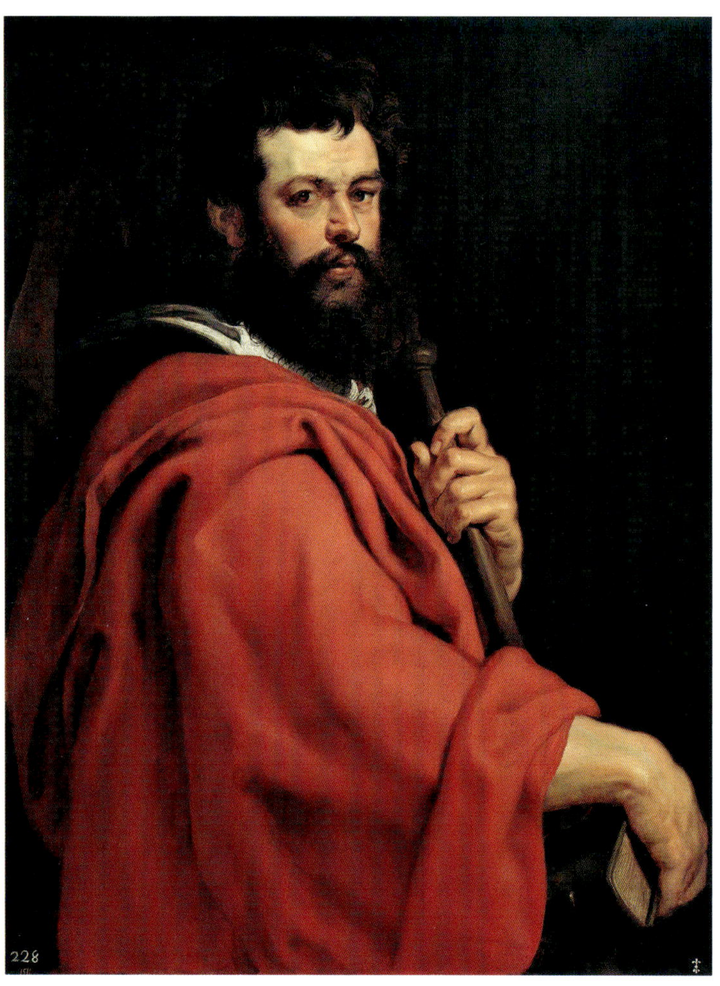

Fig 2 Peter Paul Rubens, *St. James the Greater*, 1610–12.
Oil on panel, 108 × 83 cm. Museo del Prado. P01648.

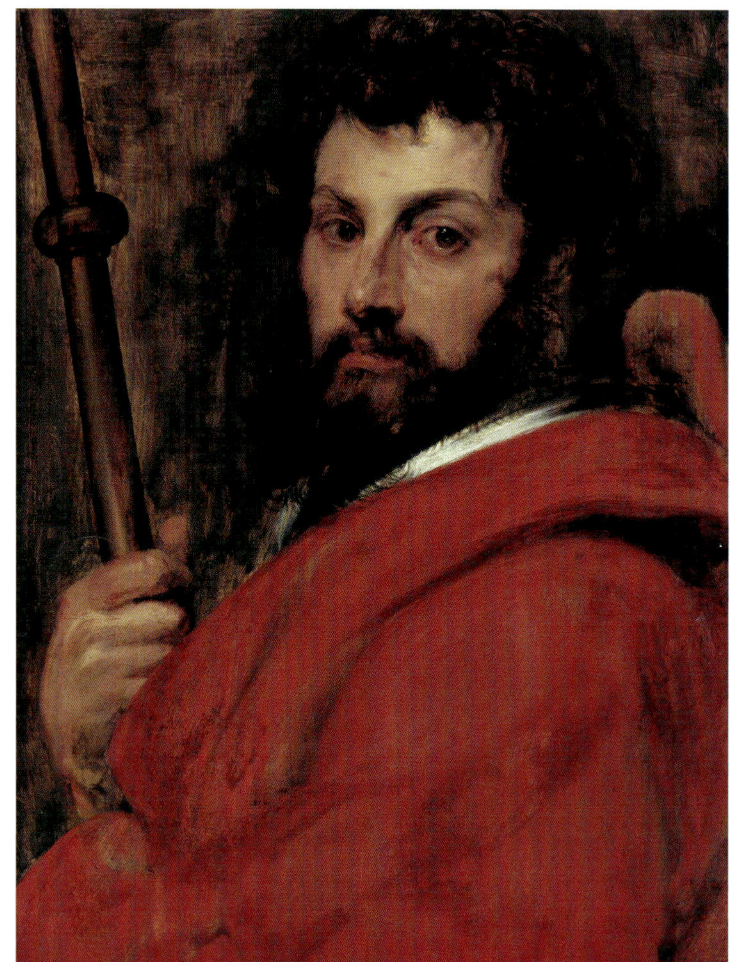

Fig 3 Anthony van Dyck, *Saint James the Greater*, 1618.
Oil on panel, 64.8 × 48.9 cm. Museum of Fine Arts, Boston. Private collection. Photograph © 2019 Museum of Fine Arts, Boston.

Fig 4 Anthony van Dyck, *Saint James the Greater*, 1619–20. Oil on panel. Private collection, Stockholm.

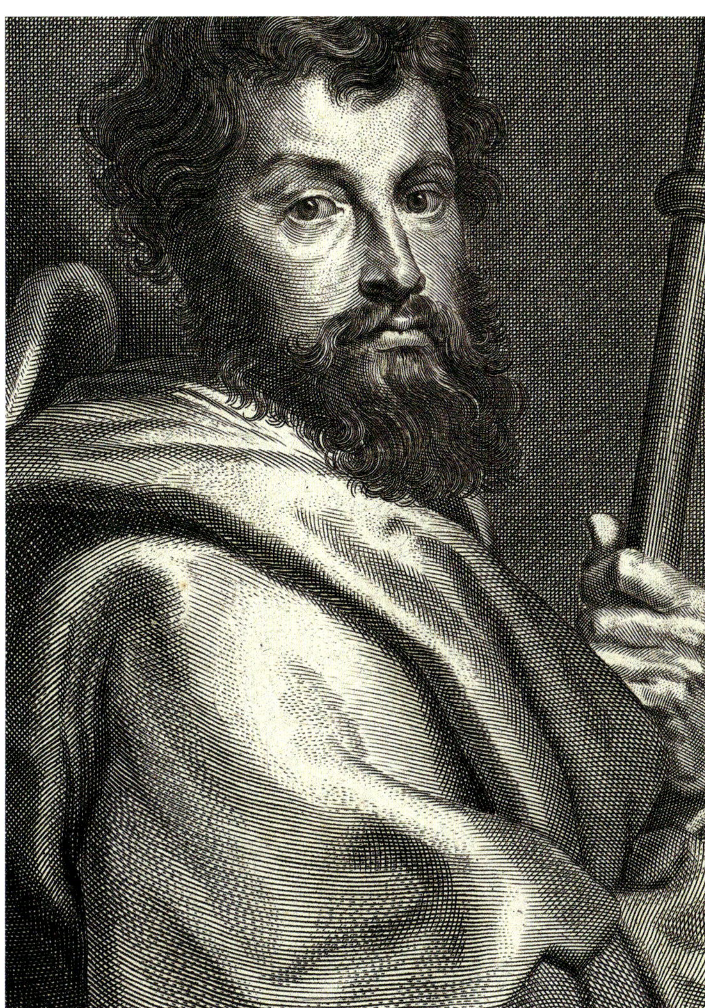

Fig 5 Cornelis van Caukercken, after Anthony van Dyck, *S. Iacobus Maior*, c. 1660–80. Engraving, 17 × 12.1 cm. Fine Arts Museums of San Francisco, Achenback Foundation for Graphic Arts. 1963.30.14133.

Peter Paul Rubens
Saints Gregory, Domitilla, Maurus, and Papianus
1606
Oil on canvas
147.3 × 120.5 cm

Staatliche Museen zu Berlin
Mü.4586

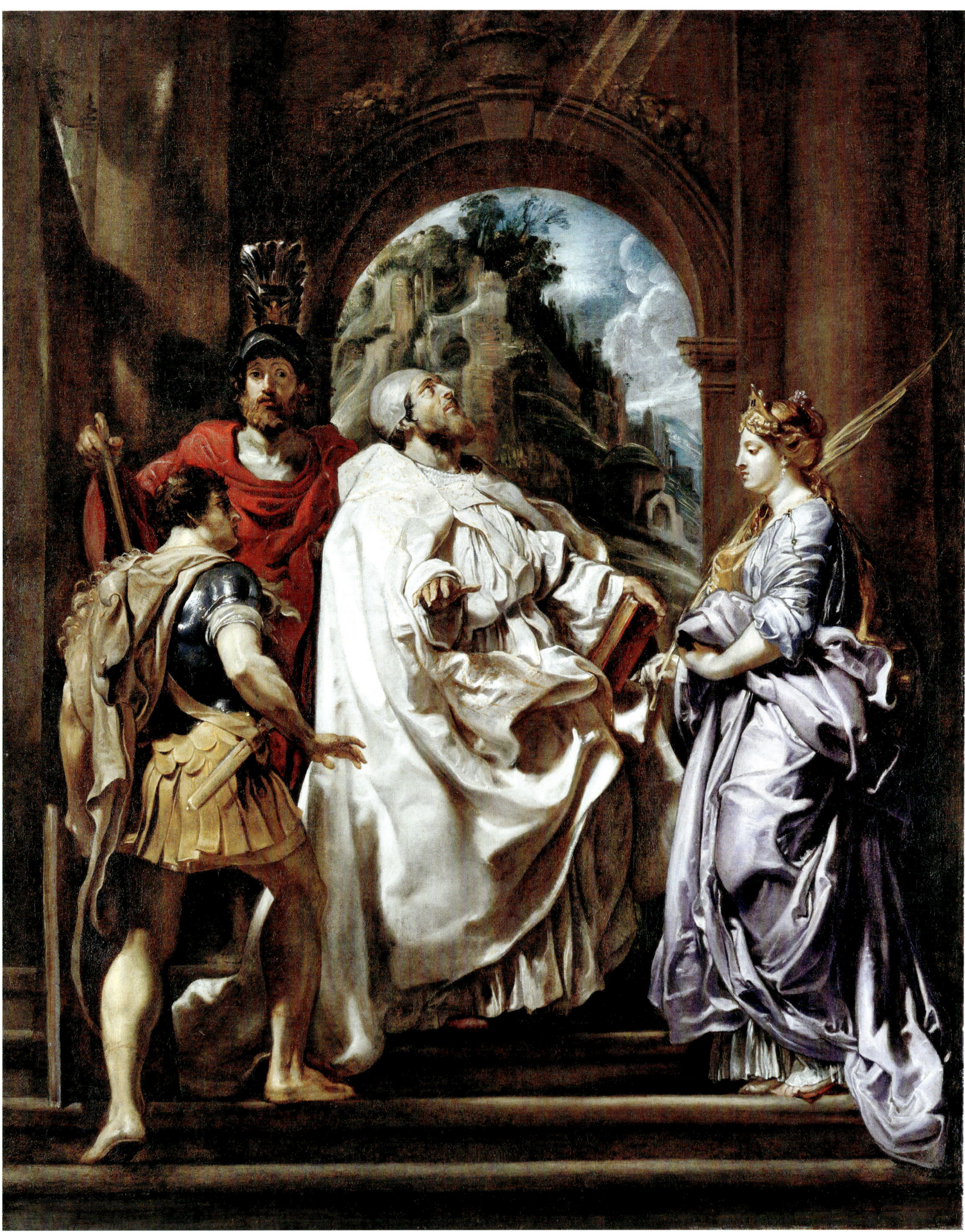

Peter Paul Rubens
Saints Gregory, Domitilla, Maurus, and Papianus

This painting relates to a commission for the high altarpiece of Rome's Chiesa Nuova (also known as Santa Maria e Gregorio in Vallicella), arguably the most significant of all Rubens's Italian projects. Born of the Counter-Reformation, the patron was the Oratorians, a secular brotherhood founded by Saint Filippo Neri in 1575. Their "new" church had been consecrated as recently as 1599. For the vast apse of the Chiesa Nuova, Rubens was asked to decorate a miracle-working late medieval icon of the Virgin and Child, transferred from a side chapel to the more prestigious high altar. Gregory, as the patron saint to whom the church was dedicated, took the privileged centre: his sacred relics were interred in that location. Rubens, aged just twenty-nine, signed a contract in September 1606 and delivered the altarpiece, now in Grenoble, in 1607.

However, the patron was dissatisfied with the first version on canvas, because it did not show well in the space, and ordered a new altarpiece painted on slate in three sections, which remains in situ on the high altar. When another buyer for the original canvas did not emerge, Rubens kept it and brought it back to Antwerp. It would be installed near his mother's burial place.

The Berlin painting had an unusual purpose. Michael Jaffé proposed that the painting, too large to be purely preparatory, was made in order to secure the commission from patrons who would not have known his style or reputation. This proposition has been generally accepted. Dating prior to the signing of the contract in 1606, the canvas is an unusually highly finished and large preamble, yet still not attempting to explore all aspects of the subject. It is different from the loosely executed oil sketches Rubens more frequently produced to spontaneously develop ideas. This hypothesis is defended by the intermediate changes from the Berlin painting to the finished altarpiece in Grenoble that can be documented in other works. Notably, all the saints were represented differently in the final altarpiece. The use of canvas better allowed for the object to be moved around, as it did not have to be permanently installed. Rubens's gesture recalls Tintoretto's celebrated bold self-confidence to complete such a work prior to formalizing a contract.

In this version, Saint Gregory is dressed in abundant white robes and a relatively informal skullcap rather than a papal tiara that, out of respect for the icon, we must imagine above his head outside the painting. Saint Domitilla—a favourite of the Oratorian Cardinal Cesare Baronio—appears as a Roman matron and early Christian martyr, with a symbolic palm frond. With less visual tradition at his disposal, Rubens imagined the iconography of the two other male saints portrayed like ancient Roman soldiers, Maurus with his back turned and Papianus making direct eye contact with the viewer, which was a conservative altarpiece convention. Like Gregory, all these saints had relics held in the high altar of the Chiesa Nuova, which accounts for their inclusion in Rubens's painting.

The towering, full-length saints, though self-absorbed as individuals, stimulate a spiritual drama in Rubens's composition. The main saint, Gregory, transmits tremendous energy in his seemingly spontaneous, inspired movements as he reacts to the icon. His sense of revelation is of a particular type, defined as "in ecstasy": a religious possession. Controlling the tonalities of

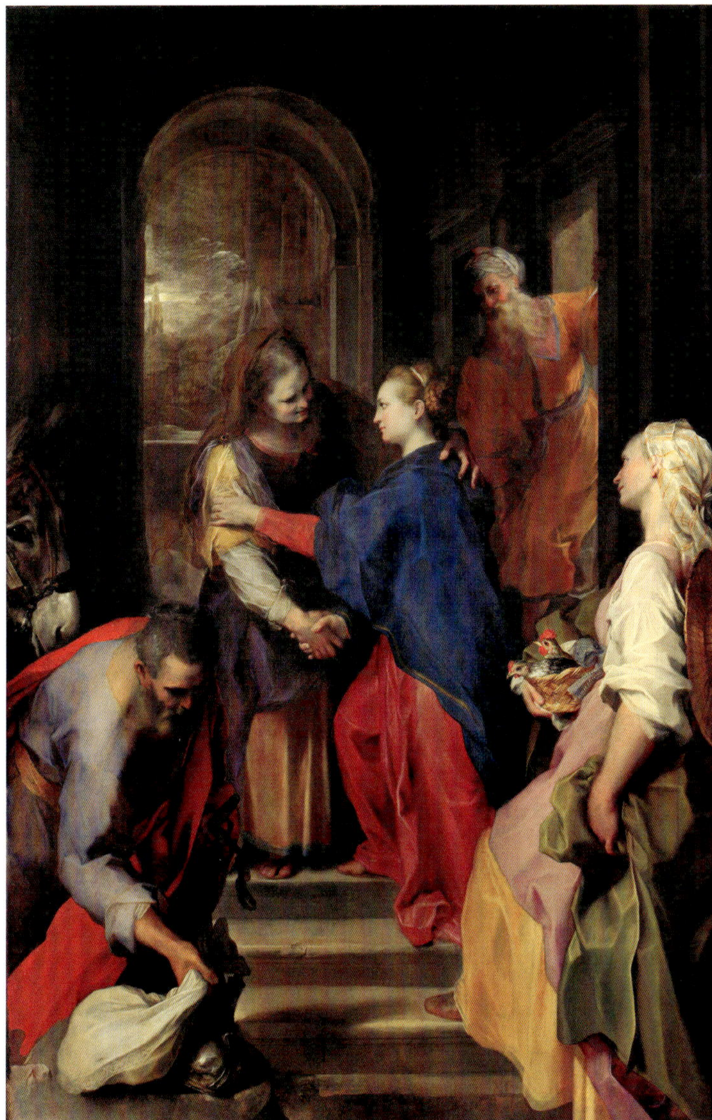

Fig 1 Federico Barocci, *Visitation*, 1583–86. Oil on canvas, 285 × 187 cm. Chiesa Nuova, Rome. Photo: Fondo Edifici di Culto – Min. dell'Interno. Photo © Scala/Art Resource, NY.

the opalescent white drapery of Gregory as it reacts to his emotion is a virtuoso performance by the painter. The overlapping density on one side of the composition, to our left, creates an imbalance that was novel and Rubens's attempt to be unpredictable—a lively electricity rustles through the sumptuous draperies. In addition to the suspended gestures in pictorial space, the dramatic range of light to dark acknowledges Caravaggio's painting of the *Deposition* in the same church. Caravaggio had just left Rome in the summer of 1606 to avoid arrest for murder, which must have further inspired Rubens to try to assert his artistic dominance in the city, in this very space.

Correggio's *Madonna and Child with Saint George,* then in Modena (now in the Gemäldegalerie in Dresden), has also been noted as a source for the composition, which seems possible for the foreground male saint, reversed from the *Saint George*. Rubens made a drawn copy after this altarpiece, which survives in the Albertina. Much closer, however, as an overall influence are Federico Barocci's two altarpieces of the *Visitation* (fig. 1) and *The Presentation of the Virgin in the Temple,* in the same Chiesa Nuova, both of which feature monumental figures standing and moving up steps, bold architecture with a central organizing arch, and draperies shimmering in evaporating light. The ever-mutable Rubens here was blatantly attempting to emulate Barocci's altarpiece to further please his patron and sustain a distinctly Oratorian pictorial style. It was an accident of his career, perhaps, that Rubens worked for newer orders like the Oratorians and the Jesuits, but the fact remains that he created unprecedented religious imagery in the first years of the seventeenth century in the Eternal City.[1]

David Franklin

1 For the selected bibliography relating to this entry, please see note 1 on page 199.

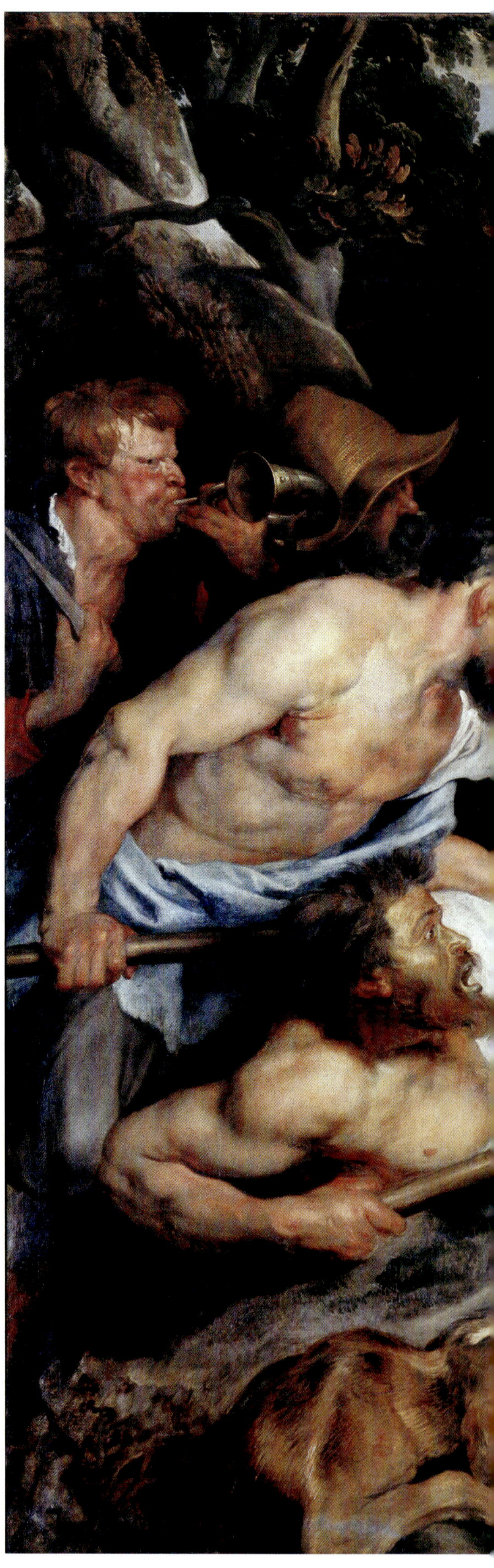

Peter Paul Rubens
The Boar Hunt
c. 1615–17
Oil on canvas
250 × 320 cm

Musée des Beaux-Arts, Marseille
BA 103

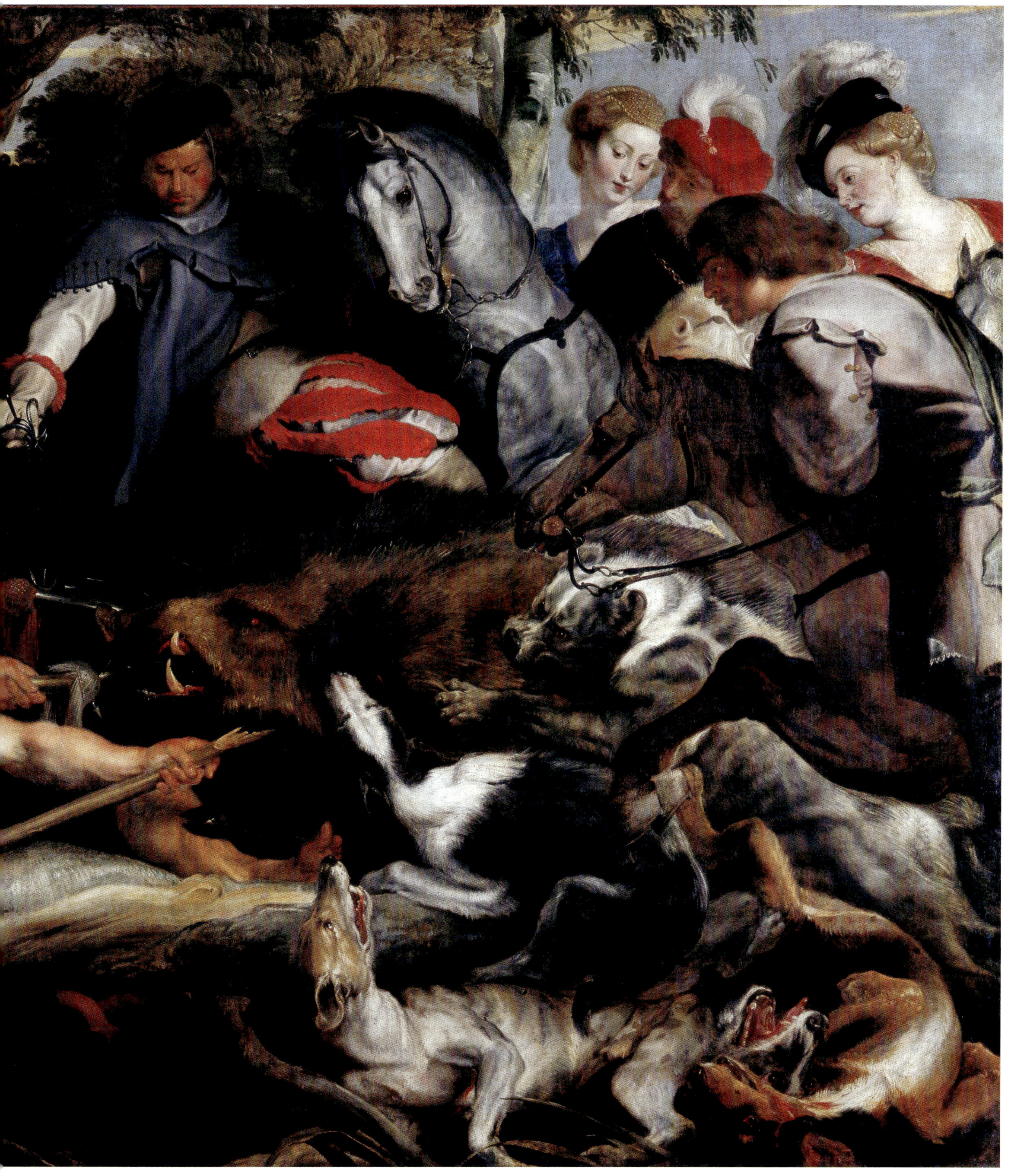

Peter Paul Rubens
The Boar Hunt

Of Rubens's four hunting paintings commissioned by Duke Maximilian I of Bavaria in 1616, *The Boar Hunt*'s claustrophobic concentration of figures and compaction of terror are unparalleled.[1] A ferocious boar takes centre stage in this graphic depiction of the savagery between predator and prey. There is literally no room for escape. He is hemmed in from all sides by adrenaline-fuelled huntsmen with javelins, a frenzied pack of hounds, and a rider on horseback, whose deadly rapier blade is about to strike. In the upper right, an entourage of aristocratic onlookers is crammed into the remaining space, leaving barely a trace of the ground or landscape, save for the glimpses of a few trees and sky.

As Hans Vlieghe discerned, Rubens's hunting pictures prior to 1620 are typically "marked by a centripetal and diagonal scheme of composition" whereby all movement, gesture, and expression are directed toward the "dramatic action."[2] Rubens boldly thrusts the viewer into the vortex of the climactic moment while the collision of dogs almost appears to tumble out the frame. The effect is stifling and compositionally discordant as the viewer attempts to disentangle and make sense of the onslaught of figures. The physicality of the combat is emphasized by tactile devices such as the broken javelin and the dog biting the ear of the boar—a motif that can be found in many Roman sarcophagi in which the boar at bay crushes a dog or the wounded Adonis under his foot. To intensify the chaos even further, Rubens effectively evokes a cacophony of sound: the snarling boar; the sweating horn-blower signalling the kill; and the two yelping, prostrate dogs. Vivid chromatic accents of red, repeated in the feathered hat of a bystander in the background and in the ruffled glove accessory and velvet panes of the main hunter's breeches, highlight the boar's bloodshot eye, positioned precisely at the picture's centre.

Once the viewer takes a moment to digest the visceral and visual impact of the scene, a psychological dichotomy emerges from the throng of dramatis personae.[3] On one end, there is the cool apathy exemplified by the motionless trio of elegantly dressed aristocrats and the dispassionate countenance of the main huntsman. On the other, there is the unbridled violence of the beaters and the wild fury of the animals. The former group's detachment typifies what Susan Walker describes as the hallmark of constancy: an "absolute mastery over the self's actions, feelings and beliefs. This necessitated resistance to the passions."[4] This contrast in the reaction and actions of the nobility contributes to the painting's push-and-pull dynamic—one that epitomizes the underlying tension in Rubens's images. However, the inclusion of the aristocratic figures stems from the fact that hunting was a popular pastime with the elite, including the ruling classes in court circles. In *The Boar Hunt*, Rubens clearly pays homage to the tradition of the Burgundian courtly style, which typically depicted aristocratic hunters and spectators in landscapes recalling gardens of love. Although these subsidiary figures from what Arnout Balis describes as a "fossilized genre" do not serve a "dramatic function,"[5] the calm, courtly composure and countenance of Rubens's iterations act as a counterpoint to the impassioned state of the beaters.

The aristocratic connection accounts for the appeal of engravings of exotic hunts among the elite and the demand for Flemish tapestries during the fifteenth and sixteenth centuries.[6] In fact, Rubens is credited as having to have retouched a drawing after one of the Mantuan hunts by Giulio Romano (a pupil of Raphael) and Baldassarre Peruzzi in the Farnesina. By the time of the Renaissance, the sport was staged like a bullfight in a portable coliseum. For example, a corralling cloth fence for the animals

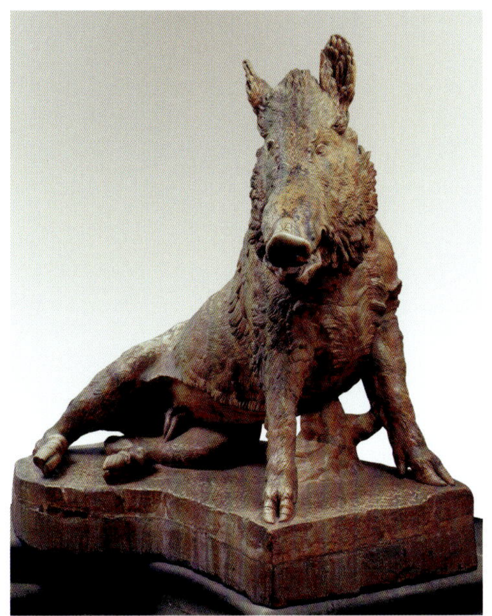

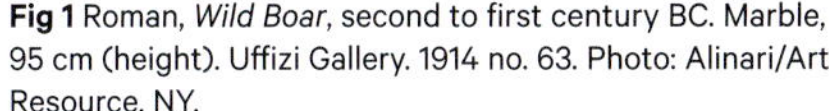

Fig 1 Roman, *Wild Boar*, second to first century BC. Marble, 95 cm (height). Uffizi Gallery. 1914 no. 63. Photo: Alinari/Art Resource, NY.

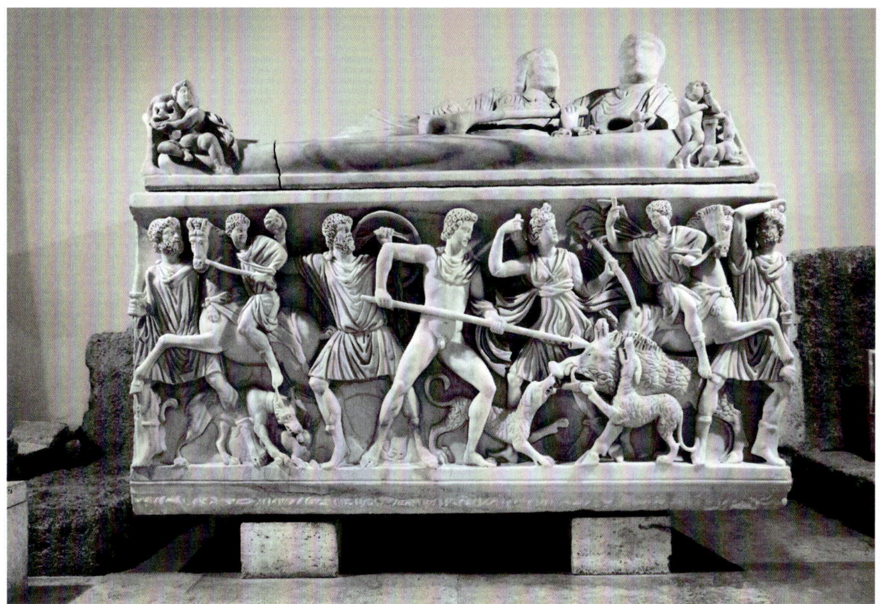

Fig 2 *The Calydonian Boar Hunt, At the Center, Meleager Hunts Calydonian, Before Artemis*, Roman sarcophagus (front panel), second century AD. Marble, 125 × 256 × 137 cm. Capitoline Museums, Rome, Italy. Inv. Scu 917. Lanmas/Alamy Stock Photo.

is visible in Diego Velázquez's portrait of *Philip IV Hunting Wild Boar* in The National Gallery in London.[7] Titian includes a deer hunt in the background of the *Pardo Venus* at the Louvre. Rubens may originally have been excited by exotic animals, sometimes on view in royal menageries, but he quickly accepted the challenge of showing the force of assailing hunters and the close combat of swords and spears.

Rubens's iconography for his epic battle also took inspiration from his reverence for ancient art and culture. During his Italian sojourn, he drew extensively from antique sarcophagi and statues, which culminated in his unpublished essay "De Imitatione Statuarum." A famous freestanding marble boar sculpture, now at the Uffizi Gallery in Florence (fig. 1), must had been known to Rubens; but the most influential source of inspiration was the celebrated sarcophagus known as *The Calydonian Boar Hunt* (fig. 2). The latter was replicated on countless sarcophagi and recounted in the *Metamorphoses* by Ovid and the *Imagines* by Philostratus the Younger.[8] The position and pose of the boar and black-and-white hound in *The Boar Hunt* mirror its sculptural counterpart. The earliest manifestation of Rubens's assimilation of this iconic ancient source is his eponymous painting from about 1611–1612, which includes the figures of Atlanta and Meleager (fig. 3). In this mythological setting, the boar's passive position, as endorsed by an antique marble then in the Medici collection, resembles a scruffy, well-behaved family dog in comparison with the tormented beast in the c. 1615–1617 painting. The sculptural handling of the huntsmen and horses, and the shallow, relief-like composition recall classical sculpture: a characteristic of Rubens's formative style.

Rubens's inventive invocation of both Burgundian images of courtly culture and antique models resonated with learned viewers and patrons and found an eager clientele. Accordingly, the artist returned to the subject of the hunt numerous times and, by the 1620s, had gravitated toward images of the goddess Diana hunting, in which animals at speed are run down by missile-like hounds, and only dogs rather than servants are caught in the line of fire. Action unfolds in a frieze-like manner in his later works, imparting a temporal dimension to the viewer's experience.[9]

Inevitably, the high demand for his hunting pictures would entail the assistance of his workshop. The most particular aspect of this genre is that once Rubens had conceptualized the paintings—probably in small oil sketches—he felt no need to execute them. Frans Synders and Paul de Vos are reputed to have contributed their hand in the painting of the animals, while the young

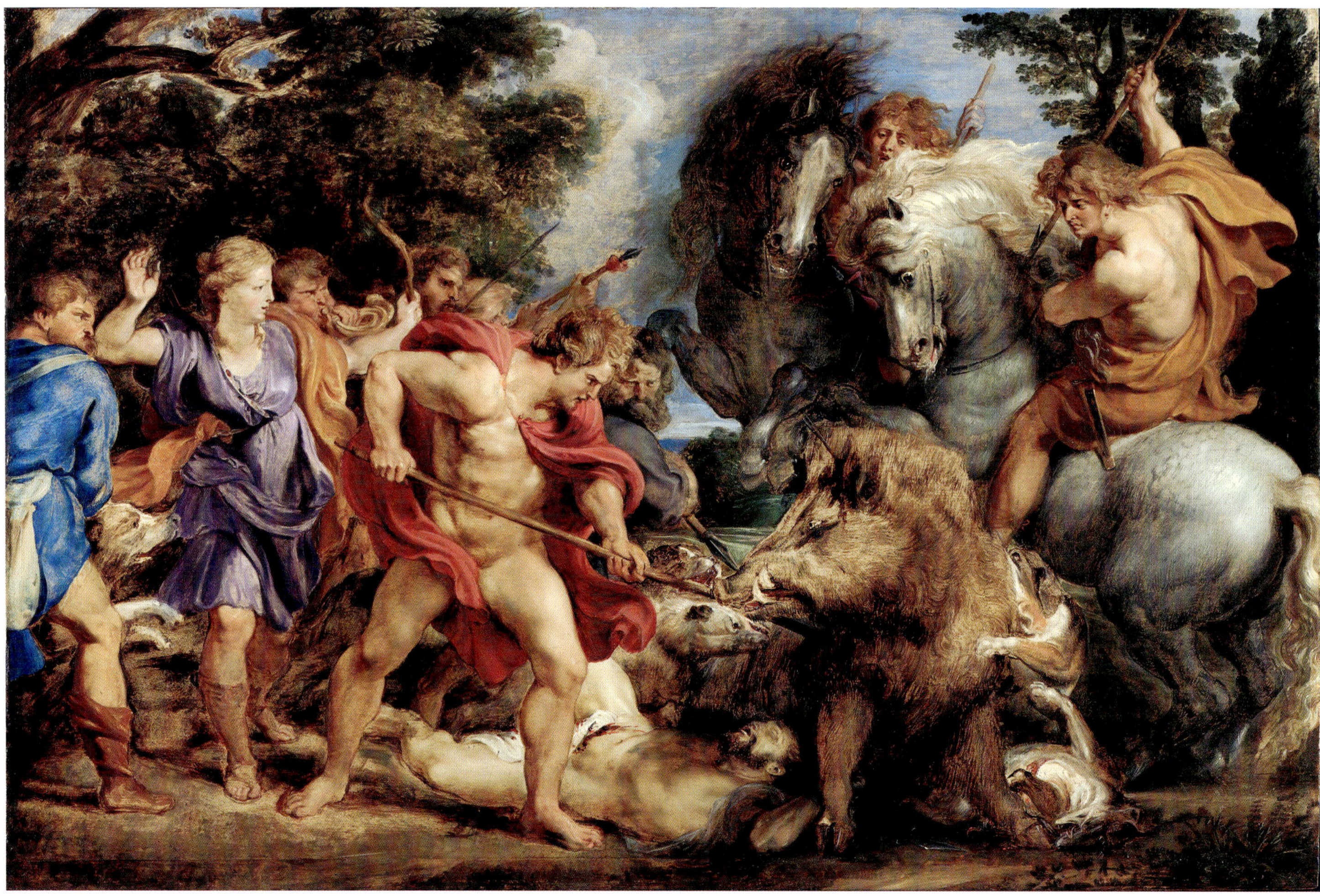

Fig 3 Peter Paul Rubens, *The Calydonian Boar Hunt*, c. 1611–12. Oil on panel, 59.2 × 89.7 cm. The J. Paul Getty Museum, Los Angeles. 2006.4.

Van Dyck most certainly executed the horn-blower and man with a straw hat—two figures that reappear in *The Boar Hunt,* c. 1618–1620, a collaboration with Snyders.[10] The master himself touched up such elements as the red highlights on the right-hand-side horse's muzzle. Further, the Rubensian style of Jacob Jordaens's *Crucifixion* in Saint Paul's Church in Antwerp suggests that he was also an assistant. Although there are several copies and versions of the four hunting scenes commissioned by Maximilian, the quality of the ones he purchased are unsurpassed, leading Balis to believe that *The Boar Hunt* and its three companions are the originals. Just as fine horsemanship projects a ruler's authority and power, so the commission was important in Rubens's positioning himself as an international artist. Almost single-handedly, the Flemish Baroque master and his prolific workshop revitalized an entire genre whose legacy would find its most potent expression in French Romantics such as Théodore Géricault and Eugène Delacroix.

Corrinne Chong and David Jaffé

1 The other three commissioned works are *Hippopotamus and Crocodile Hunt* (Alte Pinakothek, Munich), *The Lion Hunt* (Musée des Beaux-Arts de Bordeaux, now lost), and *Tiger, Lion and Leopard Hunt* (Musée des Beaux-Arts de Rennes).

2 Hans Vlieghe, *Flemish Art and Architecture, 1585–1700* (New Haven, CT: Yale University Press, 1999), 225. Also see Hans Vlieghe in Arnauld Brejon de Lavergnée, ed., *Rubens* (Gent: Snoeck, in association with Palais des Beaux-Arts de Lille, 2004), 150, exh. cat. no. 151.

3 Although there are no literary allusions or mythic heroes such as Diana from Rubens's mature period of hunting scenes, scholar Susan Walker offers a Neo-Stoic interpretation that is plausible given that Rubens was an acolyte and friend of Justus Lipsius. In his philosophical treatise *De Constantia* (1584), Lipsius exalts the virtue of self-restraint and self-command but condemns the moral dangers of the passions. Virtue, as the Humanist scholar defined it, was "a right an immovable strength of the mind, neither lifted up nor pressed down with external or casual accidents." See Susan Walker, "Composing the Passions in Rubens' Hunting Scenes," *Netherlands Yearbook for History of Art* 60, no. 1, n22.

4 Walker, *Composing the Passions* 115.

5 Vlieghe, *Flemish Art*, 225. Also see Vlieghe in Brejon de Lavergnée, ed., *Rubens*, 150, cat. no. 151.

6 According to Arnout Balis, the subject of hunting in art was apparently at its peak during the late Middle Ages but waned during the Humanistic age. See Arnout Balis, *Corpus Rubenianum Ludwig Burchard: Rubens Landscapes and Hunting Scenes, Part XVIII*, 2 vols. (New York: Oxford University Press, 1986), 2:55.

7 A similar enclosure can be seen in Antione Caron's drawing of a boar hunt c. 1576. See Ketty Gottardo, *Antoine Caron Drawing for Catherine de' Medici* (London: Courtauld Institute of Art, 2017), 68, cat. no. 10. Such French blocking nets, *tele*, were a novelty in early sixteenth-century Italy. See Jeremy Kruse, "Hunting, Magnificence and the Court of Leo X," *Renaissance Studies* 7, no. 3 (September 1993): 243–57.

8 For textual sources, see lines 267–525 in Ovid, *Metamorphoses* VIII, trans. Frank Justus Miller (London: Will Heinemann, 1946), 425–37, where the Calydonian boar's "eyes glowed with blood and fire"—an image Rubens seems to be transferring to the Marseilles painting. In Book X, lines 714–15, page 115, Ovid writes of the death of Adonis, who roused up a wild boar from his hiding place. There are many antique sarcophagi showing hunts, including the *Death of Adonis*. For two examples in Rome, Casino of Palazzo Rospigliosi, see Dagmar Grassinger, *Die Mythologischen Sarkophage*, vol. 1, *Achill-Amazonen: Die Antiken Sarkophagreliefs* (Berlin: Gebr. Mann Verlag, 1999), 211, plate 38, no. 46; and 216, plate 46, no. 62. This relief shows Venus catching Adonis's dying breath, as Rubens illustrates in his Washington drawing; for the inscribed drawing, see Jaffé in David Jaffé and Elizabeth McGrath, *Rubens: A Master in the Making* (London: National Gallery Company Ltd., 2005), 69, cat. no. 15, for Rubens description of the Rospigliosi Adonis sarcophagus no. 62: "His passing out and the last breath as it were into the mouth of Venus who approaches him to receive it." See Marjon van der Meulen, *Corpus Rubenianum Ludwig Burchard: Rubens Copies after the Antique*, 3 vols. (London: Harvey Miller, 1994), 1:84, no. 36. There is a similar Adonis sarcophagus in Palazzo Ducale Mantua, where the boar is again seated, standing on the dog, and again Venus is trying to catch his soul from his dying breath. See Grassinger, 215, plate 50, no. 55—but here, in addition, Cupid is stanching the wound as in Rubens's drawing, and the boar is charging.

9 The goddess of the hunt, Diana, was a recurrent mythical figure in the second phase of Rubens's hunting genre. In these scenes, the target of the frequently disrobed Diana was often a stag or deer—docile in comparison with the prey in his Maximilian series. For a discussion on the mature hunting scenes, see Aneta Georgievska-Shine and Larry Silver, "Hunts and the Closing Circle," in *Rubens, Velázquez, and the King of Spain* (London: Ashgate, 2014), 225–43.

10 Balis, *Corpus Rubenianum*, 117.

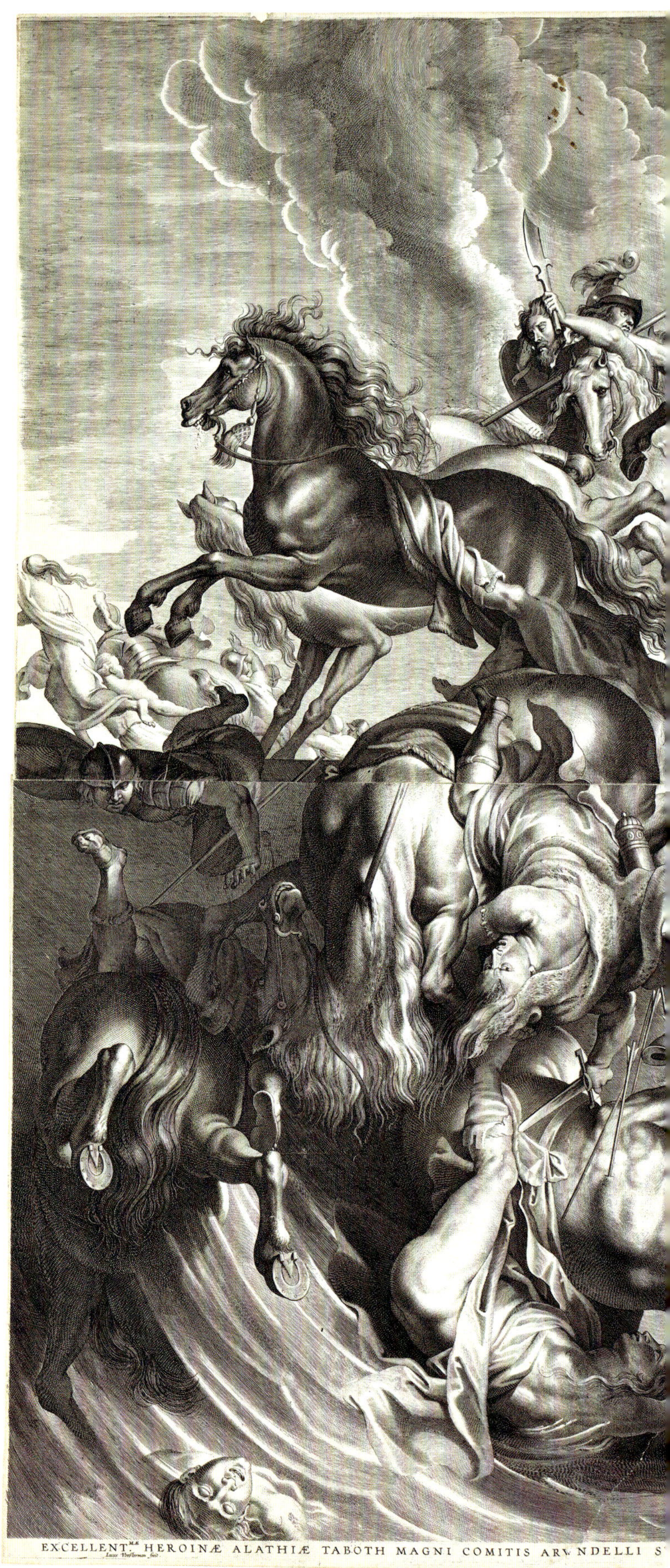

Lucas Vorsterman
born Zaltbommel, Netherlands, 1595;
died Antwerp, Belgium, 1675
after Peter Paul Rubens
Battle of the Amazons
1623
Engraving
85.7 × 120.2 cm

Rijksmuseum, Amsterdam
RP-P-OB-33.047

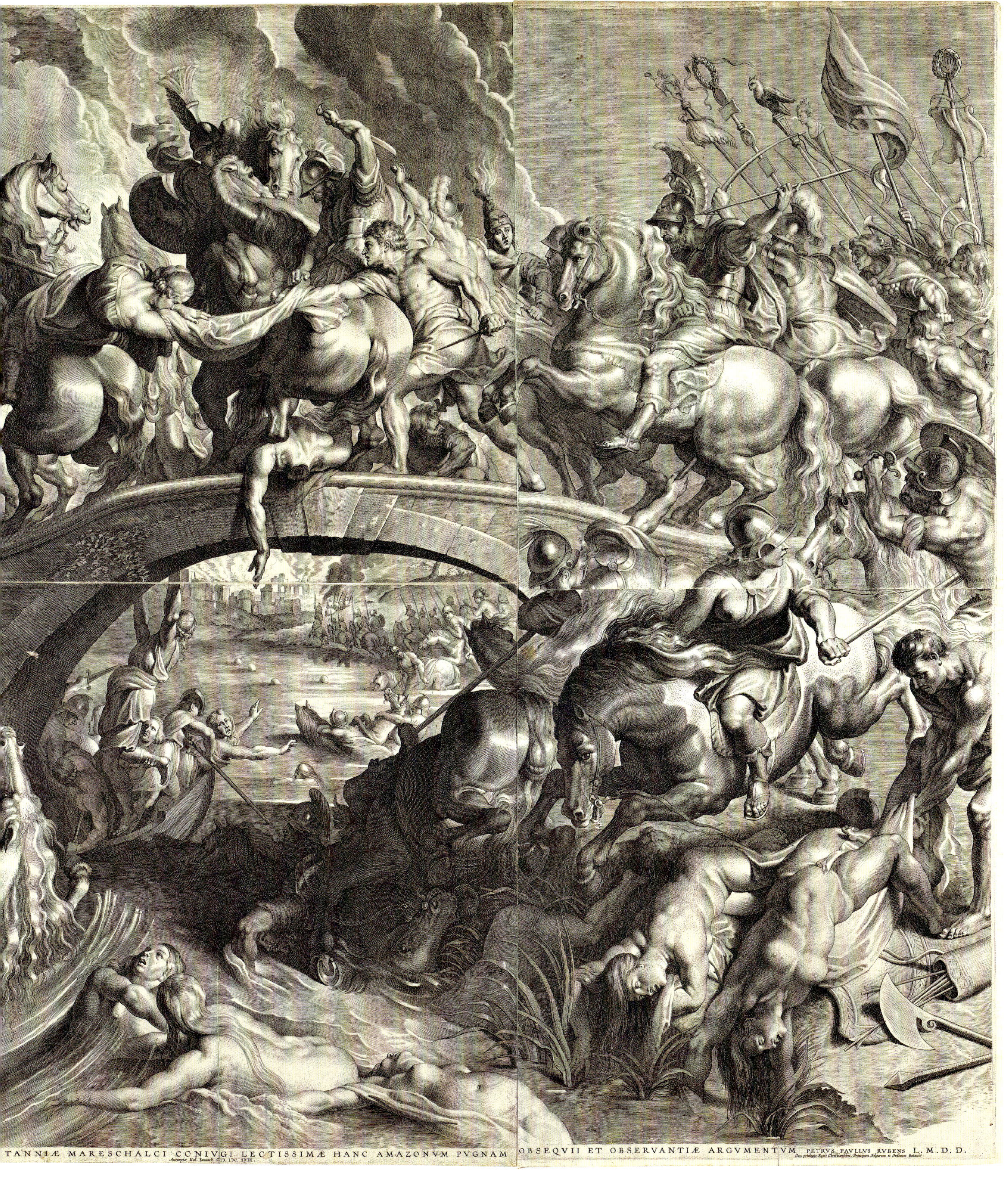
TANNIÆ MARESCHALCI CONIVGI LECTISSIMÆ HANC AMAZONVM PVGNAM OBSEQVII ET OBSERVANTIÆ ARGVMENTVM PETRVS PAVLLVS RVBENS L. M. D. D.
Antverpiæ Kal. Ianuarij CIↃ. IↃC. XXIII.
Cum privilegijs Regis Christianissimi, Principum Belgarum et Ordinum Batauiæ.

Lucas Vorsterman I
Battle of the Amazons

Marks: "Lugt 240"

Engraved in plate, below image: *EXCELLENT.MÆ HEROINÆ ALATHIÆ TABOTH MAGNI COMITIS ARVNDELLI SVPREMI BRITANNIÆ MARESCHALCI CONIVGI LECTISSIMÆ HANC AMAZONVM PVGNAM OBSEQVII ET OBSERVANTIÆ ARGVMENTVM PETRVS PAVLLVS RVBENS L.M.D.D.*

Lower left: *Lucas Vorsterman fecit*

Lower centre: *Anturpiæ Kal. Ianuarij M.DC.XXIII.*

Lower right: *Cum priuilegijs Regis Christianißimi Principum Belgarum et Ordinum Batauiæ.*

This gruesome engraving depicting the battle of the Amazons, a mythical band of female warriors, against the Greeks is closely based on Rubens's 1616–1618 painting of the same subject, today in the Alte Pinakothek, Munich. Engraved by Lucas Vorsterman I and printed from six copper plates on six sheets of paper, it was the largest engraving printed in the Netherlands up to that date. It is only one-third smaller than the actual painting, which at the time hung in a prominent place in the picture gallery of the important Antwerp collector (and supporter of Rubens's work) Cornelis van der Geest. Rubens may well have come to the idea of reproducing several of his significant paintings, in particular in a large multi-sheet format, from his exposure to prints after Titian. The Italian artist had employed many printmakers to translate his work into prints, including the massive multi-sheet woodcut *The Drowning of Pharaoh's Army in the Red Sea* (approximately 1.21 by 2.21 m).

The sheer brutality of the composition is striking. The Amazon warriors are shown in the moment of their defeat as their standard bearer, at the centre of the image, loses control of her flag. The references to Leonardo's lost *Battle of Anghiari* are impossible to miss.[1] Rubens knew the composition well, and in fact he had reworked a copy by an unknown Italian artist after the lost cartoon by Leonardo da Vinci (fig. 1).[2]

In his depiction of a subject more popular in antiquity than in the Renaissance, Rubens explores the brutality of war without blinking: a beheaded corpse hangs on the edge of the bridge at the very centre of the work while bodies float in the river below or lie trampled on the shore.[3] In many ways, the unflinching approach to violence of the scene recalls the artist's earlier *The Massacre of the Innocents* (page 176). In Rubens's *Battle of the Amazons*, no one is the victor, and in many ways, it can be read as an antiwar image, something that would have been welcome in a city and country that had recently lived through death and destruction under Spanish occupation and that was living under an uneasy armistice.[4] Creating a print of this image makes the sentiment public.

From a letter he wrote to Pieter van Veen on January 23, 1619, we know that Rubens was planning to have several of his compositions reproduced in engravings by "a well-intentioned young man," almost certainly Vorsterman.[5] Rubens could have chosen a well-established and experienced printmaker, as there were a number in Antwerp (for example the Galle family), but rather he chose to bring Vorsterman into his studio, where Rubens would have been able to shape and control his work. Rubens worked closely with all the printmakers he employed, helping them to translate his paintings into prints in a manner that would successfully share his compositions with a larger audience, thus increasing his fame. The drawing Vorsterman used as a model

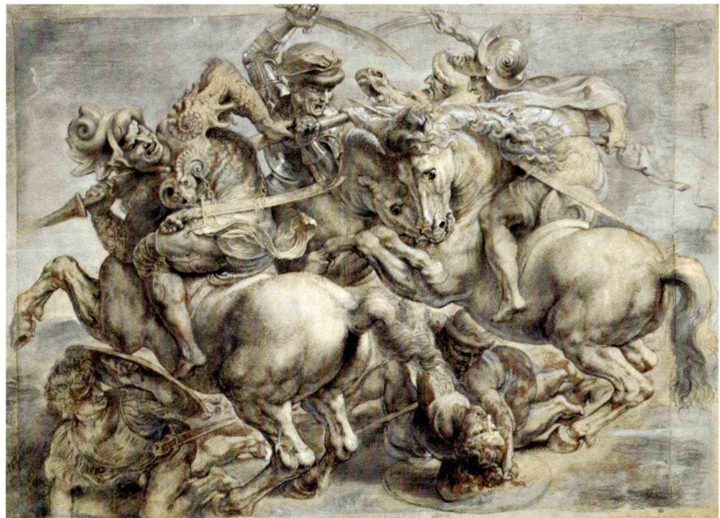

Fig 1 Peter Paul Rubens, *Copy after the Battle of Anghiari by Leonardo da Vinci*, c. 1603. Black chalk, pen in brown ink, brush in brown and grey ink, grey wash, heightened in white and grey-blue, 45.3 x 63.6 cm. Louvre Museum, Paris. INV 20271. Photo © RMN-Grand Palais/Art Resource, NY.

from which to make his engraving would have been created by a member of Rubens's studio. The black chalk drawing survives in Oxford (inv. 1857), and the engraving closely follows it.[6]

There were problems between Vorsterman and Rubens, though, and by 1622, Rubens wrote to Van Veen about "the mental disorder of my engraver."[7] Apparently, there were delays even though the print had been paid for long ago, and in the same letter Rubens wrote, "I cannot get it [the *Battle of the Amazons*] out of the hands of this fellow, though he was paid for the engraving three years ago."[8] It is not clear exactly what happened, but it seems that Vorsterman made at least one physical attack on Rubens. The artist's friends sought "a writ of protection" for him against Vorsterman that was at first rejected by the Spanish king's privy council, but later granted by the Archduchess Isabella.[9] In the summer of 1622, Vorsterman left for England. He returned in 1630 and found work with Anthony van Dyck.

Alexa Greist

1 Other sources for the composition include Titian's *Battle of Cadore* and antique sarcophagi. *Rubens in der Graphik: Rubens, Van Dyck, Jordaens und die Rubens-Stecher* (Würzburg: Martin von Wagner Museum, 1977), 104–6, cat. no. 73. Lastman's painting of the *Battle at the Milvian Bridge* (1613, private collection) was a source closer to home.

2 Louvre, inv. 20271 recto.

3 A drawing in Oxford at Christ Church (inv. 1857, 81 x 102 cm, black chalk, likely retouched by Rubens in black chalk, red chalk, grey wash, pen, and brown ink, heightened with white), sometimes attributed to Van Dyck, was the model for the engraver and shows signs of retouching by Rubens. Anne-Marie Logan-Saessesser, "Rubens Exhibitions, 1977," *Master Drawings* 15, no. 4 (Winter 1977): 403–17; 416, fig. 3.

4 Sabine Poeschel makes a convincing argument for the *Battle of the Amazons* (both the painting and the engraving) as antiwar statements by Rubens. See Sabine Poeschel, "Rubens' 'Battle of the Amazons' as a War-Picture: The Modernisation of a Myth," *Artibus et Historiae* 22, no. 43 (2001): 91–108.

5 Peter Paul Rubens to Pieter van Veen, January 23, 1619, *The Letters of Peter Paul Rubens*, ed. and trans. Ruth Saunders Magurn (Cambridge, MA: Harvard University Press, 1955), 69. In a list of seventeen individual works and a group of portraits, Rubens referred to "a battle between the Greeks and the Amazons" and "where Christ is raised on the cross."

6 The drawing was likely retouched by Rubens in black and red chalks; grey wash; pen and brown ink; and white body colour. See Jaco Rutgers and Simon Turner, eds., *The New Hollstein*, 2 vols. (Ouderkerk aan den Ijssel, Netherlands: Sound & Vision, forthcoming), 1: cat. no. 53. I offer my sincere thanks to Jaco Rutgers and Simon Turner for sharing their insights and manuscript text regarding this engraving.

7 Rubens to Van Veen, June 19, 1622, Magurn, 87.

8 Rubens to Van Veen, June 19, 1622, Magurn, 88: "Ho ancora una battaglia d'Amazoni di sei pezzi alla quale manchano pochi giorni di lavoro, che non posso cavar delle mani di costui, benché sono tre anni che l'opera è pagata." "I have also a *Battle of the Amazons* in six sheets, which requires only a few more days' work, but I cannot get it out of the hands of this fellow, although he was paid for the engraving three years ago." See *Correspondance de Rubens et documents épistolaires concernant sa vie et ses oeuvres, Codex diplomaticus Rubenianus*, ed. and trans. Max Rooses and Charles Ruelens, 6 vols. (Antwerp, 1887–1909), 2:444–45, doc. 264.

9 Paul Oppenheimer, *Rubens: A Portrait; Beauty and the Angelic* (London: Duckworth, 1999), 250.

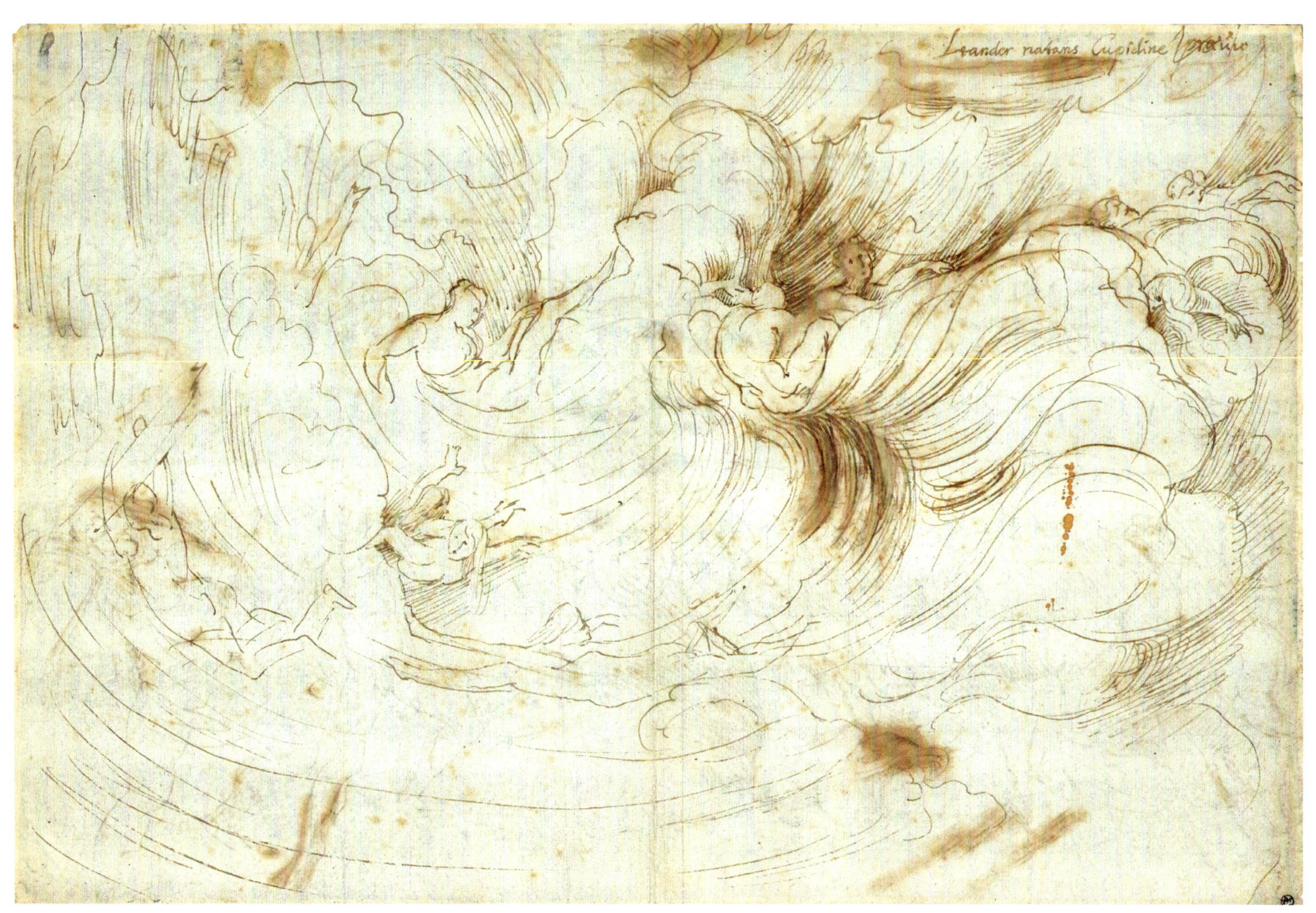

Peter Paul Rubens
Hero and Leander
1600–03
Pen and brown ink with wash on paper
20.4 × 30.6 cm

National Galleries of Scotland
D493

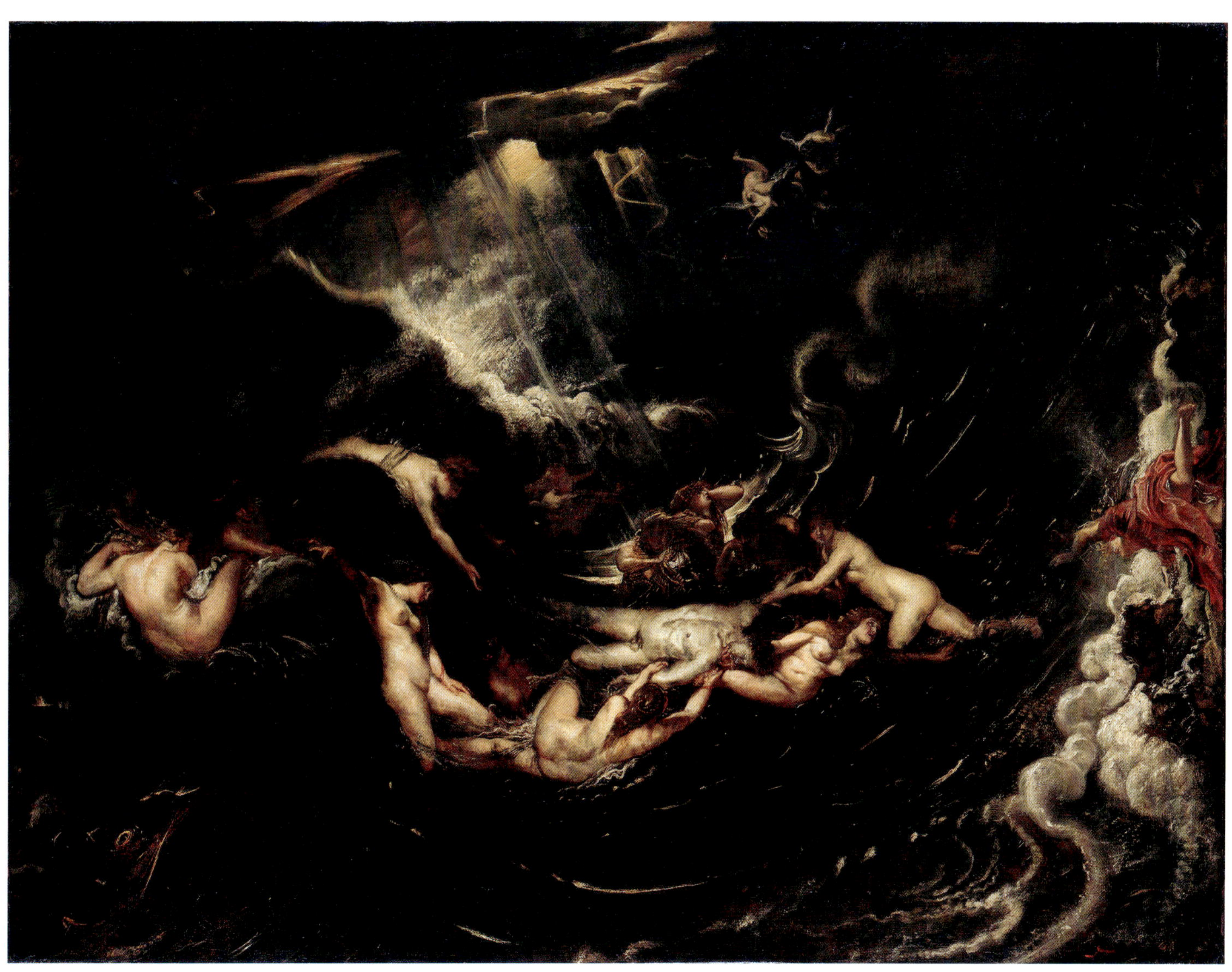

Peter Paul Rubens
Hero and Leander
c. 1604
Oil on canvas
95.9 × 128 cm

Yale University Art Gallery
Gift of Susan Morse Hilles
1962.25

Peter Paul Rubens
Hero and Leander
Yale University Art Gallery, New Haven

Peter Paul Rubens
Hero and Leander
National Scottish Gallery, Edinburgh

Inscriptions recto, at top right: *Leander natans Cupidine praevio.*

Inscriptions verso, at top left: *Sol*; at left of centre: "*ad pedes lúx clarior*; at top left of centre: "*Maxima púlvis núbis instar/aút Caliginis*; at top right of centre: "*púlvis longo tractu/a tergo albescit.*

Annotated in faint pencil at bottom centre: "*Luca Cambiaso.*

Cinematic in its composition and dramatization, Rubens's painting *Hero and Leander* depicts the tragic ending to an ancient tale of forbidden love. Each night, Leander, a youth from Abydos, swam across the treacherous waters of the Hellespont to Sestos for clandestine meetings with Hero, a virgin priestess of Aphrodite. One autumnal evening, a strong wind extinguished the flame in Hero's lantern. Leander, unable to see, was engulfed by the relentless vastness of the sea. Upon learning of his drowning, the disconsolate Hero plunged headlong from her tower into the thrashing waves to reunite with her lover in death.

Although influenced by Ovid's *Heroides* (first century BC), the chief inspiration for the scene was the elaborate account detailed in Musaeus's poem "Hero and Leander" (fifth century AD). The influence of Tuscan and Venetian artists (notably Tintoretto and Michelangelo) is also reflected in some of the composition's elements. Rubens heightens the drama by adding a twisting mass of nereids, or sea-nymphs. As noted by Michael Jaffé and Amy Golhany, among others, these figures are not included in the abovementioned classical sources.[1] In Rubens's visualization of the moralizing tale, the nereids enhance the *affetti*, or passions, through their anguished expression and contortions as they struggle to save Leander. The juxtaposition of Hero's suicide with Leander's drowning, a conflation of two separate episodes, equally underscores the artist's invention. In Musaeus's text, the former only discovers the youth's corpse the next morning. The contrast between the rigidity of Leander's garish green-grey corpse and the pliant bodies of the nymphs creates an uneasy tension—one amplified by Leander's horizontal posture versus Hero's vertiginous vertical fall. However, it is not only the passions that are incited but the spectator's senses. For example, zigzagging bolts of lightning illuminate the nocturnal sky, charging the air with a tangible electricity, while the suggestion of thunder evokes an auditory sensation. Bubbling, agitated sea foam, redolent of salt, also imparts texture, not only through its representation but through painterly application as observed in the "impasto passages."[2] Rubens thrusts the spectator directly into the vortex of his sensory storm.

The spectral nighttime effects, the interplay between the luminous and numinous, undoubtedly enthralled Rembrandt, who purchased *Hero and Leander* in 1637. Likewise, the painting inspired one of the most celebrated poets and courtiers in

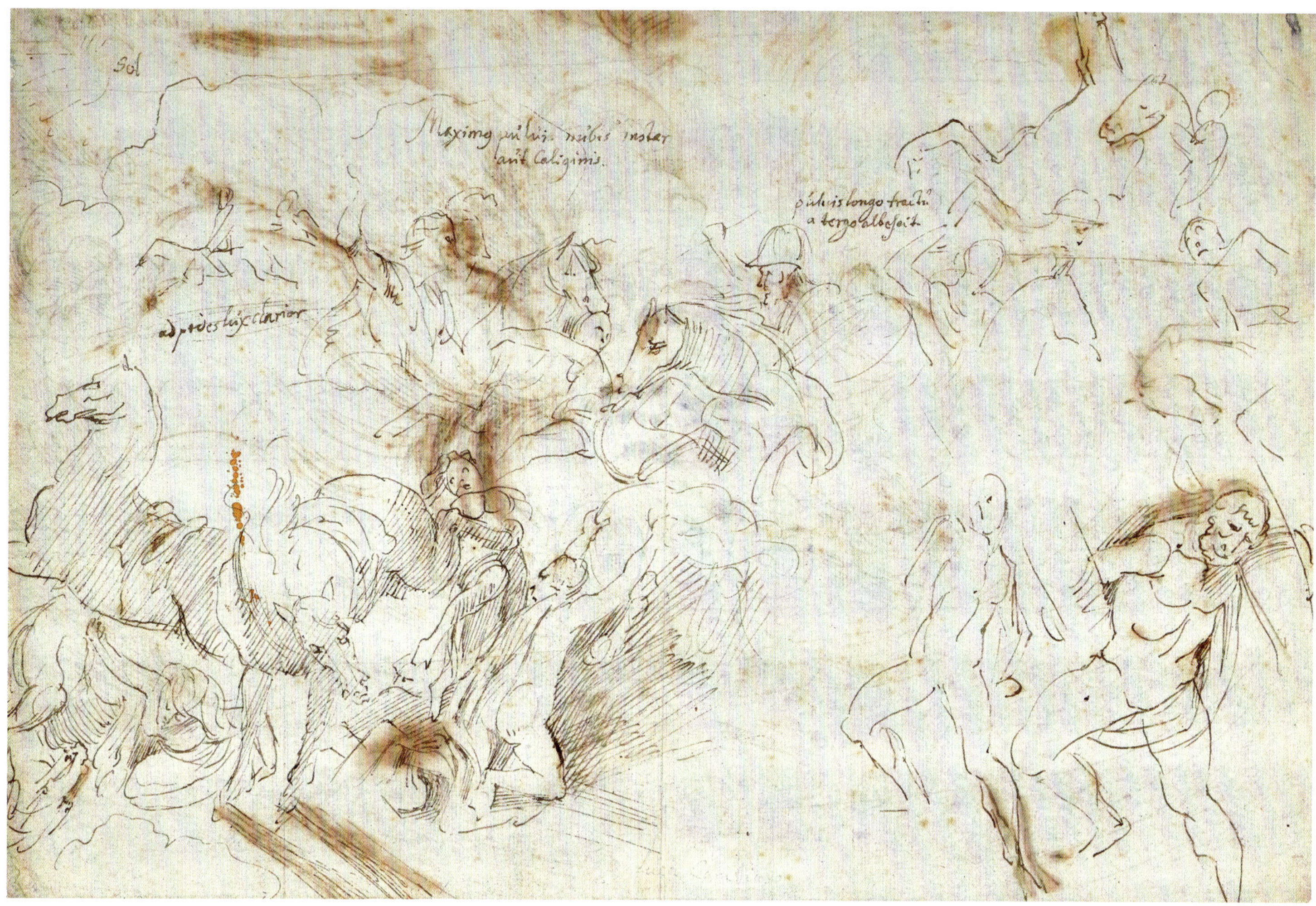

Fig 1 Peter Paul Rubens, *Studies for the Battle of the Amazons*, verso. Pen and brown ink with wash on paper, 20.4 × 30.6 cm. National Galleries of Scotland. D4936.

seventeenth-century Italy, Giambattista Marino. Rubens's work was one of the *favole* (fables) represented in Marino's acclaimed *Galeria del Cavalier Marino* (Venice, 1619/1620)—an anthology of iconic poems or verse commentaries based on famous artworks.[3] Marino had likely seen *Hero and Leander* in person at the Mantuan court, where he was employed as court poet to Gonzaga. It is generally agreed that the painting dates from Rubens's Mantuan period. Owing to the high-voltage drama and pathos in the artist's retelling of the story, "Leandro morto tra le braccia delle Nereidi" (Leander lying dead in the arms of the nereid) is one of the most affecting poetic tributes in *Galeria.* More importantly, Marino's poem provides the first written account of the work.

According to Elizabeth McGrath, the painting's subject did not originate from the classical myth but from a generic image of a storm-tossed shipwreck.[4] The evidence lies in a related pen sketch, in Edinburgh, which depicts a turbulent tempest rendered in the most cursory but dynamic and rhythmic lines. Rubens's studies for his painting *Battle of the Amazons* appear on the verso, dating the drawing to about 1600–1603 (fig. 1). As already observed in the painting, here Rubens also exults and excels in depicting the plasticity and sculptural qualities of water. The sublime terror of natural phenomena is as much the protagonist as the figures. In spite of the inscription at the top right of the page, which reads *Leander natans Cupidine praevio* (Leander swimming, urged on by

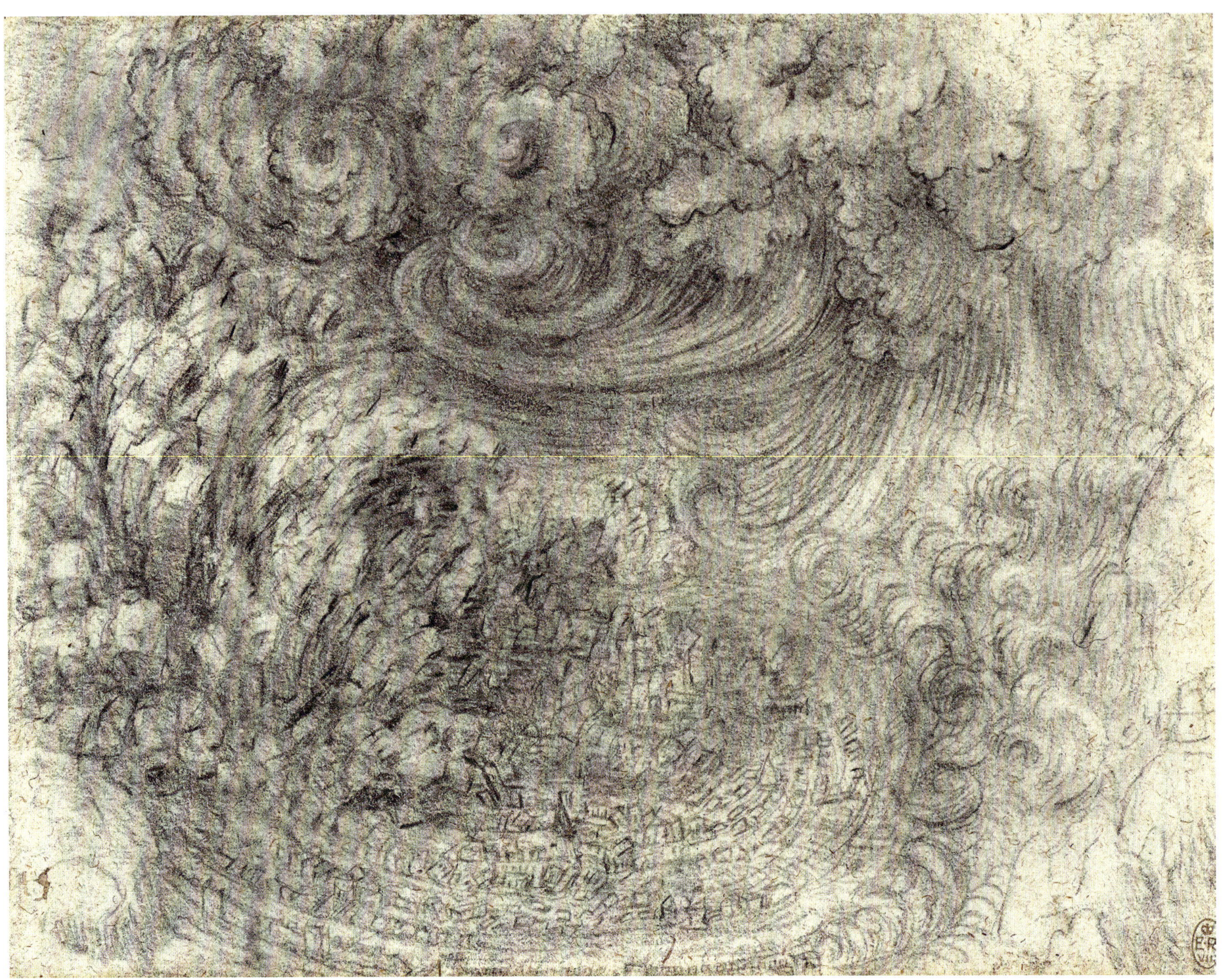

Fig 2 Leonardo Da Vinci, *A Deluge*, c. 1517. Black chalk, 15.8 × 20.3 cm. Royal Collections Trust, London. RCIN 912377. Royal Collection Trust/© Her Majesty Queen Elizabeth II 2018.

Cupid) (Ovid, *Heroides* XVII), the absence of Cupid and a clearly identifiable male protagonist has led scholars to presuppose that the inscription was added after the artist saw the composition's potential to develop into the tragic tale of the two lovers.[5] A more credible classical source, McGrath suggests, is Virgil's account of Neptune's calming of a sea storm from Book I of *The Aeneid*. However, this alternative is equally problematic, given that there is no sea god nor any of his recognizable attributes in Rubens's interpretation. Instead, other scholars have compared the drawing to Leonardo Da Vinci's powerful *Deluge* series (1513–1515)(fig 2). Rubens might have seen these works in 1603 at the home of the court sculptor Pompeo Leoni in Madrid. The link to Leonardo is also reinforced by the Latin inscriptions on the verso, which echo the Renaissance master's reflections on the reciprocal effects of light and dust in the *Libro di Pittura*.[6] Notwithstanding the ambiguity surrounding the narrative source for both the drawing and the painting, the focus should fall on the remarkable fertility of imagination and classical erudition that Rubens exercised in his mythological genre.

Corrinne Chong

1 See Michael Jaffé, "Rubens and Italy: Rediscovered Works," *Burlington Magazine* 100, no. 669 (1958): 412–22 [415–21]; Amy Golahny, "'Hero and Leander' and Its Poetic Progeny," *Yale University Art Gallery Bulletin* (1990): 20–37 [22–23]; and Jaffé in David Jaffé and Elizabeth McGrath, *Rubens: A Master in the Making* (London: National Gallery Company Ltd., 2005), 72. Wieseman suggest that a possible source for the Nereids may be the Greek poet Bion's *Lament for Adonis* (second century BC); see Marjorie E. Wieseman in Peter C. Sutton, ed., *The Age of Rubens* (Boston: Museum of Fine Arts, 1993), 226, cat. no. 23.

2 For compelling, albeit brief, discussion on Rubens application of *disegno* and *colorito*, see Golahny, "'Hero and Leander,'" 24.

3 The other painting by Rubens that inspired Marino depicts Meleager and Atlanta on the hunt for the Calydonian boar. The specific painting is unknown. The title of the poem is "Meleagro con Atalanta." Out of six hundred poems, only two Northern artists were included: Rubens and Cornelis Cort. For an in-depth analysis of literary works adapted from Rubens's paintings (nine in total), see Bert Schepers, "Mythological Scenes by Rubens in Their Intellectual Context," in *Classical Mythology in the Netherlands in the Age of Renaissance and Baroque: Proceedings of the International Conference* (Antwerp, May 19–21, 2005), ed. Carl van de Velde (Leuven: Peeters, 2009), 129–80. Also see Arnout Balis, *Corpus Rubenianum Ludwig Burchard, Part XVIII: Rubens Landscapes and Hunting Scenes*, 2 vols. (New York: Oxford University Press, 1986), 2:9n26 and 94.

4 McGrath in Jaffé and McGrath, *Rubens*, 34.

5 For example, see Christian Tico Seifert, *Rubens & Company: Flemish Drawings from the Scottish National Gallery* (Edinburgh: National Galleries of Scotland, 2016), 48, exh. cat.; and McGrath in Jaffé and McGrath, *Rubens*, 34.

6 Anne-Marie S. Logan and Michiel C. Plomp, *Peter Paul Rubens: The Drawings* (New York: Metropolitan Museum of Art; New Haven, CT: Yale University Press, 2005), 85, exh. cat.

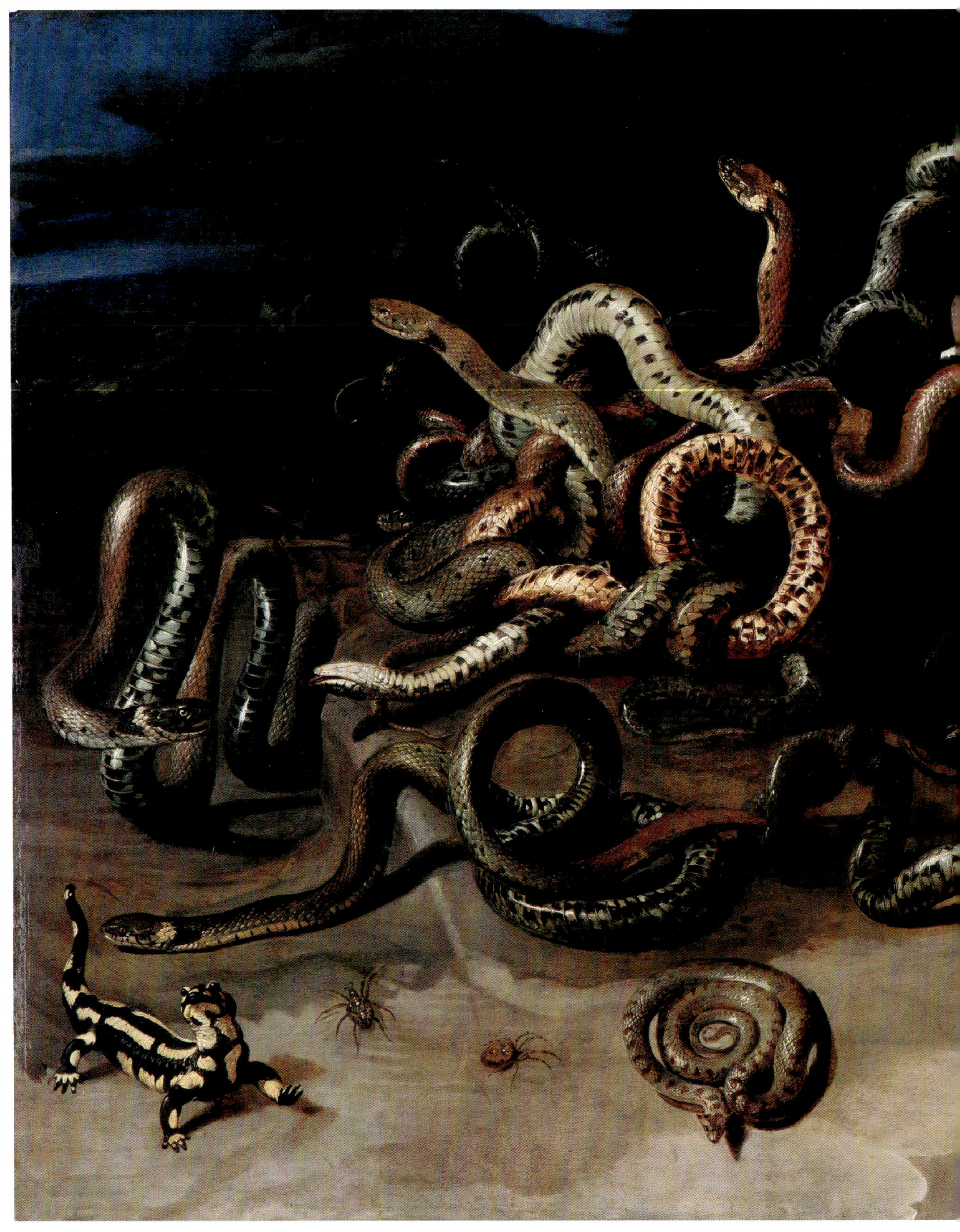

Peter Paul Rubens
Head of Medusa
c. 1617–18
Oil on oak panel
60.6 × 112 cm

Moravian Gallery, Brno
A.2

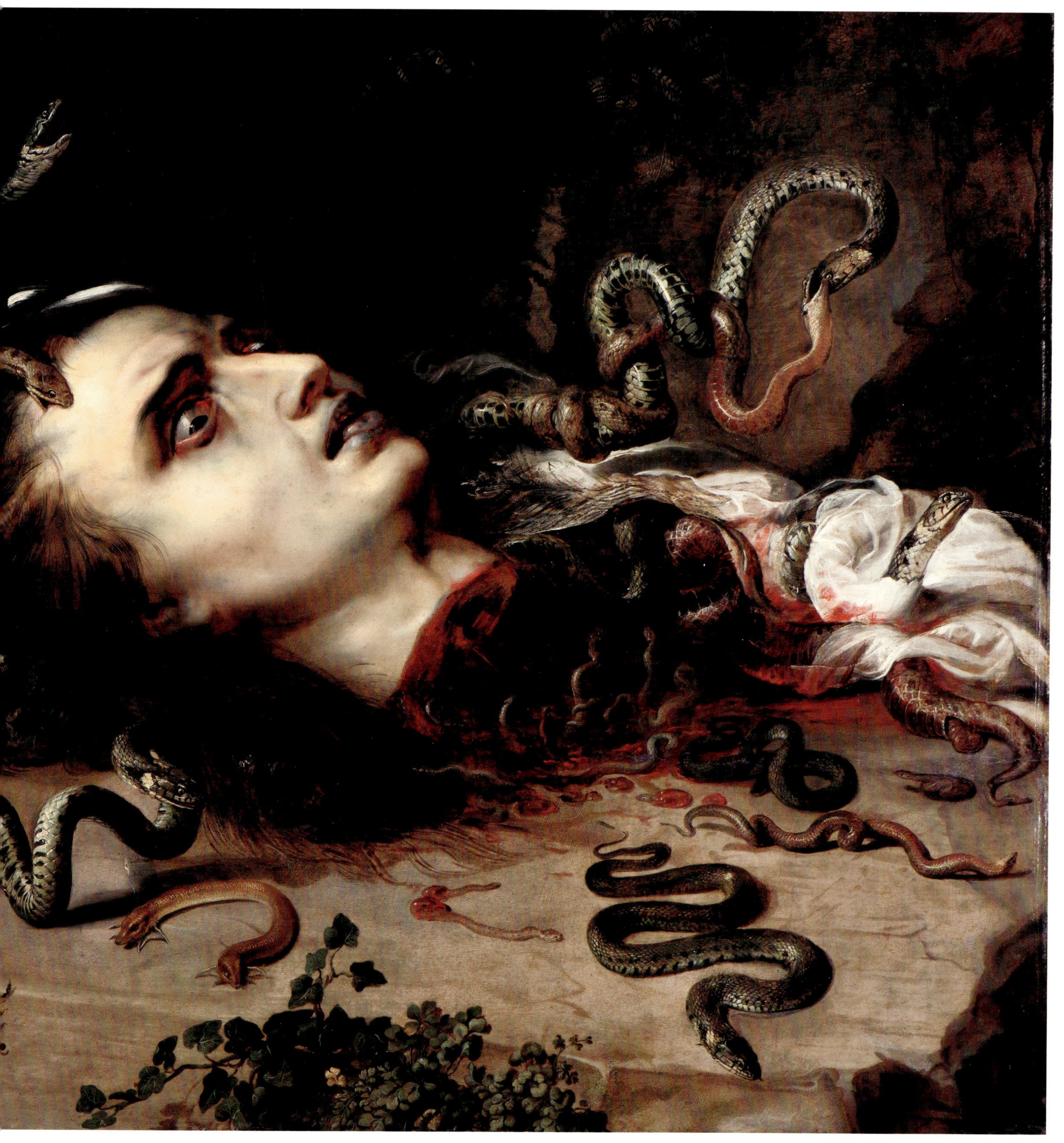

Peter Paul Rubens
Head of Medusa

Rubens's riveting *Head of Medusa* first entered the Brno museum's inventory on December 26, 1818, as *Ein Oehlgemälde das Medusenhaupt vorstellend* without an artist's attribution.[1] The painting was bequeathed to the museum by Count Joseph von Nimptsch I through the Moravian-Silesian provincial governor Count Anton Friedrich Mittrowsky.[2] Although Nimptsch's proprietary seal is preserved on the back of the painting to this day, how he acquired this work has not yet been reliably substantiated. Circumstantial evidence points to his second wife, the Countess Augusta Marcolini-Ferretti. Augusta was the daughter of Count Camillo Marcolini-Ferretti, who was the confidante and friend of the Saxon prince-elector and king, Frederick Augustus III/I. While Marcolini held the position of *Kabinettsminister* in the Dresden court, he was also the director of the Meissen porcelain manufactory from 1774 to 1814 and became the general director of the arts and art academy in Saxony in 1780.[3] For all these reasons, he had many opportunities to cultivate a collection. Considering Marcolini's artistic interests, Frederick Augustus may have presented the painting to him as a reward for his loyal service.[4] It is possible that Augusta and her husband inherited the Brno version of Rubens's *Head of Medusa*. The fact that Count Nimptsch donated the work to the museum a year after his wife's death would suggest it originally belonged to her.[5]

Head of Medusa was first publicized by the Brno doctor, scientist, and art collector Ernst Rincolini, who was appointed curator of the museum in 1822. He attributed the work to Rubens's pupil and collaborator Abraham van Diepenbeeck, while the animals surrounding Medusa's severed head were thought to have been executed by Frans Snyders.[6] Subsequently, the duo of Diepenbeeck-Snyders figured in an 1853 printed guide to the Francis Museum in Brno,[7] as well as in similar publications from later periods.[8] It was not until 1899 that, for the first time, the name Peter Paul Rubens was mentioned, albeit alongside Snyders.[9] After restorative work in the 1940s, the Brno museum's conservator Hedwig Böhm-Hajek reinforced the attribution to Rubens (again in collaboration with Frans Snyders) and posited that the Brno version originated before the Viennese variant at the Kunsthistorisches Museum. She based her evidence on pentimenti, or the changes made by the artist, and the use of a more expensive wooden framework.[10] In a modified account included in the catalogue for the first postwar exhibition,[11] Böhm-Hajek identifies Jan Brueghel the Elder as Rubens's collaborator, even though the Brno painting was still considered to be a copy of the one in Vienna in the wider art-history discourse.[12] Most recently in the scholarship, Gero Seelig presented the Moravian Gallery's *Medusa* as being solely the work of Rubens.[13]

Regardless of which version the spectator beholds, the macabre fascination in Rubens's arresting image of Medusa lies in the tension between attraction and repulsion. Emotions oscillate between delight in the vestiges of beauty remaining on the victim's face and disgust at the hyper-realistic entanglement of grisly snakes and bursting arteries. The contradictory reactions it arouses are vividly encapsulated by the Flemish statesman, Humanist, and poet Constantijn Huygens. In his autobiographical account from 1629, he describes his first impression of *Head of the Medusa* at the house of the Antwerp merchant Nicolaas Sohier:

> There is the compelling painted head of Medusa, wreathed by snakes that spring from her hair. The countenance of the extremely beautiful woman has its grace still persevered, but at the same time evokes the horrors of the fitting beginning of death and the wreath of hideous snakes. The combination is so shrewdly executed that the spectator would be shocked by the sudden confrontation ... but at the same time is moved by the lifelikeness and beauty with which the grim subject is rendered.[14]

One can imagine that the painting's psychological impact and shock value would have been heightened by its display behind a curtain—a conventional mode of presentation that worked to the subject's advantage. Upon the unveiling, the viewer would confront the Gorgon's grotesque face in all its *terribilità*, provoking the Stoic concept of the ictus.[15] Furthermore, the bloodstained white cloth in the background can be read as an extension of the real-life curtain.[16]

According to Ovid (*Metamorphoses,* 4.617–803), Medusa was the most beautiful of Phorcys's three daughters and was greatly admired for her hair. One day, an enamoured Neptune violated her in the sacred Temple of Minerva, provoking the goddess to transform Medusa's prized tresses into a loathsome crown of snakes as punishment. Thereafter, anyone who gazed at Medusa's hideous visage would turn into a stone. However, the cunning Perseus, using the reflection on his mirror-like shield as a guide, followed and decapitated her while she lay asleep. Subsequently, her head would become a resourceful weapon in his heroic adventures until he presented it to Minerva for the decoration of the aegis.

Rubens, by virtue of his expansive erudition, was undoubtedly familiar with the subject's range of allegorical interpretations and iconographical models. For example, in the seventeenth century, men of letters such as Cesare Ripa and Lodovico Dolce most often identified Medusa with her apotropaic powers or more generally with reason and logic.[17] At the same time, others interpreted her attributes in a negative, if not misogynist, light. For instance, Karel van Mander, in his treatise on *Metamorphoses*, casts Perseus as paragon of virtue while Medusa is castigated as the embodiment of licentiousness and pride. Rubens leaves the judgment of Medusa up to the viewer.

Unlike popular apotropaic depictions of Medusa on a shield or breastplate—like Caravaggio's iconic version at the Uffizi—Rubens places the brutally decapitated head on a precipice set against an ominous, nondescript void. Here, it lies haphazardly on the ground, as if it had just been freshly severed by Perseus's sword; the oblique view exposes the stump of the neck in all its gore. Rubens intensifies the violence of this sparse landscape by incorporating two vipers caught in the act of a deadly mating ritual, and a scattering of flesh-hungry snakes. Elsewhere, spiders, a lizard, and a two-headed amphisbaena add to the chaos. As Susan Koslow compellingly argues, while Ovid provided a broad narrative framework, Lucan's *Pharsalia* offered Rubens detailed descriptions of the varieties of snakes and their unique behaviours.[18] Perseus is obviously absent, leaving the narrative moment vague; however, the dry terrain evokes the poet's account of the hero's journey over the Libyan desert, during which droplets of blood, upon touching the sand, morph into snakes. The minimalist narration directs the viewer's attention to the grey-green pallor of Medusa's skin, the silent scream emanating from her gaping mouth, and the downward gaze of her bloodshot eyes toward the coagulating mass of surging arteries and snakes. The outcome is a portrait whose vivid expressiveness, verisimilitude, and virtuosic technique are indeed "unforgettable," to quote Huygens.

Corrinne Chong and Petr Tomášek

1 Haupt-Inventar über alle an das Franzensmuseum eingelangten Gegenstände in dem Jahrlaufe 1808[–1836] (manuscript), inv. no. 713, Archive of the Moravian Museum in Brno.

2 Moravian-Silesian governor Count Anton Friedrich Mittrowsky, letter, December 14, 1818, collection G 82—Agricultural society, 1796–1942, box 239, call nr. V/1, Francis Museum, donations, acquisitions to collections and others, 1815–1829, Moravian Archive Brno.

3 Compare with Friedrich August Ô-Býrn, *Camillo Graf Marcolini, Königlich Sächsischer Cabinetsminister, Oberstallmeister und Kämmerer: Eine biographische Skizze* (Dresden: Emil Schilling, 1877).

4 In 1741, the Saxon prince-elector Frederick Augustus II purchased the painting *"ein Kopf Medusiae von Rubentz"* for 100 florins (guilders) as part of a collection of 268 paintings from Duchcov (Dux) Castle by Count Franz Joseph Georg von Waldstein. See Lubor Machytka, "Zum Verkauf Waldsteinischer Bilder nach Dresden im Jahre 1741," *Jahrbuch der Staatlichen Kunstsammlungen Dresden* 18 (1986): 67–73.

5 Although there are no artworks in Augusta's estate inventory, that it was common to avoid high inheritance tax means that this hypothesis would still seem very likely. See Inventur, Uiber das angegebene und vorgefundene Verlassenschafts Vermögen der verstorbenen Frau Augustine Gräfin von Nimptsch, gebohrne Gräfin von Markoliny, . . . Wien am 27ten October 1817 (manuscript), collection G 315, box 24, inv. no. 35, Moravian Archive Brno.

6 Ernst Rincolini, "Notizen über in Mähren vorhandene vorzügliche Kunstwerke der Mahlerey," *Archiv für Geschichte, Statistik, Literatur und Kunst* 16, nos. 110–11 (1825): 668: "Furthermore, the envy, as Medusa's head allegorically surrounded by many snakes and other animals, the head is of Dippenbeck, Rubens pupil, the animals of Snyders, on wood at 2 ½ feet high, 3 ½ feet wide. As ghastly as the chosen object is, one cannot admire enough the power of colour and the most faithful imitation of the animals." This view was also shared by Franz Moriz Xaver Braumüller, who in a separate article focuses particularly on a description of the subject. See X.B. [Franz Moriz Xaver Braumüller], "Ueber ein Gemälde im Franzens-Museum, das Medusenhaupt vorstellend," *Moravia* 1, no. 86 (December 12, 1838): 344.

7 Albin Heinrich, *Das Franzensmuseum* (Brno: Rudolph Rohrer's Erben, 1853), 67, cat. no. 6.

8 Moric Trapp, *Das Franzens-Museum in Brünn* (Brno: K.K. mähr. schles. Gesellschaft, 1882), 48, cat. no. 132; Moric Trapp, *Františkovo museum v Brně* (Brno: C.k. mor.-slez. společnost, 1882), 43, cat. no. 132; Moric Trapp, *Führer durch das Franzens-Museum in Brünn* (Brno: K.k. mähr. schles.-Gesellschaft, 1890), 87, cat. no. 140; Moric Trapp, *Průvodce Františkovým museem v Brně* (Brno: C.k. mor.-slez. společnost ku zvelebení orby, přírodo- a zeměznalství, 1891), 88, cat. no. 140; Moriz Trapp, *Führer durch das Franzens-Museum in Brünn* (Brno: K.k. mähr. schles.-Gesellschaft, 1894), 85, cat. no. 140; Jaroslav Helfert, ed., *Průvodce po sbírkách Mor. zemského musea v Brně* (Brno: Moravské zemské Museum, 1924), 62, cat. no. 100 (attribution to an unnamed pupil of Rubens and Frans Snyders).

9 *Führer durch die Gemälde-Galerie des Franzens-Museums* (Brno: Franzens-Museum, 1899), 52, no. 140; *Průvodce obrazárnou Musea Františkova* (Brno: Museum Františkovo, 1899), 49, cat. no. 140.

10 Hedwig Böhm-Hajek, "Gemälde berühmter Meister in Heimatmuseen und Privatbesitz I: Das Haupt der Medusa," *Morgenpost* 79, no. 19 (January 23, 1944): 3: "But before that, our Brno Medusa may have originated. It is painted on a high quality and carefully prepared oak panel and measures 60 × 112 cm. That it is the first work to be done proves a change (a so-called pentimenti [*sic*]) to one of the serpents."

11 *Obrazárna zemského musea v Brně: Výběr význačných děl* (Brno: Zemské museum v Brně, 1946), n. p., cat. no. 60.

12 Compare with, for example, Andor Pigler, *Barockthemen 2, Profane Darstellungen* (Budapest: Akadémiai Kiadó, 1974), 173; Klaus Demus et al., *Peter Paul Rubens, 1577–1640* (Vienna: Kunsthistorisches Museum, 1977), 82; Lubomír Slavíček, ed., *Artis pictoriae amatores: Evropa v zrcadle pražského barokního sběratelství* (Prague: Národní galerie v Praze, 1993), 152.

13 Gero Seelig, *Die Menagerie der Medusa: Otto Marseus van Schrieck und die Gelehrten* (Munich: Hirmer, 2017), 42–45.

14 Anne T. Wolleett in Anne T. Woollett and Ariane van Suchtelen, *Rubens and Brueghel: A Working Friendship* (Los Angeles: J. Paul Getty Trust, 2006), 182, exh. cat. no. 24. The version described by Huygens is likely a studio copy, since the original (now in Vienna) was listed in the Duke of Buckingham's estate in 1635.

15 Ulrich Heinen, "Huygens, Rubens and *Medusa:* Reflecting the Passions in Paintings with Some Consideration of Neuroscience in Art History," *Netherlands Yearbook for History of Art* 60, no. 1 (2010): 150–77.

16 Heinen, 153.

17 See Wollett in *Rubens and Brueghel*, 182, and Marjorie E. Wieseman in Peter C. Sutton, ed., *The Age of Rubens* (Boston: Museum of Fine Arts, 1993), 245–46.

18 Susan Koslow, "'How Looked the Gorogon Then...' The Science and Poetics of *The Head of Medusa* by Rubens and Snyders," in *Shop Talk: Studies in Honor of Seymour Slive Presented on His Seventy-Fifth Birthday* (Cambridge, MA: Harvard Art Museums, 1995), 147–49.

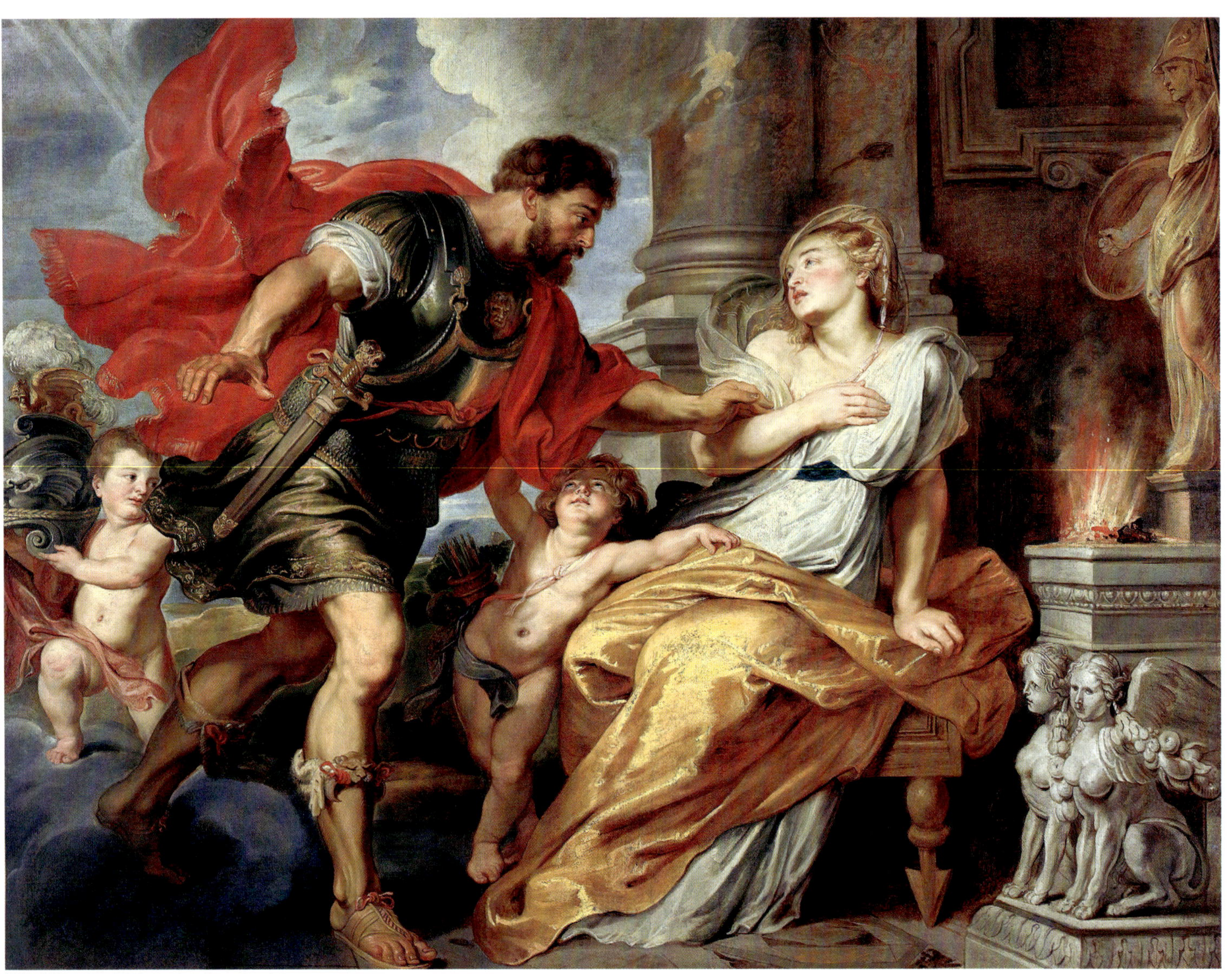

Peter Paul Rubens
Mars and Rhea Silvia
c. 1616–17
Oil on canvas
208 × 272 cm

Liechtenstein, The Princely Collections, Vaduz-Vienna
GE122

Peter Paul Rubens
Mars and Rhea Silvia

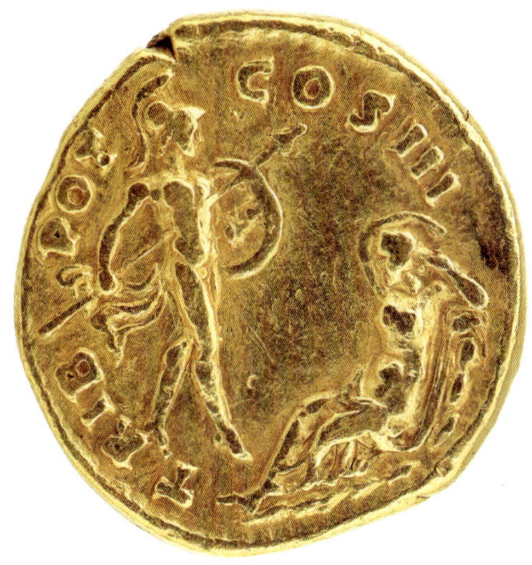

Fig 1 *Aureus coin with Mars and Rhea Silvia*, AD 140–144. Struck gold, 1.85 cm, 7.29 g. Royal Ontario Museum, Toronto. 927.18.2. With permission of the Royal Ontario Museum © ROM.

Among the narrative episodes surrounding the legendary founding of Rome by the twins Romulus and Remus, Rubens depicts the moment of their imminent conception by the god of war, Mars, and the mortal Rhea Silvia (or Ilia). To develop his iconographic program, he consulted canonical ancient literary sources such as Livy's *Ab Urbe Condita Libri* (1.4), Virgil's *Aeneid II* (272–74), and Ovid's *Fasti III* (11–42)., as well as contemporary interpretations, most notably *De Vesta et Vestalibus Syntagma* (Antwerp, 1605) by his friend and mentor, the Neo-Stoic scholar Justus Lipsius. According to the myth, Rhea Silvia, daughter of King Numitor, was forced to become a vestal virgin by her father's usurper and brother, Amulius, to thwart her future offspring from contesting the crown. In Ovid's well-known account, an enraptured Mars sexually violates Rhea Silvia while she sleeps in a sacred grove: "Sweet slumber overpowered and crept stealthily over her eyes, and her languid hand dropped from her chin. Mars saw her; the sight inspired him with desire, and his desire was followed by possession."[1] The result of her ravishment was the birth of the famous twins and her punishment, imprisonment.

In his painting—largely executed by his studio but retouched by his own hand—Rubens characteristically intensifies the drama by underscoring the physical push-and-pull between the two principal protagonists and by externalizing the psychological tension of the moment. Here, as in the *modello* (also in the Liechtenstein collections), Mars impatiently descends from a cloud and charges toward the recoiling figure of Rhea Silvia. At the same time, the vestal priestess's facial expression is one of attraction and apprehension, her left arm pliant yet protective. She is at once startled and seduced: "awake and aware of her awakening feelings," to quote Elizabeth McGrath.[2] The subsidiary actors are equally alert. For instance, Cupid, the matchmaking busybody at the centre of the composition, facilitates the disrobement of the couple, while to the far left a putto hurriedly removes the god's helmet. In *Fasti,* the god is fully disarmed, but as McGrath clarifies, Rubens's Mars is clad in armour not for the sake of decency, conformation to Renaissance models, nor identification but to "illustrate how the war-god is to be disarmed, both literally and metaphorically by love—another illustration of how *amor vincit omnia*."[3]

In the setting, Rubens demonstrates his use of Classical models as a point of departure for his reinventions. For example, he relocates the action from the woods to the Temple of Vesta, where Rhea Silvia has vowed to guard the eternal fire before the enshrined statue of Pallas Athena, the Palladium. By doing so, Rubens simultaneously portrays Mars's profanation, Rhea Silvia's negligence of duty, the breach of her oath of celibacy, and the desecration of a

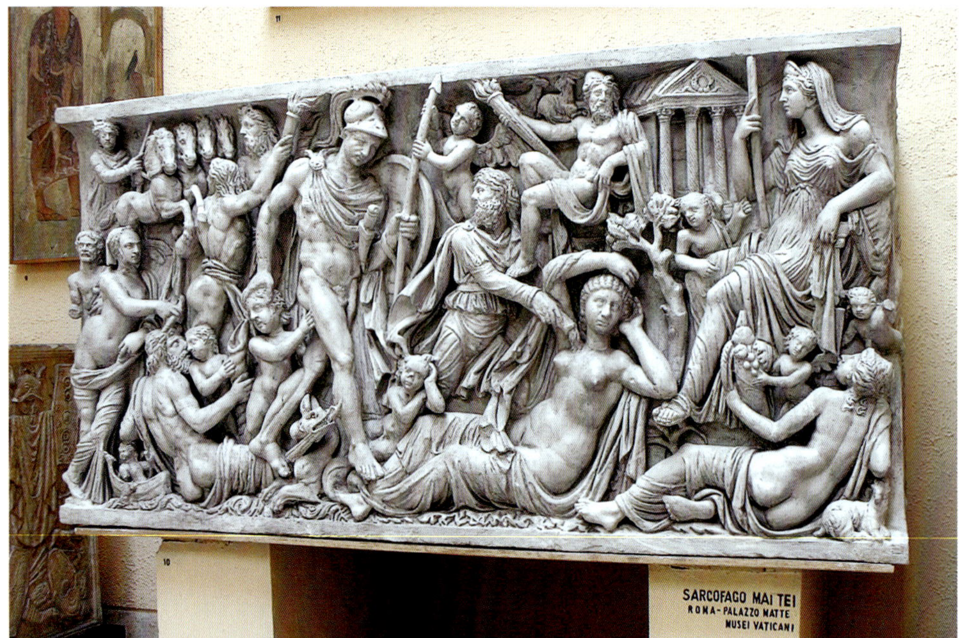

Fig 2 *Mars and Rhea Silvia*, Roman sarcophagus relief, AD 190. Palazzo Mattei, Rome. Photo by Giovanni Dall'Orto.

sacred site. Above all, this shift in setting enabled Rubens to channel his veneration of the antique. To illustrate, the altar with the sphinxes draws from his erudite knowledge of ancient architecture, and the side view of the virgin is a motif from his study of Roman numismatics (fig. 1).[4] Compositionally, the picture's shallow relief-like quality, concentration of all dramatis personae in the foreground, and placement of the protagonists are clearly inspired by a sarcophagus in the Palazzo Mattei in Rome (fig. 2).[5] As he emphatically expounded in his unfinished treatise, "De Imitatione Statuarum," artistic perfection was entwined with the profound knowledge of ancient sculpture, but its emulation must be judicious.[6] Accordingly, in Rubens's adaptation, the vestal virgin adopts the seated pose of Venus from the sarcophagus but the latter's veil is replaced by an unravelled woolen headpiece to symbolize the loss of her virginity—an Ovidian detail in the poem that was much admired by Justus Lipsius.[7]

Rubens's visualization of the iconic Palladium, on the other hand, was informed by Lipsius's text on the cult of the vestal virgins. True to Lipsius's description, the statue is shown in mid-stride with a lance in her raised hand (cut off by the compo-si-tion though visible in an earlier sketch at the Liechtenstein); here, Rubens replaced the distaff and spindle with a shield.[8] The placement of her principal attributes and those of Mars in their respective left hands indicates that the composition was to be reversed for the design of a tapestry. In the early literature, this cartoon was most often associated with the *Decius Mus* cycle. However, stylistic, thematic, and chronological inconsistencies suggest that *Mars and Rhea Silvia* was intended for a tapestry series chronicling the life of Romulus and Remus—a project that was likely abandoned when the artist took on the colossal Medici cycle.[9]

Corrinne Chong

1 Ovid, *Fasti*, Loeb Classical Library 253, trans. James G. Frazer and rev. by G.P. Goold (Cambridge, MA: Harvard University Press, 1931), 121.

2 Elizabeth McGrath, *Corpus Rubenianum Ludwig Burchard, Part XIII: I, Subjects from History*, 2 vols. (London: Harvey Miller, 1997), 1:116. The contradictory feelings exhibited by Rhea Silvia's countenance and composure are also noted by Julius S. Held. He is one of the few scholars who do not regard the finished painting as inferior to the sketch. See Julius S. Held, *The Oil Sketches of Peter Paul Rubens: A Critical Catalogue*, 2 vols. (Princeton, NJ: Princeton University Press, 1980), 1:337, cat. no. 248.

3 McGrath, *Corpus Rubenianum*, 116

4 Marjon van der Meulen, *Corpus Rubenianum Ludwig Burchard: Rubens Copies after the Antique*, 3 vols. (London: Harvey Miller, 1994), 1:89–90.

5 For an analysis of the iconography on the sarcophagus, see Phyllis Bober and Ruth Rubinstein, *Renaissance Artists and Antique Sculpture: A Handbook of Sources*, 2nd ed. (London: Harvey Miller, 2010), 72.

6 For two seminal works on Rubens's theory on the emulation of ancient art, see Jeffrey M. Muller, "Rubens's Theory and Practice of the Imitation of Art," *Art Bulletin* 64, no. 2 (June 1982): 229–47, and Steven J. Cody, "Rubens and the 'Smell of Stone': The Translation of the Antique and the Emulation of Michelangelo," *Arion: A Journal of Humanities and the Classics* 20, no. 3 (Winter 2013): 39–55.

7 Elizabeth McGrath, *Peter Paul Rubens and the Italian Renaissance*, ed. Dana Rowan (Canberra: Australian National Gallery, 1992), 118, exh. cat. no. 33.

8 Reinhold Baumstark, *Liechtenstein: The Princely Collections*, ed. John Philip O'Neill (New York: Metropolitan Museum of Art, 1985), 331, cat. no. 207.

9 For succinct notes on the relationship between the conception of *Mars and Rhea* and the *Decius Mus* cycle, see Reinhold Baumstark, *Masterpieces from the Collection of the Princes of Liechtenstein*, trans. Robert Erich Wolf (New York: Hudson Hills Press, 1981), 115–16; Nadja Lowitzsch, *Peter Paul Rubens, 1577–1640: Masterpieces from the Viennese Collections*, ed. Johann Kräftner, Wilfried Seipel, and Renate Trnek (Vienna: Christian Brandstätter Verlag, 2004), 192, cat. no. 41; and McGrath, *Peter Paul Rubens*, 118–19.

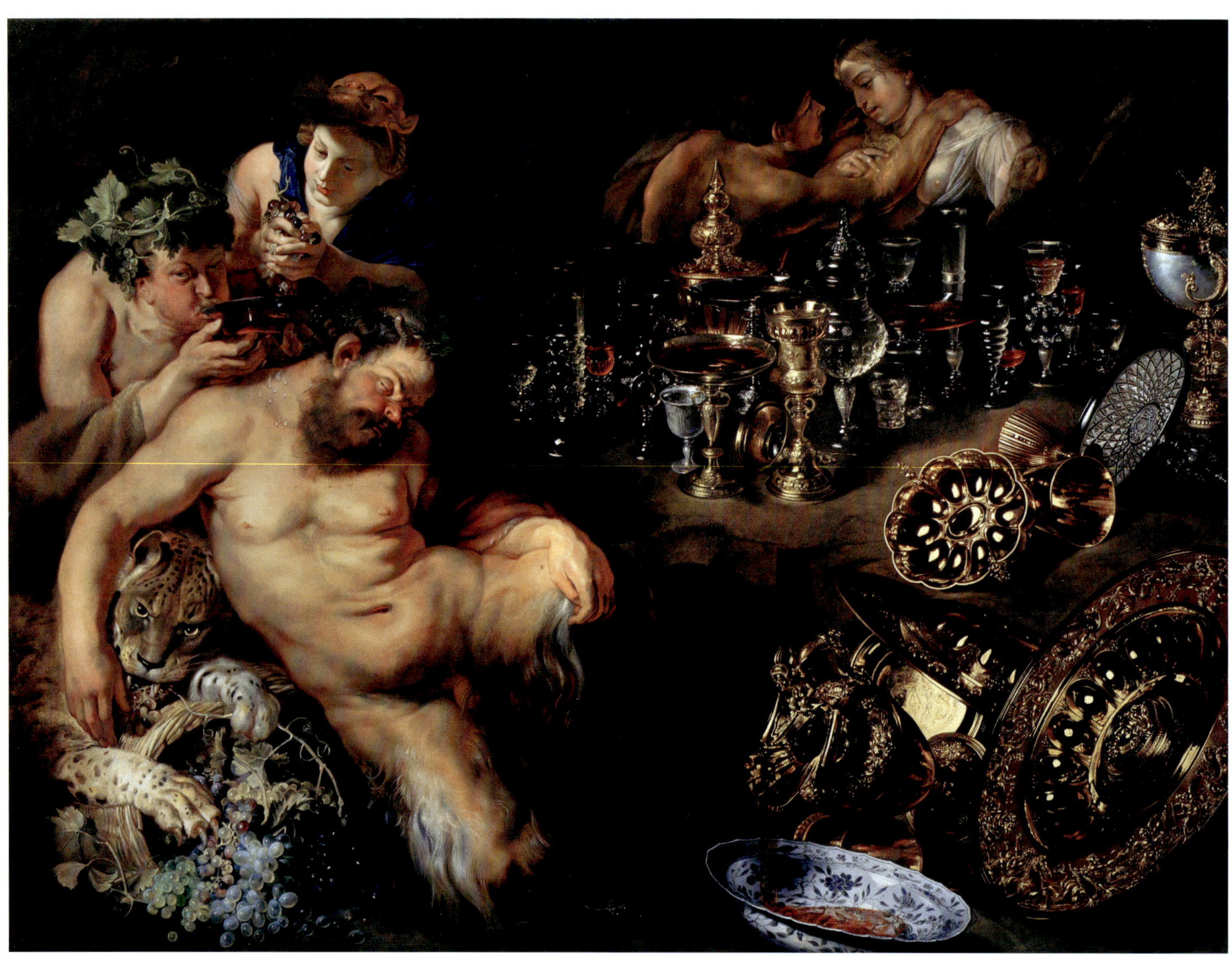

Peter Paul Rubens
The Dreaming Silenus
1610–12
Oil on canvas
158 × 217 cm

Gemäldegalerie der Akademie der bilenden Künste, Vienna
756

Peter Paul Rubens
The Dreaming Silenus

Rubens might initially have conceived this painting as a *pronkstilleven*, a genre that held particular appeal in the first decades of the seventeenth century. With incredible skill and bravura, Rubens painted a still life filled with luxurious objects. He shows off his ability by carefully rendering the different materials and textures, offering a wide array of crockery, goblets, and glassware. The shimmering quality of the metal is caught by an invisible light source in the lower left and emphasized by the many applied highlights. The transparent quality of the glassware, some of them filled with wine, is extremely convincing. One might imagine that the master, recently returned to Antwerp, felt the need to show off his technical skill in this somewhat strange hybrid between still life and mythological scene.

The viewer's attention is torn between the competing scenes—the still life on the right, and the figural group on the left. The jug that has fallen on the right, pouring wine into a porcelain bowl, is mirrored on the left by the drunken Silenus, who has fallen asleep. His reclining heavy, fleshy body is sunken against a panther clawing a basket of grapes. The panther was probably executed by Frans Snyders, a specialist in animals and hunting scenes, who collaborated with Rubens on various occasions.[1] Behind Silenus sit two youthful figures, Bacchus wearing a wreath of grape leaves while sipping wine, and a Maenad, dressed in blue, squeezing the liquid into his bowl. The mask on her head refers to the duality within humankind: rationality versus carnal instinct.[2] Two lovers recede in the background, detached from the group and preoccupied with each other. They might be the vision appearing in the dreams of Silenus. This scene of drunkenness and lovemaking clearly reveals that carnal instincts have, indeed, taken over.

The painting's strange composition and lack of focal point is the result of it being painted in two stages. Examination with X-ray revealed that the still life was conceived first and the Bacchus group included at a later stage; some of the objects are visible in the underpainting of the figural group. Whether Rubens had always intended the Bacchus group is unknown, but the mythological world of Bacchus and his followers was a theme that the painter repeatedly depicted throughout his career.[3] He had studied related scenes of classical Roman sculptures during his stay in Italy, drawing the various poses of Silenus, the figure he most often championed in these works. The pose of Silenus is copied from his own sketch (at Windsor Castle, Collection of Her Majesty the Queen of England) made during his sojourn in Italy.

Carolyn Mensing

1 Reinhild Stephan-Maaser, *Mythos und Lebenswelt: Studien zum "Trunkenen Silen" von Peter Paul Rubens* (Münster: Lit Verlag, 1992), 265.

2 Johann Kräftner, Wilfried Seipel, and Renate Trnek, *Peter Paul Rubens, 1577–1640, die Meisterwerke, die Gemälde in den Sammlungen des Fürsten von und zu Liechtenstein, des Kunsthistorischen Museums und der Gemäldegalerie der Akademie der bildenden Künste in Wien* (Vienna: Christian Brandtstätter Verlag, 2004), 60–62, cat. no. 10.

3 Lucy Jane Davis, "A Gift from Nature: Rubens' Bacchus and Artistic Creativity," *Netherlands Yearbook for History of Art* 55 (2005): 227–43; Stephan-Maaser, *Mythos und Lebenswelt*, 227.

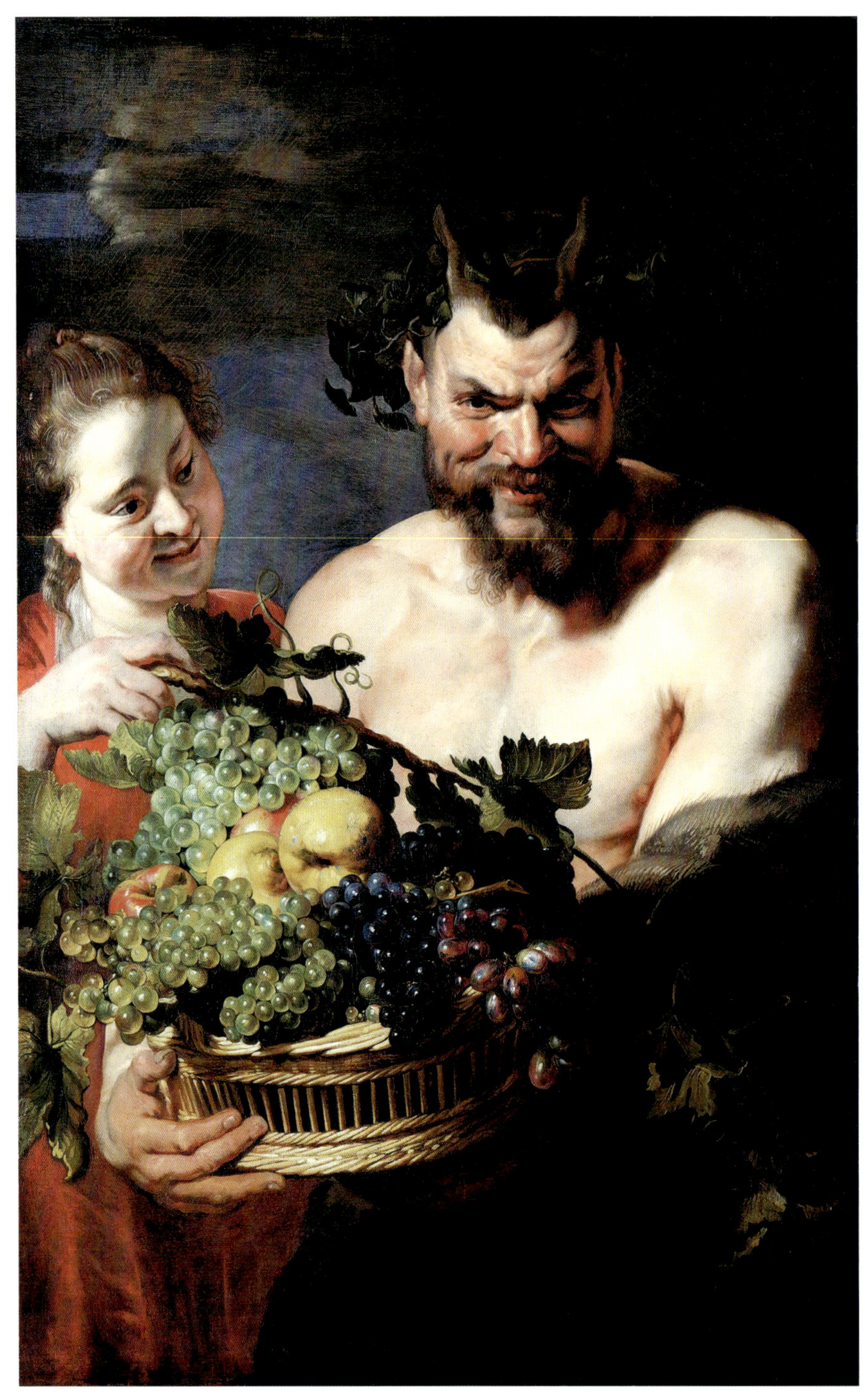

Peter Paul Rubens
Possibly with Frans Snyders
Satyr and Maid with Fruit Basket
c. 1615
Oil on canvas
113 × 71 cm

Private collection, on permanent loan to Liechtenstein,
The Princely Collections, Vaduz-Vienna
Inv.-No. G006

Peter Paul Rubens
Possibly with Frans Snyders
Satyr and Maid with Fruit Basket

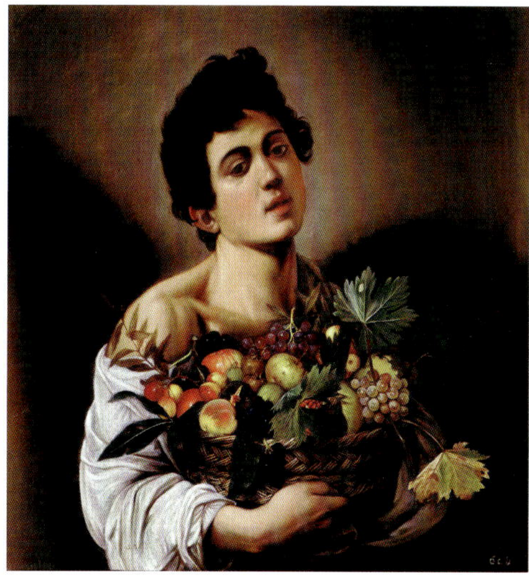

Fig 1 Michelangelo Merisi da Caravaggio, *Boy with a Basket of Fruit*, c. 1593–94. Oil on canvas, 70 × 67 cm. Galleria Borghese, Rome.

Rendered at life size, a satyr looks out of this picture directly at the viewer. He wears a garland of ivy just behind his short horns, suggesting that he is engaged in some Bacchic revelry. His loose smile and rosy cheeks confirm his slight inebriation, as does his lack of concern for the fur garment that has slipped off his shoulders. The intended destination for the fruit he carries is unclear, but he appears to be offering the basket and its contents to the viewer. Yet, at just this moment, his welcoming gesture has been curbed by a young woman—perhaps herself a bacchante—who gently reproves the satyr with the touch of a dried grape vine. In the instant before the satyr turns to rejoin his companions, the sensuously described basket of fruit hovers at the picture plane, tempting the viewer to reach out and cross the boundary of the frame.

No fewer than twenty versions of this extremely popular composition are known.[1] While the head of the young woman tends to vary, the face of the satyr remains relatively consistent across the versions and may be based on a model for which a head study exists, in the Liechtenstein collection.[2] For a composition this frequently repeated, workshop participation is nearly ensured. It has been suggested also that Rubens's frequent collaborator Frans Snyders, a specialist of flora and fauna, may have executed the basket of fruit.[3]

The painting's direct address of the viewer is striking, a feature not often encountered in Rubens's gallery pictures. If we compare *Satyr and Maid with Fruit Basket* with *Diana Returning from the Hunt*, a contemporaneous painting that depicts a very similar satyr carrying an abundance of fruit, the difference in tone is felt immediately. The horizontal orientation and shallow depth of *Diana Returning from the Hunt* evokes ancient relief sculpture and implies a larger narrative that contextualizes the scene.[4] In *Satyr and Maid with Fruit Basket*, these narrative cues are largely absent and the direct psychological confrontation with the satyr limits the perceived action nearly to the present instant. *Satyr and Maid with Fruit Basket* has been compared to Caravaggio's *Boy with a Basket of Fruit* (fig. 1),[5] and while the theme is clearly similar, it is Rubens's attempt to devise an image that would freeze viewers in their tracks before the painting that truly relates the basket-carrying satyr to Caravaggio's art.[6]

Kirk Nickel

1 Johann Kräftner, Wilfrid Seipel, and Renate Trnek, eds., *Rubens in Vienna: The Masterpieces* (Vienna: Liechtenstein Museum, Kunsthistorisches Museum Wein, Gemäldegalerie der Akademie der bildenden Künste Wien, 2004), 110, exh. cat. no. 23.

2 John Philip O'Neill, ed., *Liechtenstein: The Princely Collections* (New York: Metropolitan Museum of Art and Prince of Liechtenstein Foundation, 1985), 322–23, exh. cat. no. 203.

3 Kräftner, Seipel, and Trnek, *Rubens in Vienna*, 110.

4 On the Dresden painting and the possible relation of its fruit-carrying satyr to the type of satyr head used in *Satyr and Maid with Fruit Basket*, see Anne T. Woollett and Ariane van Suchtelen, eds., *Rubens and Brueghel: A Working Friendship* (Los Angeles: J. Paul Getty Trust, 2006), 176, exh. cat.

5 Kräftner, Seipel, and Trnek, *Rubens in Vienna*, 110.

6 During his time in Rome, Rubens was attentive to Caravaggio's art and may have come to understand his contemporary's pursuit of a visual experience that could shock a viewer into stunned silence, although Rubens did not, with very few exceptions, pursue this as a goal in his own work. On petrification as an artistic goal in early Seicento Rome, see Elizabeth Cropper, "The Petrifying Art: Marino's Poetry and Caravaggio," *Metropolitan Museum Journal* 26 (1991): 193–212.

Plantin-Moretus press
(Jan and Balthasar Moretus)
Jan Moretus
born and died Antwerp, Belgium, 1543–1610;
Balthasar Moretus
born and died Antwerp, Belgium, 1574–1641
Breviarium Romanum
1614
Printed book
34.8 × 22.5 cm

New York Public Library, New York
Spencer Coll., Neth. 1614

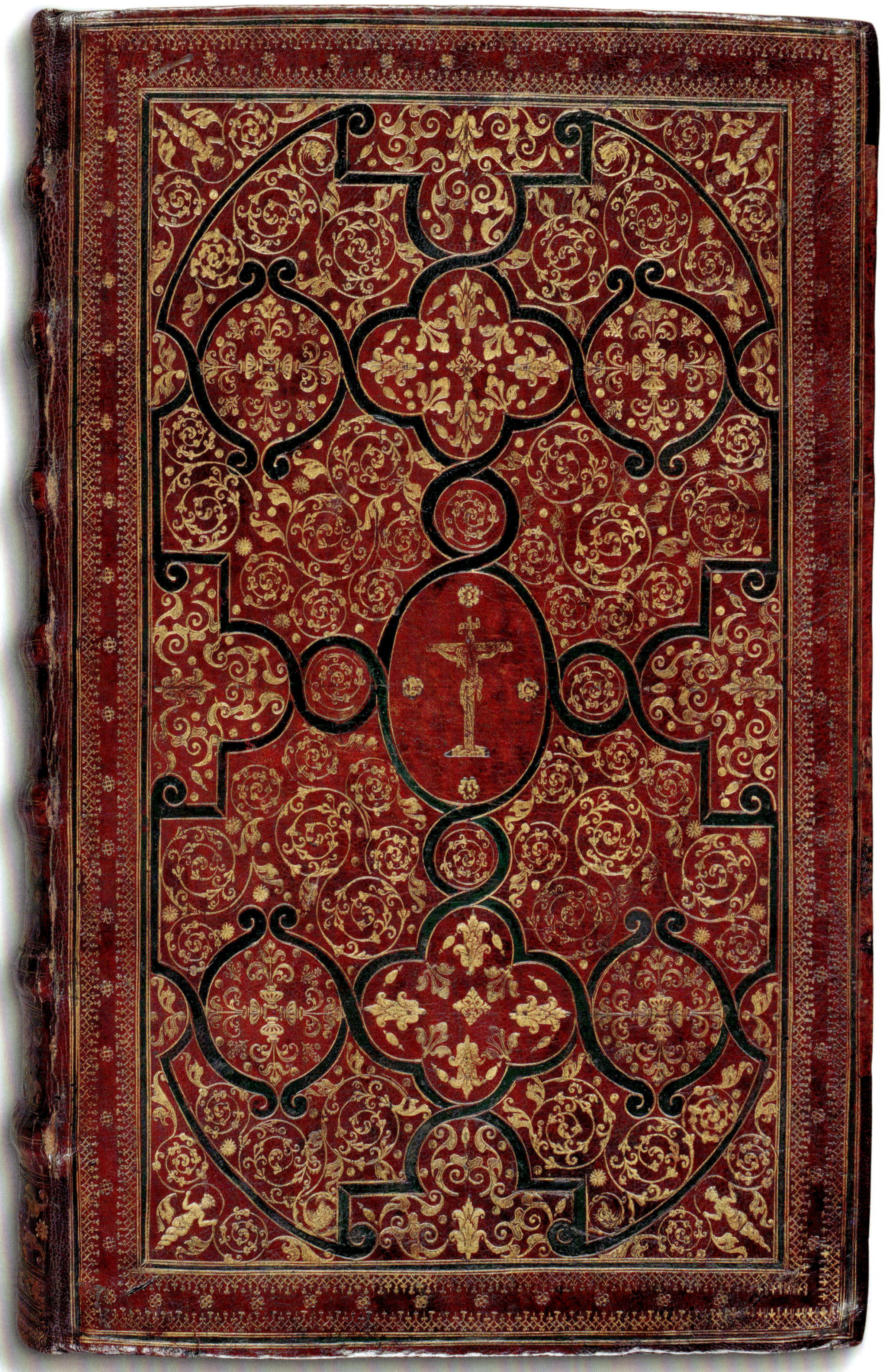

Plantin-Moretus press (Jan and Balthasar Moretus)
Breviarium Romanum

In 1612, the owners of the Plantin-Moretus press, Jan and Balthasar Moretus, the latter a close friend of Rubens since childhood, commissioned the artist to make thirteen drawings for new editions of popular liturgical books: the *Missale Romanum* (1613) and the *Breviarium Romanum*. In the years 1613 to 1616, Rubens received payment of 132 florins for his drawings for the *Breviarium* and for two drawings of the Crucifixion that were not used for the 1614 edition. In addition to eight new compositions and the title page, Moretus included in the *Breviarium* two engravings that Rubens had designed for use in the *Missale Romanum*—*The Adoration of the Magi* and *The Ascension of Christ*—and reused the engraved borders from the earlier project. Five drawings for the *Breviarium* survive: four full-page drawings and the title page. One other is known through a copy. Six corrected proofs of the engravings are extant.

The *Breviarium Romanum* commission was Rubens's largest for book illustrations. Theodoor Galle, head of the important Antwerp Galle family workshop (and brother-in-law to Moretus), engraved the designs,[1] receiving 540 florins for his work. The higher sum paid to Galle reflects the cost of the copper plates and the substantially longer time needed to engrave plates than to create drawings. The lower fee paid to Rubens also reflects that he seems to have made the drawings on Sundays and holidays, always with a long lead time. These factors reduced the price he asked for his work.[2] During his normal work week, Rubens devoted this time to the more profitable endeavour of painting.

The *Breviarium Romanum*, or *Roman Breviary*, was one of the most important liturgical books of the Catholic faith from the time of the Counter-Reformation until Pope Paul VI's reforms of 1974.[3] The breviary contained the Latin liturgical rights, including the public prayers, hymns, and psalms for daily use. Accordingly, the Plantin-Moretus press published several editions of the text during its years of operation. The 1614 version was the first new edition of a *Breviary* from the press since 1575.[4] The choice of subjects illustrated within it were the same that the press had been including for decades. The illustrations, which each precede a relevant section of the text, are

David Poenitens
The Annunciation
The Adoration of the Shepherds
The Adoration of the Magi
The Resurrection
The Ascension of Christ
Pentecost
The Last Supper
The Assumption of the Virgin
All Saints

However, the many full-page illustrations and the ornamented borders on the pages facing them make the 1614 *Breviarium* stand out from other versions of the text published by competing publishers.

Antwerp was the northern seat of Catholic religious publications during the period following the Counter-Reformation, and the Plantin-Moretus press was the major player in this market. The bulk of its publications were not scientific or literary but rather liturgical texts. The average number it printed during this period was 2,000 to 3,000 copies per edition of a breviary, and while Balthasar was in charge, the press printed 33,000 missals.

The liturgical texts were primarily for two groups of consumers: the Spanish market and the Franciscans (the former as the largest market for missals).[5] That the press's books were known to be high quality, well edited, and beautifully illustrated assured them dominance in a competitive market. The folio-sized *Breviarium Romanum* could have been purchased for sixteen guilders on mediaen paper, or for eighteen guilders on stronger, double mediaen paper.[6]

To make it stand out from other editions and to catch the attention of a profitable audience, Balthasar Moretus raised the total number of illustrations in the 1613 *Missale* by two, but more so he focused on increasing the size of the illustrations and replacing woodcuts with engravings, thus allowing for a greater degree of detail.[7] His choice of Rubens as designer also brought great value to the work. Having unusually large illustrations is only as successful as the quality of the engravings, in execution, composition, and narrative power. Rubens's compositions were undeniably beautiful, balanced, and varied, showing familiarity with both Italian and Northern predecessors. They were very much in line with the Counter-Reformation's goals for images: legibility and naturalism.

The popularity of Rubens's illustrations is undeniable: new editions were published with his designs until 1672. Even after the original copper plates were so worn that they could no longer be printed, the designs were copied onto new plates in folio and other sizes.[8]

Alexa Greist

1 Because of the differing processes for printing engravings and woodcuts, all engravings by Theodoor Galle in Plantin-Moretus editions were printed by the Galle workshop. Woodcuts were printed in-house at the Plantin-Moretus press, as they could be formatted to fit within letterpress.

2 This charming and oft-repeated detail about when Rubens created book illustrations or title plates for Moretus comes from the many letters preserved at the Plantin-Moretus house. If Rubens had done the drawings during the week, he would have charged 100 florins for each.

3 The book introduced by Pope Paul VI in 1974 is sometimes referred to as the *Breviary* but is officially called the *Liturgy of the Hours*.

4 J. Richard Judson and Carl van de Velde, *Corpus Rubenianum Ludwig Burchard, Part XXI: Book Illustrations and Title Pages*, 2 vols. (London: Harvey Miller—Heydon and Son, 1978), 1:118.

5 Karen L. Bowen and Dirk Imhof, *The Illustration of Books Published by the Moretuses* (Antwerp: Museum Plantin-Moretus, 1996), 46–47.

6 Judson and Van de Velde, *Corpus Rubenianum*, 119, 432.

7 Bowen and Imhof, *Illustration of Books*, 43. For a discussion of competitor's editions, see Bowen and Imhof, 44–45.

8 In 1631, Cornelis Galle was responsible for engraving, for the *Missale*, a new set of illustrations, including those designed by Rubens.

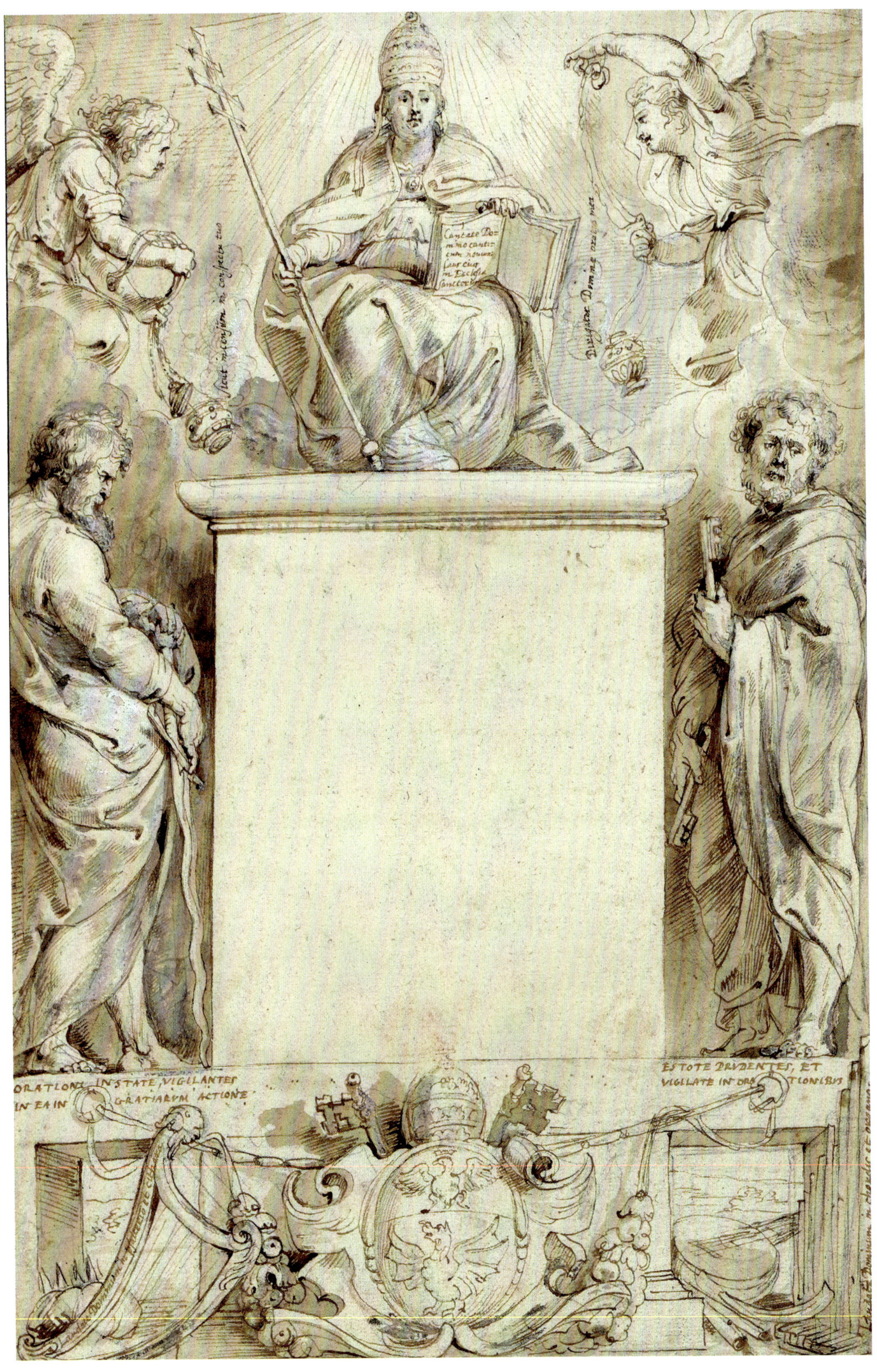
ORATIONI INSTATE, VIGILANTES
IN EA IN GRATIARUM ACTIONE
ESTOTE PRUDENTES, ET
VIGILATE IN ORATIONIBUS

Peter Paul Rubens
Title Page for the *Breviarium Romanum*

In 1612, Balthasar Moretus commissioned his long-time friend Rubens to make eight full-page folio designs and a title page for a new edition of the *Breviarium Romanum* (page 259). For the title page, Moretus provided Rubens with three diagrams of the layout and the scriptural texts that he selected for the page. As Moretus's diagrams were textural rather than figural, Rubens was given licence to envision the composition. Throughout the time Rubens worked for the press, he was allowed significant freedom to choose allegorical images for the title pages he designed, a fact that reflects the high opinion the publisher held of his friend's intelligence and learning. Not all of Rubens's title pages are signed, and there is disagreement among scholars about exactly how many he designed, but the number is somewhere between forty and fifty.

Rubens closely based his final drawing on Moretus's third original diagram (today in the Plantin-Moretus museum).[1] He made only one significant change: at the bottom of the drawing, he substituted musical instruments for what Moretus had indicated as figures playing their instruments. Flanked by censing angels, Ecclesia (the Church), wearing the papal tiara, holding the pope's staff, and with a book open at her knee, tops the image. Saints Peter and Paul stand below her, on either side of a plinth that has been left blank for the title. The papal arms of Paul V anchor the composition at the centre, with musical instruments representing Saint Catherine and King David in the bottom corners.[2]

The layout of the figures within an architectural frame is reminiscent of Italian papal tomb sculpture, although there is no direct identifiable comparison.[3] Rubens's title pages are defined by their clarity of design. His Plantin-Moretus house designs were a departure from those of the previous century, which were primarily decorative and featured highly stylized figures.[4] Elaborate architectural frames often dominated compositions, leaving room only for text and small figures. In contrast, in his second title page for Balthasar Moretus, Rubens already arranges his figures around simple architectural forms, prioritizing legibility over decoration and naturalism over Mannerism. Rubens's title page designs caused a shift in style in the north for the rest of the century.[5]

Alexa Greist

1 Museum Plantin-Moretus, Antwerp, arch. 118, fol. 427, Antwerp, 33b, 126–27.

2 Theodoor Galle received a payment to alter the papal coat of arms from that of Paul V to Urban VIII for the 1628 edition.

3 J. Richard Judson and Carl van de Velde, *Corpus Rubenianum Ludwig Burchard, Part XXI: Book Illustrations and Title Pages*, 2 vols. (London: Harvey Miller and Heydon & Son, 1978), 1:120, cat. no. 18.

4 Julius S. Held, *Rubens: Selected Drawings* (Oxford: Phaidon, 1986), 26.

5 Rubens's first title-page design for Moretus was for François d'Aguilon's *Opticorum Libri Sex* (1613).

Opposite page

Peter Paul Rubens
Title page for the *Breviarium Romanum*
1613–14
Drawing in pen and brown ink with white wash heightened with white over graphite
34.3 × 22.2 cm

British Museum, London
1881, 0611.30

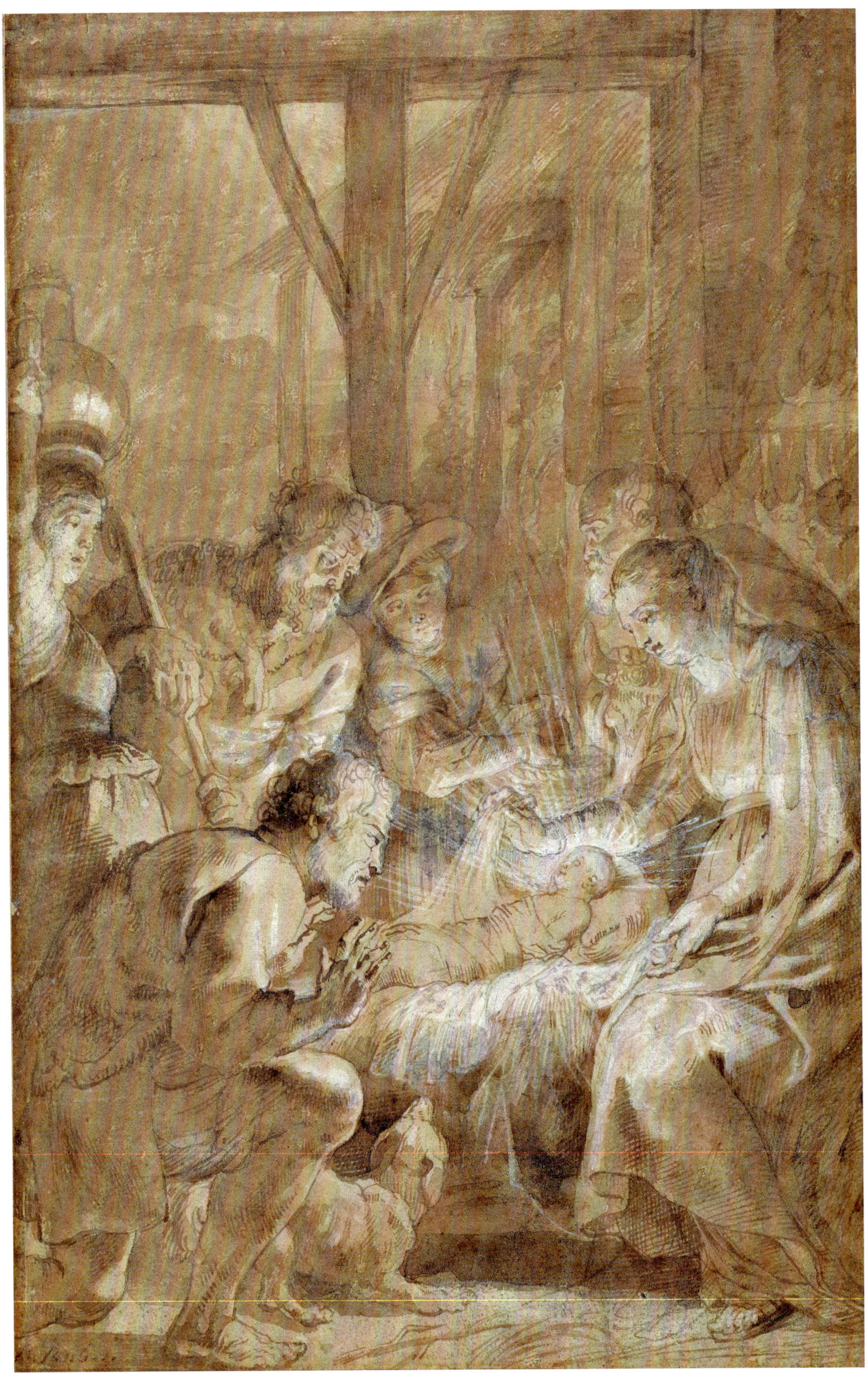

Peter Paul Rubens
The Adoration of the Shepherds for the *Breviarium Romanum*

Secondary inscription at the bottom left:
"P.P. Rub . . ." in brown ink

The heavy use of washes in this nocturnal scene is unique in the surviving drawings for the *Breviarium*. Rubens uses a brown wash across the entire design to create the darkened setting, building figures from and infusing the scene with divine light through the use of white heightening. This technique owes much to the work of two Italian artists that Rubens would have seen in Italy: Correggio and Caravaggio. But it has its origins in the north with Geertgen tot Sint Jans's *Nativity*. Rubens first painted a nocturnal *Adoration* while in Italy in 1608 and again used the convention for his painting in Saint Paul's Church in Antwerp (1609). In *The Adoration of the Shepherds* for the *Breviarium*, Rubens deviates from his earlier representations and creates an earthly setting without dramatic airborne angels. The composition is canonical in many respects but, in the shepherdess carrying a milk pitcher on her head, Rubens introduces a new type of figure to the subject.

This drawing differs from the others that Rubens created as models for the engraver, Theodoor Galle. At this point in his career, Rubens did not provide engravers with oil sketches as models, as he would later. The more detailed, less atmospheric character of the other drawings that the painter provided for the *Breviarium* is typical of the type of drawing used as a model for the inherently linear medium of engraving. In this atypical model, Rubens desired to make clear the importance of the nocturnal setting for this scene, but he must also have had faith in the professional engraver's ability to translate the tonal range effectively into line. To aid in the transfer, the engraver would have placed the model drawing face up on a prepared copper plate and then used a stylus to incise the major outlines of the composition onto it. The resulting fine lines would serve as basic guides for positioning figures and architecture. Galle would then have done most of the work freehand while looking at the drawing.

Alexa Greist

Opposite page

Peter Paul Rubens
The Adoration of the Shepherds
for the *Brevirarium Romanum*
c. 1613–14
Pen and brown ink and brown wash, white gouache heightening; incised for transfer
27.9 × 18.1 cm

J. Paul Getty Museum, Los Angeles
86 GA.592m

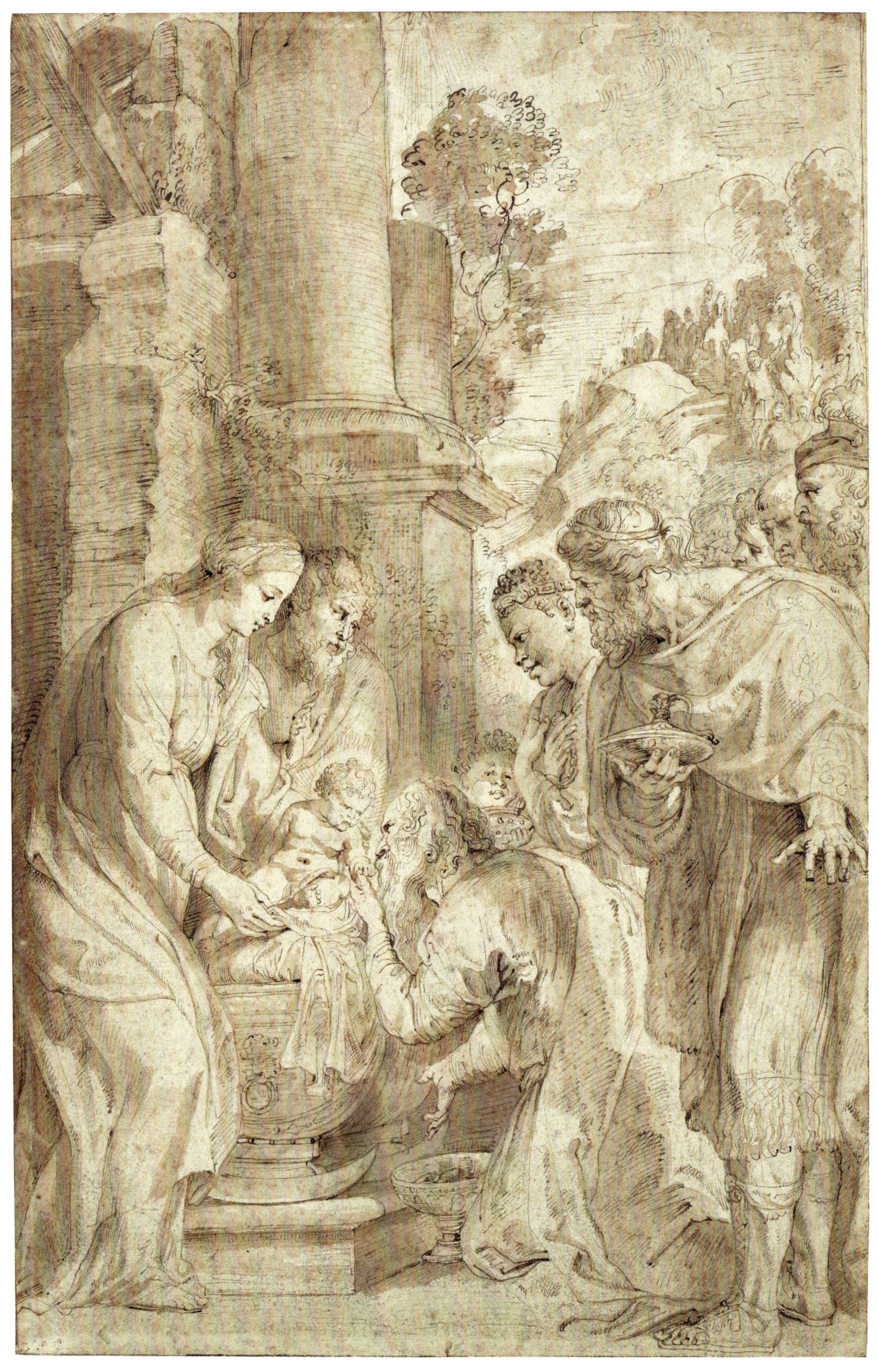

Peter Paul Rubens
The Adoration of the Magi for the *Breviarium Romanum*

In *The Adoration of the Magi*, as in almost all of his drawings for book illustrations, Rubens first marked out areas with black chalk before positioning figures with fine lines of brown ink drawn with the pen. Next, he emphasized certain lines with a broader pen, clarifying the figures in the foreground for the engraver. Rubens considered that the engraving would reproduce the drawing in reverse and planned for this by having the kneeling Magi and the Christ Child clasp each other's left hands in the drawing.

The standing position of the Virgin is unusual, but Rubens used this pose in other depictions of *The Adoration of the Magi*, including in the 1609 commission from the City Council of Antwerp (today held in the Museo Nacional del Prado, Madrid) and in a later painting for the Saint John's Church at Malines (1617–1619).[1] The choice creates a V shape that directs the movement of the scene into the luminous space of the Christ Child. In this highly finished drawing, scant details apart from the background foliage are left up to the engraver, and accordingly there are few differences between the drawing and the finished engraving. The most notable change is the addition of the Virgin's halo. In the drawing, it is possible to see where Rubens has changed the number of figures behind the Magi from four to three, obscuring the fourth man with lightly inked foliage. Engraver Theodoor Galle followed this change.

Rubens supplied drawings for the Plantin-Moretus press for more than thirty years. This drawing was one of two he had created for Moretus for the *Missale Romanum* of 1613. It was included in the *Breviarium Romanum* published the next year. The addition of full folio-sized illustrations of *The Adoration of the Magi* and *The Ascension of Christ* to the *Missale*, to supplement eight engravings from 1606 by Marten de Vos, was a first for the Plantin-Moretus press (although both subjects had been present in smaller formats earlier in the century).

Alexa Greist

1 Felice Stampfle, *Netherlandish Drawings of the Fifteenth and Sixteenth Centuries and Flemish Drawings of the Seventeenth and Eighteenth Centuries in the Pierpont Morgan Library* (Princeton, NJ: Princeton University Press, 1991), cat. no. 11.

2 Judson and Van de Velde, *Corpus Rubenianum*, 128, cat. no. 21a.

Opposite page

Peter Paul Rubens
The Adoration of the Magi
for the *Breviarium Romanum*
c. 1612–13.
Pen and brown ink with brown wash over black chalk; incised for transfer
29.2 × 19.1 cm

Pierpont Morgan Library, New York
Purchased by Pierpont Morgan (1837–1913) in 1909
Acc. no.I, 230; Call.no. F1.17.4

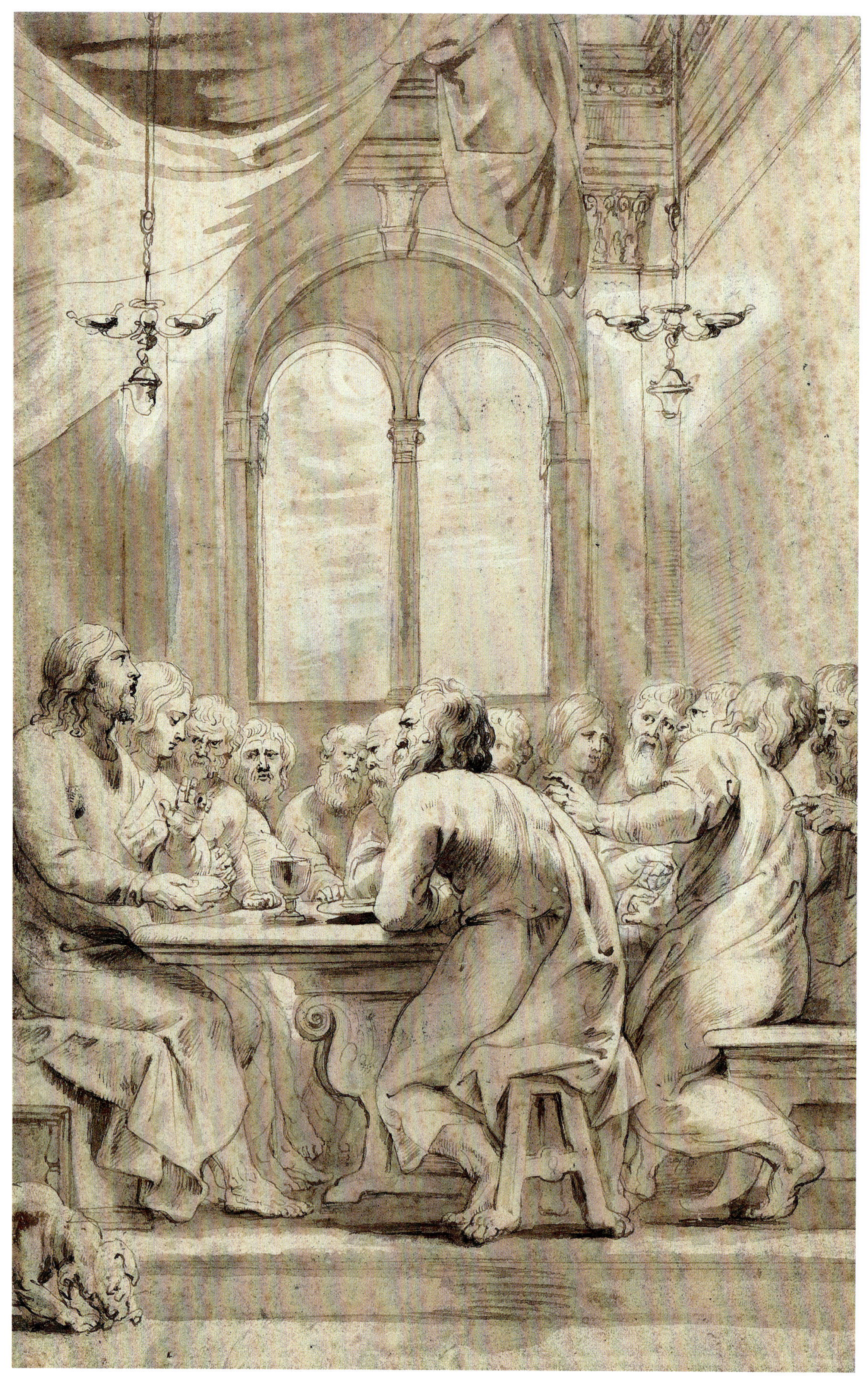

Peter Paul Rubens
The Last Supper for the *Breviarium Romanum*

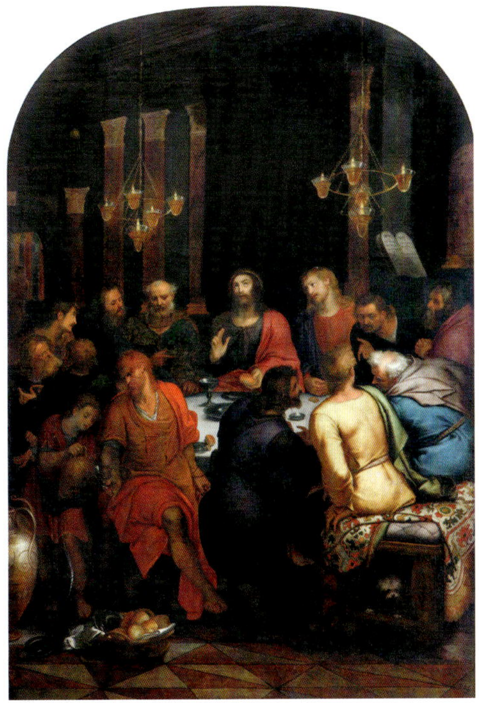

Fig 1 Otto van Veen, *Last Supper of Christ*, 1592. Cathedral of Our Lady, Antwerp. Photo © jozef sedmak/Alamy Stock Photo.

Lent by Richard and Mary L. Gray, this unusual presentation of the Last Supper shows Judas with renewed centrality, after decades of being pushed to the side in Northern representations of the subject. Placing Christ at the end of the table was a northern Italian convention that Rubens could have seen in Tintoretto's *Last Supper* in the Scuola Grande di San Rocco, Venice, or in the Italian artist's painting of the same subject in Santo Stefano, also in Venice. The architectural setting, with its arching double windows, also harkens back to Italy. Northern in feel, though, is the nocturnal setting illuminated by two lamps, which recalls an altarpiece by Rubens's master, Otto van Veen, for the Cathedral of Our Lady, Antwerp (fig. 1).[1] In Rubens's drawing, the apostles converse with each other in cohesive groups like those popularized by Leonardo and Raphael, but the figure types are similar to those Rubens painted around 1612 for his series of apostles now in the Museo Nacional del Prado in Madrid. There are also figural similarities to a drawn study for the same subject in the Devonshire Collection, Chatsworth.[2] The only significant change from the drawing to the engraving is the addition of Christ's halo.

Rubens depicts Christ in profile at the edge of the composition. This illustration faced the page of the *Breviarium* containing the Feast of Corpus Christi, which celebrates the institution of the Eucharist. In Rubens's composition, the viewer clearly sees Christ blessing the bread and wine, which is placed in an open space on the table. But this sole open space is also next to Judas. It invites the viewer both to participate in the Eucharist but also to be complicit in Judas's betrayal.

Alexa Greist

1 Suzanne Folds McCullagh, *Gray Collection: Seven Centuries of Art* (Chicago: Art Institute of Chicago, 2010), 60, cat. no. 33.

2 Judson and Van de Velde, *Corpus Rubenianum*, 140, cat. no. 26a.

Opposite page

Peter Paul Rubens
Last Supper for the *Breviarium Romanum*
c. 1613–14
Pen and brown ink and wash, heightened with white over traces of black chalk; indented for transfer
30 × 19.5 cm
Private collection

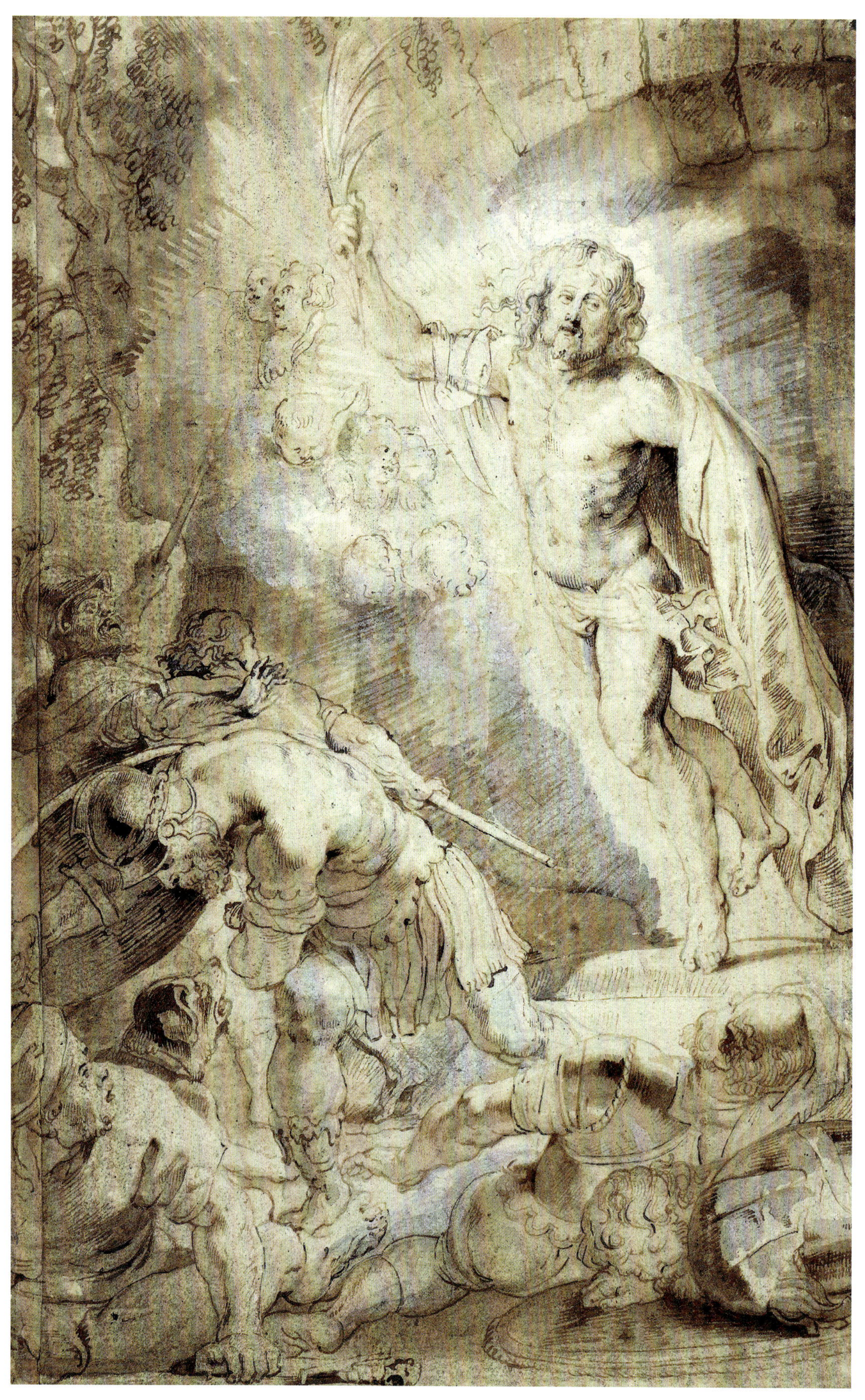

Peter Paul Rubens
The Resurrection for the *Breviarium Romanum*

Christ arises from the tomb radiating holy light that blasts the slumbering soldiers, some who have awoken and tumble away with a heaviness that contrasts the effervescent figure of the Saviour rising, his toe barely touching the Earth. Rubens created a dramatic composition using varied shades of brown washes and white heightening to define holy light. His chiaroscuro activates the scene and is the source of action both physically and visually. Engraver Theodoor Galle captured this effect using the blankness of the page and intricate webs of engraved lines.

In *The Resurrection*, Rubens combines several sources. The overall composition, as noted by Konrad Oberhuber, owes much to Jörg Breu the Younger's woodcut of the same subject. The pose of Christ may refer to Giambologna's sculpture of Mercury, while the muscular nature of Christ's torso brings to mind classical sculpture. Rubens would have seen many examples of ancient sculpture while in Italy, and during the 1610s he incorporated these figural types into several paintings. In addition, the costumes of the soldiers relate to studies he made of antique sarcophagi. He also reuses small details of his own works in the Cathedral of Our Lady in Antwerp: the barking dog from *The Raising of the Cross* and the soldier arriving from the left in *The Resurrection*.

The designs Rubens made for engravings were almost always transferred to the copper plates by means of tracing on the front of the drawing (all the drawings for the *Missale* and *Breviarium* in this catalogue show evidence of the indentations of a stylus used for this purpose). This method of transfer does not account for the reversal of the image in the drawing. Usually, Rubens considered this aspect, but in this drawing the artist did not put the palm into the left hand of Christ, as would be customary in planning for a reversal. Thus, the figure of Christ holds the palm in his left hand in the finished engraving. This is less obvious than would be having left-handed soldiers or authors, but it may well indicate an oversight.

Alexa Greist

Opposite page

Peter Paul Rubens
The Resurrection for the *Breviarium Romanum*
c. 1613–14
Drawing in pen and brown ink, touched with pen and grey ink, with brown wash heightened with white; indented for transfer
29.7 × 18.8 cm
British Museum, London
1895,0915.1049

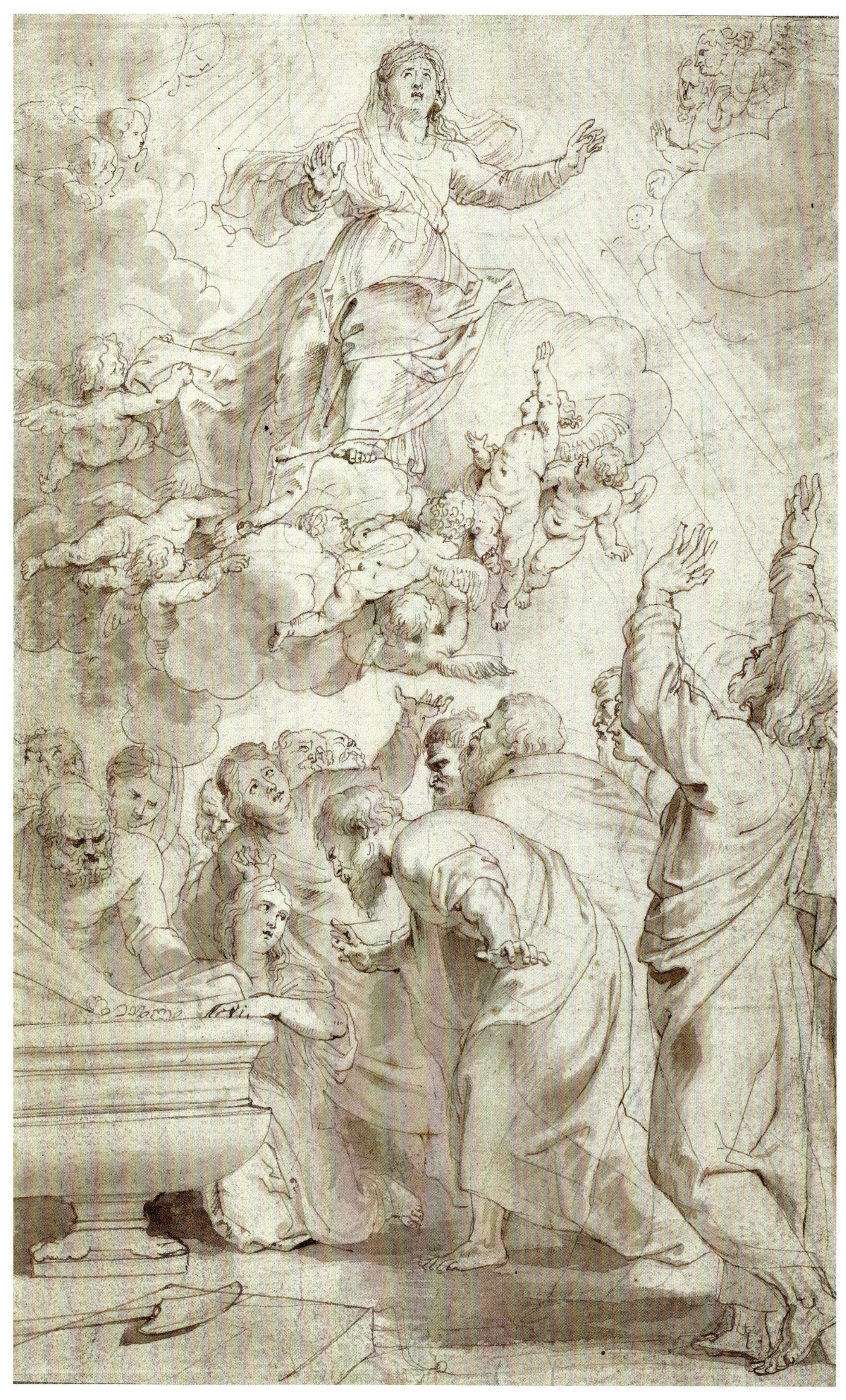

Peter Paul Rubens
The Assumption of the Virgin for the *Breviarium Romanum*

Secondary inscription, (recto) on mount, inscribed: "Rubens, no. 14" in brown ink; (verso) on mount, inscribed: "T. Philipe" in brown ink

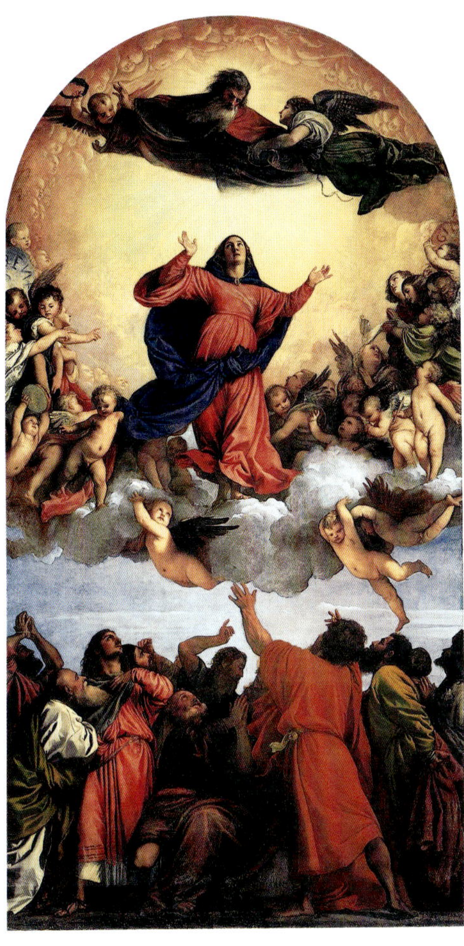

Fig 1 Titian, *Assumption of the Virgin*, 1516–18. Oil on panel, 690 × 360 cm. Santa Maria Gloriosa dei Frari, Venice.

The theme of the assumption of the Virgin was one that Rubens painted repeatedly between 1611 and 1615. The drawing for the *Breviarium* relates to a *modello* of the assumption in Buckingham Palace and a large painting of the same subject in Vienna.[1] The composition of this drawing clearly owes a debt to Titian's well-known *Assumption of the Virgin* in the Venetian church of Santa Maria Gloriosa dei Frari (fig. 1).[2] In Rubens's composition, as in Titian's, the Virgin rises on a cloud supported by Italianesque putti, her arms held aloft, while the figures below either ponder her empty tomb or gaze upward in stupefied awe. Rubens's composition also refers to a lesser-known lost Italian source that the artist saw while in Italy, that of a fresco by Pordenone in the Malchiostro Chapel of San Nicolò, Treviso.[3] Typically Northern in character, though, is the addition of women to the scene.

Because of the existence of pentimenti, in particular in the figure of the Virgin and the indentations suggesting transfer, the Getty collection website posits this was not the final drawing given to the engraver.[4] This is unlikely. There are pentimenti in other drawings that Rubens supplied to his engraver for the *Breviarium*. Also, since the pentimenti in this drawing are in black chalk, the medium used for the very first expressions on the paper that was covered over with subsequent media, they are not distracting. A seasoned engraver such as Theodoor Galle would have been able to look past pentimenti. Lastly, the indentations made by a stylus present on this drawing are in fact evidence for it being used by the engraver, as such indentations indicate transfer to a copper plate and are the same as those found on all the other sheets.

Alexa Greist

1 Held, *Rubens*, 103.

2 Judson and Van de Velde, *Corpus Rubenianum*, 144, cat. no. 27.

3 Held, *Rubens*, 103.

4 "The Assumption of the Virgin," J. Paul Getty Museum, accessed August 10, 2018, http://www.getty.edu/art/collection/objects/22/peter-paul-rubens-the-assumption-of-the-virgin-flemish-about-1613-1614/.

Opposite page

Peter Paul Rubens
The Assumption of the Virgin for the *Breviarium Romanum*
c. 1613–14
Drawing in pen and brown ink with brown wash over black chalk; incised for transfer
30 × 18.9 cm

J. Paul Getty Museum, Los Angeles
83.GG.198

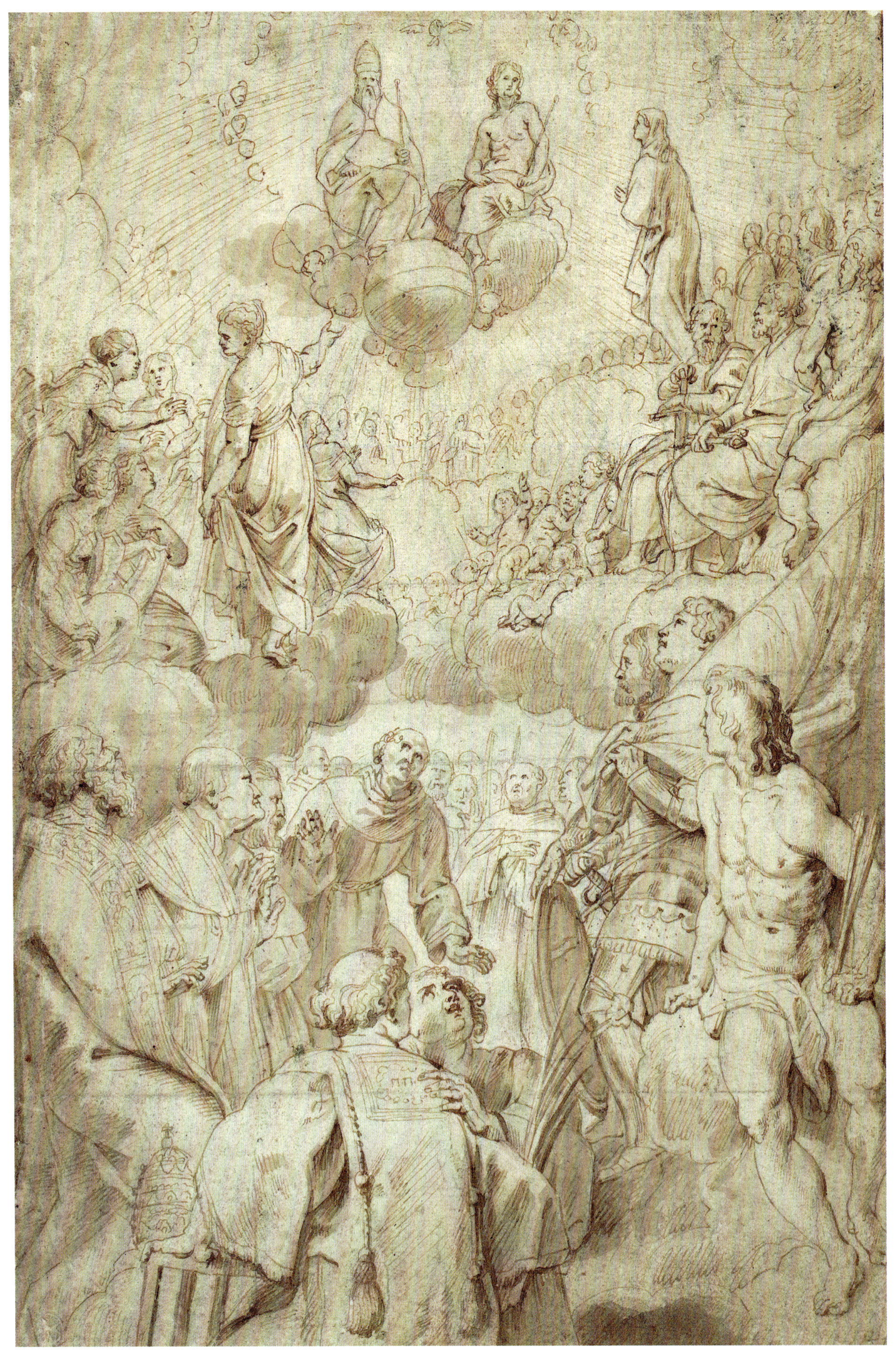

Peter Paul Rubens
All Saints for the *Breviarium Romanum*

Stamp/mark: "Fries (Lugt 2903); Herzog Albert von Sachsen-Teschen (Lugt 174)"

Rubens's design depicting the company of all the saints worshipping the Holy Trinity was the one most frequently reused by the Plantin-Moretus press for its liturgical books. The plate itself was reused (in *Missale* editions of 1616, 1618, 1619, and in 1623; in the *Breviarium* in 1628) and close copies were made and appear in a 1640 missal, a 1652 book of hours, a 1663 diurnal, and an 1823 breviary.

Rubens's composition depicts Christ and God the Father seated on a cloud with the Holy Ghost between and above, shining in divine light. The Virgin floats on a cloud to the left of Christ, bridging the realms of the Trinity and the rest of the holy figures. On the next level of cloudbanks we see the apostles and, opposite, female saints and the innocents, represented by small children. The lowest zone contains saints and monks, some of whom are easily recognizable (for example Saints Sebastian, Lawrence, and George, as well as saints in Franciscan and Dominican robes, possibly representing the founders of those orders), though most are indistinct. Theodoor Galle made no changes between the drawing and the engraving, and Rubens only made a few small adjustments of light and shadow to the proof.

The influences for the format of the multi-tiered clouds supporting saints appear to date from Rubens's exposure to Venetian painting. Both Titian's *Triumph of the Trinity*, a work that Rubens might have seen in 1603 or have been familiar with through the Cornelis Cort engraving of 1566, and Tintoretto's *Venice as Queen of the Sea* are likely precedents.[1] As with all of the drawings Rubens produced for this series, many of the figures repeat types and poses that the artist had used in works created while he was in Italy.[2] In particular, the figure of Saint Sebastian is similar to a drawing of a boy in a 1604–1605 representation of a baptism of Christ, but in reverse. The drawing of the boy was based on a fragmentary, classical nude sculpture that Rubens saw while in Italy.[3]

An oil sketch of a very similar composition exists in the Museum Boijmans Van Beuningen, Rotterdam (inv. no, 1738).[4] At 58 by 38 cm, it is larger than the drawings that served as models for the engravings in the *Breviarium*. Although it does not relate to a known altarpiece, it is close in style and execution to oil sketches Rubens made in the years 1609 and 1610. Thus, it is likely that Rubens looked to this sketch for ideas when he made the pen and ink drawing used as a model for the engraving.

Alexa Greist

1 Judson and Van de Velde credit a variety of sources for these identifications. See Judson and Van de Velde, *Corpus Rubenianum*, 147–48, cat. no. 28.

2 For an analysis of the relevant works, see Judson and Van de Velde, *Corpus Rubenianum*, 147–48, and Museum Plantin-Moretus, Antwerp, 1996–97, cat. no. 33d.

3 For a history of this identification, see Judson and Van de Velde, *Corpus Rubenianum*, 147–48, cat. no. 28.

4 Museum Plantin-Moretus, Antwerp, 1996–97, cat. no. 33c.

Opposite page

Peter Paul Rubens
All Saints for the *Breviarium Romanum*
1613–14
Pen and brown ink and grey-brown wash over graphite, traced to transfer
29.6 × 20 cm
The Albertina Museum, Vienna
8213

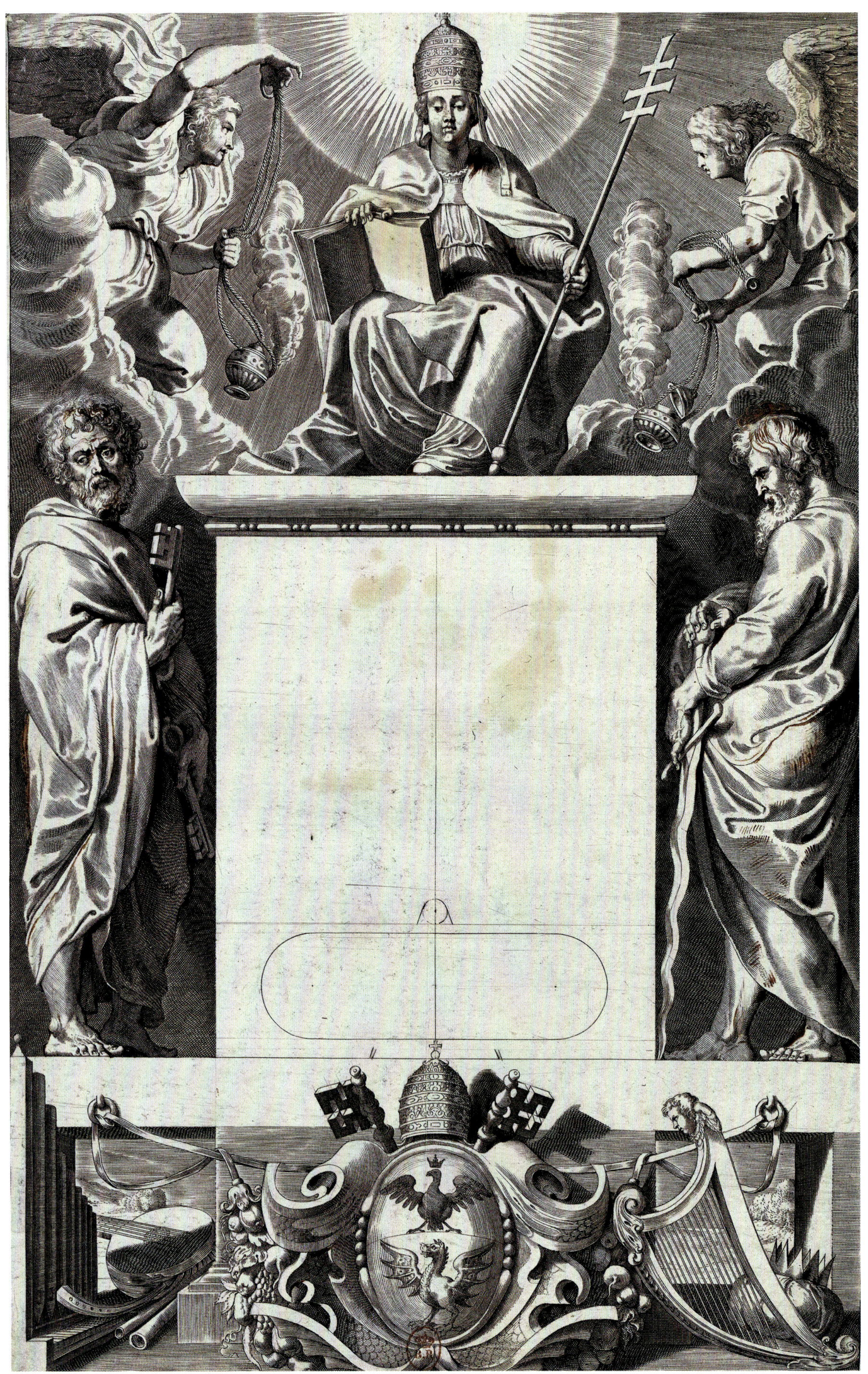

Theodoor Galle
Title Page for the *Breviarium Romanum*
The Adoration of the Shepherds for the *Breviarium Romanum*
The Adoration of the Magi for the *Breviarium Romanum*
The Last Supper for the *Breviarium Romanum*
The Assumption of the Virgin for the *Breviarium Romanum*
All Saints for the *Breviarium Romanum*

Throughout the more than thirty years that he designed book illustrations and title pages for the Plantin-Moretus press, Rubens was closely involved with the process, from the drawn model through the proof state of the engraving or woodcut. In the case of models for engravings after his paintings, Rubens often had students make drawings, correcting only light and shade and making other adjustments necessary for the translation from drawing into engraving.[1]

For book illustrations, the process was different. Until very late in his career, when he suffered from gout, Rubens drew new compositions himself and continued his direct oversight of the work by making corrections or clarifications on proofs of prints.[2] Rubens cared deeply about how all his designs were seen by the public, not just his compositions for paintings. It is likely that observing how the Plantin-Moretus press controlled its products and distribution gave Rubens a glimpse into how he could best spread his inventions and thus his reputation. When he brought engravers into his studio for the sole purpose of translating his paintings into prints, he was taking a next step that may have germinated in his mind in the years since he first worked for his friend Balthasar Moretus.[3]

Today, six proof states of Theodoor Galle's engravings with corrections by Rubens for the *Breviarium Romanum* of 1614 are extant in the collection of the Bibliothèque nationale de France in Paris. That Rubens corrected these proofs himself is secure based on the hand and what we know of the artist's working process when designing for prints. These are not the only proofs with evidence of the master's reworking. Corrections to engravings, woodcuts, and the only known print made by Rubens himself (the etched *Saint Catherine*) demonstrate that the artist regularly kept a close eye on the final print product regardless of who commissioned the work.[4]

As is evident from a comparison of the extant proof engravings with the final, printed engravings, Rubens's changes mostly emphasized shading or chiaroscuro. He used brush and pen with ink as well as a white body colour (today oxidized to blue-grey) to guide Galle in any changes. An engraving that exists in a corrected proof, *The Adoration of the Magi*, was one of two included in the *Missale Romanum* of 1613. Rubens's changes to the proof state are present only in the version printed in the *Breviarium*. No example of proof states with corrections by Rubens made before those for the *Breviarium* exist. It is possible that Rubens had not been entirely pleased with the two engravings by Theodoor Galle for the *Missale*, and thus began to take control of the proof step, but there are no documents in all the copious Plantin-Moretus archives or in Rubens's own correspondence to prove this.

These retouched engravings survived together because they were in the collection of Pierre-Jean Mariette, a famous eighteenth-century French collector and dealer of Old Master drawings and prints. Mariette was a voracious collector of interesting or unusual states of prints as well as an admirer of Rubens, and after Mariette's death, much of his collection was purchased by an early curator of the Bibliothèque nationale.

Alexa Greist

Opposite page

Theodoor Galle
born Antwerp, Belgium, 1571;
died Antwerp, Belgium, 1633
retouched by Peter Paul Rubens
Title page for the *Breviarium Romanum*
1614
Engraving retouched with pen and brush, and dark brown ink; white body colour
34.1 × 22 cm
Bibliothèque nationale de France, Paris
NQ-C059942

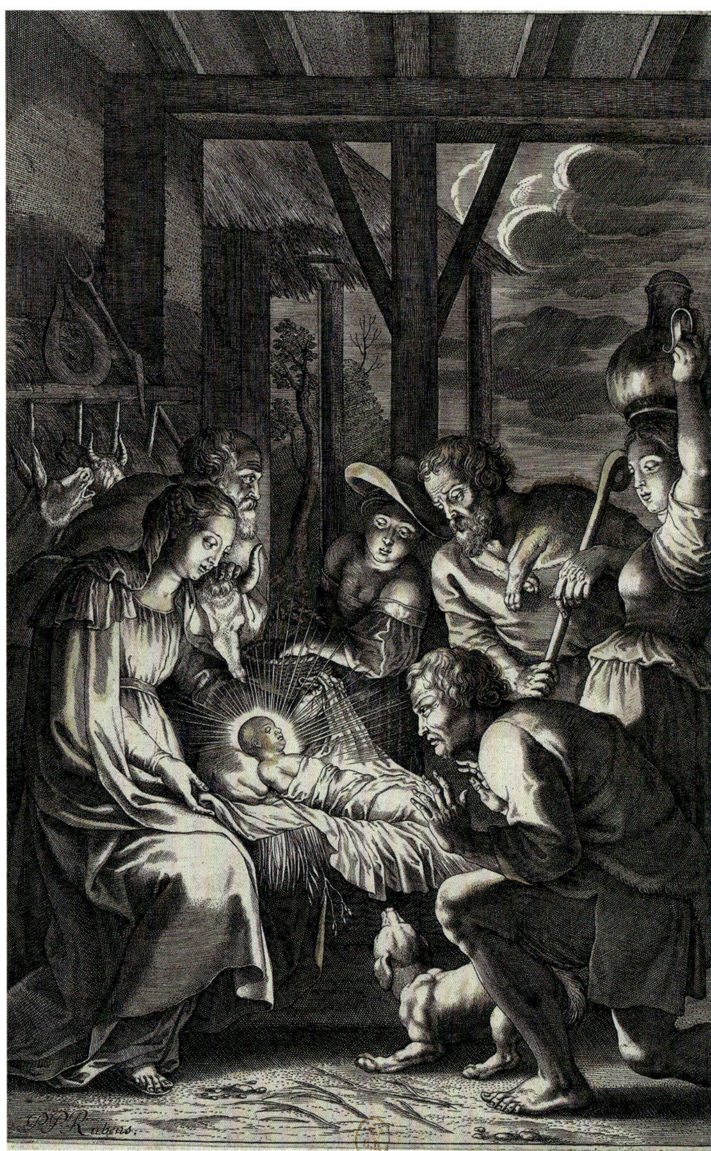

Theodoor Galle
born Antwerp, Belgium, 1571;
died Antwerp, Belgium, 1633
retouched by Peter Paul Rubens
The Adoration of the Shepherds for the *Breviarium Romanum*
1614
Engraving retouched with pen and brush, and brown ink
29.8 × 19.3 cm

Bibliothèque nationale de France, Paris
71-C-46232

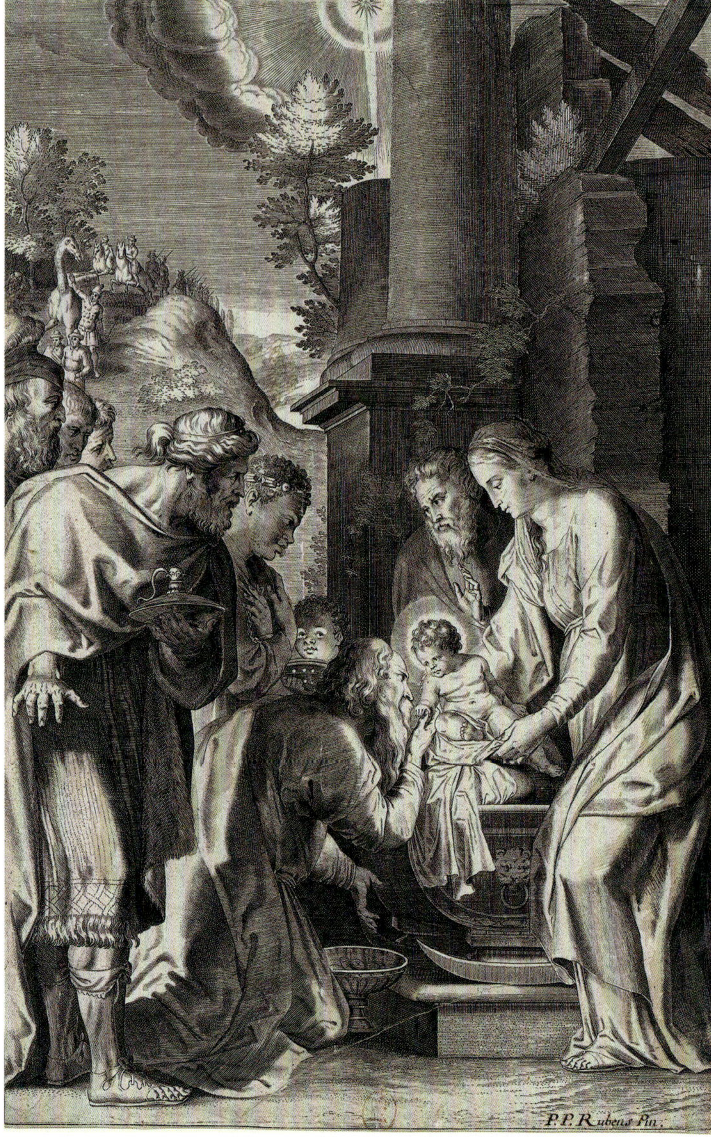

Theodoor Galle
born Antwerp, Belgium, 1571;
died Antwerp, Belgium, 1633
retouched by Peter Paul Rubens
The Adoration of the Magi for the *Breviarium Romanum*
1614
Engraving retouched with brush and brown ink
29.8 × 19.3 cm

Bibliothèque nationale de France, Paris
71-C-46233

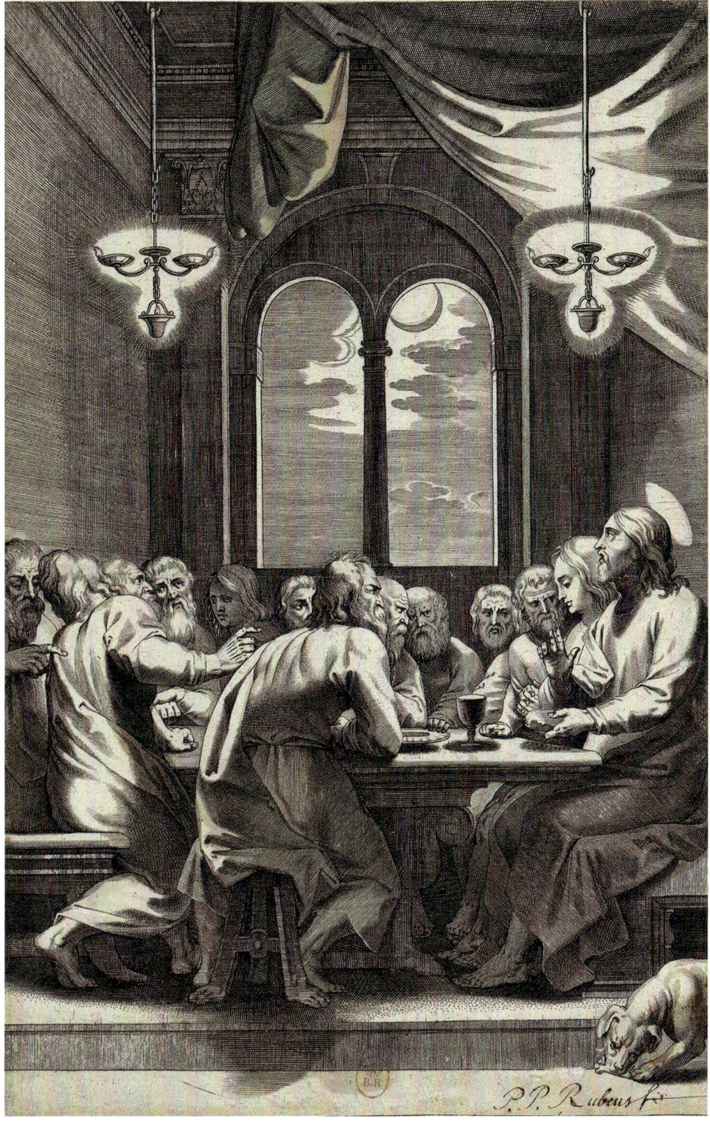

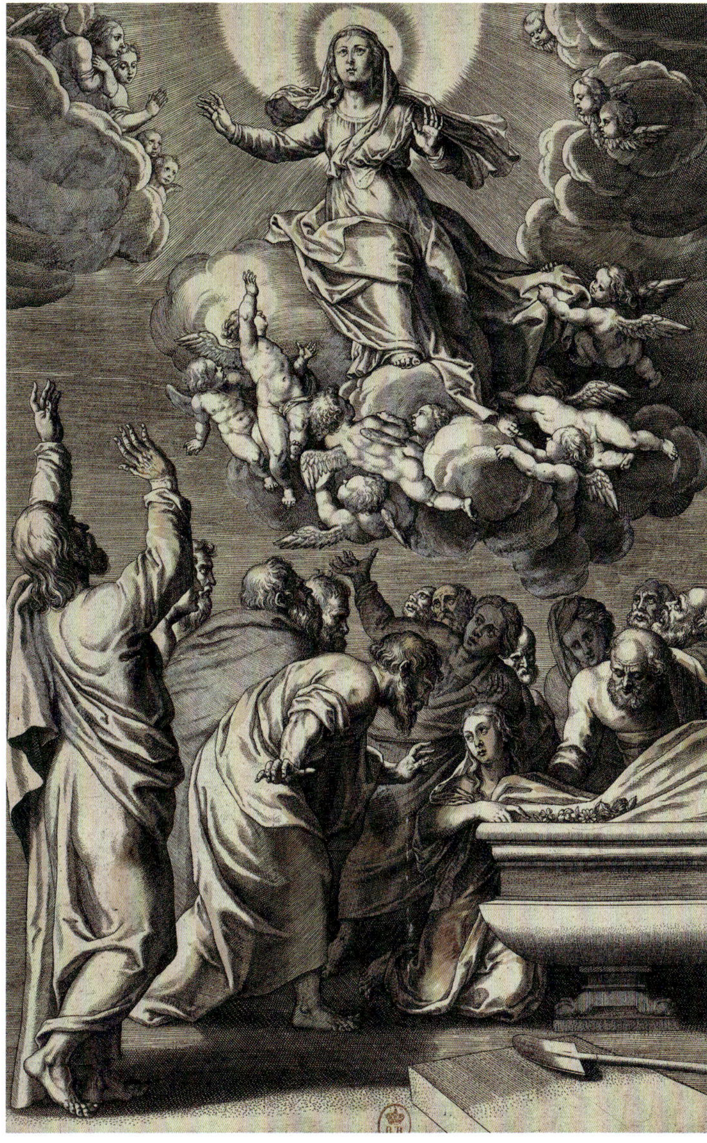

Theodoor Galle
born Antwerp, Belgium, 1571;
died Antwerp, Belgium, 1633
retouched by Peter Paul Rubens
The Last Supper for the *Breviarium Romanum*
1614
Engraving retouched with brush and brown ink
29.7 × 19.6 cm

Bibliothèque nationale de France, Paris
71-C-46234

Theodoor Galle
born Antwerp, Belgium, 1571;
died Antwerp, Belgium, 1633
retouched by Peter Paul Rubens
The Assumption of the Virgin
for the *Breviarium Romanum*
1614
Engraving retouched with brush and brown ink, and white body colour now turned blue
30.4 × 19.7 cm

Bibliothèque nationale de France, Paris
RC-A-77827

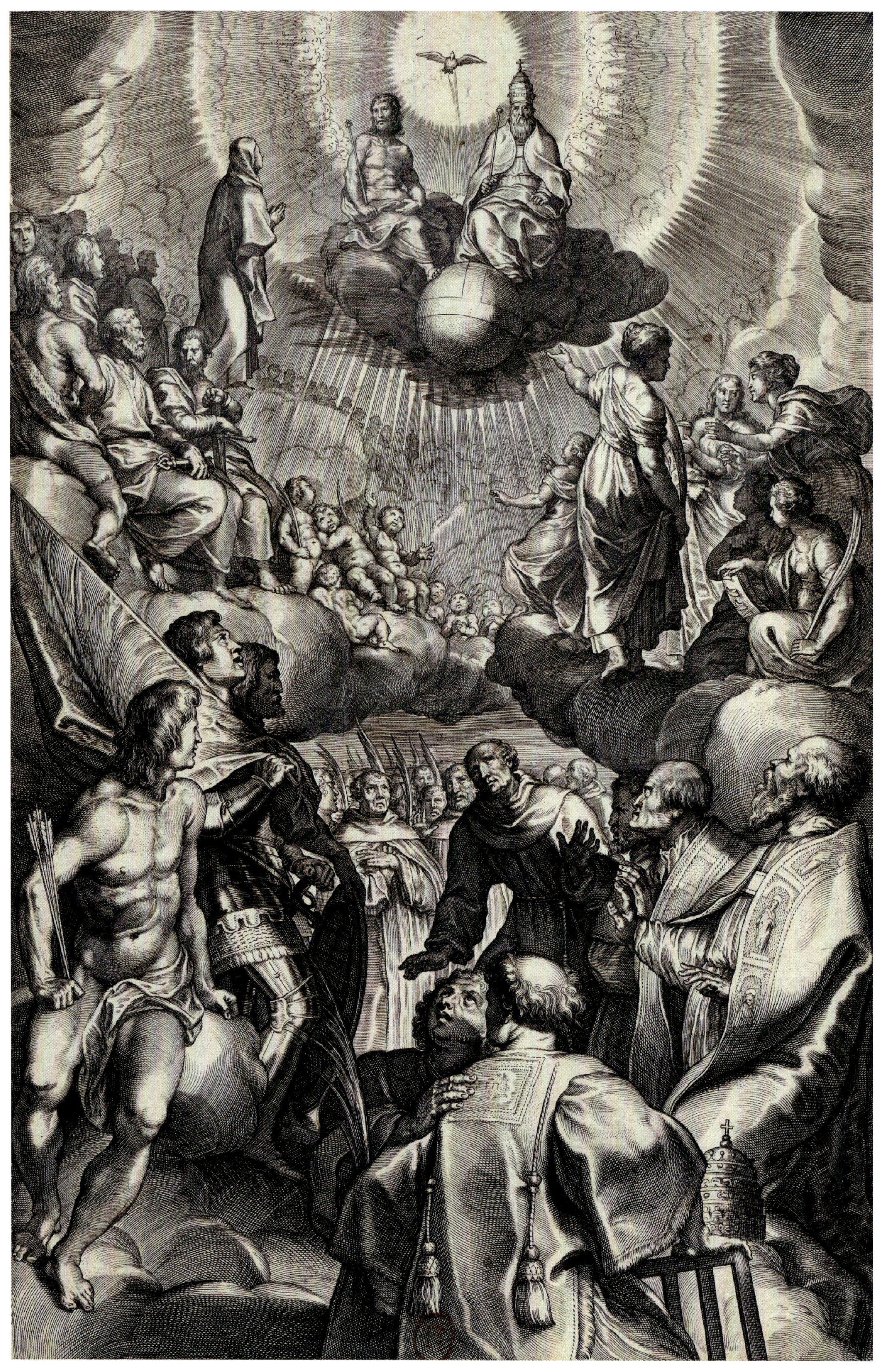

1 Julius S. Held, *Rubens: Selected Drawings* (Oxford: Phaidon, 1986), 35.

2 Held, *Rubens*, 36n33.

3 See essay in this catalogue by Jaco Rutgers, page 102.

4 For a selection of examples of Rubens's corrections to prints and to drawings after his paintings made by others as models for engravings, see the beautifully illustrated catalogue by Nico van Hout, *Rubens et l'art de la gravure* (Gand: Ludion, 2004). In a letter to Nicolas-Claude Fabri de Peiresc (1580–1637), a French Humanist with whom Rubens corresponded regularly, dated March 31, 1635, Rubens referred to his process of correcting proofs (to argue whether or not a certain engraving was made in a certain year, a year he was abroad in England): "Chera impossibile di far questo intaglio in absenza mia essendo stato rotoccho (come s'usa sempre) piu volte di mia mano." ("It was impossible to make this engraving in my absence, as it would have been retouched [as always] several times by my hand.") Quoted in Lydia Pauw-de Veen, "Rubens and the Graphic Arts," *Connoisseur*, August 1977: 243–51. (Quote translated by A. Greist.)

Opposite page

Theodoor Galle
born Antwerp, Belgium, 1571;
died Antwerp, Belgium, 1633
retouched by Peter Paul Rubens
All Saints for the *Breviarium Romanum*
1614
Engraving retouched with brush and brown ink; white body colour now turned blue
30.4 × 19.7 cm

Bibliothèque nationale de France, Paris
74-C-67109

CHRONOLOGY

Unless otherwise noted, all events in this timeline took place in Antwerp.

1608–1615

Rubens returns to Antwerp following an eight-year sojourn in Italy. The circumstances in the North are particularly favourable for a promising young artist. The Twelve Years' Truce between Spain, the Southern Netherlands, and the Dutch Republic is about to be signed; this will trigger an economic revival. Additionally, the ambitious restoration and building campaigns of the Catholic Counter-Reformation stimulated a large demand for altarpieces and paintings. Through personal connections with influential members of the state, mercantile elite, and scholarly circles, Rubens secures several major commissions soon after his arrival. These works elevate his artistic status in the Low Countries, and more commissions follow. By 1611, Rubens has become the city's foremost artist and leads a successful workshop. Some of the masters with whom Rubens collaborates in the first years of the Truce include Frans Snyders (1579–1657), a specialist in animal painting, and Jan Brueghel the Elder (1568–1625), painter of small-scale landscapes. Beginning in 1613, Rubens regularly provides designs for title pages and illustrations for books published with the prestigious Plantin press. This partnership would continue up until the painter's death. Some prints after Rubens's compositions appeared in the Northern Netherlands, but Rubens was not the initiator of these projects.

1608

October 28

In a letter addressed to Annibale Chieppio (1563–1623), the secretary of his patron Vincenzo I Gonzaga (1562–1612), Rubens announces his urgent departure from Rome upon receiving news that his mother, Maria Pyjpelinckx, was gravely ill. In fact, she had already died from a purported severe asthma attack on October 19. The artist was back in Antwerp by December 11, 1608. Rubens's pupil, Deodat del Monte (1582–1644), who had accompanied him to Italy, returns with Rubens and registers with the Guild of Saint Luke. It has been speculated that del Monte may be one of the men represented in the *Self-Portrait in a Circle of Friends at Mantua* (page 120).

December

Rubens joins the brotherhood of Saint Peter and Saint Paul.

1609

Hendrik van Balen (1575–1632), a former student of Rubens's teacher Adam van Noort (1562–1651), becomes dean of the Guild of Saint Luke. He takes on five pupils, among them Anthony van Dyck (1600–1641), who would later become the most important assistant in Rubens's studio.

Rubens is reacquainted with his childhood friend Balthasar Moretus (1574–1641). Balthasar would inherit the Golden Compass House, or Officina Plantiniana, from his grandfather Christophe in 1610. For generations, it would stand unrivalled as the most prestigious printing house of scholarly publications in Europe.

January 14

Philip Rubens (1574–1611), a preeminent Neo-Stoic scholar, political philosopher, jurist, and Peter Paul's older brother, is appointed municipal secretary of Antwerp (see Detroit portrait, page 125). This creates a direct link between the artist and the city's political elite, expanding his circle of patrons.

March 26

Marriage of Philip Rubens and Maria de Moy at the Cathedral of Our Lady. Maria was the younger sister of Clara de Moy—the mother of Rubens's future wife, Isabella Brant.

April 9

Following a period of negotiations, the Twelve Years' Truce is signed in Antwerp City Hall. The treaty was ratified in The Hague on April 21 and in Madrid on July 7. Rubens paints the *Adoration of the Magi* (1609, Museo del Prado) for the Chamber of States, where the treaty would be signed. This painting held both religious and political resonance, as it represented the triumph of Catholicism and peace between Church and State. Nicolaas Rockox (1560–1640), a distinguished Humanist, antiquarian, art collector, and lifelong friend of the artist, helped in assigning the commission to Rubens. At the time of Rubens's return in 1609, Rockox was the burgomaster—a position he also held in 1606 and 1607.

April 10

Rubens writes to Johann Faber (1574–1629) in Rome, the German doctor who cured him of pleurisy in 1606. At this point, the artist is still hesitant about returning to Italy or remaining in Antwerp. In the end, he decides to settle in the North for good (see "September 23, 1609"). Rubens never sets foot on Italian soil again.

June 29 (Saint Peter and Paul day)
Rubens is inducted into the Guild of Romanists, a collective of erudite Antwerpians who had visited Rome. They included artists and scholars as well as members from the political, religious, and mercantile elites. Membership was exclusive and limited to twenty-five people.

Before July 4
Frans Snyders returns from Italy.

July 10
Maximilian I (1573–1651), Duke of Bavaria and, after 1609, a patron of Rubens, establishes the Catholic League, a military alliance of states in present-day Germany. The intention is to counter the Protestant Union started in the North in 1608. The League was to become a key player in the Thirty Years' War (1618–1648).

September 23
Rubens is appointed painter to the court of Archdukes Albert and Isabella in Brussels. This position comes with several important privileges, the most enticing being the choice to remain in Antwerp, the right to take on the commissions of other patrons, and the exemption from registering his pupils with the Guild of Saint Luke, thereby, allowing him to instruct anyone he wished. These privileges enabled Rubens to establish a large and thriving workshop. Vigorous proponents of the arts, the Archdukes would be of vital importance for Rubens's career.

October 3
Marriage of Peter Paul Rubens and Isabella Brant (1591–1626), the eldest daughter of the alderman, municipal secretary, and Humanist scholar Jan Brant (1559–1639). The wedding takes place at Saint Michael's Abbey, the final resting place of the artist's mother. Rubens celebrates his union with Isabella in a wedding portrait known as *The Honeysuckle Bower* (1609). The couple moves into the house of Jan Brant in the Kloosterstraat, where they would live for some years. The location of Rubens's workshop at this time is unknown.

1610

Theodoor Galle (1571–1633), engraver, becomes dean of the Guild of Saint Luke.

Painters Abraham Janssen (1567–1632) and Sebastian Vranckx (1573–1647) join the Guild of Romanists.

Balthasar Moretus (1574–1641) inherits the Plantin press. Balthasar went to grammar school with Rubens, and would commission many designs from his childhood friend in the years that followed.

May 14
Henry IV of France (b. 1553) is assassinated in Paris by a Catholic fanatic. Henry's widow Marie de' Medici (1575–1642) is appointed regent, as their son Louis XIII (1601–1643) is underage.

Early June
Rubens signs the contract for his iconic *Raising of the Cross*, which will figure above the main altar of the Church of Saint Walburga. He completed the painting in the church, apparently within a span of ten months (see "March 12, 1611"). Cornelis van der Geest (1575–1638), a wealthy spice merchant, was instrumental in financing the commission. He would remain a lasting patron of Rubens.

July 18
Death of Michelangelo Merisi da Caravaggio (called Caravaggio, b. 1571) in Porto Ercole.

September 29
(Feast of Saint Michael)
Rubens installs *Saint Gregory, Surrounded by Saints, Adoring the Madonna of Vallicella* near his mother's tomb in Saint Michael's Abbey. The work was originally commissioned by the Oratorians for their church in Rome, the Santa Maria in Vallicella, but it was refused. In Antwerp, the painting showcased Rubens's command of the modern Italian style. Measuring 147 by 120 centimetres, the preparatory oil sketch featured in the exhibition (page 225) is known to be the artist's largest.

November 1
Rubens purchases an estate on De Wapper just off the Meir for the princely sum of 10,000 guilders. The sale is officially concluded January 4 of the following year. Rubens and Isabella continue to live in the Brant family residence while the artist begins renovating his newly-acquired property. The design includes a large studio in the south wing (see essay by Koen Bulckens, page 84).

Rockox commissions the artist to paint *Samson and Delilah* (1609–1610, National Gallery, London) for his town house. The oil sketch for this painting is featured in the exhibition (Cincinnati, page 166).

December 11
Death of painter Adam Elsheimer (b. 1578), who specialized in creating small works on copper, in Rome. Rubens, who had met the German painter during his Italian sojourn, expresses profound grief over his passing in a letter to Faber dated January 14, 1611.

1611

Joos de Momper II (1564–1635), painter, becomes dean of the Guild of Saint Luke.

March 12
Jan Legrand, a local merchant, writes that Rubens is referred to as "the God of Painters," adding that he executed several public works that are held in high regard. He mentions the Church of Saint Walburga (*Raising of the Cross*), the Dominican's Church (probably the *Disputa of the Holy Sacrament*), Saint Michael's Abbey (*Gregory the Great with Saints Domitilla, Maurus, and Mapianus*, Musée de Grenoble), and City Hall (*The Adoration of the Magi*, Museo del Prado). This testifies to the early popularity of Rubens's work.

March 21
Rubens's first child, Clara Serena (1611–1623), is baptized in the Church of Saint Andrew. She dies of an illness at the age of twelve. Rubens finds comfort in Stoicism and ceases correspondence.

April 22
Rubens applies for the commission for the high altar of the Cathedral of Our Lady, presenting two oil sketches to the canons. Otto van Veen (1556–1629), Rubens's former teacher and one of Antwerp's leading artists, had also submitted a design on March 24. The canons went with Rubens, but the commission would be delayed until 1626. Van Veen would move to Brussels in 1614, leaving the city in the capable hands of a younger generation of artists.

Spring
Rubens also tries to obtain the commission for the high altar of Saint Bavo's Cathedral in Ghent. He makes an oil sketch with *The Conversion of St. Bavo* (National Gallery, London) at the request of Bishop Charles Maes (1559–1612). However, Maes dies before the execution begins, and his successor is hesitant to continue the project. Rubens tries to pressure the new bishop through Archduke Albert in 1614. Still, he would obtain the green light for the commission only in 1623, when Antoon Triest (1576–1657) had become bishop of Ghent.

May 11
In a letter to draftsman and engraver Jacob de Bie (1581–1640), Rubens mentions that he has already refused over 100 students. This testifies to the early popularity and prestige of Rubens's workshop among young artists.

August 28
Philip Rubens dies suddenly at the age of thirty-seven and is buried at Saint Michael's Abbey. Rubens paints *The Four Philosophers* (page 19) as a tribute to his brother. The painting shows Philip and fellow Humanist Jan Woverius (1576–1636) alongside the philosopher Justus Lipisus (1547–1606), their mentor and friend. Peter Paul is now the sole survivor of Jan Rubens and Maria Pypelinckx's family of seven children.

September 7
Rubens receives the commission for the altar of the Harquebusiers' Guild in the Cathedral of Our Lady, for which he would paint *The Descent from the Cross*. The Harquebusiers were not a craft guild but a civic militia. Their members belonged to the upper classes and helped to guard the city. Rubens's friend and patron Rockox was headmaster of the Guild, and is depicted in the right wing of the triptych. The altar was consecrated on July 22, 1614.

September 13
Baptism of Philip Rubens II, the son of Philip and Maria de Moy, at the Cathedral of Our Lady. His godfather is Nicolaas Rockox and his godmother is Clara de Moy, Rubens's mother-in-law.

1612

Sebastian Vranckx (1573–1647), painter, becomes dean of the Guild of Saint Luke.

January 20
Death of Rudolf II of Hapsburg (b. 1552), Holy Roman Emperor, in Prague. He is succeeded by his brother Matthias (1557–1619).

February 9
Death of Vincenzo I Gonzaga in Mantua.

June
Rubens travels to the Northern Netherlands, accompanied by his friends and colleagues Hendrik van Balen and Jan Brueghel the Elder, and maybe others. They visited Haarlem, where the engraver-turned-painter Hedrick Goltzius (1558–1617) and other local artists welcomed

them. In Leiden, Rubens spoke to prominent Humanist scholars such as Dominicus Baudius (1561–1613), Daniel Heinsius (1580–1655), and Hugo Grotius (1583–1645). The trip had been in the making for some time and until recently (see essay by Jaco Rutgers, page 102), it was generally believed that Rubens's motive was to seek reputable engravers to translate his paintings into prints.

1613

Jan Collaert (1561/66–1620/28), engraver and painter, becomes dean of the Guild of Saint Luke.

Beginning of renovations in the Capuchin's Church (unspecified, until 1614) and the Cathedral of Our Lady (vaulting and entrance, until 1619).

The Jesuit scholar François d'Aguilon (1567–1617) publishes his *Opticorum Libri Sex* with the Plantin press, a monumental work on optics with a title page and illustrations by Rubens, engraved by Theodoor Galle. Rubens also delivers designs for an edition of liturgical texts, the *Missale Romanum*, which appeared with the same publisher (see essay by Jaco Rutgers, page 102).

Around May 22
Jan Wildens (1586–1653), landscape painter and collaborator of Rubens, leaves for Italy.

1614

Johannes van Keerbergen, book seller, becomes dean of the Guild of Saint Luke.

Duke Johann Ernst I of Saxe-Weimar (1594–1626) visits Antwerp on his tour of Western Europe, and mentions the "admirable" Rubens and Jan Brueghel in his travel accounts. The former, the duke writes, paints large works and makes about 100 guilders a day, while the latter paints small panels that are artful and subtle. These comments aptly characterize two parallel traditions of painting in the city.

The *Breviarium Romanum* (page 259) is published by Plantin press, including a title page and illustrations by Rubens, again engraved by Theodoor Galle.

April 1
Helene Fourment (1614–1673) is baptized at the Cathedral of Our Lady. She is the daughter of the silk and tapestry merchant Daniel I Fourment and Clara Stappaerts, and will become Rubens's second wife in 1630.

June 5
Rubens's second child, Albert (1614–1657), is baptized in the Church of Saint Andrew. Archduke Albert is appointed godfather, and presents Rubens with an ornate silver cup. Clara Brant (1599–1642), sister of Isabella, is appointed godmother.

June 29
Rubens becomes dean of the Guild of Romanists.

November 26
Rubens and Jan Brant become the legal guardians of Philip's children.

December 10
Wolfgang Wilhelm (1578–1653), Count Palatine of Neuburg, arrives in Brussels after winning the Jülich Succession Wars (1609–1614). The purpose of his visit is to thank Archduke Albert for his help in holding off Protestant troops. Wilhelm was raised in the Lutheran faith but converted to Catholicism when he married Magdalene of Bavaria (1587–1628) in 1613. Wilhelm's visit to Brussels was the beginning of a lasting relationship between two Catholic courts.

It is probably around this time that Wilhelm is first put in touch with Rubens, from whom he would commission many large altarpieces for Neuburg churches in the years that follow. Among them are *The "Great" Last Judgement* of 1617 (Alte Pinakothek, Munich), *The Pentecost* of 1619 (Bayerische Staatsgemäldesammlungen, Munich), and *The Adoration of the Shepherds* of 1619 (Neuburg Palace, Bavaria) for the Neuburg Jesuit church.

1615

Frans Francken the Younger (1581–1642), painter, becomes dean of the Guild of Saint Luke.

Jacob Jordaens (1593–1678), collaborator of Rubens, registers as a master watercolour painter.

January 9
Wolfgang Wilhelm visits Antwerp.

March 13
Cornelis I Galle (1576–1650), engraver and younger brother of Theodoor, is paid thirty-three guilders for his engraving after a drawing by Rubens of his brother Philip. The drawing was probably based on the painted portrait from the Detroit Institute of Art (page 125).

April 15
First stone of the Jesuit church is laid (completed 1621). The first plans had been drawn up by d'Aguillon, after which the architect Pieter Huyssens (1577–1637) continued the project. Rubens provided designs for architectural decorations, as well as two altarpieces and thirty-nine ceiling paintings (see "March 29, 1620").

June 25
Rubens incurs expenses for a wall between Rubens's estate and that of the adjoining shooting range of the Harquebusiers' Guild. This is the earliest archival reference to Rubens's renovations; however, they were already well underway at this point (see essay by Koen Bulckens, page 84).

August 13–27
The archdukes attend an *Ommeganck* (procession) and visit the gallery of Van der Geest. An artistic impression of the visit is depicted in a gallery picture by Willem van Haecht (1593–1637).

1616–21

The second half of the Twelve Years' Truce is a period of astounding productivity for Rubens. In response to the high demand for commissions, the output of his flourishing workshop increases and Rubens executes some of the largest and most ambitious works of his career. With his foothold firmly established in the Catholic Netherlands and the widespread recognition of his "brand" through the proliferation of his prints, his clientele becomes increasingly international, leading to commissions for courts and churches in present-day Germany, France, and Italy. Artists who have been linked to Rubens's studio during this period—albeit it with varying degrees of certainty—include Antwerpians such as Van Dyck, Jordaens (1593–1678), and Artus De Bruyn (d. 1632), and, from the Northern Netherlands, Pieter Soutman (c. 1580–1659), a painter and engraver from Haarlem; Arnout Vinckenborgh (1585/86–1620), painter from Alkmaar; and Lucas Vorsterman (1595–1675), an engraver from Zaltbommel. Apart from regular collaborations with individual specialists, Rubens also participates in two larger collaborative projects: he is one of fourteen artists who contributes a painting to the series *The Mysteries of the Rosary* for the Dominicans' Church (see "1617"), and he jointly creates two *Allegories of the Senses* (completed in 1618) with eleven other Antwerp artists for the archdukes in Brussels.

1616

Jan II Moretus (1576–1618), printer, becomes dean of the Guild of Saint Luke.

Frans Hals (1581–1666), a painter from Haarlem, visits Antwerp, as does the English ambassador to The Hague, Sir Dudely Carleton (1573–1632). The latter writes that it is not what it used to be.

Soutman settles in Antwerp. He works for Rubens from about 1616 until 1624, mainly providing designs for engravings. Soutman also paints several variants of Rubens's compositions.

Wildens returns from Italy.

Rubens paints four hunting scenes for Maximillian of Bavaria, among them *The Boar Hunt* (page 228).

Around this time, Rubens's *Judith Beheading Holofernes* is engraved by Cornelis Galle. This print, dedicated to Jan Woverius (page 133), is the first to be initiated by Rubens himself (see essay by Jaco Rutgers, page 102).

February 17
Rubens is mentioned as living on De Wapper on the funerary scroll of Martina Plantin (1550–1616), mother of Balthasar and Jan II Moretus. This implies that he moved in sometime during the previous year.

April 23
William Shakespeare dies in London.

November 2
A contract is signed for the making of a staircase in Rubens's house. This appears to be the last substantial alteration to the workshop, so we can assume that the new building is in full use from this date on (see essay by Koen Bulckens, page 84).

November 9
The contract for Rubens's first tapestry cycle is signed, which tells the story of the Roman consul Decius Mus. The series is commissioned by unnamed "Genovese gentlemen," and is woven over the course of the following year in Brussels.

1617

Peter II Goetkint (1580–1625), dealer, becomes dean of the Guild of Saint Luke.

De Bruyn is registered as a master.

Louis XIII assumes leadership of France and exiles his mother, Marie de Medici, to Blois.

Reports of bubonic plague victims in the countryside reach Antwerp. The city magistrates round up a medical council, discussing measures to prevent an outbreak. However, they would be ill-prepared in 1625 when an epidemic finally reached the city, likely causing the death of Isabella Brant in 1626.

March 10
Paolo da Cesena (1556–1638), head of the Capuchin order, laments the exuberant spending on Rubens altarpieces. He writes that expensive pictures were ordered for their churches at Cambrai (*The Entombment*) and Antwerp (possibly *St. Francis Receiving the Christ Child*), while in Lille, *The Descent from the Cross* (1616–1617 Palais des Beaux-Arts de Lille, Lille) is currently being painted.

June 29
The staunchly Catholic Ferdinand (1578–1637; later Ferdinand II, Holy Roman Emperor) is crowned King of Bohemia, and begins closing down Protestant chapels (see "May 23, 1618").

October 1
Death of Louis Finson (b. c. 1580), painter and dealer, in Amsterdam. In his estate is a painting by Caravaggio, *The Madonna of the Rosary* (1605–1607, Kunsthistorisches Museum Wien, Vienna). The work is acquired for the Dominicans' Church by a consortium of art-lovers, consisting of Rubens, Hendrik van Balen, Jan I Brueghel, and Jan Cooymans. In its new location, Caravaggio's work would figure alongside a series of fifteen paintings with *The Mysteries of the Rosary*, executed by Van Balen, Rubens, Jordaens, Van Dyck, De Vos, De Bruyn, Vinckenborgh, and other Antwerp artists.

1618

Adriaen van Stalbemt (1580–1662), landscape painter, becomes dean of the Guild of Saint Luke.

Van Dyck and Cornelis Schut (1597–1655), talented artists of a younger generation, register as master-painters. The former continues to work with Rubens. The latter leaves for Italy not long after, where he remains until 1631.

Death of the painter Ambrosius Francken (b. 1544).

January 15
Jordaens buys a house in the Hoogstraat, which he will expand in 1639.

March 17–June 1
Rubens and Carleton exchange letters (see essay by Alexandra Libby, page 72). The former has come into possession of a collection of antique marbles which he wishes to barter with Rubens for paintings; upon learning that only half the works would be executed by the master's hand alone, he expresses qualms about the transaction. In a letter dated May 12, Rubens offers tapestries in addition to "the flower of [his] stock," as part of the deal. In an earlier letter dated April 28, Rubens appended a list in which he describes the extent to which each painting was jointly executed, offering a unique glance and insight into the painter's studio practices. Among the paintings was "a Daniel, among many lions, taken from life. Original, entirely by my hand" (page 150).

March 23
Rubens's second son, Nicolaes (1614–1657), is baptized in the Church of Saint Jacob, Rubens's parish church. The Genovese Marquis Nicolo Pallavicini is his godfather and Maria de Moy, Isabella's aunt and the widow of Philip, is his godmother.

May 23
In Prague, two envoys of King Ferdinand (see "June 29, 1617") are thrown out of a window of the Bohemian Chancellery by Protestant nobles. This event, known as the Defenestration of Prague, is one of the instigators of the Thirty Years' War.

August 29
The political and religious tensions in the Northern Netherlands escalate. Maurice, Prince of Naussau (1567–1625), hereditary stadtholder of the United Provinces of the Netherlands, orders the arrest of Stadholder Johan van Oldenbarnevelt (1547–1619).

1619

Cornelis de Vos (1584–1651), portrait painter, becomes dean of the Guild of Saint Luke.

The Dutch East India Trading Company establishes the city of Batavia.

January 4
Rubens writes to Pieter van Veen (1570–1644/47), a lawyer in the Hague and brother of his teacher Otto, for help in obtaining privileges for his engravings published in the Northern Netherlands. This letter, as well as the one described below, indicates the birth of Rubens's print publishing enterprise. Van Veen proved to be of little help, and Rubens would eventually call on Carleton to settle the matter (see essay by Jaco Rutgers, page 102).

January 23
In his second letter to Van Veen, Rubens attaches a list with the subjects of his forthcoming prints, among them *Battle of the Amazons*. The artist also mentions a "well-intentioned young man" in his service, generally identified as Lucas Vorsterman. Through his labourious technique, the precocious young engraver with a keen eye for detail is able to translate Rubens's flickering paintings into print. Their collaboration leads to engravings of the highest calibre, but their relations would begin to sour around 1622. Vorsterman, who felt that his talents were not sufficiently recognized, physically attacked Rubens in April of that year. Rubens received a writ of protection (a court document aiming to keep him safe from Vorsterman) from Archduchess Isabella on April 29, 1622.

February 22
Marie de Medici escapes from Blois and joins an aristocratic revolt against Louis XIII. Armand Jean du Plessis (1585–1642), Duke of Richelieu, is asked to mediate between her and the king. She is awarded freedom in return for peace. In 1622, Marie de Medici commissions Rubens to produce a large series depicting her life, meant to decorate the galleries of the prestigious Palais de Luxembourg in Paris.

March 1
Jan Brueghel buys a larger house, named Den Bock, in the Arenbergstraat.

March 20
Death of Matthias, Holy Roman Emperor, in Vienna. He is succeeded by Ferdinand II.

May 12
Van Oldenbarnevelt is executed in The Hague, after which Prince Maurice assumes leadership of the Dutch Republic.

June
Snyders joins the Guild of Romanists.

1620

Jan van Meurs, glassmaker, becomes dean of the Guild of Saint Luke.

Three artists associated with Rubens's workshop—Vorsterman, Soutman, and De Bruyn—register pupils with the Guild. Vorsterman is also inscribed as master engraver.

Vorsterman and Soutman become citizens of Antwerp.

Seghers returns to Antwerp.

March 29
Rubens signs a contract promising to complete thirty-nine ceiling paintings for the Antwerp Jesuit church by early 1621. It is the biggest commission he had done to date, and Rubens makes the deadline. The contract specifically mentions that Van Dyck would collaborate on the series, however; he spent extensive time in London over the course of the commission.

October 1
Woverius applauds Balthasar Moretus and Rubens as Antwerp's most prominent citizens, adding that their houses attract foreign visitors, in a letter to Moretus.

November–March 1621
Van Dyck is mentioned in London, and is said to carry letters of recommendation from Rubens. He does not enter into the permanent service of King James I (1566–1625), but leaves for home and later Italy instead. In 1632, Van Dyck returns to London to work at the court of Charles I (1600–1649), where he will remain until his death in 1641.

1621

Jordaens is appointed dean of the Guild of Saint Luke by the Antwerp magistrates on September 28. The Liggeren (archives) of 1621–1622, however, mention that Karel van Mallery was dean of the Guild of Saint Luke and the chamber of Rethorics de Violieren during the period.

Rubens dedicates an engraving of *The Flight of Lot and His Family from Sodom* to Jan Brant, and one of *The Adoration of the Magi* (Musée des Beaux-Arts de Lyon) to Maximilian of Bavaria.

March 29
Death of Philip III of Spain (b. 1578) in Madrid.

April 9
The Twelve Years' Truce comes to a close and military hostilities resume. Spain had tried to renegotiate the terms of the peace treaty but Prince Maurice refused. The religious strife instigates Rubens's diplomatic activities, in an effort to restore peace in the Netherlands. At the insistence of Archduchess Isabella, the artist would attempt to negotiate a new peace at several European courts in the years that followed.

Early June
Otto Sperling (1602–1681), future physician to the Danish king, visits Rubens's workshop as an eighteen-year-old student. The account of the visit is the only account of Rubens's workshop in action. He describes a large, windowless room, with light streaming in from a hole in the ceiling. Sperling claims to have witnessed a number of artists working on various paintings, all of which, he says, were sold as Rubens's own.

July 15
Death of Archduke Albert (b. 1559), leaving Isabella in charge of the Low Countries.

September 13
In a letter to William Trumbull, the English envoy in Brussels, Rubens writes that he is "by nature, more fit to execute large works than small curiosities." The artist is soliciting for the ceiling decorations of the Banqueting Hall in Whitehall Palace. Inspired by his Jesuit church and Decius Mus series, he would create many more large cycles in the decade that followed (see also "February 22, 1619").

October
Van Dyck leaves for Italy.

December 23
Rubens expands his estate by acquiring the house Breda on Hoplandt, the first of a series of purchases. He would acquire more adjoining parcels in 1627 (six houses, three on De Wapper and three on Hoplandt) and 1628 (the house between Breda and the other three on Hoplandt). Though the property was now expanded, Rubens would spend less time there in the decade that followed, a period during which he would undertake many travels for artistic and diplomatic purposes.

Koen Bulckens and Corrinne Chong

LIST OF WORKS

Published in 2019 by the Art Gallery of Ontario and DelMonico Books•Prestel.

The Art Gallery of Ontario is partially funded by the Ontario Ministry of Culture. Additional operating support is received from the City of Toronto, the Department of Canadian Heritage, and the Canada Council for the Arts.

Contemporary programming at the Art Gallery of Ontario is supported by

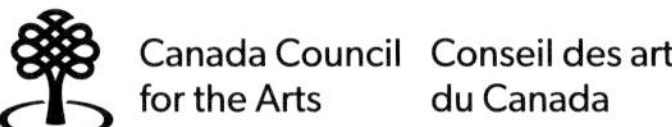

Printed and bound in Canada

10 9 8 7 6 5 4 3 2 1

Library and Archives Canada Cataloguing in Publication

Early Rubens / edited by Sasha Suda and Kirk Nickel.

Catalogue to accompany the exhibition *Early Rubens* held at the Fine Arts Museums of San Francisco from April 6 to September 2, 2019, and at the Art Gallery of Ontario from October 12, 2019 to January 5, 2020.

ISBN 978-1-988788-10-4 (hardcover : Art Gallery of Ontario)—ISBN 978-3-7913-5844-4 (hardcover : DelMonico Books)

1. Rubens, Peter Paul, 1577-1640—Exhibitions. 2. Exhibition Catalogs. I. Suda, Alexandra, editor II. Nickel, Kirk, 1979–, editor III. Art Gallery of Ontario, issuing body, host institution IV. Fine Arts Museums of San Francisco, host institution

ND673.R9A4 2019 759.9493 C2018-906369-6

Library of Congress Control Number: 2018963888

A CIP catalogue record for this book is available from the British Library.

Published in conjunction with the exhibition *Early Rubens* organized by the Art Gallery of Ontario and the Fine Arts Museums of San Francisco.

Art Gallery of Ontario
Toronto, Ontario, Canada
October 12, 2019 to January 5, 2020

Fine Art Museums of San Francisco, Legion of Honor
San Francisco, California, United States
April 6 to September 2, 2019

Art Gallery of Ontario
317 Dundas Street West
Toronto, Ontario M5T 1G4
Canada
www.ago.ca

DelMonico Books, an imprint of Prestel,
a member of Verlagsgruppe Random House GmbH

Prestel Verlag
Neumarkter Strasse 28
81673 Munich

Prestel Publishing Ltd.
14–17 Wells Street
London W1T 3PD

Prestel Publishing
900 Broadway, Suite 603
New York, NY 10003
www.prestel.com

PUBLICATION

Edited by
Sasha Suda
Kirk Nickel

Managing Editor
Jim Shedden

Production and Copy Editors
Gina Badger
Amy Lam
Kristin Li
Sarah Liss
Jason McBride
Kendra Ward

Publishing Coordinator
Robyn Lew

Proofreader
Judy Phillips

Designer
Lauren Wickware

Pre-Press
Paul Jerinkitsch

Printing and Binding
Friesens, Canada

AGO EXHIBITION

ART GALLERY OF ONTARIO

Chief Curator
Julian Cox

Curator, European Art and R. Fraser Elliott Chair, Print and Drawing Council
Sasha Suda

Project Manager
Laura Comerford

Research Assistants
Corrinne Chong
Carolyn Mensing

Interpretive Planner
Gillian McIntyre

Curatorial Administrative Assistant
Wendy Hebditch

Editor
Sarah Liss

Design and Graphics
Marilyn Bouma-Pyper
Katy Chey
Malene Hjørngaard

AGO SUPPORTERS

Generously supported by
Hans & Susan Brenninkmeyer
Robert Harding & Angel Yang

FAMSF EXHIBITION

FINE ARTS MUSEUMS OF SAN FRANCISCO

Assistant Curator of European Paintings
Kirk Nickel

Director of the Art Division
Melissa E. Buron

Curator in Charge of European Decorative Arts and Sculpture and Interim Curator in Charge of European Art
Martin Chapman

Joseph F. McCrindle Intern in European Painting
Natasha Coleman

Director of Exhibitions
Krista Brugnara

Exhibitions Manager
Hilary Magowan

Director of Education
Sheila Pressley

Chief Registrar
Kimberley Montgomery

Registrar
Nadia Ghani

Head of Paintings Conservation
Elise Effmann Clifford

Paintings Conservator
Tricia O'Regan

Exhibition Designer
Tristan Telander

Exhibition Graphic Designer
Kate Argwal

Chief Preparator
Ryan Butterfield

Director of Marketing, Communications, and Visitor Experience
Linda Butler

Director of Communications
Miriam Newcomer

FAMSF SUPPORTERS

Presenting Sponsors
John A. and Cynthia Fry Gunn
Diane B. Wilsey

Major Support
Government of Flanders
Gladyne Kenderdine Mitchell
The Bernard Osher Foundation

Significant Support
San Francisco Auxiliary of the Fine Arts Museums
The Diana Dollar Knowles Fund

Generous Support
Phoebe Cowles and Robert Girard
George and Marie Hecksher
Robert Lehman Foundation

Additional support is provided by
The Gladys Krieble Delmas Foundation

This exhibition is supported in part by an award from the National Endowment for the Arts.

The exhibition at the Legion of Honor is supported by an indemnity from the Federal Council on the Arts and the Humanities.

Following page

Peter Paul Rubens
The Annunciation (detail)
c. 1610
Oil on canvas
224 × 200 cm

Gemäldegalerie, Kunsthistorisches Museum, Vienna

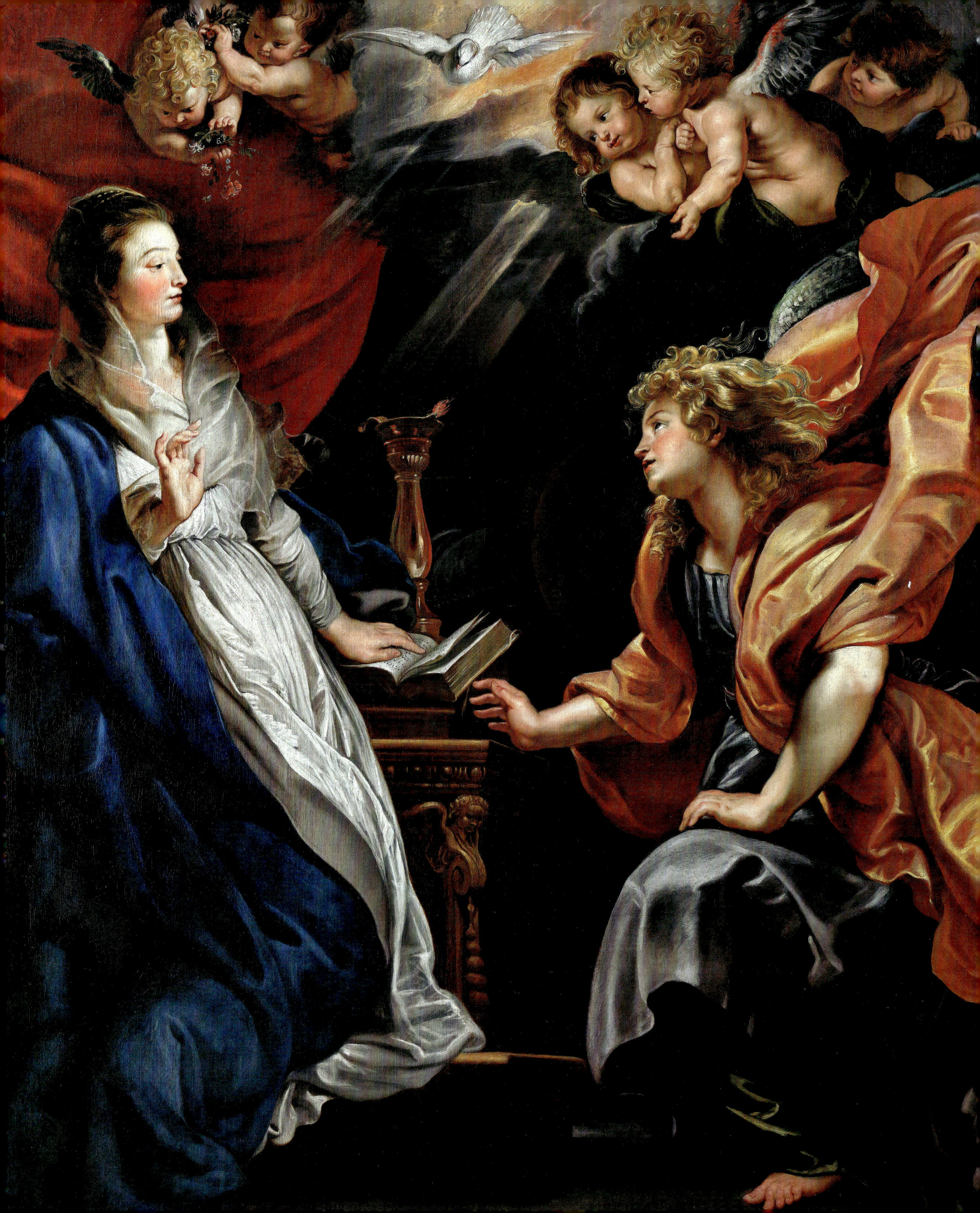